American Top 40 with Casey Kasem (The 1970's)

Pete Battistini

authorHOUSE®

AuthorHouse™
1663 Liberty Drive
Bloomington, IN 47403
www.authorhouse.com
Phone: 1 (800) 839-8640

Published by AuthorHouse 09/10/2019

ISBN: 978-1-4184-1070-4 (sc)

Print information available on the last page.

This book is printed on acid-free paper.

To my parents, Larry and Maryanne Battistini,
who provided my adolescent years with an environment
that allowed me to pursue various interests,
including an enthusiasm for Top 40 radio.

To the best wife ever, Carol Battistini, who tolerates my desire
to occasionally relive those same years.

And to the four guys who started it all,
Tom, Ron, Casey and Don.

CONTENTS

****

Preface & Introduction

****

Beginning in July 1970, *American Top 40* - the legendary weekly hit parade of contemporary music - was launched as Los Angeles renown disk jockey Casey Kasem counted down the USA's biggest and best-selling records using the Top 40 from *Billboard* magazine's Hot 100 chart. Kasem hosted the first show on the weekend of July 4, 1970 and continued as host - more than 18 years - for millions of radio listeners all over the world until August 6, 1988. The following week, disk jockey Shadoe Stevens took the reins and spotlighted the records and artists until the program ceased production with its last broadcast on January 28, 1995. But *American Top 40*, once again hosted by Casey Kasem, debuted on March 28, 1998. Due to a change administered by Premiere Radio Networks, Casey's last *AT40* broadcast aired on January 3, 2004.

With broadcasts that originated in Hollywood, *AT40* was created by Kasem and longtime friend and colleague Don Bustany, the show's producer for many years. Distributed and syndicated by Watermark Inc., Tom Rounds was the show's executive producer. And any discussion of the show's beginnings must include radio programmer Ron Jacobs who offered professional expertise, guidance, and the needed energy to bring *AT40* to reality. In addition to Casey's 1988 departure, the show's 1995 demise, and its 1998 resurrection, there are many other significant milestones in its history, including the historic media merge in 1981 between ABC Radio Enterprises and Watermark. These scenarios are well-described in Rob Durkee's best-seller *American Top 40: The Countdown of the Century*.

For the purpose of this text, however, references made to *AT40* will concentrate primarily on the decade of the 1970's.

The text that follows - from years of research in an unquestionable labor of love - originates from the author's acknowledged admission as a devoted *AT40* listener throughout the 1970's. For those at Watermark who labored to produce a quality product every week, it was work. For the author, one of millions of recipients of that product, *American Top 40* was a weekly habit of listening pleasure.

The book you are holding is divided into three primary sections. The first contains program summaries of nearly 500 *AT40* shows produced during the 1970's – from the first show on July 4, 1970 to the decade-ending special, "The Top 50 Hits of the 1970's." The second section provides an exhaustive and well-documented listing of every radio station with a program affiliation sometime between 1970 and 1979. And, in the last section, the author provides his own 'enthusiast confessions' as he pursued opportunities to listen to *AT40* on the radio. Integrate countless illustrations along with quotes from the perspective of others and you likely have more *AT40* information here than you will ever want to know. Nevertheless, it's must-have documentation for anyone who considers himself or herself an *AT40* fan.

Make a point to set aside time this Saturday or Sunday to enjoy this book – just like you did for Casey Kasem's countdown – and you may find yourself remembering *American Top 40*.

But first, to help set the tone, enjoy the following reflections.

American Top 40 Reflections

Tom Rounds

Tom Rounds was the president of Watermark Inc., the parent company and distributor of American Top 40, and AT40's executive producer.

Bill Drake deserves credit as the instigator of what became "The History of Rock and Roll." Thank goodness Rock and Roll was only about 15 years old when his suggestion to pre-record an entire New Year's weekend on KHJ, or the project would have killed Ron Jacobs, Pete Johnson, Robert W. Morgan and Bill Mouzis who put this wonderful 48 hour production together for L.A. and the rest of the RKO stations. "The History" was such an earth-shaking event for radio and popular culture that it provided the inspiration for us to position AT40 as a *weekly* history of rock and roll for the same stations who ran it in 1969. What a door-opener!

What comes through in (this text) is the total involvement of the team at Watermark. Everybody had a hand in it...not just Don Bustany and his production staff, but accounting, sales, distribution...they all had some weekly task that involved getting the show written, tracked, assembled, pressed (into vinyl) and shipped every week. After Bill Hergonson left, I took over most of the studio work starting in 1972 until I regained sanity in about 1978 when we could afford the kind of staff of which the show was worthy.

The 10 or so years covered (in this text), unearthing almost 500 time capsules, was as full of changes as the 60's (which continued to influence the entire next decade.) Consider radio moving inexorably from AM to FM, mono to stereo, and pop music going from 2 1/2 minute ditties in 1970, to complex new forms, until in 1978 the show simply had to grow from 3 hours to 4 to accommodate the entire Top 40. Also consider the transitioning from one business model to another. We were a bit too far ahead of the game when we launched the show in barter syndication, only to have to retreat back into charging the stations cash license fees in 1971. It wasn't until the mighty advertiser-oriented sales force of ABC took over in 1982 that the show went back to barter...a world it has never left.

With a few major exceptions (Boston, Washington, L.A.), American Top 40 was mainly a small market vehicle for its first years. We didn't capture New York, San Francisco, Chicago or Detroit for quite a while. In fact, AT40 was heard in Sydney, Singapore, Johannesburg, Hong Kong and, thanks to AFRTS, much of Europe, long before people could hear it in St. Louis (KIRL was in St. Charles), Miami, and Dallas. In Milan, Italy, AT40 was on the air every day!

What struck me the most is the not-too-serious tone of our communications with the subscribing stations. The stations were treated more like family than customers. Watermark ran like a self-contained radio station that happened to have not only Casey Kasem on the air, but a very talented support team that could focus their energies on doing the best damn 3 or 4 hours a week possible.

One final thought....................Tom Driscoll should be acknowledged. He was the strawberry king/investor from Northern California who backed Watermark and provided the financial security that got us through the trials and tribulations of launching a weekly syndicated show in a radio environment in which "canned" programming was held in the same esteem as toxic waste.

Pete Battistini

American Top 40 Reflections
Ron Jacobs

Ron Jacobs was the original program director of KHJ Radio in Los Angeles, co-creator of American Top 40, producer of the Cruisin' album series, and author of KHJ: Inside Boss Radio. Jacobs lives in Kaneohe, Oahu, Hawaii. He can be reached at whodaguy@lava.net.

The American Top 40 story would be incomplete without a few words about its parent company, Watermark, Inc. Initially, three radio personalities - Tom Moffatt, Tom Rounds and Ron Jacobs - worked together at KPOI Radio in Honolulu during the late 1950s and into the 1960s. In addition to their on-air work, they were involved with producing and promoting local concerts. In 1968, after leaving Moffatt in Honolulu years before, both Jacobs and Rounds were in Los Angeles and decided to promote and produce another concert - the Miami Pop Festival. At the time, Jacobs was at KHJ Radio and Rounds had recently departed KFRC in San Francisco.

The event was a pivotal point in the careers of many individuals. In fact, a Miami area kid who was inspired by the festival and the attention it generated, headed for New York where he hired key personnel and staged the event now known as "Woodstock." The November 23, 1968 edition of Billboard magazine quoted Rounds, the festival's president. "Ticket sales for the Miami Pop Festival have already soared above 5,000 and are coming in from all parts of the nation. Already, 23 major Top 40 radio stations are promoting the festival and sponsoring contests to send listeners to the event."

They financed the show with $150,000 and an equal amount from investor Tom Driscoll. Although Miami Pop was considered an artistic success, the venture lost $6,000. But more importantly it was the foundation for future collaborations. Following the December 1968 festival, Rounds, Jacobs and Driscoll formed Watermark. And in June 1969, Jacobs resigned from KHJ to join Watermark full time.

Soon after leaving KHJ, Jacobs received a call from KRLA disk jockey Casey Kasem who had an idea. Jacobs respected Kasem, not only because he was a talented deejay and successful voice-over artist, but also because of his business savvy. Kasem envisioned a nationally syndicated radio program based on a Top 40 countdown. Jacobs realized the potential for this concept based on the success of KHJ's The History of Rock & Roll, the first syndicated national pop music show, which aired in 1969. Rounds and Jacobs later met with Kasem and his partner, Don Bustany, to discuss this venture. During the meeting between the four of them, a question arose. "Why hasn't any one thought of this before?" Jacobs knew the question was a precursor to a breakthrough.

Fate - being in the right place at the right time - brought three men into the life of Ron Jacobs. He had previously developed learning relationships with Mike Joseph, Bill Gavin and Colonel Thomas A. Parker of Madison, Tennessee. Each of them had an impact on him, contributing to his professional success.

In 1958, he was the 19-year-old program director of KPOA Radio in Honolulu where he learned the basics of Top 40 radio formatics from Joseph, the first programming consultant. While at KPOA, he also worked with Gavin, then music director for the popular radio program Lucky Lager Dance Time." Gavin went on to publish The Gavin

Report and became a legend in the radio and record industries. But it was Parker who likely had the greatest impact. Jacobs first met him in 1957 and regarded Parker as his primary mentor. A radio stunt that Jacobs and Moffatt orchestrated involving the colonel's client, Elvis Presley, began on the Beach at Waikiki. It caught the colonel's eye and began a lifelong friendship. Thanks to that association, Jacobs developed Watermark's 13-hour The Elvis Presley Story radio special in 1971 along with other projects that would have otherwise been impossible.

In developing AT40, Jacobs took advantage of another relationship that proved critical to the program's evolution. In 1968, Billboard magazine invited RKO's Bill Drake to be the keynote speaker at their inaugural Radio Forum at the Waldorf Astoria Hotel in New York City. At the last moment, because of a need to supervise coverage of the Robert Kennedy assassination, Drake was unable to get to the conference and remained in Los Angeles. Billboard publisher Hal Cook and radio-TV editor Claude Hall were understandably nervous about Drake's last-minute selection of Ron Jacobs as his replacement. At the time, Jacobs was a Los Angeles program director but did not have the national recognition like Bill Drake. Fortunately, his presentation was well received and an appreciative Cook and Hall offered their assistance, if needed, in any future endeavors.

When Casey, Bustany and Jacobs first spoke, they gave little thought to a source of credible, national music data. Of course, the source was as equally important as any other AT40 program element. (Jacobs later wondered what they would have done without the Billboard "Hot 100" chart as a weekly music source.) In 1970, when Jacobs called, Hal Cook agreed to what would became a long, fruitful arrangement between "The Bible of The Music Business" and the future World's Number One Radio Program. In addition, that arrangement and relationship resulted in ad campaigns for AT40 and the Cruisin' LP series, another one of Jacobs' Watermark projects, Billboard magazine.

Here's a little-known fact: American Top 40 was almost called "National Top 40." Why? Professional football's popularity was surging in the 1960s. The sport was marketed as "The National Football League," a distinctive sobriquet for a violent activity. Tom Rounds wanted to call our new show American Top 40. Jacobs, however, somehow associated that with the American Football League, which at the time was inferior to the NFL. But he went along with Rounds who had a winning track record of hatching catchy names for promotions, disc jockeys and concerts.

Jacobs and Rounds didn't realize then, but that choice of name was another fortuitous decision. Tom Moffatt's close friend, Arthur Thurstson, chief steward of Qantas Airlines, was on a Honolulu layover. Thurston heard AT40 on KPOI, one of the show's first seven affiliates. Moffatt encouraged Thurston to take a copy of AT40 to their mutual friend in Sydney, Bob Rogers of 2UE. Rogers was Australia's most popular broadcast personality. After hearing American Top 40, the show was programmed on his country's national radio network.

The Watermark budget, or lack of one, dictated the choice of a vocal style for the AT40 jingle package. For the first and only time in Jacobs' radio career, he had a virtually unlimited budget at KHJ. The original "93 KHJ Boss Radio" jingles were written and performed by Johnny Mann, who was already considered tops in the field. The Johnny Mann Singers had released many albums and appeared on national commercials. With

Johnny, an a cappella jingle package was designed for KHJ that was recorded at RCA's Vine Street Studios. The subterranean complex was where Elvis, the Rolling Stones and other major artists recorded when in Los Angeles in the mid-60s.

For AT40's jingles, Jacobs went to Dallas, home of several important "jingle factories." Dallas was also a "right to work" (i.e., non-union) town. He had previously worked with Jim and Dennis Meeks, who owned and operated the PAMS Studios, one of the pioneer jingle firms. They created and recorded all the AT40 material in three days. The original idea of which Jacobs is proudest is one he called "split logos." ("The Hits from Coast to Coast"-pause-"American Top 40" and "Casey's Coast to Coast"-pause-"American Top 40") The jingles were a subtle but key American Top 40 element. This new mode of jingle offered AT40 station board operators two options: They could stop during the jingle pause and take a commercial break or let the show play through the jingle pause non-stop to the next segment.

In the summer of 1970, Jacobs worked with Casey and Bustany on the AT40 program format. Basically, it was a bigger and better version of what had been done on local radio since the 1950s. They began the same way, by drawing three circles - one for each hour - represented as pie charts, inserting features and commercial breaks between numbers that represented the Top 40 countdown songs. Jacobs had agreed to produce the first program, which was done with Bill Hergonson, engineer on an earlier Watermark project. Bustany, who contributed equally to the program's success, wrote the custom material that made AT40 special and Casey Kasem famous.

Then all the pieces came together to produce the first AT40 demonstration tape. From there comes a seldom-told story of American Top 40's first public performance. Tom Driscoll decided at the last minute that Watermark's management team would attend the 1970 International Music Industry Conference at Majorca, Spain. Rounds, Driscoll and Jacobs flew to the largest of Balearic Islands to promote our new venture. They were not conference exhibitors or even participants. In reality, they were "media outlaws" staying at a posh Mediterranean hotel.

A Wollensak tape recorder and a hand-lettered placard comprised their presentation gear. The AT40 "World Premiere" took place in a cold church basement. Their frantic word of mouth campaign drummed up a crowd that consisted of Nesuhi Ertegun, brother of Ahmet and co-founder of Atlantic Records, and a few young record executives with nothing much else to do. They listened to the program's demonstration tape and Rounds made his pitch. Several schoolgirls in blue uniforms wandered around. At the back of the room, Jacobs leaned against a stone wall, watching and listening. And he tried to put things in perspective. Here they were - Rounds, Driscoll and Jacobs - off the southeast coast of mainland Spain, where no one spoke English, and a world away from America, hustling an American show. They were pitching an unknown, unproven radio program to people who couldn't do a thing about it even if they liked it. Little did anyone in that room know that this was the free world's introduction to what was destined to become one of the most successful programs in radio history.

After AT40 went on the air in July 1970, Jacobs was rarely involved, other than an occasional request by Tom Rounds to pitch the show to larger market program directors that Jacobs knew. He left Watermark in 1972 and headed for San Diego to program KGB AM&FM Radio. And yet another series of adventures began.

Epilogue: "Fate" intervened one last time. It was in January 1995 at the Radio Express studios in North Hollywood. Because Jacobs had been back in Hawaii for nearly 20 years, he had never met Shadoe Stevens. On this day, Stevens was cutting voice tracks for the last AT40 broadcast. Jacobs asked engineer Brandon D'Amore to shut things down, went into the booth and introduced himself to Shadoe. "I was on hand for the birth of this baby," Jacobs told him. "That was before my daughter was born and it was an immensely big deal. Now, it's mind-blowing to be on hand when you bring down the curtain after a quarter of a century run for this creation." Shadoe and Jacobs looked at each other for a moment and pondered that. They shook hands. Then Shadoe counted down to Number One for the last time.

American Top 40 Reflections
Don Bustany

On the morning of Thursday, October 16, 1969, Casey Kasem and Don Bustany, d.b.a. Kasem-Bustany Productions, presented to Tom Rounds and Ron Jacobs, President and Vice-President, respectively, of Watermark, Inc., at Watermark's offices on LaCienega Boulevard (in Los Angeles), a fully-developed concept for the radio program that would come to be known as American Top 40. The description that Rounds and Jacobs heard that day still perfectly describes any episode of AT40 that's airing now, 33 years later. The show's working title then was National Top 40.

Two weeks later, on November 4 to be exact, Kasem and Bustany made a fuller and more formal presentation to Watermark. Present at that meeting, in addition to Rounds and Jacobs, was Watermark board chairman and principal financial backer Tom Driscoll (of the Driscoll Berry Ranches in Northern California). The Kasem-Bustany presentation that day included future plans for Country, Soul, and Album countdowns if the Top 40 version succeeded.

The basic idea of such a program--a national DJ countdown show, airing once a week and based on the Billboard chart--was strictly Casey Kasem's. Of course, Kasem has never harbored the notion that he invented the countdown. He had grown up in Detroit listening to local countdowns, and he'll tell anyone who'll listen that he was weaned on the first successful national radio countdown--"Your Hit Parade" which began in 1935 and ran until Rock & Roll knocked it off in the mid-Fifties.

Kasem first shared the idea with Bustany in late 1968 or early '69. They had formed a partnership, Kasem-Bustany Productions, and were in the business of producing radio commercials for advertisers located too far from the main production centers of New York and Los Angeles to have convenient access to the talent pools. Concurrently, K-B Productions was developing and trying to sell various packages for radio and television.

Watermark, which was about a year older than K-B, was producing concerts (the '68 Miami Pop Festival) and looking for other hills to climb in the music/recording/broadcasting industries. So, when Kasem (a top-rated deejay at KRLA) phoned Jacobs (the former PD of LA's #1 station, KHJ) in the fall of 1969, WM was ready to listen to a new idea for a syndicated show.

They bought it---figuratively and literally. K-B signed over to WM right and title in the property, retaining rights to a share in revenues. Jacobs struck a deal with Billboard for exclusive radio rights to their Pop singles chart, the Hot 100, and then lent his name (he was already a legend in Rock radio) to promoting within the industry the bizarre notion of a nationally syndicated Top 40 radio program---when everybody knew that Top 40 radio was dying.

During the early months of preparation, Rounds suggested changing the word 'National' in the working title to 'American', and everybody jumped on it. That was easy. Rounds also had the hardest part of the project---marketing American Top 40. He needed two heads, one to set up and supervise the technical production, post-production, duping, and shipping of the show and the other to get stations to carry it. In those days, syndication wasn't happening yet. Casey Kasem wasn't famous nationally, and it wasn't fashionable for music stations to carry special programming produced by somebody else. So, it was notable that Rounds had even seven stations taking this new, untried program called American Top 40 when the first show was shipped for the weekend of July 4, 1970.

AT40 was bartered its first 15 months, but not successfully. National advertisers were in the habit of buying radio time from the New York-bask networks. Not from some new little production company in Hollywood whose name implied that their main product was stationery. Finally, Rounds decided that, starting with the 4th quarter of 1971, the hundred or so stations we had by this time would begin paying cash for the show and keep all the commercial availabilities for themselves. New contracts went out and, after existing contracts had run their terms, the conversion from barter to cash was complete.

For a long time, American Top 40 operated in the red. Driscoll was willing to keep funding the operation as long as Kasem and Bustany were willing to continue producing it, because it was costing them too. (Their participation was in Net Profits and, since there were no profits, they had no revenue to cover the producing costs for which they were responsible.) It got discouraging sending out a show every week---and having to take money out of their pockets to do it. The steadily increasing number of subscribing stations was narrowing the gap between red ink and black ink, but not fast enough to keep the principals from seriously considering abandoning the project.

Jacobs, having done his part in launching the show and having other irons in the fire, went off to make more history in radio. Driscoll, Rounds, Kasem, and Bustany continued producing AT40 and periodically considered abandoning the project. Why keep investing in an unprofitable enterprise? Although the subject was broached several times, it got serious only twice---once in the spring and once in the summer of '72. Since Rounds was on salary and technically not one of the entrepreneurs, his roll was that of an interested observer. The decision to stop or go belonged to the other three. Driscoll was investing the big money--cash up front; and he prided himself on his business sense. Casey was putting in time and talent but was sensitive to Driscoll's cash investment. Bustany was putting in even more time and expressed greater passion for the viability of the project. The summer meeting was the real turning point. Driscoll wanted to stop. Casey was also tired of the non-profitable venture. Bustany was interpreting Rounds's projections on subscribing stations and revenues in the most optimistic way and predicting sure success for the show. Driscoll was affected enough by Bustany's enthusiasm and Kasem's willingness to go on to agree to continue financial support.

And the rest is history.

American Top 40 Reflections
Casey Kasem

Because we recorded each three-hour program in six 20-minute segments – one segment at a time – we would have to start the segment from the beginning if there was a reason to stop. And we stopped many times. Sometimes I would make a mistake, or Don (Bustany) would question my inflection of a particular word, or a story just didn't sound right, or we needed to confirm a chart statistic. When this occurred, we started from the segment's beginning because Ron (Jacobs) and Tom (Rounds) were concerned about the technical quality of the show – they did not want to edit or splice the recording tape. Each segment was recorded and, if necessary, re-recorded until I worked through it without making a mistake. Consequently, each three-hour show took hours and hours to record. In fact, our first program took 18 hours to produce. Obviously, we strived for a high level of quality from the very beginning.

The routine to record the show this way every week continued until Dick Clark sat in for me as a guest host in March 1972. Apparently it was his suggestion to record song introductions, artist stories – all of my voiceovers – in advance. This way, if I made a mistake, I would have to just re-read that portion of the program's script. Once I finished reading and recording the entire show, the Watermark engineer then mixed my voiceovers with the Top 40 records. The end result was the same product, and without tape splices. This suggestion made a lot of sense and, in fact, is a practice that continues today.

But it's still hard for me to believe that we recorded the program this way every week for nearly two years.

American Top 40 host Casey Kasem (right) reviews some of the material used for this book with author Pete Battistini.

American Top 40 **Reflections**
Bill "Captain Billy"* Hergonson

*"Captain Billy" is the name Casey Kasem used to call him during program recording sessions. It comes from the famous "Trouble Right Here in River City" scene from *The Music Man* which Casey was performing with a local troupe at the time.

HIRED AS *AT40*'s FIRST ENGINEER
When I graduated from Ithaca College in May 1970, along with classmate Stew Hillner, we packed up our things and headed west. My parents lived in Los Angeles where my dad (Robert W.) was working for National General Pictures. He had just completed an animated promotional film in conjunction with former KHJ Los Angeles program director Ron Jacobs and his new company called Watermark. Dad said he knew that they were starting a new syndicated radio project and that I should drop off a resume to Tom Rounds. I did that, and when I returned to the offices of National General, the receptionist said there was a message for 'Mr. Hergonson'...NOT my dad! It was from Tom Rounds, president of Watermark, who had been out to lunch when I dropped off my resume. I ran back over to Watermark where Tom said he was impressed with the fact that I had been a Top 40 DJ in a large market (WNDR, Syracuse, NY) and an engineer with major league experience (ABC Radio Networks, New York City). He explained that they were starting a new syndicated 3 HOUR radio show that would use the Billboard Hot 100 to 'count down' the Top 40 songs each week, starring Los Angeles DJ Casey Kasem. They needed a studio engineer for the show -- the guy who actually spins the records, turns the mike on and off and records the show on tape.

AT40 STUDIO SET UP
This whole (Watermark) operation was upstairs from an antiques dealer on LaCienega Boulevard in LA. The studios were the size of a large broom closet divided in half. The studio furniture, turntable pedestals, etc. had been hand crafted by an out-of-work Hollywood actor who did carpentry on the side to make ends meet. His name was HARRISON FORD. The saving grace of this 'broom closet' was that the equipment was all hand-crafted by Watermark engineer David Freese. He was an eccentric electronic genius and the sound of the studio was SUPERB and the custom gear was first rate all the way.......outstanding quality of equipment. We used brand new everything including a Scully reel-to-reel tape deck that could handle very large reels, and brand new SpotMaster cart machines. The microphone was the most expensive Neumann condenser made and even the headphones for Casey cost hundreds of dollars. We might have been in a phone booth, but it was a well equipped phone booth!

AT40 JINGLES
So the first thing that needed to be done by me, the studio engineer, was to transfer the jingles for the show onto (separate) tape cartridges...............The jingles for American Top 40 had been recorded at the famed jingle house PAMS of Dallas and supervised by Ron Jacobs, the same guy who created the famed a-cappella 'Boss Radio' jingles for KHJ with Johnny Mann. This (AT40) jingle package was a masterpiece. The famed 'Casey's Coast To Coast.......American Top 40' was called a 'split logo,' designed to allow the affiliate station to stop the jingle in the middle, play their commercials and then return to the show with the second half of the jingle, or they could let it play straight through if they had no spot break.

There were three versions of the split logo...fast, medium, and slow. This was so we could match the logo to the tempo of the song........In the end there were NINE split logos. Then, on top of that, there were singing 'numbers' for each position in the countdown...as in 'Number Twenty Three.' There was a fast and a slow of each 'number jingle.' This meant 80 carts for those alone. Plus there were the snappy Moog synthesizer themes for AT 40 and background 'sequencers' that highlighted the biographies. All in all, over 100 carts. And these had to be done ASAP! I spent literally one entire day and night doing the project. One of the main selling points for AT 40 was the studio sound quality that we promised the affiliates. So each cart had to be perfect and it had to sound exactly like the master tape......

RECORDING *AT40*'s FIRST DEMONSTRATION TAPE

We wanted to get a 'demo tape' made in time for Tom Rounds to take it to a convention (Billboard's annual radio programming forum) to stir up some business...........We then got the whole staff together to record the demo. There was Tom Rounds, Vaughn Monroe Filkins, a.k.a. 'The Live Earl Jive' who supplied the actual records and ran the timing clock, Ben Marichal who was a friend of Casey's and a walking encyclopedia of Billboard charts information, Don Bustany, who was Casey's partner and the show's writer, and Casey Kasem himself. We did a mock 'Hour Three' countdown to Number 1 which we 'telescoped' (down to) 13 minutes. This was intended to show program directors and managers how the show would sound on the air but in an abbreviated format for demonstration purposes. I recall that the chart we used for the demo had 'The Long And Winding Road' as #1 for the week, so we ended with a Beatles classic.

The final point: while I was engineer, the show was always recorded "live to tape" or in real time. Later, after I left Watermark (in January 1972), Casey would come in and "voice track" the show. I could tell the difference right away when I heard the show after I left.........however, that made NO difference to the fans and affiliates. It always seemed strange to me that AT 40's best days were the days least heard by the general public...before it became a huge hit and Casey became a super star DJ. But it all had to start somewhere, with history still in the future...and I'll always be glad I was part of the original team.

AMERICAN TOP 40
PROGRAM SUMMARY
Highlights, Errors & Points of Interest
1970 through 1979
(Information researched & compiled by Pete Battistini)

Summary Definitions

The list of definitions below will assist the reader with program summaries found in this section. The items on this page identify and define the program elements that make each *American Top 40* broadcast unique. Note, however, that not all definitions listed here apply to every program, which are arranged in chronological order on the following pages. For additional details, readers may want to refer to the appropriate *Billboard* Hot 100 chart.

Summary elements:	Summary definitions:
1. SPECIAL:	**Top 40 program with artist/record compilation different from *Billboard*'s weekly Hot 100 list**
2. GUEST HOST:	**substitute fill-in for Casey Kasem**
3. story:	**artist, record, music industry or related profile**
4. whatever happened to:	**artist update**
5. program mention:	**artist, record or background information briefly presented**
6. question:	**artist, chart or music-related question from listener**
7. question update:	**follow-up information regarding listener question**
8. odd chart stat:	**unusual chart movement or occurrence**
9. network commercial:	**national advertisement incorporated into program**
10. radio report:	**station submitting information regarding local record sales**
11. radio station edit:	**incomplete mention of station/market**
12. flipside played:	**record's B-side (of a 45) is featured instead of the A-side**
13. portion played:	**as part of a story, record is featured but not played in its entirety**
14. program offer:	**special promotion giveaway for listeners**
15. program correction:	**previous program information amended**
16. program note:	**noteworthy mention involving the program or Casey Kasem**
17. program error:	**inaccurate information provided**
18. *Billboard* report error:	**inaccurate chart information supplied to *AT40***
19. production error:	**oversight in program production**
20. production note:	**noteworthy occurrence involving the program or Casey Kasem**
21. review:	**verbal countdown of current Top 5 LPs or past Top 5 singles**
22. lyric alert:	***AT40* station notification of a record's offensive language**
23. scratchy record:	**song played with inferior broadcast quality**
24. short (edited) version:	**edited record not normally abbreviated for *AT40***
25. long version:	**extended record length not normally heard on *AT40***
26. edited long version:	**edited version of a song from an LP**
27. long distance dedication:	**record used in listener special request**
28. Book of Records:	**unusual artist, record or chart occurrence**
29. credits:	***AT40* staff mentioned by name**
30. different chart:	**weekly Top 40 chart inconsistent with *Billboard***
31. chart date/broadcast change:	**change in procedures results in new broadcast & chart date**
32. mini-quiz:	**short-lived feature which offered a multiple choice question**
33. name origin:	**description/meaning/selection of an artist's name**
34. record origin:	**description/meaning of a song**
35. oldie played:	**past Top 40 record featured**
36. LP cut played:	**current album selection featured**
37. archive #1 record played:	**chronological review and replay of a #1 record from the 1970s**
38. country chart record played:	**record spotlighted from *Billboard*'s country singles chart**

1970

1.) 07-11-70

Program #703-1
program note: first program; used *Billboard* Hot 100 chart dated July 11, 1970
program note: aired the weekend of Saturday, July 4 & Sunday, July 5
program note: Casey does not provide chart positions in outcues of any Top 40 record
story: Mark Lindsay's automobile has gold hubcaps
story: chart appearances of "It's All In The Game"
story: Ray Stevens' many talents
story: The Moody Blues' Graeme Edge competed against The Beatles
story: Bill Cosby's six Grammy Awards
story: annual record release statistics
story: Louis Armstrong bumped The Beatles out of the #1 position
story: what's a Pipkin?
story: Blood, Sweat & Tears break the Cold War
story: Melanie's overnight success
story: anti-establishment Rolling Stones
name origin: Three Dog Night
oldie played: Satisfaction - Rolling Stones
oldie played: Spinning Wheel - Blood, Sweat & Tears
oldie played: Little Ole Man - Bill Cosby
oldie played: Hello Dolly - Louie Armstrong

"If not for countdowns, I would never have taken an interest in popular music and probably wouldn't have wound up working in the music industry today. I was one of those crazy kids who knew when to find the 'Now 30,' 'Power 30,' 'Certified 35' or 'Giant 40' on any of a dozen radio signals near where I grew up -- the midpoint between Boston, Massachusetts and Providence, Rhode Island. When I wasn't listening to countdowns, I was at the local record shop perusing the under-glass copy of the week's 'Hot 100.' I saw 'American Top 40' coming during that first week in July 1970, when promotional announcements for the show's premiere were heard night and day on Boston's WMEX. And, of course, I was right there by the radio that very first Sunday, July 5th at straight-up 9am........I knew that 'American Top 40' was truly something special. A radio show from Hollywood? Imagine that. And a host who seemed to know everything about everyone making the hits? I wasn't hearing anything like that from the guy who did nights on WRKO, um, what was his name again? Oh, yeah...Shadoe Stevens."

Rich Appel, a longtime *AT40* listener

2.) 07-18-70

Program #703-2
program note: aired the weekend of Saturday, July 11 & Sunday, July 12
story: Johnnie Taylor's annoying humming
story: Tom Jones is world's Most Magnetic Male
story: "It's All In The Game" written by a U.S. vice-president
story: The Beatles are #1 with #1 records
odd chart stat: two debut records
network commercial: Increase Records (Cruisin' 1959)
network commercial: Increase Records (Cruisin' LP series)
flipside played: For You Blue - The Beatles
oldie played: It's Not Unusual - Tom Jones

3.) 07-25-70

Program #703-3
program note: aired the weekend of Saturday, July 18 & Sunday, July 19
program mention: Casey's uncertainty of Eric Burdon's "Spill The Wine"
program note: Casey does not provide chart positions in outcues of any Top 40 record, except at #1
program note: Casey mentions the important role of record producers
story: The Three Degrees' restrictions
story: Ricky Nelson's teen-age million sellers
story: rock 'n' roll's first #1 record
story: "MacArthur Park" is longest Top 10 record
record origin: Four Seasons' "Big Girls Don't Cry"
long version: MacArthur Park - Richard Harris
network commercial: Increase Records (Cruisin' LP series)
network commercial: Increase Records (Cruisin' 1961 LP)
(commercial's background music is Freddy King's "Hideaway")
oldie played: MacArthur Park - Richard Harris
oldie played: Travelin' Man - Rick Nelson
oldie played: Rock Around The Clock - Bill Haley & Comets
oldie played: Big Girls Don't Cry - Four Seasons

"My year in Saigon was more like an expatriate year than a year at war, but that is a different story for a different day. 7/18/70 was the day I stopped being short, i.e., having little time left in-country, and began my life as a soon-to-be Vietnam veteran by going home. I remember the unparalleled excitement of the ride up to Tan Son Hut AFB but little else about the plane ride to Hawaii. I was only going as far as Hawaii because I was not due at my next duty station immediately. My friend Jack's family had rented a house on Oahu for a week and had offered me the chance to stop and enjoy a couple of days of Hawaiian-style R'n'R before heading home.........The house my friends had rented was high in the hills on the back of Oahu. When I got to the house, it was empty but my friends had left me a note that I should make myself at home and that they were off playing golf. Quick as you can say Jack Robinson, I was out of my dress khakis and into a bathing suit, ready to lounge by the pool. I found a small transistor radio, copies of two hot-selling novels, **Love Story** ***and*** **The Godfather,** ***and even an ice-cold Coke. I was checking various stations to find a good station and I stumbled onto KPOI playing this top 40 countdown show hosted by a guy named Casey Kasem................I didn't catch AT40 on KPOI till Casey was up to #27, Save the Country. But I knew I had found a new home for my ears."***

Lanny Springs, a longtime *AT40* listener

4.) 08-01-70

Program #703-4
program note: aired the weekend of Saturday, July 25 & Sunday, July 26
story: The Beatles' 1964 chart statistics
story: Mountain's Leslie West is heavy
story: James Brown was 1969's top male singer
story: Ronnie Dyson inspired "Aquarias"
story: 'Goodtime' Glen Campbell's two Grammy Awards
story: Eric Burdon's four groups
story: Michael Jackson set a record
story: Hollywood Argyles' discovery
oldie played: Alley Oop - Hollywood Argyles
oldie played: I'm Walkin' - Fats Domino

4.) 08-01-70

Program #703-4 (CONTINUED)
oldie played: Gentle On My Mind - Glen Campbell
oldie played: Can't Buy Me Love - Beatles
odd chart stat: eight debut records
odd chart stat: Crosby, Stills, Nash & Young's back-to-back records
program note: Casey does not provide chart positions in outcues of any Top 40 record, except at #1
long version: Are You Ready? - Pacific Gas & Electric
network commercial: Increase Records (Cruisin' 1959 LP)
network commercial: Increase Records (Cruisin' 1961 LP)
network commercial: Increase Records (Cruisin' LP series)

5.) 08-08-70

Program #703-5
program note: aired the weekend of Saturday, August 1 & Sunday, August 2
program note: Casey provides outcue position numbers for only #29, #15 and #1
network commercial: Increase Records (Cruisin' 1956 LP)
network commercial: Increase Records (Cruisin' 1957 LP)
network commercial: Increase Records (Cruisin' LP series)
story: Melanie's LP includes recipes
story: James Brown's castle
story: "Good Vibrations" is the most expensive record
story: "Itsy Bitsy Teeny Weeny Polka Dot Bikini" is the longest title
story: Sammy Davis Jr. is Mr. Show Business
story: Andy Williams sang for Lauren Bacall
story: Freda Payne paid her dues
story: Lawrence Welk is not square
story: Eric Burdon was an artist
production error: Casey introduces "Spill The Wine" with a story about Eric Burdon, but never mentions Burdon's name
oldie played: Calcutta - Lawrence Welk
oldie played: Can't Get Used To Losing You - Andy Williams
oldie played: Itsy Bitsy Teeny Weeny Yellow Polka Dot Bikini - Brian Hyland
oldie played: Good Vibrations - Beach Boys
oldie played: Please Mr. Postman - Marvelettes

6.) 08-15-70

Program #703-6
program note: aired the weekend of Saturday, August 8 & Sunday, August 9
network commercial: Increase Records (Cruisin' LP series)
network commercial: Increase Records (Cruisin' 1960 LP)
network commercial: Increase Records (Cruisin' 1958 LP)
story: Neil Diamond's "Solitary Man" took four years to reach Top 40
story: The Coasters have most comedy hits
story: Holland-Dozier-Holland get song lyric ideas from soap operas
story: The Caravelles were French secretaries from Britain
story: Patty Duke won an Academy Award at age 14
story: U.S. President Lyndon Johnson thanked James Brown
story: Mungo Jerry nearly quit the music business
story: Guess Who performed for Prince Charles
story: Barry McGuire's "Eve of Destruction" is first #1 protest record
program note: Casey offers 'good news' from Ringo Starr
oldie played: Yakety Yak - Coasters
oldie played: I've Gotta Be Me - Sammy Davis Jr.
oldie played: Don't Just Stand There - Patty Duke
oldie played: Do You Want To Know A Secret - Beatles
oldie played: Eve Of Destruction - Barry McGuire
oldie played: You Don't Have To Be A Baby To Cry – Caravelles

7.) 08-22-70

Program #703-7
program note: aired the weekend of Saturday, August 15 & Sunday, August 16
story: Creedence Clearwater Revival's 12 gold records
story: The Mamas & Papas, millionaire hippies
story: Jackie Wilson's moustache priority
story: The Knickerbockers are not The Beatles
story: Diana Ross' first solo concert review
story: Englebert Humperdinck was laughed at
story: Desmond Dekker's #1 records in Jamaica
story: "In The Summertime" is #1 in six countries
odd chart stat: Motown Records has nine records in the Top 40
program error: Casey states in hour #1 outcue "...26 hit records to go...;" actually, after an oldie, hour #1 ended with #28
production note: program segment with Anne Murray's "Snowbird" is the shortest ever produced, with a total running time of 2:15 (see 10-06-79 for longest)
network commercial: Increase Records (Cruisin' 1961 LP)
network commercial: Increase Records (Cruisin' 1962 LP)
network commercial: Increase Records (Cruisin' LP series)
oldie played: California Dreamin' - Mamas & Papas
oldie played: Valley Of The Dolls - Dionne Warwick
oldie played: Israelites - Desmond Dekker & Aces
oldie played: Higher & Higher - Jackie Wilson
oldie played: Last Waltz - Kay Starr
oldie played: Lies - Knickerbockers

"We played the records 'live needle' for maximum sound quality, almost never on cart except for very rare occasions when a song was either so rare we dubbed it off rather than risk damaging it, or it was edited for time or content. We almost always used 45's, as supplied by Earl Jive, (because) 45's have surprisingly good sound when played with the best equipment. The same song was on both sides of a promo copy so that if one side got scratched up, you could just flip it over. Also, we wanted to be sure that we were playing the 'single version' that all the radio stations got........we didn't want to shake up the affiliates by playing a version that they never did."

Bill "Captain Billy" Hergonson, *AT40*'s original studio engineer, describing use of phonograph records during program production.

8.) 08-29-70

Program #703-8
program note: aired the weekend of Saturday, August 22 & Sunday, August 23
program note: subscribing radio station mentions begin
program note: six oldies are featured, with three between #20 & #15
program note: Casey makes references to chart movement as 'steps' and 'notches'
network commercial: Increase Records (Cruisin' LP series)
network commercial: Increase Records (Cruisin' 1959 LP)
network commercial: Increase Records (Cruisin' 1956 LP)
oldie played: Chances Are - Johnny Mathis
oldie played: She's A Heartbreaker - Gene Pitney
oldie played: Tammy - Debbie Reynolds
oldie played: Strangers In The Night - Frank Sinatra
oldie played: You Are My Sunshine - Ray Charles
oldie played: I Got You Babe - Sonny & Cher
story: Elvis Presley kissed Casey Kasem's date

8.) 08-29-70

Program #703-8 (CONTINUED)
story: Ernie is not a real person
story: James Brown shined shoes in front of a radio station he now owns
story: Debbie Reynolds' most-successful-female chart record
story: Johnny Mathis took a flying leap
story: Creedence Clearwater Revival received $500 for work in 1968
story: Frank Sinatra's dramatic comeback
odd chart stat: Ernie, a fictional *Sesame Street* TV character, debuts in the Top 40

9.) 09-05-70

Program #703-9
program note: aired the weekend of Saturday, August 29 & Sunday, August 30
story: Barbra Streisand (a.k.a. Mrs. Elliott Gould) is a combination of actress Sophia Loren & football player Y.A. Tittle
story: Ray Stevens is a great-great-grandson of a confederacy vice-president
story: The First Edition's vice-president
story: Stevie Wonder's grade-school #1 record
story: The Singing Nun's simultaneous #1 single & #1 LP
story: Diana Ross is The Jackson Five's co-manager
story: James Brown wore potato sack underwear
story: Melanie's overnight success
story: Gene Chandler's three recording names
story: Grand Funk Railroad strikes gold
network commercial: Cruisin' 1957 (Increase Records)
network commercial: Cruisin' 1958 (Increase Records)
network commercial: Cruisin' LP series (Increase Records)
program note: Casey mentions that his favorite record in Top 40 is "Tighter, Tighter"
oldie played: Second Hand Rose - Barbra Streisand
oldie played: Mr. Businessman - Ray Stevens
oldie played: Hey Little Girl - Dee Clark
oldie played: Dominique - Singing Nun
LP cut played: I Heard It Through The Grapevine - Creedence Clearwater Revival

10.) 09-12-70

Program #703-10
program note: aired the weekend of Saturday, September 5 & Sunday, September 6
story: Grand Funk Railroad's giant billboard
story: Neil Diamond's back-to-back records, both climbing up the chart
story: Paul Anka's babysitter
story: Hal Blaine played drums on five Grammy Award records
story: Rare Earth's Motown records
story: Bobby Sherman's big break
story: Elvis Presley's "O Solo Mio"
story: Dionne Warwick's diverse music styles
story: writer Carole King's hit record
story: Hotlegs' homemade "Neanderthal Man"
oldie played: A Taste Of Honey - Herb Alpert & Tijuana Brass
oldie played: It Might As Well Rain Until September - Carole King
oldie played: Diana - Paul Anka
oldie played: Do You Know The Way To San Jose - Dionne Warwick
oldie played: It's Now Or Never - Elvis Presley

11.) 09-19-70

Program #703-11
program note: aired the weekend of Saturday, September 12 & Sunday, September 13
story: Anne Murray taught physical education
story: The Beatles' break-up update

11.) 09-19-70 **Program #703-11 (CONTINUED)**
story: Terry Stafford's "Suspicion"
story: "Surfer's Stomp" was first surf song
story: "Little Darlin'" was the longest #2 record
story: disk jockey hit records
program error: Casey indicates that "In The Summertime" debuted at #22; actually it debuted at #32
program error: Casey states that "Hand Me Down World" is "....up four this week...."; actually it dropped four
program error: after #35, Casey states "...thirty-three hits to #1...."
oldie played: Surfer's Stomp - Marketts
oldie played: Suspicion - Terry Stafford
oldie played: Little Darlin' - Diamonds
oldie played: Help - Beatles
oldie played: Green Door - Jim Lowe
oldie played: Twist - Chubby Checker

12.) 09-26-70 **Program #703-12**
program note: aired the weekend of Saturday, September 19 & Sunday, September 20
story: Michael Nesmith answered a help wanted ad
story: Bob Dylan's honorary degree
story: Walter Brennan won three Academy Awards
story: Marvin Gaye's three duets
story: Smokey Robinson respected by The Beatles and Bob Dylan
story: Stevie Wonder's wedding
name origin: Connie Francis
name origin: Mungo Jerry
scratchy record: Closer To Home - Grand Funk Railroad
program mention: Linda Ronstadt sings Andy Griffith's new TV show theme
program mention: Anne Murray's "Snowbird" is #1 on *Billboard*'s Easy Listening chart
radio station edit: Lansing, Michigan
program error: Casey miscounts the number of Motown records in the Top 40
oldie played: Your Precious Love - Marvin Gaye & Tammi Terrell
oldie played: Old Rivers - Walter Brennan
oldie played: My Heart Has A Mind Of Its Own - Connie Francis
oldie played: I Second That Emotion - Smokey Robinson & Miracles
oldie played: Lay Lady Lay - Bob Dylan

13.) 10-03-70 **Program #704-1**
program note: aired the weekend of Saturday, September 26 & Sunday, September 27
story: Mungo Jerry nearly disbanded
story: Larry Verne was an advertising executive
story: The Lettermen annual income stops at $1 million
story: The New Seekers have an international base
story: Sonny James' country chart success
story: The Carpenters' commercial record
story: The Essex are five U.S. Marines
story: Creedence Clearwater Revival's Indian gift
program mention: Sesame Street's popularity
odd chart stat: The Carpenters' "We've Only Just Begun" debuts at #18
edited long version: Closer To Home - Grand Funk Railroad

13.) 10-03-70

Program #704-1 (CONTINUED)
program error: Casey mentions that Dawn's lead singer is Frankie Spinnelli, with the band comprising of two guys and three girls
program error: Casey states that "Lookin' Out My Back Door" is CCR's fourth #2 record; actually, it was their fifth
production error: Casey botches the outcue of "I Know I'm Losing You"
oldie played: Young Love - Sonny James
oldie played: Mr. Custer - Larry Verne
oldie played: Goin' Out Of My Head - Lettermen
oldie played: Easier Said Than Done - Essex
scratchy record: Young Love - Sonny James

14.) 10-10-70

Program #704-2
program note: aired the weekend of Saturday, October 3 & Sunday, October 4
story: Bobby Sherman's record sales
story: Neil Diamond's high school job was songwriting
story: Glen Campbell was near poverty
story: Kyu Sakamoto is only #1 Oriental artist
story: Poppy Family's Canadian record sales
story: "More" was nominated for an Academy Award
program mention: Capitol Records purchased "Neanderthal Man"
program mention: "Telstar" is popular in England
program mention: Stevie Wonder helped The Spinners
program error: in program recap at the end of hour #2, Casey references "Deeper & Deeper" as the week's biggest jumper; the record moved in the Hot 100 from #43 - #39
scratchy record: Long Long Time - Linda Ronstadt
review: Top 5 singles from 12-29-62
review: Top 5 singles from 02-24-68
review: Top 5 singles from 08-31-59
edited long version: Closer To Home - Grand Funk Railroad
oldie played: Sukiyaki - Kyu Sakamoto
oldie played: Love Is Blue - Paul Mauriat
oldie played: More - Kai Winding & Orchestra
oldie played: Telstar - Tornadoes
oldie played: The Three Bells - The Browns
LP cut played: I Heard It Through The Grapevine - Creedence Clearwater Revival

15.) 10-17-70

Program #704-3
program note: aired the weekend of Saturday, October 10 & Sunday, October 11
story: James Taylor's Apple Records flop
story: Eddy Arnold made money for Col. Tom Parker before Elvis Presley
story: Freda Payne was Leslie Uggams' understudy
story: Poppy Family's record cost only $355
story: Grand Funk Railroad spends $10,000 for monthly travel
story: Pat Boone wrote the book *Twixt Twelve & Twenty*
chart review: Top 5 from 07-13-68
network commercial: Tucson Arrow
network commercial: MGM Records (Burning Bridges - Mike Curb Congregation) (spot voiced by L.A. disk jockey Humble Harve)
oldie played: Make The World Go Away - Eddy Arnold
oldie played: Jumpin' Jack Flash - Rolling Stones
oldie played: Twixt Twelve And Twenty - Pat Boone
oldie played: Walk Don't Run - Ventures

16.) 10-24-70 **Program #704-4**
program note: aired the weekend of Saturday, October 17 & Sunday, October 18
story: "Love Is A Many Splendored Thing" heard every day on TV
story: Crosby, Stills, Nash & Young's non-protest record
story: Linda Ronstadt goes shoeless in concert
story: Santana's LP "Abraxas" defined
story: Simon & Garfunkel were Tom & Jerry
story: The Beatles' "Yesterday" was "Scrambled Eggs"
story: Free ignored as Blind Faith's back-up band
story: Jackson Five's early days
network commercial: Tucson Arrow
network commercial: MGM Records (Burning Bridges - Mike Curb Congregation)
(spot voiced by L.A. disk jockey Humble Harve)
chart review: Top 5 from 10-24-60
LP cut played: Black Magic Woman - Santana
oldie played: Love Is A Many Splendored Thing - Four Aces
oldie played: Yesterday - Beatles
oldie played: I Want To Be Wanted - Brenda Lee

17.) 10-31-70 **Program #704-5**
program note: aired the weekend of Saturday, October 24 & Sunday, October 25
story: Creedence Clearwater Revival, #1 jukebox artist
story: Joe Cocker's invisible guitar
story: Glen Campbell's golf addiction
story: Led Zeppelin beat The Beatles
story: James Taylor was almost a doctor
story: "Goodnight Irene" is biggest #1 record
story: "Kicks" is an anti-drug song
network commercial: MGM Records (Burning Bridges - Mike Curb Congregation)
(spot voiced by L.A. disk jockey Humble Harve)
network commercial: Tucson Arrow
review: Top 5 from 10-02-65
program error: Casey states that the group Dawn is made up of four guys - Frank, Ricky, Jim & Dave
odd chart stat: Motown Records has eight records in the Top 40
odd chart stat: The Partridge Family's "I Think I Love You" debuts at #17
oldie played: Kicks - Paul Revere & Raiders
oldie played: Hang On Sloopy - McCoys
oldie played: Goodnight Irene - Weavers
LP cut played: Immigrant Song - Led Zeppelin

18.) 11-07-70 **Program #704-6**
program note: aired the weekend of Saturday, October 31 & Sunday, November 1
network commercial: Tucson Arrow
network commercial: MGM Records (Burning Bridges - Mike Curb Congregation)
(spot voiced by L.A. disk jockey Humble Harve)
story: *Here Comes The Brides* TV star Bobby Sherman received 2 million fan letters
story: Elvis Presley breaks another record
story: David Cassidy & Shirley Jones dual relationship
story: commercial records
story: Candi Staton's one-song performance
story: "Wonderful Wonderful" & "So Rare" have longest chart runs
story: James Brown's non-Hot 100, million selling record
program note: Casey's show opening makes no reference to *American Top 40*
program error: Casey mentions the names of all members of Dawn:
Frank Spinnelli, Ricky Shannon, Jim Gregory & Dave Lavender
oldie played: So Rare - Jimmy Dorsey & Orchestra
oldie played: Wonderful Wonderful - Johnny Mathis
LP cut played: Gallows Pole - Led Zeppelin

19.) 11-14-70 **Program #704-7**
program note: aired the weekend of Saturday, November 7 & Sunday, November 8
story: Gary U.S. Bonds recruited off of the street to sing
story: The Partridge Family's Shirley Jones won an Academy Award
story: Jackson Five broke a Motown Records record
story: Eric Clapton's fellow performers
story: Dodie Stevens' record settles a military dispute
story: Christie took time from work to record
story: Elvis Presley was once paid $14-a-week
story: Led Zeppelin beat The Beatles
story: Neil Diamond's street group panhandled
network commercial: MGM Records (Burning Bridges - Mike Curb Congregation) (spot voiced by L.A. disk jockey Humble Harve)
network commercial: Tucson Arrow
oldie played: Pink Shoelaces - Dodie Stevens
oldie played: New Orleans - Gary U.S. Bonds
LP cut played: Immigrant Song - Led Zeppelin
odd chart stat: three unrelated artists with the same last name - James Taylor, R. Dean Taylor & Johnnie Taylor - are simultaneously in the Top 40 (occurred again 02-19-72, 02-24-79, 03-03-79 and 03-10-79)

20.) 11-21-70 **Program #704-8**
program note: aired the weekend of Saturday, November 14 & Sunday, November 15
story: Neil Diamond's three simultaneous Hot 100 records
story: Everly Brothers' Nashville break
story: Glen Campbell's first salary
story: #1 one-hit wonders
story: Brian Hyland's longest-titled #1 record
story: Smokey Robinson, executive
story: The Who's Tommy
story: Roger Williams was a boxer
oldie played: Autumn Leaves - Roger Williams
oldie played: In The Year 2525 - Zager & Evans
oldie played: Wake Up Little Susie - Everly Brothers
flipside played: Patch It Up - Elvis Presley
network commercial: MGM Records (Burning Bridges - Mike Curb Congregation) (spot voiced by L.A. disk jockey Humble Harve)
network commercial: Tucson Arrow
radio report: The Partridge Family is #1 at KJOY (Stockton, CA)
LP cut played: Immigrant Song - Led Zeppelin
odd chart stat: three unrelated artists with the same last name – James Taylor, R. Dean Taylor & Johnnie Taylor - are simultaneously in the Top 40 (occurred again 02-19-72, 02-24-79, 03-03-79 and 03-10-79)

21.) 11-28-70 **Program #704-9**
program note: aired the weekend of Saturday, November 21 & Sunday, November 22
program note: Casey welcomes radio programmers to Los Angeles conference
program note: Casey plays both sides of Elvis Presley's double-sided single
story: The Fifth Dimension's various backgrounds
story: The Supremes' five consecutive #1 records
story: The Kinks, one of the few remaining British Invasion acts
story: Elvis Presley's record sell-out Las Vegas concert
story: Joe Cocker dodged beer bottles
story: Shirley Jones is part-owner of a brewery
program mention: Eric Clapton formed Derek & The Dominos

21.) 11-28-70 **Program #704-9 (CONTINUED)**
flipside played: Patch It Up - Elvis Presley
oldie played: Are You Lonesome Tonight - Elvis Presley
LP cut played: Oye Como Va - Santana
network commercial: MGM Records (One Bad Apple - Osmonds)

22.) 12-05-70 **Program #704-10**
program note: aired the weekend of Saturday, November 28 & Sunday, November 29
odd chart stat: George Harrison's "My Sweet Lord"/"Isn't It A Pity" climbs from #72 to #13
flipside played: Isn't It A Pity - George Harrison
program note: George Harrison's "My Sweet Lord" is not played
story: James Brown's 300 pairs of shoes
story: Sugarloaf was Chocolate Hair
story: who is Badfinger?
story: Bobby Bloom's West Indies vacation
story: Bobby Vee fired Bob Dylan
story: James Taylor's broken hands and broken mind
story: Santana's Fillmore West star-billing
story: Smokey Robinson & The Miracles 13-year members and record label
edited long version: Black Magic Woman - Santana
program error: in introduction, Casey refers to Wilson Pickett's current chart position as #14; actually it was #19
network commercial: MGM Records (Mama - Heintje)
oldie played: Take Good Care Of My Baby - Bobby Vee
oldie played: Light My Fire - Doors

23.) 12-12-70 **Program #704-11**
program note: aired the weekend of Saturday, December 5 & Sunday, December 6
program note: Casey begins promoting the Top 80 of 1970 year-end program
story: Burton Cummings sang opera in high school
story: The Fifth Dimension rejected by Motown Records
story: Bobby Darin wrote "Splish Splash" in 12 minutes
story: Badfinger information from WKNX (Saginaw, MI) program director
story: Flaming Ember's record comes from The Bible
story: Bobby Bloom not a parental disappointment
record origin: Neil Diamond's "He Ain't Heavy....He's My Brother"
name origin: Tom Jones
radio report: The Presidents are #1 at WAIR (Winston-Salem, NC)
program error: at the end of hour #2, Casey states that the "...top 14 are coming up...."; actually, 13 records remained
network commercial: MGM Records (Mama - Heintje)
network commercial: MGM Records (Rosy's Theme [Theme from *Ryan's Daughter*] - Don Costa Orchestra)
network commercial: MGM Records (One Bad Apple - Osmonds)
network commercial: Tucson Arrow
review: Top 5 LPs
LP cut played: Oye Como Va - Santana
oldie played: Splish Splash - Bobby Darin
oldie played: Sixteen Tons - Tennessee Ernie Ford

24.) 12-19-70 **Program #704-12**
program note: aired the weekend of Saturday, December 12 & Sunday, December 13
program note: The Osmonds' "One Bad Apple" commercials produced especially for *American Top 40*

24.) 12-19-70

Program #704-12 (CONTINUED)
***Billboard* report error: "So Close" by Jake Holmes debuts at #39 on program; actually, it never reached *Billboard*'s Top 40**
story: Elton John predicted to be a star
story: Carlos Santana shuns publicity
story: Sonny James has 16 consecutive #1 country records
story: Neil Diamond would not perform a charity concert
story: Van Morrison pioneered use of the electric organ
story: Bing Crosby sold the most records
story: Brian Hyland got hired, but his group didn't
story: David Cassidy's audition for The Partridge Family
story: Barbra Streisand almost paid $8,000 to see husband Elliott Gould
odd chart stat: Neil Diamond's eight chart records in 1970
network commercial: Tucson Arrow
network commercial: MGM Records (One Bad Apple - Osmonds)
scratchy record: White Christmas - Bing Crosby
radio report: King Floyd is #1 at WAIR (Winston-Salem, NC)
radio report: Badfinger is #1 at WBBO (Forest City, NC)
radio report: George Harrison is #1 at WGAR (Cleveland) and KJOY (Stockton, CA)
LP cut played: Hope You're Feeling Better - Santana
oldie played: White Christmas - Bing Crosby
country chart record played: Endlessly - Sonny James

25.) 12-26-70

Program #704-13
program note: aired the weekend of Saturday, December 19 & Sunday, December 20
program note: Casey explains that The Guess Who's "Share The Land" (#30) is not played to allow air-time to play both sides of George Harrison's #1 "My Sweet Lord"/"Isn't It A Pity"; yet program time was made available to play two oldies
oldie played: Silent Night - Bing Crosby
oldie played: Higher & Higher - Jackie Wilson
program note: two songs are played at #1
program error: Casey's introduction of "My Sweet Lord" references that "George Harrison's parents are alive and well, living in England....;" actually, his mother passed away earlier in 1970
story: George Harrison is only Beatle to not come from a broken home
story: Bing Crosby's "Silent Night" sold more copies than any other record
story: Perry Como is in the Top 20 for first time in 12 years
story: Aretha Franklin's roller skate purchase
story: Jackie Wilson sang to buy his mother's gift
story: The Fifth Dimension's Marilyn McCoo and Florence LaRue won the same beauty contest
flipside played: Isn't It A Pity - George Harrison
flipside played: Patch It Up - Elvis Presley
network commercial: Tucson Arrow
network commercial: MGM Records (Wasn't It Easy - Bill Medley)
network commercial: MGM Records (Make Me Happy - Bobby Bloom)

Hi!

Here's the ranking by Billboard Magazine of the 80 top records of 1970. Their Charts Department complied the list ... and got it to us in time to pre-tape the show for Christmas and New Year's weekends. (That was too early for December sales figures to be included -- but, if they had been our AT40 statistician assures me that "Tears of a Clown" and "I Think I Love You" would rank among the Top 80 for 1970.)

Thanks for writing, and for listening, and I hope you have a great year!

Casey

1. BRIDGE OVER TROUBLED WATER — Simon & Garfunkel
2. CLOSE TO YOU — Carpenters
3. AMERICAN WOMAN/NO SUGAR TONIGHT — Guess Who
4. RAINDROPS KEEP FALLING ON MY HEAD — B. J. Thomas
5. WAR — Edwin Starr
6. AIN'T NO MOUNTAIN HIGH ENOUGH — Diana Ross
7. I'LL BE THERE — Jackson 5
8. GET READY — Rare Earth
9. LET IT BE — Beatles
10. BAND OF GOLD — Freda Payne
11. MAMA TOLD ME — Three Dog Night
12. EVERYTHING IS BEAUTIFUL — Ray Stevens
13. MAKE IT WITH YOU — Bread
14. HITCHIN' A RIDE — Vanity Fare
15. A B C — Jackson 5
16. THE LOVE YOU SAVE/I FOUND THAT GIRL — Jackson 5
17. CRACKLIN' ROSIE — Neil Diamond
18. CANDIDA — Dawn
19. THANK YOU/EVERYBODY IS A STAR — Sly & the Family Stone
20. SPILL THE WINE — Eric Burdon & War
21. OOH CHILD/DEAR PRUDENCE — Five Stairsteps
22. SPIRIT IN THE SKY — Norman Greenbaum
23. LAY DOWN (CANDLES IN THE RAIN) — Melanie/Edwin Hawkins Singers
24. BALL OF CONFUSION — Temptations
25. LOVE ON A TWO WAY STREET — Moments
26. ALL RIGHT NOW — Free
27. WHICH WAY YOU GOING BILLY — Poppy Family
28. I WANT YOU BACK — Jackson 5
29. JULIE, DO YA LOVE ME — Bobby Sherman
30. GREEN-EYED LADY — Sugarloaf
31. SIGNED, SEALED, DELIVERED — Stevie Wonder
32. RIDE CAPTAIN RIDE — Blues Image
33. VENUS — Shocking Blue
34. INSTANT KARMA — John Ono Lennon
35. PATCHES — Clarence Carter
36. LOOKIN' OUT MY BACK DOOR/ AS LONG AS I CAN SEE THE LIGHT — Creedence Clearwater Revival
37. RAINY NIGHT IN GEORGIA — Brook Benton
38. SOMETHING'S BURNING — Kenny Rogers & the 1st Edition
39. GIVE ME JUST A LITTLE MORE TIME — Chairmen of the Board
40. LOVE GROWS (WHERE MY ROSEMARY GOES) — Edison Lighthouse
41. LONG AND WINDING ROAD/ FOR YOU BLUE — Beatles
42. SNOWBIRD — Anne Murray
43. REFLECTIONS OF MY LIFE — Marmalade
44. HEY THERE LONELY GIRL — Eddie Holman
45. THE RAPPER — Jaggers
46. HE AIN'T HEAVY, HE'S MY BROTHER — Hollies
47. TIGHTER, TIGHTER — Alive and Kicking
48. COME AND GET IT — Badfinger
49. CECELIA — Simon & Garfunkel
50. LOVE LAND — Charles Wright & the Watts 103rd Street Rhythm Band
51. TURN BACK THE HANDS OF TIME — Tyrone Davis
52. LOLA — Kinks
53. IN THE SUMMERTIME — Mungo Jerry
54. INDIANA WANTS ME — R. Dean Taylor
55. (I KNOW) I'M LOSING YOU — Rare Earth
56. EASY COME, EASY GO — Bobby Sherman
57. EXPRESS YOURSELF — Charles Wright & the Watts 103rd Street Rhythm Band
58. STILL WATER (LOVE) — Four Tops
59. MAKE ME SMILE — Chicago
60. HOUSE OF THE RISING SUN — Frijid Pink
61. 25 OR 6 TO 4 — Chicago
62. MY BABY LOVES LOVIN' — White Plains
63. ~~LOVE OR LET ME BE LONELY~~ — Friends of Distinctio
64. UNITED WE STAND — Brotherhood of Man
65. WE'VE ONLY JUST BEGUN — Carpenters
66. ARIZONA — Mark Lindsay
67. FIRE AND RAIN — James Taylor
68. GROOVY SITUATION — Gene Chandler
69. EVIL WAYS — Santana
70. NO TIME — Guess Who
71. DIDN'T I — Delfonics
72. THE WONDER OF YOU/ MAMA LIKE THE ROSES — Elvis Presley
73. UP AROUND THE BEND/ RUN THROUGH THE JUNGLE — Creedence Clearwater Revival
74. WHY CAN'T I TOUCH YOU — Ronnie Dyson
75. I JUST CAN'T HELP BELIEVING — B. J. Thomas
76. IT'S A SHAME — Spinners
77. FOR THE LOVE OF HIM — Bobbi Martin
78. MISSISSIPPI QUEEN — Mountain
79. I WANT TO TAKE YOU HIGHER — Ike & Tina Turner & the Ikettes
80. THE LETTER — Joe Cocker

TOP 10 LP'S OF 1970

1. BRIDGE OVER TROUBLED WATER — Simon & Garfunkel
2. LED ZEPPELIN II — Led Zeppelin
3. CHICAGO — Chicago
4. ABBEY ROAD — Beatles
5. SANTANA — Santana
6. GET READY — Rare Earth
7. EASY RIDER — Soundtrack
8. BUTCH CASSIDY & THE SUNDANCE KID — Burt Bacharach/Soundtrack
9. JOE COCKER! — Joe Cocker
10. WAS CAPTURED LIVE AT THE FORUM — Three Dog Night

WATERMARK, INC. 931 N. La Cienega Blvd. Los Angeles, California 90069

During *AT40*'s first year-end countdown, Casey Kasem encouraged listeners to write-in and request a copy of the Top 80 of 1970 list.

1971

26.) 01-02-71

Program #711-1
SPECIAL: Top 80 Of 1970 (#80 - 41) (based on *Billboard*'s year-end Top 100)
program note: aired the weekend of Saturday, December 26 & Sunday, December 27
LP cut played: Keep The Customer Satisfied - Simon & Garfunkel
oldie played: Get Up I Feel Like Being A Sex Machine - James Brown
network commercial: MGM Records (Rosy's Theme [Theme from *Ryan's Daughter*] - Don Costa Orchestra)
network commercial: MGM Records (Theme from *Medical Center* - Lalo Schifrin)
network commercial: MGM Records (When I'm Dead & Gone - Bob Summers)

27.) 01-09-71

Program #711-2
SPECIAL: Top 80 Of 1970 (#40 - 1) (based on *Billboard*'s year-end Top 100)
program note: aired the weekend of Saturday, January 2 & Sunday, January 3
network commercial: MGM Records (Rosy's Theme [Theme from *Ryan's Daughter*] - Don Costa Orchestra)
network commercial: MGM Records (Theme from *Medical Center* - Lalo Schifrin)
network commercial: MGM Records (When I'm Dead & Gone - Bob Summers)
long version: Green-Eyed Lady - Sugarloaf

28.) 01-16-71

Program #711-3
program note: aired the weekend of Saturday, January 9 & Sunday, January 10
program note: Casey mentions that the show is heard Saturday nights at a Baltimore skating rink over radio station WCBM
story: Perry Como cleaned a barber shop
story: Judy Collins had polio and tuberculosis
story: Elvis Presley paid for his first recording session
story: The Lettermen, re-make kings
story: Stephen Stills is not singing "Finian's Rainbow"
odd chart stat: two debut records
network commercial: MGM Records (Wasn't It Easy - Bill Medley)
program error: Casey states that Neil Diamond's "He Ain't Heavy......" peaked at #21; actually it peaked at #20
program error: Casey points out that Dawn is made up of "....seven guys and one girl from south Philadelphia...."
program correction: Casey mentions that George Harrison's mother is deceased
radio report: Dawn is #1 at WHFM (Rochester, NY)
oldie played: Tennessee Waltz - Patti Page
oldie played: Hurt So Bad - Lettermen
oldie played: To Each His Own - Platters

29.) 01-23-71

Program #711-4
program note: aired the weekend of Saturday, January 16 & Sunday, January 17
network commercial: MGM Records (Make Me Happy - Bobby Bloom)
network commercial: MGM Records (Theme from *Medical Center* - Lalo Schifrin)
network commercial: Increase Records (Cruisin' 1956)
network commercial: Increase Records (Cruisin' 1961)
network commercial: Increase Records (Cruisin' LP series)
review: Top 5 from 01-22-66
review: Top 5 LPs
story: Barbra Streisand thought to have sung through her nose
story: Bobby Goldsboro never records music during the World Series
story: "Amazing Grace" composed 300 years ago

29.) 01-23-71

Program #711-4 (CONTINUED)
long version: Mr. Bojangles - Nitty Gritty Dirt Band
program error: Casey mentions that "Most Of All" by B.J. Thomas debuted "....last week at #40...."; actually debuted 01-09-71 at #40
program error: Casey reiterates that the group Dawn is a seven-man, one-girl group from south Philadelphia, during introduction to #1
flipside played: There Goes My Everything - Elvis Presley
oldie played: Sounds Of Silence - Simon & Garfunkel
oldie played: Wonderland By Night - Bert Kaempfert & Orchestra
LP cut played: Waiting On You All - George Harrison

30.) 01-30-71

Program #711-5
program note: aired the weekend of Saturday, January 23 & Sunday, January 24
story: The Bee Gees thought to be The Beatles
story: Carla Thomas hit the charts before her father, Rufus Thomas
story: Jerry Reed commutes from Nashville to Los Angeles
story: Elvis Presley uses karate in his nightclub act
story: The Nitty Gritty Dirt Band's kinky instruments
story: The Monkees' first two LPs sold more than eight million copies
radio report: Liz Damon's Orient Express was #1 at KPOI (Honolulu)
radio report: The Osmonds are #1 at KCPX (Salt Lake City)
radio report: The Bee Gees are #1 at WJTO (Bath, Me)
network commercial: Increase Records (Cruisin' LP series)
network commercial: MGM Records (It Was A Good Time - Eydie Gorme)
review: Top 5 from 01-30-61
review: Top 5 from 01-29-66
program note: Casey mentions that the Top 80 of 1970 year-end lists are being mailed to those requesting a copy
odd chart stat: The Osmonds' "One Bad Apple" moves from #34 to #9
oldie played: We Can Work It Out - Beatles
oldie played: I'm A Believer - Monkees
oldie played: Theme From *A Summer Place* - Percy Faith
oldie played: Will You Still Love Me Tomorrow - Shirelles

31.) 02-06-71

Program #711-6
program note: aired the weekend of Saturday, January 30 & Sunday, January 31
story: Dean Martin was a prize fighter
story: Donovan was the first from the British Isles
story: *Love Story* is breaking box office records
story: Stephen Stills' Midas touch
story: "I Wanna Be Around" was co-written by an Ohio housewife
story: Lynn Anderson was tricked
network commercial: Increase Records (Cruisin' LP series)
network commercial: MGM Records (It Was A Good Time - Eydie Gorme)
radio report: Rare Earth is #1 at WAIR (Winston-Salem, NC)
radio report: The Osmonds are #1 at KJOY (Stockton, CA)
program error: Casey states that Barbra Streisand's "People" peaked at #4; actually it peaked at #5
LP cut played: Apple Scruffs - George Harrison
flipside played: Isn't It A Pity - George Harrison
oldie played: I Wanna Be Around - Tony Bennett
oldie played: Memories Are Made Of This - Dean Martin
oldie played: Sunshine Superman - Donovan

32.) 02-13-71

Program #711-7
program note: aired the weekend of Saturday, February 6 & Sunday, February 7
story: The Osmonds were a barbershop quartet
story: Bob Dylan booed for using an electric guitar
story: The Band on the cover of *Time*
story: Peter & Gordon are the only British duo with a #1 record
story: Liz Damon is multi-national
story: Elton John's concert reviews
story: Petula Clark's successes
story: The Nitty Gritty Dirt Band bought and tailored second-hand clothes
radio report: Dave Edmunds is #1 at WQXT (Palm Beach, FL)
program error: Casey mentions that Creedence Clearwater Revival has four records that peaked at #2; actually there were five
network commercial: Increase Records (Cruisin' LP series)
network commercial: MGM Records (It Was A Good Time - Eydie Gorme)
program note: Casey was at concert where Bob Dylan was booed
program note: Casey welcomes new subscribing radio stations for first time
odd chart stat: Wadsworth Mansion's "Sweet Mary" debuts at #15
odd chart stat: Elton John's "Your Song" at #8 for four consecutive weeks
long version: Like A Rolling Stone - Bob Dylan (5:45)
oldie played: The Weight - The Band
oldie played: My Love - Petula Clark
oldie played: Like A Rolling Stone - Bob Dylan
oldie played: A World Without Love - Peter & Gordon

33.) 02-20-71

Program #711-8
program note: aired weekend of Saturday, February 13 & Sunday, February 14
odd chart stat: ten records in Top 40 are by family acts
story: Lou Christie recorded for six record labels
story: world's biggest hit of 1958
story: Janis Joplin's legacy
story: Gladys Knight's big break
story: The Mills Brothers' first hit was in 1929
story: The Osmonds' success in Japan
network commercial: MGM Records (It Was A Good Time - Eydie Gorme)
LP cut played: Superstar - Murray Head & Trinidad Singers
oldie played: Lightnin' Strikes - Lou Christie
oldie played: Cab Driver - Mills Brothers
oldie played: Volare - Domenico Modugno

34.) 02-27-71

Program #711-9
program note: aired weekend of Saturday, February 20 & Sunday, February 21
story: Janis Joplin is the biggest female artist
story: Ike & Tina Turner's concert act
story: Kris Kristofferson's songwriting talent
story: Tom Jones is England's biggest male artist
story: Frank & Nancy Sinatra's chart feat
story: MGM Records' Mike Curb is the youngest record company president
story: Diana Ross is #1 in England
odd chart stat: two brother acts are #1 and #2
odd chart stat: three versions of "Theme from *Love Story*" in the Top 40
network commercial: MGM Records (Paul Frees & The Poster People)
LP cut played: Move Over - Janis Joplin
oldie played: These Boots Are Made For Walkin' - Nancy Sinatra
oldie played: Pony Time - Chubby Checker

Released on MGM Records and advertised on *AT40*, this was the LP cover to *Paul Frees and the Poster People*. A renown voice impersonator, Paul Frees (pictured in the middle row, second from the right) offered his creative renditions of numerous celebrities including Peter Lorre, Clark Gable and Bela Lugosi.

35.) 03-06-71 **Program #711-10**
program note: aired the weekend of Saturday, February 27 & Sunday, February 28
story: MGM Records' Mike Curb identifies every Top 40 artist
story: Francis Lai's two Oscar award nominations
story: Elvis Presley is #1 in the world
story: Kay Starr's success
story: who is Mr. Bojangles?
story: Gordon Lightfoot's lower paying job
program mention: Janis Joplin's "Mercedes Benz" is an unorthodox prayer
program offer: Casey provides details on how to obtain a free wallet photo of

The Osmonds
network commercial: MGM Records (Paul Frees & The Poster People)
LP cut played: Mercedes Benz - Janis Joplin
oldie played: Rock And Roll Waltz - Kay Starr
oldie played: Suspicious Minds - Elvis Presley

36.) 03-13-71 Program #711-11
program note: aired the weekend of Saturday, March 6 & Sunday, March 7
story: "Amazing Grace" written by a slave trader
story: Glen Campbell was one of The Champs
story: Henry Mancini's Grammy Awards
story: Bobby Sherman's three ABC-TV cancellations
story: Creedence Clearwater Revival is the world's top rock group
story: Janis Joplin's voice is whiskey-soaked
network commercial: Yamaha Motorcycles
program note: Casey plays both sides of Creedence Clearwater Revival's double-sided single
flipside played: Hey Tonight - Creedence Clearwater Revival
oldie played: Lisbon Antigua - Nelson Riddle Orchestra
oldie played: Tequila - Champs
LP cut played: Buried Alive In The Blues - Full Tilt Boogie Band

37.) 03-20-71 Program #711-12
program note: aired the weekend of Saturday, March 13 & Sunday, March 14
story: Elvis Presley can earn no more than $5 million annually
story: the life of Janis Joplin
story: Wilson Pickett will quit the music business by age 30
story: Tammy Wynette's country chart success
story: 1970's top producers
story: Tommy Facenda's 28 records
story: What Is Life? (It's A Fountain)
story: Jerry Reed gave up fishing for Elvis Presley
program note: Casey mentions that it's been 9 months for "Burning Bridges"
program note: Casey mentions that The Osmonds' wallet photos are gone
program note: show's closing is unusually short
radio report: The Jackson Five are #1 on KACY (Oxnard, CA)
radio report: Jerry Reed are #1 on KJOY (Stockton, CA)
network commercial: Yamaha Motorcycles
network commercial: Dore' Records (Hangin' In There - Hudson & Landry)
oldie played: Stand By Your Man - Tammy Wynette
oldie played: High School USA - Tommy Facenda
oldie played: Surrender - Elvis Presley
LP cut played: Mercedes Benz - Janis Joplin

38.) 03-27-71 Program #711-13
program note: aired the weekend of Saturday, March 20 & Sunday, March 21
story: James Brown, as a poor child, danced for coins
story: The Temptations earned $15 for their first concert
story: Creedence Clearwater Revival's LP is certified gold prior to release
story: Partridge Family's TV show is in second place, right after *The Flip Wilson Show*
network commercial: Yamaha Motorcycles
network commercial: Dore' Records (Hangin' In There - Hudson & Landry)
program note: Casey plays both sides of Elvis Presley's double-sided single
flipside played: Rags To Riches - Elvis Presley
review: Top 5 LPs
LP cut played: My Baby - Janis Joplin
oldie played: If - Perry Como
oldie played: Blue Moon - Marcels
oldie played: Poor People Of Paris - Les Baxter

39.) 04-03-71 **Program #711-14**
program note: aired the weekend of Saturday, March 27 & Sunday, March 28
story: Glen Campbell was the voice of Steve McQueen
story: "Smoke Smoke Smoke" was an anti-cigarette record
story: highest debut record
story: Tom Jones' tonsils displayed
story: Creedence Clearwater Revival's name - past and present
story: B.J. Thomas reluctantly recorded "Raindrops Keep Falling" while ill
story: Terry Knight's pretend Top 40 radio show
program note: Casey opens show with a new station welcome
program error: Casey reports that Van Morrison's "Blue Money" ".....dropping two points....."; actually it moved up two points
review: Top 5 LPs
network commercial: Dore' Records (Hangin' In There - Hudson & Landry)
LP cut played: Move Over - Janis Joplin
oldie played: Love Me Tender - Elvis Presley
oldie played: Closer To Home - Grand Funk Railroad
oldie played: Baby Love - Supremes
oldie played: Smoke Smoke Smoke - Tex Williams

40.) 04-10-71 **Program #712-1**
program note: aired the weekend of Saturday, April 3 & Sunday, April 4
story: Brewer & Shipley's explanation of "One Toke Over The Line"
story: Marvin Gaye has Motown's biggest selling single
story: Jimmy Osmond had a gold record in Japan before The Osmonds
story: Frank Sinatra's retirement just announced
story: Jimmy Clanton's "Just A Dream" described a personal relationship
story: rock era's most popular instrumental
network commercial/program offer: The Osmonds exclusive 1971 2'x 3' poster is available to *AT40* listeners; commercial recorded by The Osmonds
odd chart stat: The Jackson Five's "Never Can Say Goodbye" debuts at #15
LP cut played: Mercedes Benz - Janis Joplin
oldie played: My Way - Frank Sinatra
oldie played: You're My Soul & Inspiration - Righteous Brothers
oldie played: Just A Dream - Jimmy Clanton
oldie played: Honky Tonk - Bill Doggett

41.) 04-17-71 **Program #712-2**
program note: aired the weekend of Saturday, April 10 & Sunday, April 11
program note: Casey's show opening includes a promo for the 05-01-71 special
***Billboard* report error: chart positions of Jackson Five's "Never Can Say Goodbye" & Cat Stevens' "Wild World" reversed on program**
story: Alice Cooper's concert audience walked out
story: Elvis Presley's first #1 record
story: Santo & Johnny is only brother group with a #1 instrumental
story: Karen Carpenter became a drummer
story: Ocean's fan mail from evangelist Billy Graham
story: Jeannie C. Riley's "Harper Valley P.T.A." is fastest selling single
story: human cannibalism of "Timothy"
story: Frankie Laine was a world record-holding marathon dancer
network commercial/program offer: Osmonds & *American Top 40* poster
oldie played: Sleepwalk - Santo & Johnny
oldie played: Mule Train - Frankie Laine
oldie played: Heartbreak Hotel - Elvis Presley
oldie played: Harper Valley PTA - Jeannie C. Riley
LP cut played: Half Moon - Janis Joplin

42.) 04-24-71 **Program #712-3**
program note: aired the weekend of Saturday, April 17 & Sunday, April 18
story: Van Morrison's first singing job
story: Johnny Cash is most successful country artist on pop chart
story: Del Shannon collects electric trains
story: first million selling LP
story: Cat Stevens' tuberculosis
story: Neil Diamond's opposition to "Solitary Man"
network commercial/program offer: Osmonds & *American Top 40* poster
network commercial: Dentyne
network commercial: Certs
review: Top 5 LPs
question: biggest upward chart jumps
program error: Casey promotes upcoming special by mentioning that "...three weeks from now....."; actually, it was two weeks
radio report: The Buoys are #1 on WNDR (Syracuse, NY)
LP cut played: Buried Alive In The Blues - Full Tilt Boogie Band
oldie played: Banana Boat (Day-O) - Harry Belafonte
oldie played: Guess Things Happen That Way - Johnny Cash
oldie played: How High The Moon - Les Paul & Mary Ford
oldie played: Runaway - Del Shannon

43.) 05-01-71 **Program #712-4**
program note: aired the weekend of Saturday, April 24 & Sunday, April 25
program note: two shows dated 05-01-71, a regular and a special program
program note: upcoming special ties in with National Music Week
program note: show's closing includes no mention of next week's special
story: Matthews' Southern Comfort's generation gap
story: Les Paul's music teacher said he had no talent
story: the meaning of "I Play And Sing"
story: "Look For A Star" had four simultaneous Top 30 versions
story: John Lennon part of the most successful songwriting team
story: Paul McCartney's desire for anonymous Beatle concerts
name origin: The Rascals
name origin: Three Dog Night
long version: Here Comes The Sun - Richie Havens
network commercial: Twenty Hits
network commercial: Certs
network commercial: Dentyne
LP cut played: I Don't Know How To Love Him - Yvonne Elliman

44.) 05-01-71 **Program #712-5**
SPECIAL: Top 40 Artists Of The Rock Era
for a complete list of records in this special, see Rob Durkee's *American Top 40: The Countdown of the Century*
program note: aired the weekend of Saturday, May 1 & Sunday, May 2
program note: The Beatles & Elvis Presley records are played back-to-back without Casey's outcue/introduction talk units

"When we were doing the show so that it aired just AS the chart was being published, we got the chart in the late afternoon of a Tuesday...they would let Earl Jive know what the new adds were and he would get the discs.....Don (Bustany) would get bio info from the labels if possible and write the intros for the new adds.......We would record, duplicate and ship the show all in one big long night! Man were we glad when we switched over to the new schedule...and <u>not one listener knew the difference</u>......"

Bill Hergonson, *AT40*'s original studio engineer, describing the transition from recording the program with advance *Billboard* chart data.

931 N. La Cienega Boulevard
Los Angeles, California 90069
(213) 659-3834

FOR WEEK ENDING: SPECIAL: MAY 1, 1971
CYCLE NO. 712 PROGRAM 5 OF 13
REEL & HOUR NO. 3-3
PAGE NO. 6

I certify that American Top 40, including each of the below listed Watermark commercials, also referred to as "Network Commercials" was broadcast on ______ from ______ until ______ on ______ ______.
CALL LETTERS — TIME STARTED — TIME ENDED — DAY — DATE AND YEAR

______
signed, ENGINEER ON DUTY

SCHEDULED START TIME	ACTUAL TIME	ELEMENT	RUNNING TIME
26:57		LOGO: AMERICAN TOP 40	:03
27:00		TALK UNIT	:44
27:41		#5 - WHERE DID OUR LOVE GO - Supremes	2:32
30:07		TALK UNIT	:07
30:19		LOGO: CASEYS COAST TO COAST	:02
30:21		LOCAL INSERT: C-6	:60
31:21		LOGO: AMERICAN TOP 40	:04
31:25		TALK UNIT	:13
31:38		#4 - WHO'S SORRY NOW - Connie Francis	2:13
33:50		TALK UNIT	:22
34:12		LOGO: CASEYS COAST TO COAST	:01
34:13		LOCAL INSERT: C-7	:60
35:13		LOGO: AMERICAN TOP 40	:03
35:16		TALK UNIT	:23
35:39		#3 - LOVE LETTERS IN THE SAND - Pat Boone	2:12
37:52		TALK UNIT	:22
38:14		LOGO: CASEYS COAST TO COAST	:03
38:17		LOCAL INSERT: C-8	:60
39:17		LOGO: AMERICAN TOP 40	:03
39:20		TALK UNIT	:14
39:34		#2 - I WANT TO HOLD YOUR HAND/LET IT BE - Beatles	
45:39		TALK UNIT	:44
46:23		NETWORK COML: DENTYNE #2	:30
46:51		NETWORK COML: 20 HITS/Cavnar Assoc.	:30
47:23		TALK UNIT	:37
48:00		#1 - DON'T BE CRUEL/NOW OR NEVER/SUSPICIOUS MINDS/- Elvis	
57:13		TALK UNIT	:27
57:40		THEME UP & UNDER	:09
57:49		TALK UNIT	:15
58:04		THEME PLAYOUT IN CLEAR TO: 59:49	
		STATION I.D.:	:10
		LOCAL INSERT:	:60

A rare look at a 1971 cue sheet containing network commercials. This is the last of six pages of cue sheets from the May 1, 1971 special, the Top 40 Artists of the Rock Era.

45.) 05-08-71 **Program #712-6**
chart date/broadcast change: preceding week's special program allowed radio stations to begin airing this show, and future shows, on the same date/week-end of *Billboard* charts; previously, *American Top 40* aired chart one week in advance of chart date
program note: aired the weekend of Saturday, May 8 & Sunday, May 9
program error: in reviewing past and present chart appearances of "I Don't Know How To Love Him," Casey states that a version by Karen Wyman was "....in the Hot 100 for several weeks a few months ago....;" actually, no version by Wyman ever appeared in the Hot 100; also no mention given to the Hot 100 appearance of the version by The Kimberleys
program error: Casey states that Dawn is from Philadelphia
story: "Chick-A-Boom" is from a Saturday morning TV show
story: *Dr. Zhivago*'s book, movie and music awards
story: Freddie Cannon likes city songs
story: Bobby Vinton's aggressive attempt to obtain a recording contract
story: Honey Cone members came from other recording acts
story: a resurrected "Superstar"
question: pop music's first million selling record
question: highest debut record
review: Top 5 LPs
network commercial: Twenty Hits
network commercial: Certs
network commercial: Dentyne
oldie played: Way Down Yonder In New Orleans - Freddy Cannon
oldie played: Somewhere, My Love - Ray Conniff
oldie played: My Blue Heaven - Fats Domino
LP cut played: Hosanna - Jesus Christ Superstar

46.) 05-15-71 **Program #712-7**
story: Paul Humphrey played on 1,000 chart recordings
story: Helen Reddy was a Catholic priest
story: Pat Boone has the most consecutive weeks on chart
story: The Mamas & Papas bought a Beverly Hills mansion
story: Mick Jagger is rock's greatest live entertainer
story: current wave of religious pop music
network commercial: Twenty Hits
network commercial: Certs
network commercial: Dentyne
program note: after three weeks on the Top 40, no information was provided for the record "Battle Hymn of Lt. Calley" to explain its meaning, who the recording artists (C Company featuring Terry Nelson) were, or how the record was certified by *Billboard* as a million seller after only one week on the chart
oldie played: I Almost Lost My Mind - Pat Boone
oldie played: Monday Monday - Mamas & Papas
oldie played: Mother-In-Law - Ernie K. Doe
LP cut played: Right Between The Eyes - Crosby, Stills, Nash & Young

47.) 05-22-71 **Program #712-8**
story: Barry Gordy's first hit record
story: Donny Osmond's phone call to radio station KCPX (Salt Lake City)
story: The Jackson Five's success
long version: What's Going On - Marvin Gaye
odd chart stat: The Carpenters' "Rainy Days & Mondays" debuts at #20
odd chart stat: three records in the Top 40 from "Jesus Christ Superstar"
review: Top 5 LPs

47.) 05-22-71 **Program #712-8 (CONTINUED)**
program error: Casey's promo for a Ricky Nelson record includes that it was #1 "...15 years ago today...;" actually, it was #1 10 years ago
network commercial: Certs
network commercial: Twenty Hits
network commercial: Dentyne
oldie played: Travelin' Man - Rick Nelson
oldie played: Money - Barrett Strong
oldie played: When A Man Loves A Woman - Percy Sledge
LP cut played: You Got To Move - Rolling Stones

48.) 05-29-71 **Program #712-9**
program note: due to complaints by Beatle fans, Casey justifies why Elvis was ranked at #1 in the recent *AT40* special countdown
program note: in answering a question, Casey mentions that he is the voice of Dexter Carter on ABC-TV's *Hot Wheels*
program note: Casey lists records falling off the Top 40, mentioning that Neil Diamond's "I Am...I Said" fell from #14 to #41
story: Murray Head's "Superstar" on Hot 100 for 27 weeks
story: Yvonne Elliman's role in *Jesus Christ Superstar*
story: Roy Orbison's start with Sun Records
story: The Rolling Stones are outrageous, ugly, violent and a travesty
story: Bobbie Gentry is only female country artist with a #1 LP
story: Eddie Holland's only hit
question: biggest Hot 100 chart fall
program error: in answering the question about the biggest Hot 100 chart fall, Casey indicates that Tony Joe White's "Polk Salad Annie" fell off the chart from position #12; actually, the record's chart fall positions were #11--#13--#28--#44
network commercial: Twenty Hits
network commercial: Certs
network commercial: Dentyne
long version: Here Comes The Sun - Richie Havens
oldie played: Running Scared - Roy Orbison
oldie played: Jamie - Eddie Holland
oldie played: Ode To Billy Joe - Bobbie Gentry

49.) 06-05-71 **Program #712-10**
program note: full-page *Billboard* advertisement reports *AT40* is #1 on radio station KRLA in Los Angeles (heard on 102 stations, as of 05-15-71)
program note: Casey relates 2 stories (Paul Humphrey/*Romeo & Juliet*) in one segment
network commercial: Twenty Hits
network commercial: Certs
network commercial: Dentyne
story: The Doors' seven gold LPs now beat Creedence Clearwater Revival
story: David Cassidy is more actor than singer
story: Barbra Streisand's daydreams
story: Three Dog Night makes $400,000 a month, weekends only
story: The Beatles were Chris Montez's back-up band in 1963
story: Aretha Franklin's record-tying record
story: Paul Humphrey played on 1,000 chart recordings
long version: Here Comes The Sun - Richie Havens
production error: running out of airtime may have contributed to a bad edit during Casey's closing of hour #1
oldie played: People - Barbra Streisand
oldie played: Paint It Black - Rolling Stones
oldie played: Love Theme From *Romeo & Juliet* - Henry Mancini
oldie played: Call Me - Chris Montez

The hottest 10 minutes In Radio Have never been On the Air.

Yet our 10 minutes have helped over 100 program directors make a rewarding decision for their stations. They've helped over 100 sales managers bring new ad revenues to their stations.

Our hot 10 minutes? The demo tape for our AMERICAN TOP 40 program. It's made some radio history in just 11 short months. And we'd like you to hear it for yourself and for your station.

With this short sample of AMERICAN TOP 40, you'll hear how our 3-hour weekly special works. You'll hear how Casey Kasem's absorbing, intelligent presentation of Billboard's weekly music survey blankets the 12-34 demographics. You'll hear for yourself why the production and content of AMERICAN TOP 40 has been so smoothly adapted to over 100 station formats and has sold over 600 local advertisers. And you'll hear a lot of things that might change your mind about syndicated programming.

Along with the demo, we'll send you facts. Ratings proof: AMERICAN TOP 40 is Number One in Los Angeles on KRLA. Our latest station line-up: 102 great stations as of 5/15—60 of the top 100 markets, 42 smaller markets. Sales testimonials: reports from stations of all sizes who are making money and happily renewing each quarter. Production data: simple and flexible ways to make the show an integral part of local programming.

AMERICAN TOP 40 is the most successful syndicated music program ever, and it's still growing, thanks to programming people like yourself. It all started with our 10-minute demo tape.

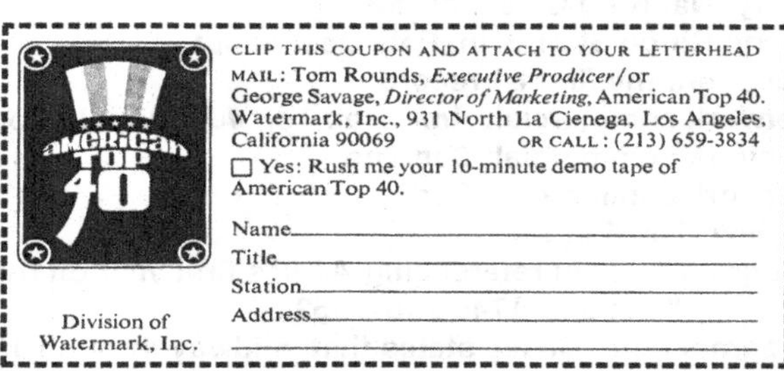

Division of
Watermark, Inc.

CLIP THIS COUPON AND ATTACH TO YOUR LETTERHEAD

MAIL: Tom Rounds, *Executive Producer*/or George Savage, *Director of Marketing*, American Top 40. Watermark, Inc., 931 North La Cienega, Los Angeles, California 90069 OR CALL: (213) 659-3834

☐ Yes: Rush me your 10-minute demo tape of American Top 40.

Name__________

Title__________

Station__________

Address__________

In an effort to create additional program awareness and recruit more radio stations to the expanding *AT40* network, this advertisement appeared in the June 5, 1971 edition of *Billboard* magazine.

50.) 06-12-71 **Program #712-11**
story: Honey Cone members came from other recording acts
story: The Beatles sold one million records every week for seven years
story: Richie Havens sold paintings in Greenwich Village
story: Pat Boone's clean-cut image
story: The Osmonds have 10 saxophones
long version: Here Comes The Sun - Richie Havens
question: record with most consecutive weeks at #1
question: Top 40 record with the most longevity
review: Top 5 LPs
network commercial: Dentyne
network commercial: Certs
network commercial: Twenty Hits
oldie played: Moody River - Pat Boone
oldie played: Paperback Writer - Beatles
oldie played: Wayward Wind - Gogi Grant

51.) 06-19-71 **Program #712-12**
network commercial: Dentyne
network commercial: Certs
network commercial: *American Top 40*'s Double Dozen LP
(a 2-LP set of oldies with stories from Casey about each recording printed on the album jacket)
(the :30 spot was voiced by *AT40* executive producer Tom Rounds, and engineered by Bill Hergonson)
program note: *American Top 40*'s origin is included in the "Double Dozen" LP
question: all-time biggest selling record
name origin: Hamilton, Joe Frank & Reynolds
story: Frank Sinatra's 20-year span between #1 records
story: Carly Simon's rave reviews
story: Jerry Reed quit high school three times
story: Isaac Hayes founded the Hayes Foundation
story: David Cassidy predicted to have one more year of popularity
story: Gary U.S. Bonds recruited off the street to sing
odd chart stat: Carole King's single & LP simultaneously hit #1
oldie played: Prisoner Of Love - Perry Como
oldie played: Quarter To Three - Gary U.S. Bonds
oldie played: Strangers In The Night - Frank Sinatra

52.) 06-26-71 **Program #712-13**
story: "Teen Angel" was a joke
story: Freda Payne sang with many jazz band greats
story: Nat King Cole's discovery
story: Ringo Starr is in, Pete Best is out
question: the first #1 record
network commercial: *American Top 40*'s Double Dozen LP
network commercial: Dentyne
network commercial: Certs
review: Top 5 LPs
program note: in referencing *AT40*'s first year on the air, Casey mentions that "...this is *AT40* show #52...."
program note: Casey states that, midway through 1971, Three Dog Night's "Joy To The World" is 1971's best seller
program note: instead of running a "Double Dozen" LP commercial, Casey read the names and artists of all songs on the album
flipside played: I Feel The Earth Move - Carole King
oldie played: Teen Angel - Mark Denning
oldie played: Too Young - Nat King Cole

Double Dozen Album of Hits, Volume 1
STEREO

Advertised on *AT40* for 14 consecutive weeks, this was the cover for the *American Top 40 Double Dozen Album of Hits, Volume 1.*

53.) 07-03-71

Program #713-1
program note: Casey mentions that *AT40* has been on the air for one year, starting on seven radio stations (now heard on 118 stations)
odd chart stat: The Rolling Stones have two records in Top 40 for the first time
story: Roberta Flack graduated from college at age 19
story: Bobby Lewis raised in an orphanage
story: Tommy James & The Shondells - one-hit wonders
story: Carly Simon's "Winkin', Blinkin' & Nod"
story: Hamilton, Joe Frank & Reynolds were The T-Bones
record origin: The Raiders' "Indian Reservation"
question: two sisters debate over The Osmonds
network commercial: Certs
network commercial: Dentyne
network commercial: *American Top 40*'s Double Dozen LP
flipside played: I Feel The Earth Move - Carole King
oldie played: Tossin' & Turnin' - Bobby Lewis

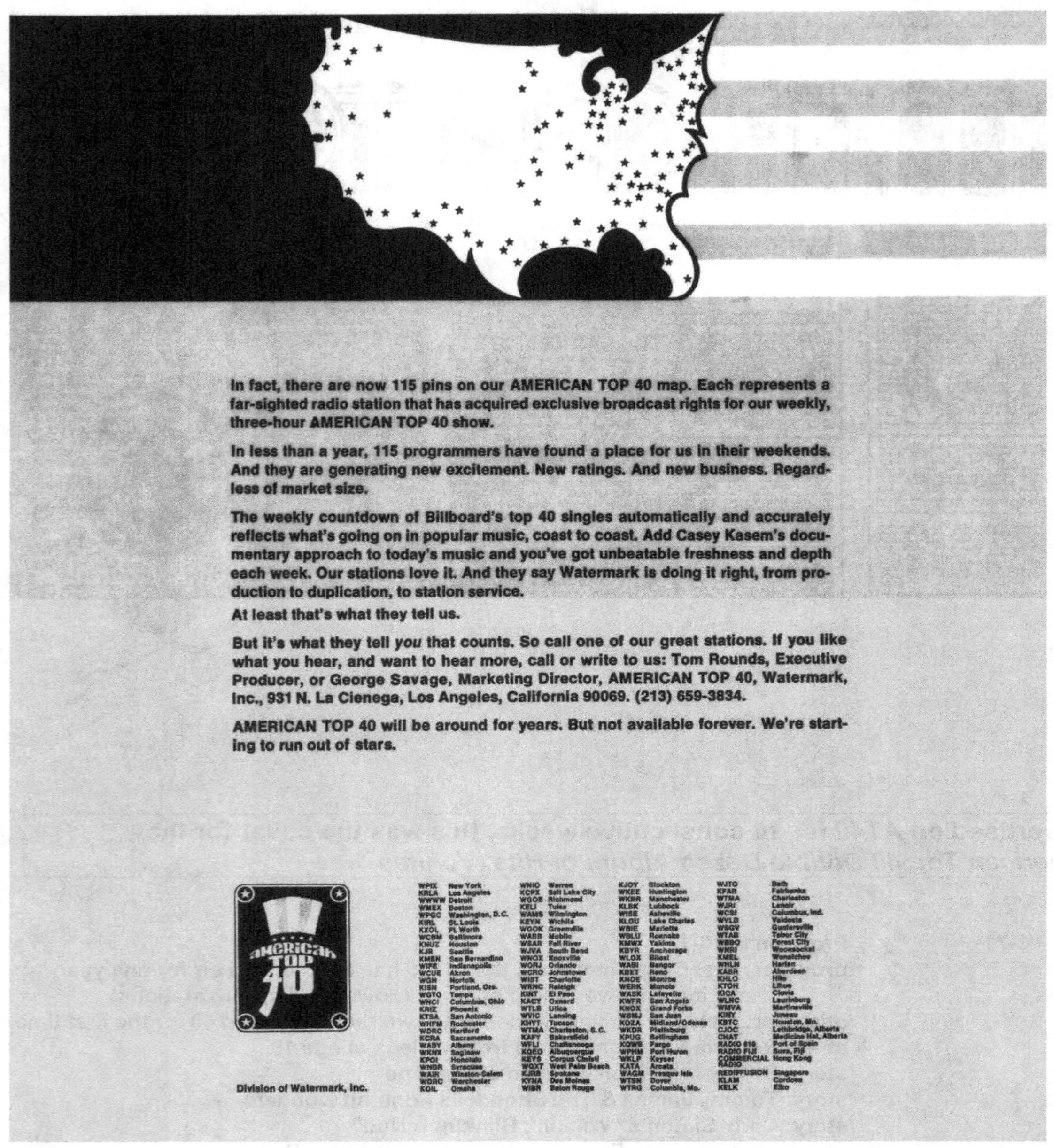

Upon its first anniversary, *AT40* ran this advertisement which appeared in the July 3, 1971 edition of *Billboard* magazine. The ad listed all radio stations carrying the weekly countdown and encouraged any contemplating station to call one on the list for a testament to the program's success.

54.) 07-10-71

Program #713-2
story: James Brown's means of transportation
story: The Ink Spots were singing janitors
story: Delaney & Bonnie's early days
story: The Beginning Of The End's commercial
story: the invention of the fuzz-tone guitar
story: Paul Williams' first song
odd chart stat: Carole King is #1 on the Hot 100 & Top LP charts for four consecutive weeks
program error: Casey mentions that Dawn is from Philadelphia
question: biggest #1 instrumental
network commercial: Dentyne
network commercial: Certs
network commercial: *American Top 40*'s Double Dozen LP
flipside played: I Feel The Earth Move - Carole King
oldie played: The Gypsy - Inkspots
oldie played: Don't Worry - Marty Robbins

55.) 07-17-71

Program #713-3
story: The Bee Gees wrote songs performed by other artists
story: The Fortunes' Coca-Cola commercial
story: The Isley Brothers' big break
story: Elvis Presley cannot give interviews
story: Roberta Flack moonlighted
story: Marvin Gaye's three duets
story: The Platters are the greatest re-make artists
review: Top 5 LPs
network commercial: *American Top 40*'s Double Dozen LP
program note: Dentyne & Certs commercials end a 13-show contract, likely resulting in a decision by Watermark to end bartering the program to radio stations
odd chart stat: Carole King is #1 on the Hot 100 & Top LP charts for five consecutive weeks
flipside played: I Feel The Earth Move - Carole King
oldie played: Harbor Lights - Platters
oldie played: I Want You, I Need You I Love You - Elvis Presley

WATERMARK IN PROMO LP DEAL

LOS ANGELES — Watermark, Inc., producers of the weekly special, "American Top 40," will unveil a new custom pop promotion album called "American Top 40's Double Dozen, Vol. 1." The two-LP set will contain 24 oldies. A special feature of the LP set, manufactured by the special products group of Custom Fidelity Company, Hollywood, will be the story of each song, written by Casey Kasem, host of the three-hour radio show. Deal for the album was completed between Watermark president Tom Rounds and Rick Donovan, product manager of Custom Fidelity.

The *American Top 40 Double Dozen Album of Hits, Volume 1* two-LP set was commercially available for $4.99 as a write-in offer to listeners. This article appeared in the July 31, 1971 edition of *Billboard* magazine.

AMERICAN TOP 40

THE CONCEPT

AMERICAN TOP 40 is a weekly, three-hour in-depth review and countdown of the nation's latest, best-selling records. Each current playlist is based on sales statistics supplied by and credited to Billboard Magazine... the nation's leading music trade publication.

The program is taped and shipped to a growing network of top radio stations in the U.S. and around the world, and it's scored spectacular successes with audiences and advertisers in markets of all sizes.

Continuity and excitement are provided by the traditional countdown... a sure-fire presentational technique that's proven itself again with the success of AMERICAN TOP 40. But what makes this program unique is the research, writing, announcing talent and production value which transform a mechanical program function into an absorbing, fast-paced, captivating documentary on American music... right now!

It all centers around the talents and energy of host, Casey Kasem. Casey's intelligent, informative presentation of popular music provides new dimension to the music most important to today's audience.

AMERICAN TOP 40 is produced weekly at Watermark, Inc., housing Los Angeles' most complete radio production facility. A full-time staff of four writer/researchers come up with new and exciting background information that adds depth and excitement to America's hottest hit records. This information is assembled and awaits the weekly relay of advance chart data from the Billboard research division. The final script is then written and production begins. Watermark's own Custom Tape Duplication Division then high-speeds each quality-controlled copy to various interstate shippers for delivery to stations. Most stations receive their 10″ or 7″ reels on Wednesdays, two days in advance of their usual weekend airplay.

AMERICAN TOP 40

THE RESULTS

- AMERICAN TOP 40 is the most successful music program on radio, carried each week by over 120 top flight stations who added the program in the first 12 months. The show is known worldwide via the American Forces Radio Network of 350 stations. An additional 200 stations have taken steps to secure exclusive broadcast rights.
- AMERICAN TOP 40 is the first three-hour contemporary block music program to find acceptance at so many dominant stations in the nation's top markets. It's also enjoyed phenomenal programming acceptance and has made money for stations in over 70 smaller markets, coast to coast, including markets under 15,000 population.
- AMERICAN TOP 40 has swept the ARB ratings in nearly every market surveyed. Average-quarter-hour-audience figures for the program showed an average increase of 65% in the 1971 April-May ARB survey. And every survey has shown repeated gains for AMERICAN TOP 40 stations. (It's the #1 music show in the time period in Los Angeles, Seattle, Omaha, Syracuse, Mobile and 36 other cities!)
- AMERICAN TOP 40 has delivered top ratings on progressive rock, Top 40, and even strict middle-of-the-road stations. It blankets the 12 to 34 demographics (85% of the audience surveyed).

Two pages from *American Top 40*'s 1971 marketing brochure provided insight to the program's early production and distribution process. Note that the show was still being distributed on reel tapes when this brochure was available, however "Sample Hour III" (next page) included no reference to network commercials.

AMERICAN TOP 40, programmed weekly as a special event, has generated new advertiser interest and station revue for previously neglected weekend time slots. Some 600 local and national advertisers are paying premium rates for AMERICAN TOP 40 avails at many stations.

AMERICAN TOP 40

WORKS FOR YOUR STATION

Watermark's Ron Jacobs and Tom Rounds have designed AMERICAN TOP 40 to be totally adaptable to the modern contemporary format. An ingenious device called the split logo allows station ID's, commercials and news with minimum loss of program continuity, and maximum simplicity. The musical split logo may be stopped mid-way for inserts or simply run through.

SAMPLE HOUR III

AVERAGE MUSIC & TALK UNIT 3:18

EACH COMMERCIAL AVAILABILITY INCLUDING LOGOS 1:06 or 2:06

TOTAL LOCAL INSERT TIME: 11:20

TOTAL PROGRAM TIME: 48:40

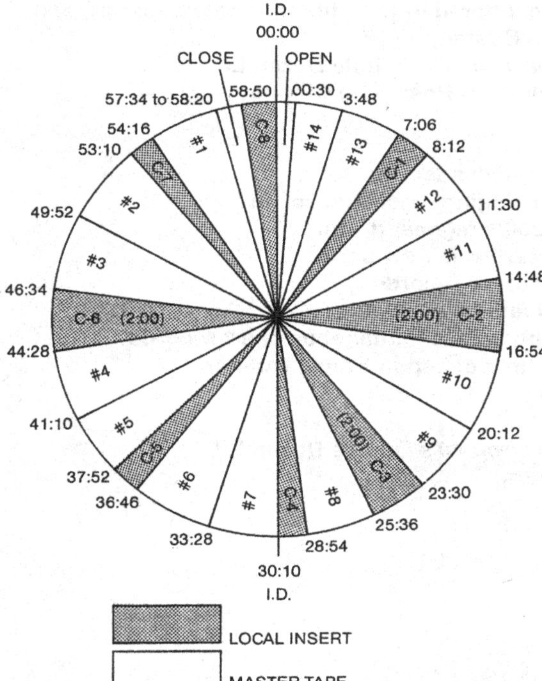

AMERICAN TOP 40, in the basic three-hour format, sets up your sales department with 33 (11 per hour) fixed position, premium-buy 60-second spots every week...or 66 30's...including one minute adjacencies each hour at :59 minute mark. This format may be expanded to carry up to 18 spots per hour, or hourly news, simply by increasing overall program time. It's a natural for exclusive sponsorships, merchandising and cross-promotion packages.

AMERICAN TOP 40's continuing contrast to local record charts emphasizes, in a new way, the importance, integrity and community service value of your station's accurate local playlist.

AMERICAN TOP 40's in-depth review of the country's top hits is a fresh sound still consistent with your station's important programming basics which hold, and build, audience loyalty. And it's exclusive for your station in your primary service area.

AMERICAN TOP 40 fills one of those hard-to-cover weekend jock shifts with one of radio's top talents for three solid hours.

AMERICAN TOP 40

A SMALL PRICE AND SHORT CONTRACT

You may schedule the program on a special 13-week trial basis for as little as $13 per hour ($39 per program). You receive three ten-inch, one-hour reels per week (or six seven-inch reels), complete with cue sheets, logging instructions, timing charts and promos, program lead-ins or feature module intros by Casey, and the free consultation services of Watermark's programming and marketing departments.

The program agreement is renewable every 13 weeks thereafter, still at the base $39.00 price for all but the Top 100 markets. Contract permits more than one broadcast per week if desired.

Delivery: The base price includes packaging, handling and delivery to your door before the close of business each Wednesday. Your only responsibility is the return of the program tapes to Watermark.

To order: Call or write Watermark's Excecutive Producer, Tom Rounds, or Marketing Director, George Savage, with start date, program times and reel requirements. Avaliability and market clearance will be verified and contracts and promo information will be forwarded to you immediately.

They're available at: Watermark, Inc.
931 North La Cienega Blvd.
Los Angeles, California 90069
(213) 659-3834.

56.) 07-24-71

Program #713-4
story: the chart longevity of Johnny Mathis' Greatest Hits LP
story: Dawn's Tony Orlando chart successes
story: Tom Clay's production of "What The World Needs Now"
story: Delaney's mom sings with Delaney & Bonnie
story: John Denver wrote "Leavin' On A Jet Plane" at a boring party
story: Paul Revere rode a motorcycle to promote "Indian Reservation"
story: The Troggs' lead singer is Presley
story: James Brown's chart longevity includes eight 1971 records
question: repeating #1 records
production note: hour #1 ends with a question from a listener
network commercial: *American Top 40*'s Double Dozen LP
oldie played: Misty - Johnny Mathis
oldie played: Wild Thing - Troggs

57.) 07-31-71

Program #713-5
story: The Carpenters are not Top 40 material
story: Freda Payne switched from jazz to rhythm & blues
story: Olivia Newton-John won a Hayley Mills look-a-like contest
story: Tom Clay arrested while broadcasting
record origin: The Raiders' "Indian Reservation"
mention: James Taylor was a Flying Machine member
review: Top 5 LPs
network commercial: Phone-X; a gadget designed to temporarily disengage a telephone mouthpiece, offered in four different colors; script read by *AT40* producer Don Bustany
network commercial: *American Top 40*'s Double Dozen LP
oldie played: Come On-A My House - Rosemary Clooney

58.) 08-07-71

Program #713-6
story: Cat Stevens could not handle success
story: Gladys Knight has been singing since age seven
story: The Platters were the 1950's biggest group
story: Creedence Clearwater Revival is now a trio
story: Marvin Gaye has more Top 10 records
story: James Taylor's musical family
question: recording act with the most simultaneous chart records
program note: hour #2 ends with a question from a listener
network commercial: Phone-X
network commercial: Certs
network commercial: *American Top 40*'s Double Dozen LP
oldie played: My Prayer - Platters

59.) 08-14-71

Program #713-7
network commercial: Phone-X
network commercial: Certs
network commercial: *American Top 40*'s Double Dozen LP
program note: Phone-X is no longer advertised after this show
story: Donny Hathaway was Donny Pitts
story: Three Dog Night's manager is Reb Foster
story: The Who shook the walls of The Met
story: John Denver performed with a broken thumb
story: The Bee Gees are the only disbanded/regrouped artist with a #1 record
program error: in the outcue of Bread's "Mother Freedom," Casey states that this is "....the first of four new songs...."; actually, there were five
program error: Casey's introduction to Rare Earth includes a reference to "Get Ready" peaking at #2 in 1970; actually it peaked at #4
flipside played: I Feel The Earth Move - Carole King
oldie played: Summer In The City - Lovin' Spoonful
program note: unusual production of hour #1; Casey plays records from #40-#26

60.) 08-21-71

Program #713-8
story: Elvis Presley is #1 on all charts
story: Janis Joplin is the biggest all-time female recording artist
story: Joe Dowell became a star as a student
story: The Jackson Five concert tour
story: James Brown's 69 non-#1 records
story: Five Man Electrical Band's Canadian success
story: Jean Knight's start in the music business
network commercial: *American Top 40*'s Double Dozen LP
network commercial: Certs
oldie played: Piece Of My Heart - Big Brother & Holding Company
oldie played: Wooden Heart - Joe Dowell

"I was stationed at Clark Air Base, Republic of the Philippines. It was around late August, 1971, and I was less than a year away from my discharge. All of a sudden, on the base AM radio station, I heard this countdown show like no other countdown show. I could tell it was a national countdown what with the host, Casey Kasem, mentioning Billboard magazine. I was only able to hear the last hour of the show because that's the way it was at the time with Armed Forces affiliates. But it was enough to get me hooked……The show might've been a week behind as heard in the USA. I thus can't pinpoint the exact date when I first heard the program. However, I believe "Uncle Albert / Admiral Halsey" by Paul and Linda McCartney was at #12, destined to go to #1 the next week. "How Can You Mend A Broken Heart" by the Bee Gees and "The Night They Drove Old Dixie Down" by Joan Baez were songs in the countdown at the time. Hearing that show made my final months at Clark Air Base go a whole lot faster."

Rob Durkee, former *AT40* statistician and writer, and author of *American Top 40: The Countdown of the Century*

'American Top 40' From Barter to $$$

LOS ANGELES — The graveyards of radio are paved with the tombstones of syndicators and the truth is that very few syndicators really make money. After almost two years, Watermark, Inc., is dropping its barter system approach to its syndicated "American Top 40" and will be charging for it. Previously, the weekly three-hour special counting down the top 40 best-selling singles in the nation, had been distributed free on an exclusive basis to major-market radio stations. Small market stations had to defray costs of the show. By Oct. 1, all stations will be paying a nominal charge for the show, based on their rate card. Some 140 stations are using the show to date.

Syndicating the special has been no easy job. For one thing, there's a natural reluctance on the part of program directors to accept outside programming, which the special represents. But, by far the biggest problem was in trying to sell the show on a national basis.

Watermark, a small group of aggressive radio people, was formed in January 1969 out of the energy left over from the Miami Pop Music Festival. The firm didn't really take shape until about July 1969 when Ron Jacobs left his position as program director of KHJ, Los Angeles, to join the organization. There's really no leader in the group. Tom Rounds said he became president because "I had the suit." Jacobs is head of Increase Records, a subsidiary, and also produced "The Elvis Presley Story," a 12-hour documentary which will be shipped Aug. 25. Thomas P. Driscoll is chairman of the board.

"Advertising executives are constantly complaining about the lack of creativity in radio, but they're also unwilling to support real creative radio. We had been trying to create a sponsorship situation for 'American Top 40' but the very thing that advertisers do all of the time in television—support an entire program—they were unwilling to do for radio," Rounds said. He spoke of having invested $250,000 trying to make the weekly special work strictly as a barter-type show. "And we came close."

The other factor Watermark had to contend with was the reluctance of program directors to let anything outside their own domain influence their station. Rounds remarked that he once felt the same way when he was programming KFRC, San Francisco, "and had been trained to generate 150 hours of programming a week and was overworked and underpaid like most program directors. But program directors feel responsible for keeping a radio station on the air and making it sound good and they feel like they're copping out if they take someone else's programming."

We've had to turn that whole prejudice around . . . many times, I came close to giving up. I guess that "The History of Rock and Roll," created by Bill Drake, paved a lot of the way for syndicated programming.

Another handicap was in convincing radio stations to pay for "American Top 40." The stations had not considered the show as "a super sales vehicle, but as a super programming item," Rounds said. Yet, "several small stations have been having to go out and generate the kind of enthusiasm with clients we have here in the office for the show. And 90 percent of them renew right along — and they've been paying for the show almost from the beginning. Casey Kasem, who hosts the show, gets fan mail sent to the stations . . . he's a 'local' deejay in markets like Wichita and Tulsa." He spoke of the manager of KLBM, La Grande, Ore., holding a party to introduce the show to local teenagers and advertising clients and selling it out on the spot.

As it is, "American Top 40 is alive and well and currently breaking even as a weekly special. The feeling is that the show will be a substantial money-maker for Watermark in the near future." And "The Elvis Presley Story" documentary has already been purchased by 107 stations and is still growing. More specials of this nature may be forthcoming. So, in spite of the pitfalls of syndication, Watermark seems set. As for "American Top 40," Rounds felt the show was already an institution. For another thing, it's a full-time job for a staff of almost a dozen people, since Watermark does its own duplicating and shipping.

THE RATINGS GAME

Watermark's "American Top 40" show has increased ratings an average of 40.35 percent among 31 stations surveyed by ARB in April/May 1971. It's estimated that the three-hour weekly special is heard by approximately a million Americans in countries overseas via the American Forces Radio-Television Service whose 466 outlets carry a version of the show. The show upped ratings 100 percent at KNUZ, Houston, over a previous ARB. KELI, Tulsa, experienced a ratings increase of 324 percent. WFLI, Chattanooga, showed ratings were up 29 percent in the show's time period. At KJOY, Stockton, Calif., ratings were up 126 percent. At WMEX, Boston, ratings were up 62.3 percent during the show's time slot.

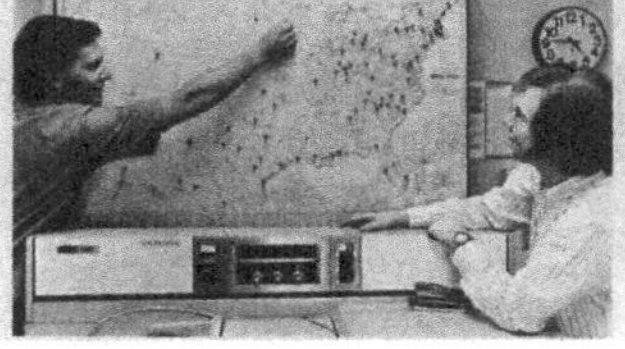

This article, which appeared in the August 28, 1971 edition of *Billboard* magazine, explained why Watermark began charging radio station subscribers a flat fee for the program. In the photo on the left, operations manager Stew Hilner watches executive producer Tom Rounds add another station to the program's map. On the right, engineer Bill 'Captain Billy' Hergonson waits for a cue from host Casey Kasem during program recording.

61.) 08-28-71 **Program #713-9**

story: Elvis Presley's signature song
story: George Harrison's Bangla Desh fund raiser
story: James Taylor's Apple Records flop
story: David Cassidy's fan mail
story: Aretha Franklin, re-make queen
story: Creedence Clearwater Revival's record sales
network commercial: *American Top 40*'s Double Dozen LP
network commercial: Certs
oldie played: Hound Dog - Elvis Presley
program mention: Carole King's Top 40 writing successes

62.) 09-04-71

Program #713-10
network commercial: *American Top 40*'s Double Dozen LP
network commercial: Certs
story: Donny Osmond indirectly persuaded by Steve Lawrence
story: Paul Stookey voted ugliest man on campus
story: The Moody Blues' Graeme Edge competed against The Beatles
story: the meteoric chart climb of "Uncle Albert/Admiral Halsey"
story: the slow chart climb of "If Not For You"
story: Rod Stewart's double recording career
question: longest stay at #1
program correction: Casey corrects an error from previous week regarding Carole King's four Top 40 compositions
odd chart stat: eight debut records
odd chart stat: "Uncle Albert/Admiral Halsey" climbs from #12--#1

63.) 09-11-71

Program #713-11
network commercial: *American Top 40*'s Double Dozen LP
network commercial: Certs
story: "Chirpy Chirpy Cheep Cheep" started as an international hit
story: Lee Michaels has tigers, cheetahs and cougars
story: Three Dog Night is only act with two #1 hits in the last 14 months
story: Supremes are #3 in #1 records
story: Aretha Franklin is #1 with gold records by a female artist
story: Paul McCartney is first former Beatle to form a new group
story: Donny Osmond is third youngest artist to have a #1 record
story: People's Choice's unusual discovery
program error: Casey states that Chicago "...dropped 14 positions this week...."; actually, it dropped four positions
odd chart stat: "Uncle Albert/Admiral Halsey" moves from #12--#1--#5 in three weeks
odd chart stat: The Carpenters' "Superstar" debuts at #17
question: longest chart run for a non-#1 record
oldie played: You Can't Hurry Love - Supremes

64.) 09-18-71

Program #713-12
production error: "I Ain't Got Time Anymore" by the Glass Bottle debuts; wrong song played: Glass Bottle's "The First Time"
story: Glass Bottle's Glass Container Institute commercial
story: The Highwaymen were fraternity brothers
story: James Brown shined shoes in front of a radio station he now owns
story: George Harrison was first Beatle to have a solo #1 record
story: Paul McCartney was second Beatle to have a solo #1 record
story: Stevie Wonder is most successful, starting at the youngest age
story: Bill Withers entered music business at age 26
story: Three Dog Night's members vote on what songs to record
story: The Carpenters are most successful brother-sister recording act
program mention: Casey references that "Superstar" by the Carpenters is their fifth million selling single
program note: after 11 weeks in the Top 40, Casey never referenced "Color My World" as the flipside to Chicago's "Beginnings," and never related a story about Chicago during "Beginnings" chart run
network commercial: *American Top 40*'s Double Dozen LP
network commercial: Certs
odd chart stat: The Osmonds at #40, Donny Osmond at #1
oldie played: Michael - Highwaymen

Released on Elektra Records and advertised on *AT40*, this was the LP cover to *Cyrus*. A would-be Top 40 performer, Cyrus Faryar's LP had an apparent Watermark connection. The album's credits listed Tom Rounds as one of 35 choir members and "Executive Producer RON JACOBS for Watermark, Inc." Other choir members credited also included David Crosby and Cass Elliott.

65.) 09-25-71

Program #713-13
production error: second week in Top 40 for Glass Bottle's "I Ain't Got Time Anymore"; wrong song played: Glass Bottle's "The First Time"
program note: this show was the last to include network commercials
network commercial: Certs
network commercial: Elektra Records (Cyrus)
program mention: after one of the Elektra Record commercials, Casey mentions that Cyrus is Cyrus Faryar, formerly with the Modern Folk Quartet
story: The Moody Blues were swindled
story: Bob Dylan fired by Bobby Vee
story: Al Green almost made the Top 40 in 1968
story: Bill Withers used the U.S. Navy
story: Honey Cone members came from other recording acts
story: Diana Ross discovered The Jackson Five
story: The Dells' early days
story: Joan Baez is the most listened-to folk singer
story: songwriters more often now sing their own material
review: chronological #1 1971 singles
oldie played: Take Good Care Of My Baby - Bobby Vee

66.) 10-02-71

Program #714-1
production correction: correct Glass Bottle song played; final week in the Top 40
question: name origin of The Bee Gees
story: The Who's Keith Moon jumped out of a restaurant window
story: Phil Spector's return from retirement
story: Freddie Hart was in the Marines at age 13
story: Tommy Roe wrote "Sheila" in the 9th grade
story: Rod Stewart is one of three British males to hit #1
story: Mac & Katie Kissoon's individual chart appearances
production error: beginning of James Brown's "Make It Funky" is edited
program error: Casey points out that The Guess Who "....have over a dozen American hits..."; actually, "Rain Dance" is their 11th Top 40 record
program note: Casey welcomes 11 new radio stations
flipside played: Reason To Believe - Rod Stewart

67.) 10-09-71

Program #714-2
story: Bobby Russell's sound-alike records
story: The Fifth Dimension came from different careers
story: Kris Kristofferson's songwriting
story: Denise LaSalle published at age 15
story: The Osmonds used saws when recording "Yo-Yo"
name origin: Ray Charles
program error: Casey indicates that there are six new radio stations to welcome, but mentions only five; one new station mentioned was welcomed on 07-17-71
flipside played: Smackwater Jack - Carole King
program note: Casey mentions that all listener letters are read by at least two of three key people - Casey, producer Don Bustany and statistician Ben Marichal
long version: The Love We Had (Stays On My Mind) – The Dells
oldie played: Hit The Road Jack - Ray Charles
LP cut played: Every Picture Tells A Story - Rod Stewart
LP cut played: (I Know) I'm Losing You - Rod Stewart

CASEY'S CORNER

This is me, Casey Kasem, greeting you again from Hollywood. I'm the emcee of a syndicated radio show called American Top 40 that reaches over 100 stations in towns and cities all over America. I hope YOUR area is one of those that pick up my show. Now let's look in Casey's notebook and see what's new this month:

Was knocked out when I got a surprise visit from DONNY and the OSMOND BROTHERS recently. Not only did they present me with their brand new MGM LPs—one by Donny and one by the group—they also gave me a copy of their fabulous program, which is available only if you happen to go to one of their concerts. . . Congrats to TINY TIM and his lovely bride VICKY on the birth of their daughter—appropriately named TULIP (as in "tip toe through—" of course) . . . Hope you've been hearing Paramount Records' new single It Ain't Easy by a group called DETROIT. It's a sensational record, but—and here's a surprise—didya know that its lead singer is none other than the famous MITCH RYDER—and that the DETROITS themselves consist of two former members of Mitch's first group, the Detroit Wheels, and three new members! Keep your eyes open for their new LP. It's on Paramount Records and it's simply called Detroit.

CASEY'S CORNER

Andy Kim

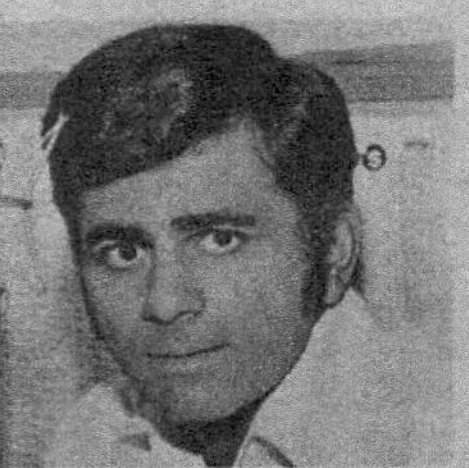

Casey Kasem

Hello from Hollywood! My name is Casey Kasem and I'm the emcee on a syndicated radio show called American Top 40. American Top 40 reaches over 100 stations, including ones in New York City, Chicago, Philadelphia, St. Louis, Providence and—oh, well, just about everywhere. Each month, I'm going to pass on a little bit of hot news I have picked up from here and there and everywhere, and salute one of my stations. So be sure to meet me in The Grapevine section of each issue of SPEC from now on—and join me for fun-time in Casey's Corner!

TERRY KNIGHT—former deejay and artist in his own right—has just announced that the MAYSLES brothers (those same two wonderful boys who brought you the ROLLING STONES' movie, Gimme Shelter) are doing a full-length film project on Capitol Records' red-hot GRAND FUNK RAILROAD—and that ought to be something worth writing home about! Twixt time, be sure to pick up on Grand Funk Railroad's newest and bestest Capitol Records' LP, Survival . . . Didja know that ROBB ROYER and JIM GRIFFIN (alias Robb Wilson and Arthur James)—both members of the fabulously successful Elektra Records' group BREAD—won an Academy Award for composing that wonderful song For All We Know, which was the theme song for the movie Lovers and Other Strangers. In case you forgot, For All We Know was a million-seller for A&M's CARPENTERS.

You are familiar with ANDY KIM as a record artist on the Steed label, but didja know that Dandy Andy is a notorious songwriter—having penned such hits as Sugar, Sugar, Jingle Jangle, Who's Your Baby?—and RON DANTE's hit Let Me Bring You Up?? . . . And speaking of Ron, he's just signed a brand new contract with Scepter Records and is now recording his first single—composed especially for him by his friend CAROLE KING. The title of Ron's first Scepter record will be Bootleg Freaks, so keep your eyes and ears tuned for that goodie!

If you have any questions or requests, you can write to me, Casey Kasem, at 8961 Sunset Blvd., Suite B, Los Angeles, Calif. 90069.

Casey's Corner, a short-lived column of music news by Casey Kasem, appeared in *SPEC* magazine. The columns represented here are from the September and October 1971 issues.

68.) 10-16-71 **Program #714-3**

program note: first show available to subscribing radio stations in boxed, LP format
production error: unusual edit of Marvin Gaye's "Inner City Blues"
production error: hour #2 opening theme 'skips'
story: Cher's family
story: Freddie Hart taught self-defense to the Los Angeles Police Department
story: Kris Kristofferson is Carly Simon's boyfriend
(see Carly Simon story on 12-16-72; married to James Taylor)
story: Mac & Katie Kissoon are a part of the West Indies invasion
program mention: The Fifth Dimension's 21 chart records
review: Top 5 LPs
LP cut played: Every Picture Tells A Story - Rod Stewart
oldie played: Don't Be Cruel - Elvis Presley
oldie played: Runaround Sue – Dion

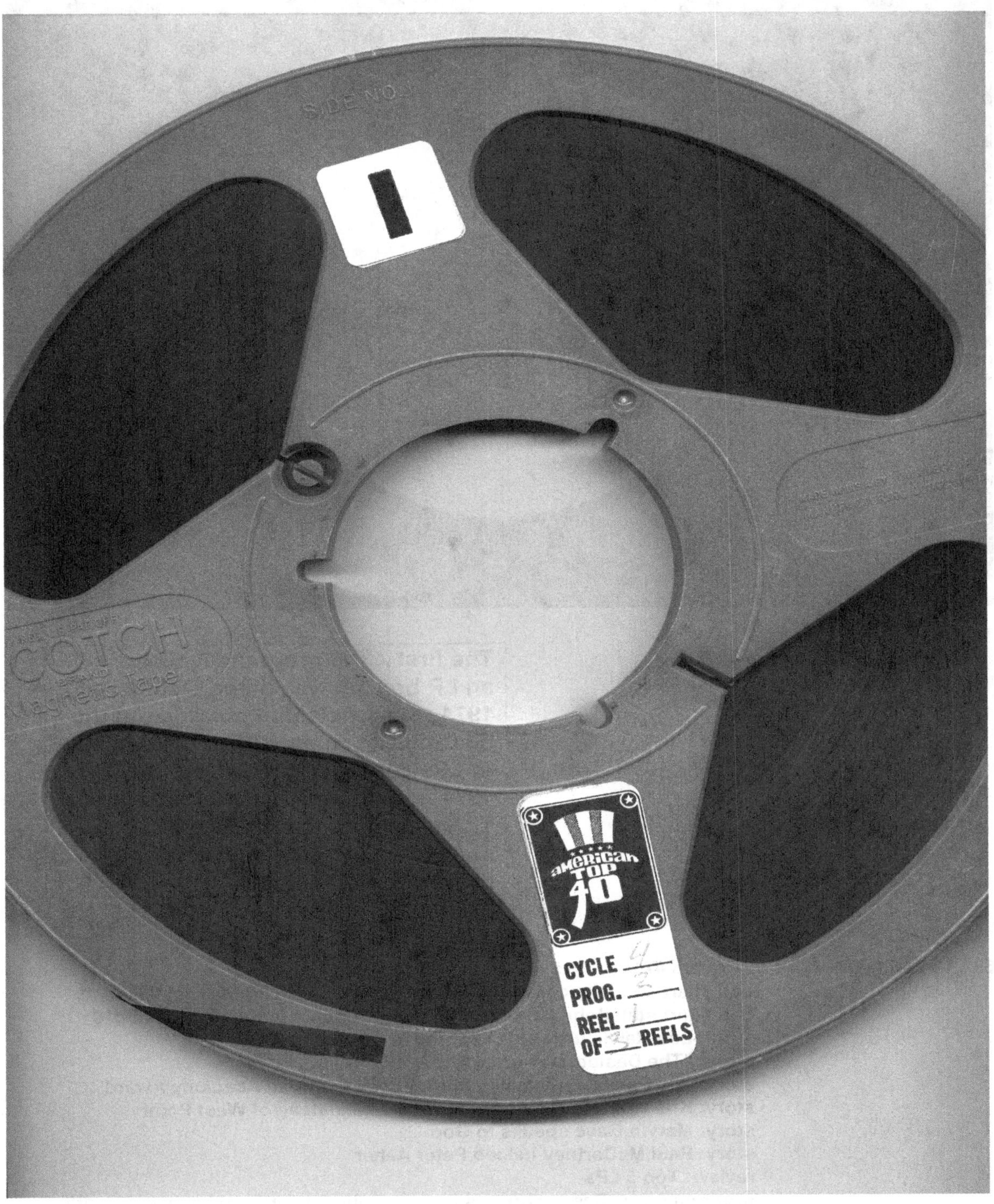

This 10½" reel, from the October 9, 1971 program (#714-2), represents Hour #1 of the last show routinely available on tape to radio stations. Exceptions to the change were made, however, if a station preferred to receive the program on reel-to-reel tapes instead of the newly implemented LP box set.

Watermark to Disk

LOS ANGELES—The Watermark syndicated "American Top 40" show, being broadcast weekends on 450-plus stations, will now be supplied on records under an agreement with Custom Fidelity here. The three-hour show was previously being provided on tape.

The first *AT40* program available in an LP box set was dated October 16, 1971. An article that pointed out the distribution change from reel tapes to LPs appeared in the October 23, 1971 edition of *Billboard* magazine. There were approximately 125 stations in the U.S. subscribing to the show at this time.

69.) 10-23-71

Program #714-4
odd chart stat: Isaac Hayes' "Theme From *Shaft*" climbs from #50 to #9
odd chart stat: John Lennon's "Imagine" debuts in the Hot 100 at #20
story: Lou Rawls urges kids to stay in school
story: "The Desiderata" great poster hoax
story: The Partridge Family's Shirley Jones won an Academy Award
story: Kris Kristofferson went to Nashville instead of West Point
story: Marvin Gaye speaks to God
story: Paul McCartney helped Peter Asher
review: Top 5 LPs
program error: Casey corrects a radio station error from two weeks earlier ("welcome to WIFE in Indianapolis") with another error; correction should have acknowledged error in welcoming WKBO in Harrisburg, PA
flipside played: Reason To Believe - Rod Stewart
oldie played: Reach Out I'll Be There - Four Tops

70.) 10-30-71

Program #714-5
story: the most mysterious group to ever hit the charts
story: James Taylor's prized pet pig Mona
story: Laura Lee helped by Della Reese
story: Carlos Santana shuns publicity
story: Isaac Hayes' image
story: Rod Stewart's simultaneous #1 U.S. and British records
program error: in record's intro, Casey mentions that Kris Kristofferson peaked at #27; outcue reads "last week at #26..."
question: zig-zag chart movements
question: *Billboard*'s first #1 record
oldie played: 96 Tears - ? & The Mysterians
LP cut played: Oh My Love - John Lennon

71.) 11-06-71

Program #714-6
GUEST HOST: Dave Hull; introduced on the program by producer Don Bustany; Hull logged 70 weeks of "emergency stand-by status" up until this program
program note: Casey missed this program due to an acting role in a movie, titled *That Lovin' Man Jesus*, later released under the title of *The Soul Hustler* (see program descriptions 11-10-73 and 11-24-73)
program note: Dave Hull uses the Hot 100 in referencing the number of weeks a record has been on the chart, not the Top 40
story: Les Crane was first network talk show host
story: Rick Hall's record producer success
story: Coven's "One Tin Soldier" single is sold by two record companies
story: Aretha Franklin weaned on gospel music
production note: Isaac Hayes' "Theme From *Shaft*" has no introduction
question: female artist's first #1 record
question: biggest leap to #1
LP cut played: Walk From Regio's - Isaac Hayes
oldie played: Big Bad John - Jimmy Dean

72.) 11-13-71

Program #714-7
story: Lou Rawls' amnesia
story: Santana managed by a barber
story: Cat Stevens' teen-age illness
story: James Taylor's mother nearly died while his father traveled
record origin: Chicago's "Questions 67 & 68"
program note: letter from an American couple in Fiji
question: oldest Top 40 recording artist
question: Stevie Wonder is Eivets Rednow
question: year with the most #1 records
LP cut played: Everything's Coming Our Way - Santana

73.) 11-20-71

Program #714-8
story: The Osmonds were a quartet at Disneyland
story: John Lennon born during a World War II air raid
story: 1971's three different "Superstars"
story: the birth of Coven's Jinx Dawson
story: Lee Michaels' 900 lb. cat collection
story: Johnny Rivers signed The Fifth Dimension to a recording contract
question: The Beatles' first hit
question: longest stay for a Top 10 record
oldie played: Poor Side Of Town - Johnny Rivers

DAVE HULL GUEST STARS FOR CASEY KASEM

Veteran Los Angeles radio personality Dave Hull is this week's special guest host of AMERICAN TOP 40. Dave, who daily occupies the 3-7 slot on 50kw top rating contender KGBS, has logged 69 consecutive weeks of emergency standby status, while Casey has made one incredible airline connection after another to make it to the Watermark studios in time for Tuesday night sessions.

This week, however, it was a different story. Casey had been on location with the crew of the motion picture, "That Lovin' Man, Jesus," somewhere in the Southern California desert. His co-starring role had him submerged in an icy swimming pool for most of the day Tuesday, and rain earlier in the week had forced a rescheduling of after dark scenes Tuesday night.

So in this 70th straight AMERICAN TOP 40 program, we're proud to introduce the incapacitated Casey's replacement, good old reliable Dave Hull, who, we think, does a great job.

A motorized convoy is standing by to bring our star back on schedule for next week's show.

This memo, which accompanied the November 6, 1971 program, alerted stations that Dave Hull was sitting in as host for Casey Kasem. This was Casey's first time away from the *AT40* microphone. Note that this was the 71st, not 70th, program.

74.) 11-27-71 **Program #714-9**
program note: Casey promos the upcoming Christmas special in show's open
question: record's longest chart run
question: artist with the longest, continuous chart run
question: highest Top 40 debut record
story: Three Dog Night's concert earnings
story: Sly & The Family Stone takes 20 dogs on concert tours
story: Chicago's "Questions 67 & 68" is a re-release
story: Isaac Hayes - rags to riches
program error: Casey references the chart jump (#39 - #14) of Three Dog Night's "Old Fashioned Love Song" as 26 notches, and the chart climb (#29 - #18) of David Cassidy's "Cherish" as nine notches
oldie played: Love Me Tender - Elvis Presley
oldie played: You Keep Me Hangin' On - Supremes

75.) 12-04-71 **Program #714-10**
story: James Brown scavenged coal as a child
story: Marvin Gaye won three NAACP awards
story: The Grass Roots replaced by P.F. Sloan
story: "The Desiderata" great poster hoax
story: The New Vaudeville Band existed without a band
story: Sly Stone was a disk jockey
question: first #1 record by a duo
question: white artists with #1 soul records
oldie played: Winchester Cathedral - New Vaudeville Band
LP cut played: Everything's Coming Our Way - Santana

76.) 12-11-71 **Program #714-11**
story: The Temptations' $15 performance
story: The Marvelettes were #1 at Motown first
story: John Lennon was too famous to be Jesus Christ
story: Melanie's overnight sensation in Holland
story: The Who's Keith Moon chartered a jet to a canceled concert
story: "I'd Like To Teach The World To Sing" is a soft drink commercial (Casey never mentions the product)
program error: Casey reviews Santana's hit singles and states that "Everybody's Everything" is their third single; actually it was their fourth
review: Top 5 LPs
question: weakest #1 record
question: The Beatles' biggest record
oldie played: Please Mr. Postman - Marvelettes
LP cut played: Batuka - Santana

77.) 12-18-71 **Program #714-12**
story: "Good Vibrations" is the most expensive record
story: James Brown loses 10 pounds when performing
story: Mickey Newbury did not write "American Trilogy"
story: David Cassidy's fans found him in the hospital
review: Top 5 LPs
question: #1 record equals a million seller
question: most #1 female artist records
question: biggest novelty record
LP cut played: Space Cowboy - Sly & Family Stone
oldie played: Good Vibrations - Beach Boys

78.) 12-25-71 **Program #714-13**
SPECIAL: Christmas Countdown
for a complete list of records in this special, see Rob Durkee's *American Top 40: The Countdown of the Century*
program offer: Casey promotes listener mail-in offer to obtain the Top 40 lists of the Christmas Countdown & the 1971 Year-End Countdown, and an *American Top 40* wall poster
production error: skip (found in the master tape) in Spike Jones' "All I Want For Christmas Is My Two Front Teeth", approximately :40 into the record

1972

79.) 01-01-72 **Program #721-1**
SPECIAL: Top 40 Of 1971 (based on *Billboard*'s year-end Top 100)
for a complete list of records in this special, see Rob Durkee's *American Top 40: The Countdown of the Century*
program offer: Casey promotes listener mail-in offer to obtain the Top 40 lists of the Christmas Countdown & the 1971 Year-End Countdown, and an *American Top 40* wall poster
long version: What's Going On – Marvin Gaye

> ***"Since it was our policy to play every song that actually made it into the Top 40 on Billboard's "Hot 100" on the show, we ran into a real problem with a song called "George Jackson" by Bob Dylan. This was a song about an inmate in California whose guilt was dubious and Dylan was "protesting" the man's incarceration. The song was NOT getting much actual airplay and made it into the Top 40 on Dylan's name alone. The problem? In the middle of the song, plain as day, he sings "He wouldn't take shit from no one...". Well this stopped the taping in its tracks! TR (Tom Rounds) asked me if I could "do something" about it. He asked me because of my reputation as one of the best tape editors in Hollywood, a fact not lost on Ron Jacobs when he later asked me to edit "The Elvis Presley Story". What I "did about it" was to take Dylan's song and re-record it on a separate reel of tape at twice the normal speed. I then went to the offending word and carefully edited out only the "shhhh" sound at the beginning and spliced it back together. When played back, it came out "He wouldn't take IT from no one..." and the edit was undetectable. Why the record label didn't issue this "edit" as a "radio version" I don't know, unless they didn't dare to try and edit out half a syllable (or maybe Dylan would have had a "shit fit"). Anyway, that's how "George Jackson" made it past the censors and out to the AT 40 stations all over the country!"***
>
> **Bill "Captain Billy" Hergonson, *AT40*'s original studio engineer, describing his creative remedy for editing offensive language out of a Bob Dylan Top 40 record, which debuted January 8, 1972.**

80.) 01-08-72

Program #721-2
story: Don McLean was a troubadour
story: Three Dog Night is 1971's #1 singles artist
story: Sonny Bono's song inspired by cookies
story: Neil Diamond thought *Fiddler On The Roof* was a loser
story: Bob Dylan's honorary doctorate
story: Charley Pride is only black artist on country chart
question: #1 record of the year by a female artist
long version: American Pie - Don McLean
LP cut played: Brighter - Carole King
production note: engineer Bill Hergonson edited Bob Dylan's "George Jackson" for program airplay, changing the offensive lyric, "...he wouldn't take **it from no one...." to "...he wouldn't take it from no one...."

81.) 01-15-72

Program #721-3
story: pre-teen Michael Jackson's many hits
story: Mickey Newbury lived in a 1954 Pontiac
story: Elton John's mother turned him onto rock 'n' roll
story: Rare Earth, all-white Motown band
story: David Cassidy is inaudible in concert
record origin: Don McLean's "American Pie"
question: white artist #1 records on soul chart
question: biggest selling instrumental
question: first foreign artist's #1 rock 'n' roll record
program error: Casey states that "Without You" is Nilsson's second Top 40 record; actually, it was his fourth
production note: engineer Bill Hergonson edited Bob Dylan's "George Jackson" for program airplay, changing the offensive lyric, "...he wouldn't take **it from no one...." to "...he wouldn't take it from no one...."

82.) 01-22-72

Program #721-4
production note: theme music at end of hours #2 & #3 is complete with cold ending
story: J. Geils Band similar to The Rolling Stones
story: The New Seekers' international base
story: Wilson Pickett's vow to quit music
story: Carly Simon's "Winkin', Blinkin' & Nod"
story: "Once You Understand" composed of teen-directed parental questions
question: commercial hits
review: Top 5 LPs
long version: American Pie - Don McLean
LP cut played: Till Tomorrow - Don McLean

83.) 01-29-72

Program #721-5
story: Fifth Dimension rejected by Motown Records
story: Joe Cocker dodged beer bottles
story: Betty Wright discovered in a record store
story: The Carpenters' producer worked on Apollo I
story: "Joy" is 250 years old
story: Guy Mitchell's background
story: Led Zeppelin beat The Beatles
review: Top 5 LPs
question: first country artist at #1 on pop chart
question: youngest #1 LP artist
flipside played: I Knew You When - Donny Osmond
LP cut played: Babylon - Don McLean
oldie played: Singin' The Blues - Guy Mitchell

84.) 02-05-72 **Program #721-6**
production error: skip (found in the master tape) in Al Green's "Let's Stay Together," approximately 1:25 into the record
story: The Hillside Singers are mostly family
story: Charley Pride's would-be baseball career
story: The Osmonds' eight gold records in 1971
story: The Supremes #1 records
story: Beverly Bremers is in *Hair*
story: The Stylistics' clothing store
question: artist with most #1 weeks in one year
question: artist with longest #2 chart stay
question: artist with most #1 consecutive weeks

85.) 02-12-72 **Program #721-7**
story: Jonathan Edwards refused to draw nude models
story: Nilsson refused to perform in public
story: Al Green was a spiritual singer
story: Johnnie Ray 'cried' to stardom
story: Cher rejected by Phil Spector
story: Charley Pride is the Jackie Robinson of country music
question: non-#1 record's highest debut
question: most active #1 record turnover
question: record with most #1 weeks
oldie played: Cry - Johnnie Ray
program note: unusual production of hour #3; Casey plays songs #15-#1

86.) 02-19-72 **Program #721-8**
lyric alert: memo from executive producer Tom Rounds which accompanied program, alerts subscribing radio stations to the potentially offensive lyric content of "Jungle Fever"
story: who was Buddy Holly?
story: Climax's Sonny Geraci recorded with The Outsiders
story: Gene Chandler's recording pseudonyms
story: Carole King's Grammy Award nominations
story: Jerry Butler's Cinderella
story: Dennis Coffey's 11 records on June 1971 Hot 100 chart
question: LP artist with most consecutive #1 weeks
question: #1 record's biggest chart fall
question: simultaneous #1 record on pop, soul & country charts
long version: Jungle Fever - Chakachas
odd chart stat: three unrelated artists with the same last name - Carly Simon, Joe Simon & Paul Simon - are simultaneously in the Top 40 (also occurred 11-14-70, 11-21-70, 02-24-79, 03-03-79 and 03-10-79)
oldie played: Duke Of Earl - Gene Chandler

87.) 02-26-72 **Program #721-9**
odd chart stat: Melanie has three records in the Top 40
story: B.J. Thomas' record sung with various artists
story: Terry Knight's start with Grand Funk Railroad
story: The Monkees created by a 'help wanted' advertisement
story: Rod Stewart's group said no to Woodstock
story: T. Rex (Rex-mania) caused concert fainting
story: Robert John was Bobby Pedrick Jr.
question: highest debut with no chart rise
question: biggest number of non-American artists in Top 10
long version: Jungle Fever - Chakachas
oldie played: I'm A Believer - Monkees

WARNING

THE DREADED "JUNGLE FEVER" HAS BROKEN INTO THE TOP 40 THIS WEEK AT #35.

THE RECORD SOUNDS LIKE GOOD CLEAN FUN TO THE AMERICAN TOP 40 CREW, BUT SOME STATIONS ARE AVOIDING IT [ALTHOUGH OUR SPOT CHECK THIS WEEK SHOWED ABOUT 50% OF THE STATIONS ADDING THE RECORD].

YOU MAY DELETE THE RECORD OR NOT ... IT'S UP TO YOU. BUT WE RECOMMEND CHECKING IT OUT.

TOM ROUNDS

Throughout the 1970s, Tom Rounds occasionally distributed memos alerting stations to potentially offensive records. The 'dreaded' "Jungle Fever" debuted on February 19, 1972.

Casey Kasem is selling shoes in Grand Forks, North Dakota.

Doing great, too.
Mork's Shoe Store signed him up for 6 more months!

Casey also works for Wards in L.A., Sears in Findlay, McDonalds in Presque Isle, Coke in Port Huron, Pepsi In New York, Pizza Palace in Lompoc, and more.

Casey gets around. His three-hour radio program, AMERICAN TOP 40, is on over 160 radio stations, every weekend. And so is his selling power.

Over 700 local and regional radio advertisers are feeling the impact of Casey's AMERICAN TOP 40 show. Their commercials within his show get maximum response and traffic and sales. And the sponsors keep on renewing.

And the radio stations keep on showing a profit for three hours of weekend time. Not bad. They also get the highest-rated, best-produced music program attraction in town.

Casey is good. But he has help to make his AMERICAN TOP 40 great. Like seven writer/researchers with six days to prepare the three-hour show. Like Billboard Magazine to supply the world's most highly accredited record chart information. And, Watermark, Inc., to produce, press and ship the program perfectly, punctually every week.

Casey is selling more shoes in more new towns every week, for as little as $39.00 a show. Best of all, he sells himself.

Clip & attach to your letterhead

Tom Rounds, Executive Producer, or
George Savage, Director of Marketing
Watermark, Inc.
931 North La Cienega Blvd.
Los Angeles, California 90069

We may have an opening for Casey.
Send demo, etc., etc., to:

Name: ______

Title: ______

Station: ______

Street: ______

City: ______ Zip: ______

With an emphasis on how *AT40* became a successful local sales tool at stations of all sizes, this advertisement appeared in the March 18, 1972 edition of *Billboard* magazine.

88.) 03-04-72

Program #721-10
story: monstrous T. Rex
story: The Osmonds were a barbershop quartet
story: Donny Osmond jammed telephone lines
story: The Addrisi Brothers' 13-year chart absence
story: Carly Simon born with a silver spoon
story: Nilsson did not write "Without You"
question: fastest rising #1 records
odd chart stat: America's "A Horse With No Name" debuts at #20
program error: Casey's introduces Robert John's "The Lion Sleeps Tonight" as the #5 record; actually, it was #6

89.) 03-11-72

Program #721-11
story: Elvis Presley breaks another chart record
story: The Rolling Stones' popularity
story: Carole King's priceless demo tapes
story: America lives in England
story: Donnie Elbert is the Howard Hughes of recorded music
story: Joe Tex's skinny legs contest
review: Top 5 LPs
question: highest one-week-on-chart, Hot 100 debut
question: song with concurrent Top 10 recordings
oldie played: Ruby Tuesday - Rolling Stones

90.) 03-18-72

Program #721-12
program note: unusual production of hour #2; Casey plays records from #26-#16
story: Bobby Vinton's daring demo session
story: The Beatles' April 1964 Top 5 chart feat
story: Cher's four hits in four months
story: The Carpenters' record company preferred their instrumentals
story: "American Pie" set record for #1 record's longest running time
long version: American Pie - Don McLean
question: one-hit, #1 record artists
question: biggest selling non-Top 40 record
oldie played: Penny Lane - Beatles

91.) 03-25-72

Program #721-13
GUEST HOST: Dick Clark; according to Rob Durkee's *American Top 40: The Countdown of the Century*, Clark suggested the idea of tape recording the program voice segments (Casey Kasem) in advance and mix in the Top 40 records later; initially, Casey recorded the entire show, including music, as a live radio broadcast
odd chart stat: Roberta Flack's "First Time Ever I Saw Your Face" debuts at #17
question: RIAA gold record awards
question: repeating #1 records
story: producer Richard Perry's success
story: Paul McCartney's banned record
story: Janis Joplin's popularity
story: Roberta Flack's pre-recording profession
story: Beverly Bremers is in *Hair*
story: Johann Sebastian Bach's "Joy"
oldie played: Me & Bobby McGee - Janis Joplin

92.) 04-01-72

Program #722-1
program note: Casey encourages listeners to register and vote
story: David Cassidy concert tickets sold for $150
story: Isaac Hayes' "El Classico" purchase
story: Aretha Franklin's roller skates purchase
story: Sonny & Cher were Caesar & Cleo
story: Connie Francis' rise to popularity
record origin: Robert John's "The Lion Sleeps Tonight"
question: most successful disk jockey record
question: artist's remake of a #1 record
oldie played: Don't Break The Heart That Loves You - Connie Francis

93.) 04-08-72

Program #722-2
program note: Casey encourages listeners to register and vote
record origin: James Brown's "King Heroin"
story: The Osmonds' hobbies
story: Don McLean's "Vincent" Van Gogh
story: Elvis Presley's truck driving job
long version: Jungle Fever - Chakachas
question: #1 LP artist
question: controversial Top 40 records
oldie played: All Shook Up - Elvis Presley

94.) 04-15-72

Program #722-3
question: longest charted non-#1 record
question: country group with #1 pop record
program note: answering a listener question, Casey explains *AT40*'s policy on playing double-sided records
program note: Casey encourages listeners to register and vote
story: J.J. Cale's trashy-looking guitar
story: Badfinger members wrote Nilsson's "Without You"
story: Paul Simon's $25 million record
story: The Beatles' solo chart action
story: pre-teen Michael Jackson's four #1 records
story: Frank & Nancy Sinatra's #1 record chart feat
oldie played: Something Stupid - Frank & Nancy Sinatra
program error: Casey's outcue on Al Green's "Look What You Done For Me" indicates that it was his "...second big hit..."; actually, it was his third

95.) 04-22-72

Program #722-4
story: Al Green has plenty of 'sole'
story: Kay Starr's comeback
story: Ringo Starr faked-name LP performances
story: Don McLean's 38 record company rejections
story: Bobby Vinton's career launched by rejection
story: Joe Tex's dancing microphone
name origin: Jo Jo Gunne
program note: Casey encourages listeners to register and vote
program error: after outcue for #29, Casey closes hour #1 with "...we have two big hours and 27 hits to go...."
production error: #27 jingle is used to introduce record #28
question: longest #1 song title
question: capsule history of *American Top 40* radio program (Casey mentions that the show was originally broadcasted in eight cities)
oldie played: Wheel Of Fortune - Kay Starr

96.) 04-29-72

Program #722-5
story: Vincent Van Gogh's artistry
story: Jackson Browne is a songwriter
story: Clint Eastwood discovered Roberta Flack's music
story: Harry Chapin nominated for an Academy Award
story: Sammy Davis Jr. dances
story: Dennis Coffey's 500 chart record appearances
program note: Casey does not identify Buffy Saint-Marie's debut record
question: #1 record's shortest chart run
question: classical-inspired #1 records
question: #1 comedy LPs

97.) 05-06-72

Program #722-6
story: Buffy Sainte-Marie's record deficiency
story: Cat Stevens' album artwork
story: Sonny & Cher's new house
story: Three Dog Night is the biggest concert attraction
story: Aretha Franklin's five Grammy Awards
program note: Casey promos upcoming special
program note: Casey announces the marriage of a KLID (Poplar Bluff, MO) disk jockey
question: biggest instrumental record
question: longest spanning #1 records
question: longest titled Top 40 hit
flipside played: Castles In The Air - Don McLean

98.) 05-13-72

Program #722-7
story: Badfinger was The Iveys
story: The Rolling Stones' one-day, 37,000 concert seat sell-out
story: The Carpenters' canceled concert series
story: Gallery's lead singer is a welder
story: the five chart appearances of "Little Bitty Pretty One"
odd chart stat: top eight positions in the Top 10 are held by soul artists
question: correlation of #1 records and Grammy Awards
question: slowest climbing #1 record
program note: Casey promos upcoming special
program note: Casey encourages listeners to register and vote
long version: Isn't Life Strange - Moody Blues

99.) 05-20-72

Program #722-8
program note: Casey encourages listeners to register and vote
program note: Casey promos upcoming special
production error: in closing hour #1 after #29, Casey states "...we have two big hours and 27 hits to go...."
story: *The Godfather* will gross more income than *The Sound of Music*
story: Jerry Lee Lewis' in-concert piano fire
story: Harry Chapin 'discovered' himself
story: "Nice To Be With You" rated 57½ on *American Bandstand*
story: Joe Tex antagonized James Brown
story: "Hot Rod Lincoln" and other car songs
story: The Rolling Stones are the only remaining British Invasion group
long version: Isn't Life Strange - Moody Blues
odd chart stat: Roberta Flack's "First Time Ever" at #1 for six consecutive weeks
question: song with second longest #1 chart run
oldie played: Whole Lotta Shakin' Goin' On - Jerry Lee Lewis

100.) 05-27-72 **Program #722-9**
story: Bill Withers' gold toilet award
story: The Moody Blues were swindled
story: Love Unlimited was retired
story: Karen Carpenter failed a music test
story: Sammy Davis Jr. forced to record "Candy Man"
story: Dr. Hook & The Medicine Show in Dustin Hoffman movie
program note: Casey promos upcoming special
long version: Walking In The Rain With The One I Love - Love Unlimited
oldie played: Stranger On The Shore - Mr. Acker Bilk

101.) 06-03-72 **Program #722-10**
story: Little Jimmy Osmond on the chart at age 9
story: Bill Withers entered music business at age 28
story: Andy Williams is most successful family member
story: Billy Preston's label credit with The Beatles
story: The Rolling Stones' 85-mile line of fans
story: The Chi-Lites' Eugene Record quit driving a taxi
edited long version: Isn't Life Strange - Moody Blues
long version: Day Dreaming - Aretha Franklin
question: artist with most non-#1, #2 records
question: oldest and youngest #1 artists
question: same-title, different-song records
program error: Casey's outcue of "Sylvia's Mother" states that it was #6; actually, it was #5

102.) 06-10-72 **Program #722-11**
story: Dr. Hook & The Medicine Show recorded a Shel Silverstein song
story: The Staple Singers dropped gospel for pop music
story: Elton John & Bernie Taupin's songwriting technique
story: Frederick Knight did not want to sing
story: Billy Preston's performance at a Mahalia Jackson concert
story: David Cassidy's voice dubbed on Partridge Family TV show
name origin: Commander Cody & His Lost Planet Airmen
program note: Casey promos upcoming special
question: first female #1 record
question: artist with most simultaneous Top 40 records

103.) 06-17-72 **Program #722-12**
story: Elton John searched for drugs
story: Sammy Davis Jr. forced to record "Candy Man"
story: Millie Jackson refused to quit her day job
story: Roberta Flack quit playing the baritone horn
story: Jimmie Castor was Frankie Lymon in concert
story: The Rolling Stones' trail of riots and mob scenes
question: biggest #1 chart fall
question: artist with most Top 10 records, in shortest time span
program note: Casey promos upcoming special
LP cut played: Rip This Joint - Rolling Stones
production note: beginning of Bill Withers' "Lean On Me" is edited

WATERMARK, INC. 931 N. La Cienega Blvd. Los Angeles, California 90069 (213) 659-3834

TO: AMERICAN TOP 40 Program Directors, Operations Managers, Traffic folks, Production guys, etc.

FROM: Tom Rounds, Watermark

RE: Final Notice... AMERICAN TOP 40 Format Change

DATE: June 30, 1972

Here it is... AMERICAN TOP 40 Program #723-2... the first show built around the new hourly format plan.

All internal split logos... C-1 through C-5... are scheduled to hold 2 minutes of commercial content; C-6, at the end of each hour, is built to hold 1 minute. The total of 11 minutes of available commercial time in each hour can be increased in the usual way, simply by the addition of a like amount of total time over 3 hours.

On the First of June, all stations subscribing to AMERICAN TOP 40 were sent replacement pages for the Operations Manual reflecting the new format layout. If you didn't receive these sheets, or if you'd like a new Operations Manual, please drop us a line and we'll be happy to send you what you require.

The continued success and quality of AMERICAN TOP 40 will be built on your continued comments and suggestions. If you have anything to contribute in the way of content suggestions, topics for the specials, our production techniques or technical quality, our methods of delivery... even if you've got an idea for a new syndicated series or special... call me collect and I'll get right back to you on the WATS line.

Thanks !

This memo described a production change that began with the July 8, 1972 program.

104.) 06-24-72

Program #722-13
production note: Tom Rounds notifies subscribing stations of changes in the show's commercial formatting
question: artist with most chart records in one year
question: record with most consecutive weeks on chart
story: Mouth & MacNeal's English hit in Holland
story: Royal Scots Dragoon Guards' soldiers-in-line-of-duty chart feat
story: The Fifth Dimension's wedding went "Up, Up & Away"
story: Neil Diamond's experience with death
story: Karen Carpenter more athletic than brother Richard
story: Roberta Flack is #1 in *Downbeat*
odd chart stat: Luther Ingram's "If Loving You Is Wrong" debuts at #19
program error: Casey's intro to "Outa-Space" promos upcoming special by mentioning "....don't forget, a couple of weeks from now...."; actually, the special was the following week; elsewhere in the show he mentions that it is "....less then 10 days away...."; no reminder is made of the special in the program closing
program note: Casey wishes Decatur, Alabama a successful "4th of July Spirit of America Festival"
oldie played: Groovin' - Young Rascals

105.) 07-01-72

Program #723-1
SPECIAL: Top 40 Records Of The Rock Era
for a complete list of records in this special, see Rob Durkee's *American Top 40: The Countdown of the Century*
credits: Tom Rounds (executive producer), George Savage, Jane Nunez, Steve Aiken, Don Bustany (producer), David Freeze (studio operations), Stew Hilner (operations manager), Larry Aiken, Larry Nixon (business manager), Tommy Whitaker, Susie Aiken & Mary Ann Gordon (production assistants), Nikki Wine, Alan Kaltman & Fred Millstein (writers & researchers), Ben Marichal (chief statistician), Tom Driscoll (security officer)

106.) 07-08-72

Program #723-2
story: Alice Cooper's concert audience walks out
story: David Cassidy's fans are life-threatening
story: Sonny & Cher removed from Rose Bowl Parade
story: Procol Harum's failed "Conquistador"
story: Carole King is most successful female songwriter
story: Elton John is first superstar of the 1970's
story: Bill Withers used the U.S. Navy
question: artist with most consecutive weeks on chart
question: artist with most Top 10 records
odd chart stat: Cornelius Brothers & Sister Rose is largest Top 10 family act
oldie played: It's Too Late - Carole King

107.) 07-15-72

Program #723-3
long version: Layla - Derek & the Dominos
story: Donny Osmond's five re-makes
story: Neil Diamond wrote poems in high school
story: The Hollies remain from the British Invasion
story: Donny Hathaway was Donny Pitts
story: Bobby Vinton's identity problem
question: female artist with most chart records
question: artist with most non-#1 chart records
question: simultaneous #1 records on pop, soul & country charts
production error: Casey's intro and outcue of 5th Dimension record stated that it was "...at #23 on our countdown..."; actually it was #33

TO: SUBSCRIBING STATION MANAGERS, SALES & PROGRAM DIRECTORS
FROM: TOM ROUNDS, AMERICAN TOP 40
RE: RATINGS
DATE: JULY 24, 1972

Not all the April-May 1972 ARB Books are in, but the first 54 books covering markets in which AMERICAN TOP 40 is broadcast looked so great we decided to go ahead and pass on the good news:

1. AMERICAN TOP 40 IS BIGGER THAN EVER!

Counting only those stations who have been with us since the last ARB's came out, the AMERICAN TOP 40 average quarter hour audience has grown by 134,900. Not counting new stations that have started airing the show since, that's 134,900 NEW LISTENERS FOR AMERICAN TOP 40 STATIONS!

By the way, we now estimate the world-wide total weekly cume audience for AMERICAN TOP 40 at more than 6,000,000!

2. AMERICAN TOP 40 STATIONS ARE BIGGER THAN EVER!

Our tabulation is based only on stations that have been broadcasting AT40 since January, 1971. Weekend Metro Shares for these stations have increased an average 43%... more evidence that AMERICAN TOP 40 tunes up the whole weekend.

3. AMERICAN TOP 40 PULLS MORE LISTENERS AWAY FROM THE COMPETITION!

Casey Kasem's special treatment of the definitive, national Top 40 single hits of the week, as reported by Billboard, leads the way in weekend programming. AMERICAN TOP 40 TOPS WEEKEND AVERAGE SHARES BY 46.4%. (Basis: a comparison of the average AT40 Metro Share with the average of all weekend Metro Shares for the 54 stations. It was assumed that AT40's audience was the same as that reported for a time period of 4 or 5 hours, e.g. "Sundays 10AM-3PM").

THANKS TO ALL OF YOU FOR GREAT SCHEDULING, GREAT PROMOTION, GREAT PRODUCTION AND GREAT TEAMWORK!

WATERMARK, INC. 931 N. La Cienega Blvd. Los Angeles, California 90069 (213) 659-3834

Executive producer Tom Rounds offered a bright ratings picture with this memo.

MEMO TO: AMERICAN TOP 40 STATION PROGRAM DIRECTORS
PROMOTION MANAGERS
FROM: TOM ROUNDS
DATE: JULY 25, 1972
RE: SURPRISE SPECIAL

WATERMARK, INC. 931 N. La Cienega Blvd. Los Angeles, California 90069 (213) 659-3834

For a slight summertime change of pace, and in recognition of another record-breaking year in Album sales, we've decided to produce a Surprise Summer Special called...

"AMERICAN TOP 40 PRESENTS THE NATIONAL ALBUM COUNTDOWN"

The Album Special will pre-empt and appear in place of the regular countdown of the Billboard Singles Chart for the week ending August 5, 1972... program #723-6. Because this AMERICAN TOP 40 Extra-Special has not been announced within preceding AT40 shows, Casey will give special emphasis to a running re-cap of the week's top 40 singles.

The National Album Countdown will present highlight cuts from the 40 top LPs of the week as reported by Billboard. Cuts will be selected by the AMERICAN TOP 40 staff on the basis of variety, popularity and airplay.

The National Album Countdown Special is actually one stage in the development of a new program concept by Watermark. In planning for more than a year now, the "LP" counterpart of AMERICAN TOP 40 should be available for licensing to stations in the very near future. As in the case of "The Elvis Presley Story" it will be offered to stations licensed to broadcast AMERICAN TOP 40 at the time on a "first refusal" basis.

We'd welcome your comments... both critical or complimentary... and any suggestions you might have in making such a program more useful to you and your station.

Tom Rounds alerted stations to a one-week-only program format change – a previously unannounced and unpromoted Top 40 special based on *Billboard*'s Top LPs.

108.) 07-22-72 **Program #723-4**
story: Sailcat re-grouped
story: Jim Croce 'shoved' into songwriting
story: Paul McCartney's "Mary Had A Little Lamb" is most popular version
story: Donna Fargo 'were a' English teacher
story: "Day By Day" written 700 years ago
story: Eric Clapton refused to use his name for Derek & The Dominos
story: Bill Withers refused to write songs for other artists
question: #1 record tie
program mention: WAIR (Winston-Salem, NC) personality corrects Casey
LP cut played: Salvation - Elton John

109.) 07-29-72 **Program #723-5**
story: Joey Heatherton not killed by *Bluebeard*
story: "Sealed With A Kiss" summertime chart appearances
story: The Osmonds break Elvis Presley & Beatles chart records
story: Nilsson's previous profession
story: Alice Cooper nearly executed on-stage
story: Looking Glass' long hair problem
story: Paul McCartney thumbed his nose with "Mary Had A Little Lamb"
question: shortest song title
question: most records by one artist
program mention: Happy 50th Birthday to WDRC (Hartford, CT)
program error: Casey mentions that Elton John's real name is Reg Swight; actually, his real name is Reg Dwight

110.) 08-05-72 **Program #723-6**
SPECIAL: National Album Countdown
for a complete list of records in this special, see Rob Durkee's *American Top 40: The Countdown of the Century*
program note: Watermark was experimenting a new LP countdown program with this show, using *Billboard*'s LP chart; because the program change was previously unannounced and unpromoted, Casey also mentioned the chart positions of all singles in the Top 40
story: Janis Joplin's voice is whiskey-soaked
story: Elvis Presley's #1 records on singles, LP, soul & country charts
story: Casey Kasem introduced The Osmonds in concert
story: The Jackson Five managed by a crane operator
story: The Rolling Stones' fans not interested in their music
question: biggest one-hit wonder

111.) 08-12-72 **Program #723-7**
story: Gary Glitter's suggested stage names
story: Barbra Streisand's turned-down apartment offer
story: Rod Argent turned down $1 million
story: Mac Davis is not Mac David
story: Nilsson did not write his Top 10 records
story: Wayne Newton slugged by a teacher
story: Gilbert O'Sullivan makes people laugh and cry
story: Sonny & Cher's beer commercial record (Casey never mentions the product)
question: advance record sales

112.) 08-19-72 **Program #723-8**
story: The Who's gold record award party
story: Nilsson is country singer Buck Earl
story: Barbra Streisand record supports U.S. presidential candidate's nomination
story: James Taylor's pet pig Mona

112.) 08-19-72

Program #723-8 (CONTINUED)
story: British publication *Melody Maker*'s depiction of Alice Cooper
question: record with longest non-Top 40 chart run
question: most recorded Beatles song by other artists
question: biggest Hot 100 chart leap
question: #1 flipside records
production error: Casey states that The Hollies' "He Ain't Heavy, He's My Brother" peaked at #7 in 1969; actually it peaked in 1970
production error: after #15, Casey closes the hour with "....the top 13 sounds in the USA coming right up...."

113.) 08-26-72

Program #723-9
story: The Bee Gees attempted to impersonate The Everly Brothers
story: The Isley Brothers' new social expression
story: Beatles-written, another-artist #1 record
story: Jim Croce wrote after being shoved again
story: Three Dog Night's assistance to unknown songwriters
story: Gilbert O'Sullivan's LP recalled
question: artist with most Hot 100, non-Top 40 records
question: artists with different-version, same-song records
question: 3rd place artist for #1 records
program mention: Happy 13th Birthday to *AT40* affiliate Hong Kong Commercial Broadcasting
oldie played: A World Without Love - Peter & Gordon

114.) 09-02-72

Program #723-10
story: Luther Ingram started in 1964
story: The Raspberries' scented LP
story: Elton John, as a 4-year-old, played at his mother's parties
story: Neil Diamond accommodated Greek Theatre fans
name origin: The O'Jays
question: Gilbert O'Sullivan's song lyrics
question: artist with most #1 consecutive weeks
question: largest Top 40 group
question: artist replacing himself at #1
production error: Casey's outcue for Bread's "The Guitar Man" reads "...after 4 weeks on *AT40*, its up to #13 - it moved 4 notches this week...."; actually, it was in its 5th week on the chart, and in position #11
odd chart stat: Gilbert O'Sullivan's "Alone Again Naturally" returns to #1

115.) 09-09-72

Program #723-11
story: Arlo Guthrie's "Alice's Restaurant"
story: Donna Fargo's double life
story: Chuck Berry is rock 'n' roll's founding father
story: Rick Springfield's Australian popularity
story: Michael Jackson's "Ben" is one of 4,000 rats
story: Neil Diamond's biggest record
story: The Carpenters disliked by the Minneapolis Symphony Orchestra
story: Argent's concert bomber
story: Chicago's LPs
question: record popularity - national vs. local hits
production error: bad edit in outcue of Joe Simon's "Power Of Love"
lyric alert: memo from Tom Rounds which accompanied program alerts subscribing stations to the potentially controversial lyrics in Chuck Berry's record
production note: to assist stations opting to delete Chuck Berry's "My Ding-A-Ling," 'one beat' pauses are edited into Casey's intro and outcue of the record

WATERMARK, INC. 931 N. La Cienega Blvd. Los Angeles, California 90069 (213) 659-3834

TO: Program Directors, AT40 Subscribing Stations

FROM: Tom Rounds, Executive Producer

RE: My Ding A Ling

September 1, 1972

By now you know that Chuck Berry's "My Ding A Ling" has debuted on Billboard's Top 40 chart at #31 and is consequently included in this AMERICAN TOP 40 episode... Program #723-11.

We point this out in accordance with our usual policy to caution program directors regarding the inclusion of "controversial" records in any AMERICAN TOP 40 program.

By now, we're sure you've made your own decision about broadcasting "My Ding A Ling." If you decide to delete the record from this AT40, we have allowed for appropriate "dump-out" points before and after the intro and outro. We'll do the same in future programs if at all possible.

Watermark was so concerned about the potentially offensive content of "My Ding A Ling" that a built-in, one-beat pause in Casey Kasem's dialogue was provided to stations to conveniently edit out the record, according to this memo. This procedure was included in every program until "My Ding A Ling" reached the #1 position. WCFL, the *AT40* affiliate in Chicago, actually edited out the pauses.

"I was a student at the University of Tulsa, in Tulsa, Oklahoma, in the early 70s and jocked on the weekends at KELI under the air name 'Jay Fredericks.' At KELI, we ran AT-40 in the 6-9 p.m. slot on Saturday night, with my shift from 9-12 midnight...............Our (station) owners were very conservative and we, like many other stations, refrained from airing 'My Ding-A-Ling' by Chuck Berry. This was especially tough in the weeks when the song was in the #1 slot on AT-40. (When 'My Ding A Ling' was #1) we cut out the song, and put in a message from either the PD or GM stating that KELI had chosen not to air the song based on the station's interpretation of local standards. That message was, therefore, followed by Casey's usual "goodbye" and theme song to close. That would end it at around 8:58 PM. I would insert an oldie that would not be misconstrued, by someone tuning in late, as being in the AT-40 countdown. That, then, took me to 9 PM to start my regular show, and answer irate listener calls who had waited three hours only to find the #1 song pre-empted............"

Fred Baur, former *AT40* board operator and disk jockey at KELI Radio

116.) 09-16-72

Program #723-12
story: Arlo Guthrie's love telegram
story: Moog Synthesizer chart appearances
story: Main Ingredient's Cleo Award
story: Elton John is *Playboy* magazine's #1 piano player
story: Gilbert O'Sullivan's music jams words
story: Three Dog Night's concert performance feat
question: city named most often in Top 40 record titles
question: posthumous #1 records
production note: to assist stations opting to delete "My Ding-A-Ling," 'one beat' pauses are edited into Casey's intro and outcue of the record
program error: in the outro to Hot Butter's "Popcorn," Casey incorrectly reverses record title and artist "...last week 18, now 23 – that's Hot Butter by Popcorn..."

117.) 09-23-72

Program #723-13
***Billboard* report error: Leon Russell's "Tightrope" and Uriah Heep's "Easy Livin'" chart positions switched**
production error: skip (found in the master tape) in Bill Withers' "Use Me," approximately :35 into the record
production note: to assist stations opting to delete "My Ding-A-Ling," 'one beat' pauses are edited into Casey's intro and outcue of the record
long version: Freddie's Dead - Curtis Mayfield
story: Leon Russell's faked performance I.D.
story: The Who's concert tour losses
story: Jim Croce's quarry truck job
story: Three Dog Night records only LPs
story: actor Rick Nelson was a psychopathic rapist
story: The Moody Blues are #1 in *Playboy*
question: artist chart longevity
question: re-released but failed #1 records

118.) 09-30-72

Program #724-1
SPECIAL: Top 40 Artists From 1967-1972
for a complete list of records in this special, see Rob Durkee's *American Top 40: The Countdown of the Century*
production note: end of hour #2 theme music contains the sound of a squeaking rubber duck

119.) 10-07-72

Program #724-2
story: Jerry Wallace's "If You Leave Me Tonight I'll Cry" is from Rod Serling's *Night Gallery* TV show
story: Joe Cocker dodged beer bottles on stage
story: Rod Stewart concert review
story: Rick Nelson is #1 with teen-age records
story: The Moody Blues' "Nights In White Satin" is a re-release
story: "Popcorn" released in 25 versions
story: The Raspberries' scented LP
story: Mel & Tim's previous profession
name origin: The Eagles
question: year/artist with the most #1 records
question: The Beatles' first hit
program note: Casey welcomes 10 new radio stations
production note: to assist stations opting to delete "My Ding-A-Ling," a 'one beat' pause is edited into Casey's outcue of the record

120.) 10-14-72

Program #724-3
question: brother-sister recording act with most #1 records
question: state named most often in Top 40 record titles
question: song with most charted versions
story: actor David Cassidy
story: James Brown lost 2,000 pounds
story: Rick Springfield's prayer
story: Rick Nelson bombed out at Madison Square Garden
story: Main Ingredient member's famous ancestor
program note: Casey mentions that all listener letters are read by at least two of three key people - Casey, producer Don Bustany and statistician Ben Marichal
production note: to assist stations opting to delete "My Ding-A-Ling," a 'one beat' pause is edited into Casey's outcue of the record

121.) 10-21-72

Program #724-4
program note: Casey thanks the program director and disk jockeys of Radio Hauraki (Auckland, New Zealand) for sending a gift to him - a canoe
question: artists with #1 debut single & LP
question: Top 40 TV themes
question: total number of charted records
odd chart stat: 1950's recording artists Chuck Berry, Elvis Presley & Rick Nelson have records in the Top 10
story: Chuck Berry's first #1 record
story: Elvis Presley rejected by *Ted Mack's Amateur Hour* TV show
story: Leon Russell's Oklahoma estate
story: Three Dog Night broke a Beatles concert record
story: The Fifth Dimension's Marilyn McCoo and Florence LaRue won the same beauty contest
story: Helen Reddy goes from concert circuit to maternity ward
production error: Casey's outcue of Johnny Nash's "I Can See Clearly Now" reads "...The Fifth Dimension move up seven big notches to #21 with that one, If I Could Reach You....."

Soon.....stereo

At last, AMERICAN TOP 40's three hours of dynamite programming will soon be produced in compatible stereo. Our weekly package of three L.P. discs will be great as ever on AM stations and double great on FM-stereo stations that carry the show. Nearly 30 of our 180 stations include the show in their FM programming. And more have asked for stereo.

AM or FM, you'll be getting the same fast-paced, entertaining countdown of the 40 biggest records in the nation. You'll be getting Casey Kasem's fact-filled bios and stories. And you'll be getting all the extra special countdown shows like the up-coming "40 Biggest Artists of the Past Five Years."

If you've never heard AMERICAN TOP 40 before, send in the coupon. We'll send you a demo, our new 8-page brochure and other stuff to help you sell the show in your market. If you've heard the show before, send in the coupon anyway. You might say AMERICAN TOP 40 sounds twice as good as ever.

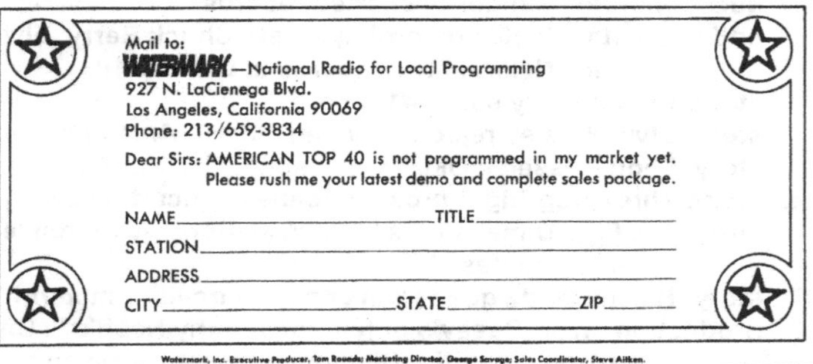
Mail to:
WATERMARK—National Radio for Local Programming
927 N. LaCienega Blvd.
Los Angeles, California 90069
Phone: 213/659-3834

Dear Sirs: AMERICAN TOP 40 is not programmed in my market yet.
Please rush me your latest demo and complete sales package.

NAME________ TITLE________
STATION________
ADDRESS________
CITY________ STATE____ ZIP____

Watermark, Inc. Executive Producer, Tom Rounds; Marketing Director, George Savage; Sales Coordinator, Steve Aitken.

The "Soon...Stereo" advertisement was included in presentation materials sent to radio stations considering the addition of *AT40* to their program schedule.

TO: Program Directors, Engineers, Subscribing AT40 Stations

FROM: David Freese, Watermark

RE: AT40 "Going Stereo"

September 1, 1972

WATERMARK, INC. 931 N. La Cienega Blvd. Los Angeles, California 90069 (213) 659-3834

An upcoming ad in Billboard will announce that "AMERICAN TOP 40 will soon be available in stereo."

To let you in on some details, and to invite your comments and suggestions, here's the plan:

----"Soon" means sometime within the next four months. We're moving our studios and corporate headquarters to a more modern and much larger building in Studio City, about five miles from our present address in West Hollywood. The new address and phone number will be announced shortly. We've decided to build the new control room "from the ground up", and rather than convert present equipment to stereo, start with brand new electronics. Around November 1, AT40 will be mastered in stereo, then mixed down to mono. Test stereo discs will be cut, and testing of these discs will take place simultaneously. When we've worked all potential bugs out of the stereo disc system, AMERICAN TOP 40 will officially be available in "compatible stereo," and we expect this to be around the first of the year.

----The major difference between AT40 stereo discs and the stereo LP's you're playing now is that ours will probably have a slightly lower reference level, a consequence of the greater length-per-side. As usual, a standard reference level will be placed at the beginning of each side to enable you to pre-set your levels.

----Possible problems will be in the capability of your equipment to handle reduced groove width. The same remedy we now recommend will apply: readjustment of tracking weight.

----If you are now broadcasting in mono nothing will change in the sound of AMERICAN TOP 40. The AT40 stereo discs will have the same degree of mono compatibility you are now enjoying with regular commercial LP releases.

-1-

. . AT40 "Going Stereo". . . . . .

----If you are now broadcasting in stereo you will probably have to do no more than put the records on your present turntables and play them in full stereo without ever having to apologize to the "stereo freaks" in your audience again.

----If you are now simulcasting. . . again, no problem depending on whether you usually originate your programming from the FM stereo studio or the AM/mono studio. If you are simulcasting, we'd like to discuss the situation; we have some new ideas on the subject and we'd also like to anticipate any unforeseen problems in this area. Call me collect. I'll be looking forward to hearing from you.

This two-page memo from studio operations manager David Freese alerted stations to an approximate start-up timetable for *AT40* stereo broadcasts. Note his reference to November 1 as a projected date to begin test mastering of the program in stereo. The reference is an indication that stereo programs may have been produced and available internally prior to the February 24, 1973 stereo start date. (See the 3-24-73 show for details.)

123.) 11-04-72

Program #724-6
story: Jim Croce's LP rejection
story: Leon Russell studied classical piano
story: Cashman & West were The Buchanan Brothers
story: flying saucer records
question: male vs. female #1 records
question: foreign artists vs. American artists
question: The Jackson Five sing on Michael Jackson's "Ben"
question: oldest Top 40 artist (corrected on 11-18-72 show)
edited long version: American City Suite - Cashman & West
long version: Nights In White Satin - Moody Blues

124.) 11-11-72

Program #724-7
question: individual Beatles #1 records
question: posthumous Top 40 records
question: highest debut position
program note: Casey promos upcoming special
story: The Temptations' lead singer change
story: "Convention '72" gives equal time
story: The Spinners' name change
story: Jim Croce's other jobs
story: The Stylistics' successful first LP
story: Lobo wrote the *Total Cereal* jingle

125.) 11-18-72

Program #724-8
story: David Bowie - bizarre, new artist
story: Chuck Berry's surfing record
story: Alice Cooper's faked performance
story: Lobo quit college for music
question: artist with longest time between Top 40 records
question: fastest dropping #1 record
question: Broadway musical with most Top 10 records
program correction: oldest Top 40 artist (from 11-04-72 show)

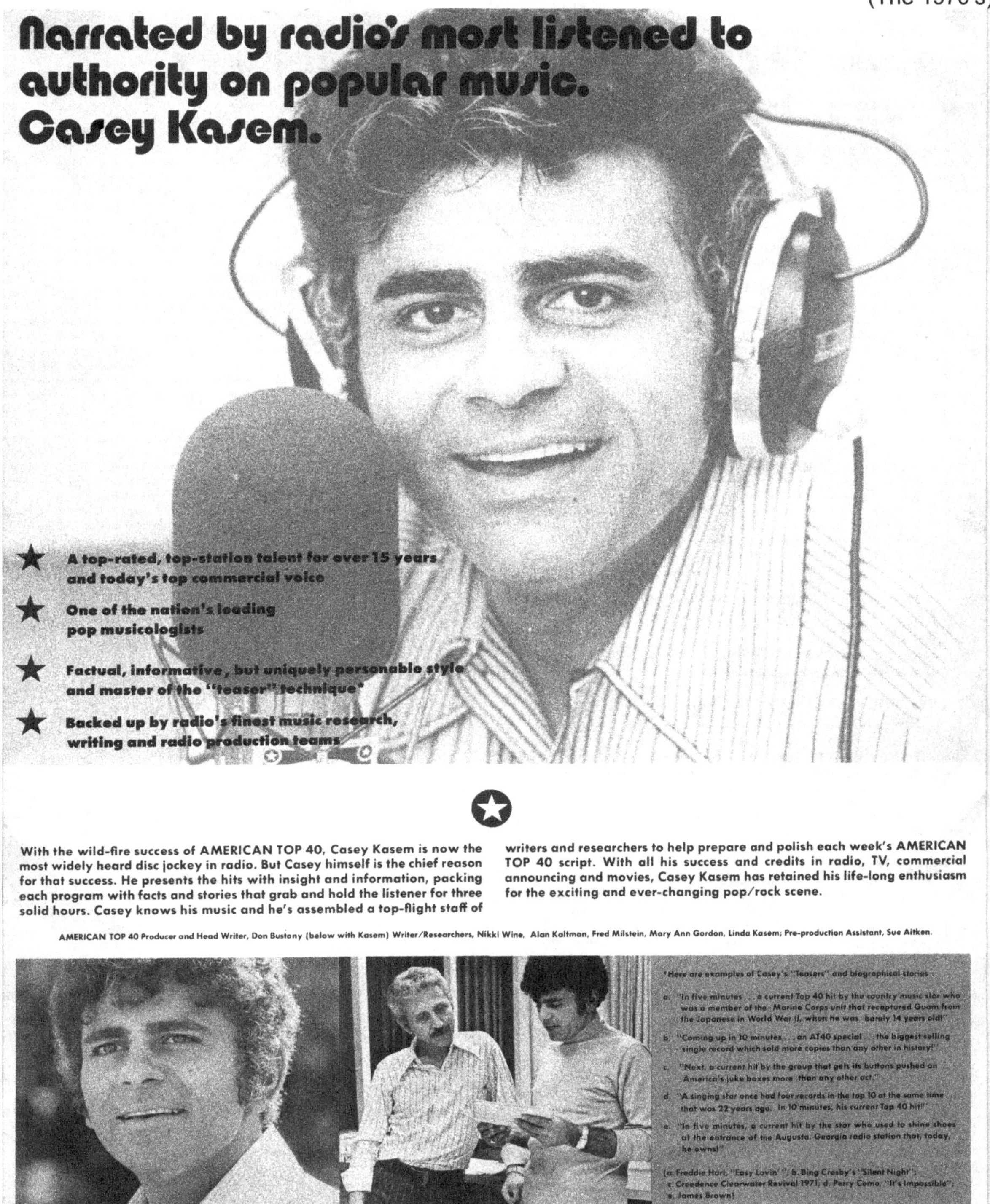

Two pages from the 1972 *AT40* marketing brochure offered insight to what made the countdown program attractive to radio stations.

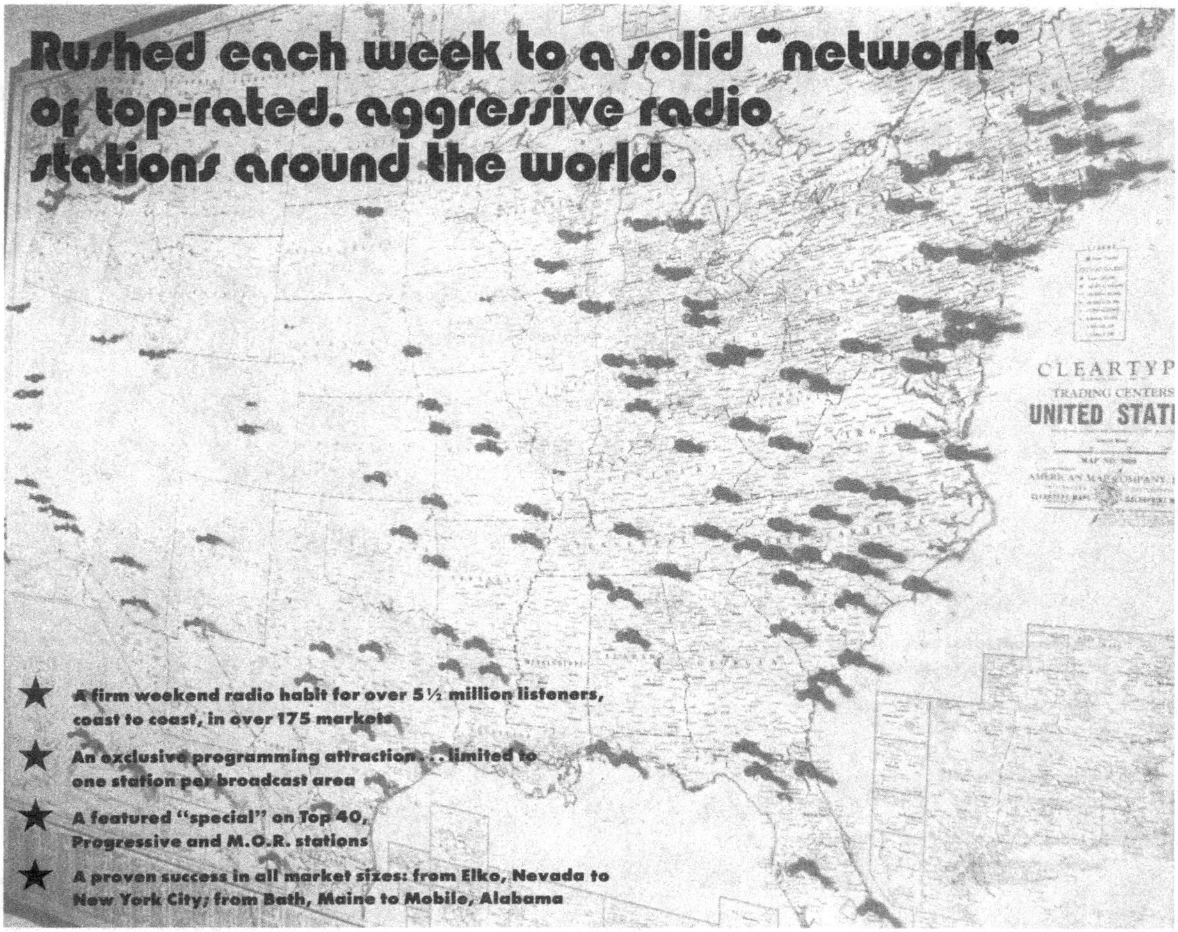

Rushed each week to a solid "network" of top-rated, aggressive radio stations around the world.

★ A firm weekend radio habit for over 5½ million listeners, coast to coast, in over 175 markets

★ An exclusive programming attraction . . . limited to one station per broadcast area

★ A featured "special" on Top 40, Progressive and M.O.R. stations

★ A proven success in all market sizes: from Elko, Nevada to New York City; from Bath, Maine to Mobile, Alabama

AMERICAN TOP 40 is a phenomenon in radio. It is the first block music program to gain acceptance, acclaim and long-term commercial success on so many of the nation's dominant radio stations. Its production sound and content have fit well with a variety of programming formats. It's gained and held audiences and sponsors in all time slots, primarily scheduled on weekends. And it has overcome all of the traditional objections to so-called *outside*, packaged programs. In addition to nearly 200 world-wide commercial-station outlets, AMERICAN TOP 40 is a top-rated feature on over 350 stations via the American Forces Radio Service. Available for exclusive licensing for 13 weeks. Over 60% of the AMERICAN TOP 40 subscribers are currently on 26-week or 52-week contracts.

126.) 11-25-72

Program #724-9
program note: Casey & staff begin weekly predictions of the following week's #1 record; #1 prediction for 12-02-72 program - Lobo's "I'd Love You To Want Me"
program note: Casey's introduction to Austin Roberts' record "Something's Wrong With Me" includes Casey performing his "Shaggy" impersonation, from the *Scooby Doo* cartoon show
production note: disks contain generic promos for upcoming special
story: The Doobie Brothers' audition tape
story: The Moody Blues' Ray Thomas gave away concert tickets
story: Alice Cooper's violent, sex appeal
question: two #1 artists on one #1 record
question: artist with #1 records on the most labels
question: pre-Beatles #1 British records
question: first #1 record by a black female artist
question: 1972's biggest hit (Casey's answer to this question points out that it has not yet been determined because 1972's year-end list "....is now being tabulated by *Billboard* magazine....."; however, for the year-end countdown, *AT40* used a list developed by statistician Ben Marichal, not *Billboard*)
long version: Walk On Water - Neil Diamond
edited long version: American City Suite - Cashman & West

127.) 12-02-72

Program #724-10
story: Albert Hammond performed as women stripped
story: Cat Stevens offends people
story: The Four Tops' formation
story: Rick Nelson bombed out at Madison Square Garden
story: Johnny Rivers is more than a singer
story: Austin Roberts kicked out of school for singing
question: same-name Top 40 artists
question: artist with most consecutive #1 records
question: #1 movie soundtrack themes
long version: Papa Was A Rolling Stone - Temptations

128.) 12-09-72

Program #724-11
story: Johnny Rivers, re-make artist
story: Jim Seals' Texas state fiddle championship
story: Bill Cosby beat Billy Paul
story: Helen Reddy preferred to not record *Jesus Christ Superstar* record
question: artist with longest Top 40 time span
question: record with longest post-#1 chart run
question: song with most versions on the chart
question: record with most on & off chart runs

129.) 12-16-72

Program #724-12
production error: "Angel" by Rod Stewart debuts; wrong song played: Rod Stewart's "Los Paraguoys"
production error: outcue for Neil Diamond's "Walk On Water" refers to chart performance from previous week
question: #1 Christmas records
question: biggest #1 LP, soul & country singles for 1972
question: artist with most one-year #1 records
question: big artists missing in the Top 40 in 1972

129.) 12-16-72 **Program #724-12 (CONTINUED)**

program error: in answering a question regarding big artists not making the Top 40 in 1972, Casey mentions numerous names, including Andy Williams who was in the Top 40 in May/June 1972 with "The Theme from *The Godfather* (Speak Softly Love)"
odd chart stat: James Taylor and Carly Simon (husband and wife) debut with solo recordings at #38 and #37 (see Carly Simon story on 10-16-71; Kris Kristofferson, boyfriend)
program note: Casey promos upcoming special
program note: new "American Top 40 - Casey's Coast-to-Coast" split logo jingles debut
story: Seals & Crofts' religion
story: Dennis Yost sang at Major League Baseball's All-Star game
story: Johnny Nash discovered on a golf course
story: Carole King was Neil Sedaka's "Oh! Carol"

> ***"I was 14 years old, it was December, 1972. My dad had one of those floor-standing console stereo hifi's. Because he wanted to listen to a New York City classical station, he bought a new roof antenna (we lived about 35 miles east of Manhattan). So I helped him hook it up and started scrolling up and down the dial to check out stations I couldn't receive previously. I stopped on 101.9, WPIX-FM, as I heard a program counting down the Top 80 songs of 1972. It sounded very professional and I liked the fact that they gave the story behind the making of a song. From that point on, I was hooked, plain and simple. I began taping the program every Sunday morning from 10am-1pm regularly and would play it back in my own bedroom "make-believe" radio show. For me, growing up with American Top 40 was like having a companion around that I could rely on to always deliver the 40 top hits of the week straight through and never miss a beat."***
> **Kurt Youngmann, a longtime *AT40* listener**

130.) 12-23-72 **Program #724-13**

SPECIAL: Top 80 Of 1972 (#80-41) (based on *AT40* staff's year-end list) for a complete list of records in this special, see Rob Durkee's *American Top 40: The Countdown of the Century*
long version: Jungle Fever - Chackachas
edited long version: Layla - Derek & The Dominos
production error: low-level false start on Sonny & Cher's "A Cowboy's Work Is Never Done"
program note: at least eight records are played where Casey does not speak over the beginning of the song

131.) 12-30-72 **Program #724-14**

SPECIAL: Top 80 Of 1972 (#40 - 1) (based on *AT40* staff's year-end list) for a complete list of records in this special, see Rob Durkee's *American Top 40: The Countdown of the Century*
edited long version: American Pie - Don McLean

TO: AT40 Station Folks
FROM: Tom Rounds
RE: Enclosed "Top 80" Printout
November 24, 1972

It started as an afterthought two years ago when requests for lists of the top records of the year began to trickle in and the AT40 crew found themselves into heavy last-minute xeroxing. Now, as 1972 nears a close, we're a bit more prepared with the enclosed souvenir edition. The sample is hot off the presses... the tabulation was based on all the Billboard '72 charts through this weekend's.

If you'd like to have a stock of these top 80 printouts on hand either for faithful listeners who drop by the station, or to mail out, or even as an extra holiday promotion for your regular sponsors, simply call us collect. Each lot of 250 is only $12.50... postpaid... that's just a nickel each. And for a penny or two more you can add your station call letters or sponsor message to the front cover.

To order your AMERICAN TOP 40 "Top 80" printouts, simply place a person-to-person collect call (if you are in the continental U.S.) to "The Operations Department" at (213) 980-9490. We'll ship all orders placed before December 8 on the 11th so you'll have them before the AMERICAN TOP 40 Year-end Special runs as scheduled on Christmas and New Year's weekends. That gives you plenty of time to distribute the charts to listeners who'd like to follow the top 80 countdown as they lock into your station for six hours.

We'll be looking forward to hearing from you... and setting you up with another merchandising AT40 extra.

WATERMARK, INC. 10700 Ventura Blvd., Los Angeles, California 91604 (213) 980-9490

In this note from Tom Rounds, multiple copies of *American Top 40*'s Top 80 of 1972 year-end list were made available to *AT40* stations and listeners.

1973

132.) 01-06-73

Program #731-1
story: War's back-up experience
story: Hurricane Smith was the Beatles' recording engineer
story: Paul McCartney's "Hi Hi Hi" banned
story: Donna Fargo's stage fright
story: James Taylor & Carly Simon's chart feat
story: John Fogerty is The Blue Ridge Rangers
question: artist with longest span from first chart record to first #1 record
question: rock 'n' roll era's longest-staying #1 record
long version: Walk On Water - Neil Diamond
program note: new chart-position number jingles debut

133.) 01-13-73

Program #731-2
long version: Walk On Water - Neil Diamond
question: record with biggest upward chart movement
question: two-version, one-artist record
question: Top 40 record's longest title
story: Hurricane Smith's three names
story: "Me & Mrs. Jones" uses part of "Secret Love"
story: the meaning of "Superfly"
story: John Denver's name change
program note: new theme music debuts, closing all three hours

134.) 01-20-73

Program #731-3
program note: letter answered from a Chicago listener (program's last broadcast on radio station WCFL in Chicago was 12-30-72, and not heard again in Chicago until 06-09-74)
story: Bobby Womack helped by Sam Cooke
story: Chuck Berry's Berry Park Rock Festival
story: Albert Hammond translated American hits in Spain
story: Timmy Thomas' composition of "Why Can't We Live Together"
question: first Motown #1 record
question: weekday found most in song titles
question: artist with most 1972 Top 40 hits
question: longest time from LP release to single release

135.) 01-27-73

Program #731-4
story: *Dr. Zhivago*'s author refused Nobel Prize
story: Mae West's advice for Elvis Presley
story: Elton John's fear of performing
story: Stevie Wonder's child labor law violation
story: King Harvest's near tragedy
story: chart appearances of "Do You Want To Dance"
name origin: Edward Bear
name origin: Jethro Tull
oldie played: Somewhere, My Love - Ray Conniff

American Top 40 presents 52 specials in '73.

So can you.

47 Weekly Countdowns.

The best of Billboard's Hot 100 hosted by today's number one commercial voice, Casey Kasem. Ratings increases book after book. 200 stations around the world. Recorded at the Watermark Studios, Hollywood's newest 8 track radio production facilities. Shipped every Friday with on time delivery guaranteed. Every show a special.

5 Super Specials.

April 7-8: "The 40 Top Hits of the Past Five Years." A fresh look at the biggest records of the contemporary era, based on Billboard charts from 1968 through 1972.

July 7-8: "The 40 Greatest Disappearing Acts of the Rock Era." Another milestone in rock trivia. What ever happened to such heavies as The Monotones, The Hollywood Argyles, The Singing Nun? They all shot to the Billboard Top 10 and then plummeted right back into obscurity.

October 6-7: "The 40 Top Artists of the Rock Era." Back to '55 again for a 17 year chart sweep that pits today's superstars against those of the 50's and 60's. A new tabulation by AT 40 statistician Ben Marichal.

December 22-23: "AMERICAN TOP 40's All-Time Christmas Countdown." A new review of the biggest holiday hits; a fresh update of one of the most popular concept specials.

December 29-30: "The 40 Top Hits of 1973." Billboard's year end compilation of the year's history making singles.

Mail To:
WATERMARK—National Radio for Local Programming
10700 Ventura Boulevard
Los Angeles, California 91604
Phone: 213/980-9490

Dear Sirs: AMERICAN TOP 40 is not yet programmed in my market. Rush me your latest demo and complete sales package, and better yet, fill me in on how 200 stations have sold the show to 850 different advertisers.

Name ______________________ Title ______________________

Station ______________________ Address ______________________

City ______________________ State ______________ Zip ______________

This advertisement appeared February 3, 1973 in *Billboard* magazine.

136.) 02-03-73

Program #731-5
story: Marvin Gaye's partners
story: Timmy Thomas' part-time jobs
story: "Reelin' & Rockin'" is not a B-side this time
story: Bette Midler is hot
story: "Dueling Banjos" lists no artists on label
story: David Cassidy's stand-in is a woman
story: John Fogerty, Fantasy Records stock boy
question: most weeks for #1 & non-#1 records
odd chart stat: *Deliverance* Soundtrack's "Dueling Banjos" debuts at #18
production note: new music theme plays out cold on LP side 3B
oldie played: Come On-A My House - Rosemary Clooney

137.) 02-10-73

Program #731-6
story: Dr. Hook will not be on *Rolling Stone* magazine's cover
story: Don McLean has most Grammy Award nominations
story: Elvis Presley's offer to become rich
story: Stevie Wonder's #1 dry spell
story: Steve Alaimo, record producer
story: James Brown loses 10 pounds when performing
question: artist with most Top 10 records
question: most versions of a Top 40 record

138.) 02-17-73

Program #731-7
story: Gallery's lead singer is no longer a welder
story: Creedence Clearwater Revival's frustration
story: Billy Paul's work with Bill Cosby
question: white artists at #1 on the soul chart
question: artist with most weeks at #1
question: foreign language #1 records
question: foreign artist ranked second in charted records

139.) 02-24-73

Program #731-8
program note: *AT40*'s first stereo broadcast; however, at least one record within this program, Elton John's "Crocodile Rock," remained in mono
story: David Bowie's "Space Oddity" bombed
story: "Give Me Your Love" is from *Superfly*
story: The Fifth Dimension will tour for no pay
story: Edward Bear's 15 drummers
story: Roberta Flack discovers "Killing Me Softly"
story: Anne Murray's previous profession
record origin: Deodato's "Also Sprach Zarathustra"
question: animal-titled #1 records
question: #1 Oscar award records

140.) 03-03-73

Program #731-9
odd chart stat: Roberta Flack's first two single releases reach #1
odd chart stat: "You're So Vain" in the Top 10 for 11 weeks
story: Diana Ross disliked Billie Holiday's music
story: Loudon Wainwright III's famous ancestor
story: Gladys Knight's early days
story: The Moody Blues were swindled
story: King Harvest was The Five Americans
question: two versions, two #1 records
question: artist with longest span of time between #1 records
program note: Casey promos upcoming special

> ***"..........Perhaps the most outrageous thing that happened when I was on 'AT-40 duty' was during one evening in 1973 when the program director left the station for a publicity event inadvertently leaving the AT-40 discs locked in his office. At KELI, we ran AT-40 in the 6-9 PM slot on Saturday night. I didn't discover the problem until around 5:57 PM, and, as a young man with weak decision making skills, I came on the air at 6 PM and announced that 'the airing of AT-40 (is) delayed -- since Casey (is) locked up in our program director's office!!' This prompted a nervous phone call from the Tulsa Police dispatcher asking if we actually had a man 'holed-up' in an office, and should they send a squad car!!....."***
> **Fred Baur, former *AT40* board operator and d.j. at KELI in Tulsa, Oklahoma**

141.) 03-10-73

Program #731-10
story: Joe Stampley failed with The Uniques
story: The Four Tops' Levi Stubbs will not record solo
story: Bette Midler's naked audience
story: The Moody Blues' Graeme Edge once competed against The Beatles
story: Loudon Wainwright III's factory work with Jonathan Edwards
story: Don McLean was a troubadour
name origin: Hurricane Smith
long version: Do It Again - Steely Dan
question: longest span from first to second versions of the same song (corrected 03-24-73)
production note: beginning of "Daddy's Home" is edited

142.) 03-17-73

Program #731-11
story: Vicki Lawrence's TV appearances
story: The Spinners' wedding causes concert tardiness
story: The Moody Blues remain from British Invasion
story: David Bowie's concert review
story: Alice Cooper is weird
story: "Dead Skunk" skunk festivals
question: Elvis Presley missing the chart
question: #1 family groups
question: male & female #1 record leaders
program note: referring to "Dueling Banjos" stay at #2 for four weeks, Casey promises next week to answer the question "what record stayed at #2 the longest, and for how long?"
program note: Casey promos upcoming special
program error: Casey's promo for upcoming special indicates that it is "...two weeks from now...."

143.) 03-24-73

Program #731-12
program error: Casey makes no mention of "what record stayed at #2 the longest....," as promised in preceding week's show
program error: outcue to "Crocodile Rock" reads "...after nine weeks in the Top 10, it moves to #13......"; actually, it was #27
program correction: longest span from first to second versions of the same song (from 03-10-73 show)
question: last male artist to have two consecutive #1 records
question: highest ranking record with biggest fall off chart
story: Alice Cooper's concert props
story: Sonny refused to allow Cher to record "The Night The Lights Went Out In Georgia"
story: "Killing Me Softly" recorded with partially deaf producer
story: "The Cover Of Rolling Stone" banned from airplay
story: Seals & Crofts changed instruments due to religion
portion played: Do You Want To Dance - Bobby Freeman

144.) 03-31-73 **Program #731-13**
program note: Casey promos upcoming special
story: "The Cover Of Rolling Stone" airplay ban update
story: Jim Croce's military basic training
story: Judy Collins had polio and tuberculosis
story: War is certified gold
story: Deodato disliked other recordings of "Also Sprach Zarathustra"
story: Vicki Lawrence's big break
question: multiple Top 5 instrumentals
question: #1--#2--#1 records
portion played: The Twelfth Of Never - Johnny Mathis
odd chart stat: Roberta Flack's "Killing Me Softly" returns to #1 position

145.) 04-07-73 **Program #732-1**
SPECIAL: Top 40 Records From 1968-1973
for a complete list of records in this special, see Rob Durkee's *American Top 40: The Countdown of the Century*

146.) 04-14-73 **Program #732-2**
story: "Sing" is from *Sesame Street*
story: Tony Orlando's solo career
story: Lou Reed's hoodlum band experience
story: Ronnie Dyson's mother-arranged audition
story: Judy Collins is "Suite: Judy Blue Eyes"
record origin: Deodato's "Also Sprach Zarathustra"
question: most amazing chart statistic
question: The Beatles' weakest chart record
question: artists replacing themselves at #1

147.) 04-21-73 **Program #732-3**
story: The Osmonds' popularity in England
story: War's free ride
story: "Tommy" hits
story: Ronnie Dyson's missed "Aquarias" opportunity
story: Neil Diamond's repeat hit
story: violence in "The Night The Lights Went Out In Georgia"
story: Helen Reddy's win/lose talent contest
question: longest staying Top 10 record
program note: Casey promos upcoming special

148.) 04-28-73 **Program #732-4**
story: the meaning of "Tie A Yellow Ribbon 'Round The Old Oak Tree"
story: New York City won't quit their day jobs
story: The Carpenters paid their father back
story: Sylvia was part of Mickey & Sylvia
story: Jud Strunk's *Laugh-In* chart feat
story: Carly Simon & James Taylor are the richest couple
story: Donny Osmond's voice change
portion played: Sweet & Innocent - Donny Osmond
question: artists with three simultaneous Top 10 records
question: most male and female hit records
program note: Watermark survey distributed to all 200 station subscribers

TO: American Top 40 Subscribers

FROM: Tom Rounds

RE: Sales and Programming Questionnaire Results
.... Part One

Friday, May 18, 1973

WATERMARK, INC. 10700 Ventura Blvd., Los Angeles, California 91604 (213) 980-9490

First of all, may we congratulate you on being the most responsive group in our memory. The two mailings of the questionnaire to 200 of our stations resulted in an 80% return.

The programming section of the questionnaire was designed to give the producers of American Top 40 a keener insight into the real meaning of the show as a programming vehicle for radio stations and how it relates to their overall strategy. Now that we have established general areas for further study, we plan to devise further surveys that will enable us to zero in on specific ways in which American Top 40 can be improved and made more totally relevant. As programmers, we all must be aware of (1) the market for contemporary radio in terms of present product to which the audience is now responding, and (2) how the needs of this audience for new information and new kinds of music and methods of presenting both.... the change factor.... can be met by gradual changes in programming itself.

We thought you'd be interested in the results of the multiple choice programming questions in the survey. Next week, we hope to present a more general analysis of the survey in terms of conclusions that we have drawn from both programming and sales considerations.

Here's how you answered the Questionnaire:

1. Timeliness of Billboard Chart Info

1. Way ahead of us:	2%
2. Slightly ahead:	11%
3. Right on:	28%
4. Slightly behind:	48%
5. Way behind:	16%

2. Compatability of Billboard Chart with Station Playlist

1. Playing all 40:	15%
2. Playing 35:	28%
3. Playing 30-35 :	31%
4. Playing 20-30:	24%
5. Playing less than 20:	2%

.....

Always seeking input from *AT40* programmers, Tom Rounds shared responses from a recent survey in this two-page memo dated May 18, 1973.

3. Chart History in AT40
   1. Love it, want more: 39%
   2. Love it, it's enough: 60%
   3. Cut it down: 1%
   4. Who cares, kill it: 0%

4. Listener Response
   1. Incredible phone & mail: 16%
   2. I hear it on the street: 52%
   3. They don't call, but I know they're out there: 31%
   4. They yawn alot: 1%
   5. We get hate mail: 0%

(note: some respondents crossed out the word "incredible" above.)

5. Chart Info as Laid out and Interpreted by Casey in AT40
   1. Important, easy to follow: 81%
   2. Not important, easy to follow: 14%
   3. Important but hard to follow: 2%
   4. Not important and confusing: 0%
   5. Too much chart info: 2%
   6. Too little chart info: 1%

6. Stories and background info as laid out by Casey in AT40
   1. They're great, but not enough of them: 34%
   2. They're great, but sufficient: 64%
   3. They're OK, but too frequent: 0%
   4. They're OK, but too long: 2%
   5. Play more music: 0%

7. Reasons I schedule AT40
   1. Purely sales: 5%
   2. Sales & Programming (ratings): 58%
   3. Programming only: 22%
   4. Weekend filler: 10%
   5. Boss likes it: 4%
   6. Boss's wife likes it: 1%

8. American Top 40 Specials
   1. I like them: 69%
   2. I don't like them: 1%
   3. I want more: 30%

We're busily analyzing these figures, and in upcoming weeks, we'll be dispensing our opinions as well as some very enlightening special comments that many of you added to your questionnaires. Meanwhile, if you have any comments on the results so far, we'd love to hear them. Call me collect.

And thanks again for your tremendous cooperation!

TR

149.) 05-05-73 **Program #732-5**
story: Elton John's record company said 'no' to "Daniel"
story: Al Green said 'no' to sexy "Pillow Talk"
story: New York City connection to The Five Satins
story: Elvis Presley beat Archie Bunker
story: Dobie Gray was as good as Elvis Presley
story: Donny Osmond, re-make artist
story: foreign country ranking #3 in Top 40 records
story: Stevie Wonder is Eivets Rednow
question: artist with most instrumentals
program error: Casey refers to New Birth's debut record as "I Can't Understand It"; actually, it was "I Can Understand It"
program note: Casey promos upcoming special

150.) 05-12-73 **Program #732-6**
story: Johnny Rivers, re-make artist
story: The Carpenters failed with a Beatles re-make
story: The Beatles' two Top 5 LPs
story: 'flying saucer' technique
story: Lobo is Kent Lavoie
story: Carly Simon's discrimination
production note: explosion sound effect heard after Casey's program closing
program note: Casey promos upcoming special
question: shortest & longest #1 record titles
portion played: Fingertips - Stevie Wonder

151.) 05-19-73 **Program #732-7**
story: "Teddy Bear Song" written by a homicide detective
story: *The Cisco Kid* was a TV show
story: Karen Carpenters plays softball better than brother Richard
story: Clint Holmes quit school to sing
story: Elton John is #1 British recording artist of the 1970's
story: Alice Cooper's near-death concert
odd chart stat: male artist (Stevie Wonder) with consecutive #1 records
portion played: Love Is Strange - Mickey & Sylvia
program note: Casey promos upcoming special

152.) 05-26-73 **Program #732-8**
odd chart stat: five foreign artists in the Top 10
story: Ohio Players will not settle for second
story: Jud Strunk's isolated home
story: Tony Orlando's early days
story: origin of *Frankenstein*
story: Perry Como's mistaken song title
story: Skylark members fired by Ronnie Hawkins
question: 1973's top record
question: #1 country & pop records
program note: Casey promos upcoming special
production note: reverb used in Casey's story of *Frankenstein*
production note: Casey and Don Bustany seek input from subscribing radio stations for research on Disappearing Acts special
production note: galloping horses sound effect is heard after Casey's program closing

153.) 06-02-73 **Program #732-9**
story: "Superfly Meets Shaft" is star-studded
story: J. Geils Band is America's Rolling Stones
story: Dr. John in prison
story: "Tie A Yellow Ribbon" popular due to Vietnam peace agreement
story: Alice Cooper's great put-down

TO: American Top 40 Subscribing Stations

FROM: Tom Rounds

RE: Paul Simon Record

May 25, 1973

The first line of this week's #28 record, "Kodachrome" by Paul Simon, (a new entry to the American Top 40) contains language that some stations may deem offensive to listeners. It is our customary practice to notify stations of possible controversial record content, but as usual, we will refrain from making a judgment or exercising any editorial control.

Such decisions are under the terms of the AT40 licensing agreements left to the discretion of the stations.

Here's another Tom Rounds memo that alerted stations to a potentially offensive record. This time it's Paul Simon's "Kodachrome" which debuted June 2, 1973.

153.) 06-02-73 **Program #732-9 (CONTINUED)**
story: the meaning of Elton John's "Daniel," from a listener question
story: Don McLean's "And I Love You So"
question: artist with most Top 40 records in one week
program note: Casey tells story of listener loyalty in Houston during program's transition from one radio station to another, as described in an article in the *Houston Post*
program note: Casey promos upcoming special
program note: a list of *AT40* radio stations and broadcast times is available for the first time to vacationing listeners (now heard on 200 stations)
production error: Barry White record contains *AT40* background music
production note: an organ sound effect is heard within Casey's closing
lyric alert: memo from executive producer Tom Rounds which accompanied program alerts subscribing radio stations to the potentially controversial lyric content of Paul Simon's "Kodachrome"

154.) 06-09-73 **Program #732-10**
different chart: Top 40 chart used was inconsistent with Hot 100 due to new *Billboard* computer system; the chart positions of only three records on this program matched *Billboard*'s Top 40; in addition, this program contained four records not on *Billboard*'s Top 40 list, including the #27 song, which was not in *Billboard*'s Hot 100 - Jud Strunk's "Daisy A Day"
program note: Casey mentioned that *Billboard*'s new computer tabulations may result in unusual chart movement
program note: Casey received a phone call from Radio Canto in Japan inquiring about the upcoming Disappearing Acts special
program note: Casey stated that Elvis Presley's "Fool" is the flipside of "Steamroller Blues," "......and if its still around next week, we'll play 'Fool'.......”; it was in the Top 40 at #28 the following week, but was not played
program note: Casey mentioned that the *AT40* radio station guide is available to vacationing listeners
program note: throughout its chart run, the running time length of Billy Preston's "Will It Go Round In Circles" varies; for this program, it is approximately 4:09
odd chart stat: "Steamroller Blues" is Elvis Presley's 129th chart hit
odd chart stat: while there were four new records in *Billboard*'s Top 40, this program's chart featured no debut records
story: Three Dog Night's non-LP release of "Shambala"
story: Billy Preston shared record label credit with The Beatles
story: Sylvia wrote, produced and performed "Pillow Talk"
story: "Tie A Yellow Ribbon" may be #1 for 1973

155.) 06-16-73 **Program #732-11**
GUEST HOST: Don Bowman; at the time, Bowman was host-in-training for Watermark's new program *American Country Countdown*; *ACC* went on the air the weekend of October 6, 1973
program note: other than the #1 record, Bowman made no mention to the previous week's position of any record in the Top 40
program note: Bowman invited listeners to send a postcard to *AT40* to receive a corrected chart list from the preceding week's show
program note: Bowman invited vacationing listeners to send a self-addressed, stamped envelope to receive a copy of the *AT40* radio station list
program note: Bowman promoted the 20th anniversary *American Bandstand* ABC-TV special
program note: Bowman promoted upcoming special

FLASH.............ALERT...........URGENT...............BULLETIN

The enclosed American Top 40 program (#732-10) is based on chart information inconsistent with the Billboard Hot 100 dated Saturday, June 9, 1973. The Top 40 presented in 732-10 was supplied to us by the Billboard Chart Department on Wednesday afternoon, May 30 at the usual time. We had been earlier warned by the chart department to expect an unusual chart because, for the first time, Billboard's long-awaited chart computer would be taking over, and that the magazine would print the results no matter how unusual. This explanation of statistical peculiarties (such as records that had been dropped in earlier charts suddenly re-appearing; records that had been moving steadily upward dropping in position, etc.) is given once an hour by Casey Kasem in program 732-10.

Then, late Thursday afternoon, May 31, we were called by Billboard and told that their chart department had discovered errors in computer methodology, that the computer was re-programmed, and that the Hot 100 for week ending June 9 had been re-tabulated. The result was a new list quite different from the one reported earlier on which this week's show was based.

By this time, the discs of program #732-10 had already been plated, pressed and packaged and were awaiting shipment on Friday to our more than 200 subscribers. Rather than risk lateness of delivery, we decided to ship the original 732-10, even though it reports a chart that will not appear in Billboard!!

Watermark prides itself in accurately reporting information, but we hope you will understand that in this one, rare case, we didn't really have a chance. In that all the records played in this week's program are pre-established hits, we do not feel that the erroneous chart will affect the listenability of this program in the slightest.

We also support Billboard's policy of taking advantage of the latest advances in computer science, and we're willing to bear with them in their transition period.

We can assure you that we will check and double check all reports from Billboard in the upcoming weeks, and that this is one problem that will not re-occur.

Thanks!

Tom Rounds
Friday, June 1, 1973

Printed on hot pink paper, Tom Rounds explained in this note an unforeseen, last-minute chart change to the June 9, 1973 program, based on an overhaul of *Billboard*'s computer system. See the program's summary for additional information.

155.) 06-16-73

Program #732-11 (CONTINUED)
program note: throughout its chart run, the running time length of Billy Preston's "Will It Go Round In Circles" varies; for this program, it is approximately 3:03
program note: the LP version of Bette Midler's "Boogie Woogie Bugle Boy" was played
program note: Bowman closed the program with "...keep your feet on the ground, and don't step on any stars...."
production note: auto brake screeching sound effect is heard after Bowman's program closing
question: same-title, different-version #1 records
portion played: Long Ago & Far Away - Perry Como
story: Clint Holmes discovered while impersonating Johnny Mathis
story: Charlie Rich's 5-year chart increments
story: Stevie Wonder's blindness
story: Alice Cooper painted by Salvador Dali

156.) 06-23-73

Program #732-12
question: longest turnover of #1 records
question: multiple and consecutive foreign record chart appearances
story: Gerry Rafferty quit Stealer's Wheel
story: The Carpenters' concert review
story: The Beatles' #1 LP
story: Clint Holmes received Michael's flowers
story: Sylvia's "Pillow Talk" recorded in the dark
story: Three Dog Night's "Liar" recorded in the men's room
portion played: Liar - Three Dog Night
program note: Casey offered *AT40*'s radio station list to vacationing listeners
program note: Casey promoted upcoming special

157.) 06-30-73

Program #732-13
story: The Spinners' needed name change
story: Barry White went to reform school
story: "Monster Mash" is back
story: Perry Como's barber shop work
story: #1 literature instrumentals
story: The Beatles' odd LP chart feat
story: Alice Cooper is different
name origin: The Stylistics
question: record with longest Top 10 chart appearance
program error: Casey stated that "Shambala" was Three Dog Night's 9th Top 10 record; actually, it was their 10th
program note: Casey promoted upcoming special
portion played: I Really Love You - Stereos
portion played: Get A Job - Silhouettes
long version: I'll Always Love My Mama - Intruders
long version: Diamond Girl - Seals & Crofts

158.) 07-07-73

Program #733-1
SPECIAL: Disappearing Acts Of The Rock Era
for a complete list of records in this special, see Rob Durkee's *American Top 40: The Countdown of the Century*

TO: American Top 40 Subscribers

FROM: Tom Rounds

RE: American Country Countdown: First Refusal

July 6, 1973

We're proud to announce a new weekly series coming soon from Watermark. It's a three-hour, weekly countdown of the Top 40 Country singles in the United States as reported by Billboard Magazine. The program, "American Country Countdown", will be hosted by top country music personality and veteran jock Don Bowman.

The complete presentation package including sales brochure, demo tape, posters and the works is in the final stage of preparation now.

On July 23 (issue dated July 28), the first full-page announcement of this new syndication event will appear in Billboard.

The first program produced for air use will be scheduled for broadcast on the weekend of October 6-7, 1973.

As is customary, we are hereby offering current American Top 40 subscribers a first refusal option to license "American Country Countdown" for broadcast on their present facilities. This option will be good for three weeks from the date you receive the full presentation package, and during those three weeks we'll hold off any and all other stations in your market, if you order the first refusal option.

But you must let us know you're interested. Just fill in the enclosed form; stick it in the enclosed envelope, and send it back right away. We'll honor any request for first refusals received by July 25, 1973. And once they're received here, we'll send you the full package, rates, etc. as soon as available. Then you'll have three weeks without worrying about the competition, without having to make any commitments.

Please be sure to send back the form... even if you think there's only a faint possibility you'd be interested in "American Country Countdown". It's worth it for our mutual peace of mind.

WATERMARK, INC. 10700 Ventura Blvd., Los Angeles, California 91604 (213) 980-9490

On July 6, 1973, Tom Rounds announced the start-up of Watermark's latest offering -- *American Country Countdown* -- and made it available first to interested *AT40* stations.

American Top 40... Much More Than Music

1. WAS GEORGE HARRISON FIRST EX-BEATLE TO HIT NUMBER ONE?
2. WHAT DO ALICE COOPER AND VINCENT FURNIER HAVE IN COMMON?
3. DID THE O'JAYS GET THEIR NAME FROM (A) A DISC-JOCKEY, (B) A FOOTBALL PLAYER, OR (C) A SQUEEZABLE FRUIT?
4. WAS IT JIM SEALS OR DASH CROFTS WHO WAS TEXAS STATE FIDDLE CHAMP AT THE AGE OF NINE?
5. WHAT CURRENT RECORDING ARTIST IS SECOND ONLY TO ELVIS IN NUMBER OF HITS?
6. WHY DID LOBO START RECORDING UNDER AN ASSUMED NAME?
7. HAVE THE TEMPTATIONS HAD THE GREATEST LEAD-SINGER TURNOVER OF ALL THE SUPERGROUPS?
8. ELTON JOHN'S "DANIEL." WHAT'S IT ALL ABOUT?
9. WHOSE PUNCH KNOCKED JIM CROCE OUT OF THE TEACHING PROFESSION?
10. DOES DIANA ROSS HAVE ANY FEMALE COMPETITION FOR MOST FREQUENT APPEARANCE IN NUMBER ONE RECORDS?
11. IS PAUL McCARTNEY THE TOP CHARTING EX-BEATLE?
12. WHY CAN'T STEALERS WHEEL DUPLICATE "STUCK IN THE MIDDLE" LIVE?
13. AT THE TENDER AGE OF 23 DOES STEVIE WONDER LEAD THE PACK FOR LONGEST RUN OF NUMBER ONE HITS?
14. CAROLE KING'S STAYED ON THE LP CHART FOR MORE THAN 2 YEARS. CAN ANYONE TOP THIS?
15. WHAT BIG BLUES SINGER TALKED CHUCK BERRY OUT OF BECOMING A HAIRDRESSER?
16. WHY DID THREE DOG NIGHT RECORD "LIAR" IN A TOILET?
17. WHAT TOOK THE DELLS 13 YEARS TO ACCOMPLISH?
18. WHY CAN'T THE MEANING OF STEELY DAN'S NAME BE EXPLAINED ON THE AIR?
19. HAS AL GREEN OUTDISTANCED RAY CHARLES IN THE RACE FOR MORE CONSECUTIVE HITS?
20. HOW DID WOMEN'S-LIBBER HELEN REDDY GET SO MILITANT?
21. WHY WERE THE SPINNERS FORCED TO RELEASE SINGLES UNDER THREE DIFFERENT NAMES?
22. WHAT RECENT DAVID BOWIE HIT BOMBED IN TWO EARLIER RELEASES IN '69 AND '70?
23. IS "SOUL MAKOSSA" THE MOST COVERED HIT OF '73?
24. DID CHARLIE RICH HIT NUMBER ONE COUNTRY WITH "MOHAIR SAM" OR "LONELY WEEKENDS" OR DID HE HAVE TO WAIT UNTIL "BEHIND CLOSED DOORS?"
25. IS BILLY PRESTON THE ONLY ARTIST TO SHARE LABEL CREDITS ON A TOP 40 BEATLE HIT?
26. WHOSE 1941 OSCAR-NOMINATED HIT SONG IS BETTE MIDLER RIDING THE CHARTS WITH?
27. DOES DAWN HAVE THE BIGGEST HIT OF '73 SO FAR?
28. DID THE STYLISTICS GET THEIR NAME FROM (A) A 19TH CENTURY ART FORM, (B) A MEN'S CLOTHING STORE OR (C) A VINTAGE AUTOMOBILE?
29. HAVE THE CARPENTERS COMPOSED ANY OF THEIR HITS?
30. IS JAMES BROWN THE FIRST CONTEMPORARY ARTIST TO HAVE A CHART GROUP NAMED AFTER HIM?
31. WHAT'S PAUL McCARTNEY'S SECRET MESSAGE TO STEVIE WONDER?
32. HAVE THE FOUR TOPS BEEN TOGETHER LONGER THAN ANY OTHER ROCK GROUP?
33. DID DR. JOHN INVENT HIS ROCK IMAGE WHILE SERVING TIME?
34. WHO IS DICKIE GOODMAN, AND WHY HAS HE BEEN CHARTING FOR 17 YEARS?
35. WHAT DID BARRY WHITE LEARN IN L.A.'s TOUGHEST REFORM SCHOOL?
36. HAS BOBBY "BORIS" PICKETT MILKED "MONSTER MASH" MORE THAN TWICE?
37. ARE GLADYS KNIGHT AND THE PIPS THE FIRST GROUP TO HAVE SIMULTANEOUS SINGLES CHART HITS SINCE THE BEATLES?
38. WHAT DID DOBIE GRAY DO IN HIS EIGHT YEARS BETWEEN HITS?
39. ARE THE SIX CORNELIUS BROTHERS AND SISTER ROSE THE BIGGEST GROUP OF SIBLINGS EVER TO HIT THE TOP TEN?
40. SYLVIA'S BACK, BUT WHAT HAPPENED TO MICKEY?

If you like our questions, you'll love our answers. AMERICAN TOP 40 delivers total music information in three dynamite hours every week. Casey Kasem's countdown of Billboard's top 40 covers the world through 225 subscribing stations. And now, as of the April-May ARB, major market AT40 network members have yet another increase in average quarter hour listeners. 52 Specials a year, including five-super specials, every show is produced in full compatible stereo and is shipped to each station on three LP discs. For 850 local, regional and national advertisers, and millions of weekly listeners, AMERICAN TOP 40 is much more than music.

MAIL TO: WATERMARK
NATIONAL RADIO FOR LOCAL PROGRAMMING
10700 VENTURA BOULEVARD
NO. HOLLYWOOD, CALIFORNIA 91604
PHONE: (213) 980-9490

Dear Sirs:
AMERICAN TOP 40 is not yet programmed in my market. Rush me your latest demo and complete sales package.

Name ______________ Title ______________

Station ______________ Address ______________

City ______________ State ______________ Zip ______________

This advertisement appeared in the July 21, 1973 edition of *Billboard* magazine.

159.) 07-14-73 **Program #733-2**

program note: Casey regularly begins mentioning program's chart date in show's closing
program note: Watermark announced the start-up of *American Country Countdown*, and gave subscribing *AT40* stations first right of refusal
question correction: "Nights In White Satin" was the fastest fall-off-the-chart record, not "Crimson & Clover"
long version: Diamond Girl - Seals & Crofts
story: Kris Kristofferson went to Nashville, not West Point
story: "Monster Mash" is a Boris Karloff imitation
story: Charlie Rich advised to play bad, like Jerry Lee Lewis
story: The Beatles & Billy Preston's consecutive #1 solo records
story: Gladys Knight, age 6, was on *Ted Mack's Amateur Hour* TV show
story: letter from *Rolling Stone*'s Paul Gambacini
story: "The Morning After" won an Oscar award

160.) 07-21-73 **Program #733-3**

story: Jeanne Pruett wrote Marty Robbins' songs, but not "Satin Sheets"
story: Chicago's special recording studio
story: Diana Ross' chart success
story: Foster Sylvers' recording of "Misdemeanor"
story: Jim Croce's teaching career ends
story: "Playground In My Mind" name change
portion played: Hey School Girl - Tom & Jerry
long version: Uneasy Rider - Charlie Daniels
program note: Casey mentioned that, since *AT40*'s staff began making #1 record predictions, they have correctly guessed 19 times and incorrectly guessed nine times

161.) 07-28-73 **Program #733-4**

story: braille on Wings' "Red Rose Speedway" LP
story: Aretha Franklin is #1 female with gold records
story: the mystery of "Shambala"
story: Al Green's concert tickets scalped for $20 each
story: another 007 movie song on the chart
story: Maureen McGovern's sex discrimination
story: Billy Preston's B-sides of his single records; story of "Will It Go Round In Circles"
program error: Casey stated that Paul Simon's first solo record was "Me & Julio Down By the Schoolyard"; actually, it was "Mother & Child Reunion"
program note: the LP version of Bette Midler's "Boogie Woogie Bugle Boy" was played

162.) 08-04-73 **Program #733-5**

story: "Soul Makossa" sells for $10
story: Bette Midler's naked audience
story: Bobby Pickett drives a New York City cab
story: Paul Simon's "Kodachrome" will not have a British release
story: the meaning of "Smoke On The Water"
name origin: Lobo
question: back-to-back #1 record-of-the-year artist

TO: AMERICAN TOP 40 SUBSCRIBERS

FROM: TOM ROUNDS

RE: The Last ARB

August 10, 1973

WATERMARK, INC. 10700 Ventura Blvd., Los Angeles, California 91604 (213) 980-9490

About 75 stations subscribing to AMERICAN TOP 40 are located in markets surveyed by ARB in April-May, 1973. All the books are in, and we've finally had a chance to analyze the results from a variety of standpoints. Because of the tremendous differences in specific markets, specific ratings results are difficult to assess. But after examining all 75, and averaging the statistics, we can draw some general conclusions. Neatly avoiding the currently raging controversy over the accuracy of ARB, especially in weekend time blocks, I feel that our analysis does reflect the listener acceptance of AMERICAN TOP 40 on a national basis. Here are the results of our computations on specific areas of information:

1. AT40 Improvement. We based our analysis on the average quarter hour figures for all persons 12+ in the total survey area, and compared the figures for April-May, 1973 to those listed for the prior ARB survey... depending on market size either January-February, 1973; October-November, 1972 or April-May 1972. We tried to determine if more, or less, people were listening to AMERICAN TOP 40 than before. In other words, is the general AMERICAN TOP 40 audience growing? 67% of individual stations' average quarter hours were up, 33% were down.

2. AT40 Improvement (based on metro shares). This is another way of arriving at the same conclusion. This time we examined the "metro share" report; in other words, the shore of the people listening to the radio during the period in which AT40 is scheduled as opposed to the total number of persons. 63% of our subscribers showed an increase in AT40 audience share; 37% showed a decrease.

3. AT40 compared to Mon-Sunday 6AM-12Midnight. Next we checked to see how AT40 fared, not in respect to the rest of the stations in the market, but in respect to the balance of the subscribers' schedules. Was there a concentration of listening while AT40 was being broadcast? The answer was "Yes". In 74% of all situations, AT40 had a higher share than the station average for the entire week, and in 26% of these cases, the AT40 share was lower.

/////

This two page memo from Tom Rounds to stations, dated August 8, 1973, highlighted *AT40*'s recent ARB April-May 1973 ratings from 75 program subscribers.

AT40 Subscribers
Re: The Last ARB
August 8, 1973.........Page 2

4. AT40 rank in market compared to subscribers'. This was another way of appraising AMERICAN TOP 40's strength as a special programming feature. Based on metro audience share, here's how it looks:

	Subscribers	AMERICAN TOP 40
Ranks Number One in Market	24 %	41 %
Ranks Number Two in Market	23 %	24 %
Ranks Number Three in Market	10 %	20 %
Ranks Number 4 or lower	26 %	32 %

Reaction to the above figures should be conditioned by the fact that the weekend time periods in which AMERICAN TOP 40 is scheduled vary greatly and are not representative of a subscriber's general standing in the market. On the weekend, everything is different, including the receptivity of the audience and the strength of competitive programming.

Other general conclusions that can be drawn include:

1. If a station is up or down in ratings, so goes AT40, although there are frequent exceptions to this conclusion.

2. The strength of demographic groups listening to AT40 is roughly parallel to that of the station's entire week. However, AT40 tends to pull heavier men and women 18-34 and slightly fewer teens, on the average.

3. Sharp increases and decreases from prior ARB reports were much more frequent in periods of overall lighter listening, such as Sundays 7PM-12Midnight. Listening from survey period to survey period was less erratic in periods of concentrated listening such as Sunday afternoons. Subscribers either ecstatic or depressed by severe changes in listening since the last rating book came out were usually those who had scheduled AT40 in a "light listening" time slot such as Sunday evenings. Some of these subscribers mentioned they felt that sample sizes became so small in "off times" that the survey results were not entirely dependable.

163.) 08-11-73 **Program #733-6**
story: Al Green's fan description
story: Karen Carpenter's 'baseball' hits
story: Helen Reddy's weekly allowance
story: Diana Ross' Japanese royalty invitation
story: Aretha Franklin's Grammy Award success
story: unusual chart appearance of "Young Love"
story: Bette Midler's *Ms.* article
program correction: artist with most Top 10 records
long version: Diamond Girl - Seals & Crofts

> ***"This is Casey Kasem on AT40 and here's that letter from a listener in Santa Monica, California asking a question that we answered on the show just a few months ago. But today we have a different answer. Alice Gardner wants to know what artist has had more records in the Top 10 than anybody else. Well Alice, a few months ago we said that it was Bing Crosby with a total of 57 Top 10 hits. But we've done some more research thanks to your letter and we've discovered that the total number of hits is actually 63 and not 57. And they all belong to Bing Crosby – still the record holder for the greatest number of hits in the Top 10. Alice, thanks a lot for your letter. And now, on with the countdown....."***
>
> ***AT40*** **host Casey Kasem making a correction on the August 11, 1973 program.**

164.) 08-18-73 **Program #733-7**
odd chart stat: first of three debut records appears in the Top 40 at #31, indicating that nine records were heard before the first debut song
production error: no outcue for Carole King's "Believe In Humanity"
program error: Casey references title of Isley Brothers' "That Lady" as "Meet The Lady"; listed on Hot 100 as "Meet That Lady"
story: Billy Preston is best with Top 10 vocal & instrumental hits
story: Al Green was biggest for 1972
story: Lobo refuses publicity
story: Paul McCartney's label credits
story: Johnnie Taylor's name trouble
story: "Uneasy Rider" lyric error
story: Bobby Womack's record company told him 'no recording'
story: Carole King helped Little Eva
question: #1 record repeat chart appearances
long version: Saturday Night's Alright For Fighting - Elton John
long version: Diamond Girl - Seals & Crofts

165.) 08-25-73 **Program #733-8**
question: #1 recording artist profession origins
story: Cat Stevens' flying saucer trip
story: The Isley Brothers' 1950's, 1960's & 1970's chart records
story: Paul Simon danced with Carole King
story: Gilbert O'Sullivan's Grammy Award embarrassment
story: Marvin Gaye is Motown's biggest artist
story: Jim Croce's "Bad Bad Leroy Brown" is real
name origin: Grand Funk Railroad
long version: Angel - Aretha Franklin

166.) 09-01-73

Program #733-9
flipside played: You Light Up My Life - Carole King
flipside played: A Million To One - Donny Osmond
long version: Diamond Girl - Seals & Crofts
long version: Angel - Aretha Franklin
story: Kris Kristofferson was Billy The Kid
story: Don Covay's songwriting success
story: War's early career goal
story: Curtis Mayfield's "Superfly" profits
story: Three Dog Night's battle with B.W. Stevenson over "Shambala"
story: repeat Top 10 records
story: Diana Ross on The Jackson Five's cartoon show
story: "Brother Louie" similar to "Society's Child"
question: back-to-back #1 female artists
program note: old numerical jingles return
program error: Casey's outcue of "Why Me" states "...at #32 this week.."; actually, it was #31
program error: in describing Don Covay's songwriting success, Casey indicated that he told of Covay's "Chain Of Fools" the preceding week; however, there was no mention of Covay's songwriting prior to this show
program error: Casey's introduction to Joe Simon's "Cleopatra Jones" listed Joe Simon's "...four big hits in the past..." but did not mention "Power Of Love" and "Step By Step"

167.) 09-08-73

Program #733-10
production note: instrumental version of Joe Simon's "Theme From *Cleopatra Jones*" played
odd chart stat: "Monster Mash" ties record for all-time total weeks
question: the reality of "Uneasy Rider"
story: Dawn successful, yet unknown
story: Elton John's concert review
story: Edgar Winter's concert review
story: Maureen McGovern's "The Morning After" has two meanings
story: Grand Funk's $40,000 donation for drug rehabilitation
story: Tyrone Davis' career saved by a three-year-old
portion played: Young Love - Tab Hunter
portion played: Young Love - Sonny James
program note: Casey promos upcoming special

168.) 09-15-73

Program #733-11
flipside played: A Million To One - Donny Osmond
long version: Gypsy Man - War
long version: Angel - Aretha Franklin
long version: Ramblin' Man - Allman Brothers Band
question: non-entertainment industry Top 40 records
program note: Casey promos upcoming special
story: Conway Twitty's chart absence
story: Sly Stone's on-stage description
story: Cher will not succeed, according to Phil Spector
story: Diana Ross is like fighter Joe Lewis
story: Allman Brothers' deaths
odd chart stat: "Monster Mash" breaks record for all-time total weeks on the Hot 100

TO: Sales, Promotion and Program Directors, AT40 Subscribers

FROM: Steve Aitken, Marketing Director

RE: Brand New Merchandising Item: AT40 Playing Cards

August 24, 1973

Here's a sample of the hit giveaway item at the Billboard Programming Forum ... a deck of AMERICAN TOP 40 Playing Cards. Each deck includes 56 cards ... the usual 52 plus 2 jokers, a Casey Kasem picture card and a card listing important facts about AMERICAN TOP 40.

Manufactured by U.S. Playing Card Co. of Cincinnati, manufacturers of "Bicycle" brand cards, the AT40 decks are the real thing.

They're available to AT40 subscribers as the latest merchandising item at Watermark's cost. Possible uses:

1. Advertiser location giveaways or premium items... at either sponsor or station cost.

2. Gifts to sponsors either presently or potentially backing AT40 broadcasts.

3. Station giveaways or contest prizes.

4. The secret Saturday night card game your chief engineer's been holding at the transmitter all these years.

5. Wherever your imagination leads you.

We have 2,000 decks in stock right now. More require a six week order, so we suggest you order a few dozen to have on hand or more if you come up with specific uses immediately. The cost... $12.00 per dozen... includes handling and shipping to U.S. radio stations. Postage will be charged to subscribers overseas.

Mail To: Steve Aitken
Watermark, Inc.
10700 Ventura Boulevard
No. Hollywood, California 91604

Steve--send me ________ dozen deck(s) of AMERICAN TOP 40 Playing Cards.
@ $12 per dozen that makes my total cost $______________.
Please make checks payable to: Watermark, Inc.

My Name:________________________________ Title:____________________

Signature:_____________________________ Station Call Letters:__________

Address:____

City:______________________State:__________________Zip:____________

A rarely seen promotional tool -- the *AT40* Playing Cards -- made available to affiliates as described in Steve Aitken's August 24, 1973 memo. Included in the deck of cards was an *AT40* fact card and a rare photo of a cigar-smoking, card-playing Casey Kasem. He, apparently, lost his shirt in the last hand.

169.) 09-22-73 **Program #733-12**
program note: program disks contain upcoming special promo announcements
program note: Casey promos upcoming special
odd chart stat: Marvin Gaye's "Let's Get It On" returns to #1 position
odd chart stat: chart of 09-15-73 makes 1973 a record year for #1 female artists
story: The Tokens are now Cross Country
story: Allman Brothers Band's record-breaking concert
story: Conway Twitty inspired *Bye Bye Birdie*
story: Elton John's introduction to Bernie Taupin
story: The Isley Brothers' big break
story: Elvis Presley's British fan club

170.) 09-29-73 **Program #733-13**
story: Bob Dylan's honorary doctorate
story: The Pointer Sisters' popularity
story: Cher's Indian image
story: Eddie Kendricks' career launched with stolen check
story: "Delta Dawn" failed twice
question: biggest selling single & LP
question correction: #1 records about real people
name origin: Dawn
program note: Casey promos upcoming special

171.) 10-06-73 **Program #734-1**
SPECIAL: Top 40 Artists Of The Rock Era (update from 05-01-71 special) for a complete list of records in this special, see Rob Durkee's *American Top 40: The Countdown of the Century*

TO: AT40 Subscribers

FROM: Tom Rounds

RE: AMERICAN TOP 40 IDEA BANK

Friday, September 14, 1973

Looks like the idea for the Idea Bank is paying off. Jerry King, PD at KVSF, Santa Fe, N. M., called today with an inspiration we're putting into action immediately.

To help promote the next upcoming special (Program #734-1, scheduled for the weekend of October 6-7), we're adding four special voice tracks to the AT40 program discs this week, for you to lift off and use outside the show.

Each of the 4 promos spots will be recorded dry (no music bed) and are designed to be run as follows:

Spot # 1-----from 10 days before your scheduled date of the special through the weekend before the special;

Spot #2-----the week before the special (refers to "this weekend");

Spot #3-----the day before the special (refers to "tomorrow");

Spot #4-----the day of the special (refers to "coming up").

We've tried to make the material as general as possible. We suggest specific times and dates be added to the Casey tracks along with as much station production as you'd like to throw in.

CONSULT THE AT40 CUE SHEET TO LOCATE THE CUTS ON THE PROGRAM DISCS.

This special is going to be really special, and it's worth special promotion, so we hope you'll find this material useful.

And thanks, Jerry.

WATERMARK, INC. 10700 Ventura Blvd., Los Angeles, California 91604 (213) 980-9490

As described in this September 14, 1973 memo from Tom Rounds, an idea to include separate LP voice tracks to promote an upcoming *AT40* special was put into action for the first time.

To: AT40 Subscribers

From: Tom Rounds

Re: Idea Input

Friday, October 5, 1973

1. From Bob Kaghan, PD at WISE, Asheville, N.C. comes this helpful household hint: why not lay 60 seconds of "in-the-clear" AT40 theme on a separate cut on one of the regular shows so stations can lift it off and use for promo B.G. or whatever?

Sounds like a good idea, so we're doing it. Following a locked groove at the end of a likely half hour side on one of this week's (734-2) AMERICAN TOP 40 discs is 60 seconds of opening theme (in mono) for your dubbing pleasure.

2. From J. J. Jordan, PD at WGRQ, Buffalo, N.Y. a potential can of worms (thanks, J. J.), but something that we feel is worthy of airing:

J. J. has mentioned a problem with music balance that usually shows up in hour I, and that is the predominance of hugh clusters of R&B material that either has (a) shown signs of crossing into general Top 40 (b) shown signs of remaining strictly music for R&B programming (c) shown signs of stiffing completely. We'll refrain from giving any examples for obvious reasons, but we agree with J. J.

Neither of us, unfortunately, has any solution to the problem. If we had the option to program the order of records played, the problem would be greatly diminished, but, of course, the countdown marches on in the precise order directed by the Billboard chart.

Setting up a mechanism whereby individual stations could eliminate product in the #31-40 range that, in their opinion, didn't justify inclusion as an established hit might help. At the moment, we just haven't figured a way to do this and preserve the "cluster" format presently in use. Any suggestions will be deeply considered.

In general, we should make the comment that Billboard has greatly increased the timliness of its chart. Because of new, rapid research methods and a reorganization that has brought the collection of data closer to the completion of the chart, Billboard is acually coming up with records in the top 40 that are so new they haven't broken in some markets.

/////

WATERMARK, INC. 10700 Ventura Blvd., Los Angeles, California 91604 (213) 980-9490

This two-page memo dated October 5, 1973 from Tom Rounds addressed correspondence from two program directors highlighting the need for access to an unedited *AT40* theme and a potential problem with music balance in the program's first hour.

To: AT40 Subscribers

Page 2.

October 5, 1973

For this reason, we're super reluctant to make a judgement ourselves as to whether a particular record does or doesn't belong in the top 40. Who knew, for example, that "Funky Worm" would become a pop hit in so many places? In other words, we don't want to single out any record or records as being deletable from the show, but we do want to remind stations that it is always their option to delete anything they feel, for whatever reason, shouldn't be played. And this doesn't just go for the typical 4-in-a-row R&B sweep that contains records that may be stiffing in a particular market. This goes for any record. The problem is how, and we're open for ideas.

On the other side, however, snap judgements can get all of us in trouble. As many times as not, a record that crept into the #38 position and looked like the all-time stiff has turned out to be a giant; whereas quite a few "sure-shots" have fizzled in the high 20's.

AT40 has many uses, and perhaps one of them is the fact that it does give quite a few records another chance on a national basis. Back in my old programming days, I missed obvious hits... everybody does. And if AT40 can smoke out consumer response for a record that fools most of us, great! Lord knows we all need all the hit record product we can find.

172.) 10-13-73

Program #734-2
production error: "You're A Special Part Of Me" by Diana Ross & Marvin Gaye debuts; wrong song played: Diana Ross & Marvin Gaye's "I Just Fall In Love With You"
program error: Casey stated that "...Joe Simon got as high as #18 - that was last week..."; actually, Joe Simon peaked at #19
story: The DeFranco Family's popularity pre-tested
story: Paul Simon's "Bridge Over Troubled Water" earned more than $3.5 million
story: Diana Ross & Marvin Gaye, super duo
story: Kool & The Gang's big break
story: two records from the movie *Cleopatra Jones*
odd chart stat: Diana Ross/Marvin Gaye duet debuts; each has a former #1 record in the Top 40
question: year with no #1 female record
question: comedy spoofs
production note: program disks contain a separate cut of *AT40* theme music

173.) 10-20-73

Program #734-3
story: Jim Croce remembered
story: Bobby Goldsboro's love of baseball
story: The Rolling Stones are the biggest rock group
story: Dawn emotional over "Tie A Yellow Ribbon"
story: Simon & Garfunkel's back-to-back solo records
story: Marie Osmond is fourth Osmond act in Top 40
story: Seals & Crofts' early days
long version: Ramblin' Man - Allman Brothers Band
production note: whistle in program theme at close of show

174.) 10-27-73 **Program #734-4**
question: #1 female artist record-of-the-year
story: Seals & Crofts' religion
story: Bob Dylan has something in common with Lawrence Welk
story: Stevie Wonder's automobile accident
story: Gladys Knight's biggest record
story: Ringo Starr hated by Pete Best fans
story: Ike & Tina Turner's concerts
portion played: Love Jones - Brighter Side of Darkness

175.) 11-03-73 **Program #734-5**
production note: crowd cheering sound effect heard after Casey's closing
odd chart stat correction: *AT40* staff was in error when they announced that "Monster Mash" broke a chart record (from 09-15-73 show)
production error: Casey introduced Roberta Flack's "Jesse" by stating "... at #33, moving up 3 notches..."; actually, it dropped three notches
story: Ike & Tina Turner described by *Life*
story: Marvin Gaye's partners
story: Stevie Wonder's practical joke on Elton John
story: Frank Sinatra discovered Harold Melvin & The Blue Notes
story: solo Temptations
story: The Carpenters' home life

176.) 11-10-73 **Program #734-6**
program note: Casey announced his upcoming personal appearance in Houston on Monday, November 19 for a movie opening - *Soul Hustler* - in which he has a starring role
story: Ringo Starr's LP reunites The Beatles
story: The Pointer Sisters buy clothes at thrift stores
story: Eddie Kendricks' solo struggle
story: Todd Rundgren was a member of Nazz
story: Paul Simon backed by The Dixie Hummingbirds
portion played: Loves Me Like A Rock - Dixie Hummingbirds
odd chart stat: eight family acts in the Top 40
question: record year for #1 records

177.) 11-17-73 **Program #734-7**
story: Bobby Goldsboro injured by his breakfast, per *The National Enquirer*
story: Tavares' "Check It Out" written by lost friend
story: Kris Kristofferson's "Why Me" almost not released
story: meaning of "Goodbye Yellow Brick Road"
story: Jim Webb wrote "All I Know" and other records
story: Marie Osmond is youngest #1 country artist
question: Top 40 movie theme records
program note: after the #1 record, Casey stated there would be no #1 record prediction for next week by explaining "....that way, we won't be wrong..."
odd chart stat: Marvin Gaye has three records in the Top 40

TO: AMERICAN TOP 40 SUBSCRIBERS

FROM: TOM ROUNDS

Friday, November 30, 1973

WATERMARK, INC. 10700 Ventura Blvd., No. Hollywood, California 91604 (213) 980-9490

***** UPCOMING SPECIALS, SHIPPING DATES, HOLIDAY HASSLES, ETC.

On Friday, December 7, the Watermark sorting, packing, sticking and stamping crew will be packing and shipping Three AT40 Shows simultaneously. This means that you will be receiving programs 734-11 (air date Dec. 15-16), 734-12 (air date Dec. 22-23) and 734-13 (air date Dec. 28-29) in one package. You should advise your people that regular shipments will, therefore, not be arriving on the weeks beginning Dec. 17 and 24. More than ever, it's important to remind the usual people to call us if the shipment has not been received or has been damaged in transit on the Wednesday prior to the first of the above air dates, Wednesday December 12. Trouble calls should be placed person to person collect to "The Operations Department" at (213) 980-9490. We'll get right back to you on the 'WATS' line to coordinate an emergency shipment via air freight.

Since 1970, we've turned out at least 15 special countdown shows dealing with a wide variety of subjects relating to chart history... all attempting to understand the significance and excitement of pop music in contemporary culture. We've all come a long way since '70, but now we're going right back to where we started on specials with show #734-12... "The All-Time Christmas Countdown". A show with this same title aired on December 20, 1970, and featured replays of the durable holiday favorites... at least the ones we could track down. This year's edition is a vast improvement. We succeeded in locating all the original records... all of them are in the show, with one exception, the quality of which was marginal. The research is much more comprehensive and the production crew went overboard to present the music in such a way that none of the different artists identified with each of the biggest Christmas songs was neglected. In any case, we hope you enjoy airing "The All-Time Christmas Countdown" as much as we enjoyed putting it together. We think it's worthy of extra promotion or special scheduling consideration.

The second of the two specials, #734-13, will be our annual countdown of "The 40 Top Hits of 1973".

With these specials in your hands 2-3 weeks prior to air time, you might want to consider lifting certain elements to create promos or special demo cassettes for the sales folks.

Extra copies are available @ $7.50 postpaid from Watermark (cash, check or gas rationing stamps) while they last.

Happy Holidays!!

_AT40_ stations were provided with delivery plans for the final three 1973 programs – including two specials – in this November 30, 1973 memo from Tom Rounds.

178.) 11-24-73 **Program #734-8**
program note: Casey thanked radio station KRLY in Houston and those attending the opening for the movie *Soul Hustler*
program note: Casey resumed #1 record predictions
story: Cher missed with "The Night The Lights Went Out In Georgia"
story: Todd Rundgren's multi-colored hair
story: Ruth Pointer marries
story: Neil Diamond & Casey Kasem in the same movie
story: Elton John introduced in concert by celebrities
question: most-named state in #1 records
question: three biggest female artists
long version: Ramblin' Man - Allman Brothers Band

179.) 12-01-73 **Program #734-9**
question: *AT40* heard in the movie *Scarecrow*
odd chart stat: Jim Croce's "Time In A Bottle" debuts at #18
odd chart stat: Jim Croce is first to have two posthumous, simultaneous Top 20 records
odd chart stat: first of three debut records appears in the Top 40 at #32, indicating that eight records were heard before the first debut song
story: Johnnie Taylor replaced Sam Cooke
story: Nutbush is not on the map
story: Sonny & Cher's ticket sales resulted in 80,000 telephone calls
story: Ringo Starr's unhealthy childhood
story: "Tie A Yellow Ribbon" is 1973's #1 jukebox record
story: Charlie Rich voted likely to succeed
program note: Casey promos upcoming specials

180.) 12-08-73 **Program #734-10**
program note: Casey & staff made their last prediction for the following week's #1 record; finishing at 15 correct and 32 incorrect predictions (see 07-21-73)
program note: Casey promos upcoming Christmas special
program note: Casey promos upcoming specials
program note: original *AT40* theme closes hours #2 & #3
story: "Time In A Bottle" is from the TV movie *She Lives*
story: movie plot of *Jonathan Livingston Seagull*
story: Brownsville Station specializes in bathroom songs
story: Billy Preston's big break
story: The Carpenters' 'sprinkled moon dust'
story: the Moog Synthesizer
portion played: Switched-On Bach - Walter Carlos
odd chart stat: three artists - Jim Croce, Gladys Knight & The Pips, Marvin Gaye - each have two records in the Top 40

181.) 12-15-73 **Program #734-11**
odd chart stat: last of 19 weeks in the Top 40 for Kris Kristofferson's "Why Me"
odd chart stat: siblings Donny Osmond and Marie Osmond have separate records in the Top 40
production error: skip (found in the master tape) in Carole King's "Corazon", approximately 1:20 into the record
program note: Casey announced that he was in Honolulu recently for a filming of *Hawaii Five-O* and thanked radio station KPOI and a *Honolulu Advertiser* newspaper writer
program note: Casey & staff correctly predicted Charlie Rich's #1 record, however no mention is made
flipside played: When I Fall In Love - Donny Osmond
long version: Hello It's Me - Todd Rundgren

181.) 12-15-73 — **Program #734-11 (CONTINUED)**
question: #1 solo Beatles LPs
program note: Casey promos upcoming specials
program note: original *AT40* theme closes hour #2
story: Loggins & Messina formation as a duo
story: War's producer prohibits songwriter interviews
story: Olivia Newton-John's early days
story: Dawn's long song titles
story: Billy Preston's work with superstars

182.) 12-22-73 — **Program #734-12**
SPECIAL: Christmas Countdown (update from 1971 special)
for a complete list of records in this special, see Rob Durkee's *American Top 40: The Countdown of the Century*
program note: original *AT40* theme closes hour #1

183.) 12-29-73 — **Program #734-13**
SPECIAL: Top 40 Of 1973 (based on *AT40* staff's year-end list)
for a complete list of records in this special, see Rob Durkee's *American Top 40: The Countdown of the Century*

The LP boxes for 1973's two year-end specials contained special artwork.

1974

184. 01-05-74 Program #741-1
program note: original *AT40* theme returned to close each hour
story: background of spoken word "Americans"
story: Al Wilson's phony talent scout
story: posthumous #1 artists
story: Todd Rundgren, record producer
name origin: Love Unlimited Orchestra
long version: Hello It's Me - Todd Rundgren
question: #2 artist to Elvis Presley
question: "Why Me" chart run
question: The Beatles re-grouping

185. 01-12-74 Program #741-2
program error: Casey introduces Grand Funk's "Walk Like A Man" and references it as their second hit single; actually, it was their fifth
program error: Casey's introduction to Merle Haggard's "If We Make It Through December" indicates that "Okie From Muskogee" was his first *American Top 40* hit; actually, "Okie" never made the Top 40
program error: Casey teases listeners with a story about Steve Miller playing the Fillmore West, however no story was told
question: female artist with most #1 records
flipside played: When I Fall In Love - Donny Osmond
portion played: You're Sixteen - Johnny Burnette
story: Brownsville Station's self-description
story: Elton John's Rocket Records party
story: Barbra Streisand's shared celebrity status
story: Loggins & Messina's big break
story: Byron MacGregor's "Americans" royalties donated to charity
story: Al Green's big-selling, non-Top 40 record
story: The Staple Singers' fans objected to their music
program note: new theme used at end of hours #1, #2 & #3
production note: use of jingle music as background for outcues of records at #39, #26 & #13
production note: new background music used for introduction of #31

186. 01-19-74 Program #741-3
flipside played: When I Fall In Love - Donny Osmond
story: Tom T. Hall, songwriter
story: Jim Stafford's big break
story: Ringo Starr's big break
story: proceeds to charity for both "Americans"
story: three times for "Hello It's Me"
story: Elton John's Jerry Lee Lewis impersonation
story: Merle Haggard on Don Bowman
name origin: Brownsville Station
question: re-grouping #1 artists
question: longest running #1 record

187. 01-26-74 Program #741-4
story: Aretha Franklin's Grammy Awards
story: Steve Miller's broken neck
story: Isaac Hayes wanted to be *Shaft*
story: Ringo Starr, furniture designer
story: Paul McCartney hints at a Beatles reunion
program mention: Gregg Allman's "Midnight Rider" is on three LPs
odd chart stat: two versions of spoken word "Americans" in the Top 40
question: artist with most consecutive weeks on LP chart

american top 40 announces 52 contemporary/gold/day-part night-part/weekday/weekend "q"/long-playlist/short-playlist adult/non-adult/hard/soft active/passive/conservative progressive specials for 1974

47 weekly countdowns

Every week Casey Kasem covers the Cream of the Crop. The 40 hottest hits from coast to coast as tabluated by the BILLBOARD Chart Department . . . the most respected music survey organization in the world today . . . combined with a multi-track analysis of the talent that makes the hits happen. Timed for simultaneous broadcast release with BILLBOARD's print publication date.

5 super specials

April 6-7: "The 40 most extraordinary British hits of the Rock Era."

From '55 through '73, these are the records from the Mother Country that made the biggest impact on the U.S. popularity charts. Casey Kasem counts down 40 classics from the nation that has had the heaviest per capita impact on the history of Rock and Roll.

July 6-7: "The 40 top artists of the Seventies."

To celebrate the 4th Anniversary of AMERICAN TOP 40 we're counting down the 40 most successful singles artists of this decade. The first "historical" countdown in which Elvis and the Beatles WON'T walk off with all the honors, this will be a wide open race for polystyrene supremacy in the Seventies.

October 5-6: "AMERICAN TOP 40 presents . . . the Producers."

From the contemporary era (1970-1973), a special breakout on the brains behind the superstars. We'll pick the hottest producers based on chart performance and trace the evolution of Rock by playing their most significant hits from the past and the present. A heavy assignment for the AT40 research staff.

December 21-22: "The 100 Top Hits of 1973 . . . Part One."

We've scrubbed our regular three hour format for a brand new FOUR HOUR presentation of BILLBOARD's Annual Chart Sweepstakes . . . No.'s 100 - 51.

December 28-29: "The 100 Top Hits of 1973 . . . Part Two."

This second four hour episode in our year end double special can be combined with "Part One" for EIGHT HOURS of non-stop holiday hit programming. Casey winds up another year with BILLBOARD's No.'s 50 - 1.

all 5 free to american top 40 subscribers

AMERICAN TOP 40—Watermark, Inc.
10700 Ventura Blvd.
No. Hollywood, Calif. 91406
(213) 980-9490

First Offer . . . Brand New
1974 Presentation Package

Send me the new AMERICAN TOP 40 Presentation Spectacular including the "Much More Than Music" brochure, recyclable demo tape, station roster, operations manual, and a poker deck of air-cushion-finish AT40 bicycles, along with the story of how AMERICAN TOP 40 makes it in over 250 different radio formats . . . and with over 1,000 different advertisers.

NAME ______________ TITLE ______________

CALL LETTERS ______ ADDRESS ______________

CITY ______________ STATE ______ ZIP ______

AMERICAN TOP 40 is produced and distributed weekly on compatible stereo LP's by Watermark, makers of American Country Countdown. ©1973, Watermark, Inc.

This advertisement appeared in the January 19, 1974 edition of *Billboard* magazine.

TUESDAY, 8:00 AM
Final rewrite of a week's research for the upcoming Top 40 Hit Singles starts the day at Watermark.

TUESDAY, 5:00 PM
Billboard's Chart Department tabulates up-to-the-minute nationwide research and reports it to Watermark.

TUESDAY, 5:30 PM
AMERICAN TOP 40 producer checks with record personality for last minute news or update.

WEDNESDAY, 10:00 AM
Casey Kasem starts actual in-studio recording of voice track elements for the latest edition of AMERICAN TOP 40.

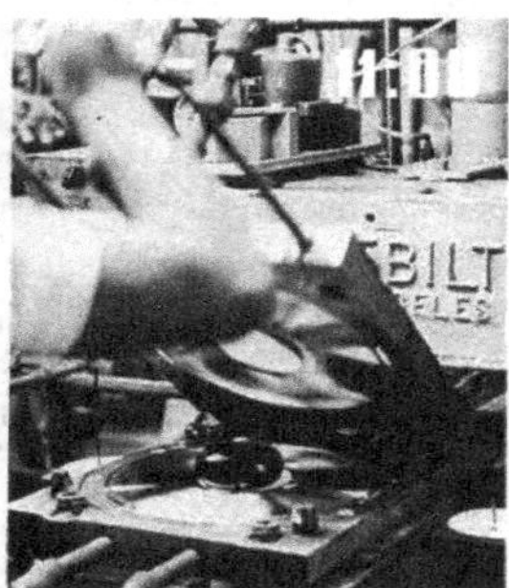

WEDNESDAY, 3:15 PM
Watermark studio technician records final audio tracks for assembly of finished tape masters.

WEDNESDAY, 6:00 PM
AMERICAN TOP 40 editor puts the finishing touches in the stereo program before sending to mastering engineer.

THURSDAY, 11:00 AM
With acetate masters cut and plated, stamping machines in a Los Angeles pressing plant turn out broadcast stereo LP discs.

FRIDAY, 9:00 AM
After exhaustive quality control procedures the complete program package is assembled for distribution to subscribers.

From the 1974 marketing brochure, a day in the production life of an *American Top 40* program.

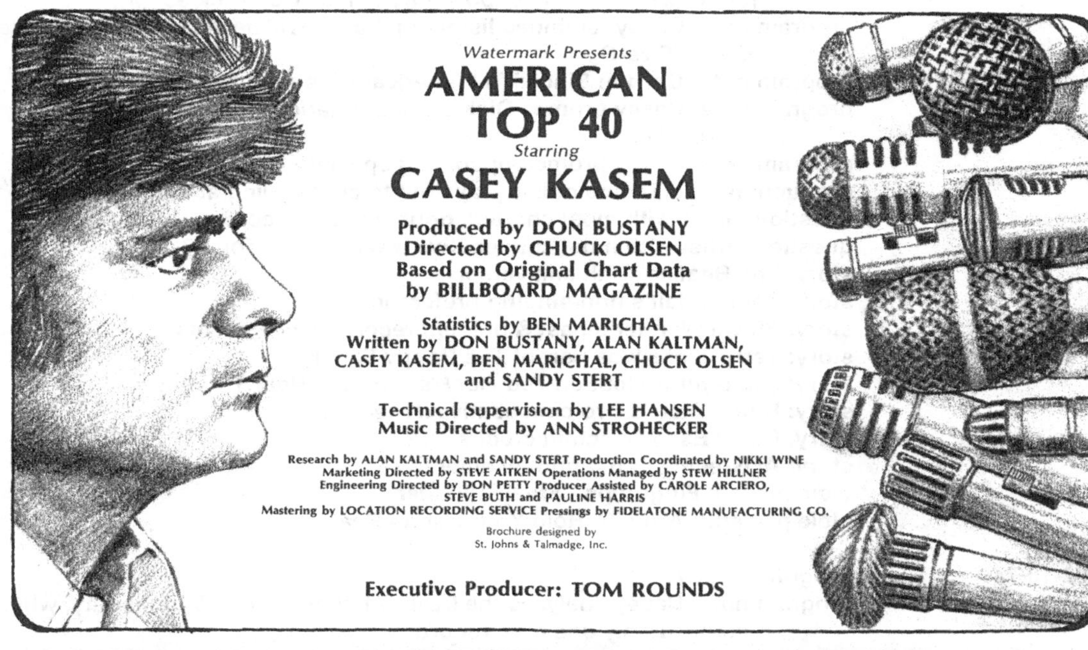

". . . continually sold out" WTLB—Utica, New York ". . . best damn money maker we've ever had" KABR—Aberdeen, S.D.
". . . most professional program ever carried" WDAL—Meridian, Miss. ". . . huge ratings . . . it sounds great" WDRC—Hartford, Connecticut
". . . tremendous audience attraction" WBSR—Pensacola, Florida ". . . consistently attracts new full-time listeners" WPIX—New York

Another page from the 1974 marketing brochure provided a credits list of all involved with program production and distribution.

188. 02-02-74 **Program #741-5**

program note: with two versions of "Americans" in the Top 40, Casey does not play Byron MacGregor's version "..since we already heard Gordon Sinclair's version...."; while both versions were in the Top 40 during the month of February, only one version was played each week
program note: song from the #1 LP played; once a common feature, this was the first time an LP cut was featured since the 08-05-72 National Album Countdown special
program note: Casey offers two different pronunciations - one during the record's tease and one during the record's introduction - to the Rolling Stones' "Doo Doo Doo Doo Doo"; Casey's introductions & outcues of the record's remaining chart appearances reference only the song's subtitle, "Heartbreaker"
program note: Casey *sings* portion of Cher's "Dark Lady" lyric
program note: Casey promos upcoming special
odd chart stat: lead singers of seven different groups in the Top 40 as solo acts
story: Al Wilson was a singing car hop
story: David Essex's big break
story: Tom T. Hall's Grammy Award
story: Helen Reddy advertises gratitude to the music industry
long version: Livin' For The City - Stevie Wonder

189. 02-09-74 **Program #741-6**
program note: regarding a televised celebrity roast, Casey thanked Dean Martin for allowing him the opportunity to kiss Don Rickles
program note: Casey reminded listeners that he will be acting in an episode of *Hawaii Five-O*
program note: Gordon Sinclair's "Americans" is not played
program note: Casey promos Dick Clark's *American Music Awards* new TV special
program note: Casey promos upcoming special
production note: theme music plays out to cold ending at end of hour #1
question: artist with most charted, double-sided records
question: artist with most consecutive weeks in the Top 40
story: The Beatles' 10th anniversary
story: Tom T. Hall's non-singing preference
story: Stevie Wonder's past & present record achievements
story: Terry Jacks was part of The Poppy Family
story: Jim Stafford lost on *Ted Mack's Amateur Hour* TV show
story: Ringo Starr's two consecutive #1 records
story: David Essex's acting credits
story: Al Green's birth announcement
oldie played: Fingertips - Stevie Wonder
oldie played: I Want To Hold Your Hand - Beatles

190. 02-16-74 **Program #741-7**
program note: Casey analyzes the 02-09-74 chart's Top 10 for variety, which included only one rock record
program note: Casey promos Dick Clark's upcoming *American Music Awards* TV special
program note: Casey promos upcoming special
program note: Byron MacGregor's "Americans" is not played, even though it is in the Top 10 at #6
odd chart stat: six Canadian acts in the Top 40
odd chart stat: Barbra Streisand's "The Way We Were" returns to #1 position
question: longest running Top 10 record
story: Lamont Dozier, successful songwriter
flipside played: When I Fall In Love - Donny Osmond
portion played: When I Fall In Love - The Lettermen
question: first Beatles #1 record
question: slowest-breaking, longest-riding #1 records
LP cut played: You Don't Mess Around With Jim - Jim Croce
story: Aretha Franklin's roller skates purchase
story: Black Oak Arkansas gives away real estate
story: Barry White, rags to riches
story: evolution of Steve Miller's "The Joker"
portion played: Gangster Of Love - Steve Miller Band
portion played: Space Cowboy - Steve Miller Band

191. 02-23-74 **Program #741-8**
story: Charlie Rich's "There Won't Be Anymore" released in 1962
story: "My Sweet Lady" from TV movie *Sunshine*
story: 'sixteen' is number most-often used in song titles
story: Spanish-born Top 40 artists
story: Paul McCartney helped Peter Asher
portion played: Mockingbird - Charlie & Inez Foxx
program error: Casey mentions that Charlie & Inez Foxx are a husband & wife duo; actually, they are brother & sister
program note: Casey promos upcoming special
question: total of records charted

192. 03-02-74 Program #741-9

production note: program's hour #3 closing theme music includes a distorted, sheep-sounding 'hey'
production note: old theme music is used to end hour #1
program error: Casey states that Charlie Rich has three records on the chart, including"The Most Beautiful Girl"; actually, "The Most Beautiful Girl" fell off of the Hot 100 chart the preceding week
program note: Casey promos upcoming special
question: most successful country record
question: shortest chart climb for a #1 record
odd chart stat: twelve foreign acts in the Top 40
odd chart stat: five re-makes in the Top 40
odd chart stat: according to the Hot 100, there were twelve gold singles in the Top 40
story: Rick Derringer's two #1 records
story: Dickie Goodman's cut-in records
story: Olivia Newton-John's background
story: Cliff DeYoung, actor & singer
story: the history of "Seasons In The Sun"
story: B.B. King works 310 days a year

193. 03-09-74 Program #741-10

production error: jingle for #21 is used during the introduction to #26
story: composer Jim Kirk tells origin of *American Top 40* theme music, as a result of a question from a KVOX Radio (Moorhead, MN) disk jockey
story: stuttering songs
story: Barbra Streisand's turned-down apartment offer
story: James Taylor & Carly Simon most successful married duo
story: John Denver's name change
story: The Moments were hot, then not
story: another nun on the chart
story: Bobby Womack's 1962 "Lookin' For A Love"
question: posthumous #1 records
program note: Casey promos upcoming special
odd chart stat: fourteen foreign artists in the Top 40

194. 03-16-74 Program #741-11

production note: program disks contain generic promos for upcoming special
program error: Casey points out that Harry Chapin had a hit "...last year with 'Taxi'..."; actually, it was in the Top 40 in 1972
program error: Casey points out that The Main Ingredient had a hit "last year called 'Everybody Plays The Fool'..."; actually, it was in the Top 40 in 1972
story: Jim Croce song title used to re-name a movie
story: Ringo Starr's first release flopped
story: Barbra Streisand sings through her nose
question: gold & platinum record awards
question: first #1 foreign record
question: most Top 40 versions of the same song

195. 03-23-74 Program #741-12

story: radio station WOLD is real
story: Sister Janet Mead's concerts
story: Charlie Rich's early days
question: oldest Top 40 artist
program note: Casey promos upcoming special

To: AT40 Subscribers

From: Tom Rounds

Re: Earth Shaking Events

March 8, 1974

1. If you'll be at the NAB in Houston, don't forget to pop in at the Hyatt Regency and say hello. Steve Aitken and I will be holding forth... get the room number (registered to Watermark) from the hotel operator.

2. Jerry Rogers, PD at WSGA, Savannah Georgia reports: "We've been saving the AT40 shows for the past year and we'll be giving them away once an hour in a special AT40 weekend giveaway. We'll be billboarding them with the date and the record that was number one. With the vinyl shortage and budget problems this might be something the other stations might like to try." Thanks, Jerry.

3. A reminder that stations needing extra copies of AT40 specials for whatever purpose may buy them from us at $7.50 per copy including postage to stations in ~~the U.S.~~ International subscribers will have to pay the extra postage.

4. Three weeks fro~~m now~~, we'll be shipping the next AT40 special "The 40 Most Extraordinary British Hits of ~~the~~ Rock Era". To celebrate this event we have included three Casey voicers as extra ~~cuts~~ on this weeks et's (741-11). Copy is as follows:

> 1. "The 40 Most Extraordinary British Hits of the Rock Era." That's the name of our next AMERICAN TOP 40 super special. This is Casey Kasem hoping you'll join me for a countdown of the 40 classics from the British Isles that had the biggest impact on the charts from 1955 till now. Coming up on our next AMERICAN TOP 40 show, right here."
>
> 2. "Hi. This is Casey Kasem getting set to count downthe 40 most extra-ordinary British hits of the rock era. Join us right here tomorrow for another AMERICAN TOP 40 super special."
>
> 3. "Coming up today on AMERICAN TOP 40, another super special on the history of the charts. This is Casey Kasem and this time we'll count down the 40 most extraordinary British hits of the rock era. A very special AMERICAN TOP 40 coming up today."

To locate the specific promos by number on the discs, please refer to this week's cue sheet. Hope you can use 'em.

5. Also, regarding the special (742-1), we've thrown an extra minute of com-merical time into part three. We hope you can put it to good use.

6. We've already shipped out several thousand of the new AT40 brochures. De-mand is so heavy we've started to ration each station's allotment, which I hope explains why we haven't been sending complete orders.

WATERMARK, INC. 10700 Ventura Blvd., No. Hollywood, California 91604 (213) 980-9490

The March 8, 1974 memo from Tom Rounds covered miscellaneous topics including an *AT40* program giveaway promotion in Savannah, Georgia.

196. 03-30-74

Program #741-13
program note: Casey acknowledges receiving #1 network radio show award from Southeastern Europe Network, a part of the American Forces Radio outlets
program note: Casey promos upcoming special
question: biggest record by a female artist
odd chart stat: Charlie Rich has two chart-climbing, back-to-back records
story: *The Exorcist* is movie of the year
story: Sami Jo failed airline stewardess school
story: Rick Derringer's big break
story: Barbra Streisand daydreamed
story: "The Lord's Prayer" is nearly 2,000 years old
story: Paul McCartney is most successful songwriter
story: Cher's two consecutive #1 records

197. 04-06-74

Program #742-1
SPECIAL: Most Extraordinary British Hits Of The Rock Era
for a complete list of records in this special, see Rob Durkee's *American Top 40: The Countdown of the Century*

198. 04-13-74

Program #742-2
***Billboard* report error: chart positions of Kool & The Gang's "Jungle Boogie" and Diana Ross & Marvin Gaye's "My Mistake Was To Love You" reversed**
story: Maria Muldaur will not be a white slave
story: Little Eva helped by Carole King
story: Billy Joel was Bill Martin
story: Cher's belly button
story: The Beatles' April 1964 Top 5 chart feat
portion played: Please Please Me - The Beatles
portion played: I Wanna Hold Your Hand - The Beatles
portion played: She Loves You - The Beatles
portion played: Twist & Shout - The Beatles
portion played: Can't Buy Me Love - The Beatles
portion played: Seasons In The Sun - Rod McKuen
story: "Seasons In The Sun" recorded by Rod McKuen
story: Bobby Womack created superstars
program note: old *American Top 40* split logo jingles return
long version: Sunshine On My Shoulder – John Denver

199. 04-20-74

Program #742-3
question: records with most weeks at #1 on the pop, soul & country charts
question: disbanded group with charted solo records
question: 'sunshine' in song titles
portion played: Lookin' For A Love - The Valentinos
portion played: Hooked On A Feeling - Jonathan King
story: Marvin Hamlisch's Academy Awards
story: Mike Oldfield fears *The Exorcist*
story: Bachman-Turner Overdrive's Guess Who roots
story: Maria Muldaur's voice
odd chart stat: according to the Hot 100, there were nine gold singles in the Top 40
program error: Casey mentions that "Jungle Boogie" was last week's #24 record; actually, it was #25
program error: Casey mentions that Chicago's "I've Been Searchin' So Long," which moved from #31 - #20, "...up nine positions..."; and credit was given to Three Dog Night's "The Show Must Go On" as the week's biggest climber, which moved from #29 - #19
program error: in answering a listener question about 'sunshine' in song titles, Casey introduces "Sunshine On My Shoulder" as the #3 record; actually, it was #6

AT40 #742-1 "40 MOST EXTRAORDINARY BRITISH HITS" OPENING Hour ONE

Hi!...Welcome to American Top 40...I'm Casey Kasem. ~~If you've heard any of our regular weekly countdowns during the past few weeks, then you probably know it's a special show we're doing today.~~

Well today's the day we do the special I've been telling you about for the past month or so.

During the Sixties, the biggest contribution to America's popular music came from people born and raised in the British Isles... Englishmen, Welshmen, Scotsmen, and Irishmen.

So AT40 has ranked--for the past 19 years--the biggest hits on Billboard's American charts by these recording artists. This is our countdown of the 40 Most Extraordinary British Hits of the Rock Era! And here it begins!

(JINGLE: #40)

INTRO Paul & Linda McCartney "UNCLE ALBERT"/"ADMIRAL HALSEY" 34

742-1

This next one may be the most unusual hit among the forty. It's two seperate songs released ~~as a~~ on a single side. One following the other without missing a beat!

Could it be symbolic of the relationship of the recording artists? The label reads... "Paul and Linda McCartney". That's man and wife...two seperate pepple...regarded by society as a single unit:...the married couple. Oh, maybe I'm making something out of nothing. The main thing is whether you like their music. I think it's great.

(JINGLE #34)

Two actual script cards used in production and recording of the April 6, 1974 "Most Extraordinary British Hits" special. Note Casey Kasem's handwritten script changes for the program opening and introduction to Paul McCartney's #34 record.

INTRO Beatles "YESTERDAY" #23

742-1

The range in styles that the Beatles covered was unbelievable.
What we just heard...and what we're about to hear...they did
only a year apart.
This Next song OPENED A LOT OF ears to the
creative brilliance of the Beatles. It has recorded
More than a hundred & 30 different recording acts have cut there version of this song.

INTRO Beatles "COME TOGETHER"/"SOMETHING" #17

742-1

Here's something a record company hates to see:
Two Number One songs...on the same disc. They miss out on sales
that way. But with the Beatles, what difference did it make?
Over half the singles they released!...hit Number One!!
This double-sided hit/of theirs ranks at Number 17 among the top hits
by the British.

That Song Hit number One And so did the flip side here it is

Additional script cards from the British program illustrate changes made to the introduction to two Beatle records, located at #23 and #17 in the special. Both sides of the #1 single -- "Come Together" & "Something" -- were played.

200. 04-27-74

Program #742-4
story: Stevie Wonder's five Grammy Awards
story: Helen Reddy's $250,000 contribution
story: origin of the phrase 'the show must go on'
story: The Jackson Five's big break
story: Joni Mitchell's word paintings
story: Gladys Knight & The Pips' early days
odd chart stat: Ray Stevens' "The Streak" debuts at #19
long version: The Show Must Go On - Three Dog Night
question: same song but different recordings at #1
production error: Casey's outcue from "Midnight At The Oasis" is from the 04-20-74 program

201. 05-04-74

Program #742-5
story: Albert Hammond performed while women stripped
story: Charlie Rich's simultaneous Top 3 LPs
story: Marvin Hamlisch's early successes
story: Stevie Wonder, 5th grader & #1 artist
story: Paul McCartney's "Live & Let Die" hoax
story: "The Locomotion" is #1 again
name origin: Three Dog Night
question: second place in most chart hits
program note: Casey mentions the record-tying chart return of Bill Haley's "Rock Around The Clock"

202. 05-11-74

Program #742-6
***Billboard* report error: chart positions of Al Green's "Let's Get Married" and Sister Janet Mead's "The Lord's Prayer" reversed**
odd chart stat: three instrumentals in Top 10
odd chart stat: according to the Hot 100, there were eleven gold singles in the Top 40
story: Gordon Lightfoot's paycut
story: "Rock Around The Clock" breaks a chart record
story: Elton John's "Bennie & The Jets" was not recorded live
story: Carole King's "Tapestry" success
story: Aretha Franklin's seven Grammy Awards
question: oldest song lyric
question: artist with most records on one chart
oldie played: Rock Around The Clock - Bill Haley & Comets

203. 05-18-74

Program #742-7
odd chart stat: two debut records
odd chart stat: according to the Hot 100, there were ten gold singles in the Top 40
story: Bo Donaldson & The Heywoods opened concerts
story: dirty ragtime music
story: many failed 'streaks'
story: Olivia Newton-John's bombed Grammy record
story: U.S. President Lyndon Johnson thanked James Brown
story: most #1 records in one year
story: Stevie Wonder's *Time* article
story: Mike Oldfield's 274 overdubs
program mention: Blue Swede members are all from Sweden
question: capsule history of *AT40* (now heard on 240 radio stations)

To: AT40 People

From: Tom Rounds

Re: Listening Directory and Station I.D.'s and Upcoming Special

Friday, June 7, 1974

WATERMARK, INC. 10700 Ventura Blvd., No. Hollywood, California 91604 (213) 980-9490

1. Enclosed, a few copies of "The American Top 40 Worldwide Listening Directory" (1974 edition). Starting with program 742-11, we'll be promoting the fact that copies of the Directory will be available at subscribing stations. We suggest you lay in a stock by writing to :

Jody Tucker
Customer Relations Rep.
Watermark, Inc.
10700 Ventura Blvd.
No. Hollywood, CA 91604

Please specify the desired quantity. You may not get all copies you asked for, but we'll do our best. We don't expect incredible response, and 50 copies will probably hold you for now. We'll be going into a second printing around July 1.

Remember the concept behind the Listening Directory: subscribing stations are actually cooperating to trade listeners as they move around the country. AT40 listeners on vacation or relocating will relate best to the station carrying AT40 in the new location.

2. The station I.D.'s we requested a couple of weeks ago are coming in at the rate of about 5 per day. We'll start using them in the show as soon as we've amassed a hundred or so. They'll be laid in over intros, etc. in collage style and should be fairly fascinating listening. Just get one of your guys to tape a typical station I.D. including call letters, town and state plus any little interesting tidbit (10 words max) about the station, territory served, etc. if you'd like. 7½ IPS, full or ½ track mono, 1½ mil tape, please. Send the I.D. tapes to Jody. Any questions, call me collect.

3. "The 40 Top Singles Artists of the Seventies". It's being produced today, for shipment June 28 and broadcast the weekend of July 6-7. The Beatles, Elvis and all the other 50's and 60's giants that have continually dominated AMERICAN TOP 40 special countdowns won't even appear. It'll be an interesting slice of contemporary rock history with plenty of surprises and grabber stories. The gimmick, of course, is a nostalgia show on the 1970's. A little strange until you realize the decade will be half gone by the end of this year.

In this June 7, 1974 memo, Tom Rounds pointed out the latest news about 1974 listening directories, the station ID effort, and the upcoming July 6, 1974 special. Stations were encouraged to provide their own IDs which were used in place of Casey Kasem's station mentions. Beginning with the June 22, 1974 program, IDs were used in each show through September 28, 1974.

204. 05-25-74 **Program #742-8**
odd chart stat: Bill Haley & Comets' "Rock Around The Clock" re-debuts in the Top 40
odd chart stat: according to the Hot 100, there were nine gold singles in the Top 40
program note: Casey's outcue of "Oh My My" includes only a lyric sample
program note: Casey promos upcoming special
long version: The Show Must Go On - Three Dog Night
story: Paul McCartney's three recent Top 10 records
story: never-released Beatles' singles
story: MFSB backed Cliff Nobles on "The Horse"
story: Scott Joplin's first million seller
story: Cat Stevens' tuberculosis
story: William DeVaughn's big break
story: James Brown is without a #1 record
story: Joni Mitchell's critic review
story: "The Locomotion" odd chart statistic

205. 06-01-74 **Program #742-9**
story: Grand Funk donates blood
story: "Hooked On A Feeling" is not obscene
story: The Carpenters' missed "Ticket To Ride"
story: Ringo Starr's *Son of Dracula* movie
story: Ray Stevens turned down "Raindrops Keep Falling On My Head"
story: Scott Joplin's Top 3 classical LPs
story: Eddie Kendricks' preference for female songwriters
story: Anne Murray's country/pop double-sided record
odd chart stat: according to the Hot 100, there were eleven gold singles in the Top 40
program note: Casey promos upcoming special
program mention: story of "Band On The Run"
question: repeating Top 5 chart

206. 06-08-74 **Program #742-10**
question: rock-era artists with most Top 40 hits
program note: Casey promos upcoming special
story: Aretha Franklin, re-make queen
story: The DeFranco Family's pre-established fame
story: Carly Simon's wealth & social status
story: The Beatles' solo hits
story: William DeVaughn quit his day job

207. 06-15-74 **Program #742-11**
name origin: The O'Jays
story: The Main Ingredient's death
story: The Righteous Brothers' reunion
story: Gladys Knight apologizes for "I Heard It Through The Grapevine"
story: national vs. local record popularity explanation
story: "You Won't See Me" is first Beatles remake
program error: Casey's intro to "You Won't See Me" states "...coming in at #19 this week...."; actually, it was #18
portion played: You Won't See Me - The Beatles
question: records on the Hot 100
program note: Casey promos upcoming special

7-13-74

To: AT40 SUBSCRIBERS

From: Tom Rounds

Re: CASEY'S ANNUAL DISAPPEARING ACT

July 5, 1974

The producers of "Hawaii Five-0" were so pleased with Casey's performance as a TV talk-show host on an earlier episode this year, they've now re-cast him in a bigger part being filmed right now in Honolulu. Casey has been upgraded from the part of the semi-crooked host of a TV talk show to that of the semi-crooked manager of a department store.

In any case, the part (and full-screen credit) will be good promotion for all of us. We'll let you know when the episode will run on CBS this fall.

We tried to talk Casey into dragging the production crew along with him, but Billboard's new Wednesday chart compilation date and other problems made the schedule too tight.

Therefore, we proudly announce our newest AT40 guest host... "Humble Harve" Miller. Humble Harve is a veteran of KHJ's golden days in the 60's and currently holds the 9AM-12Noon slot at KKDJ(FM) here in Los Angeles.

Casey returns next week.

Meantime, we're running your actual station I. D.'s off at the rate of 9 per show. We've got 54 in the can so far, meaning that about 200 stations haven't sent their tapes in yet. We all think the bit sounds great on the air, so we hope you'll put your station I. D. on tape ($7\frac{1}{2}$ IPS, $\frac{1}{4}$", mono, $1\frac{1}{2}$ mil tape) and send it in right away.

The best I. D.'s are the ones in which something touristy or crazy is included. "K. R. A. P. plays more music" really doesn't mean much on a galactic basis... but "W. W. N. R. from the coal fields of West Virginia" has great audience value. And the combination of all those voices, all those call letters and all those place names adds a lot more meaning to the program.

Important: Please include the state or the country (Anchorage, Alaska; Auckland, New Zealand). No personal names, please. Also, please put reels in boxes before putting them in the mailing envelope.

Send tapes to: Jody Tucker
Customer Service Rep.
Watermark, Inc.
10700 Ventura Blvd., No. Hollywood, CA 91604

WATERMARK, INC. 10700 Ventura Blvd., No. Hollywood, California 91604 (213) 980-9490

More news from Tom Rounds about Casey Kasem's TV role and the ID effort. The July 13, 1974 show was only the fourth time Casey was away from the *AT40* microphone – this time for a guest role in the Hawaii Five-O television series.

208. 06-22-74

Program #742-12
program note: radio stations begin to I.D. themselves
program note: Casey promos *AT40* worldwide listening directory
program note: Casey promos upcoming special
production note: program disks contain promos for upcoming special
portion played: The Locomotion - Little Eva
question: white artists at #1 on soul chart
question: artist with most non-#1 Top 40 records
name origin: The Eagles
odd chart stat: according to the Hot 100, there were six gold singles in the Top 10
story: Mac Davis' identity crisis
story: "Rock The Boat" started in discos
story: Olivia Newton-John's abbreviated Disneyland concert
story: "Rock And Roll Heaven" honors six deceased rock stars
record origin: Jim Stafford's "My Girl Bill"

209. 06-29-74

Program #742-13
different chart: listing based on statistical estimate by *AT40* staff; at the time, *AT40* was recorded on a regular basis on Wednesday mornings, with the 06-22-74 show likely tracked on Wednesday, June 12; without having to wait for *Billboard*'s 06-29-74 chart and a tracking date of Wednesday, June 19, this program was recorded as early as Thursday, June 13; Casey recorded the 07-06-74 special as early as Friday, June 14 which allowed him to leave for Hawaii (see 07-06-74 program note) and not have to return to the Watermark studios until the week of July 8; this show included ZZ Top's "LaGrange" at #33, which never reached *Billboard*'s Top 40
production error: no outcue for Jimmy Buffett's "Come Monday"
production note: closing theme music to hour #2 begins after Casey's closing, instead of usual production of 'music up & under'
program note: Casey promos upcoming special
program note: Casey promos *AT40* worldwide listening directory
story: Elvis Presley breaks another chart record
story: Abba's "Waterloo" performed at international competition
story: Joni Mitchell raised on Shakespeare
story: George McCrae swept nightclub floors
story: Ray Stevens is the pop chart comic
story: Gordon Lightfoot's purpose as a human being
story: Maria Muldaur's critic review
program mention: The Spinners were the brown Beatles
question: year with most #1 instrumentals
question: artist on the chart longest
long version: On & On - Gladys Knight & The Pips

210. 07-06-74

Program #743-1
SPECIAL: Top 40 Singles Artists Of The 1970's
for a complete list of records in this special, see Rob Durkee's *American Top 40: The Countdown of the Century*
program note: although radio stations are mentioned, self-produced I.D.'s are not used in this program

To: AT40 Subscribers

From: Tom Rounds

Re: Authentic Station I. D.'s

July 19, 1974

The actual station ID's that have been appearing in AT40 shows for the past few weeks are getting great comment, are fun to do, and help add a new significant dimension to the show. We'd like to get an ID track from every subscriber. Response, so far, has been o. k., but not overwhelming. We're not asking that much really... just go into the studio right now, cut your station ID (include call letters, city, town, state and some short typical slogan line or tourist-type phrase... no jingles, no personal names... $7\frac{1}{2}$ IPS, mono). It'll take you just a few minutes to cut the ID and mail it back to Watermark.

In case you're in doubt, these stations have NOT yet sent ID's in:

1ZN	KGAL	KQYX	WAIR	WGTO	WNOX
2ZA	KBMW	KRBC	WASK	WHBC	WORG
2ZM	KHIT	KRGN	WAYC	WHEB	WPGC
3XA	KINL	KRIZ	WBAW	WHKY	WRBC
Swazi	KINY	KRLY	WBBO	WHMT	WRCN
Kanto	KISN	KROS	WBSR	WIBM	WREL
JOTF	KISR	KRPL	WBTR	WIBR	WROM
Rediffusion	KIXS	KSDB	WBYQ	WICH	WSGA
Radio 610	KIXY	KSKG	WCIT	WINA	WSGN
3YB	KJOY	KTEE	WCSI	WINH	WSIB
3CS	KJR	KTGR	WDBC	WISE	WSKW
3KZ	KJRB	KTLK	WDCR	WJMX	WVAM
TBC	KKUA	KTSA	WDOV	WJRI	WVBS
	KLAM	KUDI	WDRC	WJTO	WVIC
KABR	KLIK	KUDL	WDXY	WKBO	WVLD
KALB	KLOM	KVOX	WEIM	WKEE	WVMI
KAYC	KLWT	KVNU	WERK	WLAP	WWCW
KBMN	KMBY	KVRO	WFMO	WLAR	WWYO
KCRA	KMEN	KVSF	WGAS	WLCY	WYNG
KDLK	KNOX	KXOL	WGCD	WLNC	WYXE
KDWB	KOSE	KYJC	WGLX	WLWL	WMIX
KERN	KOZE	KYSN	WGGG	WLVA	WKAP
KEYN	KPOD	KZFM	WGRD	WMEX	WDHP
KEYY	KPUA		WGH	WMGY	WCAI
KFAR	KPUG	WABB	WGNE	WMHI	WSIZ
KFIZ	KQEO	WACO	WGOE	WNER	WDHF

...continued...

WATERMARK, INC. 10700 Ventura Blvd., No. Hollywood, California 91604 (213) 980-9490

7/19/74

To: AT40 Subscribers

Page 2

WZAR	WICB	WFOM	WWIS	WCBA	WROD	WFFG
WYCR	CKBI	WCOK	KBUG	KUKU	KXRA	

This list will be published from time to time, and I have to type it, so please make my job easier and your reputation better by getting your name off it.

If you've already sent in your ID, thanks! It'll be coming up in a few weeks. Obviously, if everybody contributes, the rotation will take almost a year to complete, and the whole thing will sound better.

Mail the ID's in a box as well as an envelope or jiffy bag to:

Jody Tucker
Customer Service Rep.
Watermark, Inc.
10700 Ventura Boulevard
North Hollywood, CA 91604

In an effort to add to the number of stations previously submitting IDs, Tom Rounds attempted to motivate unresponsive *AT40* affiliates with a no-reply list in this memo.

211. 07-13-74

Program #743-2
GUEST HOST: Humble Harve, introduced by Casey
program note: when this program was recorded, Casey was in Hawaii acting in an episode of *Hawaii Five-O*
production note: post-production commercial break inserted between #29 & #28
portion played: Billy Don't Be A Hero - Paper Lace
story: "Billy Don't Be A Hero" #1 by different artists
story: George McCrae competes with his wife
story: Gladys Knight & The Pips' two versions of the same Hot 100 record
story: Elvis Presley's record sales
story: Holland is #3 foreign country in placing records on Hot 100
question: #1 novelty records
question: duo with most #1 records

"My only AT40 story while at KOIL (in Omaha) happened in 1974 when Casey solicited station ID's from affiliates. We were running the promo line, 'The birth place of rock and roll radio' at the time, taking credit for the top 40 format actually beginning in Omaha though it was at another station in the 1950s. So I produced a voice ID over a jingle bed that tagged out with a jingle, sent it in, and it was run in a show a couple of weeks later. I was ecstatic over having my top 40 KOIL ID appearing nationally on such a solid show. Just in time, too. The practice was quickly discontinued due to affiliate complaints. Apparently we were in the minority in not objecting to other station's IDs within the countdown show."
Carl Mann, former KOIL air personality and AT40 board operator

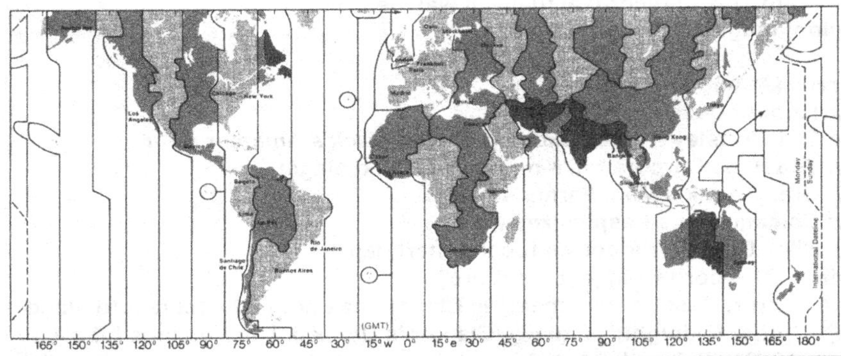

AMERICAN TOP 40 WORLDWIDE LISTENING DIRECTORY

JUNE, 1974

STATE	CITY	STATION	FREQ.	BAND	DAY AND TIME
ALABAMA	Birmingham	WSGN	610	AM	SUN 6PM-9PM
	Mobile	WABB	1480	AM	SUN 10AM-1PM
		WABB	97.5 (S)	FM	SIMULCAST
	Montgomery	WMGY	800	AM	SUN 3PM-6PM
		WMGZ	103.3 (S)	FM	SIMULCAST
ALASKA	Anchorage	KENI	550	AM	SUN 3PM-6PM
	Cordova	KLAM	1450	AM	FRI 7PM-10PM
	Fairbanks	KFAR	660	AM	SUN 3PM-6PM
	Juneau	KINY	800	AM	SAT 3PM-6PM
ARIZONA	Phoenix	KRIZ	1230	AM	SUN 6PM-9PM
ARKANSAS	Fort Smith	KISR	93.7 (S)-	FM	SAT 9PM-12MID
	Osceola	KOSE	860	AM	SAT 9AM-12NOON
		KHFO	98.1	FM	SIMULCAST
	Paragould	KHIG	104.9 (S)	FM	SAT 9PM-12MID SUN 12NOON-3PM
CALIFORNIA	Bakersfield	KERN	1410	AM	SUN 9AM-12NOON
	Crescent City	KPOD	1310	AM	SUN 12NOON-3PM
	Lompoc	KLOM	1350	AM	SUN 3PM-6PM
		KLOM	92.7	FM	SIMULCAST
	Modesto	KTRB	860	AM	SAT 9PM-12MID

STATE	CITY	STATION	FREQ.	BAND	DAY AND TIME
	Skowhegan	WSKW	1150	AM	SAT 10AM-1PM SUN 9AM-12NOON
MARYLAND	Baltimore	WCBM	680	AM	SAT 9PM-12MID
	Frederick	WMHI	1370	AM	SAT 1PM-4PM
	Leonardtown	WKIK	1370	AM	SAT 8PM-11PM
MASSACHUSETTS	Boston	WMEX	1510	AM	SUN 9AM-12NOON SUN 9PM-12MID
	Fall River	WSAR	1480	AM	SUN 10AM-1PM SUN 10PM-1AM
	Fitchburg/Leominister	WEIM	1280	AM	SUN 12NOON-3PM
	Southbridge	WESO	970	AM	SAT 9AM-12NOON
MICHIGAN	Battle Creek	WKNR	1400	AM	SUN 4PM-7PM
	Coldwater	WTVB	1590	AM	SAT 6:30PM-9:30PM
	Escanaba	WDBC	680	AM	SUN 7PM-10PM
	Grand Rapids	WGRD	1410	AM	SUN 8AM-11AM
	Jackson	WIBM	1450	AM	SAT 9AM-12NOON
	Lansing	WVIC	730	AM	SAT 6PM-9PM
		WVIC	94.9 (S)	FM	SIMULCAST
	Mt. Pleasant	WCHP	650	AM	SUN 6PM-9PM
MINNESOTA	Breckenridge	KBMW	1450	AM	SUN 7:30PM-10:30PM

212. 07-20-74 **Program #743-3**
program error: after completing the outcue to record #11, and prior to a commercial break, Casey teases listeners that he will identify two songs, each having five different versions simultaneously on the same chart; however, there was no further mention or details provided
story: John Denver is Colorado's poet laureate
story: Steely Dan's jet broke concert hall windows
story: Helen Reddy was a Catholic priest
story: Mac Davis was a hoodlum
story: Elvis Presley's simultaneous #1 record
program mention: Don Bowman wrote "Wildwood Weed"
question: longest descent for a #1 record
program note: nice note to "Uncle Casey"
program note: Casey provides mailing address to listeners for the first time

213. 07-27-74 **Program #743-4**
program note: after three radio stations identify themselves (for example, "this is Metromedia Stereo, WDHF Chicago"), Casey ID's himself as "...and this is 152 lb. Casey Kasem...."
story: Dave Loggins discovered by Dan Loggins, brother to Kenny Loggins
story: Jim Croce's record number of posthumous records
story: The Osmonds' record number of combinations
story: The Impressions' can't use Jerry Butler
story: Rufus plays crud music
program error: Casey states that Three Dog Night's "Try A Little Tenderness" never reached the Top 40; actually, it peaked at #29
program error: Casey states that Roberta Flack's "Feel Like Makin' Love" is her 4th Top 10 record; actually, it was her third
question: longest LP chart run

214. 08-03-74 **Program #743-5**
story: Lamont Dozier, songwriter
story: Elvis Presley's failed audition on *Ted Mack's Amateur Hour*
story: The Hues Corporation's no-success lead singer
story: Grand Funk's Mark Farner's hair
story: Chicago visits hospitalized fans
story: Billy 'Crash' Craddock's record chart gap
question: #1 record's biggest chart drop
program error: Casey states that Eric Clapton has not had a hit record since "After Midnight;" actually, Clapton's Derek & The Dominos hit #10 in 1972 with "Layla"

215. 08-10-74 **Program #743-6**
story: Mike Curb profile
story: The Righteous Brothers on TV's *Shindig*
story: Golden Earring's jumping drummer
story: Elton John - $8 million man
story: #1 female artists
story: Don Bowman's "Alamo Coward"
story: "Rock The Boat" started in discos
question: #1 record tie
question: *Billboard*'s first #1 record
long version: Clap For The Wolfman - Guess Who

216. 08-17-74

Program #743-7
story: Billy Preston's cost to ship instruments
story: Johnny Bristol, Motown producer
story: Paper Lace's loss to Bo Donaldson & The Heywoods
story: George McCrae beat his wife (see 07-19-75 story)
story: Don Bowman's country songwriting pledge to Casey Kasem
story: The Hollies, one of two surviving British Invasion groups
long version: Beach Baby - First Class
question: artist with most 1964 - 1974 charted records
question: biggest rock era instrumental
question: Frankie Laine vs. The Rolling Stones

217. 08-24-74

Program #743-8
question: biggest 1974 record
question: first gold record
long version: Beach Baby - First Class
story: Billy Preston's vocal & instrumental records
story: Billy 'Crash' Craddock promoted as another Elvis Presley
story: Roberta Flack's refusal to perform in Las Vegas
story: Paul Anka's chart record
story: Grand Funk's Mark Farner donated hair
story: James Brown's days of poverty

743 · 8

SPECIAL FEATURE (Most #1's in a calendar year.)

We've been keeping an eye...and a count...on the number of songs that have hit Number One so far this year. Because it looks as though 1974 may set a new record. So far, the most Number Ones in a calendar year first came together in 1966 when 27 records made it to the top position. And that number was repeated in 1973. But this year, we're sure to push past it...and set a new high. ~~Up to~~ Including this week, we've already had 23 Number Ones...and there are still 18 weeks to go in 1974.

A script card from the August 24, 1974 program illustrates Casey Kasem's changes to an accounting of the year with the most #1 records.

218. 08-31-74 **Program #743-9**
odd chart stat: seventeen foreign artists in the Top 40
odd chart stat: ten British artists in the Top 40
odd chart stat: Abba's "Waterloo" falls from #6 to #24
story: Charlie Rich needs to be like Jerry Lee Lewis
story: Jonathan King's illegal "Beach Baby" audition
story: the reality of "The Night Chicago Died"
story: Paul Anka's "Diana"
program note: Casey promos upcoming special
question: artist with most Top 10 records
question: Canadian artists with most #1 records
question: artist with most 1970 - 1974 #1 records
long version: Beach Baby - First Class

219. 09-07-74 **Program #743-10**
program note: Casey points out that the *AT40* staff is now receiving too much mail to acknowledge; prior acknowledgements used to include "at least a postcard from *AT 40*"; however, listeners are encouraged to keep writing
program note: Casey mentions that Tokyo's Radio Canto's disk jockey, Rainbow Rayco, translates the program from English to Japanese, every week
program note: Casey promos upcoming special
story: Bad Company's members profiled
story: Cat Stevens, until now, wrote & recorded his own material
story: Dionne Warwicke meets The Spinners
story: Dave Loggins took a year to write "Please Come To Boston"
story: Bo Donaldson & The Heywoods own part of the North Pole
odd chart stat: Mac Davis debuts in the Top 40 with two records
long version: Beach Baby - First Class
question: first #1 black artist
question: Top 10 debut records
question: The Rolling Stones vs. Elvis Presley & The Beatles
question: greatest see-saw record
program correction: Casey points out that Paul Anka broke Stevie Wonder's (not Dean Martin's) chart record for #1 records

220. 09-14-74 **Program #743-11**
story: Dave Loggins meets Dan Loggins
story: Mac Davis received Col. Tom Parker's advice
story: Joni Mitchell's autobiography
story: Helen Reddy's allowance
story: Charlie Rich's early days
story: Roberta Flack's #1 records
name origin: Rufus
name origin: Lynyrd Skynyrd
portion played: Another Saturday Night - Sam Cooke
program note: Casey promos upcoming special
long version: Beach Baby - First Class
program error: Casey mentions that Cheech & Chong's "Sister Mary Elephant" was their first Top 40 record; actually, their first was "Basketball Jones"
question: artist with the greatest Top 10 longevity
question: foreign language #1 records

221. 09-21-74

Program #743-12
production note: disks contain upcoming special promos
production note: hours #1 & #2 close with original theme music
question: artist with most Top 40 records in one year
question: capsule history of *AT40* (now heard on 300 radio stations)
question: youngest & oldest #1 artists
question: rock era's highest debuting LPs
question: Paul Anka's partner on "(You're) Having My Baby"
program note: Casey points out that, due to mail volume, they are no longer able to respond to each letter received
program note: Casey promos upcoming special
story: the history of Eric Clapton
story: Fancy member chooses marriage over music
story: The Miracles' first group change
story: Dawn's lost copyright cost Bell Records
story: The Tymes are back
story: timed release of "Beach Baby"
long version: Beach Baby - First Class

222. 09-28-74

Program #743-13
program note: last show where stations I.D. themselves
program note: Casey promos upcoming special
odd chart stat: Barry White's "Can't Get Enough Of Your Love, Babe" falls from #1 to #12
odd chart stat: Beach Boys' "Surfin' USA" debuts in the Top 40
long version: Beach Baby - First Class
portion played: Never My Love - Association
portion played: Never My Love - Fifth Dimension
question: record staying longest at #2
program error: Casey references The Fifth Dimension's "Never My Love" as a 1972 hit; actually, it peaked in 1971
production note: disks contain additional upcoming special promos, along with announcements for Casey's upcoming appearance on *Hawaii Five-O*
story: Jim Stafford is a 'hickie'
story: Rufus' singing guitar
story: George Martin, the fifth Beatle
story: Bo Donaldson & The Heywoods' wedding invitation to fans
story: Elton John, as a 4-year-old, performed at his mother's parties
story: Wolfman Jack profile
program mention: Jackson Five sing on Stevie Wonder's record
program mention: Casey will guest star on an upcoming episode of *Hawaii Five-O*

223. 10-05-74

Program #744-1
SPECIAL: Top 10 Producers Of The 1970's
for a complete list of records in this special, see Rob Durkee's *American Top 40: The Countdown of the Century*

224. 10-12-74 **Program #744-2**
odd chart stat: eight debut records
program note: 16 debut records are played, which include eight new records from 10-05-74 & eight debut records from the 10-12-74 chart
program note: Casey mentions that *AT40* is heard on 400 outlets of American Forces Radio, which expanded *AT40*'s airtime from 1 to 2 hours
whatever happened to: The Cowsills
long version: Beach Baby - First Class
question: Top 10 records from the 1940's
story: Donny Osmond, electronics whiz kid
story: Cat Stevens' artistry
story: Andy Kim co-wrote & sang on The Archies' "Sugar Sugar"
story: John Lennon is Dr. Winston O. Boogie
story: Mac Davis' method to 'get girls'
story: Olivia Newton-John is not a country singer

225. 10-19-74 **Program #744-3**
story: Kool & The Gang's big break
story: Wolfman Jack's early radio broadcasts
story: Carole King's success with "Tapestry" LP
story: "Life Is A Rock (But The Radio Rolled Me)" is a name-dropper
story: Ohio Players' preference for #1
story: The Raspberries' scented LP
long version: Beach Baby - First Class
program mention: Cat Stevens' charity work
question: #1 record's longest playing time
question: artist with most charted LPs, without a charted single
odd chart stat: 1974 breaks the record as year with most #1 records
odd chart stat: First Class' "Beach Baby" falls from #4 to #26
odd chart stat: Cat Stevens' "Another Saturday Night" falls from #6 to #25

226. 10-26-74 **Program #744-4**
odd chart stat: 1974 is the year with most #1 records (29, as of this week)
odd chart stat: Billy Preston's "Nothing From Nothing" falls from #1 to #15
odd chart stat: Blue Swede's "Never My Love" falls from #7 to #33
long version: Beach Baby - First Class
program note: show contains a montage of 1974's #1 records
program note: in answering a listener question, Casey sings "I Get Ideas"
story: Chicago's LP success
story: Kiki Dee's career saved by Elton John
story: Jim Weatherly's songwriting success
story: Olivia Newton-John's country music awards
story: America explains nonsensical lyrics
story: Tony Orlando's recording of "Candida"
story: John Lennon's musical roots
story: Elton John is Mickey Mouse & The Phantom of the Opera
question: longest chart run for a non-#1 record
question: Gordon Lightfoot in *The Guinness Book of World Records*

227. 11-02-74

Program #744-5
odd chart stat: 1974 is the year with most #1 records (30, as of this week)
odd chart stat: Dionne Warwicke & The Spinners' "Then Came You" falls from #1 to #15
odd chart stat: Billy Preston's "Nothing From Nothing" falls from #15 to #39
story: Harry Chapin's Academy Award nomination
story: Bobby Vinton's identity problem
story: Dionne Warwicke & The Spinners tie a chart record
story: Neil Diamond's experience with death
story: Elton John's terror with small audiences
story: Stevie Wonder's 1964-1974 success
story: John Denver, Chad Mitchell Trio member
story: Marvin Gaye speaks to God

228. 11-09-74

Program #744-6
odd chart stat: 1974 is the year with most #1 records (31, as of this week)
odd chart stat: Stevie Wonder's "You Haven't Done Nothin'" falls from #1 to #12
odd chart stat: Dionne Warwicke & The Spinners' "Then Came You" falls from #15 to #39
odd chart stat: Tony Orlando & Dawn's "Steppin' Out (Gonna Boogie Tonight)" falls out of the Top 40, from #7 to #48
odd chart stat: Lynyrd Skynyrd's "Sweet Home Alabama" falls out of the Top 40, from #8 to #44
odd chart stat: Mac Davis' "Stop & Smell The Roses" falls from #9 to #31
program mention: Prelude's "After The Gold Rush" is sung a cappella
program error: Casey states that "Kung Fu Fighting" is the first Kung Fu record to reach the Top 40; actually, Curtis Mayfield's "Kung Fu" peaked at #40 on 08-03-74
production note: program opens with old theme
production note: without explanation, a different version of Mac Davis' "Stop & Smell The Roses" is played, its last week in the Top 40
story: Elvis Presley's chart success
story: Doc Severinson's doctor prescribed "Stop & Smell The Roses"
story: Gordon Lightfoot's manager arrested for guitar smuggling
story: Gino Vanelli influenced by soul music
story: Elton John's current concert tour
whatever happened to: Brenda Lee
question: Top 3 #1 soul artists
question: #1 record with slowest chart fall (see 12-14-74 show)

229. 11-16-74

Program #744-7
odd chart stat: 1974 is the year with most #1 records (32, as of this week)
odd chart stat: Bachman-Turner Overdrive's "You Ain't Seen Nothing Yet" falls from #1 to #12
odd chart stat: Carole King's "Jazzman" falls from #2 to #11
story: a cappella records
story: Three Dog Night's chart success
story: Elton John's record collection
story: Al Green's big selling, non-Top 40 record
story: Bobby Vinton's daring demo session
story: John Lennon completes solo-Beatle #1 records
story: Carl Carlton entertained fellow students
story: Stevie Wonder violated child labor laws
portion played: You Can Have Her - Roy Hamilton
question: biggest LP producer of the 1970's
question: year with fewest #1 records

230. 11-23-74

Program #744-8
odd chart stat: 1974 is the year with most #1 records (33, as of this week)
odd chart stat: John Lennon's "Whatever Gets You Through The Night" falls from #1 to #12
odd chart stat: John Lennon's "Whatever Gets You Through The Night" is in the Top 10 for only three weeks
odd chart stat: Bachman-Turner Overdrive's "You Ain't Seen Nothing Yet" falls from #12 to #34
odd chart stat: Carl Douglas' "Kung Fu Fighting" climbs from #27 to #7
story: Harry Chapin's benefit concert philosophy
story: Latimore's definition of "Let's Straighten It Out"
story: BTO's Randy Bachman stutters on "You Ain't Seen Nothing Yet"
story: Neil Sedaka's "Oh! Carol"
story: Al Green's family had no faith
story: The Pointer Sisters on the country chart
story: Elvis Presley's double-sided records
story: Neil Diamond thought *Fiddler On The Roof* was a loser
program note: Casey promos upcoming special
question: year with most #1 Canadian records

231.11-30-74

Program #744-9
odd chart stat: Bachman-Turner Overdrive's "You Ain't Seen Nothing Yet" climbs from #34 to #8
odd chart stat: America's "Tin Man" falls from #4 to #25
program note: chart move explanation for "You Ain't Seen Nothing Yet"
program note: Casey promos upcoming special
question: LP with most weeks at #1
question: 'king' of the LP chart
story: Stevie Wonder's *Newsweek* article
story: Eric Clapton's desire to be a stained glass designer
story: The Pointer Sisters' first stage show
story: Billy Swan's applause on "I Can Help"
story: Bachman-Turner 'Overweight'
story: Andy Kim's debut nearly ruined by Chinese food

232. 12-07-74

Program #744-12
odd chart stat: 1974 is the year with most #1 records (34, as of this week)
odd chart stat: eight re-makes in the Top 40
program note: Casey promos upcoming special
program mention: J. Geils Band's Peter Wolf is married to actress Faye Dunaway
program mention: Chicago's members named
program error: Casey mentions that Jethro Tull's "Bungle In The Jungle" "....in its second week on the chart moves from #42 to #32..."
question: highest debuting, non-#1 record
story: Elton John described by Jerry Lee Lewis
story: The Righteous Brothers' return
story: Fancy's 'body' music
story: The Pointer Sisters receive an ultimatum from church
story: The Rolling Stones' chart significance of "Ain't Too Proud To Beg"
story: Harry Chapin's wife inspired "Cat's In The Cradle"
story: Carl Douglas' "Kung Fu Fighting" breaks a foreign artist chart record
story: Barry White's #1 records as vocalist and orchestra leader
story: Paul Anka wrote the *Tonight Show* theme
long version: Do It ('Til You're Satisfied) - B.T. Express

To: AMERICAN TOP 40 SUBSCRIBERS

From: Tom Rounds

Saturday, November 9, 1974

WATERMARK, INC. 10700 Ventura Blvd., No. Hollywood, California 91604 (213) 980-9490

Casey Tubes Again!

On Friday, November 15 (check the guide for local times), Casey Kasem will be appearing on his second "Dean Martin Celebrity Roast" on NBC-TV. This time the gang will be attacking Telly Savales and Casey follows up his unforgettable characterization of Adolph Hitler (done for the benefit of Don Rickles last season) with an impersonation of Columbo. We suspect the two cops will have a fun time trying to bust each other.

"Elvis" is back

The Watermark crew under the aggressive direction of Ron Jacobs is digging into our mountain of clippings, pictures, records, interviews and rare tapes on Elvis Presley in preparation for our brand new production of "the Elvis Presley Story". We're aiming for a completion date of about January 1, 1975. The special will consist of 13 51-minute chapters, and feature lots of new stuff. It'll be available in stereo, on disc (tape will also be available, but it'll cost more). At the moment, we plan to include only stereo records by Elvis that were mixed that way, and we plan to avoid any of the "electronically enhanced for stereo" records, meaning the first several hours will remain mono.

We'll keep you up on developments because we're sure you'll want first shot at "The Elvis Presley Story" for your market. National trade publicity will break around January 15, so consider yourselves forewarned and forearmed. If you want to lock it up now, call me collect, and we'll work it out.

"Top 100"

We'll be shipping all eight hours of it to you on Saturday, December 14. That means there will be no program shipment on Saturday, December 21. Remember that each half of the "Top 100 Hits of 1974" is an expanded format... four hours in length. Program #744-12 will contain #s 100-51, and 744-13 will contain #s 50-1. Lots of subscribers will run the whole eight hours twice... on the weekend of December 21-22... and again on the weekend of December 28-29. Others will pre-empt on the weekend of 21-22 and wait to run the whole thing on the 28-29. In any case, all restrictions about play dates and repeats are off... so go ahead and schedule "The Top 100" wherever you think it will be the most effective. ----Regular countdowns resume with program #751-1, scheduled for broadcast January 4-5, and shipping Saturday, December 28.

This multiple topic memo promoted Casey Kasem's appearance on a Dean Martin Celebrity Roast, an Elvis Presley Story update and the Top 100 of 1974.

To: AMERICAN TOP 40 SUBSCRIBERS

From: Nikki Wine

Re: End of Year Specials: #744-12 and 13

December 7, 1974

Each program is expanded from the normal three hours containing 40 songs to four hours containing 50 songs.

Procedure for making one eight-hour show out of the two four-hour shows is as follows:

Show #744-12 counts down the hits from #100 thru #51.

At the end of the 4th hour, between the end of the outro of song #51 and the AT40 theme (over which Casey does the regular closing) is a beat of dead air sufficient for cutting out cleanly at the board, preferably by key.

Show #744-13 counts down from #50 thru #1.

At the beginning of the 1st hour, the segue between the opening theme and song #50 is such that you can cue up to start with song #50.

So, to go from the end of the 4th hour of #744-12 to the start of #744-13, cut out of show #744-12 after the outro of song #51... and hit the first hour of show #744-13 cued up to the beginning music of song #50.

WATERMARK, INC. 10700 Ventura Blvd., No. Hollywood, California 91604 (213) 980-9490

Producer Nikki Wine provided directions and recommendations for station engineers when ending Part 1 of the Top 100 of 1974. This was the first time *AT40* stations were required to accommodate a program containing more than three hours.

233. 12-14-74 **Program #744-11**
odd chart stat: Elton John's "Lucy In The Sky With Diamonds" climbs from #36 to #9
odd chart stat: all four former Beatles - Ringo Starr, Paul McCartney, John Lennon & George Harrison - have solo records in the Top 40
production note: "Kung Fu Fighting" contains glass-breaking sound effect
production note: disks contain promos for upcoming special
production note: without explanation, a different version of Paul Anka's "One Man Woman/One Woman Man" is played
program error: Casey's introduction indicates that "One Man Woman/One Woman Man" is #30; actually, it was #24
program note: Casey promos upcoming special
program mention: Paul McCartney's record subjects
portion played: Everlasting Love - Robert Knight
story: Robert Knight update
story: Elvis Presley's $50 Christmas present
story: Neil Diamond's opposition to "Solitary Man"
story: J. Geils Band LP & concert review
story: "Angie Baby" description
story: summary of martial arts popularity
story: Kiki Dee's philosophy on the music business
name origin: Bachman-Turner Overdrive
question: #1 record with slowest chart climb (see 11-09-74 show)

"I discovered AT40 when we moved to Germany in late spring 1974. My dad was in the Air Force, and I had just turned 14. AT40 generally aired on Sunday afternoons and was heard by the American servicemen and their dependants via AFN--The American Forces Network........ I remember many times taking the radio on bike rides, hikes to the nearby castle (Hohenecken Castle, above the village near where I lived), or long hikes into one or another German town listening to AT40. The program had a HUGE influence on me. The first show I can recall that really made an impact on me was the Top 100 of 1974. I remember listening to the last 2 hours of that show and thinking, "Man, this is a really cool countdown--all the good songs are here!" And there was such a drama to the show, as you got closer and closer to the number one song of the year. And Casey made it all seem so OFFICIAL......."
Steve Orchard, a longtime *AT40* listener

234. 12-21-74 **Program #744-12**
SPECIAL: Top 100 Of 1974 (#100 - 51) (based on *Billboard*'s year-end Top 100) for a complete list of records in this special, see Rob Durkee's *American Top 40: The Countdown of the Century*
long version: Rockin' Roll Baby - Stylistics
long version: Beach Baby - First Class
long version: Clap For The Wolfman - Guess Who
long version: On & On - Gladys Knight & The Pips

235. 12-28-74 **Program #744-13**
SPECIAL: Top 100 Of 1974 (#50 - 1) (based on *Billboard*'s year-end Top 100) for a complete list of records in this special, see Rob Durkee's *American Top 40: The Countdown of the Century*
long version: Boogie Down - Eddie Kendricks
long version: The Show Must Go On - Three Dog Night
long version: Sunshine On My Shoulder – John Denver

American Top 40 became so well known and respected that it set the standard for many countdown radio shows. One of the earliest imitations - *Canadian Top 40* - was hosted by Vancouver-based Michael Morgan in 1974 and included "Morgan's Coast-to-Coast" jingles.

1975

236. 01-04-75 **Program #751-1**
story: Elvis Presley's spoken word, in-concert LP
story: Monti Rock III's talk show popularity
story: Barry Manilow's commercial jingles
story: Chaka Khan's name change
story: Beatles remake at #1
story: *Los Angeles Times* writer wrong with Beatles prediction
program note: *Los Angeles Times* story presented twice, preceding George Harrison & Ringo Starr records
name origin: The Eagles
question: most recorded Top 40 song
question: artist's #1 record replaced by same artist's #1 record
odd chart stat: this week's Top 9 records by artists with #1 records

To: AMERICAN TOP 40 SUBSCRIBERS

From: TOM ROUNDS

February 1, 1975

We're kicking off the month with a surprise guest artist filling in for Casey on AT40 #751-6. It's none other than superjock Robert W. Morgan. Currently doing morning drive on Bill Drake's K-100 in Los Angeles, Robert W. was lead-off personality at KHJ from 1965 through 1971, except for an 18 month appearance as morning man at WIND, Chicago. We're really proud and pleased that Bob was nice enough to pitch in for Casey at the last minute this week.

As for Casey, he's hobbling around doing his famous impersonation of the hunchback after slipping a disc (we think it was a Rosemary Clooney 78). Teams of medics are working round the clock to prepare the Caser for next week's show.

WATERMARK, INC. 10700 Ventura Blvd., No. Hollywood, California 91604 (213) 980-9490

This memo informed stations that guest host Robert W. Morgan was at the *AT40* microphone for the February 8, 1975 program. He hosted the countdown again on September 29, 1979.

237. 01-11-75

Program #751-2
odd chart stat: all four former Beatles - Ringo Starr, Paul McCartney, John Lennon & George Harrison (Billy Preston, too) - have solo records in the Top 40; Elton John is at #1 with "Lucy In The Sky With Diamonds"
odd chart stat: J. Geils Band's "Must Of Got Lost" falls out of the Top 40, from #12 to #44
odd chart stat: 22 artists in the Top 40 have previously had #1 records
story: Billy Joel's job application
story: Carol Douglas' lightning success
story: Al Green's manager's 'big star' promise
story: Paul McCartney's country chart record
story: singer/songwriter trends
story: Ringo Starr's "Only You" ties a Top 10 chart record
story: Linda Ronstadt's sexy image
program note: Casey thanks Dr. Demento for supplying an oldie
portion played: Rock And Roll - Boswell Sisters
question: origin of the term "rock 'n' roll"
question: total number of #1 records
flipside played: Sally G - Wings

> ***"One anecdote confirms what an AT40 nut I was: driving back across the country from my brother's home in Oregon in January 1975, I purposely stopped Saturday night in Salt Lake City just so that Sunday morning I would still be in range for the entire program before continuing eastbound."***
> **Lanny Springs, a longtime *AT40* listener**

238. 01-18-75

Program #751-3
odd chart stat: all four former Beatles have solo records in the Top 40
program error: in the outcue of "Only You," Casey indicates "...Ringo Starr is the second of four Beatles we'll hear this week...."; actually, Ringo's record was the third former Beatles record played
story: Elton John's deficiency in British #1 records
story: Harry Chapin's self-description
story: Monti Rock III's strange claim
story: Lynyrd Skynyrd stole Leonard Skinner's name
story: "Angie Baby" interpretations
story: Barry White's reform school lesson
story: Paul Anka's songwriting success
question: pre-Beatles British artists at #1
question: one-hit wonders
question: first female #1 record

239. 01-25-75

Program #751-4
story: Alan O'Day's Christmas greeting
story: Frankie Valli's falsetto voice
story: Barry White's deep-bass voice
story: Mac Davis' old boots
story: John Denver's father made aviation history
story: 1959 vs. 1975 Top 40 singer/songwriters
story: Gloria Gaynor's weight loss
story: Carole King's songwriting chart feat
odd chart stat: "Please Mr. Postman" hits #1 again
question: second time around #1 records
question: youngest #1 LP artist

240. 02-01-75

Program #751-5
story: Bachman-Turner Overdrive arrested for bubblegum possession
story: Jethro Tull's Ian Anderson received 'other instruments' award
story: Carole King's success with "Tapestry" LP
story: Stevie Wonder's Grammy Award success
story: Neil Sedaka's chart return
story: Monti Rock III talks about Monti Rock III
story: Joni Mitchell drives "Big Yellow Taxi" again
story: Electric Light Orchestra's two cellos and one violin
program mention: Billy Preston uses an arp synthesizer
question: chart performances of "Lucy In The Sky With Diamonds"
portion played: Lucy In The Sky With Diamonds - The Beatles
portion played: Morning Side Of The Mountain - Tommy Edwards
portion played: Roll Over Beethoven - Electric Light Orchestra
program error: Casey mentions that Styx was once known as Trade Winds

241. 02-08-75

Program #751-6
GUEST HOST: Robert W. Morgan
story: The Beatles' LP success
story: Carole King will appear on *The Mary Tyler Moore Show*
story: "Mandy" was "Brandy"
story: The Ohio Players' version of "Over The Rainbow" played at Judy Garland's funeral
story: The Beatles' "Lucy In The Sky With Diamonds" banned
story: Neil Sedaka kicked out of Moscow classical competition
story: Odia Coates was a teen-age fan of Paul Anka
question: 1970's #1 male artist
program error: Robert introduces "My Eyes Adored You" by indicating it "...makes the biggest leap, up 10 places..."; actually, it moved up 16
program error: Robert mentions that B.T.Express' first record went to #1; actually, it peaked at #2

242. 02-15-75

Program #751-7
story: Frankie Valli buys "My Eyes Adored You" from Motown Records
story: Al Martino in *The Godfather*
story: Love Unlimited once retired
story: The 'middle-of-the-road' Carpenters
story: Grand Funk's $12,000 gold record
story: "Don't Call Us" is only record containing a telephone call to the White House
story: Maria Muldaur is Linda Ronstadt's favorite
story: Linda Ronstadt is pop, country and rhythm & blues
story: "Lily Marlaine" stopped World War II
portion played: Lily Marlaine - Lolly Anderson
portion played: Crimson & Clover - Tommy James & The Shondells
whatever happened to: Tommy James

243. 02-22-75

Program #751-8
flipside played: Snookeroo - Ringo Starr
program mention: Phoebe Snow connected to railroad boxcars?
story: Tommy James & The Shondells' music
story: Grammy Awards dominated by female artists
story: Neil Sedaka mini-*rock*umentary
story: Joe Cocker dodged beer bottles
story: foreign female artists at #1
story: Tony Orlando's career inspired by his younger sister
story: New Zealand's Bunny Walters' recording of "Brandy" ("Mandy")
portion played: Brandy - Bunny Walters
portion played: Amazing Grace - Royal Scots Dragoon Guards
portion played: Hanky Panky - Tommy James & The Shondells
portion played: Crimson & Clover - Tommy James & The Shondells
portion played: Sweet Cherry Wine - Tommy James & The Shondells
portion played: Mony Mony - Tommy James & The Shondells
odd chart stat: foreign group instrumental at #1
program note: Casey introduces the Average White Band's #1 record with The Royal Scots Dragoon Guards' "Amazing Grace" in background

244. 03-01-75

Program #751-9
story: Elvis Presley's $850,000 payday
story: B.J. Thomas' troubles with recording "Raindrops Keep Falling On My Head"
story: David Gates' struggle with solo records
story: Shirley Goodman's 1957 risqué record
story: Sugarloaf's Jerry Corbetta's eye accident
story: Styx's resurrected "Lady"
story: LaBelle only black artist performing at The Met
story: Grand Funk panned by critics, loved by fans
production error: LP disks are mislabeled, with side 1A on same disk as 2A
flipside played: Snookeroo - Ringo Starr
portion played: You're No Good - Betty Everett
question: artist replacing himself at #1

245. 03-08-75

Program #751-10
story: The Beatles' "I Feel Fine" used in Sugarloaf's "Don't Call Us (We'll Call You)"
story: The Ohio Players' unusual LP covers
story: Neil Diamond's "Hot August Night" LP popularity in Australia
story: Bad Company's Paul Rodgers voted top British male vocalist
story: David Gates' love song to his wife
story: Shirley Goodman's comeback
odd chart stat: Olivia Newton-John joins four female artists with back-to-back #1 records
odd chart stat: Grand Funk's "Some Kind Of Wonderful" falls from #5 to #30
program note: Casey promos upcoming special
question: records leaping to #1 from outside the Top 10
whatever happened to: Lesley Gore
portion played: It's My Party - Lesley Gore
portion played: I Feel Fine - The Beatles
lyric alert: memo from executive producer Tom Rounds which accompanied program, alerts subscribing radio stations to the potentially controversial lyric content of Ringo Starr's "No No Song"

TO: AT40 SUBSCRIBERS

FROM: TOM ROUNDS

RE: RINGO'S "NO NO" AND UPCOMING SPECIAL

March 1, 1975

WATERMARK, INC. 10700 Ventura Blvd., No. Hollywood, California 91604 (213) 980-9490

"The No No Song" by Ringo Starr is double listed with "Snookeroo" at #25 this week. Our usual practice on two-sided hits is to alternate between the sides, playing one each week, and this week it's "No No's" turn.

We checked with a random sample of subscri bers last week and ascerained that a few are not playing "No No" due to lyric content. The majority of stations are playing "No No" however, and it seems to be the bigger hit.

As usual we're leaving the final decision up to you, but be advised that "The No No Song" is in AT40 this week.

The crew is hot and heavy into updating our all-time most popular special "The Greatest Disappearing Acts of the Rock Era". Special emphasis is being given to the "Where are they now" aspect. We have actually tracked down such one-hit wonders as Buzz Clifford, Joan Weber, Phil Phillips, The Elegants, Claudine Clark, the Penguins and a host of fabulous characters of a bygone era. They all had one huge hit and then never made the charts again.

When we first produced this special a few years ago stations and audiences responded very enthusiastically. The original "Disappearing Acts" was subsequently re-produced for American Airlines in-flight audio service, and turned out to be one of their all time favorites.

The brand new updated "Disappearing Acts" special is program #752-1, and it's scheduled for broadcast the weekend of April 5-6. It deserves extra promotion and the attention of your sales department.

For more information, check the ad in this week's Billboard (issue dated March 8.

Here's another Tom Rounds memo that alerted stations to a potentially offensive record, Ringo Starr's "No No Song," along with an update to the Disappearing Acts special.

246. 03-15-75 **Program #751-11**
flipside played: Snookeroo - Ringo Starr
flipside played: I Am Love, Part 2 - Jackson Five
name origin: Phoebe Snow
story: Charlie Daniels' "Uneasy Rider"
story: David Gates & Leon Russell's homemade recording
story: Al Martino's chart history
story: Chaka Khan turned down Stevie Wonder
story: Grammy Awards to female artists
story: Maria Muldaur played with the Jim Kweskin Jug Band
question: records tied at #1
question: rock artist with biggest #1 LP
portion played: I'm A Woman - Jim Kweskin Jug Band
program note: Casey promos upcoming special

247. 03-22-75 **Program #751-12**
story: Al Martino helped by Mario Lanza
story: The Beatles' caricatures
story: Freddy Fender picks
story: Chaka Khan will not reveal her real name
story: The Jackson Five managed by a crane operator
story: Olivia Newton John's slow climbing record
story: Frankie Valli's comeback
program note: Casey promos upcoming special
question: artist with most simultaneous charted LPs
oldie played: Eight Days A Week - Beatles

248. 03-29-75 **Program #751-13**
production note: disks contain promos for upcoming special
program note: Casey promos upcoming special
flipside played: Snookeroo - Ringo Starr
story: Doobie Brothers' John Hartman's unusual clothing
story: Elton John's rise to superstar status
story: Frankie Valli's new chart record
story: LaBelle's regret in recording "I Sold My Heart To The Junkman"
story: Shirley Goodman's preferences for co-singers
story: Helen Reddy shares chart feat with Roberta Flack
story: Fanny's gender accomplishment
story: Bob Dylan's comeback
name origin: Earth, Wind & Fire
long version: Tangled Up In Blue - Bob Dylan
question: artist with most #1 records on different labels
oldie played: Stop In The Name Of Love - Supremes

249. 04-05-75 **Program #752-1**
SPECIAL: Disappearing Acts (update from 07-07-73 special)
for a complete list of records in this special, see Rob Durkee's *American Top 40: The Countdown of the Century*

250. 04-12-75

Program #752-2
story: The Spinners paid $5 to stop singing
story: Al Green has plenty of 'sole'
story: Tony Orlando & Dawn's "He Don't Love You (Like I Love You)" originally titled "He Will Break Your Heart"
story: U.S. President Harry Truman's music critic threat
story: Elton John ties a Jackson Five chart record
story: Sammy Johns' phone calls of gratitude to radio stations
story: Bob Dylan's *Rolling Stone* LP review
long version: Tangled Up In Blue - Bob Dylan
question: highest debut record
question: double-sided, individually-charted #1 records

251. 04-19-75

Program #752-3
odd chart stat: debut of Paul Wynn's "Shaving Cream"
odd chart stat: Phoebe Snow's "Poetry Man" falls from #5 to #25
story: suicidal songs
story: "Shaving Cream" took 29 years
story: John Lennon's Ben E. King remake
story: Jimmy Castor was Frankie Lymon
story: Leo Sayer beat up for singing
story: Al Green's birth announcement
story: "Lovin' You" birds
portion played: Gloomy Sunday - Billie Holiday
portion played: Stand By Me - Ben E. King
question: longest chart run for a non-#1 record

252. 04-26-75

Program #752-4
story: Casey Kasem played in high school band with Donald Byrd
story: Ben E. King feared for his life due to The Drifters
story: Paul Anka almost boarded Buddy Holly's fatal flight
(see Waylon Jennings story - 04-03-76; 07-09-77)
story: Ringo Starr lacked confidence
story: Neil Sedaka's "The Immigrant" dedicated to John Lennon
story: appearances of "Beer Barrel Polka"
story: dirty "Shaving Cream"
odd chart stat: Ringo Starr's "No No Song" falls from #4 to #24
question: #1 songs with shortest chart run
program mention: 'Hot' groups
portion played: When Will I Be Loved - Everly Brothers
portion played: He Will Break Your Heart - Jerry Butler

253. 05-03-75

Program #752-5
story: Alice Cooper is not music's first male 'Alice'
story: Jimmy Castor's early days
story: Ben E. King became The Drifters' lead singer
story: Freddy Fender picks
story: Rick Hall's early production days
story: corrected artist label credit for "Shaving Cream" record
question: most recent record at #1 for more than six weeks
question: longest-titled chart record
question: artists with most Top 10 records

TO: AMERICAN TOP 40 SUBSCRIBERS

FROM: TOM ROUNDS

RE: EXTRA COPIES, "DISAPPEARING ACTS" SPECIAL

March 8, 1975

We're running off about 100 extra copies of the "DISAPPEARING ACTS" special for subscribers. If you'd like one or more extra copies, send us an order specifiying how many extras you'd like (they're $7.50 each, including postage).

We'll guarantee delivery of all orders received by Wednesday, March 26. (The special is program #752-1; broadcast dates: April 5-6, 1975) They make good presentational items for agency people, contest winners, etc...or just to keep in the archives for posterity.

At this moment, we have absolutely no backlog of any previous AT40 specials. In view of that and the fact "THE 40 GREATEST DISAPPEARING ACTS OF THE ROCK ERA" will be an especially hot item, better order now.

You can either enclose a check or ask that you be billed on the next regular invoice.

WATERMARK, INC. 10700 Ventura Blvd., No. Hollywood, California 91604 (213) 980-9490

In this memo, sent out a month in advance of the Disappearing Acts special, affiliates were given the option to purchase extra program copies for giveaway or promotional purposes.

EXCLUSIVE!

AMERICAN TOP 40 PRESENTS

THE GREATEST DISAPPEARING ACTS OF THE ROCK ERA

A brand new and completely updated edition of Casey Kasem's most popular special countdown ever! These are the 40 biggest acts . . . from the 50's, 60's and early 70's . . . who rose to the top with one tremendous hit . . . and then plummeted right back into obscurity, never to hit again. We've tracked down most of these one-hit wonders and we'll bring you right up to date on where they are now.

Whatever happened to The Fendermen, The Monotones, Joan Weber, The Penguins, Laurie London, The Elegants and a lot of others, too?

THIS SPECIAL 3 HOUR PROGRAM IS SCHEDULED FOR BROADCAST THE WEEKEND OF APRIL 5-6, 1975.

AMERICAN TOP 40
Watermark, Inc.
10700 Ventura Blvd.
No. Hollywood, Ca. 91604

Please fill me in on how I can program THE GREATEST DISAPPEARING ACTS and send along the entire, free 1975 AMERICAN TOP 40 Presentation Package including demo tape, rates and market availability.

Name ____________________ Title____________________
Call Letters____________ Address____________________
City ____________ State________________ Zip__________

This advertisement appeared in the March 8, 1975 edition of *Billboard* magazine.

WATERMARK, INC. 10700 Ventura Blvd., No. Hollywood, California 91604 (213) 980-9490

TO: AMERICAN TOP 40 SUBSCRIBERS

FROM: TOM ROUNDS

RE: 1975 SPECIAL REVIEW

April 12, 1975

It was great to see so many of you at the N.A.B. We saw a lot of good friends, made some new ones, and learned much. And several subscribers forcibly reminded us to get our act together and issue a schedule of forthcoming AT40 specials for 1975. Here it is:

Program #753-1, Scheduled for broadcast the weekend of July 4-5-6, 1975: "July Forth Nineteen Seventy: The First AT40 Broadcast."

American Top 40 celebrates its fifth anniversary of consecutive weekly programs by delving back into the archives to present our very first show. Recorded in a coat closet at 931 N. La Cienega Blvd. in Hollywood (now a Pup 'N Taco stand), this historic countdown presented some great hits from the summer of 1970. A total trip into memory-land narrated by the 1975 Casey Kasem.

Program #754-1, Scheduled for broadcast the weekend of September 6-7, 1975: "The 40 Top Rock And Roll Acts Of The Fifties."

How many can you name? Well, here's the official countdown of the 40 classiest acts of rock and roll's golden era, each presented by the biggest hit they'd cut by the end of 1959. Everybody knows who'll come in number one, but who knows where Chuck Berry, Little Richard, Pat Boone and Gale Storm will show up on our 40 rung ladder of the 50's Hall of Fame?

Programs #754-12 and 13, Scheduled for the weekends of Dec 20-21 and 27-28, 1975 "The 100 Top Hits of 1975"

Raves from all our subscribers make it our pleasure to once again present a total of eight hours (2 4-hour shows) reviewing the greatest hits of 1975. Suitable for repeat broadcasts, especially on New Years Day, 1976, the American Top 40 "Top 100" will be delivered well in advance of the holidays for blockbuster scheduling.

Tom Rounds alerted stations to the schedule of remaining 1975 specials with this memo, including the repeat of the first program.

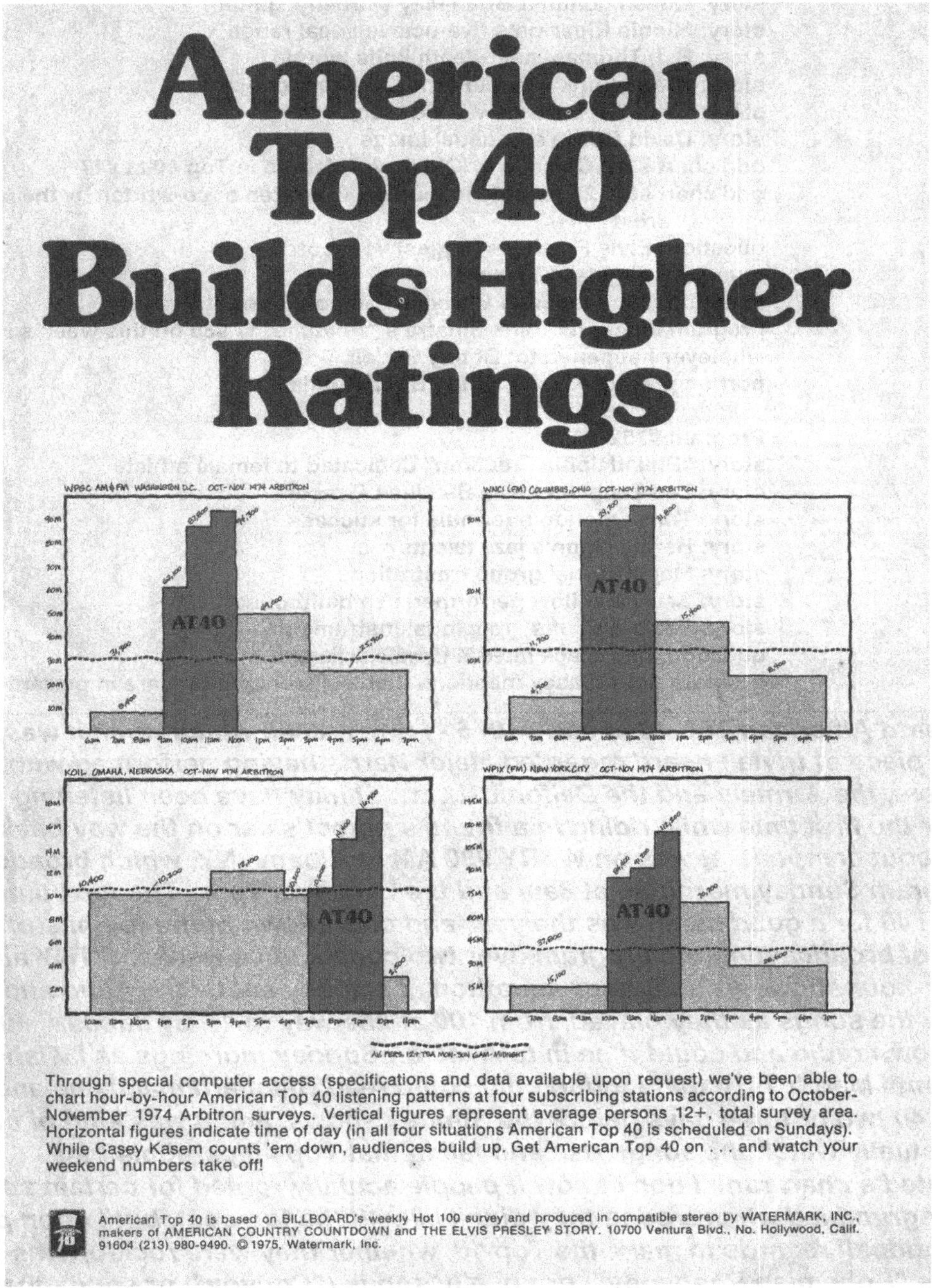

American Top 40 Builds Higher Ratings

WPGC AM&FM WASHINGTON D.C. OCT-NOV 1974 ARBITRON

WNCI (FM) COLUMBUS, OHIO OCT-NOV 1974 ARBITRON

KOIL OMAHA, NEBRASKA OCT-NOV 1974 ARBITRON

WPIX (FM) NEW YORK CITY OCT-NOV 1974 ARBITRON

AT40

Through special computer access (specifications and data available upon request) we've been able to chart hour-by-hour American Top 40 listening patterns at four subscribing stations according to October-November 1974 Arbitron surveys. Vertical figures represent average persons 12+, total survey area. Horizontal figures indicate time of day (in all four situations American Top 40 is scheduled on Sundays). While Casey Kasem counts 'em down, audiences build up. Get American Top 40 on . . . and watch your weekend numbers take off!

American Top 40 is based on BILLBOARD's weekly Hot 100 survey and produced in compatible stereo by WATERMARK, INC., makers of AMERICAN COUNTRY COUNTDOWN and THE ELVIS PRESLEY STORY. 10700 Ventura Blvd., No. Hollywood, Calif. 91604 (213) 980-9490. © 1975, Watermark, Inc.

Promoting the positive ratings that *AT40* received in a recent survey, this bar graph ad appeared in the April 19, 1975 edition of *Billboard* magazine. Specifically, ratings information was provided for for radio stations in New York City, Washington DC, Omaha, and Columbus, Ohio.

254. 05-10-75 **Program #752-6**
story: Queen guitarist Brian May's 'trashy' guitar
story: Minnie Riperton's five-octave vocal range
story: B.J. Thomas' near-death knife wound
story: Grand Funk's Mark Farner answers critics
story: Alice Cooper's new band members
story: David Bowie's unusual image
odd chart stat: Chicago's "Old Days" debuts in Top 40 at #17
odd chart stat: 27 records in the Top 40 written or co-written by the performing artist
question: Elvis Presley's biggest #1 record
question: biggest #2 record
question: simultaneous #1 record on pop & country charts
program mention: Frank Sinatra's "Anytime" is #80 on this week's Hot 100
whatever happened to: Bobby Rydell
portion played: Kissin' Time - Bobby Rydell

255. 05-17-75 **Program #752-7**
story: "Philadelphia Freedom" dedicated to female athlete
story: Led Zeppelin ties a Beatles LP record
story: Tony Orlando's formula for success
story: Herbie Mann's jazz talents
story: Major Harris' group frustrations
story: Barry Manilow performed in a bathhouse
story: Seals & Crofts' 'religious' instruments
question: first black male & female artists at #1
program note: Casey mentions that all listener letters are important

I first heard American Top 40 in early 1975 - I don't recall which week it was, but the first piece of trivia I heard regarded Major Harris having performed with the Teenagers, the Jarmels and the Delfonics...........I may have been listening to AT40 for the first time while riding in a friend's parent's car on the way back from a Boy Scout campout. It was on WTRY 980 AM in Albany, NY, which broadcasted the program Sunday mornings at 8am and then again at 7pm. The next time I heard AT40 for a good listen was the year-end countdown of the top hits of 1975. Instead of broadcasting the program over two consecutive weeks, WTRY aired the two four-hour shows as an 8-hour marathon. I actually sat by the radio and wrote down all the songs as they played, from 100 all the way to 1. By January 1976, I had my own radio and could tune in to AT40 on Sunday mornings as I wished. It wasn't until March 1976 that I found out I could read Billboard magazine and see the Top 40 two or three days before the Sunday shows, and it was kind of cool for me to actually watch the songs rise and fall in that Top 40 parabola that constituted a chart run. I don't know if people actually rooted for certain songs to hit #1 or grumbled when a song they didn't like hit the top spot, but I often pulled for the oddball records to make the Top 10, whether they were rock-operas (Queen's "Bohemian Rhapsody") or novelty songs ("Convoy") or songs that actually sounded cool (Boston's "More Than A Feeling"). I would write down the Top 40 for that week as it aired, and eventually lose the slips of paper by the time next week's installment aired. For me, American Top 40 was a chance to hear all different types of music - rock, soul, funk, country, disco, ballads - in what amounted to a true popularity contest. Songs would rise and fall depending on their longevity on the charts, and their popularity inherent therein.

Chuck Miller, author of *Warman's American Records*, writer for *Goldmine Magazine*, and a longtime *AT40* listener

AMERICAN TOP 40 IS MOVING A LOT OF BURGERS IN WATERLOO

and theater tickets in New York (WPIX), jeans in Chicago (WDHF), and stereos in L.A. (KKDJ). Best of all, it moves people, pulling highest rated time period of the week in many of its 325 markets around the world.
And we've got the facts to back it up in our new, 1975 American Top 40 marketing survey. Do yourself . . . and your radio station . . . a favor. Send in the coupon now and find out how easy it is to get your weekends moving with American Top 40.

Here's 17 year old Patty Steimel, KLEU's official American Top 40 girl. Patty appears every Saturday at one of Henry's 4 Locations in Waterloo, Iowa. She awards prizes in an American Top 40 Treasure Hunt masterminded by KLEU's Manager Bill Bundy and PD Dave Jonasen. Since Henry's has been sponsoring weekly AT40 broadcasts burgers have been moving up to 5 times faster! BELOW: AT40 host Casey Kasem interviews a burger from Henry's.

AMERICAN TOP 40
10700 Ventura Blvd.
No. Hollywood, CA 91604
(213) 980-9490

Send me your complete free presentation package including complete show, demo tape, marketing survey, sales kit and worldwide listening directory. Include price and market exclusivity information.

Name ______________________ Title ______________________

Station ____________ Address ______________________

City ______________________ State ____________ Zip ____________

American Top 40, with up-to-the-minute hit information from BILLBOARD'S Hot 100, is produced every week in compatible stereo by Watermark . . . makers of AMERICAN COUNTRY COUNTDOWN and THE ELVIS PRESLEY STORY.

This advertisement appeared in the May 3, 1975 edition of *Billboard* magazine. This ad includes a rarely seen picture of Casey Kasem "interviewing a burger" from Henry's Hamburgers.

June 21, 1975

TO: AMERICAN TOP 40 PROGRAM SUBSCRIBERS

FROM: Steve Buth

RE: AT-40 Promos for program 753-1

Included at the end of 3B of this week's AT-40 (program 752-13) are eight Casey voice promos for the upcoming special (program 753-1): "July Fourth Nineteen Seventy: The First AT-40 Broadcast." The special will be shipped June 28, 1975, and is scheduled for broadcast the weekend of July 5-6.

PROMO COPY

1. Hi, this is Casey. To celebrate American Top 40's fifth birthday, we decided to share with you something rather dusty but very dear to our hearts. From a damp, dark corner of the vault, we've brought out the original tape of the very first AT-40 countdown ever broadcast. It contains the forty most popular songs in America on the 4th of July 1970. And this week we're going to re-run it just as it ran five years ago. I hope you'll be with me.

2. Hi, this is Casey Kasem reminding you to tune in to American Top 40 this week for a time trip back to the 4th of July, 1970. We're re-running the original tape of the first AT-40 countdown.

3. American Top 40 is five years old and this is Casey inviting you to our birthday celebration. It's tomorrow and we're going to re-run the first AT-40 countdown ever broadcast. Hope you'll join us.

4. Hi, this is Casey Kasem reminding you to tune in to American Top 40 tomorrow for a time trip back to the 4th of July, 1970. We're re-running the original tape of the first AT-40 countdown that we ever did. That's tomorrow. I hope you'll be there.

5. Coming up in just a little while on American Top 40 is that piece of the past I've been telling you about. This is Casey and in celebration of our fifth birthday...this is the day we re-run the first AT-40 countdown ever broadcast. Keep listening.

6. A piece of the past is coming up on American Top 40. This is Casey reminding you to tune in for the unprecedented, even un-necessary, re-run of the original tape of the first AT-40 countdown we ever did. It happened exactly five years ago and it's happening again today. Don't miss it.

7. Same copy as #6 with tag changed to TOMORROW.

8. Same copy as #6 with tag changed to THIS WEEK.

WATERMARK, INC. 10700 Ventura Blvd., No. Hollywood, California 91604 (213) 980-9490

_AT40_ stations were provided with 5th anniversary promotional announcements with the June 28, 1975 show, as described in this memo from Steve Buth.

256. 05-24-75

Program #752-8
program error: Casey's introduction of "Misty" states that Ray Stevens has had two #1 songs – "The Streak" and "Ahab The Arab"; actually, "The Streak" and "Everything Is Beautiful" were #1; "Ahab" peaked at #5
question: biggest Top 10 artist of the 1970's
program mention: Supertramp's "Bloody Well Right" flipside
whatever happened to: Jimmy Clanton
portion played: Just A Dream - Jimmy Clanton
story: B.J. Thomas' "(Hey Won't You Play) Another Somebody Done Somebody Wrong Song" broke longest-title chart record
story: Elton John is #1 with LPs
story: Major Harris should have become a doctor
story: Paul Anka only #1 artist in 1950's & 1970's
story: John Denver voted great by Miss America contestants
story: Alice Cooper painted by Salvador Dali

257. 05-31-75

Program #752-9
program error: Casey corrects previous week's Ray Stevens error with another error by stating that he had two #1 songs - "The Streak" and "Mr. Businessman"; actually, "Mr. Businessman" peaked at #28
production error: Bad Company's "Good Lovin' Gone Bad" debuts; wrong song played: Bad Company's "Whiskey Bottle"
story: Jessi Colter took name from a Jesse James gang member
story: Linda Ronstadt provoked by a concert photographer
story: Alice Cooper's concert audience walked out
story: Roger Whittaker's "Last Farewell" was a record store problem
story: Freddy Fender's "Before The Next Teardrop Falls" ties a chart record
story: Chicago's LP success
whatever happened to: Dick And Deedee
portion played: The Mountain's High - Dick And Deedee
flipside played: My Ship - Tavares
question: most successful artist using a stage name
question: 1975's most popular British artist

258.06-07-75

Program #752-10
story: 250 records annually reach the Top 40
story: award winning "The Way We Were"
story: Jim Seals, fiddle champion
story: Chicago's non-#1 chart record
story: Ray Stevens' "Misty" remake unlike original
odd chart stat: Elton John's new LP debuts at #1
odd chart stat: since January, five Top 40 records drop from #1 to #7
question: artist with most consecutive #1 records
question: The Beatles' chart records
whatever happened to: Linda Scott
portion played: I've Told Every Little Star - Linda Scott
portion played: Misty - Johnny Mathis
program mention: Monti Rock III's 'Sir' distinction
program mention: Bachman-Turner Overdrive pronunciation correction

TO: AMERICAN TOP 40 SUBSCRIBERS

FROM: TOM ROUNDS

RE: SENSATIVE MATERIAL??

July 26, 1975

WATERMARK, INC. 10700 Ventura Blvd., No. Hollywood, California 91604 (213) 980-9490

By now you will have realized our solution to the now famous Isley Brothers' "Fight The Power" record. We simply inserted some assorted grunts and drumkicks found lying around the studio for the offending reference to a vital byproduct of our cattle industry. We felt the T-neck (Columbia) label's solution was substandard and simply went ahead and provided our own.

Now get ready for the next one:

We were sure the Z.Z. Top record "Tush" would make the forty this week, but it didn't quite. In that it will inevitably appear on AT40 in upcoming weeks, and if there's anybody out there that isn't aware of it, "Tush" is defined in the "Random House Dictionary of the English Language" thusly: ...from the Hebrew..." 'Tushie' (toosh'ee, n.) (informal, babytalk). The buttocks.

If you wish to delete this reference to something that is normally beneath us, it's your option.

Here's another Tom Rounds memo that alerted stations to two records containing "sensitive material." Two 1975 *AT40* shows, July 12 and July 19, contained unedited versions of the Isley Brothers record as described in the program summaries.

259. 06-14-75 **Program #752-11**
story: Tanya Tucker's father misses prediction
story: Freddy Fender busted for playing guitar while on guard duty
story: Toni Tennille's backstage problem with The Beach Boys
story: John Denver's image
story: Van McCoy's inspiration for "The Hustle"
whatever happened to: SSgt. Barry Sadler
portion played: The Ballad Of The Green Beret - SSgt. Barry Sadler
program error: Casey's introduction of Earth, Wind & Fire's "Shining Star" indicates that it's "...down to #13 this week..."; actually, it was #16
question: highest ranking comedy team record

260. 06-21-75 **Program #752-12**
question: group & solo member simultaneously in Top 10
question: queen of the charts
question: most successful family act
story: Elvis Presley's simultaneous #1 record on pop, soul & country charts
story: War's free ride
story: The Doobie Brothers' post-tour accommodations
story: The Captain & Tennille are rare #1 married duo
program note: Casey promos upcoming special
whatever happened to: Mel Carter
portion played: Hold Me, Thrill Me, Kiss Me - Mel Carter

261. 06-28-75 **Program #752-13**
whatever happened to: Freddy Cannon
portion played: Palisades Park - Freddy Cannon
odd chart stat: Top 5 records same as chart of 06-21-75
story: Seals & Crofts' use of nepotism
story: Glen Campbell's voice used for actor Steve McQueen
question: record with most charted versions, prior to its climb to #1
question: Beatles & Rolling Stones material used prior to chart appearance
question: artist with most records simultaneously on chart
program note: Casey promos upcoming special
program note: program disks contain upcoming special promo announcements
program error: in the intro to the Average White Band's "Cut The Cake," Casey mentions that there were back-to-back records by two groups from Scotland, but incorrectly identifies the band Pilot as Magic; the song "Magic" was performed by Pilot

262. 07-05-75 **Program #753-1**
SPECIAL: First *AT40* Program re-broadcast; chart date - July 11, 1970 (see 07-11-70 program description for details)

263. 07-12-75 **Program #753-2**
production error: The Isley Brothers' "Fight The Power" debuts, with an unedited version played; contains offensive language ("......by all this b*s*** goin' down..."); heard on approximately 300 subscribing radio stations**
***Billboard* report error: chart positions of Janis Ian's "At Seventeen" and Michael Jackson's "Just A Little Bit Of You" are reversed**
story: Van McCoy's songwriting success
story: Jessi Colter swallowed a hummingbird
story: Ray Stevens laughed at himself for his TV show
story: Alice Cooper's bicentennial party
whatever happened to: Lou Christie
portion played: The Gypsy Cried - Lou Christie
question: biggest selling record, 1955-1975
question update: group & solo member simultaneously in Top 10
question: all-British Top 10 chart

264. 07-19-75 **Program #753-3**
production error: unedited version of The Isley Brothers' "Fight The Power" airs again; contains offensive language ("......by all this b*s*** goin' down..."); heard on approximately 300 subscribing radio stations**
odd chart stat: James Taylor's "How Sweet It Is" debuts in the Top 40 at #20
odd chart stat: since January, six Top 40 records have fallen from #1 to #8
question: record with most weeks in Top 40
question: artists replacing themselves at #1
story: Janis Ian's one-hit wonder status
story: War's Hollywood burlesque party
story: 10cc's members
story: Paul McCartney's Top 5 aliases
story: Tony Orlando & Dawn broke show attendance records in Las Vegas
story: James Taylor's Apple Records flop
story: Gwen McCrae beats her husband (see 08-17-74 story)
whatever happened to: Jack Scott
portion played: My True Love - Jack Scott
program mention: Bachman-Turner Overdrive's "Hey You" is a compilation

265. 07-26-75 **Program #753-4**
story: Waylon Jennings & Jessi Colter's motor home
story: Michael Murphy married on an Indian reservation
story: the recordings of "How Sweet It Is"
story: male solo artists with most #1 LPs
story: Three Dog Night's 18 consecutive Top 20 singles
story: Elton John is third most successful LP artist
program mention: The Eagles' music theme
program mention: 'Hot' groups
portion played: Try A Little Tenderness - Three Dog Night
portion played: How Sweet It Is - Marvin Gaye
portion played: How Sweet It Is - Jr. Walker & The All Stars
question: Australian artists at #1
question: group with longest chart longevity

266. 08-02-75 **Program #753-5**
lyric alert: memo from executive producer Tom Rounds which accompanied program indicates that *AT40* has created their own censored version of the Isley Brothers' "Fight The Power" because T-Neck Record Company's version is unacceptable
lyric alert: in the same memo, Tom Rounds alerts subscribing radio stations to the potentially controversial lyric content and the impending arrival of ZZ Top's "Tush" to the Top 40; a definition of 'tush' is included
story: Judy Collins had polio and tuberculosis
story: "Love Will Keep Us Together" dedicated to Neil Sedaka
story: Tony Camillo produced Gladys Knight's "Midnight Train To Georgia"
story: Ambrosia tested new Hollywood Bowl equipment
story: Janis Ian, a former child prodigy
story: Elton John's *Time* article produced celebrity letters
name origin: Frankie Valli
portion played: Love Will Keep Us Together - Neil Sedaka
portion played: Peppermint Twist - Joey Dee & The Starliters
whatever happened to: Joey Dee & The Starliters
question: #1 TV theme show records

267. 08-09-75 **Program #753-6**
story: Three Dog Night's bathroom recording of "Liar"
story: The Captain & Tennille's Spanish "Love Will Keep Us Together"
story: Freddy Fender's 25,000 hours of labor
story: Elton John's 106 consecutive weeks on Hot 100
story: Mike Post's arm wrestling success
story: Marvin Hamlisch's three-Oscar-award night
odd chart stat: Top 3 records by British artists
portion played: Liar - Three Dog Night
portion played: Por Amor Vivivemos - Captain & Tennille
program note: Casey mentions *AT40*'s appreciation of listener mail

268. 08-16-75 **Program #753-7**
story: Stevie Wonder makes more money than Elton John
story: Travis Wammack smuggled into nightclub by Bill Black's Combo
story: Tony Orlando & Dawn invested $800,000 into image
story: Frank Sinatra back on Hot 100
story: James Taylor's prized pet pig Mona
story: Neil Sedaka's big break
record origin: Amazing Rhythm Aces' "Third Rate Romance"
portion played: All Or Nothing - Frank Sinatra
odd chart stat: Captain & Tennille's "Love Will Keep Us Together" on Hot 100 in two different languages
odd chart stat: Van McCoy's "The Hustle" falls from #11 to #34
odd chart stat: 29 records in the Top 40 written or co-written by the performing artist

269. 08-23-75 **Program #753-8**
program note: new "American Top 40 - Casey's Coast-to-Coast" split logo jingles debut
production error: The Osmonds' "The Proud One" debuts; wrong song played: The Osmonds' "The Last Day Is Coming"
production error: Casey both teased and introduced a Johnny Rivers' story by stating "......I have a debut song by a singer....."; actually, Rivers was in the Top 40 for three weeks
whatever happened to: Dee Dee Sharp
story: ZZ Top's advice to other musicians
story: Hamilton, Joe Frank & Reynolds were The T-Bones
correction: Casey acknowledges additional chart statistics from radio station WPCC in Clinton, SC in regards to chart longevity question
question: Elton John's LP dedication
question: country group at #1
odd chart stat: Tony Orlando & Dawn's "Mornin' Beautiful" falls out of the Top 40 from #14 to #45
portion played: Mashed Potato Time - Dee Dee Sharp

270. 08-30-75 **Program #753-9**
odd chart stat: John Denver's "I'm Sorry" debuts in the Top 40 at #20
odd chart stat: Melissa Manchester's "Midnight Blue" falls out of the Top 40 from #12 to #41
odd chart stat: 10cc's "I'm Not In Love" falls out of the Top 40 from #14 to #43
question: longest charted record
story: The Temptations were The Primes
story: The Pointer Sisters' Houston rescue
story: America justifies their music
story: Barry Manilow's 'sweet Melissa'
story: Glen Campbell's Hollywood success
story: David Geddes gave up music for law school
story: Elton John's expensive eyewear
portion played: Help Me Rhonda - Beach Boys

WATERMARK, INC. 10700 Ventura Blvd., No. Hollywood, California 91604 (213) 980-9490

To: AT40 Subscribers

From: Tom Rounds

Re: Wink In, Casey Out

October 4, 1975

Casey's up for a long overdue extended vacation during the remainder of October, and this week we welcome the first of three consecutive guest stars: Wink Martindale.

Star of CBS-TV's show "Gambit", Watermark's own "Elvis Presley Story", and daily host of the mid-day show on L. A.'s giant KMPC, Wink is also one of the most musically knowledgeable of broadcast personalities.

We'll have other surprise guests occupying the Casey Kasem chair of musicology on programs 754-3 (weekend of October 18-19) and 754-4 (weekend of October 25-26).

Casey will be back in action on program #754-5 (weekend of November 1-2).

And a reminder: We're once again producing "The Top 100". 1975's year-end tabulation by Billboard will be the subject of two special four-hour countdowns scheduled for the last weekend of December (27-28) and the first weekend of January (3-4). The entire 8 hours will be shipped on December 13.

Thanks.

In addition to this memo informing stations that guest host Wink Martindale was at the *AT40* microphone for the October 11, 1975 program, it also informed stations that Casey Kasem would be out for the rest of the month. However, Casey returned the following week.

271. 09-06-75 **Program #753-10**
question: artist with most Hot 100, non-Top 40 records
odd chart stat: four 1975 #1 country records crossover to become #1 on the Hot 100
story: James Taylor's *Time* article
story: War's automobile collection
story: Muhammad Ali's poetic LP
story: Aretha Franklin's Grammy Award success
portion played: Respect - Aretha Franklin
portion played: Chopin's Prelude In C Minor - Claudio Arau

272. 09-13-75 **Program #753-11**
program mention: Larry Graham played with Sly & The Family Stone
program mention: The Osmonds' riddle
portion played: Dance To The Music - Sly & The Family Stone
story: box office receipts from the movie *Jaws*
story: Leon Russell, legendary songwriter and musician
story: James Taylor's broken hands and broken mind
story: David Bowie intimidated by success
story: Freddy Fender's near-miss "Wasted Days And Wasted Nights"
story: Janis Ian's thoughts about her music
question: artist with most Top 10 records in shortest time
question: record with most versions
odd chart stat: Glen Campbell's "Rhinestone Cowboy" simultaneously #1 on Hot 100 and country chart
program error: Casey's outcue to Jefferson Starship's "Miracles" indicates that it's "....at #35 this week....."; actually, it was #34

273. 09-20-75 **Program #753-12**
whatever happened to: Nino Tempo & April Stevens
portion played: Deep Purple - Nino Tempo & April Stevens
story: KC & The Sunshine Band nearly missed European tour
story: Johnny Wakelin's thoughts on Muhammad Ali
story: The Spinners' lost talent contest prize
story: Dickie Goodman's record forte
story: David Bowie popularized glitter rock
story: Earth, Wind & Fire's philosophy
story: Paul Simon's "Bridge Over Troubled Water" earned $25 million
program note: Casey promos upcoming special
question: #1 records - men vs. women

274. 09-27-75 **Program #753-13**
question: artist with most top 10 records
question: 1975's biggest hit so far
production note: disks contain promos for upcoming special
story: Phoebe Snow was a homely teenager
story: Dickie Goodman's record label error
story: Janis Ian's "At Seventeen" is real
story: John Denver's concert popularity
story: Simon & Garfunkel update

275. 10-04-75 **Program #754-1**
SPECIAL: Top 40 Rock & Roll Acts Of The 1950's
for a complete list of records in this special, see Rob Durkee's *American Top 40: The Countdown of the Century*
program note: "Shuckatoom," *American Top 40*'s new theme music debuts in program closing
production error: skip (found in the master tape) in Chuck Willis' "C.C. Rider", at the very end of the record

276. 10-11-75

Program #754-2
GUEST HOST: Wink Martindale; according to memo accompanying the show, Casey would be gone the entire month of October, but returned 10-18-75
odd chart stat: nine debut records
odd chart stat: Olivia Newton-John's "Something Better To Do" debuts at #19
story: John Fogerty's one-person Blue Ridge Rangers
story: Elton John's chart record ends
story: Glen Campbell on TV's *Shindig*
story: Jefferson Airplane reincarnated
story: Natalie Cole is Nat King Cole's daughter
story: John Denver is the 'Avis' of the LP chart
story: Helen Reddy's Brentwood home
program mention: Linda Ronstadt's double-sided record
program mention: Bruce Springsteen's philosophy on Elvis Presley
whatever happened to: Gary U.S. Bonds
portion played: New Orleans - U.S. Bonds
portion played: I Only Have Eyes For You - The Flamingos
program error: Wink listed all the #1 records during the 1970's that returned to #1, but did not mention Roberta Flack's "Killing Me Softly"
question: longest chart run of a non-#1 record

277. 10-18-75

Program #754-3
flipside played: Calypso - John Denver
whatever happened to: Timi Yuro
portion played: Hurt - Timi Yuro
question: #1 record with two versions, simultaneous chart runs
question: longest chart run for a Top 10 record
question: biggest LP-with-no-singles artist
program mention: Freddy Fender's three Hot 100 records
program mention: Glen Campbell's "Rhinestone Cowboy" has longest 1975 chart run
story: The Four Seasons' continued popularity
story: Bruce Springsteen's critical acceptance
story: Esther Phillips' underage talent contest win
story: The Captain & Tennille's storybook romance
story: Neil Sedaka's six Hot 100 records in 1975

278. 10-25-75

Program #754-4
program mention: Austin Roberts worked on TV's *Scooby Doo*
story: Melissa Manchester's college professor was Paul Simon
story: Frank & Nancy Sinatra's chart feat
story: Bruce Springsteen's press biography
program note: airing on Halloween, Casey promos and acts in ABC-TV's production of *War of the Worlds*
odd chart stat: twelve foreign acts in the Top 40
odd chart stat: Elton John's "Island Girl" climbs from #36 to #8
flipside played: Love Is A Rose - Linda Ronstadt
flipside played: Calypso - John Denver
question: biggest record adapted from classical music
question: biggest instrumental artist
question: biggest Top 10, non-#1 artist
oldie played: Something Stupid - Frank & Nancy Sinatra

279. 11-01-75 **Program #754-5**
flipside played: Calypso - John Denver
flipside played: Peace Pipe - B.T. Express
question: artist with most #1 records, most consecutive years
question: record with most Top 10 weeks
question: record with longest #2 stay
story: The Beatles' "Yesterday" bridges the generation gap
story: Orleans' nonexistent psychologist
story: Frankie Valli singing on "Who Loves You?"
story: Simon & Garfunkel reunited
record origin: The Raiders' "Indian Reservation"
program mention: "I Only Have Eyes For You" first heard in 1934 movie
odd chart stat: Elton John's "Island Girl" climbs from #8 to #1, 4 weeks on the Hot 100
odd chart stat: Sweet's "Ballroom Blitz" falls from #9 to #33
program note: last show where original *AT40* theme music opens program
oldie played: Yesterday - Beatles
oldie played: Indian Reservation - Raiders

280. 11-08-75 **Program #754-6**
program note: "Shuckatoom," new *AT40* theme music, opens program
flipside played: Calypso - John Denver
flipside played: Peace Pipe - B.T. Express
question: highest debut, non-#1 record
question: shortest & longest song titles
question: record charting most often
name origin: Jigsaw
program mention: Bay City Rollers' 'roller mania'
story: John Fogerty's #2 records
story: The Bee Gees disband & re-group
story: Dion, a forgotten has-been
story: Kyu Sakamoto's "Sukiyaki" is only #1 Oriental record
story: Morris Albert's mother forbid piano playing
story: Elton John's LP debuts at #1
portion played: What A Diff'rence A Day Makes - Dinah Washington
oldie played: Abraham, Martin & John - Dion
oldie played: Sukiyaki - Kyu Sakamoto

281. 11-15-75 **Program #754-7**
story: The Four Seasons were The Wonder Who
story: "Calypso" & Jacques Cousteau
story: Neil Sedaka's reason to write & record music
story: Joan Baez was going broke
story: Natalie Cole's meeting with Harry Belafonte
story: Paul Simon advised Carole King
story: Melissa Manchester's encounters with record company president Clive Davis
name origin: Captain (of Captain & Tennille)
flipside played: Calypso - John Denver
flipside played: Peace Pipe - B.T. Express
production note: commercial break added, prior to Abba's "SOS"
whatever happened to: Gene McDaniels
question: double-sided record replacing itself at #1
oldie played: Don't Think Twice - Wonder Who
oldie played: Hundred Pounds Of Clay - Gene McDaniels

ACC/AT40 PRODUCTION SCHEDULE 754-8 THRU 761-1 (TR 10-7-75)

ALL RECORDING TIMES: 9AM
RECORDS FOR AT40 SPECIALS DUE: 11/7
RECORDS FOR ACC SPECIALS DUE: 11/21

SUNDAY	MONDAY	TUESDAY	WEDNESDAY	THURSDAY	FRIDAY	SATURDAY
NOV 9	NOV 10	NOV 11 ACC 754-8 TRACK+ASSEMBLE	NOV 12	NOV 13 AT40 754-8 TRACK+ASSEMBLE	NOV 14	NOV 15 AT40 754- TRACK+ASSEMBLE (SPECIAL)
NOV 16	NOV 17	NOV 18 ACC 754-9 TRACK+ASSEMBLE	NOV 19	NOV 20 AT40 754-9 TRACK+ASSEMBLE	NOV 21	NOV 22 AT40 761-1 TRACK+ASSEMBLE (SPECIAL)
NOV 23	NOV 24	NOV 25 ACC 754-10 TRACK+ASSEMBLE	NOV 26 AT40 754-10 TRACK+ASSEMBLE	NOV 27 THANKSGIVING	NOV 28 ACC 754-13 TRACK+ASSEMBLE (SPECIAL)	NOV 29
NOV 30 ACC 761-1 TRACK+ASSEMBLE (SPECIAL)	DEC 1	DEC 2 ACC 754-11 TRACK+ASSEMBLE	DEC 3	DEC 4 AT40 754-11 TRACK+ASSEMBLE	DEC 5	DEC 6
DEC 7	DEC 8	DEC 9 ACC 754-12 TRACK+ASSEMBLE	DEC 10	DEC 11 AT40 754-12 TRACK+ASSEMBLE	DEC 12	DEC 13 SHIP 754-12 754-13 761-1 BOTH SHOWS

NEXT AT40 TRACKING: WED DEC 31   NEXT ACC TRACKING: TUES DEC 30

Prepared by Tom Rounds, here's a production schedule for both Watermark shows -- *American Top 40* and *American Country Countdown*. It included recording dates for all remaining programs for 1975 beginning with the November 22 show and concluding with the year's Top 100.

282. 11-22-75

Program #754-8
flipside played: Calypso - John Denver
question: biggest family act of the 1970's
question: highest 1975 debut record
odd chart stat: Pete Wingfield's "Eighteen With A Bullet" is at position #18 'with a bullet'
odd chart stat: Silver Convention's "Fly Robin Fly" climbs from #16 to #2
story: Otis Redding's posthumous success
story: The Staple Singers' angry gospel fans
story: Hank Williams' big break
story: Bay City Rollers' Eric Faulkner's optimism
whatever happened to: Billy Joe Royal
portion played: Down In The Boondocks - Billy Joe Royal
oldie played: Sittin' On The Dock Of The Bay - Otis Redding

283. 11-29-75

Program #754-9
odd chart stat: The Eagles' "Lyin' Eyes" falls from #12 to #39
story: Carole King's "Tapestry" LP success
story: Freddy Fender worked in a car wash in 1974
story: Frankie Valli's pseudonyms
story: KC & The Sunshine Band's Harry Wayne Casey cleaned record studios
story: Simon & Garfunkel's "My Little Town" reunion
record origin: David Geddes' "The Last Game Of The Season"
record origin: Four Seasons' "Big Girls Don't Cry"
program note: Casey promos upcoming special
question: Abba's "SOS" is a palindrome
question: slowest & fastest falling #1 records
question: rock era artist with most Top 10 records
question: first #1 Canadian artist
program error: after playing #15, Casey closes the hour with "...we have the Top 13 best-selling songs yet to come....."
oldie played: It's Too Late - Carole King

284. 12-06-75

Program #754-10
odd chart stat: two debut records
story: Glen Campbell's first guitar
story: Paul McCartney is #1 in #1's
story: Natalie Cole not like Nat King Cole
story: Kiss' Gene Simmons burned in concert
story: Joan Baez's social movement theme
story: possible chart record with 1975's #1 records (34, as of this week)
story: Simon & Garfunkel won all music awards in 1970
question: top artists of the 1970's
question: artists with most weeks at #1
portion played: Heat Wave - Martha & The Vandellas
portion played: We Shall Overcome - Joan Baez
oldie played: The Night They Drove Old Dixie Down - Joan Baez
edited long version: Who Loves You – Four Seasons
production note: disks contain promos for upcoming special
program note: Casey promos upcoming special
program note: statistician Ben Marichal's last show

285. 12-13-75

Program #754-11
production note: disks contain promos for upcoming special
question: female artist with most #1 records
question: artist with most #1 records on soul and country charts
story: "Volare" is lucky for Italian singers
story: War's non-violent image
story: Ohio Players pre-concert screaming
story: Al Green's big selling, non-Top 40 record
story: Elton John's deficiency in British #1 records
story: David Ruffin's top vocal-range note
story: Silver Convention's back-up musicians quit
program note: Casey promos upcoming special
long version: I Love Music - O'Jays
odd chart stat: C.W. McCall's "Convoy" climbs from #82 to #29
portion played: Secret Love - Doris Day

286. 12-20-75

Program #754-12
production note: disks contain promos for upcoming special
story: Average White Band's debut #1 single & LP
story: Jackie Wilson's Christmas gift to his mother
story: "Convoy" is theme to speeding highway travelers
story: Gladys Knight & The Pips' two debut records
story: Jose Feliciano's "Star-Spangled Banner" controversy
story: The Bee Gees attempted to impersonate The Everly Brothers
program mention: Olivia Newton-John sings on John Denver's "Fly Away"
program mention: Donna Summer's "Love To Love You Baby" is gold
question: biggest Top 10, non-#1 record
program note: Casey promos upcoming special
program note: Casey mentions his upcoming appearance on the ABC-TV movie, *Mr. & Ms. Bandstand Murders*
program error: after #7, Casey states ".......the four biggest hits.......are next....."
odd chart stat: three weeks after leaving the #1 position, KC & The Sunshine Band's "That's The Way I Like It" returns to #1
oldie played: Jingle Bell Rock - Bobby Helms
oldie played: Feliz Navidad - Jose Feliciano

287. 12-27-75

Program #754-13
SPECIAL: Top 100 Of 1975 (#100 - 51) (based on *Billboard*'s year-end Top 100) for a complete list of records in this special, see Rob Durkee's *American Top 40: The Countdown of the Century*
long version: Do It ('Til You're Satisfied) - B.T. Express

1976

288. 01-03-76

Program #761-1
SPECIAL: Top 100 Of 1975 (#50 - 1) (based on *Billboard*'s year-end Top 100) for a complete list of records in this special, see Rob Durkee's *American Top 40: The Countdown of the Century*
program note: show's closing credits include all of *AT40* staff identifying themselves
long version: Lucy In The Sky With Diamonds - Elton John
long version: Fire - Ohio Players
long version: Boogie On Reggae Woman - Stevie Wonder

289. 01-10-76

Program #761-2
story: The Who's unchanged membership
story: "Teen Angel" was a joke
story: Paul Anka record audience-tested
story: The Bay City Rollers 'blasted' by Soviet journal
story: Neil Sedaka's two versions of "Breaking Up Is Hard To Do"
story: Johnnie Ray 'cried' to stardom
portion played: Cry - Johnnie Ray
odd chart stat: 24 Top 40 records written or co-written by the performing artist
odd chart stat: 20 Top 40 records move up two notches
question: male & female artist's record longevity
question: all-female Top 10
question: week with no debut records
question: soundtrack LP's chart longevity
oldie played: Teen Angel - Mark Denning

290. 01-17-76

Program #761-3
story: Janis Joplin's 'full-tilt' life
story: KC & The Sunshine Band's Harry Wayne Casey cleaned record studios
story: Bob Dylan has something in common with Lawrence Welk
story: Neil Sedaka kicked out of Moscow classical competition
story: The Who's Keith Moon jumped out of a restaurant window
story: Barry McGuire's "Eve Of Destruction" is first #1 protest record
long version: Evil Woman - Electric Light Orchestra
program mention: Paul Simon wrote "50 Ways To Leave Your Lover" for his 3-year-old son
question: year with most #1 Canadian records
oldie played: Eve Of Destruction - Barry McGuire
oldie played: Me & Bobby McGee - Janis Joplin

291. 01-24-76

Program #761-4
story: Linda Ronstadt is the remake queen
story: The Eagles carry on from the Buffalo Springfield
story: "Baby Face" popular in the 1920's, 30's, 40's, 50's, 60's & 70's
story: Donovan's image & first #1 record
story: Kiss helped Michigan high school football team
story: C.W. McCall's advertising success
name origin: Bay City Rollers
whatever happened to: The Monkees
program mention: Glen Campbell's award nominations
question: artists using surnames
oldie played: Sunshine Superman - Donovan
oldie played: Last Train To Clarksville - Monkees

" When I was in 8th grade (Fall of 1975), our science teacher let us listen to the radio in class, he had it turned to an FM station that was automated and didn't talk over a song's intro. I liked the station and began listening to it at home..........and then I heard a Casey Kasem promo for AT40, about each week counting down the 40 biggest hits of the week. While thinking of our local station's playlist I had tacked to the wall with 27 songs on it, I thought, "40 songs? There's 40 songs out each week? I have to hear this show.".........So then came the big moment on Sunday night February 1, 1976, on came the AT40 theme music, the intro, and then the #40 jingle (I thought, wow that jingle's cool, I love this already), and on came "December 1963 (Oh What A Night)" by the 4 Seasons, a song I never heard before. Our stations were still playing "Who Loves You". Next was Art Garfunkel..then the Spinners..etc etc. I was hearing songs I've never heard before, and loved it. Then Casey played the "Sounds Of Silence" by Simon & Garfunkel and called it an AT40 extra. I thought he said 1840, I thought 1840? I wrote the song down (even though I knew it was old), then realized what he was talking about. I feel foolish thinking about that today........After listening to the old shows on tape, I realized that Casey had introduced our local station KRNQ in Des Moines, Iowa to the AT40 family of stations on the 1-17-76 show...."

John Jayne, a longtime *AT40* listener

To: AMERICAN TOP 40 SUBSCRIBERS

From: Tom Rounds

January 31, 1976

Casey's on vacation this week (show #761-6), and it's our pleasure to welcome Jerry Bishop as our guest host.

Jerry is presently simulcasting on KIIS here in L. A.

He comes from a long background in contemporary radio on both coasts; does lots of commercials and was voted disc jockey of the year in '69 by the Los Angeles Times.

Casey will be back next week.

* * * * * * * * * * *

Memo to PD's:

Every ARB season we anonymously call subscribers in surveyed markets to double check on the AT40 broadcast schedule. Recently, we've noticed more and more station switchboard operators have either inaccurate information or no information whatever on the AMERICAN TOP 40 broadcast schedule.

It might be helpful if we again point out the fact that over 325 stations now carry the show. Many newcomers in your market will be looking for AMERICAN TOP 40. When they call your station for information it would be constructive if your phone people were right on top of your AT40 schedule.

Thanks.

WATERMARK, INC. 10700 Ventura Blvd., No. Hollywood, California 91604 (213) 980-9490

This memo informed stations that guest host Jerry Bishop was at the *AT40* microphone for the February 7, 1976 program.

292. 01-31-76

Program #761-5
program error: Casey plays two oldies, one in Hour #1, between songs #31 and #30 (Simon & Garfunkel's "Sounds of Silence"), the other in Hour #2, between songs #25 & #24 (The Beatles' "We Can Work It Out"), introducing both as the #1 song from 10 years ago
story: chart feat of "Deep Purple"
story: The Miracles' chart history
story: The Beatles' April 1964 Top 5 chart feat
story: Barry Manilow assisted Bette Midler
story: Simon & Garfunkel's big break
question: artist names in record titles
question: female artists with most Top 10 records
question: third best artist with most #1 records in one year
program mention: John Denver's pre-music professions
oldie played: We Can Work It Out - Beatles
oldie played: Sounds Of Silence - Simon & Garfunkel

293. 02-07-76

Program #761-6
GUEST HOST: Jerry Bishop
flipside played: I Feel Like A Bullet - Elton John
story: Frankie Valli did not sing lead on The Four Seasons' "December 1963"
story: The Bee Gees are not The Beatles
story: The Spinners' four-year chart feat
story: The Eagles are the Oakland A's of rock 'n' roll
story: Neil Sedaka's first million selling record
story: Barbra Streisand's turned-down apartment offer
odd chart stat: Paul Simon's "50 Ways To Leave Your Lover" climbs from #10 to #1
odd chart stat: Kiss' "Rock And Roll All Night" falls out of the Top 40 from #12 to #47
question: female artist's record with most #1 weeks
question: artist with longest name
oldie played: People - Barbra Streisand

294. 02-14-76

Program #761-7
portion played: Vesti La Giubba - Enrico Caruso
story: first million selling record
story: Neil Sedaka's songwriting success
story: Diana Ross' success
story: The Captain & Tennille's wedding
story: Sam Cooke's singing style
story: Paul Simon's self-description
question: year with most #1 female records
question: married couples with husband & wife solo Top 40 records
program mention: citizen band radio popularity
oldie played: Cupid - Sam Cooke
oldie played: Someday We'll Be Together - Diana Ross & Supremes

295. 02-21-76

Program #761-8
flipside played: I Feel Like A Bullet - Elton John
odd chart stat: The Ohio Players' "Love Rollercoaster" falls from #7 to #33
odd chart stat: 29 Top 40 records written or co-written by the performing artist
question: former Beatle with the most Top 10 records
question: biggest #1 instrumental
question: youngest contemporary singer
name origin: Dr. Hook
story: Larry Groce's Christian Science LP
story: Eric Carmen dropped classical music training for rock 'n' roll
story: Helen Reddy's surprise fund raising party
oldie played: Mr. Tambourine Man - Byrds
oldie played: Signed, Sealed, Delivered, I'm Yours - Stevie Wonder

296. 02-28-76

Program #761-9
story: Bachman-Turner Overdrive's gesture for fans injured at concert
story: "Good Vibrations" is most expensive record
story: MGM Records' Mike Curb's accomplishments
story: Al Jolson, the legend
story: Gary Wright assisted by George Harrison
odd chart stat: "Theme From *SWAT*" represents rare #1 occurrence
question: Top 40 artists using only their first name
question: artist with most Top 40 records in 1975
question: actors/actresses with Top 40 records
portion played: Tracks Of My Tears - Smokey Robinson & The Miracles
long version: Golden Years – David Bowie
edited version: The Bay City Rollers' "Money Honey"; edited to 1:34
oldie played: Good Vibrations - Beach Boys

297. 03-06-76

Program #761-10
story: legend of Jim Reeves
story: The Osmond Family recording combinations
story: Arlo Guthrie's "Alice's Restaurant"
story: Tony Orlando's early days
story: "Baby Face" popular in the 1920's, 30's, 40's, 50's, 60's & 70's
program note: "Baby Face" montage featured
program note: Casey reads a letter from a U.S. native in Jamaica
portion played: He'll Have To Go - Jim Reeves
portion played: Baby Face - Al Jolson
portion played: Baby Face - Little Richard
portion played: Baby Face - Bobby Darin
odd chart stat: Elton John's "Grow Some Funk Of Your Own" falls out of the Top 40 from #14 to #42
odd chart stat: Miracles' "Love Machine" takes 20 weeks to climb to #1
question: longest chart-riding, non-Top 10 record
question: biggest #1 records of the 1970's
question: year with most Beatle records at #1
oldie played: City Of New Orleans - Arlo Guthrie

To: American Top 40 Subscribers

From: Tom Rounds

Re: 1976 Specials

March 13, 1976

WATERMARK, INC. 10700 Ventura Blvd., No. Hollywood, California 91604 (213) 980-9490

Your requests have brought forth this list of AT40 specials for 1976. The actual advertising copy is included. Please save this list for your own promotional purposes, and be sure to pass a copy along to the sales department. We intend to publish it in a full page ad in Billboard in the near future.

American Top 40 Specials for 1976

American Top 40's Bicentennial Special: The Fourth of July's Greatest Hits (July 3-4, 1976; program #763-1)

Casey Kasem presents all the hits that were number one on the Fourth of July for the past 40 years. Guy Lombardo and His Royal Canadians get it all started with the unforgettable "It Looks Like Rain In Cherry Blossom Lane", Billboard's #1 on July 4, 1937... we'll groove through the 40's with hits like "Comin' In On A Wing And A Prayer" (July 4, 1943) and "Chi-Baba Chi-Baba" (July 4, 1947)... move into the 50's with "Cherry Pink And Apple Blossom White" (July 4, 1955) and "Purple People Eater" (July 4, 1958)... rock into the 60's with "Quarter To Three" (July 4, 1961) and "Paperback Writer" (July 4, 1966)... right up through July 4, 1975. Casey covers each one of the 40 Fourths and tops it off with some of his own personal bicentennial minutes in pop history.

An American Top 40 Time Capsule: The 40 Top Hits of the Beatle Years (1964-1970) (October 2-3, 1976; program #764-1)

We've picked one of the most exciting episodes of the rock era and pulled out the forty biggest chart hits. The Beatles themselves occupy four of the forty positions, including number one. The period witnessed the first hit by the Carpenters and the last by Otis Redding. The Supremes make the list, so do the Doors, the Stones and Roy Orbinson. But what about the Mamas and Papas, the Beach Boys, and Dylan? Find out when Casey counts 'em all down ... the Beatles and their stiffest competition... the 40 top hits of the Beatle years... all the way from "I Want To Hold Your Hand" to "The Long and Winding Road".

... more...

In this two-page correspondence, Tom Rounds prepared stations for the rest of 1976 with a schedule of the year's specials which including the Fourth of July's Greatest Hits Bicentennial program.

To: American Top 40 Subscribers

March 13, 1976

American Top 40 Presents the Top 100 of 1976
(December 25-26, 1976 and January 1-2, 1977; programs #764-13 and 771-1)

This is our traditional eight hour countdown of the biggest hits of the year. Based on Billboard's official tabulation, Casey Kasem rounds up all the memorable pop events of 1976 and counts down the records that made it ... from #100 to #1. A double special worth double scheduling over the holidays.

298. 03-13-76 **Program #761-11**
story: Carole King is the songwriting queen
story: *Ode To Billie Joe* movie promo
story: Queen guitarist Brian May's 'trashy' guitar
story: Wayne Newton's Las Vegas success
story: The Four Seasons return to #1
story: Larry Groce married his English professor
story: Sweet's bubblegum image dumped
question: The Beatles' solo records on the same Top 40 chart
question: record with most songwriters
odd chart stat: ten British artists in this week's Top 40
name origin: Nazareth
oldie played: Daddy Don't You Walk So Fast - Wayne Newton
oldie played: Ode To Billy Joe - Bobbie Gentry

299. 03-20-76 **Program #761-12**
story: Aerosmith's "Dream On" is not representative of their music
story: Seals & Crofts' donation assists Guatemala earthquake relief
story: high schools producing the most songwriters & recording artists
story: Natalie Cole de-throned Aretha Franklin
story: Neil Sedaka's songwriting accomplishment
program mention: 1960s discos vs. 1970s discos
question: #1 record re-makes becoming #1 records
question: solo artist with most weeks at #1
question: stage production with most Top 40 records
oldie played: Diamond Girl - Seals & Crofts

300. 03-27-76 **Program #761-13**
portion played: Please Please Please - James Brown
story: James Brown's non-Hot 100, million selling record
story: Johnny Mercer's career
story: The Raspberries' scented LP
story: Neil Diamond's experience with death
story: Motown Records' first million selling record
story: Carole King opened Grammy Award doors
question: top British solo artist
question: year with more British artists at #1
program mention: Natalie Cole represented U.S. in international competition
program mention: Casey reads a letter from a listener in Mexico
oldie played: Shop Around - Smokey Robinson & The Miracles
oldie played: I Am I Said - Neil Diamond

301. 04-03-76 **Program #762-1**
whatever happened to: The Shirelles
story: Chaka Khan turned down Stevie Wonder
story: Waylon Jennings almost boarded Buddy Holly's fatal flight
(see Paul Anka story - 04-26-75)
story: The Sylvers are largest recording family act
story: Carole King's success with "Tapestry" LP
story: Marvin Gaye's "I Heard It Through The Grapevine"
question: same-title, different-record #1 records
question: fastest climbing #1 record
oldie played: Will You Still Love Me Tomorrow - Shirelles
oldie played: I Heard It Through The Grapevine - Marvin Gaye

302. 04-10-76 **Program #762-2**
odd chart stat: John Sebastian's "Welcome Back" debuts at #20
odd chart stat: twelve records remain in the same position as previous week
question: #1 record with shortest Top 10 stay
question: year with only groups at #1
question: slowest climbing record
story: The Carpenters' big break
story: Dr. Hook fools concert audience
story: The Everly Brothers' early days
story: Abba's "Waterloo" performed at international competition
oldie played: All I Have To Do Is Dream - Everly Brothers

303. 04-17-76 **Program #762-3**
whatever happened to: songwriter Gerry Goffin
question: artist with no-single, #1 LP
question: #1 foreign female artists
question: artists' names starting with 'z'
story: "Shannon" was a dog
story: Tommy James & The Shondells' big break
story: Gary Wright's instrumental line-up
story: Fleetwood Mac's stolen name
oldie played: Hanky Panky - Tommy James & Shondells

304. 04-24-76 **Program #762-4**
story: Kiss make-up used by Cadillac, MI officials
story: The Beatles' re-released records in current British Top 50
story: songwriter Al Kasha's success formula
story: Peter Frampton's two *Rolling Stone* issues
story: The Mamas & Papas brought respect to hippie image
program mention: Bay City Rollers' bass guitarist quits
question: artist with longest running soul chart record
question: food in #1 record titles
long version: Shout It Out Loud - Kiss
oldie played: California Dreamin' - Mamas & Papas
oldie played: The Morning After - Maureen McGovern

305. 05-01-76 **Program #762-5**
story: Al Wilson's big break
story: Bellamy Brothers' Larry Williams drove Neil Diamond's truck
story: Diana Ross' career gamble
story: Fleetwood Mac's "Rhiannon" explained
story: Fats Domino's success
story: one-song, three-title record
portion played: O Solo Mio - Enrico Caruso
portion played: There's No Tomorrow - Tony Martin
portion played: It's Now Or Never - Elvis Presley
long version: Silly Love Songs - Wings
question: rock era group with most members
question: movie theme on the chart most weeks
oldie played: Blueberry Hill - Fats Domino

306. 05-08-76 **Program #762-6**
program error: Casey states that "Bohemian Rhapsody" is Queen's ".....first American hit....;" actually its their second
odd chart stat: The Rolling Stones' "Fool To Cry" debuts at #20
portion played: In The Year 2525 - Zager & Evans
whatever happened to: Zager & Evans
story: Elvis Presley's three-chart feat
story: Olivia Newton-John's foreign-artist chart feat
story: John Sebastian, then and now
story: Electric Light Orchestra sued by Great Britain's prime minister
story: Neil Sedaka's big break
question: biggest Top 10, non-#1 record of the 1970's
question: foreign artist-dominated Top 10
oldie played: Do You Believe In Magic - Lovin' Spoonful

307. 05-15-76 **Program #762-7**
whatever happened to: Roy Orbison (updated 10-06-79)
story: Doobie Brothers' Jeff Baxter had an offer to work for Elton John
story: Steve Barry produced four contemporary TV show themes
story: Bad Company was too well known
story: Rolling Stones are #1 in LP sales
story: Elvin Bishop's move to the ghetto
question: youngest artist to make the Top 40
question: leap year chart date
question: non-#1 record to become #1 song of the year
flipside played: For The Heart - Elvis Presley

Based on the syndication success of *American Top 40*, one-time *AT40* guest host Humble Harve was inspired to launch the *National Album Countdown* in the mid-1970s. The three hour countdown profiled the Top 30 albums from *Record World* magazine.

308. 05-22-76

Program #762-8
story: Casey Kasem played in high school band with Donald Byrd
story: Al Wilson fired for performing too well
story: Dorothy Moore's big break
story: The Beatles' weekly record sales
flipside played: For The Heart - Elvis Presley
question: biggest medley
question: biggest answer song
question: biggest disk jockey record
whatever happened to: Jim Lowe
portion played: The Green Door - Jim Lowe
program note: Casey reads poem from listener

309. 05-29-76 **Program #762-9**
production error: question answered regarding 'biggest answer song' repeated from previous week; same letter writer & origin, same question and answer from 05-22-76
program error: Casey's closing of "I'll Be Good To You" states "......at #38, moving up eight....."; actually, it was #30
record origin: Jimmy Dean's "I.O.U."
whatever happened to: Bobby Lewis
story: Chubby Checker's dance records
story: Diana Ross' #1 record chart feat
story: special Australian distinction of "Waltzing Matilda"
story: Johnny Cash's early days
question: biggest #1 record
question: biggest answer song
program note: Casey promos upcoming special
odd chart stat: 18 first-time-on-chart artists in the Top 40
oldie played: Tossin' & Turnin' - Bobby Lewis
oldie played: Twist - Chubby Checker
oldie played: Waltzing Matilda - Jimmie Rogers

310. 06-05-76 **Program #762-10**
whatever happened to: Doris Troy
story: The Brothers Johnson's early days
story: The Coasters' humorous, danceable records
story: Gary Wright, an American, led an all-British group
story: Gerry & The Pacemakers' chart feat
story: The Rolling Stones' Top 10 LP streak
story: John Sebastian's part in "Creeque Alley"
story: Diana Ross' invitation to Japan's Imperial Palace
question: pre-Beatles British artists at #1
portion played: Young Blood - The Coasters
portion played: Creeque Alley - The Mamas & Papas
program note: Casey promos upcoming special
oldie played: Don't Let The Sun Catch You Crying - Gerry & Pacemakers

311. 06-12-76 **Program #762-11**
story: Eric Carmen's 'homemade' audition
story: Starland Vocal Band's connection to John Denver
story: Pratt & McClain's commercial origin
story: Bob Marley special report
portion played: I Shot The Sheriff - Bob Marley & The Wailers
portion played: Oh! Susanna - The Singing Dogs
program note: Casey promos upcoming special
program note: Casey promos *AT40* radio station directory
question: non-human Top 40 artists
question: foreign language #1 records
question: group with most #1 LPs
odd chart stat: Wings' "Silly Love Songs" returns to the #1 position
production error: the first second of *AT40* theme at start of program is missing
oldie played: I Shot The Sheriff - Eric Clapton

312. 06-19-76 **Program #762-12**
question: duo replacing another duo at #1
question: records with shortest & longest titles
question: biggest record moving in & out & into the Top 10
whatever happened to: Claudine Clark
portion played: Party Lights - Claudine Clark
story: Keith Carradine's "I'm Easy" resurrected
story: name origin of B.B. King's guitar
story: *Baretta*'s Robert Blake was a Little Rascal
program note: Casey promos upcoming special
program note: program disks contain upcoming special promo announcements
odd chart stat: The Beatles' "Got To Get You Into My Life" debuts at #29
odd chart stat: 19 first-time-on-chart artists in the Top 40
odd chart stat: Paul McCartney performs and sings lead with two different groups in the Top 40
program error: in show closing, chart date that Casey provides is 06-12-76
oldie played: The Thrill Is Gone - B.B. King

313. 06-26-76 **Program #762-13**
whatever happened to: Paul Revere & The Raiders
question: oldest Top 40 artist
question: most successful #1 duos
question: records with most weeks at #1
story: Neil Diamond's Las Vegas salary
story: The Manhattans' big break
edited version: Kiss And Say Goodbye - Manhattans; spoken word beginning was edited out
program note: Casey promos upcoming special
program mention: The Beach Boys' presence in four Top 40 records

314. 07-04-76 **Program #763-1**
SPECIAL: Fourth Of July's Number One Records, 1937-1976
for a complete list of records in this special, see Rob Durkee's *American Top 40: The Countdown of the Century*
production error: 1938's Harriet Hilliard with Ozzie Nelson's "Says My Heart" was introduced by Casey but the wrong song was played; instead, listeners heard Ozzie Nelson's "Whoa Babe"

315. 07-10-76 **Program #763-2**
program error: in show closing, chart date that Casey provides is 07-11-76
program error: Casey's outcue on Led Zeppelin's "Whole Lotta Love" indicates that it "....went to #4 in 1969..."; it actually peaked at #4 on 01-31-70
production error: featured as an extra, the mono version of Led Zeppelin's "Whole Lotta Love" is played
story: Walter Murphy's "A Fifth Of Beethoven" begins with four well-known musical notes
story: Abba's Australian popularity disliked by one Australian
story: Led Zeppelin has biggest LPs with fewest single records
story: The Beatles are close to breaking Elvis Presley chart record
story: America represents U.S. in Soviet Union
question: biggest TV theme
question: biggest live-recording single record
program note: Casey promos listener radio station directory
odd chart stat: two-man, two-woman quartet's record at #1
odd chart stat: two brothers in separate duos (England Dan & John Ford Coley; Seals & Crofts) on two separate records in the Top 40
oldie played: Whole Lotta Love - Led Zeppelin

STATE	CITY	STATION	FREQ.	BAND	DAY & TIME
ALABAMA	Birmingham	WSGN	610	AM	SUN 6PM-9PM
	Carrollton	WAQT	94.1	FM	SAT 9AM-12N
	Gadsden	WGAD	1350	AM	SUN 3PM-6PM
	Guntersville	WGSV	1270	AM	SUN 1PM-4PM
	Mobile	WABB	1480	AM	SUN 10AM-1PM
		WABB-FM	97.5(S)	FM	SIMULCAST
	Montgomery	WHHY	1440	AM	SUN 8AM-11AM (AM & FM)
		WHHY	102(S)	FM	SAT 10AM-1PM (FM only)
	Huntsville	WAAY	1550	AM	SUN 3PM-6PM
ALASKA	Anchorage	KENI	550	AM	SUN 3PM-6PM
	Fairbanks	KFAR	660	AM	SAT 3PM-6PM
	Kodiak	KVOK	560	AM	SAT 2PM-5PM
	Sitka	KIFW	1230	AM	SAT 1PM-4PM
ARIZONA	Phoenix	KBBC	98.7	FM	SUN 9AM-12N
ARKANSAS	Fort Smith	KISR	93.7(S)	FM	SUN 5PM-8PM
	Harrison	KHOZ	900	AM&FM	SUN 2PM-5PM
	Little Rock	KLAZ	98.5(S)	FM	SAT 9AM-12N
	Paragould	KHIG	104.9(S)	FM	SAT 9PM-12M
					SUN 12N-3PM
	Pine Bluff	KOTN	1490	AM	SUN 2PM-5PM
	Springdale	KCIZ	104.9(S)	FM	SUN 2PM-5PM
CALIFORNIA	Bakersfield	KERN	1410	AM	SUN 9AM-12N
	Lompoc	KLOM	1330	AM	SUN 3PM-6PM
		KLOM-FM	92.7	FM	SIMULCAST
	Los Angeles	KIIS-FM	102.7	FM	SUN 6PM-9PM
		KIIS-AM	1150	AM	SUN 6:05PM-9PM
	Oxnard	KACY	1520	AM	SUN 9AM-12N
					SAT 10PM-1AM
	Sacramento	KXOA (K-108)	107.9(S)	FM	SUN 9AM-12N
	San Diego	KGB	1360	AM	SUN 9AM-12N
	San Francisco	KYA-AM	1260	AM	SUN 9AM-12N
		KYA-FM	93.3(S)	FM	SIMULCAST
	Stockton	KJOY	1280	AM	SUN 9AM-12N
COLORADO	Colorado Springs	KYSN	1460	AM	SUN 1PM-4PM
	Grand Junction	KQIX-FM	93.1	FM	SUN 6PM-9PM
CONNECTICUT	Danbury	WINE-AM	940	AM	SUN 1PM-4PM
		WINE-FM	95.1(S)	FM	SUN 1PM-4PM
	Hartford	WDRC	1360	AM	SUN 7:30PM-10:30PM
		WDRC-FM	103(S)	FM	SIMULCAST
	Norwich	WICH	1310	AM	SUN 5PM-8PM
WASHINGTON, D.C.	Bladensburg, MD	WPGC-AM	1580	AM	SUN 10AM-1PM
		WPGC-FM	95.5(S)	FM	SIMULCAST
FLORIDA	Cocoa Beach	WCKS	101.1	FM	SUN 9AM-12N
	Daytona Beach	WMFJ-AM	1450	AM	SUN 4PM-7PM
	Fort Pierce	WOVV	95.5(S)	FM	SUN 7PM-10PM
	Gainesville	WGGG	1230	AM	SUN 12N-3PM
	Jacksonville	WAPE	690	AM	SUN 10AM-1PM
	Lakeland	WQPD	1430	AM	SUN 12N-3PM
	Live Oak	WNER	1250	AM	SUN 2PM-5PM
					SAT 2PM-5PM
	Miami	WGBS	710	AM	SUN 3PM-6PM
					SAT 6PM-9PM
	Orlando	WLOF	950	AM	SUN 12N-3PM
					MON 3AM-6AM
	Ocala	WWKE	1370	AM	SUN 12N-3PM
	Palatka	WWPF	1260	AM	SUN 1PM-4PM
					MON 8:30PM-11:30PM
	Panama City	WGNE	1480	AM	SUN 10AM-1PM
	Pensacola	WBSR	1450	AM	SAT 6PM-9PM
					SUN 10AM-1PM

STATE	CITY	STATION	FREQ.	BAND	DAY & TIME
ILLINOIS	Belleville	WIBV	1260	AM	SAT 4PM-7PM
					SUN 3PM-6PM
	Charleston	WEIC	1270	AM	SUN 1PM-4PM
					SIMULCAST
	Chicago	WDHF	95.5(S)	FM	SUN 9AM-12N
	Mt. Vernon	WMIX-FM	94.1(S)	FM	SAT 4PM-7PM
		WMIX	940	AM	SIMULCAST
	Rockford	WROK	1440	AM	SUN 6PM-9PM
INDIANA	Columbus	WCSI	1010	AM	SUN 3PM-6PM
	Evansville	WGBF	1280	AM	SUN 6PM-9PM
	Indianapolis	WIFE	1310	AM	SUN 7PM-10PM
	Kokomo	WIOU	1350	AM	SAT 2PM-5PM
	Lafayette	WASK	1450	AM	SAT 9PM-12M
					SUN 9PM-12M
	South Bend	WRBR	103.9	FM	SUN 10AM-1PM
	Muncie	WERK	990	AM	SUN 11AM-2PM
	Terre Haute	WBOW	1230	AM	SUN 7PM-10PM
IOWA	Davenport	KSTT	1170	AM	SUN 9AM-12N
	Dubuque	WDBQ	1490	AM	SUN 2PM-5PM
	Des Moines	KRNQ	102.5	FM	SUN 9AM-12N
					SUN 7PM-10PM
	Sioux City	KSEZ	97.9(S)	FM	SUN 9AM-12N
	Waterloo	KLEU	850	AM	SAT 1PM-4PM
KANSAS	Hutchinson	KWHK	1260	AM	SUN 11AM-2PM
					SUN 7PM-10PM
	Salina	KSKG-FM	99.9(S)	FM	SUN 9AM-12N
					SUN 9PM-12M
	Topeka	KEWI	1440	AM	SUN 9AM-12N
					SUN 9PM-12M
	Wichita	KEYN	103.7	FM	SUN 3PM-6PM
KENTUCKY	Corbin	WCTT	680	AM	SUN 4PM-7PM
	Lexington	WLAP	630	AM	SAT 9PM-12M
	Moorhead	WMOR	1330	AM&FM	SAT 1PM-4PM
LOUISIANA	Alexandria	KALB	580	AM	SUN 7PM-10PM
	Baton Rouge	WIBR	1300	AM	SUN 6PM-9PM
	Ferriday	KFNV	1600	AM&FM	SAT 2PM-5PM
	Houma	KJIN	1490	AM	SAT 6PM-9PM
	Lake Charles	KLOU	1580	AM	SUN 12N-3PM
	Monroe	KMLB	1440	AM	SAT 9AM-12N
	New Orleans	WNOE	1060	AM	SUN 9PM-12M
MAINE	Bangor	WABI	910	AM	SAT 9AM-12N
					SUN 1PM-4PM
	Bath	WJTO	730	AM	SAT 9AM-12N
					SUN 10AM-1PM
		WJTO-FM	95.3	FM	SIMULCAST
	Calais	WQDY	1230	AM	SAT 11AM-2PM
					SUN 9:30AM-12:30PM
		WQDY-FM	92.7	FM	SAT 11AM-2PM
					SUN 9:30AM-12:30PM
	Houlton	WHOU	1340	AM	SAT 10:30AM-1:30PM
		WHOU-FM	100.1(S)	FM	SUN 7PM-10PM
					SIMULCAST
	Norway	WOXO	92.7	FM	SAT 10AM-1PM
					SUN 6PM-9PM
MARYLAND	Baltimore	WCAO	600	AM	SUN 6PM-9PM
	Frederick	WZYQ	1370	AM	SAT 1PM-4PM
		WZYQ-FM	103.9(S)	FM	SIMULCAST
	Leonardtown	WKIK	1370	AM	SAT 9PM-12M
	Salisbury	WBOC	960	AM	SUN 8PM-11PM
MASSACHUSETTS	Fall River	WSAR	1480	AM	SUN 10AM-1PM

Free for the asking, the *AT40* Listening Directory for 1976, partially pictured, listed information about every radio station that carried the program – city, state, call letters, frequency, and broadcast day and time – for traveling listeners.

To: AT40 Subscribers

From: Tom Rounds

Re: Promos for the Bicentennial Special

June 12, 1976

Casey has recorded six short voice-only (so you can add music, run 'em over record intros or run 'em as is) promos for the upcoming bicentennial special: "The Fourth of July's Greatest Hits".

The promos are located as separate cuts on this week's show (762-12). Check your cue sheet for the actual location, transfer them to tape or cart and schedule them to run June 28 through July 3/4 to prepare your listeners for the special countdown (program #763-1).

"The Fourth of July's Greatest Hits" presents the 40 records that were number one on July 4th for the past 40 years. We start out with July 4, 1937 and end up at July 4, 1976.

Because of the tremendous range in the types of music presented, the special will be an unusual and fascinating study of the evolution of the pop hit. It is quite a departure from familiar contemporary programming, especially in the first hour. For this reason, we recommend plenty of pre-promotion to clue in your listeners, who may be a bit surprised when they dial in and hear a Glenn Miller record on your frequency.

The American Top 40 Bicentennial Special undoubtedly represents the greatest departure we've ever made... or ever will make... from a contemporary sound. But... after all... this is our one and only bicentennial. Proper and ample promotion will make it all work... and that's up to you.

If you need any more info, please call. We now have an incoming Wats (toll-free) line that operates Monday-Friday 8AM-5PM Pacific time: (800) 423-2502.

Thanks!

WATERMARK, INC. 10700 Ventura Blvd., No. Hollywood, California 91604 (213) 980-9490

Tom Rounds pointed out to stations that there were Bicentennial promos included in the June 19, 1976 program and recommended that stations use them due to the special's "departure...from a contemporary sound." The Glenn Miller record, along with other music from that time period, was threatening enough for at least one radio station, Chicago's WDHF, which refused to broadcast it.

TIMOTHY

To: AMERICAN TOP 40 SUBSCRIBERS

From: Chuck Olsen, Vice President, Watermark, Inc.

Re: The July 4th Special

This is embarrassing but I'll get right to it. There's a mistake in show #763-1, "The Fourth of July's Greatest Hits". The second record in the program is listed as "Says My Heart" sung by Harriet Hilliard with the Ozzie Nelson orchestra. A gremlin slipped into the assembly session and a wrong cut from the LP was played. It is Ozzie Nelson but you won't hear Harriet - it's an instrumental entitled "Whoa Babe". It's too late to make a repair and you may not even hear about it from your listeners, so this is just to let you know about it in case you get any calls. Just blame it on us... and the chastising has already happened.

Sincerely (and humbly)

WATERMARK, INC. 10700 Ventura Blvd., No. Hollywood, California 91604 (213) 980-9490

It's likely that only a handful of listeners were able to identify the error with the 1938 record in the Bicentennial special, as described in Chuck Olsen's memo.

316. 07-17-76

Program #763-3
portion played: Rock And Roll Music - Chuck Berry
portion played: Rock And Roll Music - The Beatles
portion played: Little Darlin' - The Diamonds
production note: an incomplete version of The Beach Boys' "Rock And Roll Music" was heard in order to create a medley of the song with other versions
question: biggest non-#1, #2 record
question: artists with biggest double-sided records
odd chart stat: seven duos in the Top 40
odd chart stat: Paul McCartney sings lead on two back-to-back Top 40 records, performed by different groups
odd chart stat: two brothers in separate duos (England Dan & John Ford Coley; Seals & Crofts) on two separate records in the Top 40
story: Beethoven's victory music
story: The Carpenters' producer worked on Apollo I
story: The Rolling Stones are the loudest rock band in the world
program error: Casey's outcue for Seals & Crofts' "Get Closer" reads "....at #18......."; actually, it was #16
program error: Casey's introduction for Natalie Cole's "Sophisticated Lady" indicated "...at #29, moving up three notches...."; and Casey's outcue read "...moving up eight notches this week..."; actually, it moved from #31 to #29
program error: Casey points out that Paul McCartney performs on three Top 40 records, and mentions that Melanie "...back in 1964..." had three records in the Top 40; actually, Melanie's three simultaneous Top 40 records were in 1972; there is no mention of Marvin Gaye's three records in the Top 40 the week of 11-17-73
program error: in introducing The Manhattan's "Kiss And Say Goodbye," Casey pointed out "...here's the first Top 40 hit for The Manhattans..."; actually, it was their second
program error: Casey's introduction to Aerosmith's "Last Child" mentions "Dream On" as their other hit record, with no mention of "Sweet Emotion"
program mention: "Misty Blue" was a country record
program note: in show closing, Casey provides no chart date
oldie played: Brown Sugar - Rolling Stones

"On Sunday, July 18, 1976, I was spinning the dial of my portable radio and heard, my favorite song 'More, More, More' by the Andrea True Connection on 95BBF in Rochester, New York. As the final chorus faded out, I heard a voice that I'd never heard before outroing the song. (Because) the song was #4 that week, there was only twenty minutes left (in the countdown). But I was hooked. Week after week, I listened to Casey Kasem and kept track of the songs in a notebook. By 1978, I wanted to know ahead of time what songs were where and started a subscription to Billboard magazine.....(More than) 27 years later, I still listen to American Top 40 every week, I still get Billboard magazine and, sadly, 'More, More, More' is still my favorite song."

Jim Kiehle, a longtime *AT40* listener

ARB RESULTS

These unsolicited comments from ARBITRON RADIO diaries placed in Charlotte, Columbus, Minneapolis-St. Paul, Hartford and San Antonio, for the period of October/November 1975, show that CASEY KASEM has been given the vote as America's #1 write-in personality.

HARTFORD, CONNECTICUT . . . I like WDRC but wish they would have the top 40 survey finishing earlier. I wish I could hear more Bruins and Celtics games . . . I listen to WDRC FM at home alot and when I'm in my car it's on WDRC AM or WABC, WRLR. I listen to Casey Casem on Sunday night which I think is good. I listen to the radio all the time; it's constantly going when I'm home and on the road . . . I enjoy "American Top 40" Sunday night on WDRC . . . Casey Kasem Top 40. Like good concisive news coverage of local, national, and world events . . . American Top 40, Kasey Kasup . . . A favorite program of mine which I did not listen to this week is "Top 40" with Kasey Kasem as host. "Top 40" is based on Billboard's top 40 and is played on more than one station but I listen to it Sundays on WDRC from 7:30-10:30PM.

SAN ANTONIO, TEXAS . . . I enjoy the Top 40 countdown on KTSA on Sunday morning . . . I look forward to the top 40 on KTSA 9:00-12:00 . . . I listen to the radio every night while I go to sleep and I wake up to music. On Sundays, I like to listen to Casey Cason's Top 40 Countdown played on KTSA from 9AM-12Noon . . . Only look forward to Casey Cason's Top 40 countdown on Sundays 9:00-12:00 on KTSA! . . . KTSA's top 30 on Friday starting at 3:00PM. Casey's Coast to Coast (American Top 40) 9:00AM to NOON . . . It's my favorite radio station. I especially like to listen on Sundays because that's when Kasey Kason's program is on. The American Count Down of the top 40 songs. I like helping you in this survey. Thank you . . . Sunday Morning, Top 40 Countdown AM-KTSA 9:00-12:00. Monday Nights, Interview FM-KRMH 10:30-12:30. Weekdays, David Jarrot AM-KNOW 7:00-9:00 . . . I listened, but anyway, Casey Cason's American Top Forty, Saturday mornings 9-12 is the best show on radio . . . One of my favorite radio programs is American Top 40 . . . K.C. Kazen—very good program to listen to. They play all the top 40 records every week.

CHARLOTTE/GASTONIA, NORTH CAROLINA . . . WBT-AM on Sunday mornings around 9:30 or 10:00AM. They start counting down the 40 hits . . . I think one of the best programs on the air is Sunday the top 40 hits on WBT-AM 1110 . . . When I am in the car I jump from station to station listening to songs I like to hear. I tried to be as accurate as possible. I missed Casy Casem but I love that program Sun. at 10:00AM-1:00PM WBT . . . WBT 10:00AM to 1:00 Casey Cason's Top 40 . . . I listen to CBS news reports on the hour wherever I travel. I normally listen to American Top Forty on WBT Sunday Mornings but I missed it this week . . . American Top 40 is one program I missed that I enjoy.

MINNEAPOLIS/ST. PAUL . . . I like to listen to American Top 40 on KDWB which I didn't this week . . . Another problem with the radio is on most stations they have the weather on every half-hour. Sure you can have news but not so often—otherwise the radio is pretty good. My favorite program is KDWB top forty on Sunday nights . . . I especially like American Top 40 from Hollywood. It plays on KDWB. I like that station . . . American Top 40 Sunday . . . My favorite program is American Top 40 on Sunday nights at 8:00 on KDWB . . . I really like "the top 40" with Casey Kasen Sunday nights on KDWB. I didn't listen to it this week but I hope they keep it on . . . I like American Top 40 on KDWB Sunday at 8:00PM. I also like Paul Harvey . . . They should have the KDWB top 40 Saturday (same time) night instead of Sunday because a lot of people can't stay up till 11:00 if they have school the next day. I know I would listen to it every Saturday if they changed it . . . The Top 40 on KDWB is good. But I think most stations play too many commercials at one time . . . Sunday night on KDWB I listen to Casey Casum's countdown "Top 40 Hits." Every morning I listen to Charlie Bush and Chuck Knapp . . . I like the top 40 countdown on KDWB on Sundays at 8:00PM until 11:00PM. I like to listen to music before I go to bed . . . KDWB Top 40 8:00 to 11 pm Sunday . . . American Top 40 8:00-11:00PM Sundays . . . My favorite station is KDWB. My favorite program is the top 40 on Sunday nights on KDWB . . . Radio—I like listening and I really get into music—and I like listening to the countdown on Sundays on station KDWB . . . I like Casey Cason real well. I just wish it was on more stations.

COLUMBUS, OHIO . . . I like to listen to WNCI on Sunday mornings, especially from 9:00AM to 12:00AM. That's when they count to 40 top hits . . . I like the American Top 40 with Casey Kasem . . . I like Casey Casum's countdown on Sundays . . . I enjoy Casey's Top 40 count down and most music on WNCI . . . I love WNCI's top 40 hits program on Sunday mornings . . . I have a converter in my car, so I take FM with me wherever I go. I really like the "mini-chart" at WNCI. I listen to Casey Kasem (WNCI) every Sunday . . . But my favorite station is WNCI. They also play the top 40 hits on Sunday mornings 9-12 . . . Yes, I really like WNCI when they have the 40 top hits and tell something about the artist and the song . . . I like American Top 40 on Sundays . . . My favorite radio station is WNCI, I like all the songs on it. I always listen to the Top 40 songs of the week on Sunday mornings. I have my own radio and it's usually on WNCI. Thank you.

AMERICAN TOP 40 is heard weekly in the above markets on WDRC, KTSA, WBT, KDWB and WNCI respectively as well as 346 other stations from coast to coast and around the world.

American Top 40 – Watermark, Inc.

10700 VENTURA BLVD., NO. HOLLYWOOD, CA 91604 • (213) 980-9490

All right, I'm impressed. Please send me all the free details on American Top 40 including a complete three hour program, Sales and Marketing Guide, the AT40 descriptive brochure, "Much More Than Music" and the AT40 demo tape.

Name ______________ Title ______________

Call Letters ______________ Address ______________

City ______________ State ______________ Zip ______________

This advertisement appeared in the July 31, 1976 edition of *Billboard* magazine.

317. 07-24-76 **Program #763-4**
production note: Wings' "Let 'Em In" record begins playing prior to beginning of segment, prior to the *AT 40* jingle
odd chart stat: two debut records
odd chart stat: Wings' "Silly Love Songs" falls from #9 to #34
odd chart stat: two brothers in separate duos (England Dan & John Ford Coley; Seals & Crofts) on two separate records in the Top 40
story: Ludwig von Beethoven, musical genius
story: John Travolta, high school drop-out
story: Chicago's platinum LPs
story: The Beatles' April 1964 Top 5 chart feat
story: Karen Carpenter's love of baseball
story: Andrea True's Jamaican earnings
story: The Manhattans' death premonition
story: Pat Boone's chart feat
portion played: Shop Around - Smokey Robinson & The Miracles
portion played: April Love - Pat Boone
program note: no listener questions answered on this show

318. 07-31-76 **Program #763-5**
story: Neil Sedaka's secret marriage
story: Steve Miller's broken neck
story: Three Dog Night's chart feat
whatever happened to: Joan Weber
portion played: Let Me Go Lover - Joan Weber
odd chart stat: ten disco records in the Top 40
odd chart stat: two brothers in separate duos (England Dan & John Ford Coley; Seals & Crofts) on two separate records in the Top 40
question: biggest classical hit record
question: left-handed artist with most #1 records
question: state most mentioned in record titles
oldie played: One - Three Dog Night

319. 08-07-76 **Program #763-6**
GUEST HOST: Sonny Melendrez
story: The Drifters' "On Broadway" is star-studded
story: Dan Seals overtaken by older brother Jim Seals' religion
story: Chicago's near-misses chart record
story: Candi Staton's one-song performance
story: Elton John climbs to #1 on British chart
record origin: Starland Vocal Band's "Afternoon Delight"
edited version: Kiss And Say Goodbye - The Manhattans; spoken word beginning was edited out
program mention: The Brothers Johnson 10-foot mural
odd chart stat: two brothers in separate duos (England Dan & John Ford Coley; Seals & Crofts) on two separate records in the Top 40
oldie played: On Broadway - Drifters

320. 08-14-76 **Program #763-7**
story: Earth, Wind & Fire elected by God
story: Silver's lead singer crippled by polio
story: Aretha Franklin's gold record accomplishment
story: Sonny James' country chart feat
story: Starbuck hand-delivered "Moonlight Feels Right" to radio stations
story: George Benson's LP #1 on pop, soul and jazz charts
story: Elton John & Kiki Dee's unusual chart feat

320. 08-14-76 **Program #763-7 (CONTINUED)**
question: biggest husband & wife record
program error: Casey identifies Starbuck's "Moonlight Feels Right" as the week's biggest dropping record - from #3 to #18; however, Parliament's "Tear The Roof Off The Sucker" dropped from #15 to #36
program mention: Walter Murphy's early days
program mention: Neil Diamond's hot L.A. ticket
portion played: Young Love - Sonny James
odd chart stat: two brothers in separate duos (England Dan & John Ford Coley; Seals & Crofts) on two separate records in the Top 40

321. 08-21-76 **Program #763-8**
program note: Casey mentions his presence in an article in the September edition of *The Saturday Evening Post*
portion played: Fraulein - Bobby Helms
story: Bobby Helms' country chart feat
story: Dr. Hook's bankruptcy
story: Blood, Sweat & Tears started jazz-rock
story: Lou Rawls' amnesia
story: Cliff Richard's British success
name origin: Starbuck
question: biggest recording artist sibling
question: #1 records with no mention of title in lyric
question: first *Billboard* #1 record & capsule history of *American Top 40* (now heard on 350 radio stations)
program note: Casey promos upcoming special
odd chart stat: with two separate records in the Top 10, two brothers in separate duos (England Dan & John Ford Coley; Seals & Crofts)
oldie played: Spinning Wheel - Blood, Sweat & Tears

322. 08-28-76 **Program #763-9**
odd chart stat: one debut record
odd chart stat: with two separate records in the Top 10, two brothers in separate duos (England Dan & John Ford Coley; Seals & Crofts)
odd chart stat: four records on this week's chart have the same title, but different lyrics, of previous hit records (e.g., "Lowdown" by Chicago & Boz Scaggs)
program note: program opens with a story about Red Sovine
program note: Casey promos upcoming special
story: Elton John's $5,000 Monopoly game
story: Jim Seals is youngest Texas fiddling contest winner
story: Red Sovine's wife died before "Teddy Bear" release
story: Chuck Berry's influence on musicians
story: Shel Silverstein paid 39 cents for "A Little Bit More"
question: recording artist in second place with charted records
question: one-hit wonder artists peaking at #40
program error: answeing a question on records peaking at #40, Casey made reference to the artist "Gardner & Dyke Ashton"; actually, "Resurrection Shuffle", which peaked at #40 in 1971, was performed by Ashton, Gardner & Dyke
whatever happened to: Tiny Tim
portion played: Tip-Toe Thru' The Tulips With Me - Tiny Tim
record origin: Starland Vocal Band's "Afternoon Delight"
long version: She's Gone - Hall & Oates
edited version: Kiss And Say Goodbye - Manhattans; spoken word beginning was edited out

TO: AMERICAN TOP 40 Subscribers

FROM: Tom Rounds

DATE: September 11, 1976

WATERMARK, INC. 10700 Ventura Blvd., No. Hollywood, California 91604 (213) 980-9490

We're two shows away from "The 40 Top Hits of the Beatle Years". On program #764-1, scheduled for the first weekend of October, Casey will count down the 40 records that ranked the highest in the period that began in 1964 with "I Want to Hold Your Hand" and ended in 1970 with "The Long and Winding Road". Every record on this special chart breakout was number one; ironically, the Beatles lead off... at #40 with "She Loves You", and top the countdown at #1. But we'll also hear from all the other late-sixties biggies: Sly and the Family Stone... The Doors... The Supremes... the 5th Dimension as we recapture a special part of the rock era.

Casey promos for this special will be included on next week's show... program #763-13. Check your cue sheet for the special cuts on next week's program discs.

Tom Rounds provided a quick preview to the Beatles special in this memo.

323. 09-04-76

Program #763-10
program note: Casey promos upcoming special
program mention: Seals & Croft's Carolyn Willis was with Honey Cone
story: Chicago's special recording studio
story: history of radio station airplay
story: Paul McCartney loves his doorbell
story: Walter Murphy taught by NBC musician Rosa Rio
story: pop music careers launched by street singing
story: The Browns' chart feat
portion played: Three Bells - The Browns
program error: Casey's outcue to Candi Staton's "Young Hearts Run Free"
reads "...survey song #33, falling two notches....";
actually, it climbed two positions
odd chart stat: two brothers in separate duos (England Dan & John Ford Coley;
Seals & Crofts) on two separate records in the Top 40

324. 09-11-76

Program #763-11
program note: Casey promos upcoming special
program mention: Alan Parsons Project's LP based on Edgar Allen Poe writings
program mention: Fleetwood Mac personnel changes
odd chart stat: two debut records
odd chart stat: two brothers in separate duos (England Dan & John Ford Coley;
Seals & Crofts) on two separate records in the Top 40
story: War's steps to success
story: The Beach Boys influenced by Chuck Berry
story: The Bee Gees change to disco
story: Olivia Newton John's beautiful handicap
story: Heart is lead by women
story: James Taylor nearly ruined by *Time* cover
story: KC & The Sunshine Band's #1 records
story: The Temptations' soul chart feat
question: youngest artist with a #1 record
oldie played: (I Know) I'm Losing You - Temptations

325. 09-18-76

Program #763-12
portion played: The Ballad of Davy Crockett - Bill Hayes
whatever happened to: Bill Hayes
program mention: Ohio Players' concert gimmicks
program mention: gag writers on Elton John-Kiki Dee record
question: biggest Canadian record
question: artist replacing himself at #1
story: Lou Rawls' back-up singing on Sam Cooke record
story: Steve Miller goes unrecognized
story: Wild Cherry's lead singer re-groups
story: Helen Reddy's kidney disease
program note: Casey promos upcoming special
oldie played: Bring It On Home To Me - Sam Cooke

326. 09-25-76 **Program #763-13**
story: Rick Dees & "Disco Duck"
story: Cliff Richard's impersonation of Elvis Presley
story: The Beach Boys' early days
story: Linda Ronstadt, re-make queen
story: origin of Silver's "Wham Bam"
story: Wild Cherry's #1 soul chart record
record origin: Gordon Lightfoot's "The Wreck of The Edmund Fitzgerald"
production note: disks contain promos for upcoming special
production note: hour #2 closes with an edited outcue
program note: Casey promos upcoming special
question: artist with longest name
question: first country record to reach #1 on pop chart
portion played: Smoke Smoke Smoke - Tex Williams
program mention: Fleetwood Mac's addition of Christine McVie

327. 10-02-76 **Program #764-1**
SPECIAL: Top 40 Records Of The Beatle Years, 1964 - 1970
for a complete list of records in this special, see Rob Durkee's *American Top 40: The Countdown of the Century*

328. 10-09-76 **Program #764-2**
story: John Denver urged to finish school
story: Abba's Australian chart feat
story: singer/songwriter Bobby Gosh's dream come true
story: "Nadia's Theme" popularized through summer Olympics
story: records adapted from classical music
question: greatest #1 position turnover
question: biggest dance record
question: American group with biggest #1 record
portion played: I Only Want To Be With You - Dusty Springfield

329. 10-16-76 **Program #764-3**
whatever happened to: Gene Pitney
portion played: The Man Who Shot Liberty Valance - Gene Pitney
story: Peter Frampton injured at concert performance
story: Hall & Oates' "She's Gone" released four times
name origin: Blue Oyster Cult
long version: She's Gone - Hall & Oates
program mention: Stevie Wonder debuts on LP chart at #1
question: artists originating from non-entertainment professions
question: first Black artist at #1

330. 10-23-76 **Program #764-4**
story: Kiss' disguises protect member identity
story: Roger Williams' legacy
story: England Dan & John Ford Coley's big break
story: Jefferson Airplane's influence & comeback
story: Chicago's first #1 record
story: Buddy Holly's influence
question: biggest Motown record
question: artist using most record label aliases
odd chart stat: two debut records
portion played: Autumn Leaves - Roger Williams
portion played: A Little Bit More - Bobby Gosh
program mention: Casey congratulates KWHK (Hutchinson, KS) on their 30th birthday

331. 10-30-76

Program #764-5
story: the world's first disk jockey
story: Alice Cooper is shock-rock pioneer
story: Cliff Richard's British chart success
story: origin of *Frankenstein*
story: Linda Ronstadt, re-make queen
story: Bobby 'Boris' Pickett update
odd chart stat: duo with first two releases simultaneously in the Top 40
odd chart stat: both Orleans' "Still The One" & Boz Scaggs' "Lowdown" fall 21 notches, back-to-back, within the Top 40
program mention: Rick Dees is back on the air as a disk jockey
question: solo artist with most #1 LPs
oldie played: Frankenstein - Edgar Winter Group
oldie played: Monster Mash - Bobby 'Boris' Pickett

332. 11-06-76

Program #764-6
story: Bill Withers' gold toilet award
story: John Valenti 'beats' a pizza parlor patron
story: Harry Wayne Casey & Rick Finch's songwriting success
story: Peter Frampton, rags-to-riches
story: Marilyn McCoo & Billy Davis Jr.'s chart feat
story: Gordon Lightfoot's Canadian popularity
record origin: Heart's "Magic Man"
question: most successful Irish act
question: The Beatles' most unsuccessful record
question: male artist with biggest LP
oldie played: Ain't No Sunshine - Bill Withers
program note: Casey plays a different version of The Ritchie Family's "The Best Disco In Town"

333. 11-13-76

Program #764-7
record origin: Hall & Oates' "She's Gone"
story: Leo Sayer hit by concert goer
story: Herb Alpert & The Tijuana Brass' LP chart feat
story: Chicago's LP chart feat
story: Elvis Presley chart feat
question: producer of biggest LP of the 1970's
question: non-entertainment-profession Top 40 artists
question: foreign artist with most consecutive weeks at #1
question: solo artist with most #1 LPs
portion played: Don't Be Cruel - Elvis Presley
program error: question answered regarding 'solo artist #1 LPs' repeated from 10-30-76 show; same letter writer & origin, same question & answer
oldie played: Lonely Bull - Herb Alpert & Tijuana Brass

334. 11-20-76

Program #764-8
story: Rick Dees makes world's largest ice cream sundae
story: Aretha Franklin's soul chart success
story: Norman Connors' dedication to music
whatever happened to: Gary Lewis & The Playboys
portion played: This Diamond Ring - Gary Lewis & The Playboys
odd chart stat: Walter Murphy's "A Fifth Of Beethoven" on the Top 40 chart for 21 consecutive weeks
question: day-of-the-week appearing in most #1 record titles
question: first white solo artists at #1 on soul chart
program note: in answering a letter regarding white artists on soul chart, Casey made first-time reference to the *American Top 40* Book of Records
program mention: Elton John's future plans
oldie played: Since You've Been Gone - Aretha Franklin

> ***"American Top 40...the mere mention of that phrase for anyone who followed pop music in the 1970's evokes nostalgia of Americana as much as the phrase baseball, hot dogs and apple pie.***
>
> ***My first exposure to AT40 came in the fall of 1976, November to be exact. I was 12 at the time and just 'discovering' music. I heard that first broadcast on KCRV -FM out of Caruthersville, MO. The program aired on Saturday nights and from the first time I tuned in, I was hooked. I kept waiting for 'Wreck of the Edmund Fitzgerald' by Gordon Lightfoot to hit number 1. While it never happened, thanks to Rod Stewart and that Rubberband Man, I was hooked! AT40 became a weekly ritual for me and was until the mid-80's.***
>
> ***In the past few years I have rediscovered the magic of AT40. I've been fortunate to make the acquaintance of several former Watermark employees, staff writers, and Casey himself. More importantly, I have discovered there are a lot of us fellow junkies out there who share the same types of stories of how AT40 was an expected way of life each weekend.***
>
> ***I listen to the old broadcasts now and have a deeper appreciation for the production that had to take place on a weekly basis. You cannot help but to be taken back as you listen. For the staff to pull off the stories, editing, production and distribution is nothing short of amazing when you consider this was a time prior to digital editing, Federal Express or the internet."***
>
> **Shannon Lynn, a longtime *AT40* listener**

335. 11-27-76

Program #764-9
story: Eric Clapton update
story: 'Edmund Fitzgerald' & other Lake Superior tragedies
story: 'commercial' records
story: Alice Cooper not the first male musician named 'Alice'
story: capsule history of *AT40* (now heard on 380 radio stations)
story: Faron Young's country chart feat
story: Yvonne Elliman's gimmick for concert attention
odd chart stat: two debut records
odd chart stat: Walter Murphy's "A Fifth Of Beethoven" on the Top 40 chart for 22 consecutive weeks
question: #40 to #1 records
question: #1 disk jockey records
portion played: Hello Walls - Faron Young
program note: Casey promos upcoming special
oldie played: We've Only Just Begun - Carpenters

TO: AMERICAN TOP 40 Subscribers

FROM: Tom Rounds

November 20, 1976

EXTRA HOLIDAY PROGRAMMING

Because Christmas falls on a weekend this year we've decided to re-issue a 1973 American Top 40 special titled "The All Time Christmas Countdown". Several subscribers inspired the re-issue idea; they had decided to hold off the 8-hour "Top 100 of 1976" special until New Year's weekend and asked if we had anything to run on Christmas weekend, in place of #764-13 on December 25-26. So we've pulled the master tape out of the archives and we're pressing a limited number of copies of "The Christmas Countdown". It runs according to the standard 3-hour AT40 format. All 1973 references have been deleted, and the music and stories are timeless.

To order the American Top 40 "All Time Christmas Countdown", tear off the coupon and get it to us no later than December 1. License fee is $50, and we'll add the amount to your bill for January shows. Questions or late orders? Call Jeff, Brian or Steve at (800) 423-2502 or (213) 980-9490.

- -

Watermark, Inc.
10700 Ventura Boulevard
North Hollywood, California 91604

Please send us "The American Top 40 All-Time Christmas Countdown". We understand that the license fee is $50 and is payable on or before December 15, 1976 with our invoice for January shows.

Name________________ Title________ Signature____________

Call letters________________ City or Town________________

In this November 20, 1976 memo, Tom Rounds alerted stations of their option to add another *AT40* special to their 1976 year-end programming – the recyled 1973 Christmas Countdown – which was available for a $50 licensing fee.

336. 12-04-76 **Program #764-10**
record origin: Barry DeVorzon & Perry Botkin Jr.'s "Nadia's Theme"
story: Bread reunion creates chart feat
story: Abba's Australian record sales
story: Sly Stone married at a Sly & The Family Stone concert
story: The Bee Gees' songs recorded by other artists
name origin: Englebert Humperdinck
Book of Records: The Ventures' LP sales
question: biggest #1 female artist LP
question: non-vocal, non-instrumental & non-spoken word Top 40 records
program note: Casey promos upcoming special
odd chart stat: 28 Top 40 records written or co-written by the performing artist
oldie played: Family Affair - Sly & Family Stone

337. 12-11-76 **Program #764-11**
Book of Records: white artist at #1 on soul LP chart
program mention: Jackson Five now have eight members
story: The Bar Kays survived plane crash
story: Elton John's overnight success
story: Foster Sylvers popular before The Sylvers
story: The Captain & Tennille's royal flap
story: Eric Clapton celebrated The Band's farewell
program note: Casey promos upcoming special

338. 12-18-76 **Program #764-12**
production note: disks contain promos for upcoming special
question: foreign artist with biggest record of the 1970's
question: biggest comedy LP
question: biggest Christmas record
odd chart stat: The Bee Gees' "Love So Right" falls from #3 to #21
odd chart stat: 29 Top 40 records written or co-written by the performing artist
odd chart stat: fourteen disco records in the Top 40
program note: Casey promos upcoming special
Book of Records: record with biggest climb to #1
story: Electric Light Orchestra's concert theatrics
story: Burton Cummings' "Stand Tall" has personal meaning
record origin: Gene Autry's "Rudolph The Red-Nosed Reindeer"
oldie played: Rudolph The Red Nosed Reindeer - Jackson Five

339. 12-25-76 **Program #764-13**
SPECIAL: Top 100 Of 1976 (#100 - 51) (based on *Billboard*'s year-end Top 100)
for a complete list of records in this special, see Rob Durkee's *American Top 40: The Countdown of the Century*
long version: She's Gone - Hall & Oates
long version: Wake Up Everybody - Harold Melvin & The Blue Notes
long version: Baby I Love Your Way - Peter Frampton

> ***".....All I can remember about AT40 is that I listened and loved it......I remember it was where I first heard songs like 'Afternoon Delight' and 'Shannon' and 'Dream On' - all around 1976. Actually, a friend here made me a set of tapes of the AT40 countdown of the Top 100 from 1976 and I just loved it! I couldn't believe 'Silly Love Songs' had been the number one song of the year in the USA. Here in Australia it was Abba's 'Fernando.' From an Australian perspective, AT40 gave me a chance as an impressionable, music-loving teenager to hear a lot more songs than we were getting on Australian radio. Some were terrible, but at least I was hearing them all!"***
>
> **Debbie Kruger, an *AT40* listener from Sydney, New South Wales, Australia**

1977

340. 01-01-77

Program #771-1
SPECIAL: Top 100 Of 1976 (#50 - 1) (based on *Billboard's* year-end Top 100)
for a complete list of records in this special, see Rob Durkee's *American Top 40: The Countdown of the Century*
long version: Turn The Beat Around - Vicki Sue Robinson
long version: Love Rollercoaster - Ohio Players
program note: show's closing credits include all of *AT40* staff indentifying themselves

341. 01-08-77

Program #771-2
story: George Harrison's "My Sweet Lord" vs. "He's So Fine" lawsuit
story: Aerosmith is 1976's #1 LP act
story: Freddie Perren, 1976's #1 singles producer
Book of Records: Tammy Wynette, first lady of the country chart
whatever happened to: The Platters
question: biggest spoken word record
question: biggest female artist #1 record
portion played: Big Bad John - Jimmy Dean
portion played: He's So Fine - The Chiffons
portion played: My Sweet Lord - George Harrison
portion played: Only You - The Platters
program note: *Billboard* did not publish an issue dated 01-01-77, consequently records on the 12-25-76 Hot 100 stayed in the same position for two weeks; Casey referred to 12-25-76 record positions as "last week" and included 01-01-77 chart in weeks-on-chart total; no mention was made of *Billboard*'s non-published charts
odd chart stat: Marilyn McCoo & Billy Davis Jr.'s chart feat

342. 01-15-77

Program #771-3
story: Mary MacGregor's "Torn Between Two Lovers" recorded in a bathroom
story: rose named Englebert Humperdinck
story: Barbra Streisand's awards
story: Queen guitarist Brian May's 'trashy' guitar
Book of Records: The Beatles ranked as *Billboard*'s #1 recording act
question: #1 records by artists from non-English speaking countries
question: #1 'not written by The Beatles' Beatles record
question: female artist with most Top 10 records
odd chart stat: Lynyrd Skynyrd's "Free Bird" is one of three records to reach the Top 40 with live & studio versions
odd chart stat: two debut records
production error: no outcue for Rod Stewart's "Tonight's The Night"

343. 01-22-77

Program #771-4
Book of Records: Elvis Presley's soul chart feat
question: oldest artist with a #1 record
question: biggest non-Beatle-written Beatles record
portion played: Tie Me Kangaroo Down, Sport - Rolf Harris
whatever happened to: Rolf Harris
story: Stevie Wonder's #1 record chart feat of the 1970's
story: The Spinners failed at Motown Records
story: Electric Light Orchestra member drops cello during concert
story: Bernie Taupin's trash-can career start
story: The Eagles' LP chart feat
program note: in show closing, Casey provides no chart date
program note: Casey promos Dick Clark's *American Music Awards* TV special

344. 01-29-77 **Program #771-5**
odd chart stat: 30 Top 40 records written or co-written by the performing artist
story: Gene Cotton's near-tragic automobile accident
story: Kenny Nolan failed music class
story: Barbra Streisand has most Top 10 LPs
story: Abba's "Dancing Queen" #1 worldwide
story: The Sylvers' performed on Groucho Marx TV program
story: Rose Royce lead singer's big break
question: LP act with longest name
question: #1 LP one-hit wonders

345. 02-05-77 **Program #771-6**
story: Kansas' image problem
story: 25th anniversary of Dick Clark's *American Bandstand*
story: Michael Jackson's animal collection
story: Kiss' Ace Frehley nearly electrocuted in concert
story: Fleetwood Mac's LP chart feat
story: Mary MacGregor emulated Janis Joplin
program note: Casey extends a special hello to two blind engineers at WAKY in Louisville
odd chart stat: Elvis Presley's 133rd chart record debuts
portion played: *American Bandstand* Theme - Barry Manilow
question: disbanded group with #1 record, and ex-member with #1 record
question: #1 novelty records

346. 02-12-77 **Program #771-7**
story: Elvis Presley's Top 10 records chart feat
story: Abba's worldwide record sales
story: Bread's Larry Knechtel performed on many hit records
story: Leo Sayer's impromptu recording session
portion played: Blinded By The Light - Bruce Springsteen
Book of Records: The Temptations are biggest soul group
whatever happened to: Jimmie Rodgers
question: record company with most #1 records
question: #1 record with most charted weeks

347. 02-19-77 **Program #771-8**
question: foreign artist with most #1 records
question: most successful record with non-singing, named-on-label artist
question: most successful first-name-only artists
Book of Records: Eddy Arnold, king of the country chart
story: Boston's Tom Scholz did not pay dues
story: Bread's David Gates 'won' the Trans-Pacific Yacht Race
story: Tin Pan Alley special report
story: Paul McCartney's Wings' gold record distinction
story: Brick's horn player holds a musical note indefinitely
program mention: Elvis Presley's #1 country record
program mention: Fleetwood Mac's lead singer change

348. 02-26-77 **Program #771-9**
story: Kiss vs. Dr. Doom
story: Frankie Valli's deafness is cured
story: Elton John's rise to superstar status
story: The Eagles' chart success
story: Abba's mail-order ticket sale
story: Leo Sayer beat up for singing
story: Tom Jones is back
whatever happened to: Tommy Roe
question: biggest foreign duo
oldie played: Swearin' To God - Frankie Valli

349. 03-05-77

Program #771-10
Book of Records: The Del-Vikings' chart feat
Book of Records: Charlie Rich's country chart success
story: The Bee Gee's career saved by bridge sound in "Jive Talkin'"
story: Barry Manilow's concert act followed Bette Midler
story: David Soul sings soft and hits hard
story: Al Green is a practicing minister
story: Barbra Streisand's popularity
story: Olivia Newton-John's grandfather was Albert Einstein's best friend
story: Natalie Cole lacked a singing desire
portion played: Come Go With Me - Del-Vikings
portion played: Jive Talkin' - Bee Gees
oldie played: Let's Stay Together - Al Green

350. 03-12-77

Program #771-11
program note: Casey mentions that "*Billboard* just called" with three changes involving new chart positions for Elton John, Stevie Wonder and Olivia Newton-John records
question: biggest #1 LP
story: Stevie Wonder's lucrative recording contract
story: birth of soul chart
story: Lucille Ball's television programs
story: Fleetwood Mac's stolen name
story: Paul McCartney's *Rolling Stone* awards
story: Kenny Nolan 'dreams' song lyrics
portion played: The First Cut Is The Deepest - Cat Stevens

351. 03-19-77

Program #771-12
Book of Records: The Four Seasons' soul chart appearance
question: artist with most #1 records in one year
question: Top 40 Dutch artists
question: same-name, same-title records
story: The Bee Gees' songwriting feat
story: The Eagles' interaction with concert fans
story: Bob Seger's popularity in Detroit
story: Electric Light Orchestra's Jeff Lynne hates classical musicians
oldie played: Love Hangover - Diana Ross

352. 03-26-77

Program #771-13
question: pre-Beatles, British #1 records
story: The Eagles' origin
story: William Bell's big break
story: Mary MacGregor's out-house
story: Latimore earns money from spelling
story: Steve Miller learned guitar from Les Paul
odd chart stat: *I Love Lucy* TV show theme takes 26 years to reach the Top 40
Book of Records: Perez Prado's #1 record chart feat
portion played: Cherry Pink And Apple Blossom White - Perez Prado

353. 04-02-77

Program #772-1
program mention: Ambrosia's "Magical Mystery Tour" is from an unmentioned movie
Book of Records: The Statler Brothers are most successful country group
question: number of #1 LPs; act with most #1 LPs
question: artist with the most #2 but no #1 records
question: artist with #1 instrumental & #1 vocal records
name origin: Chaka Khan
story: Jim Webb's songwriting tips
story: Enchantment's lead singer arrested for jay walking
story: Glen Campbell's studio musician success
story: Abba is England's #1 act in 1976
program error: Casey states that Glen Campbell "....finally made it into the Top 40 for the first time in 1968....with 'Gentle On My Mind'...."; actually, he had three prior Top 40 records

354. 04-09-77

Program #772-2
odd chart stat: Q is the shortest name of a Top 40 recording artist
Book of Records: Creedence Clearwater Revival's gold records
question: artist with most consecutive Top 10 weeks
question: biggest artist using an alias
question: former group members replacing themselves at #1
story: The Captain & Tennille's wedding
story: Abba's concert policy
story: Barbra Streisand (former Mrs. Elliott Gould) is a combination of actress Sophia Loren and football player Y.A. Tittle
oldie played: At Seventeen - Janis Ian

355. 04-16-77

Program #772-3
story: Linda Ronstadt's assistance to Andrew Gold
story: Kansas' barroom brawl in Iowa
story: Kenny Nolan's revengeful act
story: Stevie Wonder's Grammy Awards
story: "Philadelphia Freedom" dedicated to athlete
odd chart stat: actor David Soul reaches the #1 position
question: biggest TV-created group
question: #1 records becoming #1 re-makes
Book of Records: Frank Sinatra's LPs
oldie played: Philadelphia Freedom - Elton John

"My earliest memories of American Top 40 go hand-in-hand with becoming a huge Beatles fan in the 1976-1978 period. I realized Casey's show was my easiest method of tracking the latest Wings or George Harrison singles, and I planned my Sunday afternoons around listening to the show on Gainesville, Georgia's WFOX-FM..........Music is a powerful tool in recapturing favorite memories in incredibly detailed ways. Its ability to link us with long ago and far away events is matched by no other art form. The great thing about AT40 shows is that they are THE REAL THING - not strategic and cynical marketing tools from the 21st century - that place us back in the exact same places when we listen again. Each week's show is a joyous time capsule and the songs (whether marvelously profound or hilariously trite) are all still there to take us on our individual, magical journeys."

Ken Ott, a longtime *AT40* listener

356. 04-23-77 **Program #772-4**
story: Marvin Gaye's partners
story: Alan Freed's concert fiasco
story: Paul McCartney's four #1 aliases
story: Thelma Houston's 'shack' guitarist
story: Jennifer Warnes' need for solitude
question: #1 record-of-the-year by female artists
question: artists re-recording and re-releasing records
question: #1 one-hit wonders

357. 04-30-77 **Program #772-5**
name origin: Marshall Tucker Band
story: Hot's lead singer was a private eye
story: Captain & Tennille's first record produced in a garage
story: Fleetwood Mac wins *Playboy* award
story: Stevie Wonder is in third place
story: Glen Campbell started with a 1957 Chevy
question: artist with the most #1, pre-1955 records
question: game show theme in the Top 40
Book of Records: The Jackson Five's soul chart feat
portion played: Spanish Flea – Herb Alpert & The Tijuana Brass

358. 05-07-77 **Program #772-6**
Book of Records: The Coasters' soul chart feat
portion played: Young Blood - The Coasters
portion played: Searchin' - The Coasters
story: KC & Sunshine Band's Harry Wayne Casey gambled his life
story: The Eagles are the Oakland A's of rock 'n' roll
story: Starz lead singer's bad luck
story: *Rocky* is a new national hero
story: Joe Tex gave up music for Muslims
story: Yvonne Elliman's profit-sharing decision
question: oldest group with a Top 40 record
program note: Casey promos upcoming special

359. 05-14-77 **Program #772-7**
story: Leo Sayer beat up for singing
story: Isaac Hayes, rags-to-riches-to-rags
story: John Denver's father made aviation history
story: Sylvester Stallone held out for *Rocky*
story: Holland-Dozier-Holland's songwriting success
question: origin of LP chart, first #1 LP
question: fastest rising #1 records
program note: Casey promos upcoming special
odd chart stat: Thelma Houston's "Don't Leave Me This Way" falls from #5 to #24
Book of Records: The Miracles' chart feat
portion played: Jamie - Eddie Holland
oldie played: Theme From *Shaft* - Isaac Hayes

360. 05-21-77

Program #772-8
whatever happened to: Hank Ballard
story: Addrisi Brothers' songwriting success
story: Kiss' Gene Simmons nearly killed in concert
story: Jennifer Warnes' first public performance
story: Vincent Van Gogh's gift
story: Stevie Wonder's #1 record chart feat
program note: Casey promos upcoming special
question: artist with multiple Top 10 debut records
question: youngest Top 40 artist
question: artist most often replacing The Beatles at #1
oldie played: Vincent - Don McLean

361. 05-28-77

Program #772-9
story: Stevie Wonder violated child labor laws
story: Andy Gibb's wish
story: Foreigner's Mick Jones snubbed by The Beatles
story: Simon Soussan owns world's biggest disco record collection
question: same song-different version, back-to-back #1 records
question: instrumental artist with biggest records
portion played: Rebel-'Rouser - Duane Eddy
odd chart stat: two versions of "Gonna Fly Now (Theme from *Rocky*)" in the Top 40
program note: Casey promos upcoming special
production error: unedited version of The Eagles' "Life In The Fast Lane" debuts and contains offensive language ("......we've been up and down this highway, haven't seen a gd*** thing..."); heard on more than 400 radio stations**

362. 06-04-77

Program #772-10
story: the recording of "Three Minutes of Silence"
story: Fleetwood Mac's divorces
story: Addrisi Brothers' song rejected by Barbra Streisand
story: Abba's single-release policy
program mention: origin of Maynard Ferguson's recording of "Gonna Fly Now"
question: most successful re-united groups
question: most successful TV soundtrack
question: most successful American group on LP chart
whatever happened to: Barbara Lewis
program note: Casey promos upcoming special
portion played: Three Minutes Of Silence - Hamilton O'Hara & Don Foster
odd chart stat: nineteen male solo artists in the Top 40
odd chart stat: two versions of "Gonna Fly Now (Theme from *Rocky*)" in the Top 40
production error: unedited version of The Eagles' "Life In The Fast Lane" contains offensive language ("......we've been up and down this highway, haven't seen a gd*** thing..."); heard on more than 400 subscribing radio stations**

363. 06-11-77

Program #772-11
portion played: Alfie - Eivets Rednow
story: Eivets Rednow is Stevie Wonder
story: Richard Perry - The Hit Doctor
story: Helen Reddy's surprise fund raising party
story: Glen Campbell's early days
story: KC & The Sunshine Band's chart feat
program note: Casey promos upcoming special
production error: unedited version of The Eagles' "Life In The Fast Lane" contains offensive language ("......we've been up and down this highway, haven't seen a gd*** thing..."); heard on more than 400 subscribing radio stations**
question: most successful former-group-member, solo artist
question: artist in second place for most chart records
Book of Records: Henry Mancini's Grammy Award feat
odd chart stat: two versions of "Gonna Fly Now (Theme from *Rocky*)" in the Top 40

AMERICAN TOP 40
WORLDWIDE LISTENING DIRECTORY
June 1977 © Watermark, Inc

STATE	CITY	STATION	FREQ.	BAND	DAY & TIME
ALABAMA	Birmingham	WSGN	610	AM	SUN 6PM-9PM
	Carrollton	WAQT	94.1	FM	SAT 9AM-12N
	Enterprise	WKMX	107	FM	SUN 7PM-10PM
	Gadsden	WQEN	104	FM	SUN 12N-3PM
	Guntersville	WGSV	1270	AM	SUN 1PM-4PM
	Hunstville	WAAY	1550	AM	SUN 3PM-6PM
	Marion	WJAM	1310	AM	SUN 1PM-4PM
	Mobile	WABB (AM)	1480	AM	SUN 10AM-1PM
		WABB (FM)	97.5	FM	SIMULCAST
	Montgomery	WHHY	1440	AM	SUN 12N-3PM
		WHHY (FM)	102	FM	SAT 11AM-2PM
ALASKA	Anchorage	KENI	550	AM	SUN 3PM-6PM
	Fairbanks	KFAR	660	AM	SAT 6PM-9PM
	Juneau	KJNO	630	AM	SUN 9AM-12N
	Kodiak	KVOK	560	AM	SAT 2PM-5PM
	Sitka	KIFW	1230	AM:	SAT 1PM-4PM
ARIZONA	Flagstaff	KFLG	92.9	FM	SUN 1PM-4PM TUES 7PM-10PM
	Globe	KIKO	1340	AM	SUN 3PM-6PM
	Phoenix	KRIZ	1230	AM	SUN 9AM-12N
	Willcox	KWCX	98.3	FM	SUN 6PM-9PM
	Tucson	KTKT	990	AM	SUN 7PM-10PM
ARKANSAS	El Dorado	KELD	1400	AM	SUN 2PM-5PM
	Fort Smith	KISR	93.7	FM	SUN 5PM-8PM
	Hardy	KSRB	1570	AM	SUN 2PM-5PM
	Harrison	KHOZ	900	AM	SUN 2PM-5PM
		KHOZ (FM)	102.9	FM	SAT 9PM-12M
	Little Rock	KLAZ	98.5	FM	SAT 9AM-12N
	Mountain Home	KTLO	1240	AM	SUN 1PM-4PM
		KTLO (FM)	98.3	FM	SIMULCAST
	Paragould	KHIG	105	FM	SAT 9PM-12M

STATE	CITY	STATION	FREQ.	BAND	DAY & TIME
	Des Moines	KRNQ	102.5	FM	SUN 9AM-12N SUN 7PM-10PM
	Dubuque	WDBQ	1490	AM	SUN 2PM-5PM
	Marshalltown	KFJB	1230	AM	SAT 7PM-10PM SUN 1PM-4PM
		KFJB (FM)	101.1	FM	SIMULCAST
	Mason City	KRIB	1490	AM	SUN 1PM-4PM
	Mt. Pleasant	KKSI	1130	AM	SUN 1PM-4PM
	Sioux City	KSEZ	97.9	FM	SUN 9AM-12N
	Waterloo	KLEU	850	AM	SAT 1PM-4PM
KANSAS	Hutchinson	KWHK	1260	AM	SUN 11AM-2PM SUN 7PM-10PM
	Manhattan	KSDB	88.1	FM	SAT 9AM-12N SUN 12N-3PM
	Salina	KSKG	99.9	FM	SUN 9AM-12N SUN 9PM-12M
	Topeka	KEWI	1440	AM	SUN 9AM-12N SUN 9PM-12M
	Wichita	KEYN	103.7	FM	SUN 3PM-6PM
KENTUCKY	Corbin	WYGO	1330	AM	SAT 8AM-11AM SUN 2PM-5PM
		WYGO (FM)	99.3	FM	SIMULCAST
	Harlan	WHLN	1410	AM	SUN 2PM-5PM
	Lexington	WLAP	630	AM	SAT 9PM-12M
	Louisville	WAKY	790	AM	SUN 7AM-10AM
	Middlesboro	WFXY	1560	AM	SAT 9AM-12N
	Moorhead	WMOR	1130	AM	SAT 1PM-4PM
	Paintsville	WSIP	1490	AM	SUN 8PM-11PM
		WSIP (FM)	98.9	FM	SIMULCAST
	Pikeville	WPKE	1240	AM	SAT 1PM-4PM
	Russellville	WAKQ	101.1	FM	SUN 7PM-10PM

The *AT40* Listening Directory for 1977, partially pictured here, was free to vacationing listeners. It provided information about every station that carried the program – city, state, call letters, frequency, and broadcast day and time.

364. 06-18-77 **Program #772-12**
story: Kenny Rogers' unconventional recording sessions
story: Fleetwood Mac's 10th anniversary
story: Alice Cooper's violent concerts are fun
story: Stevie Wonder's chart feat with "Sir Duke"
story: The Sylvers' mother lost her voice
story: Jimmy Buffet beat up by Sheriff Buford Pusser
story: Maynard Ferguson's snake bite
program note: Casey promos upcoming special
question: biggest #1 LP of the 1970's
question: duo with most #1 records
program mention: "Back Together Again" inspired by comeback artists
production error: unedited version of The Eagles' "Life In The Fast Lane" contains offensive language ("......we've been up and down this highway, haven't seen a gd*** thing..."); heard on more than 400 subscribing radio stations**
odd chart stat: two versions of "Gonna Fly Now (Theme from *Rocky*)" in the Top 40

365. 06-25-77 **Program #772-13**
story: Boston's LP sales
story: Joe Tex intentionally ruins his voice
story: Marvin Gaye's fear of performing live
story: Barry & Andy Gibb were strangers
question: #1 record with fewest weeks on chart
question: most successful family act
question: slowest peaking chart record
portion played: Battle Of Swing - Duke Ellington
program note: Casey promos upcoming special
program note: in an effort to improve subscribing station alliance with listeners, beginning this week, following Casey's standard program closing, he added: "...and keep your radio tuned right where it is...."
production error: unedited version of The Eagles' "Life In The Fast Lane" contains offensive language ("......we've been up and down this highway, haven't seen a gd*** thing..."); heard on more than 400 subscribing radio stations**
odd chart stat: two versions of "Gonna Fly Now (Theme from *Rocky*)" in the Top 40

366. 07-02-77 **Program #773-1**
SPECIAL: Top 40 Girls Songs (inspired by, or dedicated to women) for a complete list of records in this special, see Rob Durkee's *American Top 40: The Countdown of the Century*

TO: American Top 40 Subscribers

FROM: Tom Rounds

RE: Controversial Sides

July 2, 1977

The regular weekly countdown resumes this week with program #773-2 and not one, but two, records that may cause problems for you. They are Rod Stewart's "The Killing of Georgie" at #36 and Mary Wilson's "Telephone Man" at #34.

The last time we checked, the Stewart record was being played in a majority of markets and there is no doubt it will continue to climb the charts.

The Mary Wilson record, however, has caused much greater concern among programmers in markets where sexual double entendre in records causes complaints.

We suggest that you review both records, if you haven't already done so, and if you think they may cause you difficulty, dub the program segments in which they occur to tape and remove them from the context of the program.

As always, American Top 40 will always play everything reported on Billboard's chart. We leave the censorship of material up to you as representative of the Licensee of your station.

/sh

WATERMARK, INC. 10700 Ventura Blvd., No. Hollywood, California 91604 (213) 980-9490

Here's another memo that alerted stations to two records containing "controversial sides," Rod Stewart's "The Killing of Georgie" and Mary (sic) Wilson's "Telephone Man."

TO: AMERICAN TOP 40 Subscribers

FROM: Tom Rounds

RE: Guest Star This Week: Program #773-3

July 9, 1977

While Casey vacations in Michigan this week, we're proud to welcome Bruce Phillip Miller to the AMERICAN TOP 40 mike. Bruce is presently morning man at the Los Angeles AT40 affiliate: KIIS AM&FM. He's also one of the up and coming national commerical artists in town; you may have heard him recently on the Rollercoaster movie spots and seen him on camera for Busch Beer. Bruce is familiar to radio audiences in California's Orange County (KWIZ); San Antonio's WOAI and Cincinnati's WLW. He's also heard daily on the 400 AFRTS stations with an hour show called "Coffee Break". The Caser will be back in his regular spot next week.

/ynt

WATERMARK, INC. 10700 Ventura Blvd., No. Hollywood, California 91604 (213) 980-9490

Tom Rounds distributed this memo to alert stations that Casey Kasem was away and Bruce Phillip Miller was host for the July 16, 1977 program.

367. 07-09-77

Program #773-2
story: 100th anniversary of the phonograph
story: Alice Cooper LPs recalled by U.S. government
story: Waylon Jennings almost boarded Buddy Holly's fatal flight (see Paul Anka story - 04-26-75)
story: live recordings of #1 singles
story: fantasy records at #1
story: Peter McCann questioned producer Andrew Oldham's credibility
story: Crosby, Stills & Nash's break-ups & reunions
long version: The Killing of Georgie - Rod Stewart
question: biggest British female artist
question: LP artists replacing themselves at #1
lyric alert: memo from executive producer Tom Rounds which accompanied program, alerts subscribing radio stations to the potentially controversial lyric content of Rod Stewart's "The Killing Of Georgie" and Meri Wilson's "Telephone Man"
portion played: Mary Had A Little Lamb - Thomas Alva Edison
program mention: Casey gives the recipe to make a Margarita

368. 07-16-77

Program #773-3
GUEST HOST: Bruce Phillip Miller
long version: The Killing of Georgie - Rod Stewart
question: biggest record to win an Oscar award
question: song titles containing numbers
question: artist with longest time span between #1 records
story: Dean Friedman's piano sculpture
story: Rod Stewart's group & solo success
story: Abba's success comparable to The Beatles
story: The Eagles' LP chart feat
story: "Gonna Fly Now" songwriter has *Rocky*-like struggle
program mention: Shaun Cassidy & David Cassidy's #1 first-time records
odd chart stat: seventeen solo male artists in the Top 40
production error: unedited version of The Eagles' "Life In The Fast Lane" contains offensive language ("......we've been up and down this highway, haven't seen a gd*** thing...."); heard on more than 400 subscribing radio stations**

369. 07-23-77

Program #773-4
program mention: Fleetwood Mac's back-to-back records
whatever happened to: Jan & Dean (updated 10-20-79)
question: family act with the most 1970's records
story: celebrities vacationing in Luckenbach, TX
story: The Sylvers' high school competition
story: Hal Blaine, successful sessions musician
story: Rita Coolidge is the 'Delta Lady'
portion played: Delta Lady - Joe Cocker
portion played: Surf City - Jan & Dean
long version: The Killing Of Georgie - Rod Stewart

370. 07-30-77

Program #773-5
program note: Casey mentions his upcoming TV appearances on *Police Story*

and *Quincy*
story: monetary value of the record "Stormy Weather"
story: Dan Seals overtaken by older brother Jim Seals' religion
story: Jackie Wilson condition update
story: The Brothers Johnson's scented record
story: Helen Reddy, rags-to-riches
story: Brian Wilson's early days
question: biggest LP of the 1970's
program error: question answered regarding 'the biggest LP of the 1970's' is repeated from 06-18-77 program, same letter writer & origin
portion played: Stormy Weather - Five Sharps
portion played: Da Doo Ron Ron - The Crystals
oldie played: I Get Around - Beach Boys

371. 08-06-77

Program #773-6
story: Alice Cooper interviewed snakes
story: Supertramp's millionaire
story: England's Elvis Presley Fan Club traveled to Indianapolis
story: Steve Miller 'borrows' music
story: Heart is lead by women
story: Peter McCann's early days
odd chart stat: two debut records
portion played: Rock'n Me - Steve Miller Band
portion played: All Right Now - Free
portion played: Higher & Higher - Jackie Wilson
Book of Records: Marie Osmond's country chart feat
question: artists with most consecutive years with a #1 record

372. 08-13-77

Program #773-7
story: B.J. Thomas injured by mugger
story: Barry Manilow's chart feat
story: Rita Coolidge's success due to husband Kris Kristofferson
story: *Star Wars* income
story: Electric Light Orchestra sued by Great Britain's prime minister
story: Bay City Rollers' member losses
story: Ledbelly's chart feat
question: most successful female artist on LP chart
program mention: Helen Reddy is the 'queen of housewife rock'

373. 08-20-77

Program #773-8
story: Alice Cooper's great put-down
story: Mac McAnally's overnight success
story: The Emotions produced by admirer & fan Maurice White
story: The Brothers Johnson's big break
story: Barbra Streisand's chart feat
portion played: Vaya Con Dios - Les Paul & Mary Ford
question: first Canadian #1 record
question: biggest soul record of the 1970's
question: most successful married couple
question: artist with double-sided record with individual #1 flipsides
program note: Elvis Presley is the answer to a listener question regarding double-sided records but, due to advance program production, no mention was made of his death which occurred on 08-16-77
program note: Casey congratulates graduating engineer from Hanover, NH station at Dartmouth College
odd chart stat: Barbra Streisand's "My Heart Belongs To Me" falls from #6 to #27
oldie played: Let's Stay Together - Al Green

374. 08-27-77

Program #773-9
story: Elvis Presley tribute

story: James Taylor saved by Carly Simon
story: anonymous recording of "Don't Worry Baby"
story: Carole King's songwriting chart feat
story: Johnny Rivers' record company signed The Fifth Dimension
story: Fleetwood Mac's LP chart feat
Book of Records: London Symphony Orchestra's chart feat
question: records with slowest chart climbs to #1
portion played: Up, Up & Away - Fifth Dimension
odd chart stat: The Bay City Rollers' "You Made Me Believe In Magic" falls from #10 to #33
LP cut played: Suspicious Minds (live version) - Elvis Presley

375. 09-03-77 Program #773-10
story: Alice Cooper's concert audience walked out
story: James Taylor not helped by The Beatles
story: Foreigner's Mick Jones injured playing tennis
story: Elvis Presley popularity poll
program note: Elvis Presley's "Way Down" re-debuts in the Top 40
question: group with longest span of time between #1 records
question: first all-female group at #1
portion played: Boogie Woogie Bugle Boy - Bette Midler
odd chart stat: James Taylor & Carly Simon (husband & wife) have solo records in the Top 40
odd chart stat: The Emotions' "Best Of My Love" reaches #1, matching the chart climb of The Eagles' "Best Of My Love"; same title, different song
oldie played: Don't Go Breaking My Heart - Elton John & Kiki Dee

376. 09-10-77 Program #773-11
story: Phil Spector answers Elvis Presley's critics
story: Sanford-Townsend Band's big break
story: Rita Coolidge's Top 40 struggle
story: Carole King was Neil Sedaka's "Oh! Carol"
story: Meco preferred big band music over rock 'n' roll
story: Harry Chapin awarded for campaigning against hunger
question: year with more #1 British records
question: biggest #1 TV show theme
question: rock era's biggest Canadian group
program mention: Leo Sayer wrote songs for The Who's Roger Daltrey
program mention: Stephen Bishop's big break
program mention: George Benson's music business motivator
oldie played: Cat's In The Cradle - Harry Chapin

377. 09-17-77 Program #773-12
production note: no #40 jingle
story: Stevie Wonder is most honored artist of the 1970's
story: Ted Nugent, wild game hunter
story: Ronnie Milsap's pre-country chart success
story: The Beatles' April 1964 Top 5 chart feat
story: George Lucas is most successful creative talent
story: The Brothers Johnson unknowingly signed first contract
story: Joan Baez's social movement theme
story: B.J. Thomas' drug habit
question: country artist with most LPs on pop LP chart
odd chart stat: four weeks after leaving the #1 position, Andy Gibb's "I Just Want To Be Your Everything" returns to #1
oldie played: The Night They Drove Old Dixie Down - Joan Baez
oldie played: Can't Buy Me Love – Beatles

378. 09-24-77

Program #773-13
story: The Spinners recognized on the Hollywood Walk of Fame
story: "Surfin' USA" reaches the Top 40 again
story: Elvis Presley tribute record
story: The Emotions' meeting with Stevie Wonder
story: Sanford/Townsend Band 'recycled' pop bottles
story: Rita Coolidge benefited from recording artist Booker T. Jones
story: 'time capsule' chart re-cap of 1975
story: Wild Cherry lead guitarist nearly abandoned group
odd chart stat: London Symphony Orchestra's "Star Wars" falls from #10 to #36
odd chart stat: The Emotions' "Best Of My Love" returns to #1 position
program mention: title of Brothers Johnson's "Strawberry Letter 23" defined
program mention: Casey promotes his appearance on ABC-TV's *The Hardy Boys/Nancy Drew Mysteries*

379. 10-01-77

Program #774-1
story: classical Top 10
story: Stevie Wonder carried off stage
story: Mac Davis' method to 'get girls'
story: Fleetwood Mac breaks Elvis Presley chart record
story: Shaun Cassidy's weekly allowance
story: Ronnie McDowell's recording of "The King Is Gone"
story: classical conductor Leopold Stokowsky releases LP at age 95
program mention: Casey promotes his appearance on ABC-TV's *The Hardy Boys/Nancy Drew Mysteries*
odd chart stat: two debut records
odd chart stat: The Floaters' "Float On" falls from #2 to #19
program error: in show closing, chart date Casey provides is 09-24-77
oldie played: A Fifth of Beethoven - Walter Murphy & Big Apple Band
oldie played: Baby Don't Get Hooked On Me - Mac Davis

380. 10-08-77

Program #774-2
GUEST HOST: Mark Elliott
program note: Dick Clark's upcoming ABC special is promoted
program note: Casey's TV appearances on *Hardy Boys* and *Switch* are promoted
story: Andy Gibb record may be #1 for 1977
story: Ben E. King's first break nearly cost him his life
story: Elvis Presley's two paychecks upon discharge from Army
story: Steve Miller earned $400/month in the early 1950's
story: Marvin Gaye recorded "I Heard It Through The Grapevine" in 1965
story: Brick's horn player holds a musical note for 30 minutes
story: Stevie Wonder LP debuted at #1
story: Barry White's #1 records as vocalist and orchestra leader
program error: during the outcue to Dave Mason's "We Just Disagree," Mark Elliott states that Dave Mason "....has been in the Top 40 in the past as a member of the popular British group Traffic....."; actually, Traffic never had a Top 40 record
odd chart stat: B.J. Thomas' "Don't Worry Baby" falls from #17 to #39
odd chart stat: while Debby Boone's "You Light Up My Life" climbs from #15 to #3, Fleetwood Mac's "Don't Stop" falls from #3 to #15
oldie played: Supernatural Thing - Ben E. King

381. 10-15-77 **Program #774-3**
story: Dave Brubeck's "Take Five"
story: Barry Manilow's recording of "Mandy"
story: Ronnie McDowell's fascination with Elvis Presley
story: Michael Jackson's #1 'rat'
story: Fleetwood Mac's group changes
story: Eric Carmen's expensive LP
story: Chicago's LP chart feat
odd chart stat: two *Star Wars* theme versions simultaneously in the Top 40
odd chart stat: Andy Gibb's "I Just Want To Be Your Everything" in the Top 10 for 16 consecutive weeks
odd chart stat: Judy Collins' "Send In The Clowns" re-debuts in the Top 40 after a two-year absence
oldie played: Mandy - Barry Manilow
oldie played: Take Five - Dave Brubeck Quartet
oldie played: Ben - Michael Jackson

382. 10-22-77 **Program #774-4**
production error: unedited version of Jimmy Buffett's "Changes In Latitudes, Changes In Attitudes" contains offensive language ("......goodtimes and riches and son of a bitches.....")
odd chart stat: Debby Boone's "You Light Up My Life" is seventh movie theme record to reach the #1 position
question: soul artist with most charted LPs
question: group with most consecutive #1 weeks on LP chart
story: Linda Ronstadt disobeys Boy Scout code
story: Peter Frampton's LP sales
story: Paul Nicholas uses singing for acting
story: female artist averages in Top 40
oldie played: Lucy In The Sky With Diamonds - Elton John
oldie played: Bad Bad Leroy Brown - Jim Croce

383. 10-29-77 **Program #774-5**
production error: no outcue for Stephen Bishop's "On And On"
odd chart stat: Linda Ronstadt's two chart-climbing Top 40 records
odd chart stat: five records - in positions #21, #20, #19, #18 and #17 - were all re-makes
story: Soviets ban Neil Sedaka
story: Pat & Debby Boone's chart feat
story: Bing Crosby special report
story: The Bee Gees are not The Beatles
story: Ringo Starr's childhood diseases
story: Peter Brown deceived by his record producer
story: Ronnie Milsap expelled from music class
question: largest Top 40 group
portion played: Battle Hymn Of The Republic - Mormon Tabernacle Choir
oldie played: You're Sixteen - Ringo Starr
oldie played: If You Leave Me Now - Chicago
oldie played: Laughter In The Rain - Neil Sedaka

Fast becoming an institution within an institution, the annual 8-hour, Top 100 of the year countdown was appealing to both listeners and radio stations. This advertisement for 1977's year-end special appeared in the November 12, 1977 edition of *Billboard* magazine.

384. 11-05-77

Program #774-6
story: James Taylor's mother nearly died while his father traveled
story: Paul Davis' first place lesson
story: The Commodores' early days
story: Lynyrd Skynyrd's plane crash
story: Chicago goes unrecognized
story: Stevie Wonder's co-writer credit on "Signed, Sealed And Delivered"
story: Linda Ronstadt's five million-selling LPs
question: highest non-#1 debut record
question: The Beatles first British #1 record
program mention: Casey provides ingredients to a diamatica cocktail
program mention: Barry Manilow celebrates Marie Osmond's birthday
oldie played: Sweet Home Alabama - Lynyrd Skynyrd

385. 11-12-77

Program #774-7
story: Boone family's three generations of #1 records
story: Barry Manilow The Recluse
story: Leo Sayer's nervous breakdown
story: James Taylor's *Time* article
story: Freddy Fender's marijuana arrest
story: Mark Hamill directed to *Star Wars* by automobile accident
story: Nitty Gritty Dirt Band's Russian performance
production error: in opening hour #3, Casey welcomes four new stations, but mentioned only three
question: biggest record of the 1970's
program mention: Casey lists groups named after cities
portion played: Chattanooga Shoeshine Boy - Red Foley
portion played: I Almost Lost My Mind - Pat Boone
oldie played: Wasted Days & Wasted Nights - Freddy Fender
oldie played: Mr. Bojangles - Nitty Gritty Dirt Band

386. 11-19-77

Program #774-8
story: Debby Boone's #1 record chart feat
story: Peter Brown's do-it-yourself record
story: Paul McCartney's income from Buddy Holly's music
story: Steve Miller's broken neck
story: Dolly Parton's talent questioned by Chet Atkins
story: Carly Simon's stammering
program note: Casey promos upcoming special
question: longest span of time between one record's two Top 40 appearances
program mention: Fleetwood Mac's "Rumours" LP chart feat
oldie played: Someday We'll Be Together - Diana Ross & Supremes
oldie played: My Little Town - Simon & Garfunkel

387. 11-26-77

Program #774-9
story: Chicago visits two hospitalized fans
story: Debby Boone's #1 record chart feat
story: Pat Boone's Hot 100 record chart feat
story: James Taylor & Carly Simon's husband-and-wife chart feat
story: the mystery of "Calling Occupants Of Interplanetary Craft"
story: James Taylor's broken hands and broken mind
story: Bob Welch's bad timing
question: female artists with fastest & slowest rising #1 records
program note: Casey promos upcoming special
odd chart stat: female artists have nine records in the Top 40
odd chart stat: Linda Ronstadt's two chart-climbing Top 10 records
portion played: April Love - Pat Boone
oldie played: Then Came You - Dionne Warwick & Spinners

oldie played: Mockingbird - James Taylor & Carly Simon

388. 12-03-77 **Program #774-10**
GUEST HOST: Mark Elliott
program note: Mark promos upcoming special
question: biggest record with a one-word title
question: artist with most Top 10 records in the shortest time
story: Rod Stewart hates the music business
story: Paul Simon advised Carole King
story: The Rolling Stones' violent reputation
story: Steve Miller goes unrecognized
story: The Bee Gees songs recorded by other artists
story: Debby Boone's #1 record chart feat
story: Heatwave member faked soul music talent
oldie played: Honky Tonk Woman - Rolling Stones

389. 12-10-77 **Program #774-11**
program note: Casey mentioned his appearance on NBC-TV's "*Billboard*'s #1" show
program note: Casey promos upcoming special
record origin: Fleetwood Mac's "Rhiannon"
story: Player member joined group for no pay
story: Billy Swan's recording of "I Can Help"
story: Electric Light Orchestra member drops cello during concert
story: The Doobie Brothers' first recording contract
story: Barry White predicted his own success
story: Elvis Presley's multi-chart, #1 record chart feat
story: Linda Ronstadt is first female with two simultaneous Top 10 songs
story: Debby Boone's #1 record chart feat
portion played: Hey School Girl - Tom & Jerry
portion played: Don't Be Cruel - Elvis Presley
oldie played: Long Train Running - Doobie Brothers
oldie played: Rhiannon - Fleetwood Mac
oldie played: I Can Help - Billy Swan

390. 12-17-77 **Program #774-12**
production note: disks contain promos for upcoming special
edited version: Barry White's "It's Ecstasy......"; edited to 1:15
odd chart stat: two debut records
odd chart stat: sixteen Top 40 records move up two notches
question: biggest solo artist using an alias
story: Elvis Presley's $50 Christmas present
story: Debby Boone's #1 record chart feat
story: The Hardy Boys' popularity
story: Kansas' road crew was paid more than the group
story: High Inergy's big break
story: Fleetwood Mac's Top 10 chart feat
program note: Casey plays three Christmas records as program extras
program note: Casey promos upcoming special
oldie played: White Christmas - Bing Crosby
oldie played: Blue Christmas - Elvis Presley
oldie played: Little St. Nick - Beach Boys

391. 12-24-77

Program #774-13
SPECIAL: Top 100 Of 1977 (#100 - 51) (based on *AT40* staff's year-end list)
for a complete list of records in this special, see Rob Durkee's *American Top 40: The Countdown of the Century*
long version: Year Of The Cat - Al Stewart
edited version: Donna Summer's "I Feel Love"; edited to 2:18
production error: a montage of 1977's #1 records, played between #52 & #51, contains a portion of Andy Gibb's "I Just Want To Be Your Everything" played backwards

392. 12-31-77

Program #781-1
SPECIAL: Top 100 Of 1977 (#50 - 1) (based on *AT40* staff's year-end list)
for a complete list of records in this special, see Rob Durkee's *American Top 40: The Countdown of the Century*

1978

393. 01-07-78

Program #781-2
story: Gladys Knight's apology for "I Heard It Through The Grapevine"
story: Samantha Sang's big break
story: War represents peace
story: Kansas member washed windows
story: Dion DiMucci's success
portion played: Runaround Sue - Dion
question: biggest name-change artist
question: biggest movie soundtrack LP
oldie played: Why Can't We Be Friends - War
oldie played: Midnight Train To Georgia - Gladys Knight & The Pips

394. 01-14-78

Program #781-3
whatever happened to: Sam The Sham
portion played: Wooly Bully - Sam The Sham & The Pharaohs
story: Billy Joel's creative job application
story: Barry Mann & Cynthia Weil's songwriting success
story: chart records broken by Debby Boone's "You Light Up My Life"
story: Melissa Manchester's college professor was Paul Simon
story: Stevie Wonder's numerous awards
question: artists with separate #1 records, with separate groups
oldie played: Midnight Blue - Melissa Manchester

395. 01-21-78

Program #781-4
question: most successful Canadian artist
question: artist in third place with most Top 10 records
question: biggest female re-make artist
story: Neil Diamond's dreams
story: Dan Hill failed singing in high school
story: Santana discovered by a barber
story: the satire of "Short People"
story: Lynyrd Skynyrd's LP jacket cover changed
whatever happened to: The Rascals
oldie played: Evil Ways - Santana
oldie played: People Got To Be Free - Rascals

TO: AT40 Subscribers, ESP. GM's, PD's, Sales and Promotion People

FROM: Tom Rounds, Watermark

January 21, 1978

By popular demand, we're adding another special countdown in 1978. For the past few years, we'd been producing, in addition to the year end Top 100, just one special on July 4 weekend.

This year, two specials will pre-empt the regular weekly countdown, and they'll happen on the April 1 and July 1 weekends.

Ads will run in the Trades in the next few weeks announcing all this to the world; we wanted you to know first, so here's the ad copy:

SOME VERY SPECIAL AMERICAN TOP 40'S FOR 1978

April 1-2: (782-1) AT40 GOES TO THE MOVIES. The very weekend before the Oscars, Casey Kasem counts down the 40 biggest hits from the Silver Screen since 1960. Casey covers the movie stars and the movie stories...and plays the 40 most successful hits the movies made - from #40 to 1.

July 1-2: (783-1) THE 40 BIGGEST ACTS OF THE 70'S. Casey Kasem celebrates AT40's eighth birthday by stacking up and ranking the hit careers of the biggest superstars of the decade so far. Elton John, Stevie Wonder, Wings, Eagles, Fleetwood Mac. They'll all appear...but where? Another special American Top 40 tabulation - from #40 to #1.

Dec. 23-24: Dec. 30-30 (784-12 & 784-13) THE TOP 100 OF 1978. Casey Kasem's traditional holiday special. The greatest hits of the year and the fascinating stories behind them as AT40's format expands to a two-weekend, eight-hour, gift-wrapped bonanza ready to take on a basketful of year-end assignments.

In other news, we're happy to report another recurrence of an every-seven-years phenomenon: 1978 has 53 weekends in it. To adjust for this, we have declared the third calendar quarter (July-August-September) a 14-weekend quarter, so programs for this period will be numbered 783-1 through 783-14 (instead of the usual 13).

WATERMARK, INC. 10700 Ventura Blvd., No. Hollywood, California 91604 (213) 980-9490

Tom Rounds' January 21, 1978 two-page memo notified stations of 1978's *AT40* special programs including a "Movies" special scheduled to broadcast at the Academy Awards time of year.

Page Two

Watermark has commissioned several hour-by-hour Arbitron breakouts to chart the performance of AT40 on the weekends (when individual hours are not broken out in the books). We're happy to report that AT40 is up at least a couple of percentage points in most books in the Oct-Nov survey as compared to April-May. Special congratulations to KIIS AM&FM, Los Angeles, (AT40 is #1 teens and total persons... ahead of KHJ and everybody else), WPIX, New York; KYA (AM), San Francisco; WZGC, Atlanta; KGW, Portland, WPGC AM&FM, Washington; WMET, Chicago; WNCI, Columbus...to name a few.

If you'd like ratings details, we'll be happy to share them with you if we have them. Just call us at (800) 423-2502 or (213) 980-9490.

396. 01-28-78 **Program #781-5**
story: Queen's elaborate concert stage description
story: Steely Dan's jet broke concert hall windows
story: The Bee Gees disband and re-group
story: Dobie Gray answered Sonny Bono's advertisement
story: Maria Muldaur will not be a white slave
story: Leif Garrett grateful to Shaun Cassidy
question: foreign country ranking third in artists reaching the Top 40
question: artist with most pre-Top 10 records
oldie played: You Ain't Seen Nothin' Yet - Bachman-Turner Overdrive
oldie played: Midnight At The Oasis - Maria Muldaur
oldie played: Drift Away - Dobie Gray

397. 02-04-78 **Program #781-6**
story: street corner singing
story: producer & songwriter Joe Brooks' movie ventures
story: Lou Rawls' amnesia
story: Marvin Hamlisch's Academy Award feat
story: Paul Davis' recording contract permitted studio sleeping
story: John Williams' profitable movie success
question: artist with most Hot 100 records in one year
program error: Casey's introduction to "Lovely Day" pointed out that Bill Withers' first Top 40 record, "Ain't No Sunshine", was in 1972; actually, it was 1971
production error: closing of Con Funk Shun's "Ffun" continues under Casey's introduction of the next record
odd chart stat: four Top 10 records are written by Bee Gees member Barry Gibb
odd chart stat: Bee Gees replace Player at #1, after Player replaced The Bee Gees

398. 02-11-78 **Program #781-7**
story: Donna Summer saved Casablanca Records from Johnny Carson fiasco
story: The Bee Gees #1 record chart feat
story: The Bee Gees three-record chart feat
story: Dan Hill's true confessions
story: Neil Diamond is Las Vegas' highest paid performer
story: The Commodores' summer vacation
story: George Benson's first guitar
story: Abba receives vegetables instead of cash
odd chart stat: 32 Top 40 records written or co-written by the performing artist
odd chart stat: The Bee Gees have three records in the Top 10
question: artists with most Top 10 records
oldie played: This Masquerade - George Benson

Spotlighting the upcoming specials for the year, this advertisement appeared in the February 4, 1978 edition of *Billboard* magazine.

399. 02-18-78

Program #781-8
odd chart stat: The Bee Gees have three records in the Top 10
story: three solo recording artists perform on "What A Wonderful World"
story: David Gates a 'winner' in the Trans-Pacific Yacht Race
story: the history of Eric Clapton
story: Chic's "Dance, Dance, Dance" rejected & reprinted
story: Stevie Wonder's practical joke on Elton John
story: Odyssey encouraged by Duke Ellington
story: Rod Stewart is 1977's #1 singles artist
question: #1 3-LP sets
question: duos with #1 LPs
program error: Casey points out that War's "Galaxy" is a debut record; actually, it was in its second week in the Top 40
oldie played: You Haven't Done Nothin' - Stevie Wonder

400. 02-25-78

Program #781-9
record origin: Eric Burdon & War's "Spill The Wine"
story: Neil Sedaka's "Breaking Up Is Hard To Do" chart feat
story: Samantha Sang's wasp incident
story: Raydio's Ray Parker Jr. hung up on Stevie Wonder
story: LeBlanc & Carr almost boarded Lynyrd Skynyrd's fatal flight
program note: Casey promos upcoming special
odd chart stat: The Bee Gees' "How Deep Is Your Love" in the Top 10 for 16 consecutive weeks
odd chart stat: The Bee Gees have three records in the Top 10
question: most #1 records in shortest time period
question: year with most #1 instrumentals
oldie played: Spill The Wine - Eric Burdon & War
oldie played: Breaking Up Is Hard To Do - Neil Sedaka

401. 03-04-78

Program #781-10
story: Lou Rawls is no one-hit wonder
story: Peter Asher, producer
story: The Temptations' chart success
story: Barry Manilow's gold record income
story: Paul Davis pleaded for no release of "I Go Crazy"
story: The Eagles go unrecognized
program mention: Kansas' use of the violin
question: group with most Top 10 LPs
portion played: The Way You Do The Things You Do - Temptations
odd chart stat: four records in the Top 40 from the movie *Saturday Night Fever*
odd chart stat: artist (Andy Gibb) replaces a relative (The Bee Gees) at #1
odd chart stat: The Bee Gees' "How Deep Is Your Love" in the Top 10 for 17 consecutive weeks
odd chart stat: The Bee Gees have three records in the Top 10
program note: Casey promos upcoming special
oldie played: Take It To The Limit - Eagles

402. 03-11-78 **Program #781-11**
question: origin of *Billboard*'s disco chart
question: year since 1964 with no English #1 records
story: Chicago's best-forgotten chart record
story: Nat King Cole's pre-rock era success
story: Kansas' image problem
story: *Saturday Night Fever* soundtrack LP daily sales
story: Andy Gibb's early days
story: Gene Cotton's near-tragic automobile accident
Book of Records: The Four Seasons' chart feat
program note: Casey promos upcoming special
oldie played: If You Leave Me Now - Chicago
odd chart stat: The Bee Gees have three records in the Top 40

403. 03-18-78 **Program #781-12**
Book of Records: Marie Osmond's country chart feat
story: The Bee Gees faked first record sales
story: Yvonne Elliman's gimmick for concert attention
story: Billy Joel becomes "The Piano Man"
story: Gene Cotton borrowed $5,000 for first record
story: David Gates 'won' his wife
odd chart stat: The Bee Gees have records in the #1 & #2 positions
odd chart stat: The Bee Gees have three records in the Top 40
odd chart stat: two debut records
program note: Casey promos upcoming special
question: artist with most consecutive years on chart
question: most successful record company president & Top 40 artist

404. 03-25-78 **Program #781-13**
odd chart stat: six records in the Top 40 from the movie *Saturday Night Fever*
odd chart stat: The Bee Gees have three records in the Top 40
odd chart stat: RSO Records has most consecutive #1 records
program note: Casey promos upcoming special
question: female country artist with pop & country #1 record
question: highest-peaking, shortest-span-of-time Top 40 record
question: different Top 40 artists with the same name
story: Natalie Cole's poolside meeting with Harry Belafonte
story: Enchantment's member recruitment lie
story: Stargard's dream of Norman Whitfield
story: Kansas' favorite story
production note: disks contain promos for upcoming special

405. 04-01-78 **Program #782-1**
SPECIAL: *American Top 40* Goes To The Movies
for a complete list of records in this special, see Rob Durkee's *American Top 40: The Countdown of the Century*

406. 04-08-78

Program #782-2
story: Raydio's Ray Parker Jr. walked out on Stevie Wonder
story: Eric Clapton's desire to be a stained glass designer
story: Chuck Mangione's father invites jazz performers home
story: Parliament and Funkadelic are the same, different band
story: KC & The Sunshine Band's Harry Wayne Casey cleaned record studios
story: rock era's slowest moving Top 10 record
Book of Records: The Ventures' LP chart feat
odd chart stat: Wings' "With A Little Luck" debuts in the Top 40 at #17, up from #57 the previous week
odd chart stat: RSO Records has six records in the Top 10
program error: during program introduction, Casey pointed out that Wings' "With A Little Luck", which debuted at #17, is the highest debut record ever in *AT40*'s history; during the record's introduction, Casey references the #20 debut of John Lennon's "Imagine" as the highest previous debut; actually, since July 1970, numerous other records debuted at #20 or higher, including George Harrison's "My Sweet Lord" which debuted at #13 on 12-05-70; Isaac Hayes' "Theme from *Shaft*" debuted at #9 on 10-23-71, and Wadsworth Mansion's "Sweet Mary"debuted at #15 on 02-13-71; ironically, "Imagine" debuted in the Top 40 the same week as "Shaft"

407. 04-15-78

Program #782-3
story: The Bee Gees attempted to impersonate The Everly Brothers
story: Lou Rawls was a paratrooper
story: Eddie Money arrested by rock promoter Bill Graham
story: Andy Gibb ties Elvis Presley chart record
story: Rubicon started at the top
question: artist with pre-Beatles song
question: real people in #1 record titles
question: disbanded Top 40 groups with members becoming Top 40 artists
portion played: From Me To You - Del Shannon

408. 04-22-78

Program #782-4
Book of Records: Gerry & The Pacemakers' British chart feat
story: Tavares helped by a non-released Bee Gees record
story: The Trammps' "Disco Inferno" charts again
story: Olivia Newton-John's grandfather was Albert Einstein's best friend
story: Paul McCartney's chartered news conference
question: artist with #1 record in most consecutive years
question: group with #1 LP with no charted records
question: highest Top 40 debut record

409. 04-29-78

Program #782-5
story: Elton John's LP chart feat
story: Parliament members were barbers
story: Zela Lehr helped by a non-released Dolly Parton record
story: Sweet's Brian Conley's throat injury
story: Olivia Newton-John's dolphin-killing protest
story: RSO Records' Robert Stigwood pledged $100,000 to telethon
story: Wings' "Mull Of Kintyre" biggest British record
portion played: Mull Of Kintyre - Wings
question: #1 record preventing most #2 records from #1 position
question: artist with longest time from debut to #1 record
program mention: Eddie Money borrows from Doris Day's "Que Sera Sera"

410. 05-06-78 **Program #782-6**
Book of Records: Fats Domino's non-#1 chart feat
story: Shaun Cassidy's show business family
story: Electric Light Orchestra's Jeff Lynne hates classical musicians
story: Eddie Money was a policeman
story: The Bee Gees' manager almost received a million birthday greetings
story: Jefferson Starship member joined for less pay
story: Abba's concert ticket orders
question: record on chart longest without hitting #1
question: country group with most successful pop hit

411. 05-13-78 **Program #782-7**
GUEST HOST: Mark Elliott
short version: Let's All Chant - Michael Zager Band
story: 12" disco records
story: Meatloaf's oxygen use at concerts
story: Abba's "Waterloo" performed at a worldwide competition
story: Eric Clapton's concert insecurity
story: John Travolta, high school drop-out
story: Yvonne Elliman's image problem
question: group with biggest #1 record
question: palindrome records
question: #1 records with no title mention

> ***"Waking up on a Sunday morning back in '78, I put the radio on just like always but heard something different on 99X in New York City....I can't be 100% certain but it must've been (May 14, 1978) because that was my regular station at the time and I always turned it on every morning, Sundays included.......What I heard was quite intriguing on several levels. First, it was the voice. I knew I had heard it a whole bunch of times in other places but now I knew his name -- Casey. Second, the stories very much humanized the artists that were performing the songs. Third, and maybe most important, were the songs being played early on in the show, many I heard for the first time. Over time, I became a regular weekly American Top 40 listener and began logging the chart information past and present."***
> **Doug Bowden, a longtime *AT40* listener**

412. 05-20-78 **Program #782-8**
odd chart stat: one debut record
odd chart stat: Paul Davis' "I Go Crazy" ties Hot 100 longevity chart record
odd chart stat: duos hold consecutive chart positions at #2, #3 & #4
(Roberta Flack & Donny Hathaway, Johnny Mathis & Denise Williams and John Travolta & Olivia Newton-John)
story: Atlanta Rhythm Section paid to not perform
story: the world's first disk jockey
story: Top 40 monsters
story: Linda Ronstadt, re-make queen
story: Abba's translator
story: Paul McCartney's #1 record chart feat
question: non-Top 40 artist with most Hot 100 records
question: oldest, most chart-active artists
question: ex-group member replacing another ex-member at #1

413. 05-27-78 **Program #782-9**
story: Jimmy Buffett's invisible concert band
story: Bonnie Tyler's vocal cord surgery
story: Eddie Money's traffic accident autograph session
story: Jefferson Starship member's mountain lion encounter
whatever happened to: Brook Benton
portion played: It's Just A Matter Of Time - Brook Benton
portion played: Rainy Night In Georgia - Brook Benton
portion played: The Lovliest Night Of The Year - Mario Lanza
question: longest chart run of a non-#1 Top 40 hit
question: two #1 artists co-singing a #1 record
question: female artist with most Top 10 records

414. 06-03-78 **Program #782-10**
story: Linda Ronstadt's backstage encounter with Mick Jagger
story: The Trammps booed for their tramp image
story: Paul Davis' "I Go Crazy" sets chart record
name origin: Meatloaf
program note: Casey promos upcoming special
question: Top 40 movie record with longest chart run
question: #1 record repeating at #1
question: youngest and oldest artists with #1 records
question: slowest climbing #1 LP
odd chart stat: Johnny Mathis & Deniece Williams, two established solo artists, reach #1 as a duo
oldie played: I Go Crazy - Paul Davis

415. 06-10-78 **Program #782-11**
story: Atlanta Rhythm Section's drummer played professionally at age 15
story: The Beach Boys' Mike Love formed another band
story: origin of term 'rock 'n' roll'
story: The Bee Gees' 1975-78 chart success
name origin: The O'Jays
question: biggest #1 medley
question: record with most weeks at #1
question: biggest 1970's Top 10 record
program note: Casey promos upcoming special
odd chart stat: John Travolta & Olivia Newton-John, two established solo artists, reach #1 as a duo
portion played: Rock And Roll - Boswell Sisters

416. 06-17-78 **Program #782-12**
story: Andy Gibb's #1 record chart feat
story: Sweet's bubblegum image dumped
story: Jimmy Buffet beat up by Sheriff Buford Pusser
story: Meatloaf struck in the head with a shotput
story: Barry Manilow's eleven-record chart feat
story: Johnny Mathis' LP chart feat
program note: Casey promos upcoming special
odd chart stat: Player's "This Time I'm In It For Love" falls from #10 to #36
odd chart stat: two jazz artists - George Benson and Chuck Mangione - have back-to-back Top 10 records
question: artists with self-made re-make records
question: artists with most simultaneous charted records
question: Top 40 family acts including children and one parent

STATE & CITY	STATION	FREQ.	BAND	DAY & TIME
Nevada				
Carson City	KKBC	97	FM	SUN 7PM-10PM
Las Vegas	KFMS	101.9	FM	SAT 9AM-12N
Winnemuca	KWNA	1400	AM	SAT 3PM-6PM
New Hampshire				
Franklin	WFTN	1240	AM	SAT 9AM-12N
Hanover	WDCR	1340	AM	SAT 9AM-12N
Portsmouth	WHEB	750	AM	SAT 9AM-12N
				SUN 10AM-1PM
New Jersey				
South Vineland	WMVB	1440	AM	SUN 6PM-9PM
	WMVB	97.3	FM	SAT 10AM-1PM
New Mexico				
Albuquerque	KQEO	920	AM	SUN 9AM-12N
Clovis	KTQM	99.9	FM	SAT 1PM-4PM
Farmington	KRAZ	96.9	FM	SAT 9AM-12N
Gallup	KYVA	1230	AM	SUN 1PM-4PM
Santa Fe	KVSF	1260	AM	SUN 4PM-7PM
New York				
Buffalo	WYSL	1400	AM	SUN 12N-3PM
Corning	WCBA	1350	AM	SAT 1PM-4PM
Fulton	WKFM	104.7	FM	SUN 8AM-11AM
Gloversville	WENT	1340	AM	SAT 7PM-10PM
Latham	WTRY	980	AM	SUN 10AM-1PM
				SUN 6PM-9PM
Olean	WMNS	1360	AM	SAT 10AM-1PM
Plattsburg	WIRY	1340	AM	SAT 9AM-12N
Potsdam	WPDM	1470	AM	SUN 1PM-4PM
Riverhead	WRCN	1570	AM	SUN 10AM-1PM
	WRCN	104	FM	SIMULCAST
Rochester	WBBF	950	AM	SUN 10AM-1PM
Seneca Falls	WSFW	99.3	FM	SAT 12:30PM-3:30PM
Wash. Mills	WTLB	1310	AM	SUN 9AM-12N

STATE & CITY	STATION	FREQ.	BAND	DAY & TIME
Oklahoma				
Bartlesville	KWON	1400	AM	SUN 6PM-9PM
Henryetta	KHEN	1590	AM	SUN 2PM-5PM
	KHEN	99.5	FM	SIMULCAST
Oklahoma City	KOFM	103.7	FM	SUN 1PM-4PM
Oregon				
Bend	KBND	1110	AM	SUN 1PM-4PM
Coos Bay	KYNG	1420	AM	SUN 12N-3PM
Corvallis	KFLY	1240	AM	SUN 6PM-9PM
Eugene	KBDF	1280	AM	SUN 9AM-12N
Klamath Falls	KAGO	1150	AM	SUN 4PM-7PM
Medford	KYJC	1230	AM	SUN 6PM-9PM
Newport	KNPT	1310	AM	SUN 7PM-10PM
Pendleton	KTIX	1240	AM	SUN 12N-3PM
Portland	KGW	620	AM	SUN 10:30AM-1:30PM
Salem	KSLM	1390	AM	SAT 7PM-10PM
				SUN 1PM-4PM
Tillamook	KTIL	1590	AM	MON 6:30PM-9:30PM
Pennsylvania				
Altoona	WVAM	1430	AM	SAT 12N-3PM
				SUN 6PM-9PM
Bedford	WAYC	1600	AM	SAT 9AM-12N
				SUN 1PM-4PM
Clarion	WWCH	1300	AM	SUN 1:30PM-4:30PM
Clearfield	WCPA	900	AM	SUN 1PM-4PM
Erie	WJET	1400	AM	SUN 5PM-8PM
Hanover	WYCR	98.5	FM	SAT 9AM-12N
				SUN 12N-3PM
Harrisburg	WKBO	1230	AM	SUN 12N-3PM
Honesdale	WDNH	1590	AM	SUN 1PM-4PM
Lafayette Hill	WZZD	990	AM	SUN 8AM-11AM
Latrobe	WQTW	1570	AM	FRI 2PM-5PM
Lykens	WQIN	1290	AM	SAT 1PM-4PM
New Castle	WKST	1280	AM	SAT 9AM-12N

Partially pictured here, *AT40*'s 1978 Listening Directory, was available free to listeners and provided information about every subscribing radio station – city, state, call letters, frequency, and broadcast day and time.

417. 06-24-78 **Program #782-13**
Book of Records: The Temptations & Jackson Five share a soul chart feat
program note: Casey promos upcoming special
story: Frankie Valli's voice and group changes
story: Barry White's Midas touch
story: Holland-Dozier-Holland's songwriting success
story: Abba receives Soviet Union permission for record release
story: Andy Gibb is only 1970's solo artist to have 3 consecutive #1 records
story: Michael Johnson's worst year
program mention: Paul McCartney's mood setting for "With A Little Luck"
question: biggest TV theme record
question: capsule history of *AT40* (now heard on more than 500 stations)

418. 07-01-78 **Program #783-1**
SPECIAL: Top 40 Superstars Of The 1970's
for a complete list of records in this special, see Rob Durkee's *American Top 40: The Countdown of the Century*

TO: AMERICAN TOP 40 PROGRAM DIRECTORS

FROM: Tom Rounds, Watermark

June 16, 1978

I've asked our creative consultant Don Bustany to draft a statement regarding the Billy Joel record presently in the countdown. Here's Don's report:

> There's an interesting song in the countdown now that we want to call to your attention. It's interesting because, without even the hint of an off-color utterance, it could be controversial depending upon your audience and your community. The song is "ONLY THE GOOD DIE YOUNG" by Billy Joel. He censures the Catholic Church on certain counts and he argues against premarital chastity.
>
> In keeping with our policy, we don't omit records from the countdown for editorial reasons. But if any seem to be potentially offensive or too controversial, we do call such matters to your attention. What happens after that is strictly, and properly, up to you, the Licensee.

WATERMARK, INC. 10700 Ventura Blvd., No. Hollywood, California 91604 (213) 980-9490

Accompanying the June 24, 1978 program was this note from Tom Rounds with a comment from Don Bustany regarding Billy Joel's "Only The Good Die Young." The potentially offensive record debuted on *AT40* on June 17, 1978.

AMERICAN TOP 40

presents

The Four Hour Countdown

an idea whose time has come

On the weekend of
October 7-8, 1978,
American Top 40 and its
entire 486 station
network will join the age
of the 3½ minute single
and the 12 minute
commercial hour.

Nothing endures but change
Plato 378 B.C.

And the countdown continues
Casey Kasem 1978 A.D.

WATERMARK 213/980-9490

A milestone announcement in *AT40*'s history, this advertisement appeared in the August 5, 1978 edition of *Billboard* magazine.

419. 07-08-78 **Program #783-2**
GUEST HOST: Mark Elliott
story: The Rolling Stones' LP chart feat
story: Barry Manilow's LP sales feat
story: Steely Dan refuses public appearances
story: Steve Martin is hottest new comedian
story: Eric Clapton's heroin addiction
question: artist with #1 record in most consecutive years
question: married duos with most Top 10 hits
odd chart stat: eight debut records
program note: 16 debut records are played, which include eight new records from 07-01-78 & eight debut records from 07-08-78 chart
portion played: Chattanooga Choo Choo - Glenn Miller
program error: Mark answers a question regarding artists with #1 records for most consecutive years; exact letter/writer from 04-22-78 program

420. 07-15-78 **Program #783-3**
whatever happened to: Tony Sheridan
story: Copacabana Night Club profile
story: *Grease* soundtrack sales
story: Barbra Streisand opposes a nose job
story: Foreigner member goes deaf
story: foreign country with most *Billboard* #1 records
program mention: scalped ticket prices for a Rolling Stones concert
portion played: Will You Still Love Me Tomorrow - The Shirelles
portion played: My Bonnie - The Beatles with Tony Sheridan
question: biggest artist from a non-English speaking country
question: #1 record titles containing food
question: most common pre-Top 40 artist profession
odd chart stat: 18 male artists in the Top 40
program error: during the outcue of Walter Egan's "Magnet And Steel," Casey stated "...at #36, moving up five..."; actually, it was at #26

421. 07-22-78 **Program #783-4**
story: Quincy Jones' talent extended to other artists
story: Roberta Flack is Rubina Flake
story: Foreigner's identity problem
story: The Singing Nun faces possible jail time
story: RSO records artists having unprecedented chart performance
story: Abba's net profit greater than auto manufacturer Saab
story: Meatloaf's "Two Out Of Three Ain't Bad" used Elvis Presley record
portion played: I Want You, I Need You, I Love You - Elvis Presley
question: group and female artist with most #1 LPs
question: female artist with LP on chart for longest span of time
odd chart stat: RSO Records' artists in #1 position for 29 out of 32 weeks

422. 07-29-78 **Program #783-5**
story: Steve Martin sold Disneyland guidebooks
story: The Rolling Stones' good & bad image
story: Quincy Jones profile
story: Motown Records special report
story: Todd Rundgren does it himself
story: Jefferson Starship's skateboarding guitarist
odd chart stat: Gerry Rafferty's "Baker Street" at #2 for six consecutive weeks
Book of Records: Pat Boone's consecutive-weeks-in-Top 40 chart feat
question: second time around Top 40 records
question: second most successful Top 40 group
program note: after this program, due to pending four-hour format change, Casey no longer uses the in-program promo "...three hours once a week, and you know where your favorite songs are....."

423. 08-05-78 Program #783-6
story: Paul McCartney's pet chicken taxi ride
story: The Rolling Stones chart performance
story: Bob Seger saxophonist's concert attraction
story: Quincy Jones' 1977 Grammy Award
story: similarity of "Rivers of Babylon" & "How Dry I Am"
story: Olivia Newton-John saved the dolphins
question: biggest live recording to reach the Top 40
question: artist with most novelty records
Book of Records: Top 40's longest leap into #1 position

424. 08-12-78 Program #783-7
story: Jefferson Starship caused a riot
story: Electric Light Orchestra's Hollywood billboard
story: The Rolling Stones' concert income
story: The Gibb's are the most successful Top 40 family
record origin: Peter & Gordon's "A World Without Love"
Book of Records: Gerry Rafferty's "Baker Street" chart feat
program note: Casey corrects himself for crediting Phil Spector as the producer of The Shirelles' "Will You Still Love Me Tomorrow"
question: Top 10 debut records
question: artists with more than one #1 record-of-the-year

425. 08-19-78 Program #783-8
odd chart stat: Top 14 positions remain unchanged from previous week
story: first anniversary memorial of Elvis Presley's death
story: King Tut's touring tomb
story: "Baker Street" saxophonist received recording contract
story: three Bible-producing records
long version: Macho Man - Village People
whatever happened to: Wilson Pickett
question: youngest artist with a Top 40 record
question: 1970's recording act with most Top 10 records
oldie played: Mystery Train - Elvis Presley

INTRO ONLY CHART EXPLANATION

Now let me mention something that the Chart Buffs among you have already noticed.

~~By the way, you may have noticed that many songs during the past hour~~ The Hits From Back at Number 14 on up through number 2 — stayed in the same position as last week. Well, when we tallied it up... we discovered that the Top 14 positions in the survey remain the same.

And when we checked with the Director of Billboard's Chart Department, Bill Wardlow, he confirmed it for us: never before in the 38-year history of the CHART have so many songs at the top of the SURVEY held the same position for two weeks in a row. The reason for it now is the big sales and frequent airplay all of these songs are getting.

Well, now...before we hear the Number One song on the pop chart, let's see what's at the top of the other charts:

With his own handwritten changes, here's one of Casey Kasem's script cards used in recording the August 19, 1978 show. A rare chart occurrence made this show extra special – the previous week's Top 14 records remained unchanged.

426. 08-26-78 **Program #783-9**
program note: Casey reads a listener letter and plays the first Long Distance Dedication; encourages other listeners to write
long distance dedication: Desiree - Neil Diamond
story: Cheryl Ladd's fame due to commercials
story: Barry Manilow's breakfast treat
story: recorded music popularity special report
story: Barry Gibb's one-year #1 songwriting feat
story: Donna Summer's disco chart feat
story: Anne Murray's singing attitude
question: artist with same-title, different-version chart records
question: biggest #1 comedy LP

427. 09-02-78 **Program #783-10**
GUEST HOST: Larry McKay
***Billboard* report error: three records, coincidentally by solo female artists in the first hour - Rita Coolidge, Cheryl Ladd and Barbra Streisand - were in the wrong chart positions**
odd chart stat: three Beatle re-makes in the Top 40
story: Barbra Streisand's acting and singing feat
story: Boston debut LP challenges The Beatles
story: Walter Egan's full moon
story: Foreigner's Mick Jones snubbed by The Beatles
Book of Records: Herb Alpert & The Tijuana Brass' LP sales feat
question: biggest LP of the 1970's
question: artist with most consecutive #1 LPs

I remember being the P.D. at W.E.R.K. in 1965 when we first signed on the air that Valentine's Day......(We) soon had the opportunity to sign-on as an affiliate to the growing AT40 worldwide network. Or course we jumped on it and became, I believe, one of the pioneer stations to join.........Imagine my delight when I was asked to fill-in for Casey when I was at KIIS-AM in L.A. to be guest host on the Labor Day '78 show. Wow, was I full of myself, or what? I recall going to their studio on Cahuenga Blvd. West in Hollywood and working with associate producer Nikki Wine for approximately 3 or 4 hours. She was great (as) Don Bustany's "right-hand" who obviously did all the "detail" work on the show. (During the program's production) they let me hear the intros to all the songs on the countdown so I could get a "feel" for the tempo and "flow" of the music I was presenting. This really helped me "get into it." I also remember listening to (that) Labor Day performance while vacationing in Laguna Beach, California with the girl who would bcome my wife less than two years later. Tragically, I learned that Nikki Wine (who was a guiding force behind AT40's success back then) died of leukemia in her mid 40's sometime in the early '90's. Very sad. I received a vinyl copy of that show and later my son, who by-the-way is now the production director of alternative rock, "The Buzz" in West Palm Beach, Florida, transferred the recording to compact disc for me. So, luckily, I have a pristine copy of the entire show.

Larry McKay, one-time *AT40* guest host and former program director at *AT40* affiliate WERK in Muncie, Indiana

428. 09-09-78

Program #783-11
story: Toni Tennille's backstage problem with The Beach Boys
story: Chuck Berry, living legend
story: Anne Murray's gold record feat
story: Kenny Loggins' lack of solo artist success
story: A Taste Of Honey's multi-chart feat
story: The Beatles' "Got To Get You Into My Life" chart feat
question: record with most consecutive weeks in Top 40
question: American male group with most #1 records
long distance dedication: If You Leave Me Now – Chicago

429. 09-16-78

Program #783-12
odd chart stat: two debut records
story: A Taste Of Honey's female lead musicians
story: Gerry Rafferty refuses concert tours
story: Bill Graham special report
story: Andy Gibb's #1 record chart feat
story: Robin Gibb's "Sesame Street Fever" LP
story: The Who's odd chart feat
question: female artist with most charted LPs
question: twins in the Top 40
portion played: When - Kalin Twins (also see 01-13-79)
lyric alert: memo from executive producer Tom Rounds which accompanied program alerts subscribing radio stations to the potentially controversial lyric content of Meatloaf's debut record "Paradise By The Dashboard Light"
edited long version: Paradise By The Dashboard Light - Meatloaf
long distance dedication: Sometimes When We Touch - Dan Hill

430. 09-23-78

Program #783-13
story: Linda Ronstadt, re-make queen
story: Foxy banned from playing "Get Off"
story: Alicia Bridges was a 13-year-old disk jockey
long distance dedication: Summer Nights - John Travolta & Olivia Newton-John
Book of Records: Hal Blaine's gold record feat
question: biggest record with male name in title
question: artist with most Top 40 instrumental records
edited long version: Paradise By The Dashboard Light - Meatloaf

431. 09-30-78

Program #783-14
story: Carly Simon's failed sister duet
story: Bob Seger's difficult Detroit departure
story: The Who's Keith Moon remembered by Pete Townshend
story: The Captain & Tennille nearly ruined by TV
story: Exile's record label instability
story: The Rolling Stones' Top 10 LP chart feat
long distance dedication: You Needed Me - Anne Murray
portion played: Winkin' Blinkin' & Nod - Simon Sisters
question: artists using Mr., Miss or Mrs. in their name
question: artist with most different recordings of the same song
question: youngest #1 artist of the 1970's

TO: AT40 SUBSCRIBERS

FROM: TOM ROUNDS, WATERMARK

SEPTEMBER 9, 1978

Good old Meatloaf is back with an 8 minute record that could bring the wrath of some of your more outspoken listeners down upon you. We have edited it down to 5:00, but I guarantee you if played in any length it will get all kinds of response, some of which may be rather nasty.

We always play everything that makes the Forty and we advise you to exercise your own discretion in exorcizing this demon from the Countdown. You'll find it conveniently located, this week at least, at number 40... first record in the show.

As a reminder, there are just three weeks to go until AT40 enlarges to a four hour show. There'll be lots of new ingredients in the Countdown, and we're eager for your reaction.

Thanks!

WATERMARK, INC. 10700 Ventura Blvd., No. Hollywood, California 91604 (213) 980-9490

Here's another Tom Rounds memo that alerted stations to a potentially offensive record. This time it's Meatloaf's "Paradise By The Dashboard Light" which debuted September 16, 1978.

WATERMARK, INC. 10700 Ventura Blvd., No. Hollywood, California 91604 (213) 980-9490

TO: AT40 SUBSCRIBERS

FROM: Tom Rounds

September 23, 1978

Casey, Nikki, Don, Sandy, Peter and I finished AT40 tracking late Wednesday night (Casey's been filming a "Charlie's Angels" episode this week) and we all wanted to go out and drink a toast to all you guys who have given us so much support over the years. You see, it was program #783-14, the final three hour AMERICAN TOP 40, something like 431 consecutive countdowns since July 4, 1970. But we, and the 12 or so other people who take an active part in getting AT40 together every week, decided instead just to keep you in our thoughts...and get a good night's sleep, in preparation for a final week of finishing touches on the new 4-hour show.

But we wanted you to know that you are the reason for the incredible success of AMERICAN TOP 40...your handling of it, getting it on the air, promoting, selling, feedback complimentary and critical, your talking it up in the business, your faith in and commitment to good radio.

We just wanted to share our excitement over our new beginning and renew our pledge to give you a production you're proud to air... every week. Program #784-1...the first four hour AMERICAN TOP 40... is scheduled for broadcast the weekend of October 7-8.

Thanks!

This Tom Rounds memo commemorates the last production and recording session for the 3-hour version of *AT40*. Note that he correctly identified the September 30, 1978 show as being #431.

432. 10-07-78

Program #784-1
program note: *American Top 40* expands to a weekly, four-hour program
program note: Casey begins archiving the #1 records of the 1970's, three per week; feature continues until completed 06-21-80
long distance dedication: Sunshine On My Shoulders - John Denver
long distance dedication: One Tin Soldier - Coven
question: American artist with most #1 records since 1970
story: Elton John's duet
story: Carly Simon's stuttering problem
story: Boston's Tom Scholz worked for Polaroid
story: The Everly Brothers used tom-toms first
story: Mick Jagger's live entertainer claim
story: songs with numbers in title
story: Linda Ronstadt's LP sales feat
story: Debby Boone's support for deaf children
story: Fleetwood Mac's success with "Rumours"
story: Olivia Newton-John's Top 10 record feat
story: Aerosmith guitarist Steve Tyler's automobile accident
archive #1 record played: Raindrops Keep Falling On My Head - B.J. Thomas
archive #1 record played: I Want You Back - Jackson Five
archive #1 record played: Venus - Shocking Blue
oldie played: Don't Go Breaking My Heart - Elton John & Kiki Dee
oldie played: Dreams - Fleetwood Mac
oldie played: Til I Kissed You - Everly Brothers
oldie played: You Light Up My Life - Debby Boone

433. 10-14-78

Program #784-2
story: Boz Scaggs' *Saturday Night Fever* loss
story: The Who's Keith Moon chartered a jet to a canceled concert
story: Santana managed by a San Francisco barber
story: "Almost Like Being In Love" is from *Brigadoon*
story: Commodores' "Three Times A Lady" inspired by Lionel Richie, Sr.
story: Loggins & Messina's partnership
question: Top 40 record with the most up and down chart movements
question: artist with most charted LPs without a Top 40 record
program note: Casey mentions that he has a role in this week's episode of TV's *Charlie's Angels*
Book of Records: Carole King's singer/songwriter success
long distance dedication: Afternoon Delight - Starland Vocal Band
long distance dedication: Knowing Me Knowing You - Abba
oldie played: Bad Bad Leroy Brown - Jim Croce
oldie played: Lowdown - Boz Scaggs
oldie played: Evil Ways - Santana
archive #1 record played: Thank You - Sly & Family Stone
archive #1 record played: Bridge Over Troubled Water - Simon & Garfunkel
archive #1 record played: Let It Be - Beatles

434. 10-21-78

Program #784-3
story: *Saturday Night Fever* soundtrack update
story: Paul Davis slept on the studio floor
story: white artists' soul chart feat
story: songwriter Jim Webb given Hollywood advice
story: Mick Jagger has no house, no cars, no yacht
portion played: Tequila - The Champs
question: fewest number of words sung on a #1 record
question: longest span of time on chart for non-#1 record
question: record on Hot 100 longest without making the Top 40

TO: AT40 SUBSCRIBERS

FROM: Tom Rounds

September 23, 1978

Here's the first of the four hour AMERICAN TOP 40's...fatter, jucier, smoother and, in our opinion, better listening than ever.

Now, we'd like your feedback. We're especially interested in getting your comments on pacing, extras (oldies), and anything having to do with the feel of the show. Drop us a line or call Brian, Jeff, Gary or me at (800) 423-2502 or (213) 980-9490.

And please pass this information on to your board person: There is a new closing theme at the end of hours one, two and three. We're letting the entire cut play out to its conclusion... about 1:00 after end of voice. End of voice now comes at 47:30 (counting recommended local commercial inserts) instead of the old 48:30.

The new closing theme is there if you want to play it, however, we suggest you use it as emergency fill only and dump out after :15 or :20 following end of voice.

And it wouldn't hurt if you once again reminded everyone...traffic, sales, etc., that AMERICAN TOP 40 hours now allow for 12 minutes of commercial.

Thanks!

This memo accompanied the first 4-hour *AT40* program which was dated October 7, 1978. As noted, the show included a new closing theme.

434. 10-21-78

Program #784-3 (CONTINUED)
long distance dedication: Hey Deannie - Shaun Cassidy
long distance dedication: Colour My World - Chicago
program note: a jingle is used to introduce the long distance dedications
archive #1 record played: ABC - Jackson Five
archive #1 record played: American Woman - Guess Who
archive #1 record played: Everything Is Beautiful - Ray Stevens
oldie played: This Will Be - Natalie Cole
oldie played: Stayin' Alive - Bee Gees
oldie played: Superstition - Stevie Wonder

435. 10-28-78

Program #784-4
story: Randy Newman relatives receiving Academy Award nominations
story: Diana Ross & The Supremes' chart performances
story: Player's drummer quit the Ice Follies
story: The Captain & Tennille's wedding
story: *American Top 40*'s first #1 record
story: Foreigner member's tennis injury
story: The Beatles' farewell song
long distance dedication: Those Were The Days - Mary Hopkin
long distance dedication: Best Thing That Ever Happened To Me - Gladys Knight & The Pips
program note: jingle is not used to introduce the long distance dedications
question: female singer with most Top 10 LPs
question: #1 record taking longest amount of time to fall off chart
odd chart stat: "Hot Child In The City" completes a 21-week chart climb to #1
oldie played: Someday We'll Be Together - Diana Ross & Supremes
oldie played: Short People - Randy Newman
archive #1 record played: The Long & Winding Road - Beatles
archive #1 record played: The Love You Save - Jackson Five
archive #1 record played: Mama Told Me - Three Dog Night

436. 11-04-78

Program #784-5
story: The Commodores' big break
story: "You Needed Me" writer tore up first draft
story: promotion of "Rock Around The Clock"
story: Barry Gibb wrote songs with five co-writers
story: Bread disbanded and re-grouped
record origin: Barbra Streisand & Neil Diamond's "You Don't Bring Me Flowers"
question: soul record during the 1970's with most weeks at #1
question: recording artists with shortest & longest names
question: family act with most Top 40 records during the 1970's
long distance dedication: The Way We Were - Barbra Streisand
long distance dedication: Even Now - Barry Manilow
oldie played: Rock Around The Clock - Bill Haley & Comets
archive #1 record played: Close To You - Carpenters
archive #1 record played: Make It With You - Bread
archive #1 record played: War - Edwin Starr

One week in 1978, I was living at my aunt's house and she was not a fan of Sunday morning radio, even if it was AT40. Not wanting to miss the show, I asked if there was a radio somewhere in the house so I could listen to the program without disturbing her. She mumbled something about the car radio, so I took her car keys and went outside and listened to AT40 in her car. All four hours of it. And yes, I caught holy hell when they tried to start the car that afternoon and discovered that I had drained the battery.

Chuck Miller, author of *Warman's American Records*, writer for *Goldmine Magazine*, and a longtime *AT40* listener

437. 11-11-78 **Program #784-6**
Book of Records: Jim Reeves' country chart feat
story: Foxy's drummer threw out toy drums
story: The Beach Boys' lead vocalist changes
story: origin of the San Diego Chicken
story: Diana Ross' #1 record feat
story: Motown Records' success
program note: Casey relates only one story ("Foxy's drummer.........") that pertains to current Top 40
question: most Top 40 appearances by different artists with the same record
odd chart stat: Donna Summer's back-to-back #1 records
long distance dedication: The Right Thing To Do - Carly Simon
long distance dedication: Easy - Commodores
archive #1 record played: Ain't No Mountain High Enough - Diana Ross
archive #1 record played: Cracklin' Rosie - Neil Diamond
archive #1 record played: I'll Be There - Jackson Five
oldie played: Sloop John B - Beach Boys
oldie played: I Heard It Through The Grapevine - Marvin Gaye

438. 11-18-78 **Program #784-7**
story: Paul Anka's romance with Annette Funicello
story: reminiscing Woodstock
story: posthumous #1 records
story: Eric Carmen's 'homemade' audition
story: Dr. Hook, riches to rags
story: the death of Chicago's Terry Kath
story: Gino Vanelli's desperation to record
odd chart stat: The Who's "Who Are You" falls out of the Top 40, from #14 to #52
odd chart stat: The Bee Gees' "Too Much Heaven" debuted on the Hot 100 at #35
question: three artists hit #1 with same record
long version: MacArthur Park – Donna Summer
long version: YMCA - Village People
production error: drag on Casey's outcue of "YMCA"
long distance dedication: If - Bread
long distance dedication: Can't Smile Without You - Barry Manilow
oldie played: Sittin' On The Dock Of The Bay - Otis Redding
oldie played: Woodstock - Crosby, Stills, Nash & Young
archive #1 record played: I Think I Love You - Partridge Family
archive #1 record played: Tears Of A Clown - Smokey Robinson & Miracles
archive #1 record played: My Sweet Lord - George Harrison

439. 11-25-78 **Program #784-8**
story: The Beatles' "Sgt. Pepper" LP picture disk
story: The Edwin Hawkins Singers' gospel group chart feat
story: Village People member nearly died on *What's My Line?* TV show
story: Chaka Khan turned down Stevie Wonder
story: Donna Summer's single & LP chart feat
long distance dedication: Goodbye Girl - David Gates
long distance dedication: You Can't Hurry Love – Supremes
odd chart stat: Chic's "Le Freak" climbs from #37 to #6
odd chart stat: Kenny Loggins' "Whenever I Call You Friend" falls from #9 to #35
odd chart stat: Exile's "Kiss You All Over" falls from #7 to #33
question: family act with most Top 40 records
program note: Casey promos upcoming special
program note: Casey mentions that he will be riding the *American Top 40* float in the televised Hollywood Christmas Parade on November 26

439. 11-25-78 **Program #784-8 (CONTINUED)**
oldie played: Oh Happy Day - Edwin Hawkins Singers
oldie played: Handy Man - James Taylor
oldie played: Satisfaction - Rolling Stones
LP cut played: Sgt. Pepper's Lonely Hearts Club Band - Beatles
archive #1 record played: Knock Three Times - Tony Orlando & Dawn
archive #1 record played: One Bad Apple - Osmonds
archive #1 record played: Me & Bobby McGee - Janis Joplin

440. 12-02-78 **Program #784-9**
story: Rick Nelson is most successful TV actor turned pop star
record origin: Barbra Streisand & Neil Diamond's "You Don't Bring Me Flowers"
story: Paul McCartney's songwriting success
story: Kiss members released solo LPs
story: Elton John's LP chart feat
story: Fleetwood Mac's LP chart feat
story: Anne Murray's pop & country chart feat
story: Alicia Bridges' slow-climbing chart feat
story: Alice Cooper committed to alcohol clinic
program note: Casey promos upcoming special
long distance dedication: So Into You - Atlantic Rhythm Section
archive #1 record played: Just My Imagination - Temptations
archive #1 record played: Joy To The World - Three Dog Night
archive #1 record played: Brown Sugar - Rolling Stones
oldie played: Garden Party - Rick Nelson
oldie played: Over My Head - Fleetwood Mac
oldie played: Yesterday - Beatles

441. 12-09-78 **Program #784-10**
story: The Fifth Dimension's "Aquarias/Let The Sunshine In" chart feat
story: Chicago goes unrecognized
story: Abba's "Waterloo" performed at international competition
story: The Captain & Tennille's success with Greenfield-Sedaka songs
story: Carly Simon's controversial "You're So Vain"
story: Elton John's Beatle-like success
program note: Casey promos upcoming special "...two weeks from today..."
odd chart stat: Billy Joel has three records from "The Stranger" LP simultaneously on the Hot 100
question: artist with first three LPs at #1
long distance dedication: Precious & Few - Climax
long distance dedication: Just Remember I Love You - Firefall
archive #1 record played: Want Ads - Honeycone
archive #1 record played: It's Too Late - Carole King
archive #1 record played: Indian Reservation - Raiders
oldie played: You're So Vain - Carly Simon
oldie played: Tracks Of My Tears - Smokey Robinson & The Miracles
oldie played: Waterloo - Abba
oldie played: Aquarius/Let The Sunshine In - Fifth Dimension

WATERMARK, INC. 10700 Ventura Blvd., No. Hollywood, California 91604 (213) 980-9490

TO: AMERICAN TOP 40 Subscribers

FROM: Steve Buth - Watermark Operations

RE: THE TOP 100 HITS OF 1978 - Eight Hour Version

December 9, 1978

For those stations electing to air program #784-12 (#100 - #51) and program #784-13 (#50 - #1) back to back, here is a suggestion for accomplishing this feat. At the end of side 4B on program #784-12, Casey does the outro for #51 Imaginary Lover by the Atlanta Rhythm Section. There is a beat between the end of the outro and the beginning of the closing theme. It is at this point that you should cut away from the program and go to a commercial, a station jingle or whatever you have planned. I strongly suggest that you listen to the disc in advance.

For those stations that do not plan to run all eight hours at once, just let the disc track after the outro for #51. The theme will hit, Casey will close the show and invite everyone to join him next week for the second half of "THE TOP 100 HITS OF 1978".

HAVE A HAPPY HOLIDAY SEASON

In this memo Steve Buth provided suggested directions for station engineers to coordinate the transition of Part 1 and Part 2 of the Top 100 of 1978.

A page from the 1978 marketing brochure provided a list of those credited with producing, distributing, and making *AT40* an overall success.

442. 12-16-78

Program #784-11
program note: original version of "You Don't Bring Me Flowers," produced by radio station WAKY (Louisville, KY) program director, is featured at #1
program note: Casey promos upcoming special
program note: Casey plays six Christmas records as program extras
long distance dedication: This One's For You - Barry Manilow
story: "The Christmas Song" written in untraditional setting
story: Glen Campbell is most successful studio musician turned singer
story: "Step Into Christmas" is Elton John's only non-chart feat
story: Queen's elaborate concert stage description
story: The Carpenters' "Merry Christmas Darling" record sales
story: The Beach Boys' early days
story: Bing Crosby's "White Christmas" record sales feat
story: the "Oh Holy Night" Christmas miracle
question: most successful instrumental LP artist
oldie played: Christmas Song - Nat King Cole
oldie played: Little St. Nick - Beach Boys
oldie played: Oh Holy Night - Nat King Cole
oldie played: White Christmas - Bing Crosby
oldie played: Step Into Christmas - Elton John
oldie played: Merry Christmas Darling - Carpenters
archive #1 record played: You've Got A Friend - James Taylor
archive #1 record played: How Can You Mend A Broken Heart - Bee Gees
archive #1 record played: Uncle Albert/Admiral Halsey - Paul & Linda McCartney

443. 12-23-78

Program #784-12
SPECIAL: Top 100 Of 1978 (#100 - 51) (based on *Billboard*'s year-end Top 100) for a complete list of records in this special, see Rob Durkee's *American Top 40: The Countdown of the Century*
long version: Deacon Blues - Steely Dan

444. 12-30-78

Program #784-13
SPECIAL: Top 100 Of 1978 (#50 - 1) (based on *Billboard*'s year-end Top 100) for a complete list of records in this special, see Rob Durkee's *American Top 40: The Countdown of the Century*

1979

445. 01-06-79

Program #791-1
GUEST HOST: Mark Elliott
long distance dedication: When Will I See You Again - Three Degrees
long distance dedication: Feels So Good - Chuck Mangione
production error: memo accompanying show to radio stations gives instructions to edit out Andy Gibb's "An Everlasting Love", which was played by mistake in place of "(Our Love) Don't Throw It All Away"
flipside played: Fat Bottom Girls - Queen
odd chart stat: The Eagles' "Please Come Home For Christmas" is the highest debuting Christmas song in 18 years
story: George Benson's morally offensive LP lawsuit
story: The Blues Brothers' *Saturday Night Live* origin
story: Rod Stewart hates the music industry
story: Donna Summer's "MacArthur Park" chart feat
story: Paul Simon's aliases
story: artists at #1 during the 1970's
question: demographics of 513 #1 records
oldie played: Loves Me Like A Rock - Paul Simon
oldie played: On Broadway - George Benson
oldie played: Promised Land - Elvis Presley
oldie played: How Deep Is Your Love - Bee Gees
archive #1 record played: Go Away Little Girl - Donny Osmond
archive #1 record played: Maggie May - Rod Stewart
archive #1 record played: Gypsies, Tramps & Thieves - Cher

446. 01-13-79

Program #791-2
story: YMCA unhappy with The Village People
story: Barry Manilow The Recluse
story: Alan Freed's concert fiasco
story: records with number in title
story: biggest hit recorded by two recording acts
story: Cheryl Lynn's *Gong Show* big break
story: Kenny Rogers' recording studio policy
story: Creedence Clearwater Revival's #2 chart feat
story: Linda Ronstadt's 1968 feat
whatever happened to: Kalin Twins
portion played: When - Kalin Twins (see 09-16-78)
long distance dedication: You Made Me Believe In Magic - Bay City Rollers
long distance dedication: Love Is Here And Now You're Gone - Supremes
program note: Casey's reading of a letter from a long distance dedication writer includes 'soap opera' background music
odd chart stat: Andy Gibb's "(Our Love) Don't Throw It All Away" is in position #9 for fifth consecutive week
archive #1 record played: Theme From *Shaft* - Isaac Hayes
archive #1 record played: Family Affair - Sly & Family Stone
archive #1 record played: Brand New Key - Melanie
oldie played: #9 Dream - John Lennon
oldie played: I'm Gonna Make You Love Me - Supremes & Temptations
oldie played: Different Drum - Stone Poneys
oldie played: Lookin' Out My Back Door - Creedence Clearwater Revival

447. 01-20-79

Program #791-3
odd chart stat: Chic's "Le Freak" returns to #1 for the third time
long distance dedication: My Way - Elvis Presley
long distance dedication: Ready To Take A Chance Again - Barry Manilow
program note: Casey's reading of a letter from a long distance dedication writer includes 'soap opera' background music
story: Christmas records with post-holiday chart runs
story: Barry Manilow's hamburger sales
story: the meaning of "The Wreck of the Edmund Fitzgerald"
story: RSO Records' Robert Stigwood is master showman
story: Rose Royce's lead singer nearly joined Undisputed Truth
story: longest playing #1 record
story: The Carpenters disliked by the Minneapolis Symphony Orchestra
question: Top 40 game show theme
question: biggest rock era duet
archive #1 record played: American Pie - Don McLean
archive #1 record played: Let's Stay Together - Al Green
archive #1 record played: Without You - Nilsson
oldie played: Superstar - Carpenters
oldie played: The Wreck Of The Edmund Fitzgerald - Gordon Lightfoot

448. 01-27-79

Program #791-4
story: Nigel Olsson out of Elton John's shadow
story: Talking Heads' boredom with painting
story: The Bee Gees' 'mining disaster'
story: Nicolette Larson's *Rolling Stone* feat
story: Evelyn 'Champagne' King's janitor work
story: Marvin Gaye's female partners
question: artist in third place with Top 40 records
question: artist with most 1978 hits
long distance dedication: Looks Like We Made It - Barry Manilow
long distance dedication: Back In The U.S.A. - Linda Ronstadt
archive #1 record played: Heart Of Gold - Neil Young
archive #1 record played: A Horse With No Name – America
archive #1 record played: First Time Ever I Saw Your Face - Roberta Flack
oldie played: Neither One Of Us - Gladys Knight & The Pips
oldie played: Shame - Evelyn 'Champagne' King
oldie played: You're All I Need To Get By - Marvin Gaye & Tammi Terrell
oldie played: New York Mining Disaster 1941 - Bee Gees

UREGENT---READ THIS BEFORE JANUARY 5, 1979

TO: AMERICAN TOP 40 SUBSCRIBERS
FROM: Tom Rounds, Watermark
RE: Repairs to be made in #791-1

January 2, 1979

There is an unfortunate error in this weekends show, #791-1, scheduled for broadcast the weekend of January 6-7, 1979.

In the <u>first segment</u> (between the opening and C-1) of hour 4-A, the second record (#9) is the <u>incorrect cut</u>. Instead of playing "OUR LOVE DON'T THROW IT ALL AWAY" by Andy Gibb, we played Gibb's "AN EVERLASING LOVE".

We would very much appreciate your taking steps to correct this error by playing "OUR LOVE DON'T THROW IT ALL AWAY" at #9.

There are two ways to pull this off:

1. Dub the two-record segment to tape and edit in "OUR LOVE..."

2. Cue "OUR LOVE..." up and segue into it cold from the end of Mark Elliot's intro, which reads:

"...Here's Andy with OUR LOVE DON'T THROW IT ALL AWAY".

(There's a convenient hole to get out of "EVERLASTING LOVE" with).

Coming out, just delete the outro of the record and go to:

..."For Casey Kasem this is Mark Elliott".

We regret the error and hope you'll understand that these things just happen sometimes. We promise not to do it again unitl 1984.

Happy New Year!

JAY - I'VE RECORDED THAT FIRST SEGMENT OF SIDE 4A. IT'S [illegible] ATTACHED TO THE AT 40 BOX (UNIQUE COAST TO COAST SINGLE)

WATERMARK, INC. 10700 Ventura Blvd., No. Hollywood, California 91604 (213) 980-9490

The January 2, 1979 memo was urgently sent to stations (in an envelope marked "IMPORTANT") after it was determined that the wrong Andy Gibb record had been mixed into the January 6, 1979 program. While this was not the first time an incorrect song was played and wrongly identified, this was the first time an effort was made to ask stations to recitify the problem. The handwritten notation on the memo came from a program director with correction instructions for the station's *AT40* engineer.

449. 02-03-79

Program #791-5
story: The Isley Brothers' longevity chart feat
story: "The Gambler" songwriter's psychic incident
story: Bobby Caldwell's heart-shaped record
story: biggest American group LP debut
story: Chic's "Le Freak" danced by few
story: Herb Alpert's biggest record
story: John Belushi's TV, film and recording success
story: *Animal House* revived "Louie Louie"
question: biggest commercial record
question: biggest foreign language record
long distance dedication: Daddy Don't You Walk So Fast - Wayne Newton
long distance dedication: The Way We Were - Barbra Streisand
archive #1 record played: Oh Girl - Chi-Lites
archive #1 record played: I'll Take You There - Staple Singers
archive #1 record played: Candy Man - Sammy Davis Jr.
oldie played: Louie Louie - Kingsmen
oldie played: New Kid In Town - Eagles
oldie played: That Lady - Isley Brothers
oldie played: This Guy's In Love With You - Herb Alpert

450. 02-10-79

Program #791-6
program note: last show produced by Nikki Wine
program note: Casey plays oldies by Elvis Presley, The Beach Boys, The Temptations and, in artist introductions, mentions each artist's all-time Top 3 records; the biggest of the three is played
archive #1 record played: Song Sung Blue - Neil Diamond
archive #1 record played: Lean On Me - Bill Withers
archive #1 record played: Alone Again (Naturally) - Gilbert O'Sullivan
oldie played: I Can't Get Next To You - Temptations
oldie played: I Can't Help Myself - Four Tops
oldie played: Respect - Aretha Franklin
oldie played: I Get Around - Beach Boys
oldie played: Ain't No Mountain High Enough - Diana Ross
oldie played: All Shook Up - Elvis Presley
story: Aretha Franklin's eight consecutive Grammy Awards
story: Earth, Wind & Fire is 1978's #1 soul band
story: Poco's persistence pays
story: Little Richard gives up rock 'n' roll
story: Billy Joel's popularity credited to radio
story: Diana Ross' solo career success
long distance dedication: Hot Child In The City - Nick Gilder
long distance dedication: Stayin' Alive - Bee Gees
odd chart stat: The Bee Gees' "Tragedy" debuts on the Hot 100 at #29

451. 02-17-79

Program #791-7
story: Rod Stewart censored
story: Santana managed by a barber
story: Dolly Parton's rags-to-riches dream
story: Paul Anka's "One Man Woman" test-marketed
story: Michael Jackson chart appearances
program mention: "Fire" chart appearances
odd chart stat: Ace Frehley's "New York Groove" falls from #13 to #35
long distance dedication: Someday We'll Be Together - Diana Ross & The Supremes
long distance dedication: California Nights - Lesley Gore
question: oldest Top 40 artist
program note: two Diana Ross/Supremes records are played
program correction: Casey reads a letter acknowledging an error in the 01-20-79 program regarding Donna Summer's "Heaven Knows" singing partner
long version: Got To Be Real - Cheryl Lynn
archive #1 record played: Brandy - Looking Glass
archive #1 record played: Black & White - Three Dog Night
archive #1 record played: Baby Don't Get Hooked On Me - Mac Davis
oldie played: Devil Woman - Cliff Richard
oldie played: Got To Be There - Michael Jackson
oldie played: Love Child - Diana Ross & Supremes
oldie played: One Man Woman, One Woman Man - Paul Anka

452. 02-24-79

Program #791-8
program note: Casey introduces a new feature which provides a recap of previous week's Top 3 records, prior to playing the #40 record
program mention: Ian Matthews was Matthews' Southern Comfort lead singer
long distance dedication: You Should Be Dancin' - Bee Gees
long distance dedication: We Are The Champions - Queen
odd chart stat: Dolly Parton's "Baby I'm Burnin'" is the first record simultaneously listed on pop, country and disco charts
odd chart stat: Earth, Wind & Fire's "September" falls from #11 to #35
odd chart stat: three unrelated artists with the same last name - Rod Stewart, Al Stewart & Amii Stewart - are simultaneously in the Top 40 (also occurred on 11-14-70, 11-21-70, 02-19-72, 03-03-79 and 03-10-79) (updated mention 04-28-79)
odd chart stat: fourteen foreign artists in the the Top 40
question: record with most weeks at #2
question: record with most weeks at #1 on country chart
question: youngest Top 40 group
story: Olivia Newton-John questioned success and attractiveness
story: The Bee Gees' true-life prophecy
story: Chicago members hate Chicago IV LP
story: Neil Diamond's college scholarship for athletics
long version: Got To Be Real - Cheryl Lynn
archive #1 record played: Ben - Michael Jackson
archive #1 record played: My Ding-A-Ling - Chuck Berry
archive #1 record played: I Can See Clearly Now - Johnny Nash

453. 03-03-79

Program #791-9
production error: hour #2's closing theme contains the sound of a telephone busy signal
long distance dedication: So Far Away - Carole King
long distance dedication: Please Mr. Postman - The Carpenters
story: The Bee Gees disband and re-group
story: Suzi Quatro's rise to fame
story: The Pointer Sisters' country chart record
story: Nick The Greek's high-stakes card game
story: Nicolette Larson recorded "Lotta Love" on roller skates
question: most successful family act
question: parent's Top 40 appearance after child's appearance
question: solo artist with most Top 40 records in one year
archive #1 record played: Papa Was A Rolling Stone - Temptations
archive #1 record played: I Am Woman - Helen Reddy
archive #1 record played: Me & Mrs. Jones - Billy Paul
oldie played: Bye Bye Love - Everly Brothers
odd chart stat: Barry Manilow's "Somewhere In The Night" falls from #9 to #31
odd chart stat: three unrelated artists with the same last name - Rod Stewart, Al Stewart & Amii Stewart - are simultaneously in the Top 40 (also occurred on 11-14-70, 11-21-70, 02-19-72, 02-24-79 and 03-10-79) (updated mention 04-28-79)

TO: AMERICAN TOP 40 SUBSCRIBERS
FROM: Tom Rounds, WATERMARK

February 17, 1979

WATERMARK, INC. 10700 Ventura Blvd., No. Hollywood, California 91604 (213) 980-9490

We're installing a new feature in the AMERICAN TOP 40 format this week. At the beginning of the show (hour one), Casey begins with a recap of last week's top three songs. (#40 actually occurs after the first commercial break...about 12 minutes in.

We point this out so that programmers and jocks can avoid playing those three songs (in this week's case Rod Stewart, Village People and Olivia Newton-John) near the beginning of AT40.

A quick look at the AT40 log by the preceeding air shift will avoid repetition.

A new feature – replaying the Top 3 records from the previous week's show -- was introduced to subscribing stations in the *AT40* program dated February 24, 1979, as described in this memo.

TO: PROGRAM DIRECTORS, AT40 SUBSCRIBERS

FROM: Don Bustany, Producer, AT40

RE: Song Lyric Content Advisory for #791-11

March 9, 1979

Please check out the lyrics on record #37, "SUPERMAN" by jazz star Herbie Mann.

A couple of lines---sung by an uncredited female group--may be sensitive, depending upon standards in your community and/or your station image.

This isn't to advocate one stand or another regarding this lyric, but simply to alert you to the presence of even the most remotely sensitive program content.

WATERMARK, INC. 10700 Ventura Blvd., No. Hollywood, California 91604 (213) 980-9490

Accompanying the March 17, 1979 program was this note from Don Bustany regarding Herbie Mann's "Superman" which debuted on *AT40* that week.

454. 03-10-79

Program #791-10
question: days-of-the-week in song titles
story: Frank Mills' "Music Box Dancer" played in error
story: Eddie Rabbitt's Elvis Presley decision
story: Bobby Caldwell's songwriting inspiration
story: Neil Diamond's 15-cent check
story: Richard Perry, record producer & hit doctor
story: Doobie Brothers' extracurricular activities
long distance dedication: Time In A Bottle - Jim Croce
long distance dedication: I Just Wanna Stop - Gino Vanelli
archive #1 record played: You're So Vain - Carly Simon
archive #1 record played: Superstition - Stevie Wonder
archive #1 record played: Crocodile Rock - Elton John
odd chart stat: thirteen disco records in the Top 40
odd chart stat: three unrelated artists with the same last name - Rod Stewart, Al Stewart & Amii Stewart - are simultaneously in the Top 40 (also occurred on 11-14-70, 11-21-70, 02-19-72, 02-24-79 and 03-03-79) (updated mention 04-28-79)

455. 03-17-79

Program #791-11
lyric alert: memo from producer Don Bustany which accompanied program alerts subscribing radio stations to the potentially controversial back-up singer lyric content of Herbie Mann's debut record "Superman"
story: Kenny Rogers' music industry book
story: Gloria Gaynor stimulated a soccer win
story: Hollywood's psychiatrist for rock artists
story: Heart's origin
story: The Babys' music video
odd chart stat: Cheryl Lynn's "Got To Be Real" produced by a father-son team
whatever happened to: The Mamas & Papas
program note: Casey re-caps Frank Mills and Bobby Caldwell stories from previous week
question: artist with most Top 40 records during the 1970's
question: record taking the most time to reach the Top 40
program error: in show closing, chart date Casey provides is 03-10-79
long distance dedication: Always & Forever - Heatwave
program mention: Evelyn 'Champagne' King was 'Bubbles'
archive #1 record played: Killing Me Softly - Roberta Flack
archive #1 record played: Love Train - O'Jays
archive #1 record played: Night The Lights Went Out In Georgia - Vicki Lawrence

456. 03-24-79

Program #791-12
odd chart stat: two debut records
odd chart stat: ten female artists in the Top 40
program note: Casey thanks listeners for their long distance dedications, however 'thousands and thousands' have been received, making it impossible to respond to all
long distance dedication: Nights Are Forever Without You - England Dan/John Ford Coley
long distance dedication: Just The Way You Are - Billy Joel
whatever happened to: Creedence Clearwater Revival
story: Anne Murray's profession change
story: The Bee Gees tie with The Rolling Stones
story: Billy Joel credits his wife for his success
story: Barbra Streisand's LP success
story: Judy Davis, celebrity voice teacher
story: Olivia Newton-John's producer auditions 10,000 songs annually
question: group with biggest #1 soul record
portion played: Sixty Minute Man - Dominoes

TO: AT40 SUBSCRIBERS

FROM: TOM ROUNDS, WATERMARK

MARCH 24, 1979

WATERMARK, INC. 10700 Ventura Blvd., No. Hollywood, California 91604 (213) 980-9490

Here's an insider's pre-release announcemnet on upcoming AT40 specials you can file under "4th of July" and "Year-End" programming.

AMERICAN TOP 40 program #793-1, scheduled for broadcast the weekend of July 7-8, 1979, will be a special titled "The 40 Biggest Hits of the Disco Era." On the occasion of AMERICAN TOP 40's ninth anniversary, Casey Kasem goes back to May 25, 1974, the date that "Rock The Boat" by the Hues Corporation first appeared on the Billboard chart. This event marked the first time a record that was already a hit on the disco floor leapt into America's pop mainstream. In the five years since, hundreds of hits driven by the disco beat have appeared on AMERICAN TOP 40. Now, Casey Kasem counts down the 40 biggest...from #40 to #1.

AMERICAN TOP 40 program #794-13, scheduled for broadcast the weekend of December 29-30, 1979 presents the top half of our traditional year end special. New Year's weekend, Casey Kasem counts down the 50 top hits of 1979 in an information packed 4-hour review from #50 to #1.

And AMERICAN TOP 40 program #801-1, scheduled for broadcast the weekend of January 5-6, 1980, presents the seventies' cream of the crop...the 50 top hits of the decade. Our survey period begins January 1, 1970 and covers every memorable Billboard chart year through '79. Almost 2500 records made AMERICAN TOP 40 in the seventies, and these are the 50 biggest.

(Programs 794-13 and 801-1 can be combined into a 8-hour holiday programming package. Re-runs are permitted and recommended).

Tom Rounds' March 24, 1979 memo notified stations of the special AT40 programs scheduled for later that year.

456. 03-24-79 **Program #791-12 (CONTINUED)**
program error: in show closing, chart date Casey provides is 03-17-79
oldie played: Stoney End - Barbra Streisand
archive #1 record played: Tie A Yellow Ribbon 'Round The Old Oak Tree - Dawn
archive #1 record played: You Are The Sunshine Of My Life - Stevie Wonder
archive #1 record played: Frankenstein - Edgar Winter Group

457. 03-31-79 **Program #791-13**
program note: Paul McCartney and George Harrison are featured on both debut and archive records
odd chart stat: The Babys' "Every Time I Think Of You" falls from #13 to #37
odd chart stat: fifteen disco records in the Top 40
odd chart stat: Olivia Newton-John in the Top 40 for 48 weeks in one year
long distance dedication: If You Love Me (Let Me Know) - Olivia Newton-John
long distance dedication: Thank You For Being A Friend - Andrew Gold
story: Deborah Harry is former Playboy bunny
story: Herb (Peaches & Herb) Fame's walk to New York City
story: Dire Straits' first radio airplay of "Sultans Of Swing"
whatever happened to: Lloyd Price
portion played: Personality - Lloyd Price
question: female artist with greatest length of time from debut to #1 records
archive #1 record played: My Love - Paul McCartney & Wings
archive #1 record played: Give Me Love - George Harrison
archive #1 record played: Will It Go Round In Circles - Billy Preston

458. 04-07-79 **Program #792-1**
GUEST HOST: Bumper Morgan
lyric alert: memo from executive producer Tom Rounds which accompanied program alerts subscribing radio stations to the potentially controversial lyric content of The Police's debut record "Roxanne"
portion played: Please Please Me - The Beatles
portion played: I Want To Hold Your Hand - The Beatles
portion played: She Loves You - The Beatles
portion played: Twist & Shout - The Beatles
portion played: Can't Buy Me Love - The Beatles
portion played: The Desiderata - Les Crane
portion played: Deteriorata - National Lampoon
story: Melissa Manchester's *National Lampoon* recording
story: Herb (Peaches & Herb) Fame shot by his road manager
story: Pink Floyd's LP chart feat
story: Rod Stewart's 1970's #1 chart feat
story: The Beatles' April 1964 Top 5 chart feat
story: Australian concert scene
story: The Doobie Brothers' new civic-minded image
story: Poco's concert warm-up-act frustration
question: Top 40 records with the same record title and artist name
question: same-title, different-song records
question: biggest non-singing songwriters
question: biggest fall from #1 position
archive #1 record played: Bad Bad Leroy Brown - Jim Croce
archive #1 record played: The Morning After - Maureen McGovern
archive #1 record played: Touch Me In The Morning - Diana Ross
oldie played: Money - Pink Floyd
odd chart stat: two different records in the Top 40 with the same title: Crazy Love
odd chart stat: Gloria Gaynor's "I Will Survive" returns to #1

TO: AT40 SUBSCRIBERS
FROM: TOM ROUNDS, WATERMARK
MARCH 31, 1979

WATERMARK, INC. 10700 Ventura Blvd., No. Hollywood, California 91604 (213) 980-9490

Jetting in from the Big Apple to relieve the vacationing Casey Kasem this week on AMERICAN TOP 40 is none other than Bumper Morgan. Hailing from Vestal Center, New York, population 923, Bumper left home at an early age to join the Navy, not to sail the seven seas, but to become a communications technician. Which led him directly to the all-night shift at America's only station-in-a-sugar-cane-field, KAHU, Waipahu, Hawaii. Former PD and jock at such stations at WKOP, WENE, WNBF and WINR, Bumper is one of the ace personalities now featured at 99-X, WXLO, New York. He, his wife, Anne, and their two daughters, Candace and Barbara, reside in residential Paramus, New Jersey. Casey returns to the AT40 mike and the Arbitron Spring sweep next week.

LYRIC ALERT

The lyrics in "Roxanne" by the group, Police, may be sensitive in certain markets. The record comes on at #40 this week (Hour 1-A).

The March 31, 1979 memo served two purposes – to introduce Bumper Morgan as guest host for the April 7, 1979 AT40 program and yet another "Lyric Alert" for The Police's "Roxanne."

459. 04-14-79

Program #792-2
long distance dedication: When I Need You - Leo Sayer
long distance dedication: Guitar Man - Bread
story: Amii Stewart's missed acting opportunity
story: Pointer Sisters threatened with church expulsion
story: Rod Stewart impostor
story: analysis of rock star income
story: Herb (Peaches & Herb) Fame's record store recording contract
story: Johnnie Ray cried up the charts
portion played: Cry - Johnnie Ray
question: artists replacing themselves with back-to-back #1 records
odd chart stat: fifteen disco records in the Top 40
archive #1 record played: Brother Louie - Stories
archive #1 record played: Let's Get It On - Marvin Gaye
archive #1 record played: Delta Dawn - Helen Reddy

460. 04-21-79

Program #792-3
long distance dedication: Piano Man - Billy Joel
long distance dedication: Colour My World - Chicago
story: Teddy Pendergrass' women-only concerts
story: Chic's two leaders hate disco
story: Herb (Peaches & Herb) Fame burned money at the U.S. mint
odd chart stat: The Bee Gees' "Love You Inside Out" debuts on the Hot 100 at #37
odd chart stat: twenty-one groups in the Top 40
odd chart stat: sixteen disco records in the Top 40
question: artist with most consecutive weeks in the Top 40
question: most successful country artist on the pop chart during the 1970's
program error: Casey's introduction to Blondie's "Heart Of Glass" reads ".....jumping from #8 last week to #5......"; actually, it was at #3
program error: Casey's introduction to The Bee Gees' "Love You Inside Out" references high debut records and mentions "...back at the beginning of 1970, the last three singles ever released by The Beatles, while they were still together, each debuted on the Hot 100 all the way up in the 40...."; actually, there were only two records
program note: Casey promos his TV appearance on Tom Snyder's *Tomorrow* program
whatever happened to: The Turtles
oldie played: Close The Door - Teddy Pendergrass
archive #1 record played: We're An American Band - Grand Funk Railroad
archive #1 record played: Half Breed - Cher
archive #1 record played: Angie - Rolling Stones

461. 04-28-79

Program #792-4
story: The Allman Brothers in life & death
story: The Jackson Five spanked by their manager
story: The Byrds return to the Top 40
story: Paul McCartney's $20 million recording contract
story: Blondie discovered first in Europe
story: Walter Carlos' sex change to Wendy Carlos
portion played: Switched-On Bach - Walter Carlos
program mention: Rod Stewart impostor caught
program note: listener provides another example of three artists with the same last name simultaneously in Top 40 (02-19-72: Carly Simon, Joe Simon & Paul Simon) (update from 02-24-79 program)
long distance dedication: Think It Over - Cheryl Ladd
long distance dedication: Ready To Take A Chance Again - Barry Manilow

461. 04-28-79 **Program #792-4 (CONTINUED)**
production error: no outcue for Peaches & Herb's "Reunited"
program error: Casey's outcue of Randy Vanwarmer's "Just When I Needed You Most" pointed out "....with one of the hottest songs in the countdown, last week it debuted at 28, this week it moves up ten..."; actually, it was at #28 and had moved up from its debut at #38
odd chart stat: 13 Top 40 records move up two notches
archive #1 record played: Midnight Train To Georgia - Gladys Knight & The Pips
archive #1 record played: Keep On Truckin' - Eddie Kendricks
archive #1 record played: Photograph - Ringo Starr

462. 05-05-79 **Program #792-5**
long distance dedication: Everything I Own - Bread
long distance dedication: I Will Survive - Gloria Gaynor
program note: Casey introduces a new feature, a music trivia mini-quiz, and gives multiple choices for listeners to chose from to determine Elton John's real name
story: April Wine 'smoke-screened' Rolling Stones concert fans
story: The Pointer Sisters stranded
story: Canadian artists special report
story: Cher does not get asked out for a date
story: Frank Mills' basic business skills
question: record with most weeks in the Top 40
question: record with most weeks in the Top 10
whatever happened to: Barry McGuire
archive #1 record played: Top Of The World - Carpenters
archive #1 record played: The Most Beautiful Girl - Charlie Rich
archive #1 record played: Time In A Bottle - Jim Croce
oldie played: Eve Of Destruction - Barry McGuire

463. 05-12-79 **Program #792-6**
lyric alert: memo which accompanied program alerts subscribing radio stations to the potentially offensive lyrics to Rod Stewart's debut record "Ain't Love A Bitch"
odd chart stat: eight debut records
odd chart stat: Donna Summer's "Hot Stuff" climbs from #20 to #3
long distance dedication: The Closer I Get To You - Roberta Flack & Donny Hathaway
long distance dedication: Fire - Pointer Sisters
story: Village People created from newspaper classified ad
story: Herb (Peaches & Herb) Fame's police & music industry pressures
story: G.Q.'s Bronx audition
story: George Harrison's retirement-ending inspiration
story: disco saved New York City
story: Gary U.S. Bonds recruited off the street to sing
portion played: Quarter To Three - Gary U.S. Bonds
mini-quiz: Ringo Starr's real name
program note: Casey promos his appearance on Dinah Shore's TV show
archive #1 record played: The Joker - Steve Miller Band
archive #1 record played: Show And Tell - Al Wilson
archive #1 record played: You're Sixteen - Ringo Starr

This advertisement appeared in the April 28, 1979 edition of Billboard Magazine.

TO: AT40 SUBSCRIBERS
FROM: TOM ROUNDS, WATERMARK
MAY 5, 1979

WATERMARK, INC. 10700 Ventura Blvd., No. Hollywood, California 91604 (213) 980-9490

Casey's doing another TV appearance...this time it'll be on the "Dinah Shore Show" on either of two Tuesdays. He mentions this fact in this week's show in hour II, inside the commercial slot between halves of the split logo indicated by "C-5" on cue sheet 2-B. We left enough space for you to get cleanly out of the mention, if you'd like.

Since Elton John entered the word into the rock and roll lexicon a few years back, we have not been blesses with the word "bitch" again until this week. Rod Stewart's "Ain't Love A Bitch" enters the countdown, and will very likely become Top 10. We mention this fact in case there are subscribers who feel the title and record would offend in markets where there are no bitches.

This week, in hour II, between #'s 25 and 24, there is a feature on disco saving New York. If yours is a station violently opposed to the subject (disco, not New York) check it out.

Here's a memo that covers multiple topics – another Casey Kasem TV appearance, another concern about song lyrics, and a reminder that not all radio stations and radio listeners favored disco music during the late 1970s.

TO: AMERICAN TOP 40 SUBSCRIBERS
FROM: TOM ROUNDS, WATERMARK
DATE: MAY 12, 1979

Here it is...the first annual edition of THE AMERICAN TOP 40 YEARBOOK. We hope you enjoy your complimentary copy.

At Watermark, we're always on the lookout for items that can be used by our subscribers to attract sponsors, through merchandising and promotion, to AMERICAN TOP 40. The yearbook happens to be about the most perfect item for that purpose we can imagine.

We've worked out a cost efficient deal with the publishers of the yearbook, Grossett and Dunlap, whereby you may acquire additional copies of the book, in any quantity, at a 40% discount...$2.97 per copy..off the printed retail price of $4.95.

As with any book, the major effort presently being devoted by Watermark and the publishers of the yearbook is centered around distribution. Brochures and other material on the book have been presented to booksellers and distributors nationwide. A special effort is being made to get the yearbook into record stores as well. We're sure, however, that many record and book stores will miss the book entirely, and this fact creates a commercial opportunity for your station. The book may be used as an introduction to the station for record and book store sponsors....present or potential.

There are about 98 other reasons that the station may want to acquire a quantity of books either for sales or promotional reasons...anything.. for contest prizes, location giveaways, gifts to sponsors...who knows... you may even want to get into the book business.

For this reason, we've enclosed an order blank which you can use in ordering THE AMERICAN TOP 40 YEARBOOK direct from the publisher. Extra order blanks are available at Watermark from your regional sales manager at (800) 423-2502 or (213) 980-9490.

Please be aware that delivery will take at least three weeks.

The publishers may be buying time from stations in certain major markets. For this reason, Casey Kasem has already voiced radio commercials. The two 60-second spots are available free from Watermark for use by any AT40 subscriber. Just give us a call.

Thanks for your support; we hope your imagination will lead to plenty of uses for THE AMERICAN TOP 40 YEARBOOK.

WATERMARK, INC. 10700 Ventura Blvd., No. Hollywood, California 91604 (213) 980-9490

Tom Rounds announced another AT40 promotional tool, THE AMERICAN TOP 40 YEARBOOK, which provided artist, record and Top 40 chart data from November 1977 to October 1978.

464. 05-19-79 **Program #792-7**
long distance dedication: Theme From *Romeo & Juliet* - Henry Mancini
long distance dedication: Theme From *A Star Is Born* - Barbra Streisand
story: Livingston Taylor's inspiration for "I Will Be In Love With You"
story: Roger McGuinn saved by religion
story: music of the future
story: Cher's first record rejection
story: Sister Sledge's "We Are Family" recorded in hostile environment
story: Roger Voudouris' self-assurance will further his music career success
question: biggest #1 record on disco chart
question: successful singing disk jockeys
portion played: Chase - Giorgio Moroder
archive #1 record played: The Way We Were - Barbra Streisand
archive #1 record played: Love's Theme - Love Unlimited Orchestra
archive #1 record played: Seasons In The Sun - Terry Jacks
oldie played: I Will Be In Love With You - Livingston Taylor

465. 05-26-79 **Program #792-8**
program mention: Van Halen financially backed by Kiss' Gene Simmons
long distance dedication: Baby Come Back - Babys
long distance dedication: Killing Me Softly With His Song - Roberta Flack
story: Paul McCartney & George Harrison's efforts to see *Blackboard Jungle*
story: bodily injuries caused by disco
story: Blondie assists in nabbing a radio station thief
story: origin of phrase 'knock on wood'
story: Atlanta Rhythm Section's high-speed record sounds like Fleetwood Mac's Stevie Nicks
story: producer Mike Chapman's song inspirations
question: male artist with greatest length of time from debut record to #1 record
portion played: Imaginary Lover - Atlanta Rhythm Section
archive #1 record played: Dark Lady - Cher
archive #1 record played: Sunshine On My Shoulders - John Denver
archive #1 record played: Hooked On A Feeling - Blue Swede

466. 06-02-79 **Program #792-9**
story: Dr. Hook's "Sylvia's Mother" voted worst record of all time
story: James Brown shined shoes
story: contemporary music raises the Iron Curtain
story: Kenny Rogers rejected Karen Carpenter's talents
story: England Dan & John Ford Coley's big break
story: Robin Gibb's car, train & boat accidents
odd chart stat: Sister Sledge's "He's The Greatest Dancer" falls from #14 to #39
long distance dedication: Long & Winding Road - Beatles
long distance dedication: Can't Smile Without You - Barry Manilow
question: female artist with most #1 records
archive #1 record played: Bennie & The Jets - Elton John
archive #1 record played: T.S.O.P. (The Sound Of Philabelphia) - MFSB
archive #1 record played: Loco-Motion - Grand Funk
oldie played: Papa's Got A Brand New Bag - James Brown

467. 06-09-79 **Program #792-10**
GUEST HOST: Bruce Phillip Miller
long distance dedication: Desperado - Linda Ronstadt
long distance dedication: Goodbye Girl - David Gates
odd chart stat: The Bee Gees tie Diana Ross & Supremes and The Beatles' chart record of six consecutive #1 records
question: artist with greatest length of time between #1 records
question: artist with most charted records during 1970's
whatever happened to: Bill Haley
program note: Bruce promos upcoming special
story: Doobie Brothers pre-concert troubles
story: producer Snuff Garrett sold Bibles with his grandfather
story: Electric Light Orchestra souvenir injures concert goer
story: Rickie Lee Jones worked in an empty store
archive #1 record played: The Streak - Ray Stevens
archive #1 record played: Band On The Run - Paul McCartney & Wings
archive #1 record played: Billy, Don't Be A Hero - Bo Donaldson & The Heywoods
oldie played: Rock Around The Clock - Bill Haley & Comets

468. 06-16-79 **Program #792-11**
story: Kiss helped Michigan high school football team
story: Olivia Newton-John, animal rights activist
story: Anita Ward refused to quit teaching
story: Dr. Hook's two-band, one concert performance
story: Herb (Peaches & Herb) Fame's walk to New York City
story: Cheap Trick's popularity in Japan
question: recording act with most Top 10, no #1 records
question: professional athletes on Top 40 records
portion played: I Love Mickey - Teresa Brewer
long distance dedication: I Will Still Love You - Stonebolt
long distance dedication: We Are The Champions - Queen
program note: Casey promos upcoming special
archive #1 record played: Sundown - Gordon Lightfoot
archive #1 record played: Rock The Boat - Hues Corporation
archive #1 record played: Rock Your Baby - George McCrae

469. 06-23-79 **Program #792-12**
long distance dedication: I.O.U. - Jimmy Dean
long distance dedication: Be True To Your School - Beach Boys
story: disco and the economy
story: Styx, the mythical river
story: first artist with million selling record
story: Casablanca Records president Neil Bogart's near suicide
story: Stevie Wonder made The Emotions cry
story: Kyu Sakamoto's "Sukiyaki" re-titled for U.S. release
portion played: Sukiyaki - Kyu Sakamoto
odd chart stat: Donna Summer equals Linda Ronstadt and Olivia Newton-John chart feats with two simultaneous Top 5 records
program note: Casey promos upcoming special
question: The Beatles vs. Diana Ross & Supremes
program mention: Abba will finally tour North America
archive #1 record played: Annie's Song - John Denver
archive #1 record played: Feel Like Makin' Love - Roberta Flack
archive #1 record played: The Night Chicago Died - Paper Lace

As the number of AT40 subscribing stations increased every year throughout the 1970s, so did the size of the Listening Directory. The 1979 edition listed more than 500 broadcasting outlets where listeners tuned for the weekly countdown.

TO: PROGRAM DIRECTOR, AMERICAN TOP 40 SUBSCRIBING STATIONS
FROM: TOM ROUNDS, WATERMARK
DATE: JUNE 16, 1979

According to the most recent Arbitron surveys, AMERICAN TOP 40 is the highest rated (according to average quarter hour shares) time period at better than 50% of our subscribing stations in Arbitron-rated markets. In almost 90% of these markets, AT40 delivers a higher average quarter hour share than does the station on the average, Monday-Sunday 6AM-Midnight.

We think this is great, and much of the credit goes to you for positioning, promoting and scheduling AT40 where it does the most good.

It has recently come to our attention, though, that a number of subscribing stations are not taking advantage of one of our earlier recommendations to use spot breaks within AMERICAN TOP 40 to promote your regular schedule of events and personalities.

You're really missing a bet if you don't schedule short promos featuring your jocks and special programming inside AT40 on a regular basis every week.

Remember, AT40 does attract listeners other than your regulars, and you need to influence every one of them to make your station a listening habit.

I know that a number of you are already taking advantage of this perfect promotional showcase, so consider this a suggestion to update and rethink how you're using AT40 to promote the station.

And if others have lapsed, right now's the time to get it together in the production studio. Don't miss the opportunity.

Thanks.

WATERMARK, INC. 10700 Ventura Blvd., No. Hollywood, California 91604 (213) 980-9490

In addition to offering more positive ratings information in this memo, Tom Rounds highly recommended using AT40 to promote "the regular schedule of events and personalities" of subscribing stations.

CASEY KASEM
Give this man a summer job . . . he'll work weekends!

Hear Casey's special AT40 countdown, "The 40 Biggest Hits of the Disco Era, 1974-1979" the weekend of July 7-8 on American Top 40 affiliates.

Summertime . . . longer listening . . . more sponsor action . . . and now the first special programming sale in Watermark's history . . . perfect conditions to launch American Top 40 in your market.
Call Watermark at (213) 980-9490 and find out how easy it is to get AT40 working for you this summer.

AMERICAN TOP 40 hosted by Casey Kasem is a weekly, 4 hour countdown of the 40 top hits in the USA as reported by **BILLBOARD'S** Hot 100 and is produced and distributed in compatible stereo by Watermark.

WATERMARK □ 10700 Ventura Blvd., No. Hollywood, CA 91604 □ 213/980-9490

This advertisement appeared in the June 9, 1979 edition of Billboard Magazine.

TO: AMERICAN TOP 40 SUBSCRIBERS

FROM: TOM ROUNDS, WATERMARK

JUNE 23, 1979

Next week, AMERICAN TOP 40 presents a four-hour special: "The 40 Top Hits of the Disco Era....the songs that made it in America's disco's and on the pop singles charts."

To come up with this special tabulation, the AT40 research and statistics people analyzed each week's Billboard Hot 100 for the period beginning July, 1974 (when "Rock the Boat" hit number one) through June, 1979. Casey will count down the 40 biggest disco hits in this five year period that represents the birth and formative years of the disco era.

To help you promote the special, which is show #793-1, scheduled for broadcast the weekend of June 30-July 1, 1979, we have included four promos on this week's program discs.

Here's how to find them:

> Refer to the log for show #792-13. The promos are banded at the end of side 4B.

The times are as follows:

Promo #1 :23
Promo #2 :20
Promo #3 :17
Promo #4 :23

We suggest your dubbing the four promos to cart and laying in a heavy on-air schedule starting June 25 through air time for your broadcast of the special.

Be sure to keep #793-1 in your files. It's the first four-hour emergency replacement show AT40 has produced; something perfect to have on hand when the winter winds begin to howl once again!

WATERMARK, INC. 10700 Ventura Blvd., No. Hollywood, California 91604 (213) 980-9490

To take advantage of disco music's popularity, a special countdown was produced and aired on July 7, 1979 -- AT40's 9th anniversary. The special's tabulation period and promotional announcements are described in this June 23, 1979 memo.

470. 06-30-79

Program #792-13
production note: disks contain promo announcements for upcoming special
program note: Casey promos upcoming special
long distance dedication: The Greatest Love Of All - George Benson
long distance dedication: Undercover Angel - Alan O'Day
odd chart stat: all Top 5 records are performed by female artists
odd chart stat: Donna Summer is the only female artist to ever have two records simultaneously in the Top 3
story: Blondie cocktail napkin offer to producer Mike Chapman
story: Herb (Peaches & Herb) Fame still mops a beauty salon floor
story: Elton John's Soviet Union tour
story: Kiss' Gene Simmons hair caught fire again
story: Kenny Rogers' #1 record prediction
question: months named in titles of Top 40 records
archive #1 record played: You're Having My Baby - Paul Anka
archive #1 record played: I Shot The Sheriff - Eric Clapton
archive #1 record played: Can't Get Enough Of Your Love, Babe - Barry White

471. 07-07-79

Program #793-1
SPECIAL: Top 40 Of The Disco Era
for a complete list of records in this special, see Rob Durkee's *American Top 40: The Countdown of the Century*

472. 07-14-79

Program #793-2
long distance dedication: Always & Forever - Heatwave
long distance dedication: You Are The Sunshine Of My Life - Stevie Wonder
odd chart stat: two debut records
story: Rex Smith started a food fight
story: Carly Simon saved James Taylor's life
story: disco dancing illegal in Henrietta, OK
story: McFadden & Whitehead worked in record company stockroom
story: Eric Clapton wedding creates reunion of The Beatles and Cream
story: Maurice White's 'Emotional' dream
program mention: Kiss lasers inspected by the government
long version: Shine A Little Love - Electric Light Orchestra
archive #1 record played: Rock Me Gently - Andy Kim
archive #1 record played: I Honestly Love You - Olivia Newton John
archive #1 record played: Nothing From Nothing - Billy Preston

473. 07-21-79

Program #793-3
long distance dedication: How Much Love - Leo Sayer
long distance dedication: We've Only Just Begun - Carpenters
story: David Naughton's desire to perform Shakespeare
story: Van Halen's David Lee Roth exaggerates tour diet
story: Peter Frampton's quick rise from debt to wealth
story: FBI vs. record business crime
story: James Taylor's Apple Records flop
story: John Stewart makes his own artificial teeth
story: Supertramp interrupts Seattle concert for maternity ward visit
program mention: The Knack named 'Rookies of the Year'
program error: Casey mistakingly introduced the #34 record, The Knack's "My Sharona", by stating "....here's the last of our three debut songs....."; and later introduced the #29 record, Blondie's Top 40 re-debut "One Way or Another", by concluding its chart movement re-cap with "....it then dropped out of the countdown altogether last week to #41…this week it's back at 29....."
long version: Shine A Little Love - Electric Light Orchestra
archive #1 record played: Then Came You - Dionne Warwick & Spinners
archive #1 record played: You Haven't Done Nothin' - Stevie Wonder
archive #1 record played: You Ain't Seen Nothin' Yet – Bachman-Turner Overdrive

474. 07-28-79

Program #793-4
odd chart stat: Rickie Lee Jones' "Chuck E's In Love" falls from #12 to #40
story: The Cars' LP cover painted by Vargas
story: Electric Light Orchestra's Jeff Lynne searches for perfect sound effects
story: rock artists' contract lawyers
story: Kansas' favorite story
story: Elton John's record collection contains 100,000 LPs & 75,000 45s
long distance dedication: Reminiscing - Little River Band
long distance dedication: I Will Survive - Gloria Gaynor
program mention: Dionne Warwicke is Dionne Warwick again
program mention: re-cap of two groups on one record
program mention: Atlanta Rhythm Section is like President Carter
question: record with the biggest jump into the #1 position
archive #1 record played: Whatever Gets You Through The Night - John Lennon
archive #1 record played: I Can Help - Billy Swan
archive #1 record played: Kung Fu Fighting - Carl Douglas

475. 08-04-79

Program #793-5
story: Pink Lady's popularity is #1 in Japan
story: Abba's income is #1 in Sweden
story: Arthur Fiedler's accomplishments
story: Atlanta Rhythm Section drummer sneaks out at night
story: McFadden & Whitehead interview saved their lives
story: Kingston Trio ripped off by a kangaroo
long distance dedication: Lean On Me - Bill Withers
long distance dedication: You Made Me Believe In Magic - Bay City Rollers
program note: Casey promos listening directory
portion played: I Want To Hold Your Hand - Arthur Fiedler's Boston Pops Orchestra
question: record falling off the chart from #1 position
archive #1 record played: Cat's In The Cradle - Harry Chapin
archive #1 record played: Angie Baby - Helen Reddy
archive #1 record played: Lucy In The Sky With Diamonds - Elton John

476. 08-11-79

Program #793-6
odd chart stat: Electric Light Orchestra's "Don't Bring Me Down" climbs from #41 to #18
odd chart stat: Donna Summer is in the #1 position for five consecutive weeks and eight out of 11 weeks
odd chart stat: three artists - Electric Light Orchestra, Earth, Wind & Fire and Donna Summer - each have two records in the Top 40
story: record industry groupies
story: Patrick Hernandez is first French singer to reach the Top 40
story: The Knack's first LP compared to success of "Meet The Beatles"
story: Maxine Nightingale chose career over marriage
story: Donna Summer threatened to quit disco
story: Little River Band was previously Mississippi
long distance dedication: My Man - Barbra Streisand
long distance dedication: Time In A Bottle - Jim Croce
program note: Casey promos listening directory
archive #1 record played: Mandy - Barry Manilow
archive #1 record played: Please Mr. Postman - Carpenters
archive #1 record played: Laughter In The Rain - Neil Sedaka

TO: AMERICAN TOP 40 SUBSCRIBERS (ROUTE TO PD'S & GM'S)

FROM: TOM ROUNDS, WATERMARK

8-25-79

NEW JINGLES! They actually started in last week's show, but we wanted to be sure you noticed! Produced by our old friend, Jim Kirk, at TM in Dallas, these new split logos are now included in the program in stereo. To accomplish this, AT40 is being assembled with six 2-track machines and the new system allows us to tighten Casey's walk-ups to the logo vocals. We think there's a big difference in the pace and technical quality of the show, comments welcome. In 2-3 weeks, we'll be introducing a new theme for American Top 40, retiring the present "Shuckatoom" theme after 3 years service.

LISTENING DIRECTORY RESPONSE. Two invitations to write in for a free copy of the American Top 40 Listening Directory were included in show #793-7. So far, more than 20,000 listeners have sent in their self-addressed, stamped envelopes for this item (copies of which you received a few weeks ago). The last time this offer was made, in 1976, we pulled about 5,000.

FALL ARBITRON SWEEP ALERT! It has come to our attention that several stations surveyed in the April-May 1979 Arbitron DID NOT LIST AMERICAN TOP 40 IN THE ARBITRON FACILITIES FORM. Or they listed incorrect times. Or they didn't return the form at all. The most flagrant example was an AM/FM simulcaster in a major market in the Northeast. Arbitron will not assign American Top 40 mentions in diaries unless AT40 is listed by the station in the facilities form posted prior to the survey period. If AT40 is not listed or listed incorrectly you will definitely lose share, average quarter hour and cume points in the Arbitron book, not only for the time AT40 is broadcast, but across the board. PLEASE GET THIS HANDLED BEFORE THE NEXT SURVEY STARTS!

WATERMARK, INC. 10700 Ventura Blvd., No. Hollywood, California 91604 (213) 980-9490

Tom Rounds used the August 25, 1979 correspondence to stations to highlight new jingles and listener response to the 1979 listening directory. He also reprimanded those stations (including "an AM/FM simulcaster in a major market in the Northeast") that failed to recognize AT40's influence in station ratings.

477. 08-18-79

Program #793-7
question: female artist with most Top 40 records in one year
whatever happened to: Mitch Ryder & The Detroit Wheels
story: Cheap Trick attacked on-stage
story: Donna Summer locked into a bathroom audition
story: LP art on the chart
story: Ray Parker Jr.'s big 'bone' break
story: Bonnie Pointer scats like Louis Armstrong
portion played: Blueberry Hill - Louis Armstrong
long distance dedication: You Needed Me - Anne Murray
long distance dedication: Take A Chance On Me - Abba
program mention: The Cars' fans beat up a car
program mention: Kiss' new pinball machine
archive #1 record played: Fire - Ohio Players
archive #1 record played: You're No Good - Linda Ronstadt
archive #1 record played: Pick Up The Pieces - Average White Band

478. 08-25-79

Program #793-8
story: picture disks & odd-shaped records
story: John Stewart's fans assist with recording contract
story: Patrick Hernandez's career change influenced by The Beatles
story: Dionne Warwick's peculiar accolade
story: Spyro Gyra disbands & re-groups
story: Charlie Daniels $10,000 bet with jazzman Stan Kenton
story: stuttering at #1 (update in 10-13-79 show)
portion played: Bennie & The Jets - Elton John
portion played: You Ain't Seen Nothin' Yet - Bachman-Turner Overdrive
program mention: Elton John's manager interrupts robbery
program mention: Robert Palmer taught to swim by Johnny Weissmuller
long distance dedication: To Sir With Love - Lulu
long distance dedication: The Gambler - Kenny Rogers
archive #1 record played: Best Of My Love - Eagles
archive #1 record played: Have You Never Been Mellow - Olivia Newton-John
archive #1 record played: Black Water - Doobie Brothers

479. 09-01-79

Program #793-9
whatever happened to: Chuck Berry
odd chart stat: Kiss' "I Was Made For Lovin' You" falls from #16 to #49
long distance dedication: Tragedy - Bee Gees
long distance dedication: You And Me Against The World - Helen Reddy
question: solo artist with most Top 10, non-#1 records
story: Nick Lowe affiliated with embarrassing Brinsley Schwarz
story: The Knack emulate The Beatles
story: recording artists named after foods and drinks
story: The Commodores' early days
story: Elton John's manager breaks ankles at a discotheque
program mention: Casey's introduction of Spyro Gyra's "Morning Dance" includes reference to *AT40* statistician Matt Wilson's hometown
archive #1 record played: My Eyes Adored You - Franki Valli
archive #1 record played: Lady Marmalade - LaBelle
archive #1 record played: Lovin' You - Minnie Ripperton

TO: AT40
FROM: TOM ROUNDS, WATERMARK, INC.
SEPTEMBER 1, 1979

WATERMARK, INC. 10700 Ventura Blvd., No. Hollywood, California 91604 (213) 980-9490

Casey's on summer vacation this week, and his absence provides us with a unique opportunity to share the talent of Gordon Elliott as guest host of AMERICAN TOP 40.

I first heard Gordon in Sydney Australia last June when he was sitting in for John Laws on the morning show at 2UW. (Laws, the #1 "Breakfast" personality in Sydney for the past umpteen years, has now retired and Gordon has moved into that coveted spot, managing to hold the audience in the survey taken since the switch.) Elliott was invited to guest for Casey if vacations schedules matched. They did. And here he is...the first Non-American voice at the AT40 helm in 9½ years. We think Gordon Elliott is a super talent, and I think you'll agree. And this occasion gives us a chance to acknowledge our Australian AMERICAN TOP 40 subscribers for their fantastic loyalty and support over the years. AT40 is heard in 25 markets in Australia and Tasmania; quite an honor in consideration of the high standards in the Australian Broadcast Industry.

Casey returns next week for program #793-11.

Another reminder: Two big specials are set for the end of the year: program #794-13 is "The 50 Top Hits of 1979". Broadcast dates: Dec. 29-30. Program #801-1 is "The 50 Top Hits of the 70's". Dates: Jan. 5-6. Program 12,13 and 1 will all be shipped on Dec. 15 so domestic subscibers will have all three shows by Dec. 19.

In this memo, Tom Rounds alerts stations to another guest host -- Australian Gordon Elliott, "the first Non-American voice at the AT40 helm in 9½ years."

480. 09-08-79

Program #793-10
GUEST HOST: Gordon Elliott
story: Fleetwood Mac's Peter Green mentally committed due to record royalties
story: Dr. Hook booked as headliner at soul concert
story: Dionne Warwick heeds astrological advice, career fails
story: Robert Palmer wants everything to record
whatever happened to: Grand Funk
long distance dedication: Sharing The Night Together - Dr. Hook
long distance dedication: Three Times A Lady - Commodores
long version: Philadelphia Freedom - Elton John Band
archive #1 record played: Philadelphia Freedom - Elton John
archive #1 record played: (Hey Won't You Play) Another Somebody Done Somebody Wrong Song - B.J. Thomas
archive #1 record played: He Don't Love You - Tony Orlamdo & Dawn

481. 09-15-79

Program #793-11
program error: Casey's introduction to Spyro Gyra's "Morning Dance" pointed out that ".....the song at #34 falls ten notches this week...."; actually, it dropped one notch
long distance dedication: Can't Smile Without You - Barry Manilow
long distance dedication: That Lady - Isley Brothers
question: song titles most often seen on the chart
question: fastest climbing #1 record
program mention: Amtrak's New York-to-Montreal disco train
story: producer Mike Chapman's thrifty LP philosophy
story: Island Records' Chris Blackwell was millionaire grocer
story: Eddie Rabbitt's "Suspicions" written in five minutes
story: Leo Sayer's career change was therapeutic
story: Night's Chris Thompson in the right place
archive #1 record played: Shining Star - Earth, Wind & Fire
archive #1 record played: Before The Next Tear Drop Falls - Freddy Fender
archive #1 record played: Thank God I'm A Country Boy - John Denver
oldie played: You Make Me Feel Like Dancing - Leo Sayer

482. 09-22-79

Program #793-12
program note: new *AT40* theme music debuts in program opening; program cue sheets indicate that the "Shuckatoom" theme music opens the program, however it is not used for this program
program mention: Jennifer Warnes' "I Know A Heartache When I See One" reaches the Top 40 in its 13th week in the Hot 100; average time typically taken for a record to reach the Top 40 is six weeks
story: Fleetwood Mac's Peter Green update
story: producer Mike Chapman's single-year, four #1 records
story: Maxine Nightingale uncertain about "Right Back Where We Started From"
story: physical trainer Richard Norton's rock star efforts
story: Barbra Streisand's public performance fear
story: laser uses in rock concerts
story: The Doobie Brothers' success due to pancreatitis
long distance dedication: If My Friends Could See Me Now - Linda Clifford
long distance dedication: Best Thing That Ever Happened To Me - Gladys Knight & The Pips
archive #1 record played: Sister Golden Hair - America
archive #1 record played: Love Will Keep Us Together - Captain & Tennille
archive #1 record played: Listen To What The Man Said - Paul McCartney

483. 09-29-79 **Program #793-13**
GUEST HOST: Robert W. Morgan
program note: Robert W. Morgan, a last minute fill-in for an ailing Casey Kasem, is morning man at Los Angeles' KMPC, a radio competitor to KIIS-FM which is the *AT40* station in Los Angeles
whatever happened to: The Doors
story: Maureen McGovern's contact with disaster
story: Michael Johnson's worst year
story: Chic's producers turned down Bette Midler
story: Dionne Warwick turned down Barry Manilow
story: Herb Alpert is in *The Guinness Book of World Records*
long distance dedication: Lady - Little River Band
long distance dedication: Since I Don't Have You - Skyliners
question: Australian artists at #1
program error: Robert's outcue of Electric Light Orchestra's "Don't Bring Me Down" pointed out that it was "...slipping six notches this week to #10...."; actually, it was in position #10 the previous week
archive #1 record played: The Hustle - Van McCoy & Soul City Symphony
archive #1 record played: One Of These Nights - Eagles
archive #1 record played: Jive Talkin' - Bee Gees
oldie played: Light My Fire - Doors

484. 10-06-79 **Program #794-1**
program error: Casey introduced Bob Dylan's "Gotta Serve Somebody" by mentioning that its been 2½ years since Dylan has been on the chart; actually, it had been 3½ years
whatever happened to: Roy Orbison (update from 05-15-76)
production note: program contains the longest non-stop, no-commercial segment, with a total running time of 15:41 (see 08-22-70 for shortest segment)
story: KC & The Sunshine Band nearly missed European tour
story: Maxine Nightingale's father influenced her career
story: Earth, Wind & Fire's belief in astrology
story: God vs. The Devil on the charts
story: Sniff & The Tears' Paul Roberts is famous painter
story: concerts in Japan
long distance dedication: You're Sixteen - Ringo Starr
long distance dedication: Wishing You Were Here - Chicago
odd chart stat: Robert John's "Sad Eyes" ties chart record for slowest climb to the #1 position
oldie played: Pretty Woman - Roy Orbison
archive #1 record played: Fallin' In Love - Hamilton, Joe Frank & Reynolds
archive #1 record played: Get Down Tonight - KC & The Sunshine Band
archive #1 record played: Rhinestone Cowboy - Glen Campbell

485. 10-13-79 **Program #794-2**
odd chart stat: The Eagles' "Heartache Tonight" climbs from #52 to #15
portion played: Please Please Please - James Brown
portion played: White Bucks & Saddle Shoes - Bobby Pedrick Jr.
long distance dedication: Reunited - Peaches & Herb
long distance dedication: You're My Best Friend - Queen
program mention: Bob Dylan's religious conversion
program mention: Paul McCartney's world record medal
question: LP with most weeks on chart
story: legendary songwriter Stephen Foster died penniless
story: Donna Summer saved Casablanca Records from Johnny Carson fiasco
story: Moon Martin's visit to the Wrigley mansion

485. 10-13-79 **Program #794-2 (CONTINUED)**
story: Mary MacGregor's desire to be like Janis Joplin
story: James Brown's non-Hot 100, million selling record
story: Robert John was Bobby Pedrick Jr.
program note: stuttering #1 records update (from 08-25-79 show; see 11-17-79)
archive #1 record played: Fame - David Bowie
archive #1 record played: I'm Sorry - John Denver
archive #1 record played: Bad Blood - Neil Sedaka

486. 10-20-79 **Program #794-3**
program note: "Shuckatoom" theme returns to open program after not being used since 09-15-79
odd chart stat: The Commodores' "Still" climbs from #38 to #10
odd chart stat: Fleetwood Mac's "Tusk" climbs from #40 to #15
odd chart stat: Fleetwood Mac's "Tusk" is recorded by 130 performers, which included 125 members of the University of Southern California marching band
odd chart stat: Kermit The Frog, a *Sesame Street* TV show character, debuts in the Top 40
odd chart stat: Electric Light Orchestra's "Don't Bring Me Down" falls from #13 to #39
question: records with biggest chart jumps
question: biggest American artist of the 1970's
long distance dedication: Precious & Few - Climax
whatever happened to: Jan & Dean (update from 07-23-77)
story: Bob Dylan's honorary doctorate
story: The Knack's criticisms are answered
story: Herb Alpert's chart drought ends
story: producer Freddie Perren profile
archive #1 record played: Island Girl - Elton John
archive #1 record played: That's The Way I Like It - KC & The Sunshine Band
archive #1 record played: Fly Robin Fly - Silver Convention
oldie played: Surf City - Jan & Dean

487. 10-27-79 **Program #794-4**
long distance dedication: When Will I See You Again - Three Degrees
long distance dedication: Does Your Mother Know - Abba
story: Jimmy Buffett and The Eagles' Glenn Frey cannot escape fans
story: Michael Jackson's animal collection
story: Barry Manilow's father appears after 30-year absence
story: recording artist's hair stylist
story: Lobo is a nickname
story: Fleetwood Mac's name stolen
program note: disk jockey records update
portion played: Did You Boogie With Your Baby - Flash Cadillac & The Continental Kids
question: duo with most Top 40 records in one year
odd chart stat: two unrelated, similar-titled records in the Top 40 - Lauren Wood's "Please Don't Leave" and KC & The Sunshine Band's "Please Don't Go"
archive #1 record played: Let's Do It Again - Staple Singers
archive #1 record played: Saturday Night - Bay City Rollers
archive #1 record played: Convoy - C. W. McCall

488. 11-03-79 **Program #794-5**
story: Bob Dylan parody
story: Robert John is bitter
story: profile of feisty, little Stiff Records
story: road managers special report
story: The Eagles dumped Linda Ronstadt
story: Elton John & Rod Stewart's soccer competition
story: Brenda Russell inspired by great-grandmother
question: most often named city & state in song titles
question: re-recorded #1 record making the Top 10
long distance dedication: My Guy - Mary Wells
portion played: Stuck In The Middle With You - Stealers Wheel
portion played: Breaking Up Is Hard To Do - Neil Sedaka (1962)
portion played: Breaking Up Is Hard To Do - Neil Sedaka (1976)
odd chart stat: Barbra Streisand & Donna Summer's "No More Tears" climbs from #33 to #10
archive #1 record played: I Write The Songs - Barry Manilow
archive #1 record played: Theme From *Mahogany* - Diana Ross
archive #1 record played: Love Rollercoaster - Ohio Players

489. 11-10-79 **Program #794-6**
program note: Casey provides an explanation of *Billboard*'s Hot 100 tabulation to determine the #1 record, and states that "....*Billboard* gathers sales reports from record stores all over the country, and airplay reports from radio stations. And with the aid of their computer, they tabulate the rankings." Casey then implied that the #1 record is based on sales by pointing out that "....the #1 record in any given week is simply the biggest seller that week." No explanation is provided into determining how radio station airplay is calculated into #1 record tabulation. *Billboard*'s tabulation explanation of the Hot 100 from the 11-10-79 chart reads "A reflection of National Sales and programming activity by selected dealers, one-stops and radio stations as compiled by the Charts Dept. Of *Billboard*."
question: #1 records remade into a #1 record
question: Top 40 German artists
question: *Billboard*'s tabulation process
story: Bob Dylan's $400 LP
story: Stevie Wonder record is biggest live record
story: The Crusaders are successful session musicians
story: Foreigner drummer goes deaf
story: The Commodores' internal lie
story: Kenny Rogers' first record was written by soda jerk Mickey Newbury
name origin: Pablo Cruise
long distance dedication: Run For Home - Lindisfarne
long distance dedication: How Deep Is Your Love - Bee Gees
portion played: Fingertips, Pt. 2 - Stevie Wonder
archive #1 record played: Fifty Ways To Leave Your Lover - Paul Simon
archive #1 record played: Theme From *SWAT* - Rhythm Heritage
archive #1 record played: Love Machine - Miracles

490. 11-17-79

Program #794-7
program mention: stuttering #1 record update correction (from 10-13-79)
portion played: Jive Talkin' - Bee Gees
portion played: Turn Turn Turn - Byrds
story: "Turn Turn Turn" lyrics are oldest
story: Anne Murray's difficult disposition
story: Kermit The Frog gave Edgar Bergen's eulogy
story: Electric Light Orchestra's expensive concert stage
story: Barry Manilow's solo artist achievement
story: The Eagles challenge *Rolling Stone* magazine
story: producer Giorgio Moroder inspired by Paul Anka
long distance dedication: Blinded By The Light - Manfred Mann
long distance dedication: You're In My Heart - Rod Stewart
archive #1 record played: December 1963 - Four Seasons
archive #1 record played: Disco Lady - Johnnie Taylor
archive #1 record played: Let Your Love Flow - Bellamy Brothers

491. 11-24-79

Program #794-8
public service: read by Casey, program disks include Project Hunger announcements for subscribing radio stations' optional use
question: Dutch artists in the Top 40
question: artist with most charted singles and #1 records
long distance dedication: We Are The Champions - Queen
long distance dedication: Lodi - Creedence Clearwater Revival
program note: Casey's introduction to the #1 record points out that there have been 665 #1 records in the history of the charts; a few demographics were mentioned
odd chart stat: Barbara Streisand & Donna Summer, the first two-woman duo to reach #1
story: Michael Jackson's pre-teen chart achievement
story: Herb Alpert's fear of performing
story: Dr. Hook strips on Scandinavian TV
story: whims of Top 40 artists
archive #1 record played: Welcome Back - John Sebastian
archive #1 record played: Boogie Fever - Sylvers
archive #1 record played: Silly Love Songs - Wings

492. 12-01-79

Program #794-9
portion played: Rock Your Baby - George McCrae
portion played: Willie And The Hand Jive - Johnny Otis Show
whatever happened to: Johnny Otis
story: Kenny Loggins performed with 'cheap' Electric Prunes
story: Lauren Wood's pet connection
story: "You Decorated My Life" songwriter's other life
story: Fleetwood Mac's "Tusk" from expensive LP
story: KC & The Sunshine Band's Harry Wayne Casey cleaned record studios
long distance dedication: If - Bread
long distance dedication: Just Remember I Love You - Firefall
program note: Casey promos upcoming specials
program note: during Rupert Holmes' introduction, Casey provides a Pina Colada recipe
question: Top 10 chart with no American artists
archive #1 record played: Love Hangover - Diana Ross
archive #1 record played: Afternoon Delight - Starland Vocal Band
archive #1 record played: Kiss And Say Goodbye - Manhattans

TO: AMERICAN TOP 40 SUBSCRIBERS

FROM: TOM ROUNDS, WATERMARK

DATE: DECEMBER 15, 1979

Here's our Annual Giant Package of enough American Top 40's to cover you from the weekend of December 22-23, 1979 all the way through January 5-6, 1980. Included are shows 794-12 (the last regular countdown for 1979), 794-13, "THE TOP 50 HITS OF 1979" and 801-1, "THE TOP 50 HITS OF THE 70'S."

Because Christmas and New Year's days fall on Tuesdays this year, we decided it was appropriate to schedule the two specials for the weekends following. This means you have the following options: (A) leave the schedule the way it is and run the specials as you normally would on the weekends of the 29th and 5th, (B) add a repeat of the "THE TOP 50 HITS OF 1979" on New Year's Eve and New Year's Day.

We strongly recommend against airing the "THE TOP 50 HITS OF THE 70'S" until the weekend of the 5th. We don't think this high-content show should be exposed on a Holiday and then re-run in the normal American Top 40 slot. Remember, the next regular countdown won't be until the weekend of the 12th.

Also, be sure to save both specials for use-in-case-of-an-emergency later in the year.

Promos for each special are included on the appropriate program disc.

HAPPY HOLIDAYS!

WATERMARK, INC. 10700 Ventura Blvd., No. Hollywood, California 91604 (213) 980-9490

This memo from Tom Rounds -- packaged with the December 22, 1979 regular show, the Top 50 of 1979, and the Top 50 of the 1970s -- offered a few suggestions for scheduling AT40's two year-end specials.

493. 12-08-79

Program #794-10
whatever happened to: Bobby Vinton
long distance dedication: To Love Somebody - Bee Gees
question: song with most simultaneous chart versions
question: artist with most consecutive weeks in Top 40
program note: Casey promos upcoming specials
odd chart stat: The Eagles' "The Long Run" debuts in the Hot 100 at #33
story: Spike Jones' musical mayhem
story: Styx will not provide LPs for critic review
story: Marvin Hamlisch's Academy Award achievement
story: Cliff Richard's lack of stardom
story: songwriter Ian Hunter's LP bad luck
story: Casablanca Records president Neil Bogart was singer Neil Scott
portion played: Bobby - Neil Scott
portion played: Right In The Fuhrer's Face - Spike Jones
portion played: Cocktails For Two - Spike Jones
archive #1 record played: Don't Go Breaking My Heart - Elton John & Kiki Dee
archive #1 record played: You Should Be Dancing - Bee Gees
archive #1 record played: Shake Your Booty - KC & The Sunshine Band

494. 12-15-79

Program #794-11
long distance dedication: Knock On Wood - Amii Stewart
long distance dedication: Can't Smile Without You - Barry Manilow
program note: Casey promos upcoming specials
Book of Records: seven-time, seven-year #1 LP
story: Abba's palindrome
story: audio dinosaurs
story: different-named celebrity siblings
story: Anne Murray was Elvis Presley's favorite singer
story: Donna Summer & Barbra Streisand jockey for top billing
question: four solo Beatles with simultaneous Top 40 records
archive #1 record played: Play That Funky Music - Wild Cherry
archive #1 record played: A Fifth of Beethoven - Walter Murphy & Big Apple Band
archive #1 record played: Disco Duck - Rick Dees

"Growing up in Allen Park, Michigan, a downriver Detroit suburb, I first started listening to Top 40 radio in 1971 (but) I didn't have the luxury of hearing the early AT40s. If my memory serves me right, I don't think that the AT40 program played in Detroit until 1979............Somewhere along the line I remember hearing about Casey Kasem's American Top 40 radio show and how it was the 'standard' in weekly Top 40 radio countdown shows. It could have been Casey's 1974 appearance on Hawaii 5-0 that brought my attention to the American Top 40 radio program. I seem to remember seeing a newspaper ad promoting Casey's appearance in Hawaii 5-0 and a mention of his AT40 radio program......The first AT40 show I heard was part of the Top 50 of the '70s on WDRQ during the New Years Day holiday festivities (1/1/80). After hearing a variety of radio countdown shows through the years -- the weekly Top 30 countdown shows produced by CKLW, the year end countdown shows produced by the various Detroit Top 40 radio stations (CKLW, WDRQ, WXYZ, WMJC, WNIC), as well as a couple out of Chicago (WLS, WCFL) -- I was finally listening to American Top 40 by Casey Kasem. I remember the jubilation I felt as I listened to Casey counting down the top hits of the '70s. I also remember thinking 'now I know why American Top 40 is the standard for radio countdown shows.'"

Rick Martinez, a longtime AT40 listener

495. 12-22-79 **Program #794-12**
odd chart stat: Herb Alpert has the most Top 40 instrumentals
long distance dedication: Three Times A Lady - Commodores
program note: Casey promos upcoming specials
portion played: Teen Angel - Mark Denning
portion played: Nuttin' For Christmas - Barry Gordon
portion played: Santa Claus Is Coming To Town - Bing Crosby
portion played: Winter Wonderland - Bing Crosby
portion played: Rudolph The Red-Nosed Reindeer - Gene Autry
portion played: White Christmas - Bing Crosby
portion played: Oh Susannah - Singing Dogs
portion played: Jingle Bells - Singing Dogs
story: Singing Dogs' origin
story: John Mellencamp blackmailed into John Cougar
story: "Teen Angel" was a joke
story: four biggest selling records are Christmas records
story: Barry Manilow's father appears after 30-year absence
story: "No More Tears" needed water
program mention: Stevie Wonder's LP is scented
question: youngest artist in the Top 40
long version: Ladies Night - Kool & The Gang
archive #1 record played: If You Leave Me Now - Chicago
archive #1 record played: Rock'n Me - Steve Miller Band
archive #1 record played: Tonight's The Night - Rod Stewart
oldie played: White Christmas - Bing Crosby

496. 12-29-79 **Program #794-13**
SPECIAL: Top 50 Of 1979 (based on *Billboard*'s year-end Top 100)
for a complete list of records in this special, see Rob Durkee's *American Top 40: The Countdown of the Century*

497. 01-05-80 **Program #801-1**
SPECIAL: Top 50 Of The 1970's (based on *AT40* staff list)
for a complete list of records in this special, see Rob Durkee's *American Top 40: The Countdown of the Century*

AMERICAN TOP 40
<u>RADIO STATION SUMMARY</u>
On-Air Mentions of Subscribing Stations
1970 through 1979

(Information researched & compiled by Pete Battistini)

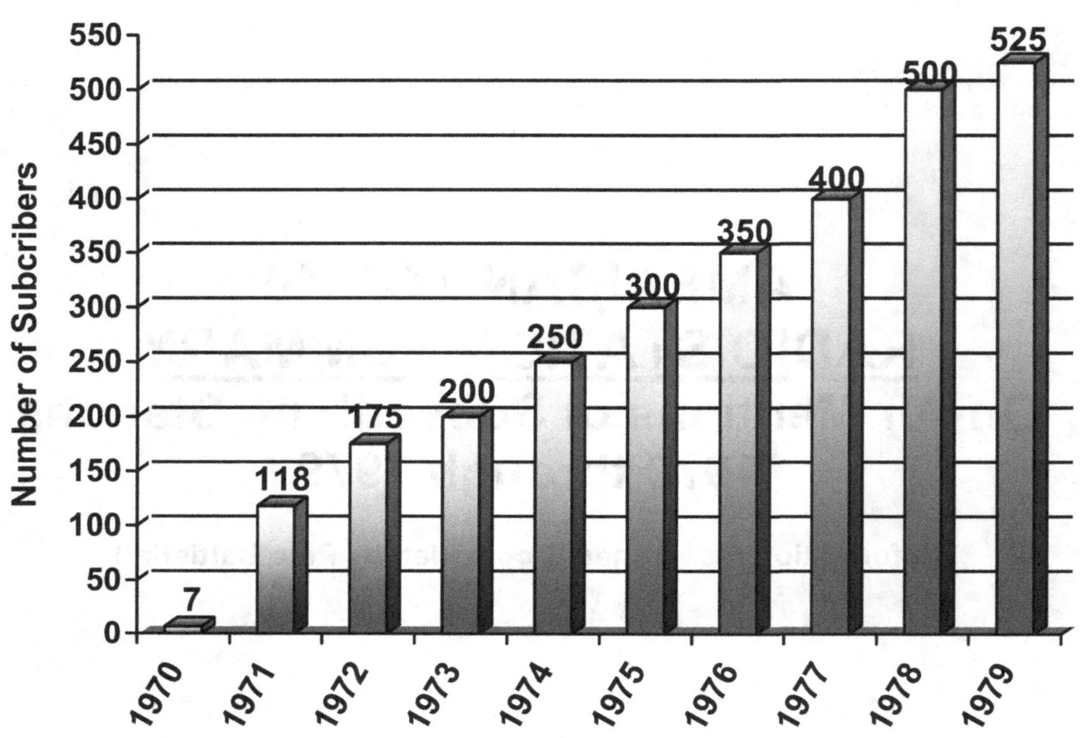

Reference key

1970 - representing the July 4, 1970 debut program; noted in Rob Durkee's *American Top 40: The Countdown of the Century*

1971 - mentioned during the 7-3-71 program

1972 - noted in 7-15-72 *Billboard Magazine* article

1973 - mentioned during the 6-2-73 program

1974 - noted in 7-5-74 memo to stations

1975 - noted in *AT40*'s 5th anniversary (7-5-75) news release

1976 - mentioned during the 8-21-76 program

1977 - noted in 8-27-77 *Billboard Magazine* article

1978 - mentioned during the 6-24-78 program

1979 - noted in 2-26-80 memo to stations

Note: station numbers from 1972-1979 do not include American Forces Radio.

NOTES:

1. The following pages list AT40's radio stations, markets and dates of station mentions or reasons for recognition. Radio station dates documented originate from all programs produced during the 1970s, each time Casey Kasem (or a substitute host) stated, "American Top 40 is heard coast-to-coast and around the world on great radio stations like......." The stations are listed under alphabetized states and cities. All dates noted reference a station's on-air mention as an AT40 affiliate unless otherwise indicated.

sample

Indianapolis	WIFE	4-17-71 (new); 6-12-71; 7-3-71 (listed in *Billboard* ad)

2. Other information for this list was obtained from advertisements for the program in *Billboard* magazine, AT40 Worldwide Listening Directories published annually during the mid-to-late 1970s, and the 1975 AT40 Sales & Marketing Guide. The phrase "listed in *Billboard* ad", for example, indicates that Watermark, American Top 40's parent company, ran an ad in the magazine that week and listed many, if not all, subscribing stations.

3. Dates marked "(new)", in most cases, indicate the approximate first time AT40 was heard on the designated station and/or in that market. It is not possible to note the last time a program was heard on a station, or in a market, because there is no reference available to program discontinuation.

4. When AT40 debuted the weekend of July 4, 1970, there were seven subscribing stations. According to Rob Durkee's book, *American Top 40: The Countdown of the Century*, the original markets were San Diego (El Cajon), Boston, Washington DC, Las Vegas, Honolulu, San Bernadino, and Tucson.

5. Station mentions began within the program dated 8-29-70. The first station recognized was KMEN in San Bernadino, California. The last program documented for this list is dated 12-22-79.

6. Within programs from late 1970 & early 1971, Casey occasionally mentioned record sale reports provided by subscribing stations. (Example: "...KPOI reports that Liz Damon's '1900 Yesterday' is #1 in Honolulu.") This type of mention is noted here as "radio report".

7. The most new station 'welcomes' at one time within one program occurred during the 10-2-71 show - 11 new affiliates.

8. For AT40 programs dated from 6-22-74 through 9-28-74, station mentions were prerecorded and submitted by affiliates. In many cases, verbal recognition originated from the station's top-of-the-hour I.D. This was an idea suggested by Casey Kasem.

9. During the 70s, AT40 was not heard for years in many of radio's Top 25 markets. Those cities included: Detroit, Chicago, Philadelphia, Miami, Milwaukee, Minneapolis/St. Paul, Atlanta, Louisville, Cincinnati, New Orleans and St. Louis. (See individual markets for specific information.) It is worth noting here that at least one Top 50 media market – Dayton, OH – never had a radio station carry AT40 during the 1970s.

10. Many station mentions were limited to once a year, sometimes near the station's contract renewal date. However, New York City's WPIX was the exception and was the most mentioned radio station from 1971-1977. Averaging ten mentions per year, or once every six weeks, WPIX was referenced as an AT40 affiliate at least 63 times in six years.

STATE

Market	*Calls*	*Air Date Mentions*
ALABAMA		
Birmingham	**WSGN**	**6-24-72 (new); 7-15-72; 11-11-72; 2-17-73; 4-21-73; 9-15-73; 12-29-73; 6-1-74; 10-12-74; 8-23-75; 11-29-75; 4-3-76; 7-24-76; 12-18-76; 9-24-77; 5-6-78; 5-19-79**
Carrollton	**WAQT**	**2-1-75 (new); 5-24-75; 1-17-76; 5-29-76; 3-5-77; 8-6-77; 10-7-78; 10-6-79**
Decatur	**WAJF**	**5-27-72 (bumper sticker welcome); 6-24-72 (4th of July Festival); 6-23-73 (new); 9-1-73; 11-17-73**
Dothan	**WDIG**	**11-15-75**
Enterprise	**WIRB**	**6-1-73 (never mentioned on show; listed in 1973 Vacation Listening Guide)**
	WKMX	**1-29-77 (new); 5-14-77; 11-5-77; 1-7-78; 11-11-78; 11-3-79**
Florence	**(see Muscle Shoals, AL)**	
Gadsden	**WGAD**	**1-17-76 (new); 7-17-76**
	WQEN	**5-7-77 (new); 7-9-77; 2-10-79**
Greenville	**WKXN**	**1-28-78 (new); 11-11-78; 11-3-79**
Guntersville	**WGSV**	**4-24-71 (new); 7-3-71 (listed in *Billboard* ad); 7-17-71; 10-2-71; 11-6-71; 11-13-71 (listed in *Billboard* ad); 3-11-72; 9-8-73; 11-24-73; 4-20-74**
	WGSV	**1-17-76 (new); 12-4-76; 12-10-77; 3-4-78; 10-28-78**
Huntsville	**WVOV**	**11-13-71 (never mentioned in program, but listed as subscribing station in *Billboard* ad)**
	WAAY	**10-11-75 (new); 8-7-76; 7-14-79**
Marion	**WJAM**	**4-16-77 (new); 9-3-77**
Mobile	**WABB-FM**	**3-13-71 (new); 6-5-71; 7-3-71 (listed in *Billboard* ad); 9-4-71; 11-13-71 (listed in *Billboard* ad); 5-13-72; 7-8-72; 10-7-72; 11-25-72; 3-10-73; 6-2-73(2x); 7-21-73; 2-16-74; 2-23-74; 10-19-74; 4-12-75; 5-31-75; 9-20-75; 5-8-76; 7-31-76; 5-21-77; 2-25-78; 12-16-78**
Monroeville	**WMFC**	**4-21-79 (new)**
Montgomery	**WMGY/WAJM**	**5-18-74 (new); 11-23-74 (mentioned as WMGZ)**
	WHHY	**3-27-76 (new); 8-14-76; 7-8-78; 2-3-79**
Muscle Shoals	**WOWL**	**1-8-72 (new); 3-11-72**
Selma	**WAMA**	**12-2-72 (new); 1-13-73; 1-4-75 (new)**
	WMRK	**6-24-78 (new); 5-5-79; 7-14-79 (1st on-air anniversary)**
Sylacauga	**WMLS**	**4-19-75**
Talladega	**WHTB**	**11-27-76 (new)**
Troy	**WTUB**	**8-9-75 (new)**

'American Top 40' Gets 26 Stations

LOS ANGELES — Twenty-six stations have launched "American Top 40," the weekly series of specials produced by Watermark, Inc., reported Watermark president Tom Rounds. The three-hour series features a countdown of Billboard's Hot 100 Chart and is rush-released to the stations so that it arrives in advance of the Billboard. The show is designed to be broadcast on Sunday afternoon. Casey Kasem is host.

Stations now featuring the show include KJR in Seattle, KJOY in Stockton, Calif.; KRUX in Phoenix; KEYN in Witchita, Kan.; WGAR in Cleveland, WAIR in Winston-Salem; WFLI in Chattanooga; WNOX in Knoxville; WCBM in Baltimore; WMEX in Boston; WPGC in Washington; WVIC in Lansing, Mich.; WKBR in Manchester, N.H.; KMEN in San Bernardino, Calif.; KACY in Oxnard, Calif.; KHYT in Tucson; KCPX in Salt Lake City; KQEO in Albuquerque, N.M.; KINT in El Paso; KTSA in San Antonio; KNUZ in Houston; KIRL in St. Louis; KEYS in Corpus Christi; KPOI in Honolulu, and WWWW-FM in Detroit.

All these stations are already carrying the show—free to the top 100 radio markets—or are slated to launch it this week. In addition, at least 10 more stations will begin carrying the weekly specials in the next three weeks.

After only three months on the air, *AT40* executive producer Tom Rounds reported that the program was now heard on 26 radio stations, according to this article which appeared in the October 10, 1970 edition of *Billboard Magazine*.

In Anchorage, KBYR's Tunedex weekly record survey for February 10, 1972 promoted *AT40* with Casey Kasem's photograph.

STATE

Market	*Calls*	*Air Date Mentions*
ALASKA		
Anchorage	KBYR	2-13-71 (new; mentioned as KBTR); 2-20-71 (corrected from 2-13-71); 5-29-71; 7-3-71 (listed in *Billboard* ad); 9-4-71; 11-13-71 (listed in *Billboard* ad); 1-8-72; 4-15-72; 12-23-72; 3-3-73; 6-16-73; 7-28-73; 1-12-74 (mentioned as WBYR)
	KENI	5-18-74 (new); 8-3-74; 11-9-74; 6-21-75; 9-20-75; 5-8-76; 7-24-76; 12-18-76; 12-10-77; 1-6-79; 6-23-79; 12-15-79
Barrow	KBRW	1-20-79 (new); 12-8-79
Cordova	KLAM	7-3-71 (listed in *Billboard* ad); 11-13-71 (listed in *Billboard* ad); 2-5-72
	KLAM	8-4-73 (new); 10-20-73; 4-13-74; 11-30-74
Fairbanks	KFAR	2-13-71 (new); 5-22-71; 7-3-71 (listed in *Billboard* ad); 11-13-71 (listed in *Billboard* ad); 12-4-71; 11-18-72; 3-3-73; 9-1-73; 12-1-73; 3-16-74; 12-7-74; 3-29-75; 4-19-75; 1-17-76; 6-12-76; 7-31-76; 5-14-77; 5-13-78; 2-3-79
Juneau	KINY	2-13-71 (new); 4-24-71; 7-3-71 (listed in *Billboard* ad); 7-31-71; 10-30-71; 11-13-71 (listed in *Billboard* ad); 1-15-72; 2-12-72; 10-21-72; 2-3-73; 3-3-73; 8-18-73; 10-20-73; 3-23-74; 1-4-75; 4-26-75
	KJNO	7-23-77 (new); 2-25-78
Kodiak	KVOK	11-29-75; 2-21-76; 8-7-76; 5-19-79
Kotzebue	KOTZ	8-5-78 (new); 3-24-79
Sitka	KIFW	12-13-75 (new); 8-14-76; 12-4-76; 6-24-78; 6-16-79; 10-27-79

STATE

Market	*Calls*	*Air Date Mentions*
ARIZONA		
Apache Junction	KSTM	5-24-75 (new)
Bisbee	KSUN	7-17-76 (new); 12-4-76
Bullhead City	KRHS	7-21-79 (new)
Casa Grande	KBFE	9-24-77 (new)
Flagstaff	KFLG	8-7-76 (new)
	KNAU	10-29-77 (new)
	KNAU	9-16-78 (new)
	KNAU	9-8-79 (new); 11-10-79
Globe	KWJB	8-23-75 (new); 2-21-76
	KIKO	6-12-76 (new); 7-24-76; 12-18-76; 12-10-77; 1-7-78; 1-20-79
Phoenix	KRUX	10-10-70 (never mentioned; listed only in *Billboard* article)
	KRIZ	4-3-71 (new); 6-12-71; 7-3-71 (listed in *Billboard* ad); 9-11-71; 11-13-71 (listed in *Billboard* ad); 1-15-72 (listener question); 3-4-72; 7-15-72; 10-28-72; 1-6-73; 5-12-73; 6-9-73; 9-22-73; 12-1-73; 6-8-74; 1-18-75; 5-24-75
	KBBC	8-16-75 (new); 10-11-75; 3-20-76; 8-7-76
	KRIZ	1-22-77 (new); 3-5-77; 9-3-77; 11-5-77
	KOY	8-19-78 (new); 4-21-79 (listener question)
Tucson	KHYT	9-5-70 (2x: program & listed in *Billboard* ad); 10-24-70; 1-2-71; 2-6-71 (listed in *Billboard* ad); 5-8-71; 7-3-71 (listed in *Billboard* ad); 10-9-71; 11-13-71 (listed in *Billboard* ad); 5-13-72; 8-25-73
	KIKX	12-15-73 (new); 3-23-74
	KTKT	6-11-77 (new); 5-19-79
Willcox	KWCX	9-18-76 (new); 12-4-76
	KWCX	3-25-78 (new)
Yuma	KBLU	8-13-77 (new); 5-6-78; 4-14-79
ARKANSAS		
Clinton	KGFL	4-14-79 (new; mentioned as Clinton, Arizona); 4-28-79 (new; corrected)
El Dorado	KDMS	8-7-71 (new); 9-11-71; 10-23-71; 11-13-71 (listed in *Billboard* ad); 11-27-71; 3-4-72; 6-23-73; 3-9-74
	KELD	2-12-77 (new); 9-3-77; 3-4-78; 10-7-78; 10-13-79
Fayetteville	KKEG	4-26-75 (new); 10-25-75
Fort Smith	KISR	4-22-72; 10-14-72; 1-6-73; 4-14-73; 5-12-73; 7-21-73; 3-30-74; 1-25-75; 11-8-75; 12-11-76; 5-13-78; 10-27-79
Hardy	KSRB	2-26-77 (new); 10-15-77; 3-10-79
Harrison	KHOZ	1-17-76; 11-20-76; 11-5-77; 10-14-78; 10-27-79
Heber Springs	KAWW	8-28-76 (new); 12-18-76
Hot Springs	KBHS	10-1-77 (new); 7-8-78
	KSPA	(listed in 1979 Listening Directory)
Jonesboro	KHIG-FM	4-29-72 (acknowledged new 5-6-72); 8-5-72; 11-11-72; 5-12-73; 9-29-73; 11-3-73; 3-23-74; 8-10-74; 2-15-75; 7-12-75; 12-20-75; 5-28-77; 8-5-78; 8-11-79
Little Rock	KLAZ	2-7-76 (new); 4-10-76; 7-31-76; 3-5-77; 1-7-78; 6-9-79
Mountain Home	KTLO	10-16-76 (new); 5-21-77; 9-23-78; 9-22-79
Osceola	KOSE/KHFP	5-11-74 (new); 2-1-75; 5-31-75; 1-31-76
Paragould	(see Jonesboro, AR)	
Pine Bluff	KOTN	10-26-74 (new); 2-22-75; 8-2-75; 1-24-76; 5-29-76; 7-24-76; 5-13-78; 9-9-78
Springdale	KCIZ	4-24-76 (new); 5-22-76 (new); 11-13-76; 7-15-78; 1-6-79; 7-21-79
Texarkana	KOSY	4-15-78 (new); 2-3-79

KBBC NOTES

HELLO AGAIN...The Super Season is coming to KBBC. Already, the mornings and evenings have new shows. Steve Martin does 6-10am and Mark James does 6-10pm. Also, Casey Kasem brings his American Top 40 to FM 99 soon. The fall line-up includes Sunday specials, and many contests and promotions to help make our station your station.

NEW MUSIC this week includes...GET DOWN TONIGHT by K.C. & The Sunshine Band; FEELINGS by Morris Albert; DEPARTMENT OF YOUTH by Alice Cooper; and IF YOU THINK YOU KNOW HOW TO LOVE ME by Smokey...... that's it for this week...take care....tony booth........

KBBC TOP ALBUMS

		ARTIST	LABEL
1.	One Of These Nights	Eagles	Asylum
2.	Capt Fantastic	Elton John	MCA
3.	Venus & Mars	Wings	Capitol
4.	Cut the Cake	AWB	Atlantic
5.	Why Can't We Be Friends?	War	UA
6.	Disco Baby	Van McCoy	Avco
7.	Made In The Shade	Rolling Stones	Atlantic
8.	Gorilla	James Taylor	Warner Bros.
9.	Between The Lines	Janis Ian	Columbia
10.	The Original Soundtrack	10 CC	Mercury

Join Casey Kasem this Sunday morning at 9 o'clock for the premier of AMERICAN TOP 40... part of the SUPER SEASON on KBBC.

KBBC MUSIC GUIDE WEEK OF 7/21/75

LW	TW		ARTIST	LABEL
1.	1.	Someone Saved My Life Tonight	Elton John	MCA
2.	2.	Listen To What The Man Said	Wings	Capitol
3.	3.	Jive Talkin'	Bee Gees	RSO
4.	4.	One Of These Nights	Eagles	Asylum
5.	5.	Fallin In Love	Hamilton, Joe Frank & Reynolds	Playboy
6.	6.	The Hustle	Van McCoy	Avco
10.	7.	Why Can't We Be Friends?	War	UA
9.	8.	Dynomite	Bazuka	A&M
11.	9.	Holdin' On To Yesterday	Ambrosia	20th Century
7.	10.	I'm Not In Love	10 CC	Mercury
12.	11.	At Seventeen	Janis Ian	Columbia
13.	12.	Rockin' Chair	Gwen McCrae	CAT
26.	13.	Could It Be Magic	Barry Manilow	Arista
8.	14.	Please Mr. Please	Olivia Newton-John	MCA
15.	15.	Love Will Keep Us Together	Capt & Tennille	A&M
22.	16.	'Til The World Ends	Three Dog Night	ABC
19.	17.	Move A Little Closer	Douglas Alan Davis	Capitol
17.	18.	Swearin' To God	Frankie Valli	Private Stock
20.	19.	Mornin' Beautiful	Tony Orlando & Dawn	Elecktra
23.	20.	How Sweet It Is	James Taylor	Warner Bros.
14.	21.	Magic	Pilot	Capitol
28.	22.	Tush	ZZ Top	London
16.	23.	Rockford Files	Mike Post	MGM
25.	24.	I Don't Know Why	Rolling Stones	ABKO
18.	25.	I'm On Fire	Dwight Twilley Band	Shelter
29.	26.	Help Me Rhonda	Johnny Rivers	Epic
31.	27.	Daisy Jane	America	Warner Bros.
32.	28.	Feel Like Makin' Love	Bad Co.	Swan Song
21.	29.	The Way We Were/Try To Remember	Gladys Knight & The Pips	Buddah
24.	30.	Funny How Love Can Be	First Class	UK
—	31.	Rhine Stone Cowboy	Glen Campbell	Capitol
—	32	That's The Way Of The World	Earth, Wind & Fire	Columbia
—	33.	There's Nothing Stronger Than Our Love	Paul Anka & Odia Coates	UA
—	34.	Third Rate Romance	Amazing Rhythm Aces	ABC
—	35.	The Proud One	Osmonds	MGM

KBBC NEW MUSIC

Get Down Tonight	K.C. & The Sunshine Band	TK
Feelings	Morris Albert	RCA
If You Think You Know How To Love Me	Smokey	MCA
Department of Youth	Alice Cooper	Atlantic

PHOENIX MUSIC GUIDE SURVEY

Although Casey Kasem did not welcome radio station KBBC in Phoenix as a new station until August 16, 1975, *AT40*'s actual debut was in mid-July according to this July 21, 1975 survey.

This advertisement appeared in the September 5, 1970 edition of *Billboard Magazine*. Note the testimonial from the general manager of all-oldies WWWW-FM which yielded to *AT40*'s contemporary sound on Sunday afternoons.

CALIFORNIA

Apple Valley	**KAVR**	**8-20-77 (new); 1-7-78; 12-9-78; 4-28-79 (25th B-day)**
Arcata	**KATA**	**6-12-71 (new); 7-3-71 (listed in *Billboard* ad)**
Bakersfield	**KAFY**	**12-26-70; 2-6-71 (listed in *Billboard* ad); 5-15-71; 7-3-71 (listed in *Billboard* ad); 7-17-71; 10-9-71; 11-13-71 (listed in *Billboard* ad); 5-6-72**
	KERN	**7-8-72 (new); 1-20-73; 12-30-72; 5-19-73; 8-18-73; 2-9-74; 10-12-74; 4-19-75; 12-13-75; 4-3-76; 7-24-76; 1-8-77 (listener question); 3-5-77; 7-9-77; 1-14-78; 1-13-79; 6-30-79; 12-15-79**
Barstow	**KWTC**	**6-17-78 (new); 4-7-79**
Bishop	**KIBS**	**3-10-73 (new); 4-14-73**
	KIOQ	**8-2-75 (new)**
Carmel	**KRML**	**8-25-79 (new); 9-1-79 (new)**
Chino	**KCIM**	**7-15-72 (new)**
Crescent City	**KPOD**	**5-18-74 (new); 10-19-74**
El Cajon	**KDEO**	**(never mentioned on program or in a *Billboard* ad; one of the first seven stations)**
El Centro	**KAMP**	**9-14-74 (new); 9-28-74; 11-23-74**
Eureka	**KRED**	**7-29-72; 10-28-72**
Fresno	**KFYE**	**10-16-76 (new); 12-4-76; 7-29-78; 6-2-79**
Lancaster	**KAVL**	**1-13-79 (new); 10-6-79**
Lompoc	**KLOM**	**1-8-72 (new, and listed in *Billboard* ad); 2-5-72; 7-29-72; 11-11-72; 3-3-73; 5-5-73; 8-18-73; 11-3-73; 2-2-74 (profiled in *Billboard* ad); 4-13-74; 11-16-74; 5-3-75; 12-20-75; 2-12-77; 7-30-77; 3-31-79**
Los Angeles	**KRLA**	**10-24-70; 1-9-71; 2-6-71 (listed in *Billboard* ad); 6-5-71 (mentioned in *Billboard* ad); 6-19-71; 7-3-71 (listed in *Billboard* ad)**
	KGBS-AM/FM	**10-2-71 (new); 10-30-71; 11-13-71 (listed in *Billboard* ad); 1-15-72; 2-5-72; 4-8-72; 5-20-72; 6-10-72; 7-8-72; 8-12-72; 10-14-72; 11-4-72; 11-18-72; 12-2-72; 12-30-72; 1-13-73; 2-10-73; 3-10-73; 3-17-73; 6-30-73; 8-4-73; 8-18-73; 9-8-73**
	KKDJ	**3-29-75 (new); 5-3-75 (listed in *Billboard* ad)**
	KIIS	**11-1-75; 4-17-76; 7-31-76; 10-16-76; 12-4-76; 12-18-76 (listener question); 4-2-77; 11-5-77; 12-17-77; 2-18-78; 4-15-78; 5-20-78; 8-19-78; 9-2-78; 11-25-78; 1-13-79; 6-2-79; 6-30-79; 11-24-79**
Mammoth Lakes	**KMMT**	**1-21-78 (new)**
Modesto	**KTRB**	**3-30-74 (new)**
Monterey	**KMBY**	**4-15-72 (acknowledged new 5-6-72); 8-19-72; 12-2-72; 3-10-73; 5-26-73; 8-18-73; 1-19-74; 4-20-74**
Oakland	**(see San Francisco, CA)**	
Oxnard	**KACY**	**9-12-70; 1-2-71; 2-6-71 (listed in *Billboard* ad); 3-20-71 (radio report); 5-8-71; 7-3-71 (listed in *Billboard* ad); 10-9-71; 11-13-71 (listed in *Billboard* ad); 4-15-72; 10-7-72; 11-25-72; 2-24-73; 5-26-73; 8-4-73; 8-18-73; 1-12-74; 2-23-74; 7-27-74; 11-30-74; 4-12-75; 11-29-75; 7-10-76; 5-21-77; 8-13-77; 5-13-78; 1-6-79; 12-8-79**
Palm Springs	**KPSI**	**7-29-72**
Paradise	**KNVR**	**1-14-78 (new); 3-4-78; 11-4-78; 3-31-79**
Redding	**KXSO**	**2-10-79 (new); 11-24-79**
Riverside	**(see San Bernadino, CA)**	
Sacramento	**KCRA**	**5-15-71 (new); 7-3-71 (listed in *Billboard* ad); 7-17-71; 9-4-71; 10-16-71; 11-13-71 (listed in *Billboard* ad); 12-25-71; 3-11-72; 9-23-72; 10-7-72; 10-28-72; 1-13-73; 5-5-73; 6-9-73; 6-30-73; 8-18-73; 12-8-73; 3-2-74; 12-14-74**
	KXOA	**1-11-75 (new); 9-6-75; 10-25-75; 2-28-76; 8-7-76; 11-18-78; 6-23-79; 12-8-79**
Salinas	**KBUL**	**10-19-74 (new)**
	(also see Monterey, CA)	
San Bernadino	**KMEN**	**8-29-70; 11-7-70; 12-26-70; 2-6-71 (listed in *Billboard* ad); 7-3-71 (listed in *Billboard* ad); 8-7-71; 11-13-71 (listed in *Billboard* ad); 11-20-71; 1-29-72; 2-12-72; 9-23-72; 10-7-72; 11-4-72; 1-6-73; 4-14-73; 5-5-73; 8-4-73; 8-18-73; 11-24-73; 4-27-74**
	KOLA-FM	**11-16-74 (new); 8-2-75; 9-20-75**
	KHNY	**1-7-78 (new); 4-8-78; 10-28-78**
San Diego	**KGB**	**3-4-72 (new) 1-19-74 (new); 2-2-74 (listed in *Billboard* ad); 3-16-74; 3-23-74; 6-29-74; 7-6-74; 1-18-75; 5-24-75; 9-13-75; 1-17-76; 6-26-76; 8-14-76; 5-14-77; 8-5-78; 11-10-79; 12-8-79**
	(also see El Cajon, CA)	

CALIFORNIA (cont'd)

San Francisco	**KNEW**	**10-9-71 (new); 11-6-71; 11-13-71 (listed in *Billboard* ad); 1-22-72; 2-5-72; 6-3-72; 7-22-72; 8-19-72**
	KYA	**7-12-75 (new); 12-6-75; 5-15-76; 8-28-76; 12-18-76; 5-21-77; 12-10-77; 8-19-78; 11-18-78; 5-26-79; 6-23-79; 11-17-79**
San Jose	**KSJO**	**8-17-74 (new); 9-14-74 (new); 1-25-75; 8-16-75 (mentioned as KSUO)**
San Luis Obispo	**KSLY**	**1-29-77 (new); 9-3-77; 11-25-78; 6-23-79; 11-24-79**
Stockton	**KJOY**	**10-17-70; 10-31-70; 11-21-70 (radio report); 12-19-70 (radio report); 2-6-71 (radio report & listed in *Billboard* ad); 3-20-71 (radio report); 6-5-71; 7-3-71 (listed in *Billboard* ad); 9-25-71; 11-13-71 (listed in *Billboard* ad); 9-2-72; 12-2-72; 1-27-73; 5-5-73; 8-18-73; 1-12-74; 2-8-75; 4-26-75; 10-25-75; 8-21-76; 11-13-76; 9-24-77; 5-13-78; 2-3-79**
Ukiah	**KUKI**	**2-17-79 (new); 12-1-79**
Ventura	**(see Oxnard, CA)**	
Yuba City	**KOBO**	**7-14-79 (new)**

310 Tenth Street, Sacramento, California, 95814 · 916/441-5272

December 1, 1972

Thomas E. Rounds
Watermark, Inc.
10700 Ventura Boulevard
Los Angeles, CA 91604

Dear Tom:

Enclosed is our signed agreement to carry American Top 40 for another year. I find myself getting redundant. The program improves every year but remains consistent in high quality and interest.

You may be interested in knowing that our week-end ratings are higher than ever. I attribute much of this success to American Top 40 and I am grateful to your organization.

Sincerely,

Johnny Hyde
Program Director

JH/js

This December 1, 1972 letter from a KCRA (Sacramento, California) program director praising *AT40* was included in *American Top 40* presentation packages to other radio stations.

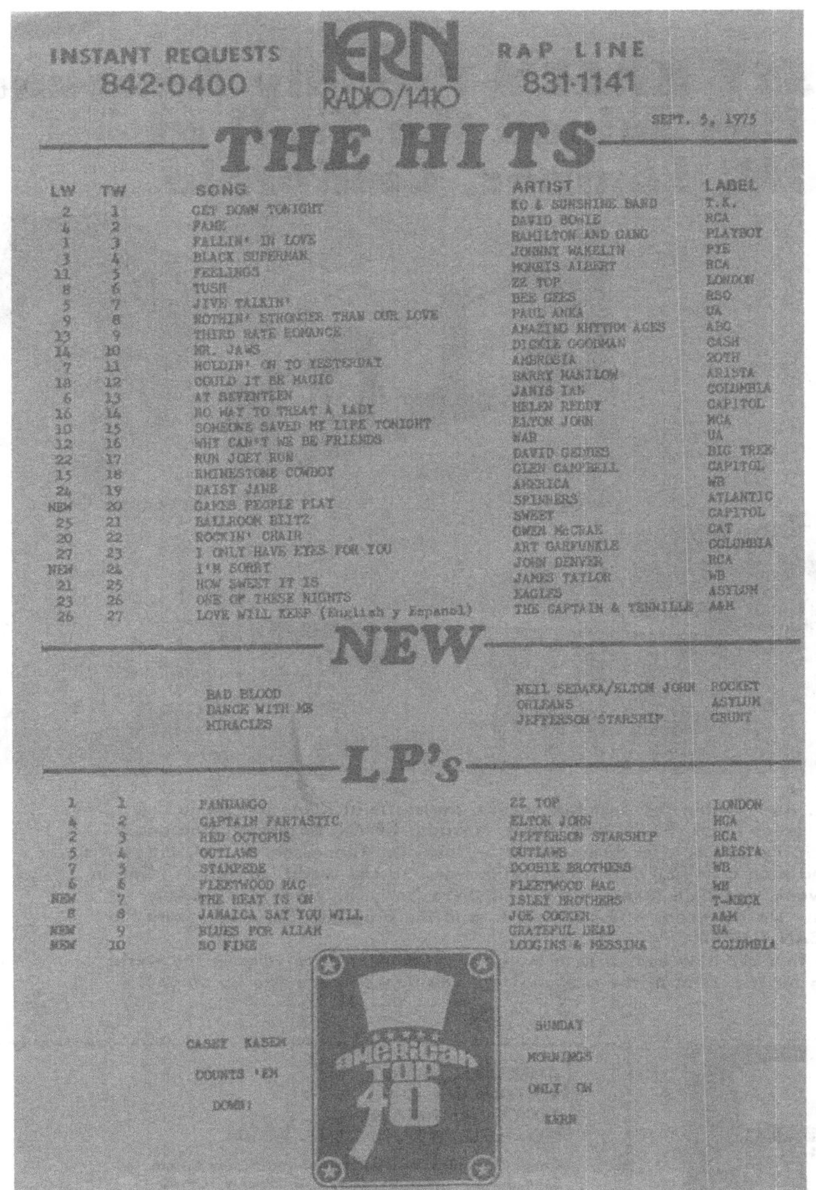

INSTANT REQUESTS 842-0400

KERN RADIO/1410

RAP LINE 831-1141

SEPT. 5, 1975

THE HITS

LW	TW	SONG	ARTIST	LABEL
2	1	GET DOWN TONIGHT	KC & SUNSHINE BAND	T.K.
4	2	FAME	DAVID BOWIE	RCA
1	3	FALLIN' IN LOVE	HAMILTON AND GANG	PLAYBOY
3	4	BLACK SUPERMAN	JOHNNY WAKELIN	PYE
11	5	FEELINGS	MORRIS ALBERT	RCA
8	6	TUSH	ZZ TOP	LONDON
5	7	JIVE TALKIN'	BEE GEES	RSO
9	8	NOTHIN' STRONGER THAN OUR LOVE	PAUL ANKA	UA
13	9	THIRD RATE ROMANCE	AMAZING RHYTHM ACES	ABC
14	10	MR. JAWS	DICKIE GOODMAN	CASH
7	11	HOLDIN' ON TO YESTERDAY	AMBROSIA	20TH
18	12	COULD IT BE MAGIC	BARRY MANILOW	ARISTA
6	13	AT SEVENTEEN	JANIS IAN	COLUMBIA
16	14	NO WAY TO TREAT A LADY	HELEN REDDY	CAPITOL
10	15	SOMEONE SAVED MY LIFE TONIGHT	ELTON JOHN	MCA
12	16	WHY CAN'T WE BE FRIENDS	WAR	UA
22	17	RUN JOEY RUN	DAVID GEDDES	BIG TREE
15	18	RHINESTONE COWBOY	GLEN CAMPBELL	CAPITOL
24	19	DAISY JANE	AMERICA	WB
NEW	20	GAMES PEOPLE PLAY	SPINNERS	ATLANTIC
25	21	BALLROOM BLITZ	SWEET	CAPITOL
20	22	ROCKIN' CHAIR	GWEN McCRAE	CAT
27	23	I ONLY HAVE EYES FOR YOU	ART GARFUNKLE	COLUMBIA
NEW	24	I'M SORRY	JOHN DENVER	RCA
21	25	HOW SWEET IT IS	JAMES TAYLOR	WB
23	26	ONE OF THESE NIGHTS	EAGLES	ASYLUM
26	27	LOVE WILL KEEP (English y Espanol)	THE CAPTAIN & TENNILLE	A&M

NEW

SONG	ARTIST	LABEL
BAD BLOOD	NEIL SEDAKA/ELTON JOHN	ROCKET
DANCE WITH ME	ORLEANS	ASYLUM
MIRACLES	JEFFERSON STARSHIP	GRUNT

LP's

LW	TW	ALBUM	ARTIST	LABEL
1	1	FANDANGO	ZZ TOP	LONDON
4	2	CAPTAIN FANTASTIC	ELTON JOHN	MCA
2	3	RED OCTOPUS	JEFFERSON STARSHIP	RCA
5	4	OUTLAWS	OUTLAWS	ARISTA
7	5	STAMPEDE	DOOBIE BROTHERS	WB
6	6	FLEETWOOD MAC	FLEETWOOD MAC	WB
NEW	7	THE HEAT IS ON	ISLEY BROTHERS	T-NECK
8	8	JAMAICA SAY YOU WILL	JOE COCKER	A&M
NEW	9	BLUES FOR ALLAH	GRATEFUL DEAD	UA
NEW	10	SO FINE	LOGGINS & MESSINA	COLUMBIA

CASEY KASEM COUNTS 'EM DOWN!

American Top 40

SUNDAY MORNINGS ONLY ON KERN

From Bakersfield, California, this KERN radio survey dated September 5, 1975 points out that "Casey Kasem counts 'em down! Sunday mornings only on KERN."

CASEY KASEM Proudly Announces He Has Joined the Staff at KLOM, Lompoc, California.

. . . And, within the past few weeks, the staffs at KGB, San Diego, KIXS, Killeen, Texas; KGRN, Las Vegas, Nevada; KBMN, Bozeman, Montana; WLCY, St. Petersberg, Florida and WBYQ, Nashville, Tennessee. In fact, Casey is a weekend man on about 250 radio stations around the world. Job offers come in every week, and he'll take every one of them (sorry, only one per market).

Your station needs a Casey Kasem, and the program that comes with him, AMERICAN TOP 40.

To find out how easy it is to have the most listened to voice in the world working for you, send in the coupon. Until you do, Lompoc's one up on you.

AMERICAN TOP 40
WATERMARK, INC.
10700 VENTURA BLVD.
NO. HOLLYWOOD, CALIF. 91604

I might just have an opening for your Casey Kasem. Send me the entire, free, 1974 AMERICAN TOP 40 Presentation Package, rates and market availability.

NAME __________ TITLE ______
CALL LETTERS ______ ADDRESS __________
CITY __________ STATE ______ ZIP ______

AMERICAN TOP 40 is a 3 hour weekly review of current events in America's most popular music as reported by BILLBOARD. Produced and distributed on compatible stereo discs (made of precious virgin vinyl!) by Watermark, makers of AMERICAN COUNTRY COUNTDOWN.

©1974, WATERMARK, INC.

To address the problem some stations experienced with filling weekend announcer slots, this advertisement pointed out that "your station needs a Casey Kasem...." The ad appeared in *Billboard Magazine* on February 2, 1974.

STATE

Market	*Calls*	*Air Date Mentions*
COLORADO		
Colorado Springs	KYSN-AM	7-8-72; 12-2-72; 1-27-73; 5-19-73; 9-22-73; 1-19-74; 2-2-74; 2-15-75; 3-6-76; 5-22-76; 8-14-76; 12-11-76; 3-31-79
Craig	KRAI	8-27-77 (new); 1-7-78
Denver	KIMN	1-30-71; 2-6-71 (listed in *Billboard* ad)
	KTLK	9-16-72 (new); 5-5-73; 6-9-73; 6-30-73; 8-4-73; 11-24-73; 6-1-74; 2-22-75; 5-17-75
	KIMN	8-14-76 (new); 4-30-77; 5-13-78; 9-16-78 (long distance dedication); 9-30-78; 6-2-79; 10-13-79; 12-22-79
Durango	KDGO	9-17-77 (new); 3-4-78; 7-22-78; 12-16-78
Estes Park	KSIR	6-19-76 (new); 7-31-76; 2-12-77; 12-10-77
Fort Collins	KIIX	9-4-76 (new)
Fort Morgan	KFTM	11-9-74 (new); 6-28-75
Glenwood Springs	KGLN	10-16-76 (new); 3-5-77
Grand Junction	KQIL/KQIX	1-10-76 (new)
	KQIX	2-11-78 (new); 11-18-78; 11-17-79
Greeley	KFKA	4-8-78 (new); 1-13-79
Montrose	KUBC	2-25-78 (new); 2-24-79
Pueblo	KDJQ	9-11-76 (new); 11-13-76 (mentioned as WDJQ)
Vail	KVMT	12-9-78 (new)
CONNECTICUT		
Bloomfield	(see Hartford, CT)	
Danbury	WINE	6-21-75 (new); 3-6-76; 6-26-76; 7-24-76; 8-28-76 (listener question); 12-11-76
	WINE/WRKI	1-7-78; 4-21-79; 6-16-79
Hartford	WDRC	6-5-71; 7-3-71 (listed in *Billboard* ad); 11-6-71 (listener question); 11-13-71 (listed in *Billboard* ad); 12-18-71; 3-25-72; 7-29-72 (50th B-day); 11-18-72; 2-24-73; 5-26-73; 9-15-73; 12-15-73; 3-23-74; 3-30-74; 3-8-75; 4-19-75; 9-13-75; 2-14-76; 8-7-76; 2-12-77; 3-5-77; 6-18-77; 7-28-79
New Briton	(see Hartford, CT)	
Norwich	WICH	4-22-72 (acknowledged new 5-6-72); 9-9-72; 9-1-73; 11-17-73; 4-27-74; 3-15-75; 4-26-75; 3-20-76; 7-31-76; 11-13-76; 3-24-79

"In 1975, when I was at WFEC in Harrisburg, PA, Casey (Kasem) was across town at WKBO. When I moved to KAFY in Bakersfield, CA in 1976, AT40 was on KERN. And in 1978 when I got to KROY in Sacramento, it was on KXOA-FM. I guess I could say that I always felt like I was day late and a dollar short when it came to American Top 40. Casey was on wherever I went, but he was always on the competition!"

Top 40 aficionado Richard "Uncle Ricky" Irwin, former WFEC, KAFY and KROY program director and founder of REELRADIO, Inc. and the original radio aircheck website.

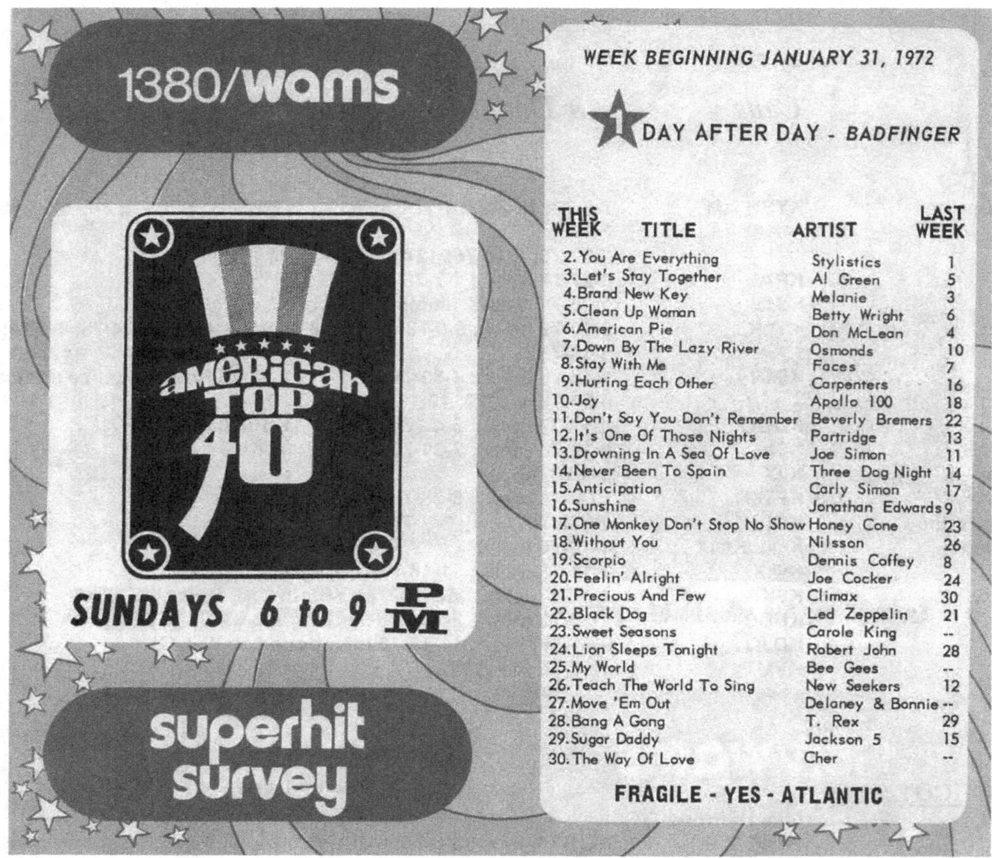

From January 31, 1972, a WAMS survey promotes *AT40* and its Sunday evening broadcast time in Wilmington, Delaware.

STATE

Market	*Calls*	*Air Date Mentions*
DELAWARE		
Dover	**WDOV**	**10-7-72 (new); 10-27-73; 3-16-74; 9-21-74; 9-28-74; 10-12-74; 6-5-76**
Wilmington	**WAMS**	**2-6-71 (2x: radio & listed in *Billboard* ad); 7-3-71 (listed in *Billboard* ad); 9-18-71; 1-8-72 (listed in *Billboard* ad)**
DISTRICT OF COLUMBIA		
Washington, DC	**WPGC**	**9-5-70 (listed in *Billboard* ad); 9-19-70; 12-5-70; 2-6-71 (listed in *Billboard* ad); 4-3-71 (mentioned as Bladensburg, MD); 7-3-71 (listed in *Billboard* ad); 7-10-71 (listener question); 8-21-71; 10-23-71; 11-20-71 (radio, & listed in *Billboard* ad); 1-22-72; 2-12-72; 5-6-72; 5-27-72; 6-17-72; 7-22-72; 8-26-72; 12-9-72; 1-27-73; 4-21-73; 8-11-73; 10-27-73; 2-16-74; 3-2-74; 5-25-74; 6-15-74 (William DeVaughn home); 10-19-74; 4-19-75 (listed in *Billboard* ad); 7-19-75; 11-8-75; 7-24-76; 11-13-76; 1-29-77; 3-5-77; 11-12-77; 1-7-78; 8-26-78; 6-16-79; 8-25-79; 12-22-79**

STATE

Market	*Calls*	*Air Date Mentions*
FLORIDA		
Chiefland	WLQH	8-21-76 (new); 12-11-76
		6-16-79 (new)
Cocoa Beach	WCKS	3-13-76 (new); 9-3-77; 2-18-78; 3-4-78; 1-20-79
Cypress Gardens	WGTO	5-8-71 (new); 7-3-71 (listed in *Billboard* ad); 7-24-71; 11-20-71 (listed in *Billboard* ad); 11-27-71; 2-26-72; 6-10-72; 10-14-72; 1-6-73; 6-30-73; 7-14-73; 10-13-73; 1-19-74; 2-2-74; 4-20-74
Daytona Beach	WOGO	9-1-73 (new; mentioned as New Smyrna Beach); 1-12-74
	WROD	11-2-74 (new); 8-16-75; 1-10-76
	WMFJ	5-15-76 (new); 7-24-76; 12-18-76; 10-1-77
	WQXQ	9-1-79; 10-6-79 (new)
Dunnellon	WTRS	12-8-73; 6-15-74; 6-29-74; 11-23-74
Fort Myers	WCAI	5-25-74 (new); 11-16-74
Fort Pierce	WOVV	4-17-76 (new); 7-31-76; 3-12-77; 10-15-77; 3-17-79
Fort Walton Beach	WNUE	6-19-76 (new); 5-28-77; 11-12-77; 5-5-79
Gainesville	WGGG	1-8-72 (new, & listed in *Billboard* ad); 5-20-72 (welcome back); 12-23-72;
		3-31-73; 6-16-73; 8-4-73; 12-15-73; 3-30-74; 6-21-75; 2-21-76; 6-19-76; 2-26-77; 12-10-77; 10-21-78; 10-20-79
Jacksonville	WAPE	4-3-76 (new); 8-21-76; 5-28-77; 4-8-78; 3-3-79
Lakeland	WQPD	9-28-74 (new); 11-30-74; 7-26-75; 9-20-75
	WQPD	12-15-79 (new)
Live Oak	WNER	1-8-72 (new, & listed in *Billboard* ad); 2-12-72; 2-19-72; 7-22-72; 4-14-73; 10-20-73; 12-14-74; 5-10-75; 11-22-75; 1-14-78; 3-17-79
Marathon	WFFG	9-14-74
	WFFG	9-8-79 (new)
Melbourne	WMEL	11-20-71 (listed in *Billboard* ad)
		3-29-75 (new)
Miami	WGBS	5-22-76; 8-28-76; 1-15-77; 3-12-77; 7-9-77
	WQAM	5-20-78 (new); 5-27-78; 9-2-78; 12-2-78; 2-24-79; 4-28-79; 9-22-79; 10-13-79 (long distance dedication); 12-15-79
Naples	WRGI	5-13-78 (new)
New Smyrna Beach	(see Daytona Beach, FL)	
Ocala	WWKE	8-30-75 (new); 3-13-76; 5-28-77; 5-19-79
Orange Park	(see Jacksonville, FL)	
Orlando	WORJ	5-29-71; 7-3-71 (listed in *Billboard* ad)
	WLOF	9-23-72 (new); 1-6-73; 8-4-73; 5-4-74; 7-13-74; 8-31-74; 1-4-75; 5-10-75; 10-18-75; 3-13-76; 8-7-76; 3-5-77; 7-15-78; 9-1-79
Palatka	WWPF	9-27-75 (new)
Palm Beach	WQXT	2-13-71 (radio report); 3-20-71
		7-3-71 (listed in *Billboard* ad as West Palm Beach)
	(also see West Palm Beach, FL)	
Panama City	WGNE	12-8-73; 4-13-74; 1-18-75; 7-26-75; 2-28-76; 8-14-76; 8-19-78
Pensacola	WNEL	10-2-71 (new); 11-20-71 (listed in *Billboard* ad)
	WBSR	2-10-73 (new); 6-16-73; 9-22-73; 1-12-74; 3-2-74; 1-10-76 (new); 1-7-78 (new); 1-14-78; 10-14-78; 10-13-79
St. Petersburg	(see Tampa, FL)	
Sarasota	WSPB	1-29-77 (new)
	WYND	1-21-78 (new)
Sebring	WJCM	8-14-76 (new); 11-13-76
Stuart	WSTU	2-5-72 (new); 5-13-72; 5-20-72; 8-5-72
Tallahassee	WONS/WGBM	3-13-76 (new)
	WGLF	1-7-78 (new); 4-7-78
	WBGM	7-14-79 (new)
Tampa	WILZ	6-1-73 (listed in 1973 Vacation Listening Guide; first public acknowledgement as a subscribing station); 8-4-73 (new); 11-24-73
	WLCY	1-19-74 (new); 2-2-74 (listed in *Billboard* ad); 5-11-74; 5-18-74; 7-6-74; 2-8-75; 12-13-75; 9-4-76
	WYNF	7-30-77; 5-13-78; 11-11-78; 6-30-79; 12-1-79
Wauchula	WAUC	3-17-79 (new)
West Palm Beach	WJNO	1-24-76 (new); 11-27-76; 1-15-77; 8-26-78; 8-4-79; 12-8-79
	(also see Palm Beach, FL)	
Winter Haven	WZNG	3-12-77 (new); 9-30-78

STATE

Market	*Calls*	*Air Date Mentions*
GEORGIA		
Albany	**WALG**	**1-6-73; 6-23-73; 8-11-73; 12-15-73**
	WWCW-FM	**2-16-74 (new); 2-15-75; 9-6-75**
	WQDE	**11-27-76 (new); 7-9-77; 11-18-78; 11-10-79**
Americus	**WDEC-AM/FM**	**1-20-79 (new); 10-20-79**
Atlanta	**WIIN**	**7-21-73 (new); 11-10-73; 4-27-74**
	WZGC	**2-5-77 (new); 8-13-77; 9-9-78; 11-18-78; 6-30-79; 11-10-79**
Augusta	**WAKN**	**12-2-72**
	WAUG	**1-31-76 (new); 7-31-76; 11-20-76**
Bainbridge	**WAZA**	**1-22-77 (new); 3-12-77; 5-7-77; 7-30-77**
	WJAD	**4-22-78 (new)**
Baxley	**WUFE**	**8-11-79 (new)**
Brunswick	**WGIG**	**10-2-71 (new); 11-20-71 (listed in *Billboard* ad); 12-4-71 6-7-75 (new); 10-11-75; 1-7-78 (new); 3-4-78; 10-28-78**
	WSBI	**11-24-79**
	WPIQ	**12-15-79 (new)**
Carrollton	**WBTR**	**12-8-73; 3-9-74**
	WPPI	**12-6-75 (new); 12-11-76; 10-1-77**
	WBTR	**10-13-79 (new)**
Columbus	**WWRH**	**12-13-75; 8-7-76; 3-19-77**
	WCGQ	**8-27-77 (new); 7-22-78; 7-21-79**
Cordele	**WMJM**	**7-29-78 (new)**
Dalton	**WTTI**	**1-13-73 (new); 9-8-73; 12-1-73; 6-15-74; 8-17-74; 2-22-75; 8-30-75; 11-1-75; 4-24-76; 11-27-76; 11-12-77**
Dublin	**WKKZ**	**8-4-79 (new)**
Eastman	**WUFF**	**7-23-77 (new); 4-8-78**
Gainesville	**WFOX**	**5-18-74 (new); 8-17-74; 10-12-74; 6-21-75; 2-14-76; 5-28-77; 12-10-77; 8-19-78; 8-11-79**
Griffin	**WKEU**	**9-10-77 (new); 1-21-78; 8-25-79**
Jesup	**WIFO**	**2-4-78 (new); 11-4-78**
Lyons	**WBBT**	**7-8-78 (new); 4-7-79**
Marietta	**WBIE**	**6-19-71 (new); 7-3-71 (listed in *Billboard* ad); 7-24-71**
	WFOM	**10-19-74; 6-21-75**
Metter	**WMAC**	**6-1-73 (listed in 1973 Vacation Listening Guide; first public acknowledgement as a subscribing station); 6-8-74; 7-27-74; 11-23-74; 6-28-75; 6-4-77**
	WHCG	**5-13-78; 10-14-78 (new); 8-11-79**
Milledgeville	**WXLX**	**10-30-76 (new); 1-8-77; 1-14-78; 9-23-78; 9-22-79**
Ocilla	**WSIZ**	**6-1-74 (new); 11-16-74; 8-23-75; 12-20-75; 6-26-76; 11-13-76; 3-10-79**
Rome	**WROM**	**7-28-73; 12-29-73; 6-8-74; 9-7-74; 11-30-74; 8-16-75; 11-22-75; 5-12-79**
Savannah	**WSGA**	**5-13-72 (new); 5-20-72; 8-12-72; 3-10-73; 6-16-73; 1-19-74; 2-2-74; 6-8-74; 6-22-74; 12-14-74; 8-23-75; 9-27-75; 5-15-76; 6-25-77; 9-3-77; 5-12-79**
Thomasville	**WPAX**	**8-9-75 (new); 11-1-75**
Valdosta	**WVLD**	**7-3-71 (listed in *Billboard* ad); 8-28-71; 11-20-71 (listed in *Billboard* ad); 11-27-71 (listener question); 3-4-72; 9-1-73; 12-8-73; 1-4-75; 5-17-75; 6-5-76**
Vienna	**WWWN**	**11-10-79 (new)**
Warner Robins	**WRBN**	**11-3-79 (new)**
Waycross	**WAYX**	**7-30-77 (new); 4-7-79**
West Point	**WRLD**	**8-30-75 (new); 5-28-77; 5-20-78; 11-25-78**
Wrens	**WRNZ**	**6-2-79 (new)**

In Honolulu, KPOI's weekly record survey for September 29, 1970 alerted listeners to tune in Sundays from 9-noon to hear Casey Kasem and *AT40*.

HAWAII		
Hilo	KHLO	4-10-71 (new); 7-3-71 (2x: radio & listed in *Billboard* ad); 7-17-71; 9-25-71; 11-20-71 (2x: radio & listed in *Billboard* ad); 2-19-72
	KPUA	7-28-73 (new); 11-3-73; 5-11-74; 5-18-74; 1-18-75; 4-10-76
	KIPA	4-28-79 (new)
Honolulu	KPOI	9-5-70 (2x: radio & listed in *Billboard* ad); 10-31-70; 1-23-71; 1-30-71 (radio report); 2-3-71 (listed in *Billboard* ad); 4-24-71; 7-3-71 (listed in *Billboard* ad); 7-31-71; 11-20-71 (listed in *Billboard* ad); 1-8-72; 11-18-72; 2-10-73; 7-28-73; 12-15-73 (2x, *Hawaii Five-O*)
	KKUA	4-27-74 (new); 5-11-74; 1-25-75; 7-12-75; 11-22-75; 6-26-76; 8-28-76; 9-25-76; 3-12-77; 1-14-78; 2-24-79; 12-15-79
Lihue	KTOH	5-8-71 (new); 7-3-71 (listed in *Billboard* ad); 9-18-71; 11-20-71 (radio & listed in *Billboard* ad)
	KIVM	2-19-72; 2-3-73; 6-23-73; 8-11-73; 11-10-73
Wailuku	KMVI	8-21-76 (new); 11-6-76; 10-22-77; 4-8-78; 6-9-79
IDAHO		
Boise	KBBK	3-9-74 (new); 8-31-74; 6-7-75
	KFXD	4-24-76 (new; mentioned as Nampa, ID); 10-15-77; 2-10-79
Grangeville	KORT	6-1-73 (listed in 1973 Vacation Listening Guide; first public acknowledgement as subscribing station); 5-4-74; 2-15-75; 1-8-77; 7-9-77
Idaho Falls	KTEE	4-13-74 (new); 2-22-75; 8-23-75 (referred to as Idaho Falls, Iowa); 2-21-76; 8-7-76; 3-12-77; 10-22-77; 2-17-79
Lewiston	KOZE	7-15-72; 1-27-73; 6-23-73; 11-10-73; 3-1-75; 1-24-76; 7-17-76; 6-4-77; 5-20-78; 5-12-79
Montpelier	KVSI	5-22-76 (new; mentioned as KDSI); 6-4-77
	KVSI	5-12-79 (new)
Moscow	KRPL	1-13-73 (new); 3-3-73; 5-5-73; 9-29-73; 11-3-73; 9-14-74; 3-8-75; 5-17-75; 12-6-75; 6-19-76; 12-18-76; 2-17-79
Mountain Home	KFLI	9-13-75 (new); 9-27-75; 6-5-76; 8-14-76
	KFLI	12-3-77 (new); 1-14-78
Nampa	(see Boise, ID)	
Orofino	KLER	6-1-73 (listed in 1973 Vacation Listening Guide; first public acknowledgement as a subscribing station); 3-15-75; 11-6-76
Pocatello	KSNN	5-11-74 (new); 8-10-74; 3-22-75
		5-13-78 (new); 2-17-79
St. Anthony	KIGO	10-9-71 (new); 10-30-71; 11-20-71 (listed in *Billboard* ad); 1-15-72; 2-12-72
Sand Point	KSPT	1-17-76 (new); 11-27-76; 9-3-77
Twin Falls	KMTW	11-1-75 (new); 8-21-76; 3-4-78; 8-19-78; 6-16-79 (5 years w/AT40); 9-8-79

ILLINOIS

Belleville	**WIBV**	**5-1-76 (new); 3-12-77; 8-13-77; 4-8-78; 1-27-79**
Bloomington	**WIHN**	**6-28-75 (new); 3-6-76; 5-8-76**
	WBNQ	**9-25-76 (new); 1-8-77; 10-1-77; 7-15-78; 6-9-79; 7-21-79**
Carbondale	**WCIL**	**7-10-76 (new); 8-21-76; 3-19-77; 10-22-77; 4-7-79**
Champaign	**WLRW**	**9-15-73 (new)**
Charleston	**WEIC**	**1-17-76 (new); 6-5-76; 11-27-76; 12-17-77; 10-21-78; 10-20-79**
Chicago	**WCFL**	**7-8-72 (new); 7-15-72; 8-19-72; 9-2-72; 11-11-72; 11-25-72; 12-23-72**
	WDHF	**6-22-74 (new); 9-14-74; 10-12-74; 4-19-75 (listed in *Billboard* ad); 5-3-75 (listed in *Billboard* ad); 6-14-75; 9-13-75; 1-31-76; 5-22-76; 8-21-76; 8-28-76 (listener question); 10-23-76; 10-30-76**
	WMET	**12-11-76; 4-16-77; 5-21-77; 7-9-77; 11-12-77; 1-14-78**
	WBBM-FM	**5-12-79 (new); 5-26-79; 8-18-79; 10-6-79; 12-22-79**
Chillicothe	**WCLL**	**6-30-79 (new)**
Decatur	**WSOY**	**1-22-77 (new); 6-4-77; 12-2-78**
Eldorado	**WKSI**	**(listed in 1979 Listening Directory)**
Galesburg	**WGIL**	**9-24-77 (new)**
Geneva	**(see St. Charles, IL)**	
Kankakee	**WBYG**	**1-21-78 (new); 5-20-78; 10-14-78; 10-13-79**
Kewanee	**WJRE**	**9-18-76 (new)**
Monmouth	**WRAM**	**9-4-76 (new); 6-4-77**
Mt. Vernon	**WMIX**	**10-19-74; 6-25-75; 11-6-76**
Normal	**(see Bloomington, IL)**	
Olney	**WSEI/WVLN**	**1-13-79 (new); 11-24-79 (WSEI)**
Pekin	**WSIV**	**12-5-70; 2-6-71 (listed in *Billboard* ad)**
Rockford	**WROK**	**5-27-72; 8-26-72; 12-2-72; 1-20-73; 9-15-73; 1-19-74; 6-8-74**
	WRRR	**6-7-75 (new); 11-8-75**
	WROK	**5-8-76 (new); 8-14-76; 9-23-78; 2-24-79**
St. Charles	**WGSB**	**6-1-74 (new); 11-23-74**
Salem	**WJBD**	**7-16-77 (new); 3-11-78; 11-4-78; 8-18-79**
Springfield	**WCVS**	**10-13-79**
Taylorville	**WTIM**	**10-19-74 (new)**
Tuscola	**WITT**	**9-16-72 (new)**

"Re AT40, I used to get each week's show after it was played. Paul Kirby, then the PD, passed 'em on to me. They came on three 10 1/2 inch reels, not discs. WCFL would physically edit in the commercial breaks.....The AT40's on tape were on Scotch reels and had stickers marked 1, 2 and 3 for each hour and another AT40 sticker identifying the program cycle and program...."

Tom Konard, former WCFL public service director and current operator of The Aircheck Factory

'American Top 40' to WCFL

CHICAGO—WCFL, 50,000-watt Top 40 operation here, added "American Top 40," the weekly Watermark three-hour special based on the Billboard Magazine's Hot 100 Chart, on June 25. Tom Rounds, chief of the radio syndication firm, reported that this brings the total to 175 stations coast-to-coast and around the world featuring the show, which is hosted by veteran air personality Casey Kasen.

The show features a countdown of chart tunes. Billboard supplies advance information and the show heard over the air either Saturday evening or Sunday on most stations is a presentation of the major-selling records as they show up in the trade paper's chart the following Monday.

WEEKENDS ON

wask radio

Saturday 7 p.m. - Sunday 9 p.m.

For Week Ending APRIL 10, 1971

THIS WEEK	LAST WEEK	TITLE / Artist
1	1	JUST MY IMAGINATION (Temptations)
2	5	WHAT'S GOING ON (Marvin Gaye)
3	11	JOY TO THE WORLD (Three Dog Night)
4	4	SHE'S A LADY (Tom Jones)
5	3	FOR ALL WE KNOW (Carpenters)
6	2	ME AND BOBBY MCGEE (Janis Joplin)
7	7	DOESN'T SOMEBODY WANT (Partridge Family)
8	10	ANOTHER DAY (Paul McCartney)
9	6	PROUD MARY (Ike & Tina Turner)
10	16	ONE TOKE OVER THE LINE (Brewer & Shipley)
11	12	WILD WORLD (Cat Stevens)
12	8	HELP ME MAKE IT (Sammi Smith)
13	9	LOVE STORY (Andy Williams)
14	14	WHAT IS LIFE (George Harrison)
15	57	NEVER CAN SAY GOODBYE (Jackson Five)
16	31	PUT YOUR HAND IN HAND (Ocean)
17	21	NO LOVE AT ALL (B. J. Thomas)
18	13	OYE, COMO VA (Santana)
19	26	I AM, I SAID (Neil Diamond)
20	15	TEMPTATION EYES (Grass Roots)
21	25	LOVE'S LINES, ANGLES (Fifth Dimension)
22	27	EIGHTEEN (Alice Cooper)
23	23	BLUE MONEY (Van Morrison)
24	32	WE CAN WORK IT OUT (Stevie Wonder)
25	33	STAY AWHILE (Bells)
26	19	YOU'RE ALL I NEED TO GET BY (Aretha Franklin)
27	28	HEAVY MAKES YOU HAPPY (Staple Singers)
28	39	IF (Bread)
29	29	SOUL POWER (James Brown)
30	44	I PLAY AND SING (Dawn)
31	22	CRIED LIKE A BABY (Bobby Sherman)
32	34	DREAM BABY (Glen Campbell)
33	35	WHERE DID THEY GO, LORD (Elvis Presley)
34	18	ONE BAD APPLE (Osmonds)
35	38	BABY, LET ME KISS YOU (King Floyd)
36	17	AMOS MOSES (Jerry Reed)
37	20	FREE (Chicago)
38	47	FRIENDS (Elton John)
39	41	CHICK-A-BOOM (Daddy Dewdrop)
40	73	POWER TO THE PEOPLE (John Lennon)

From April 10, 1971, the complete *American Top 40* survey was provided by Lafayette, Indiana radio station WASK.

From Indianapolis, Indiana, the cover of the WIFE-AM record survey, dated November 5, 1975, promoted "WIFE's AT-40 Host" Casey Kasem's acting role in the 1975 ABC Movie-of-the-Week, *The Night That Panicked America*.

STATE

Market	*Calls*	*Air Date Mentions*
INDIANA		
Batesville	WRBI	1-8-77 (mentioned as Batesville, IL); 5-7-77 (new); 7-9-77
Columbia City	WFDT	12-10-77 (new, mentioned as Columbus, IN); 3-11-78
Columbus	WCSI	5-15-71 (new); 7-3-71 (listed in *Billboard* ad); 11-20-71 (listed in *Billboard* ad); 12-4-71; 3-11-72; 5-19-73; 9-8-73; 12-1-73; 11-16-74; 4-12-75; 1-31-76; 3-12-77; 10-1-77 (mentioned as WOSI); 1-14-78; 1-13-79
Evansville	WGBF	6-7-75 (new); 11-29-75; 5-1-76; 8-21-76; 3-19-77; 10-22-77; 4-21-79; 10-20-79
Fort Wayne	WMEE	6-10-78 (new); 4-28-79
Indianapolis	WIFE	4-17-71 (new); 6-12-71; 7-3-71 (listed in *Billboard* ad); 10-2-71; 10-23-71 (mentioned in error); 11-20-71 (listed in *Billboard* ad); 11-27-71; 2-26-72; 9-16-72; 11-4-72; 1-6-73; 4-14-73; 5-5-73; 7-14-73; 10-13-73; 12-1-73; 4-27-74; 7-13-74; 8-31-74; 11-30-74; 4-26-75; 3-6-76; 9-4-76; 3-19-77; 8-13-77; 4-28-79; 5-26-79
Kokomo	WIOU	7-27-74 (new); 9-7-74; 9-21-74; 12-14-74; 8-9-75; 11-15-75; 9-11-76; 11-6-76; 3-19-77
	WZWZ	12-17-77; 5-20-78; 2-24-79
Lafayette	WASK	12-19-70; 2-6-71 (listed in *Billboard* ad); 2-13-71; 7-3-71 (listed in *Billboard* ad); 7-31-71; 11-2-71 (listed in *Billboard* ad); 4-8-72; 12-23-72; 3-31-73; 6-16-73; 7-28-73; 12-15-73; 2-23-74; 1-4-75; 4-12-75; 6-12-76; 6-4-77; 1-6-79
Mishawaka	(see South Bend, IN)	
Muncie	WERK	3-20-71 (new); 6-19-71; 7-3-71 (listed in *Billboard* ad); 11-20-71 (listed in *Billboard* ad); 6-17-72; 10-21-72; 6-30-73; 7-28-73; 1-5-74; 3-23-74; 1-18-75; 6-14-75; 11-8-75; 8-28-76; 4-21-79
Rensselaer	WRIN	6-30-79 (new)
Richmond	WRIA	1-14-78 (new); 1-21-78; 11-25-78; 5-12-79
South Bend	WJVA	6-12-71; 7-3-71 (listed in *Billboard* ad)
	WRBR	2-14-76 (new); 9-4-76; 3-17-79
Terre Haute	WTHI	2-6-71 (listed in *Billboard* ad); 4-17-71
	WBOW	1-17-76 (new); 8-28-76; 9-10-77

STATE

Market	*Calls*	*Air Date Mentions*
IOWA		
Ames	**KASI**	**9-16-72 (new); 12-9-72; 3-24-73**
Cedar Rapids	**KLWW**	**10-9-76 (new); 1-8-77; 7-9-77; 1-28-78; 8-12-78; 2-3-79**
Clinton	**KROS**	**4-27-74 (new)**
Davenport	**KSTT**	**11-22-75 (new); 11-29-75 (new); 7-31-76 (d.j. question); 8-14-76; 3-19-77; 11-25-78; 6-23-79; 11-24-79**
Des Moines	**KYNA-FM**	**7-3-71 (listed in *Billboard* ad); 7-24-71**
	KRNQ-FM	**1-17-76 (new); 8-28-76; 11-27-76; 9-3-77; 1-21-78; 5-12-79; 5-26-79**
Dubuque	**WDBQ**	**7-22-72 (new); 12-9-72; 3-31-73; 6-23-73; 8-11-73; 12-15-73; 3-16-74; 8-17-74; 2-8-75; 4-19-75; 2-14-76; 5-22-76; 9-4-76; 12-16-78; 7-28-79**
Fort Dodge	**KTGA**	**1-7-78 (new); 3-11-78; 12-2-78**
Marshalltown	**KFJB**	**4-16-77 (new); 8-13-77; 1-13-79**
Mason City	**KRIB**	**2-5-77 (new); 3-11-78; 5-12-79**
Mount Pleasant	**KKSI**	**11-27-76 (new); 10-21-78**
Ottumwa	**KLEE**	**11-23-74 (new)**
Red Oak	**KOAK**	**11-12-77 (new); 5-20-78; 9-2-78; 3-31-79**
Sioux City	**KSEZ**	**6-5-76 (new); 9-11-76; 11-6-76; 10-1-77; 11-18-78; 5-19-79; 11-17-79**
Waterloo	**KLEU**	**3-31-73; 6-30-73; 7-28-73**
		12-14-74 (new); 5-3-75 (listed in *Billboard* ad); 7-19-75; 11-1-75; 4-17-76; 9-11-76; 11-20-76; 10-21-78; 11-3-79
KANSAS		
Arkansas City	**KSOK**	**9-8-79 (new)**
Dodge City	**KEDD**	**4-8-78 (new); 1-13-79**
Emporia	**KRHA**	**11-18-78 (new); 3-10-79**
Fairway	**(see Kansas City, KS)**	
Goodland	**KLOE**	**10-1-77 (new); 5-27-78; 8-5-78**
Hays	**KAYS**	**2-4-78 (new); 10-7-78; 10-6-79**
Hoisington	**KHOK**	**11-25-78 (new); 10-13-79**
Hutchinson	**KWHK**	**1-10-76 (new); 8-21-76; 10-23-76; (30th b-day); 11-27-76; 11-12-77; 4-8-78; 12-2-78; 12-8-79**
Kansas City	**KUDL**	**9-4-71 (new; mentioned as Shawnee Mission, KS); 11-27-71; 12-4-71 (listed in *Billboard* ad, as Kansas City, MO); 12-11-71 (listener question); 2-19-72; 9-16-72; 11-4-72; 2-24-73; 5-5-73; 7-14-73 (Bloodstone's home); 8-4-73; 10-27-73; 11-17-73; 6-15-74; 9-28-74; 1-11-75; 2-15-75; 3-29-75 (re-new)**
Kiawatha	**KNZA**	**10-22-77 (new); 1-21-78**
Liberal	**KSCB**	**1-20-79 (new); 11-17-79**
Manhattan	**KSDB**	**1-19-74 (new); 6-8-74; 8-31-74 (new); 3-1-75; 8-30-75 (new); 8-28-76 (new); 2-7-76; 9-3-77 (re-new)**
Salina	**KSKG**	**2-10-73 (new); 11-17-73; 6-8-74; 3-8-75; 8-23-75; 10-18-75; 5-29-76; 8-28-76; 3-19-77; 11-18-78; 11-24-79**
Shawnee Mission	**(see Kansas City, KS)**	
Topeka	**KEWI**	**9-16-72 (new); 1-27-73; 6-30-73; 9-22-73; 1-26-74; 8-10-74; 3-15-75; 6-21-75; 9-20-75; 6-26-76; 9-4-76; 12-17-77; 7-15-78; 6-2-79; 7-28-79**
Wichita	**KEYN**	**10-3-70; 1-16-71; 2-6-71 (listed in *Billboard* ad); 5-15-71; 7-3-71 (listed in *Billboard* ad); 9-25-71; 4-15-72; 10-7-72; 11-25-72; 1-20-73; 6-2-73; 8-18-73; 2-16-74; 3-22-75; 4-19-75; 11-1-75; 9-11-76; 11-6-76; 1-20-79**

TO: AMERICAN TOP 40 BROADCASTERS

FROM: TOM ROUNDS, AT40 EXECUTIVE PRODUCER

SUBJECT: ARB RATINGS (APRIL-MAY, 1971)

The three-hour AMERICAN TOP 40 program scored audience gains for the second consecutive rating period.
The national average increase in Average Quarter Hour Listeners in April-May was 40.35%. Below I've compared the April-May survey results against the same AT40 time periods in the previous ARB survey for each station. Here goes:

Station	City	New A. Q. H. For AT40	% Increase Over Previous ARB
WPIX	NEW YORK CITY	33,900	+154.0%
WMEX	BOSTON	34,400	+ 62.3%
WPGC	WASHINGTON D. C.	23,800	+ 6.7%
WCBM	BALTIMORE	16,700	+ 47.0%
KIRL	ST. LOUIS	14,200	+ 46.4%
KOIL	OMAHA	19,800	+ 24.5%
KMEN	SAN BERNARDINO	9,000	+ 32.4%
WDRC	HARTFORD-NEW BRITAIN	21,200	+ 20.5%
WNOX	KNOXVILLE	13,300	+ 66.0%
WABB	MOBILE	11,700	+ 38.0%
KQEO	ALBUQUERQUE	9,200	+ 4.5%
WGOE	RICHMOND, VA.	5,300	+ 89.3%
KNUZ	HOUSTON	9,600	+100.0%
KJOY	STOCKTON, CALIF.	4,300	+126.0%
WIBR	BATON ROUGE	1,300	+ 30.0%
KELI	TULSA	7,200	+324.0%
WABY	ALBANY	3,600	+ 50.0%
WORJ	ORLANDO	4,400	+214.0%
WFLI	CHATTANOOGA	5,300	+ 29.0%
WAMS	WILMINGTON	4,900	+ 32.4%

*NATIONAL AVERAGE INCREASE IN AT40 LISTENERS +40.35%

*The national average includes 11 stations that showed reductions in A. Q. H. Listeners. AMERICAN TOP 40 is still the Number 1 music program in the time period in Los Angeles. (KRLA - Sunday's, 9 to Noon)

For more information, contact me or George L. Savage, Director of Marketing, Watermark, Inc.

TR.

WATERMARK, INC. 931 N. La Cienega Blvd. Los Angeles, California 90069 (213) 659-3834

With *AT40* less than a year old, this 1971 memo from Tom Rounds delivered the "audience gain" news about the program's ARB ratings in 20 markets.

STATE

Market	*Calls*	*Air Date Mentions*
KENTUCKY		
Ashland	(See Huntington, WV)	
Berea	WKXO	5-26-73 (new); 9-8-73; 11-24-73
Corbin	WCTT	8-3-74 (new); 10-12-74; 6-7-75; 10-25-75; 4-17-76
	WYGO	9-11-76 (new); 3-26-77; 7-16-77; 9-30-78; 9-29-79
Harlan	WHLN	5-8-71 (new); 7-3-71 (listed in *Billboard* ad); 11-20-71 (listed in *Billboard* ad)
	WHLN	5-13-72 (new); 6-10-72; 8-19-72; 6-1-73 (listed in 1973 Vacation Listening Guide)
	WHLN	1-8-77 (new); 8-13-77; 10-28-78; 11-24-79
Hodgenville	WLCB	6-14-75 (new); 10-18-75
Lexington	WLAP	11-6-71 (new); 11-20-71 (listed in *Billboard* ad); 4-22-72; 5-27-72; 3-17-73; 9-22-73; 1-19-74; 2-2-74; 5-11-74; 5-18-74; 9-14-74; 10-26-74; 11-2-74; 3-27-76; 7-10-76; 9-11-76; 10-1-77; 5-20-78; 9-2-78; 8-25-79
Louisville	WAKY	8-21-76 (new); 1-8-77; 11-12-77; 3-11-78; 1-6-79
Madisonville	WTTL	11-4-78 (new); 9-22-79
Middlesboro	WFXY	7-31-76 (new); 9-10-77; 10-21-78; 4-21-79
Morehead	WMOR	1-10-76 (new); 11-6-76; 1-28-78
Paducah	WDXR	3-17-73; 6-23-73
	WDXR	3-10-79 (new)
Paintsville	WSIP	1-15-77 (new); 1-21-78; 11-25-78; 12-1-79
Pikeville	WPKE	11-27-76 (new); 2-3-79 (mentioned as Pineville, KY); 2-10-79
Russellville	WAKQ	1-29-77 (new); 10-7-78; 10-6-79
Somerset	WSFC	1-20-79 (new); 11-24-79
Whitesburg	WTCW	10-7-72 (new)
LOUISIANA		
Alexandria	KALB	1-12-74; 2-23-74; 10-12-74; 5-31-75; 11-29-75; 3-26-77; 9-10-77; 7-8-78; 7-14-79
Baton Rouge	WIBR	2-6-71 (listed in *Billboard* ad); 4-17-71; 6-5-71; 7-3-71 (listed in *Billboard* ad); 7-24-71 (listener question); 11-20-71 (listed in *Billboard* ad); 4-29-72; 9-2-72; 12-2-72; 1-20-73; 7-28-73; 2-9-74; 4-27-74; 10-26-74; 11-2-74; 4-26-75; 3-6-76; 6-4-77; 2-3-79
Crowley	KAJN	4-14-73 (new); 9-8-73; 11-24-73
Ferriday	KFNV	11-29-75 (new)
Franklin	KFRA	2-3-79 (new)
Hammond	WFPR	4-29-72 (new)
Houma	KJIN	1-11-75 (new); 7-12-75; 10-11-75; 10-1-77; 3-11-78; 1-20-79
Lafayette	KTDY	8-20-77 (new); 9-16-78; 9-15-79
Lake Charles	KLOU	3-13-71 (new); 7-3-71 (listed in *Billboard* ad); 8-7-71; 2-7-76; 9-11-76; 11-6-76; 8-12-78; 8-25-79
Lake Providence	KLPL	5-4-74 (new)
	KLPL	1-6-79 (new)
Leesville	KLLA	7-16-77 (new); 1-21-78; 4-28-79
Monroe	KNOE	5-8-71 (new); 7-3-71 (listed in *Billboard* ad); 7-31-71; 11-20-71 (listed in *Billboard* ad); 4-8-72
	KMLB	8-9-75 (new); 1-31-76; 5-5-79
Natchitoches	KNWD	2-5-77 (new); 9-24-77; 1-28-78
	KNOC	7-8-78 (new); 5-5-79; 11-10-79
New Orleans	WNOE	3-27-76 (new); 9-4-76; 1-8-77; 4-30-77; 7-16-77; 5-27-78; 2-17-79; 9-8-79
Ruston	KLPI	11-12-77
Shreveport	KEEL	3-4-72 (listed in *Billboard*'s Vox Jox column as an AT40 station) 10-30-76 (new); 8-13-77; 7-8-78; 1-6-79; 12-15-79
Ville Platte	KVPI	7-23-77 (new); 5-26-79

STATE

Market	*Calls*	*Air Date Mentions*
MAINE		
Bangor	**WABI**	**4-10-71 (new); 6-5-71; 7-3-71 (listed in *Billboard* ad); 9-4-71; 11-27-71 (listener question); 12-4-71 (listed in *Billboard* ad); 12-18-71; 4-8-72; 6-24-72; 12-23-72; 3-31-73; 4-21-73; 7-28-73; 1-5-74; 2-23-74; 8-17-74; 11-23-74; 5-24-75; 1-17-76; 6-19-76; 9-4-76; 11-20-76; 10-7-78; 10-6-79**
Bath	**WJTO**	**9-5-70 (listed in *Billboard* ad); 10-10-70; 11-28-70; 1-30-71 (radio report); 2-6-71 (listed in *Billboard* ad); 3-13-71; 7-3-71 (listed in *Billboard* ad); 8-21-71; 12-4-71 (listed in *Billboard* ad); 12-18-71; 4-15-72; 6-3-72; 10-14-72; 3-31-73; 6-30-73; 7-21-73; 1-26-74; 5-11-74; 11-16-74; 8-9-75; 3-27-76**
	WIGY	**3-19-77**
	WJTO	**3-26-77**
	WIGY	**12-17-77; 5-27-78; 1-27-79**
Calais	**WQDY**	**6-28-75 (new); 1-10-76; 4-24-76; 9-11-76; 6-11-77; 5-5-79**
Caribou	**(see Presque Isle, ME)**	
Houlton	**WHOU**	**11-22-75 (new); 10-30-76; 1-21-78; 3-24-79**
Norway	**WNWY-FM**	**1-17-76 (new)**
	WOXO	**4-10-76 (new); 7-10-76**
Presque Isle	**WAGM**	**7-3-71 (listed in *Billboard* ad); 7-24-71; 12-4-71 (listed in *Billboard* ad); 12-11-71; 3-18-72**
	WDHP	**7-20-74 (new); 11-30-74; 6-14-75**
	WDHP	**7-23-77 (new); 4-21-79**
Skowhegan	**WGHM**	**5-8-71 (new)**
	WSKW	**4-14-73 (new); 6-23-73; 9-1-73; 11-17-73; 6-1-74; 12-14-74; 9-13-75; 11-8-75**
MARYLAND		
Baltimore	**WCBM**	**11-14-70; 12-12-70; 2-6-71 (listed in *Billboard* ad); 2-20-71; 7-3-71 (listed in *Billboard* ad); 9-18-71; 12-4-71 (listed in *Billboard* ad; 2-12-72; 2-19-72; 5-6-72; 6-24-72; 9-16-72; 11-4-72; 2-3-73; 4-21-73; 8-11-73; 11-3-73; 3-9-74; 4-20-74**
	WLPL	**10-26-74 (new); 6-28-75**
	WCAO	**11-8-75 (new); 5-8-76; 9-18-76; 1-15-77; 3-26-77; 10-1-77; 1-21-78; 7-22-78; 2-17-79 (Donna Summer error); 6-9-79; 7-21-79**
Braddock Heights	**(see Frederick, MD)**	
Cumberland	**WCUM**	**12-4-71 (listed in *Billboard* ad); 12-11-71; 1-6-73 (25th birthday mention)**
	WUOK	**7-21-73 (new)**
Frederick	**WMHI**	**2-3-73; 9-29-73; 10-27-73; 5-25-74; 1-11-75; 6-28-75**
	WZYQ	**6-11-77; 12-1-79**
Leonardtown	**WKIK**	**5-11-74; 7-6-74; 1-4-75 (new); 1-18-75; 8-16-75; 3-27-76; 10-30-76; 11-11-78; 3-24-79**
Oakland	**WMSG**	**6-23-73 (new); 7-14-73; 10-13-73; 12-29-73**
Ocean City	**WETT**	**6-23-73 (new); 7-14-73; 10-13-73 12-7-74 (new)**
	WKHI	**9-9-78 (new); 8-25-79**
Salisbury	**WBOC**	**1-10-76 (new); 11-20-76; 5-27-78; 10-14-78; 10-13-79**

STATE

Market	*Calls*	*Air Date Mentions*
MASSACHUSETTS		
Boston	WMEX	9-5-70 (listed in *Billboard* ad); 9-12-70; 11-21-70; 2-6-71 (listed in *Billboard* ad); 3-20-71; 7-3-71 (listed in *Billboard* ad); 8-14-71; 8-21-71; 10-16-71; 10-30-71; 11-27-71 (listener question); 12-4-71 (listed in *Billboard* ad); 1-15-72; 4-22-72; 5-27-72; 7-29-72; 8-26-72; 12-9-72; 2-3-73; 4-21-73; 6-9-73; 6-30-73; 8-11-73; 10-27-73; 3-9-74; 5-4-74; 2-1-75; 6-28-75
	(also see Lawrence, MA)	
Brockton	WCAV	4-22-78 (new); 1-6-79
Cape Cod	WCOD-FM	5-6-72 (new); 6-24-72; 7-22-72; 10-28-72; 3-3-73; 4-14-73; 9-29-73; 10-27-73
	WCOD	11-17-79 (new)
Fall River	WSAR	2-6-71 (listed in *Billboard* ad); 7-3-71 (listed in *Billboard* ad); 8-28-71; 12-4-71 (listed in *Billboard* ad); 1-8-72; 5-20-72; 8-5-72; 3-24-73; 5-12-73; 9-22-73; 11-3-73 (Tavares' hometown); 6-8-74; 2-8-75; 5-10-75; 11-15-75; 4-24-76; 9-18-76
Fitchburg	WEIM	6-17-72; 11-25-72; 3-10-73; 5-12-73; 8-25-73; 12-15-73; 3-23-74; 2-15-75; 4-19-75
Hyannis	(see Cape Cod, MA)	
Lawrence	WCGY	9-11-76 (new); 10-30-76 (mentioned as Boston, MA); 12-17-77; 4-15-78; 7-22-78; 1-13-79; 6-9-79; 7-21-79
Southbridge	WESO	5-25-74 (new); 7-20-74; 3-1-75; 6-14-75; 1-10-76; 3-26-77
Springfield	WTXL	7-24-71 (new)
West Yarmouth	WOCB	10-21-78 (new)
Worcester	WORC	2-6-71 (listed in *Billboard* ad); 3-27-71; 7-3-71 (listed in *Billboard* ad); 8-21-71; 12-4-71 (listed in *Billboard* ad); 5-13-72
	WFTQ	9-9-78 (new); 6-16-79; 8-4-79
MICHIGAN		
Alpena	WHSB	5-26-79 (new)
Ann Arbor	WAAM	6-21-75 (new); 1-10-76
Battle Creek	WKNR	5-18-74 (new); 6-22-74; 10-12-74; 5-24-75; 12-13-75; 5-8-76; 9-18-76; 10-30-76; 7-16-77; 2-4-78; 2-10-79
Big Rapids	WFRS	2-5-72 (new)
Cadillac	WATT	7-10-76 (new); 9-18-76; 1-15-77; 7-30-77; 3-11-78; 4-7-79
Charlevoix	WVOY	6-4-77 (new); 8-20-77
Coldwater	WTVB	6-8-74 (new)
Detroit	WWWW(W4)	9-5-70 (2x: radio & listed in *Billboard* ad); 2-6-71 (listed in *Billboard* ad); 4-3-71; 7-3-71 (listed in *Billboard* ad)
	WCAR	7-24-71 (new); 9-11-71; 11-6-71
	WDRQ	3-25-78 (new); 1-20-79; 6-16-79; 9-8-79; 12-22-79
Escanaba	WDBC	6-1-73 (listed in 1973 Vacation Listening Guide; first public Acknowledgement as a subscribing station); 9-29-73; 11-17-73; 3-16-74; 10-26-74; 11-2-74; 6-14-75; 2-21-76; 5-29-76; 3-26-77; 9-10-77 (w/WFNN); 7-29-78; 8-11-79 (WFNN)
Flint	WTRX	11-12-77 (new); 1-28-78; 8-12-78; 6-16-79; 9-22-79
Grand Rapids	WGRD	3-9-74 (new); 11-23-74; 7-26-75; 2-28-76; 7-10-76; 4-2-77; 10-8-77; 5-27-78; 1-27-79; 8-11-79
Iron Mountain	WMIQ	8-12-78 (new); 4-28-79 (mentioned as WMLQ)
Ironwood	WUPM	11-4-78 (new); 9-22-79
Jackson	WIBM	3-4-72 (listed in *Billboard*'s Vox Jox column as an AT40 station); 6-10-72; 10-14-72; 2-3-73; 6-30-73; 7-21-73; 4-20-74; 9-28-74; 11-16-74; 12-7-74; 3-29-75; 4-26-75; 6-12-76; 6-11-77; 10-22-77; 1-20-79
Lansing	WVIC	9-26-70 (Lansing radio station is referenced, but call letters are edited out); 2-6-71 (listed in *Billboard* ad); 7-3-71 (2x: radio & listed in *Billboard* ad); 6-2-73 (re-new); 8-18-73; 2-16-74; 12-14-74; 8-30-75; 3-13-76; 9-25-76; 6-11-77; 11-19-77; 4-8-78; 3-3-79
Marquette	WUUN	1-11-75 (new; mentioned as Marquette, MO); 8-30-75; 10-11-75 (mentioned as Marquette, WI); 12-4-76
	WDMJ	10-21-78 (new)
	WUUN	12-9-78
	WDMJ	1-6-79; 7-28-79

MICHIGAN (cont'd)

Midland	WMPX	6-1-73 (listed in 1973 Vacation Listening Guide; first public acknowledgement as a subscribing station); 9-15-73; 12-8-73
Mount Pleasant	WCHP	10-23-71 (new); 10-30-71; 12-4-71 (listed in *Billboard* ad); 1-15-72; 2-12-72; 2-19-72; 10-14-72 (Central State College); 1-13-73 (Central MI University); 10-20-73; 3-9-74 9-28-74 (new); 1-11-75; 6-7-75
	WCEN	10-16-76 (new)
	WINO	9-11-76 (new); 9-3-77 (new)
Munising	WQXO	1-27-79 (new)
Petoskey	WJML	3-31-79 (new)
Port Huron	WPHM	4-24-71 (new); 7-3-71 (listed in *Billboard* ad); 7-10-71; 9-18-71; 12-4-71 (listed in *Billboard* ad); 2-26-72
Saginaw	WKNX	12-12-70 (Badfinger information); 2-6-71 (listed in *Billboard* ad); 3-13-71; 7-3-71 (listed in *Billboard* ad); 8-14-71; 12-4-71 (listed in *Billboard* ad); 4-22-72; 6-3-72; 8-12-72
St. Ignace	WIDG	1-28-78 (new)
Tawas	WIOS	5-14-77 (new); 1-27-79
Three Rivers	WLKM	6-11-77 (new)
Traverse City	WTCM	1-20-79 (new)
West Branch	WBMB	4-26-75 (new); 1-24-76

"Without a doubt, before the radio dial was awash with dozens of copy-cat countdown shows, the one that seemed to have started it all was Casey Kasem and 'American Top 40.' His show jingle echoed from (in those days in the early 1970's) mostly AM stations. My AT40 station was Ann Arbor's WAAM (AM) 1600. I recall when the program seemed to segue over to more and more FM's. One of the things I remember most is how the program was one of the first, although not a network show, to be heard nationwide. It made you feel 'at home' no matter where you were...and still does!..........Like so many, who have had the pleasure, I've gotten to know Casey very well. Since he's from Detroit, we had much in common. In 2001, he left a glowing review on my voice mail about a video presentation I produced for WABC in New York. Even though I dubbed it to a cassette tape, I simply can't bring myself to erasing it on the voice mail hard drive. It's still there, and probably will be for a long time."

Art Vuolo, well-known radio videographer and "Radio's Best Friend"

MINNESOTA

Alexandria	KXRA	(never mentioned on program; listed in 1975 Sales & Marketing Guide)
Austin	KAUS	6-14-75 (new); 11-22-75; 6-11-77
Bemidji	KKBJ	11-19-77 (new); 3-11-78; 10-21-78
Blue Earth	KBEW	7-19-75 (new); 11-22-75; 5-15-76; 9-18-76; 4-2-77; 7-16-77; 7-21-79
Brackenridge	KBMW	6-11-77; 8-20-77
Cambridge	KABG	3-13-76 (new)
Duluth	WEBC	2-21-76 (new); 9-25-76; 9-10-76; 9-10-77; 2-4-78; 12-16-78
Luverne	KQAD	6-14-75 (new); 11-8-75; 11-27-76
Mankato	KTOE	10-16-76 (new); 1-15-77; 9-23-78; 9-22-79
Minneapolis/St.Paul	KDWB	1-5-74 (new); 3-9-74; 4-6-74; 5-18-74; 2-1-75; 6-14-75; 9-27-75; 6-19-76; 9-25-76; 10-30-76; 10-22-77; 1-28-78; 9-16-78; 10-14-78; 6-30-79; 12-15-79
Montevideo	KDMA	9-1-79 (new)
Moorhead	(see Fargo, ND)	
Owatonna	KRFO	5-12-79 (new)
Princeton	WQPM	5-24-75 (new)
Rochester	KWEB	5-31-75 (new); 2-28-76; 4-17-76
St. Cloud	WJON	5-27-78; 11-4-78; 11-3-79
Wadena	KWAD	6-10-72 (new); 7-15-72; 10-21-72; 8-12-78; 4-7-79
Willmar	KQIC	6-1-73 (listed in 1973 Vacation Listening Guide; first public acknowledgement as a subscribing station); 11-10-73; 5-25-74; 7-13-74; 7-20-74; 8-24-74; 2-15-75; 8-9-75; 2-14-76; 9-16-78; 9-8-79
Windom	KDOM	9-10-77 (new); 7-29-78; 1-6-79; 7-28-79

The famous weekly continuing American Top 40 station list (watch it grow)

CONTINUED FROM LAST WEEK

STATE	CITY	STATION
MAINE	Bangor	WABI
	Bath	WJTO
	Presque Isle	WAGM
MARYLAND	Baltimore	WCBM
	Cumberland	WCUM
MASSACHUSETTS	Boston	WMEX
	Fall River	WSAR
	Worcester	WORC
MICHIGAN	Mt. Pleasant	WCHP
	Port Huron	WPHM
	Saginaw	WKNX
MISSOURI	Columbia	KTGR
	Kansas City	KUDL
	Poplar Bluff	KLID
MONTANA	Great Falls	KUDI
NEBRASKA	Grand Island	KRGI
	Omaha	KOIL
NEVADA	Elko	KELK
	Reno	KBET
NEW HAMPSHIRE	Claremont	WTSV
	Portsmouth	WHEB

CONTINUED NEXT WEEK

The famous American Top 40 coupon request for details on radio's hottest weekly special program attraction.

(send it now)

AMERICAN TOP 40

Fill out below and attach to your letterhead.

Mail to: Tom Rounds, Executive Producer, or George Savage, Director of Marketing/AMERICAN TOP 40/Watermark, Inc./ 931 N. LaCienega/Los Angeles, California 90069.

Yes! Rush me a demo tape or sample show (now on L.P. discs) of AMERICAN TOP 40. Send facts on production, ratings results, audience response and my low fee for this weekly, three-hour special. Tell me how Casey Kasem's absorbing, informative presentation of BILLBOARD MAGAZINE'S hottest 40 hits has made radio history and how it will work for me. Send me brochures and sales aids to help us sell it profitably and exclusively in our market (before someone else does).

I am: ☐ Station Manager ☐ Program Director ☐ Sales Manager

NAME ____________________

STATION ____________

ADDRESS ____________________

____

This advertisement, which appeared in the December 4, 1971 edition of *Billboard Magazine*, was part of a series of ads that featured all *AT40* stations in alphabetical order by state.

MISSISSIPPI

City	Station	Dates
Amory	WAMY	9-9-78 (new)
Biloxi	WLOX	2-6-71 (listed in *Billboard* ad); 3-27-71; 7-3-71 (listed in *Billboard* ad); 8-14-71; 8-21-71
	WVMI	10-7-72 (new); 10-21-72; 3-31-73; 4-21-73; 7-28-73; 1-5-74; 6-15-74; 3-1-75
	WQID	5-17-75; 12-6-75; 4-17-76; 4-2-77; 4-15-78; 2-10-79
Carthage	WWYN	12-15-79 (new)
Centreville	WZZB	4-8-78 (new)
Clarksdale	WKDL	9-5-70 (listed in *Billboard* ad); 11-21-70; 2-6-71 (listed in *Billboard* ad) 10-9-76 (new)
Columbus	WACR	9-20-75 (new); 1-17-76; 4-3-76; 6-11-77; 11-19-77
Fulton	WFTA	8-11-79 (new)
Gulfport	(See Biloxi, MS)	
Indianola	WNLA	4-27-74 (new); 8-24-74
	WNLA	7-9-77 (new); 2-4-78; 9-1-79
Jackson	WRBC	3-9-74 (new); 3-8-75; 8-16-75
	WJDX	6-26-76 (new); 9-18-76; 6-18-77; 9-10-77; 6-3-78; 4-28-79
Laurel	WNSL	1-15-77 (new); 11-18-78; 11-10-79
Meridian	WDAL	7-28-73; 10-13-73; 12-1-73; 4-6-74; 6-22-74; 3-15-75; 6-14-75; 2-7-76; 4-14-79
Starkville	WKOR	12-10-77 (new); 1-21-78 (new); 11-11-78; 11-3-79
Vicksburg	WJFL	1-14-78 (new); 1-28-78; 11-4-78; 3-24-79
Waynesboro	WABO	4-10-76 (new); 4-24-76; 10-30-76; 1-6-79

MISSOURI

City	Station	Dates
Cameron	KMRN	9-10-77 (new)
Cape Girardeau	KGMO-AM & FM	3-8-75 (new); 9-6-75; 1-17-76; 7-17-76
Caruthersville	KCRV	3-3-73 (new); 9-29-73; 11-3-73; 3-9-74; 10-12-74; 4-12-75; 11-15-75; 4-10-76; 4-2-77; 10-8-77; 12-16-78
Columbia	KTGR	7-3-71 (new; also listed in *Billboard* ad as KTRG); 7-24-71; 12-4-71 (listed in *Billboard* ad); 12-11-71; 4-1-72; 8-26-72; 3-31-73; 5-19-73; 8-11-73; 12-29-73; 6-1-74; 10-26-74; 11-2-74; 8-30-75
	KFMZ	9-11-76 (new); 4-9-77; 10-29-77; 7-29-78; 6-2-79
Fredericktown	KFTW	6-24-78 (new)
Houston	KBTC	7-3-71 (never mentioned on show; listed only in *Billboard* ad)
	KBTC	9-11-76 (new)
Jackson	KJAS	11-25-72 (new); 2-3-73
	KJAS	10-9-76 (new); 1-15-77; 11-19-77; 3-18-78; 8-5-78; 8-11-79
Jefferson City	KLIK	2-5-72 (new); 8-12-72; 2-3-73; 11-10-73; 4-13-74; 11-9-74; 11-16-74 (mentioned as KJFF); 7-19-75; 10-25-75; 5-15-76; 11-20-76; 10-21-78; 11-3-79
Joplin	KQYX-AM	4-29-72 (new); 8-26-72; 3-17-73;
	KSYN-FM	6-2-73; 6-23-73; 8-11-73; 12-29-73; 12-7-74 (KQYX); 12-14-74 (KSYN); 3-29-75 (KQYX); 5-10-75; 1-31-76(KQYX); 6-18-77 (KQYX); 12-17-77; 1-28-78; 2-10-79
Kansas City	KBEQ	8-23-75 (new); 1-10-76; 6-18-77; 9-10-77; 6-3-78; 4-7-79; 5-26-79
Lebanon	KLWT	3-3-73; 9-29-73; 10-27-73; 4-20-74
Poplar Bluff	KLID	10-2-71 (new); 10-16-71; 11-13-71; 12-4-71 (listed in *Billboard* ad); 1-29-72; 2-12-72; 5-6-72 (d.j. wedding); 8-12-72; 4-21-73; 11-10-73; 4-13-74; 7-13-74; 7-20-74
Rolla	KTTR	8-7-76 (new); 8-28-76
	KCLU	1-21-78 (new); 10-7-78; 10-6-79
St. Charles	(see St. Louis, MO)	
St. Joseph	KKJO	2-5-72 (new); 7-22-72; 3-10-73
	KKJO	4-15-78 (new); 2-3-79
St. Louis	KIRL	9-5-70 (listed in *Billboard* ad); 9-19-70; 2-6-71 (listed in *Billboard* ad); 6-26-71; 7-3-71 (listed in *Billboard* ad)
	KIRL	7-23-77 (new)
	KSLQ	10-21-78 (new); 6-9-79; 9-22-79; 12-22-79
Sedalia	KSIS	10-23-76 (new)
	KCBW	7-15-78
Sikeston	KMPL	10-23-76 (new); 2-4-78; 8-12-78; 9-8-79
Springfield	KBUG	6-22-74 (new); 7-13-74; 7-20-74; 8-24-74 (2x); 2-1-75; 6-7-75
	KWTO-FM	2-21-76 (new); 4-17-76; 6-5-76; 10-30-76; 3-3-79; 9-29-79
Warrensburg	KOKO	8-14-76 (new); 8-20-77; 12-10-77; 5-5-79

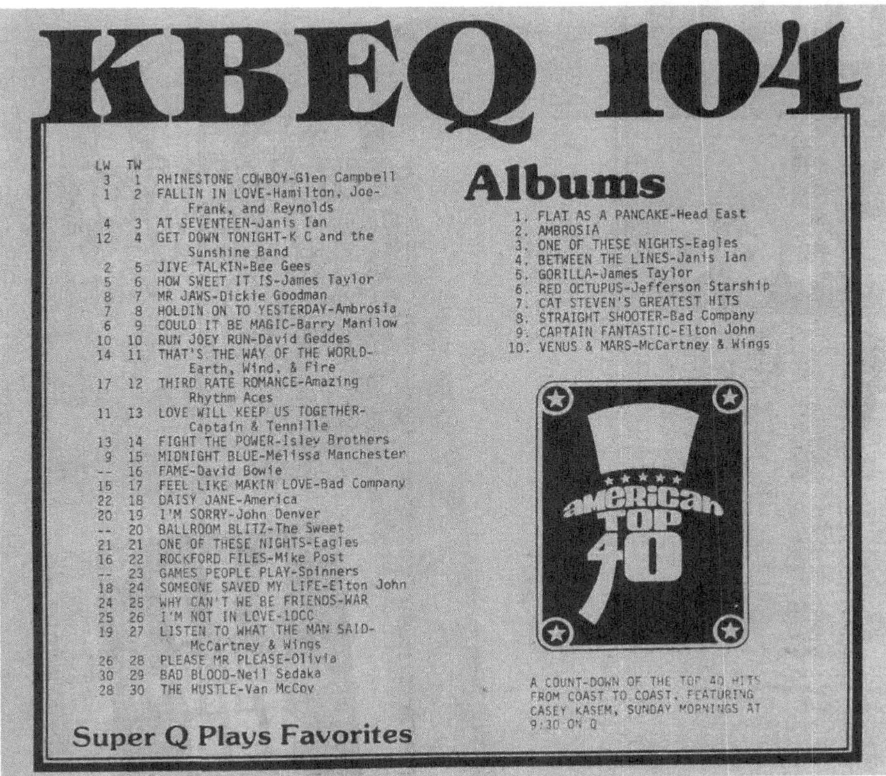

KBEQ 104

LW	TW	
3	1	RHINESTONE COWBOY-Glen Campbell
1	2	FALLIN IN LOVE-Hamilton, Joe-Frank, and Reynolds
4	3	AT SEVENTEEN-Janis Ian
12	4	GET DOWN TONIGHT-K C and the Sunshine Band
2	5	JIVE TALKIN-Bee Gees
5	6	HOW SWEET IT IS-James Taylor
8	7	MR JAWS-Dickie Goodman
7	8	HOLDIN ON TO YESTERDAY-Ambrosia
6	9	COULD IT BE MAGIC-Barry Manilow
10	10	RUN JOEY RUN-David Geddes
14	11	THAT'S THE WAY OF THE WORLD-Earth, Wind, & Fire
17	12	THIRD RATE ROMANCE-Amazing Rhythm Aces
11	13	LOVE WILL KEEP US TOGETHER-Captain & Tennille
13	14	FIGHT THE POWER-Isley Brothers
9	15	MIDNIGHT BLUE-Melissa Manchester
--	16	FAME-David Bowie
15	17	FEEL LIKE MAKIN LOVE-Bad Company
22	18	DAISY JANE-America
20	19	I'M SORRY-John Denver
--	20	BALLROOM BLITZ-The Sweet
21	21	ONE OF THESE NIGHTS-Eagles
16	22	ROCKFORD FILES-Mike Post
--	23	GAMES PEOPLE PLAY-Spinners
18	24	SOMEONE SAVED MY LIFE-Elton John
24	25	WHY CAN'T WE BE FRIENDS-WAR
25	26	I'M NOT IN LOVE-10CC
19	27	LISTEN TO WHAT THE MAN SAID-McCartney & Wings
26	28	PLEASE MR PLEASE-Olivia
30	29	BAD BLOOD-Neil Sedaka
28	30	THE HUSTLE-Van McCoy

Albums

1. FLAT AS A PANCAKE-Head East
2. AMBROSIA
3. ONE OF THESE NIGHTS-Eagles
4. BETWEEN THE LINES-Janis Ian
5. GORILLA-James Taylor
6. RED OCTUPUS-Jefferson Starship
7. CAT STEVEN'S GREATEST HITS
8. STRAIGHT SHOOTER-Bad Company
9. CAPTAIN FANTASTIC-Elton John
10. VENUS & MARS-McCartney & Wings

A COUNT-DOWN OF THE TOP 40 HITS FROM COAST TO COAST, FEATURING CASEY KASEM, SUNDAY MORNINGS AT 9:30 ON Q

Super Q Plays Favorites

Listeners of KBEQ-FM in Kansas City, Missouri heard Casey Kasem's countdown beginning at 9:30 on Sunday mornings according to this 1975 record survey.

STATE **Market**	**Calls**	**Air Date Mentions**
MONTANA		
Billings	**KOOK**	**9-13-75 (new); 12-20-75; 5-8-76; 9-25-76; 10-23-76; 2-4-78; 9-2-78; 3-24-79**
Bozeman	**KBMN**	**1-5-74 (new); 2-2-74 (listed in *Billboard* ad); 2-8-75 (new); 6-7-75**
Butte	**KBOW**	**10-6-79 (new); 12-22-79**
Dillon	**KDBM**	**7-14-79 (new)**
Great Falls	**KUDI**	**8-28-71 (new); 10-9-71; 12-4-71 (2x: radio & listed in *Billboard* ad); 2-10-73; 4-21-73; 1-26-74; 6-15-74**
	KQDI	**10-9-76 (new); 1-15-77 (mentioned as KUDI); 8-5-78 (mentioned as KGDI); 3-3-79**
Helena	**KCAP**	**1-15-77 (new); 4-9-77; 4-14-79**
Livingston	**KYBS**	**2-18-78 (new)**
Missoula	**KDXT**	**3-11-78 (new); 1-13-79**
Plentywood	**KATQ**	**9-29-79 (new)**

THIS WEEK	JANUARY 23, 1971	LAST WEEK
1.	IF I WERE YOUR WOMAN.... KNIGHT/PIPS	5
2.	LONELY DAYS.................. BEE GEES	1
3.	REMEMBER ME................ DIANA ROSS	6
4.	ONE BAD APPLE................ OSMONDS	10
5.	I HEAR YOU KNOCKIN'... DAVE EDMUNDS	18
6.	LET YOUR LOVE GO................ BREAD	8
7.	MY SWEET LORD...... GEORGE HARRISON	4
8.	YOUR SONG................ ELTON JOHN	2
9.	I REALLY DON'T WANT TO KNOW.... ELVIS	11
10.	KNOCK THREE TIMES................ DAWN	3
11.	ROSE GARDEN.......... LYNN ANDERSON	9
12.	MAMA'S PEARL............ JACKSON FIVE	29
13.	IMMIGRANT SONG.......... LED ZEPPELIN	13
14.	STONEY END.......... BARBRA STREISAND	7
15.	IF YOU COULD..... GORDON LIGHTFOOT	23
16.	MR. BOJANGLES...... NITTY GRITTY DIRT	22
17.	HAVE YOU SEEN RAIN/TONITE..... C C R	30
18.	GREEN GRASS........... WILSON PICKETT	24
19.	HANG ONTO YOUR LIFE..... GUESS WHO	28
20.	THEME FROM "LOVE STORY".... MANCINI	26
21.	LOVE THE ONE YOU'RE WITH.. STEVE STILLS	16
22.	FRESH AS A DAISY......... EMITT RHODES	--
23.	1900 YESTERDAY............... LIZ DAMON	20
24.	SOMEBODY'S WATCHIN' U... LITTLE SISTER	21
25.	WATCHIN' SCOTTY.... BOBBY GOLDSBORO	--
26.	SWEET MARY...... WADSWORTH MANSION	27
27.	PRECIOUS, PRECIOUS...... JACKIE MOORE	--
28.	SHE'S A LADY................. TOM JONES	--
29.	DEAD & GONE......... McGINNES FLINT	--
30.	JUST 7 NUMBERS............... FOUR TOPS	--

Sunday 9-12

Billboard's

TOP 40

WITH CASEY KASEM
COUNTING IT DOWN ON KIRL

EVERY SUNDAY MORNING 9-12 N

Two Midwest Top 40 stations -- KIRL in St. Louis and KOIL in Omaha -- featured *American Top 40* on Sundays. Listeners to Casey Kasem's countdown in St. Louis in 1971 adjusted their weekend schedules to accommodate the program's morning broadcast time, while in Omaha the show was heard Sunday evenings.

8901 INDIAN HILLS DRIVE, OMAHA, NEBRASKA 68114
TELEPHONE (402) 397-1290

KOIL OMAHA
KOIL FM-STEREO OMAHA
KISN PORTLAND
WIFE INDIANAPOLIS
WIFE FM-STEREO INDIANAPOLIS

DON W. BURDEN, CHAIRMAN OF THE BOARD

January 17, 1973

Pete Battistini
5461 Fillmore Street
Merrillville, Indiana 46410

Pete:

American Top 40 has been broadcast on KOIL in the Sunday, 7 to 10 pm, time slot for two years. Each program is used once and then is kept or given away to any of the station personnel who may want it for "posterity". The program has become somewhat of an "institution" here, so extensive promotion of it is not necessary. The personality on the air, preceding the program merely mentions, two or three times, that "The rock rolls on with Casy Kasem and American Top 40 at seven!" The program is broadcast off of three, 12-ince, double-sided records. As far as ratings are concerned, the show is very successful in the tenns and 18-24 categories. (I don't have the ARB book in front of me right now, so I can't quote exact figures.)

In regard to information about KOIL, it is 5000 watts, 24 hours, non-directional day, directional signal at night. The station went on the air in 1925, therefore being two years from it's "golden" anniversary. Programming could be most accurately described by the often-vague term "contemporary". Our target listeners are from 18 to 35 years of age.

I hope this is sufficient information. Enclosed is a copy of our music survey. Thanks for your interest.

Sincerely,

Scott

Scott Carpenter
Music Director
KOIL, Omaha

Enclosure

This January 17, 1973 letter from KOIL's music director offered insight to the station's *AT40* broadcast in response to a note from the author. Further details of this letter are offered in Section Three, "Confessions of an AT40 Enthusiast."

STATE Market	Calls	Air Date Mentions
NEBRASKA		
Alliance	KCOW	6-24-72 (new); 10-21-72; 2-3-73; 4-14-73; 8-18-73; 10-20-73; 3-2-74; 8-3-74; 2-8-75; 4-12-75; 9-20-75; 4-3-76; 1-22-77; 11-19-77; 7-21-79
Council Bluffs	(see Omaha)	
Grand Island	KRGI	10-2-71 (new); 11-27-71; 12-4-71 (listed in *Billboard* ad); 3-4-72; 9-9-72; 3-24-73; 9-1-73; 11-24-73; 5-25-74; 6-29-74; 2-15-75; 5-10-75; 1-31-76; 4-24-76; 4-9-77; 4-15-78; 3-10-79
Kearney	KRNY	12-9-78 (new); 11-17-79
Lincoln	KLMS	1-4-75 (new); 7-26-75; 11-8-75; 11-20-76; 10-28-78; 11-10-79
McCook	KBRL	2-5-77 (new)
North Platte	KODY	3-5-77 (new)
	KAHL	4-15-78 (new); 1-6-79
Ogallala	KIBC	7-10-76 (new); 9-25-76; 1-22-77
	KIBC	6-24-78 (new); 4-28-79
Omaha	KOIL	4-17-71 (new); 7-3-71 (listed in *Billboard* ad); 9-25-71; 12-4-71 (listed in *Billboard* ad); 4-8-72; 9-9-72; 11-25-72; 2-10-73; 5-26-73; 7-14-73; 10-13-73; 5-4-74; 8-10-74; 8-31-74; 3-1-75; 3-8-75; 4-19-75 (listed in *Billboard* ad); 5-3-75; 11-8-75; 6-5-76
	KFAB	9-25-76 (new); 10-23-76
	KGOR	2-4-78; 7-29-78; 6-2-79; 7-28-79
Scottsbluff	KOLT	6-2-79 (new)
York	KAWL	1-10-76 (new; mentioned as KWAL); 1-24-76
NEVADA		
Carson City	KPTL (also see Reno, NV)	(listed in 1979 Listening Directory)
Elko	KELK	6-26-71 (new); 7-3-71 (listed in *Billboard* ad); 7-17-71; 10-30-71; 12-4-71 (listed in *Billboard* ad); 1-15-72; 10-21-72; 3-24-73; 4-14-73; 8-18-73; 10-20-73; 3-9-74; 6-29-74; 3-15-75; 5-31-75
Las Vegas	KRGN-FM	1-5-74 (new); 2-2-74 (listed in *Billboard* ad); 5-25-74; 9-7-74
	KFMS	8-9-75; 9-27-75; 5-8-76; 1-22-77; 4-15-78; 10-21-78; 6-23-79; 10-6-79
Reno	KBET	5-1-71 (new); 7-3-71 (listed in *Billboard* ad); 7-10-71; 7-17-71; 12-4-71 (listed in *Billboard* ad); 12-18-71
	KKBC	12-11-76 (new); 4-9-77; 5-5-79; 5-26-79
Winnemucca	KWNA	4-9-77 (new); 2-4-78; 2-24-79
NEW HAMPSHIRE		
Berlin	WMOU	10-7-72 (new); 2-17-73
	WMOU/WXLQ	4-10-76 (new)
Claremont	WTSV	10-9-71 (new); 10-30-71; 12-4-71 (listed in *Billboard* ad); 1-15-72; 2-19-72; 5-20-72; 8-12-72
Dover	WTSN	2-6-71 (listed in *Billboard* ad); 4-10-71; 7-3-71 (listed in *Billboard* ad)
Franklin	WFTN	8-7-76 (new); 4-9-77; 4-21-79
Hanover	WDCR	6-23-73 (new); 7-14-73; 10-13-73; 11-24-73; 3-16-74; 10-12-74; 6-14-75; 1-31-76; 5-15-76; 6-18-77; 8-20-77 (graduating engineer); 2-11-78; 4-14-79
Manchester	WKBR	12-5-70; 2-6-71 (listed in *Billboard* ad); 3-13-71; 7-3-71 (listed in *Billboard* ad)
	WKBR	1-18-75 (new); 8-9-75; 3-20-76; 11-27-76
Newport	WCNL	9-8-73 (new); 11-17-73
Plymouth	WPCR	3-17-73 (new); 10-20-73; 5-25-74; 9-7-74 (new); 7-19-75; 10-18-75 (new)
Portsmouth	WHEB	10-9-71 (new); 12-4-71 (listed in *Billboard* ad); 4-1-72; 6-10-72; 7-29-72; 11-11-72; 5-5-73; 9-29-73; 11-3-73; 4-20-74; 10-26-74; 11-2-74; 4-19-75; 11-1-75; 4-17-76; 5-29-76; 6-3-78; 3-31-79

STATE Market	Calls	Air Date Mentions
NEW JERSEY		
Asbury Park	WJLK	6-24-78 (new); 4-21-79
Lakewood	WHLW	4-12-75 (new); 11-29-75 (new); 4-17-76
Millville	(see Vineland, NJ)	
Newton	WNNJ	10-13-79 (new)
Parsippany	WBIO	10-28-78 (new)
Trenton	WBUD	10-2-71 (new); 12-11-71 (listed in *Billboard* ad); 4-29-72
	WTNJ	3-16-74 (new)
Vineland	WMVB	4-29-72 (new); 5-27-72; 12-23-72; 3-31-73; 4-21-73; 7-28-73; 1-5-74; 5-25-74; 8-24-74; 11-9-74; 5-10-75; 10-18-75; 10-23-76; 2-3-79
	WWBZ	5-26-79 (new)
Washington	WCRV	9-9-72; 11-18-72; 2-3-73; 9-1-73; 12-1-73
NEW MEXICO		
Albuquerque	KQEO	10-31-70; 1-23-71; 2-6-71 (listed in *Billboard* ad); 5-29-71; 7-3-71 (listed in *Billboard* ad); 9-25-71; 12-11-71 (listed in *Billboard* ad); 5-6-72; 12-30-72; 3-10-73; 5-19-73; 6-23-73; 8-25-73; 2-9-74; 5-4-74; 11-16-74; 5-3-75; 12-13-75; 4-3-76; 11-19-77; 3-10-79; 12-15-79
Carlsbad	KAVE	1-19-74 (new); 2-23-74
Clovis	KICA	7-3-71 (listed in *Billboard* ad); 7-10-71 (new); 7-17-71; 7-31-71
	KTQM	3-12-77 (new); 6-3-78; 2-17-79
Farmington	KRAZ	1-17-76 (new); 6-12-76 6-18-77 (new); 3-17-79
Gallup	KYVA	4-17-76 (new); 4-24-76; 10-23-76; 2-11-78; 3-3-79
Las Cruces	KRWG-FM	9-2-72; 10-14-72; 1-13-73 (New Mexico State University); 10-20-73
	KGRT	8-31-74 (new); 12-7-74; 3-29-75; 6-28-75
Portales	KENU	10-27-73 (new)
Sante Fe	KVSF	1-13-73 (new); 1-27-73; 3-24-73; 6-23-73; 7-7-73; 9-8-73; 11-24-73; 12-14-74; 9-6-75; 2-21-76; 4-24-76; 11-27-76; 12-9-78; 12-1-79
NEW YORK		
Albany	WABY	12-5-70; 1-30-71; 2-6-71 (2x: radio & listed in *Billboard* ad); 7-3-71 (listed in *Billboard* ad); 7-31-71
	WTRY	3-17-73 (new); 5-26-73; 8-11-73; 12-29-73; 6-15-74; 8-3-74; 8-31-74; 1-11-75; 8-30-75; 12-20-75; 12-9-78; 6-23-79; 12-1-79
Binghamton	WENE	11-4-72 (new); 2-24-73; 8-25-73; 2-9-74; 3-23-74;
	WENE	8-23-75 (new); 2-14-76
Buffalo	WGRQ-FM	1-13-73 (new); 2-24-73; 5-5-73; 6-2-73; 6-23-73; 9-22-73; 11-17-73; 4-13-74; 5-4-74; 6-29-74; 1-18-75
	WYSL	3-1-75 (new); 9-6-75; 9-27-75; 4-10-76; 1-22-77; 8-20-77; 3-18-78
Canandaigua	WCGR	10-2-71 (new); 12-4-71; 12-11-71 (listed in *Billboard* ad)
Corning	WCBA	9-7-74; 2-1-75; 6-7-75; 1-17-76; 7-17-76; 4-16-77 (mentioned as WCBQ); 7-16-77; 4-15-78; 1-6-79
Endicott	(See Binghamton, NY)	
Fredonia	WBUZ	6-23-73 (new); 7-14-73
Fulton	WKFM	6-3-78; 8-26-78; 8-25-79
Geneva	WECQ	11-3-79 (new)
Glens Falls	WWSC	9-8-73 (new); 11-17-73; 7-6-74; 8-17-74; 2-8-75
Gloversville	WENT	8-20-77; 8-12-78
Ithaca	WICB	8-28-71 (new); 10-9-71; 11-6-71; 12-11-71 (listed in *Billboard* ad); 1-22-72; 9-2-72 (re-new); 10-14-72; 1-13-73 (Ithaca College); 10-20-73; 4-27-74; 9-7-74 (re-new); 2-22-75; 9-6-75 (re-new); 3-20-76; 9-3-77 (re-new); 9-17-77; 2-11-78
Jamestown	WKSN	9-18-76 (new); 10-8-77 2-17-79 (new)
Latham	(see Albany, NY)	
Middletown	WALL	11-1-75 (new)

STATE Market	Calls	Air Date Mentions
NEW YORK (cont'd)		
New York City	WPIX	5-8-71 (new); 5-15-71; 6-19-71; 7-3-71 (listed in *Billboard* ad); 9-18-71; 10-16-71; 10-30-71; 12-4-71 (listener question); 12-11-71 (listed in *Billboard* ad); 1-15-72; 2-5-72; 4-22-72; 5-13-72; 5-20-72; 6-10-72; 7-15-72; 8-5-72; 9-9-72; 10-14-72; 10-28-72; 11-18-72; 12-2-72; 12-9-72; 12-23-72; 12-30-72; 1-6-73; 2-3-73; 2-24-73; 3-17-73; 4-14-73; 5-12-73; 6-9-73; 6-16-73; 7-7-73 (Ernie Maresca mention); 7-21-73; 8-4-73; 9-15-73; 9-22-73; 10-20-73; 2-9-74; 2-16-74; 2-23-74; 3-16-74; 5-25-74; 6-1-74; 6-22-74; 10-26-74; 3-1-75; 4-19-75 (listed in *Billboard* ad); 4-26-75 (Benny Bell's home); 5-3-75 (listed in *Billboard* ad); 5-10-75; 9-13-75; 12-6-75; 3-20-76; 6-5-76; 6-26-76; 9-25-76; 10-23-76; 1-8-77; 3-19-77; 9-10-77 (Meco mention); 10-22-77
	99X(WXLO)	5-20-78 (new); 7-29-78; 9-23-78; 12-2-78; 2-17-79; 3-31-79; 5-12-79; 6-2-79; 6-23-79; 8-11-79; 9-15-79; 10-13-79 (stuttering #1 records); 12-22-79
Newark	WACK	6-1-74 (new); 8-3-74
Olean	WMNS	1-8-77 (new); 10-29-77; 11-11-78; 11-3-79
Oneonta	WSRK	12-15-79 (new)
Oswego	WOCR	10-2-71 (new); 12-11-71 (listed in *Billboard* ad, as WORC); 12-25-71; 3-25-72; 1-13-73 (Oswego State University); 10-20-73; 5-18-74
Plattsburg	WKDR	3-13-71 (new); 6-12-71; 7-3-71 (listed in *Billboard* ad)
	WIRY	5-29-76 (new); 11-19-77
Potsdam	WPDM	11-9-74 (new); 7-19-75; 11-1-75; 9-9-78; 9-8-79
Riverhead,Long Is.	WRCN	3-30-74 (new); 8-16-75; 10-11-75; 3-6-76; 6-5-76; 3-17-79
Rochester	WHFM	1-16-71 (radio report); 2-6-71 (listed in *Billboard* ad); 2-27-71; 4-24-71; 7-3-71 (listed in *Billboard* ad); 7-31-71
	WBBF	8-2-75 (new); 1-31-76; 2-26-77; 4-7-79; 5-26-79
Rome	(See Utica, NY)	
Salamanca	WGGO	6-14-75 (new); 11-15-75
Saranac Lake	WNBZ	9-20-75 (new)
Schenectady	(see Albany, NY)	
Seneca Falls	WSFW	1-8-77 (new); 6-10-78
Southampton	WSCR	11-17-73 (new)
Syracuse	WNDR	3-6-71 (new); 4-24-71 (radio report); 7-3-71 (listed in *Billboard* ad); 8-21-71; 10-23-71; 12-11-71 (listed in *Billboard* ad); 1-8-72; 3-25-72; 5-27-72; 10-7-72; 11-18-72; 2-17-73; 5-5-73; 9-15-73
	WFBL	3-16-74 (new); 8-10-74; 4-10-76
	WKFM	9-4-76 (new); 7-30-77; 9-29-79
Ticonderoga	WIPS	3-1-75 (new); 8-9-75
Troy	(see Albany, NY)	
Utica	WTLB	4-10-71 (new); 7-3-71 (2x: radio & listed in *Billboard* ad); 10-9-71; 10-30-71; 12-11-71 (listed in *Billboard* ad); 5-6-72; 5-20-72; 2-24-73; 5-19-73; 8-25-73; 2-16-74; 6-1-74; 8-17-74; 8-23-75; 11-29-75; 5-1-76; 6-3-78; 12-2-78; 6-23-79; 12-1-79
Warsaw	WCJW	6-16-79 (new)
Washington Mills	(see Utica, NY)	

RADIO PARK, FULTON, N.Y. 13069
TELEPHONE: SYRACUSE (315) 695-2165

January 28, 1978

Mr. Tom Rounds
Watermark, Inc.
10700 Ventura Blvd.
North Hollywood, CA 91604

Dear Tom:

American Top Fourty continues to contribute to the rating increases of WKFM here in the Syracuse, New York market.

When we signed on with the program over a year ago I thought it would be difficult to improve on the TM Stereo Rock format we air in any time period. So we picked Sunday morning coming out of a religion and public affairs block to generate an interest by our audience to encourage them to tune in the station earlier than normal on Sundays. We put AT/40 on the air strictly as a programming move and it has done an excellent job.

The program gives WKFM its highest listening level of the week in the time slot 8A.M. to 11A.M. Sundays. It draws mail and audience from over twenty Central New York counties plus Canada. Even though the TM Stereo Rock format continues to push WKFM ratings up (now up six ARBs and six Pulses in a row) American Top Fourty shows better than our average listening level.

Thanks to Casey Kasem and all of you folks at AT/40 for your part in moving WKFM to the top in the Central New York radio market.

Cordially,

Bob Rooney

Robert L. Rooney
Vice President & General Manager

A strong testimonial from the WKFM general manager pointed out that *AT40* passed the Sunday morning test in an effort to generate a post-public affairs audience in Syracuse, New York. This letter accompanied program materials in Watermark presentation packages to other radio stations.

NORTH CAROLINA

Ashboro	WZOO	9-18-76 (new); 4-16-77; 7-30-77
Asheville	WISE	3-6-71 (new); 6-12-71; 7-3-71 (listed in *Billboard* ad); 12-11-71 (listed in *Billboard* ad); 1-8-72; 4-22-72; 6-10-72; 8-5-72; 1-27-73; 4-21-73; 7-21-73; 1-26-74; 5-4-74; 8-9-75; 3-6-76; 4-3-76; 10-16-76 (listener question); 4-16-77; 8-6-77; 6-3-78; 11-4-78; 3-24-79 (listener question); 10-27-79
Brevard	WPNF	2-8-75 (new); 7-19-75; 12-13-75; 11-27-76; 8-20-77; 11-18-78; 11-10-79
Burgaw	WVBS	5-11-74 (new)
Burlington	WBBB	5-17-75 (new); 2-7-76; 2-26-77; 9-17-77; 3-18-78; 12-9-78
Chapel Hill	WCHL	12-9-72; 5-26-73; 7-21-73
Charlotte	WIST	2-6-71 (listed in *Billboard* ad); 2-27-71; 6-26-71; 7-3-71 (listed in *Billboard* ad); 12-11-71 (listed in *Billboard* ad); 4-15-72; 6-10-72; 9-2-72; 10-28-72; 1-6-73; 7-21-73
	WBT	4-19-75 (new); 10-11-75; 6-5-76; 9-25-76; 1-22-77; 10-8-77; 3-18-78; 7-8-78; 6-9-79; 7-14-79
Clinton	WCLN	7-23-77 (new); 4-14-79; 10-13-79
Durham	WDNC	1-5-74 (new); 3-16-74
	WSSB	5-11-74 (new); 7-27-74; 8-23-75; 9-27-75
Elizabeth City	WCNC	1-29-77 (new); 6-18-77; 10-29-77; 2-11-78; 10-14-78; 10-13-78
Fairmont	WFMO	2-10-73 (new); 7-21-73; 12-1-73; 9-14-74; 6-21-75; 11-8-75; 6-18-77; 11-5-77; 8-19-78; 8-4-79
Fayetteville	WFLB	6-3-72 (new); 7-8-72 (new); 7-22-72; 12-2-72; 3-24-73; 5-12-73
	WFNC	10-12-74 (new); 6-21-75; 9-27-75
	WQSM	4-23-77; 11-12-77
Forest City	WBBO	12-19-70 (radio report); 2-6-71 (listed in *Billboard* ad); 2-13-71; 7-3-71 (listed in *Billboard* ad); 9-11-71; 10-16-71 (1st anniversary w/AT40); 11-27-71; 1-8-72 (listed in *Billboard* ad); 3-4-72; 4-21-73; 7-21-73; 11-24-73; 5-31-75; 1-31-76; 11-20-76; 11-19-77; 10-7-78; 10-6-79
Franklin	WRFR	8-11-79 (new)
Gastonia	(see South Gastonia, NC)	
Goldsboro	WYNG	11-25-72 (new); 2-17-73; 5-12-73; 7-21-73; 11-3-73; 7-6-74; 5-17-75; 6-25-77; 11-26-77; 3-3-79
Greenville	WOOW	4-9-77 (new)
Havelock	WKVO	9-9-72 (new); 11-18-72; 12-1-73; 5-11-74; 8-10-74; 8-31-74
Henderson	WIZS	6-3-72; 8-12-72; 7-21-73; 11-10-73
	WHNC	1-13-79 (new); 10-27-79
Hendersonville	WHVL	11-25-78 (new); 8-18-79
Hickory	WHKY	2-24-73 (new); 4-21-73; 7-21-73; 10-27-73; 4-20-74; 8-2-75; 3-20-76; 11-27-76; 10-28-78
Jacksonville	WXQR	9-6-75 (new)
	WJNC	1-28-78 (new); 11-4-78
Laurinburg	WLNC	4-17-71 (new); 7-3-71 (2x: radio & listed in *Billboard* ad); 10-2-71; 11-6-71; 12-11-71 (listed in *Billboard* ad); 1-22-72; 2-26-72; 6-3-72; 7-29-72; 11-11-72; 8-4-73 (re- new); 10-27-73; 5-11-74; 5-18-74; 6-21-75; 11-15-75
	WLNC	7-9-77 (new); 4-29-78; 6-3-78; 4-28-79
Lenoir	WJRI	5-29-71 (new); 7-3-71 (listed in *Billboard* ad); 8-14-71; 10-23-71; 12-11-71 (listed in *Billboard* ad); 3-11-72; 11-18-72; 7-21-73; 12-1-73; 5-11-74; 9-7-74; 5-3-75; 3-13-76; 8-25-79
New Bern	WRNB	4-12-75 (new)
	WHIT	12-17-77 (new); 3-18-78; 10-28-78; 3-31-79; 8-11-79
Oxford	WCBQ	9-11-76 (new); 10-23-76
Raleigh	WRNC	2-6-71 (listed in *Billboard* ad); 3-27-71; 7-3-71 (listed in *Billboard* ad)
	WKIX	9-18-76 (new); 9-2-78; 6-16-79; 8-25-79; 9-29-79
Reidsville	WFRC	2-9-74 (new); 8-10-74; 10-12-74
Roanoke Rapids	WCBT	1-24-76 (mentioned as Roanoke, NC)
Rockingham	WLWL	12-11-71 (listed in *Billboard* ad); 2-26-72; 5-27-72; 8-26-72; 10-21-72 (concert story); 7-21-73; 11-17-73; 5-4-74; 10-26-74; 11-2-74; 5-10-75 9-13-75 (new); 1-10-76
	WAYN	7-8-78 (new); 4-7-79

STATE Market	Calls	Air Date Mentions
NORTH CAROLINA (cont'd)		
Rocky Mount	WEED	8-24-74 (new)
Sanford	WFJA	10-23-76 (new); 8-12-78; 8-4-79
South Gastonia	WGAS	4-20-74 (new)
Spruce Pine	WTOE	1-14-78 (new); 4-15-78; 12-2-78
Sylvia	WMSJ	9-27-75 (new)
Tabor City	WTAB	3-20-71 (new); 5-8-71; 7-3-71 (listed in *Billboard* ad); 11-27-71; 12-11-71 (listed in *Billboard* ad); 3-11-72
Warrentown	WARR	4-13-74 (new); 6-22-74
Washington	WEEW	3-11-78 (new); 1-20-79
Wilkesboro	WWWC	11-6-76 (new); 7-16-77
Wilmington	WHSL	10-19-74 (new)
	WHSL	4-23-77 (new); 1-20-79; 8-18-79
Wilson	WVOT	1-22-77 (new); 7-16-77 (new); 2-26-77; 6-10-78
Winston-Salem	WAIR	9-5-70 (listed in *Billboard* ad); 9-19-70; 11-14-70; 12-12-70 (radio report); 12-19-70 (radio report); 2-6-71 (radio report & listed in *Billboard* ad); 7-3-71 (listed in *Billboard* ad); 8-7-71; 12-11-71 (listed in *Billboard* ad); 6-24-72; 11-18-72; 2-24-73; 5-26-73; 7-21-73; 2-23-74; 11-9-74; 5-24-75; 1-17-76; 6-10-78
	WSEZ	2-24-79
NORTH DAKOTA		
Bismark	KFYR	2-12-77 (new); 4-22-78
	KYYY	12-8-79
Dickinson	KDIX	6-16-79 (new)
Fargo	KQWB	7-3-71 (never mentioned on show; listed only in *Billboard* ad)
	KVOX	2-17-73; 5-12-73; 7-28-73; 1-26-74; 3-9-74 (d.j. question); 6-15-74; 11-16-74; 2-8-75; 5-24-75; 12-6-75; 5-15-76; 6-26-76; 3-10-79
Grand Forks	KNOX	4-24-71 (new); 7-3-71 (listed in *Billboard* ad); 7-10-71; 9-11-71; 12-11-71 (2x: radio & listed in *Billboard* ad); 4-1-72; 8-19-72; 2-10-73; 6-2-73; 8-18-73; 12-8-73; 4-27-74; 9-28-74
	KYTN	12-7-74; 3-29-75
	KNOX	4-24-76 (new); 10-23-76; 3-31-79
Minot	KTYN	5-24-75 (mentioned as KYTN)
	KKOA	1-8-77 (new); 2-26-77
	KIZZ	1-27-79 (new); 10-27-79
Valley City	KVOC	10-7-72 (new); 10-21-72
Wahpeton	KBMW	10-7-72 (new); 11-11-72; 5-12-73; 12-14-74; 4-12-75; 1-10-76; 4-10-76; 1-22-77; 12-16-78
OHIO		
Akron	WCUE	7-3-71 (listed in *Billboard* ad); 7-10-71 (new); 8-28-71
Ashtabula	WFUN	10-21-78 (new)
Athens	WATH	8-17-74 (new); 9-14-74 (new); 1-11-75; 5-31-75; 1-17-76
Bellefontaine	WTOO	4-30-77 (new); 7-23-77; 2-10-79
Bellevue	WNRR	10-11-75
Bowling Green	WAWR	7-29-72
Bryan	WBNO	11-12-77 (new); 2-11-78; 7-15-78; 10-13-79
Cambridge	WILE	8-24-74 (new); 8-31-74 (new); 2-1-75; 8-2-75; 3-20-76; 4-24-76; 4-23-77; 8-6-77; 8-19-78; 8-18-79
Canton	WINW	11-25-72
	WHBC	2-24-73 (new); 3-10-73 (WINW mention); 5-19-73; 8-25-73; 9-8-73; 2-16-74; 4-20-74; 1-25-75; 8-2-75; 2-28-76; 6-12-76; 6-25-77; 8-20-77; 6-10-78; 10-28-78; 10-27-79
Chillicothe	WBEX	9-18-76 (new)
Cincinnati	WSAI	10-18-75 (new); 10-30-76 (welcome back); 1-22-77; 2-11-78

OHIO (cont'd)

Cleveland	**WGAR**	**11-21-70; 12-19-70 (radio report); 2-6-71 (listed in *Billboard* ad)**
	WIXY	**10-2-71 (new); 10-23-71; 11-20-71**
	WNCR	**9-8-73; 11-10-73**
	WIXY	**2-15-75 (new); 8-9-75; 3-27-76; 11-13-76**
	WMGC	**3-19-77; 8-13-77**
	WGCL	**4-15-78 (new); 1-27-79**
Columbus	**WNCI-FM**	**3-6-71 (new); 6-26-71; 7-3-71 (listed in *Billboard* ad); 10-2-71; 12-4-71; 12-11-71 (listed in *Billboard* ad); 3-4-72; 5-27-72; 9-23-72; 10-7-72; 10-28-72; 1-13-73; 6-9-73; 6-30-73; 9-8-73; 12-8-73; 5-25-74; 6-22-74; 4-19-75 (listed in *Billboard* ad); 6-28-75; 10-18-75; 3-18-78; 11-4-78; 6-23-79; 9-1-79; 11-3-79**
Findlay	**WFIN**	**3-11-72; 5-13-72; 6-17-72; 11-18-72; 3-17-73; 9-8-73; 12-1-73; 3-30-74; 8-3-74; 9-14-74; 9-21-74**
Galion	**WGLX**	**4-13-74 (new); 2-8-75 (mentioned as guest host's hometown); 7-26-75**
Hamilton	**WOKV**	**10-14-78 (new); 3-17-79; 12-8-79**
	(also see Oxford, OH)	
Lima	**WCIT**	**9-16-72 (new); 10-14-72; 3-3-73; 6-30-73; 7-21-73; 9-8-73; 1-5-74; 3-9-74**
Mansfield	**WMAN**	**1-17-76 (new); 10-16-76; 9-17-77**
Marion	**WDIF**	**1-10-76 (new); 7-17-76; 11-20-76; 10-8-77; 10-14-78; 10-20-79**
Middleport	**WMPO AM & FM**	**10-8-77 (new); 3-18-78; 9-2-78; 9-1-79**
Newark	**WCLT**	**3-17-73; 8-4-73; 9-8-73; 12-15-73; 6-22-74; 3-1-75; 6-7-75; 1-24-76; 10-29-77; 4-14-79**
Niles	**WNIO**	**2-6-71 (listed in *Billboard* ad, as Warren, OH); 4-3-71; 7-3-71 (listed in *Billboard* ad, as Warren, OH); 8-21-71**
Ottawa	**WPNM**	**5-14-77 (new)**
Oxford	**WOXR**	**5-26-73 (new); 7-14-73; 9-8-73; 10-13-73; 1-12-74**
Portsmouth	**WPAY**	**4-1-72**
Springfield	**WIZE**	**10-23-76 (new); 2-26-77; 6-10-78; 8-26-78; 6-16-79; 8-18-79**
Steubenville	**WSTV/WRKY**	**10-8-77 (new); 9-16-78; 9-15-79**
Toledo	**WOHO**	**6-26-76 (new); 6-10-78; 5-5-79; 6-2-79**
Warren	**(see Niles, OH)**	
Waverly	**WIBO**	**4-15-78 (new); 1-27-79**

OKLAHOMA

Ardmore	**KVSO**	**3-15-75 (new); 12-13-75; 5-8-76; 10-16-76**
Atoka	**KEOR**	**4-21-79 (new)**
Bartlesville	**KWON**	**9-3-77 (new); 2-11-78; 9-30-78**
Blackwell	**KLTR**	**11-10-79 (new)**
Henryetta	**KHEN**	**8-13-77 (new); 6-10-78**
Hobart	**KQTZ**	**6-16-79 (new)**
Lawton	**KSWO**	**4-21-79 (new)**
McAlester	**KTMC**	**10-13-79 (new)**
Norman	**KNOR**	**12-14-74 (new); 5-22-76 (new)**
Oklahoma City	**KLEC**	**5-26-73**
	KTOK	**2-19-77 (new)**
	KOFM	**1-14-78 (new); 3-18-78; 11-4-78; 6-23-79; 11-10-79**
Stillwater	**KVRO**	**6-1-73 (listed in 1973 Vacation Listening Guide; first public acknowledgement as a subscribing station); 11-10-73; 6-15-74; 3-15-75**
Tulsa	**KELI**	**1-16-71; 2-6-71 (listed in *Billboard* ad); 6-5-71; 7-3-71 (listed in *Billboard* ad); 9-25-71; 12-11-71 (listed in *Billboard* ad); 9-9-72; 11-25-72; 2-10-73; 9-15-73; 3-9-74; 8-3-74; 3-22-75; 4-19-75; 11-29-75; 5-22-76; 7-31-76 (listener question); 1-29-77**

"….Listeners quite often called 'to speak with Casey' or 'to make a request to Casey' thinking the program was live and local. That was testimony to the high level of success the producers had at giving the program the 'immediacy' of a local show."

Fred Baur, former *AT40* board operator and d.j. at KELI in Tulsa, Oklahoma

STATE Market	Calls	Air Date Mentions
OREGON		
Albany	KRKT	9-11-71 (new); 12-4-71; 12-25-71 (listed in *Billboard* ad)
	KGAL	9-23-72 (new); 12-9-72; 3-24-73; 9-1-73; 12-1-73; 3-16-74; 10-19-74
Astoria	KAST	10-2-71 (new); 11-13-71; 1-22-72; 2-26-72
Bend	KBND	1-10-76 (new); 5-1-76; 10-16-76; 11-20-76; 7-23-77; 12-9-78
Burns	KRNS	7-22-78 (new); 5-19-79
Coos Bay	KYNG	2-1-75 (new); 9-6-75; 2-28-76; 6-26-76; 1-29-77; 10-8-77; 6-10-78; 9-29-79
Corvallis	KFLY	9-17-77 (new); 2-18-78; 7-22-78
Eugene	KASH	8-10-74 (new); 10-26-74; 11-2-74; 7-19-75; 11-15-75
	KBDF	5-21-77 (new); 4-7-79; 5-26-79
Klamath Falls	KAGO	12-6-75; 2-26-77; 11-26-77; 7-8-78
La Grande	KLBM	7-10-71 (new); 7-24-71; 11-6-71; 12-25-71 (listed in *Billboard* ad)
Medford	KYJC	10-13-73 (new); 9-6-75; 3-6-76; 5-29-76; 4-23-77; 9-29-79
Newport	KNPT	6-4-77 (new); 6-17-78; 10-28-78; 3-31-79
Pendleton	KTIX	5-7-77 (new); 9-23-78; 3-10-79
Portland	KISN	4-17-71 (new); 7-3-71 (2x: radio & listed in *Billboard* ad); 12-4-71; 12-25-71 (listed in *Billboard* ad); 3-4-72; 9-16-72; 11-4-72; 1-6-73; 4-14-73; 5-12-73; 7-14-73; 10-13-73; 12-1-73; 3-23-74; 11-30-74; 4-26-75; 1-17-76
	KGW	9-11-76 (new); 5-28-77; 8-6-77; 2-11-78; 7-22-78; 6-2-79; 7-21-79; 9-1-79
Roseburg	KRSB	7-8-78 (new); 5-19-79
Salem	KBZY	1-8-72 (listed in *Billboard* ad); 4-22-72; 10-14-72; 1-6-73
	KSLM	6-30-73; 7-14-73; 10-13-73; 1-12-74
	KORI	5-11-74; 8-17-74; 12-7-74; 3-29-75
	KSLM	4-22-78 (new); 2-17-79
	KSKD	4-14-79 (new)
Tillamook	KTIL	1-14-78 (new); 3-25-78; 12-2-78; 12-1-79
PENNSYLVANIA		
Allentown	WKAP	7-20-74 (new; mentioned as Whitehall, PA); 12-14-74; 8-9-75; 10-25-75; 7-10-76; 1-29-77
Altoona	WVAM	12-25-71 (listed in *Billboard* ad); 4-15-72; 3-10-73; 4-21-73; 9-22-73; 1-26-74; 1-11-75; 5-17-75; 11-8-75 (new); 4-24-76; 4-23-77; 7-23-77; 3-25-78; 3-3-79
	WFBG	10-20-79 (new)
Ambridge	WMBA	7-17-71 (new); 7-24-71
Bedford	WAYC	8-10-74 (new); 8-17-74 (new); 1-25-75; 5-31-75; 1-24-76; 4-30-77; 8-6-77; 6-17-78; 7-8-78; 7-14-79
Clarion	WWCH	7-24-76 (new); 4-30-77; 8-27-77; 5-19-79
Clearfield	WCPA	10-9-76 (new); 1-29-77; 4-30-77; 9-17-77; 4-22-78; 12-9-78; 7-28-79
Erie	WRIE	11-9-74 (new); 8-16-75
	WWGO/WCCK	2-12-77 (new); 6-17-78 (WCCK)
	WJET	4-29-78 (new); 7-8-78; 2-3-79
Hanover	WYCR-FM	5-25-74 (new); 2-1-75; 9-6-75; 9-30-78; 9-22-79
Harrisburg	WKBO	7-17-71 (new); 8-28-71; 10-9-71 (new?); 12-25-71 (listed in *Billboard* ad); 4-15-72; 9-2-72; 10-28-72; 1-6-73; 8-18-73; 2-16-74; 5-4-74; 2-8-75; 5-3-75; 3-13-76; 6-25-77; 10-29-77; 2-3-79
Honesdale	WAEN	4-9-77 (new)
	WDNH	1-13-79
Huntingdon	WQRO	1-6-79 (new); 11-17-79
Johnstown	WCRO	2-6-71 (listed in *Billboard* ad); 2-20-71; 7-3-71 (listed in *Billboard* ad); 7-31-71
Lafayette Hill	(see Philadelphia, PA)	
Latrobe	WQTW	9-3-77 (new); 9-16-78; 2-10-79
Lewistown	WMRF	3-10-79 (new)
Lykens	WQIN	1-15-77 (new); 2-18-78; 11-25-78
New Castle	WKST	3-27-76 (new); 4-28-79
Philadelphia	WIBG	7-7-73 (Turbans mention); 7-14-73; 7-28-73; 8-11-73; 9-1-73; 9-22-73; 9-29-73; 10-13-73; 10-27-73; 12-1-73
	WZZD	2-4-78 (new); 8-26-78

PENNSYLVANIA (cont'd)

Pittsburgh	**WIXZ**	**10-2-71 (new); 11-20-71; 12-25-71 (listed in *Billboard* ad)**
	WPEZ	**9-18-76 (new); 2-19-77; 8-20-77; 11-26-77; 3-24-79; 8-25-79; 12-15-79**
Pottsville	**WPAM**	**5-15-76 (new)**
Sharon	**WPIC**	**6-30-73 (new); 7-14-73; 10-13-73**
State College	**WRSC**	**12-13-75 (new); 10-16-76; 3-25-78; 11-25-78; 11-24-79**
Waynesboro	**WEEO**	**9-25-76 (new); 8-5-78; 8-4-79**
Wellsboro	**WNBT**	**4-15-78 (new)**
Whitehall	**(see Allentown, PA)**	
Wilkes-Barre	**WILK**	**2-6-71 (listed in *Billboard* ad); 12-25-71 (listed in *Billboard* ad); 5-6-72; 6-3-72; 2-10-73 (26th B-day); 3-10-73; 5-19-73; 8-25-73; 2-9-74; 4-27-74; 8-17-74; 2-22-75; 8-2-75; 8-26-78; 8-18-79**
Williamsport	**WILQ**	**10-11-75 (new); 7-17-76; 8-26-78; 8-18-79**
York	**WYCR**	**12-3-77**

RHODE ISLAND

Providence	**WPRO**	**1-28-78 (new); 11-11-78; 3-3-79 (new); 12-8-79; 12-22-79**
Woonsocket	**WNRI**	**3-13-71 (new); 5-29-71; 7-3-71 (listed in *Billboard* ad); 10-2-71**

SOUTH CAROLINA

Aiken	**WAKN**	**3-24-73; 8-25-73**
	WLOW	**4-16-77 (new); 7-23-77; 6-17-78; 2-3-79**
Barnwell	**WBAW**	**2-17-73 (new); 8-25-73; 10-27-73 (mentioned as WBAM); 3-1-75; 4-12-75; 11-15-75; 1-29-77; 8-27-77**
Beaufort	**WSIB**	**8-25-73; 11-24-73; 6-1-74 (mentioned as WSIB/Beaumont, TX)**
Camden	**WPUB**	**5-31-75 (new); 5-15-76; 4-23-77; 10-15-77; 3-25-78; 2-10-79**
Charleston	**WTMA**	**6-19-71 (new); 7-3-71 (listed twice in *Billboard* ad); 8-28-71; 12-25-71 (listed in *Billboard* ad); 5-6-72; 5-20-72; 12-30-72; 5-26-73; 8-25-73; 2-9-74; 6-15-74; 7-13-74; 7-20-74; 8-24-74; 3-8-75; 8-23-75; 12-20-75; 4-30-77; 8-6-77; 12-2-78; 6-30-79; 11-24-79**
Chester	**WGCD**	**10-7-72 (new); 12-9-72; 2-17-73; 5-26-73; 8-25-73; 11-10-73; 3-15-75; 2-21-76; 4-30-77; 11-26-77; 2-18-78; 12-16-78**
Clinton	**WPCC**	**7-12-75 (new); 8-23-75 (question correction); 9-20-75**
Columbia	**WCOS**	**5-12-73 (new); 8-25-73; 8-3-74; 3-22-75; 1-31-76; 7-10-76; 10-16-76; 9-17-77; 1-13-79**
Florence	**WJMX**	**7-31-71 (new); 9-11-71; 12-25-71 (listed in *Billboard* ad); 6-3-72; 3-31-73; 5-12-73; 8-11-73; 8-25-73; 12-29-73; 5-11-74; 3-22-75; 5-3-75; 3-13-76; 5-7-77; 2-3-79**
Gaffney	**WFGN**	**11-23-74 (new)**
	WFGN	6-11-77 (new)
	WFGN	**3-35-78 (new)**
Georgetown	**WINH**	**5-4-74 (new); 9-28-74; 10-19-74; 8-2-75; 3-27-76**
	WGMB	**(listed in 1976 Listening Directory)**
	WGMB	**(listed in 1977 Listening Directory)**
	WGMB	**1-20-79**
Greenville	**WQOK**	**4-10-71 (new); 7-3-71 (listed in *Billboard* ad); 7-17-71; 9-18-71; 12-25-71 (listed in *Billboard* ad)**
	WQOK	**10-30-76 (new); 1-29-77; 9-9-78; 9-15-79**
Greenwood	**WCRS**	**9-10-77 (new); 7-29-78**
	WSCZ	**3-10-79; 9-22-79**
Lancaster	**WAGL**	**8-14-76 (new)**
Myrtle Beach	**WTGR**	**9-6-75 (new); 4-10-76**
Newberry	**WKDK**	**11-26-77 (new); 4-22-78; 11-11-78;**
No. Myrtle Beach	**WNMB**	**1-7-78 (new); 3-25-78; 11-11-78; 3-24-79**
Orangeburg	**WORG**	**3-16-74 (new); 9-14-74; 9-21-74; 10-26-74; 11-2-74; 7-12-75; 10-25-75**
	WDIX	**1-21-78 (new); 10-14-78**
Pageland	**WCPL**	**10-22-77 (new); 4-22-78; 7-22-78; 12-16-78**
Rapid City	**KTOQ**	**9-10-77 (new)**
	KTOQ	**12-9-78 (new); 12-1-79**
Sumter	**WDXY**	**2-9-74 (new); 3-23-74; 7-6-74; 11-9-74; 5-24-75; 2-7-76; 8-5-78; 1-13-79; 8-4-79**
	WSSC	**12-22-79 (new)**
Union	**WBCU**	**9-4-71 (new); 11-20-71; 12-25-71 (listed in *Billboard* ad); 3-2-74; 6-29-74; 11-30-74**
Walterboro	**WALD**	**5-31-75 (new)**

DRAWER T•GREENVILLE, SOUTH CAROLINA 29610•DIAL (803) 246-2112

April 26, 1971

Mr. Thomas Rounds
Watermark, Inc.
931 N. La Cienega Boulevard
Los Angeles, California 90069

Dear Tom:

Again, I would like to thank you for a great program! American Top 40 has steadily built interest over the last 5 weeks among listeners and sponsors.

As Program Director, I want to notify Watermark, Inc. that WQOK is hereby exercising its option to renew American Top 40 for the third cycle and all subsequent cycles of the program until you are notified otherwise.

The program will continue to run from Noon until 3:00 PM on Sunday afternoons.

Best regards,

WQOK, INC.

Dave Dannheisser
Program Director

DD/ed

From WQOK in Greenville, South Carolina, this letter confirmed an *AT40* contract renewal.

November 13, 1972

Mr. Tom Rounds
President-Watermark, Inc.
10700 Ventura Blvd.
Los Angeles, Calif. 91604

Dear Tom:

Sign us up! The first year of AT40 has shown its worthiness and stability as a great show beyond our greatest expectations and, believe me, we had great expectations! It has stayed sold-out consistently with prospective sponsors knocking on the door. We are very pleased, so much so that we don't hesitate at all in signing for a full year!

We're looking forward to the holiday specials and you will be hearing from us about the "Top Eighty of 1973" surveys.

Our listening audience is growing on Sunday afternoons, especially in nearby Nashville and Casey lures the listeners to 'COR from all over the midstate.

Thanks again for all your help and here's to our continued mutual success.

Sincerely yours,

Terry Climer
Music Director

TDC/bb

According to this November 13, 1972 letter from a WCOR (Lebanon, Tennessee) music director, *AT40* generated an audience in Nashville. It would be at least a year before a Nashville station signed on to broadcast Casey Kasem's countdown.

STATE Market	Calls	Air Date Mentions
SOUTH DAKOTA		
Aberdeen	KABR	3-6-71 (new); 7-3-71 (listed in *Billboard* ad); 7-17-71; 9-25-71; 11-20-71; 12-25-71 (listed in *Billboard* ad); 2-26-72; 8-19-72; 2-17-73; 11-10-73; 2-23-74; 12-7-74; 3-29-75; 5-31-75; 11-15-75; 6-12-76; 2-5-77; 10-7-78; 9-29-79; 10-6-79
Huron	KOKK	11-18-78 (new); 9-8-79
Mitchell	KMIT	8-20-77 (new); 5-5-79
Sioux Falls	KKRC	10-14-78 (new); 8-11-79
Winner	KWYR	8-13-77 (new); 2-18-78
Yankton	KYNT	1-17-76 (new); 10-16-76
TENNESSEE		
Athens	WLAR	5-25-74 (new); 6-21-75 (new)
	WENR	9-16-78 (new); 1-20-79
	WJSQ	12-15-79 (new)
Chattanooga	WFLI	10-17-70; 11-14-70; 2-6-71 (listed in *Billboard* ad); 2-27-71; 7-3-71 (listed in *Billboard* ad); 7-31-71; 12-25-71 (listed in *Billboard* ad); 4-29-72
	WDEF	7-16-77 (new); 3-25-78
	WGOW	1-27-79 (new); 6-23-79
Columbia	WKRM	1-29-77 (new); 5-7-77; 8-27-77; 2-18-78; 11-11-78; 11-3-79
Cookeville	WHUB	3-20-76; 2-5-77; 11-26-77; 6-17-78; 3-24-79; 8-18-79
Cowan	WZYX	1-22-77 (new)
Etowah	WCPH	5-14-77 (new)
Hendersonville	(see Nashville, TN)	
Humboldt	WHMT	8-19-72 (new); 12-9-72; 12-8-73; 4-20-74; 1-11-75
Jamestown	WDEB	11-4-78 (new; mentioned as WDEV); 7-28-79
Jellico	WJJT	9-9-72 (new); 12-9-72
Johnson City	WETB	9-21-74 (new); 1-25-75; 6-21-75; 10-18-75; 6-25-77; 8-12-78; 8-4-79
Knoxville *Billboard*	WNOX	11-28-70; 2-6-71 (listed in *Billboard* ad); 3-20-71; 7-3-71 (listed in ad); 8-21-71; 10-23-71; 12-25-71 (listed in *Billboard* ad); 10-7-72; 10-28-72; 3-10-73; 6-2-73; 8-18-73; 2-16-74; 5-18-74; 2-1-75; 7-12-75; 1-10-76; 4-22-78
Lebanon	WCOR	6-24-72; 8-26-72; 3-3-73
Martin	WCMT	10-12-74 (new)
Memphis	WMC-FM	9-30-78 (new); 6-16-79; 8-18-79
Morristown	WAZI	8-28-76 (new)
Murfreesboro	WGNS	10-7-72 (new); 12-9-72; 5-12-73; 9-29-73; 11-3-73; 4-13-74; 6-22-74; 2-15-75; 4-19-75; 3-6-76; 7-17-76; 2-19-77
Nashville	WBYQ	2-2-74 (listed in *Billboard* ad); 2-22-75; 5-31-75; 1-31-76; 6-12-76; 11-20-76; 7-23-77; 10-14-78; 10-13-79
Oneida	WBNT	7-9-77 (new)
Rockwood	WOFE	6-2-79 (new)
Tullahoma	WBGY	3-11-78 (new)
	WBGY	11-25-78 (new); 7-14-79
Union City	WENK	10-25-75 (new); 10-9-76; 8-5-78; 8-4-79
TEXAS		
Abilene	KRBC	12-23-72; 3-17-73; 6-16-73; 7-28-73; 12-15-73; 5-18-74; 3-1-75; 5-10-75; 12-13-75; 7-17-76; 3-26-77; 7-23-77; 2-18-78; 2-10-79
Amarillo	KPUR	1-13-73 (new); 2-24-73; 6-16-73
Austin	KTAP-AM/KHFI-FM	12-19-70; 1-23-71; 2-6-71 (listed in *Billboard* ad) 6-15-74 (new; KHFI); 7-20-74 (new); 10-19-74; 6-28-75; 1-24-76; 4-3-76; 10-16-76; 8-6-77; 4-22-78; 10-21-78
Ballinger	KRUN	8-19-72 (new); 10-21-72; 3-3-73
	KRUN	5-20-78 (new)
Beaumont	KAYC	11-6-71 (new); 12-25-71 (listed in *Billboard* ad); 5-6-72; 12-30-72; 1-20-73; 4-21-73; 6-23-73; 8-25-73; 2-9-74; 2-23-74; 6-1-74 (mentioned as WSIB/Beaumont, TX); 3-15-75; 4-12-75; 12-20-75; 10-9-76; 8-27-77; 12-9-78

TEXAS (cont'd)

Bellville	**KACO**	**8-21-76; 3-12-77; 8-6-77; 9-17-77**
Big Spring	**KBST**	**10-28-78 (new); 7-14-79**
Borger	**KQTY**	**3-3-79 (new)**
Brady	**KNEL**	**3-1-75 (new); 9-13-75; 5-22-76**
Brownwood	**KLSN-FM**	**11-10-73 (new); 4-13-74; 6-29-74; 3-22-75; 7-26-75; 11-1-75**
	KBWD	**11-13-76 (new); 4-2-77; 11-5-77**
	KBWD	**4-21-79 (new); 4-28-79 (new)**
Bryan	**KORA**	**8-19-72; 1-20-73**
	KTAM	**6-1-74; 8-10-74; 8-24-74; 3-22-75**
	KTAM	**8-14-76 (new); 4-2-77; 11-5-77; 3-10-79**
Canyon	**KHBJ**	**11-19-77 (new); 3-25-78; 7-29-78**
Coleman	**KSTA**	**3-11-78 (new)**
Corpus Christi	**KEYS**	**2-6-71 (listed in *Billboard* ad); 5-1-71; 7-3-71 (listed in *Billboard* ad)**
	KZFM	**9-22-73 (new); 1-19-74; 2-2-74; 7-6-74; 9-28-74; 10-26-74; 11-2-74; 9-6-75; 2-28-76; 4-10-76; 4-9-77; 11-19-77; 3-31-79**
Crockett	**KIVY**	**4-19-75 (new); 11-29-75; 12-4-76 (listener question; Oakwood,TX); 4-16-77; 11-12-77**
Dallas	**KLIF**	**2-21-76 (new); 7-31-76 (listener question)**
	(also see Fort Worth, TX)	
Del Rio	**KDLK**	**6-8-74 (new); 11-9-74; 6-14-75; 11-15-75; 5-1-76**
Eagle Pass	**KINL**	**1-5-74 (new); 3-23-74**
	KEPS	11-30-74
El Paso	**KINT-AM/FM**	**10-24-70; 11-14-70 (listener question); 1-16-71; 2-6-71 (listed in *Billboard* ad); 5-29-71; 7-3-71 (listed in *Billboard* ad)**
	KELP	**1-4-75 (new); 6-21-75; 1-10-76; 6-12-76; 11-20-76; 10-8-77**
	KSET	9-9-78 (new); 6-9-79; 9-15-79
Fort Worth	**KXOL**	**4-10-71 (new); 7-3-71 (2x: radio & listed in *Billboard* ad); 12-25-71 (listed in *Billboard* ad); 7-8-72; 11-11-72; 2-17-73; 5-12-73; 9-15-73; 11-3-73; 9-6-75**
	KFJZ	**3-19-77 (new); 10-29-77; 2-3-79; 6-2-79; 7-14-79**
Freeport	**KGOL**	**2-18-78 (new); 10-14-78**
Houston	**KNUZ**	**2-6-71 (listed in *Billboard* ad); 6-12-71; 7-3-71 (listed in *Billboard* ad); 7-31-71; 10-16-71; 11-13-71; 12-25-71 (listed in *Billboard* ad); 1-29-72; 5-13-72; 9-16-72; 11-4-72; 2-3-73**
	KRLY-FM	**5-26-73 (new); 6-2-73; 8-4-73; 9-22-73; 11-3-73; 11-10-73; 11-24-73; 5-25-74; 9-14-74; 12-7-74; 3-29-75; 8-16-75; 2-14-76; 7-10-76; 2-5-77; 6-11-77; 10-15-77; 9-23-78; 3-10-79; 5-12-79; 6-30-79; 9-15-79**
Kerrville	**KERV**	**1-22-77 (new); 11-26-77**
Kilgore	**KOCA**	**4-29-78 (new)**
Killeen	**KIXS**	**1-19-74 (new); 2-2-74 (listed in *Billboard* ad); 7-6-74; 1-4-75; 5-31-75; 9-27-75; 4-16-77; 12-3-77; 4-29-78**
Lake Jackson	**KGOL**	**6-17-78; 7-22-78**
Lamesa	**KPET**	**6-3-78 (new); 6-10-78**
Laredo	**KVOZ**	**7-8-72; 2-10-73; 9-15-73; 1-19-74 (new); 7-6-74; 7-13-74; 7-20-74; 1-11-75; 8-30-75; 10-11-75**
	KOYE	**4-23-77; 6-24-78; 9-9-78; 9-8-79**
Longview	**KFRO**	**9-29-79 (new); 12-22-79**
Lubbock	**KSEL**	**9-5-70 (listed in *Billboard* ad); 9-12-70; 11-7-70**
	KLBK	**5-15-71 (new); 7-3-71 (listed in *Billboard* ad); 8-7-71**
Lufkin	**KLUF**	**8-27-77 (new)**
McAllen	**KRIO**	**2-10-73 (new); 6-16-73; 7-14-73; 10-13-73; 1-5-74 (Brownsville Station); 6-8-74; 7-27-74; 1-25-75; 5-17-75; 2-7-76; 4-30-77; 8-12-78 (Toby Beau's home); 9-15-79**
McKinney	**KMMK**	**9-27-75 (new)**
Midland	**(see Odessa, TX)**	
Monahans	**KVKM**	**3-26-77 (new)**
Nacogdoches	**KEEE**	**10-26-74 (new); 2-1-75; 6-14-75**
	KEEE	**6-24-78 (new); 4-14-79**
Odessa	**KOZA**	**3-13-71 (new); 6-26-71; 7-3-71 (listed in *Billboard* ad, as Midland/Odessa)**
	KRIG	**11-2-74 (mentioned new as KIRG); 8-16-75**
	KOZA	**3-11-78 (new)**

STATE Market	Calls	Air Date Mentions
TEXAS (cont'd)		
Ozona	**KRCT**	**3-26-77 (new); 4-29-78; 2-17-79**
Plainview	**KVOP/KPLA**	**10-25-75 (new); 5-7-77; 11-19-77 (re-new); 12-2-78**
San Angelo	**KWFR/KIXY-FM**	**4-10-71 (new); 5-22-71; 7-3-71 (listed KWFR in *Billboard* ad); 9-4-71; 12-25-71 (listed KWFR in *Billboard* ad); 7-8-72; 1-20-73; 6-2-73; 9-22-73; 12-8-73; 3-30-74; 9-7-74; 9-21-74; 2-15-75; 4-26-75; 9-20-75; 3-31-79**
San Antonio	**KTSA**	**9-5-70 (listed in *Billboard* ad); 9-26-70; 11-7-70; 1-30-71; 2-6-71 (listed in *Billboard* ad); 7-3-71 (listed in *Billboard* ad); 8-7-71; 12-11-71; 12-25-71 (listed in *Billboard* ad); 3-11-72; 6-3-72; 7-8-72; 8-12-72; 10-28-72; 1-13-73; 5-12-73; 9-22-73; 12-8-73; 6-1-74; 2-22-75; 5-24-75; 2-21-76; 8-7-76; 6-25-77; 6-17-78; 3-10-79; 9-15-79**
Sherman	**KRRV**	**6-1-74 (new); 8-3-74**
	KIKM	**8-21-76 (new); 2-19-77**
Texarkana	**KTFS**	**1-8-72 (new, & listed in *Billboard* ad); 12-23-72; 1-20-73; 8-11-73; 12-15-73; 6-1-74**
Tyler	**KTYL**	**9-18-76 (new)**
	KDOK	**4-8-78 (new)**
Victoria	**KVIC**	**7-8-72; 8-16-75 (new); 5-6-78; 5-19-79**
Waco	**WACO**	**10-21-72 (new); 1-20-73; 6-16-73; 7-14-73; 10-13-73; 1-26-74; 2-23-74; 9-21-74; 9-28-74; 3-8-75; 4-12-75; 9-13-75; 11-22-75; 2-19-77; 9-24-77; 7-8-78; 7-14-79**
Wichita Falls	**KNIN**	**4-22-78 (new)**
UTAH		
Cedar City	**KBRE**	**10-16-76 (new); 2-5-77; 7-15-78; 7-14-79**
Delta	**KDLT**	**8-13-77 (new)**
Logan	**KVNU**	**10-13-73 (new); 6-15-74; 3-15-75; 8-30-75; 2-14-76; 4-3-76; 9-30-78; 9-29-79**
Manti	**KMTI**	**4-14-79 (new)**
Price	**KOAL**	**1-14-78 (new); 4-22-78; 4-29-78; 11-4-78; 3-31-79**
Provo	**KEYY**	**1-12-74; 4-6-74; 4-19-75; 1-10-76; 5-22-76; 2-19-77**
	KAYK	**9-16-78 (new); 7-21-79; 12-8-79**
St. George	**KDXU**	**2-26-77 (new); 12-16-78**
Salt Lake City	**KCPX**	**10-17-70; 1-9-71; 1-30-71 (radio report); 2-6-71 (listed in *Billboard* ad); 5-1-71; 7-3-71 (listed in *Billboard* ad); 9-4-71; 10-16-71; 1-8-72 (listed in *Billboard* ad); 9-16-72; 11-25-72; 2-24-73; 5-5-73; 5-26-73; 9-15-73; 3-2-74; 7-13-74; 7-20-74; 3-22-75; 6-7-75; 10-25-75; 5-29-76; 10-9-76; 6-4-77; 9-17-77; 2-18-78; 10-7-78; 6-16-79; 9-29-79**
VERMONT		
Brattleboro	**WTSA**	**11-30-74 (new); 8-30-75; 12-6-75; 5-29-76; 10-9-76**
Rutland	**WSYB**	**2-8-75 (new); 8-23-75; 2-19-77; 6-24-78; 12-2-78 (WSYV)**
	WHWB	**1-13-79 (new); 10-27-79**

KIXS NUMBER 1
24 HOURS A DAY

LAST WEEK	THIS WEEK	TITLE	ARTIST	LABEL	WKS. ON SURVEY
7	1	NO NO SONG/SNOOKEROO	RINGO STARR	APPLE	4
2	2	HAVE YOU NEVER BEEN MELLOW	OLIVIA NEWTON-JOHN	MCA	8
12	3	CHEVY VAN	SAMMY JOHNS	GRC	4
16	4	PHILADELPHIA FREEDOM	ELTON JOHN	MCA	4
6	5	LADY MARMALADE	LaBELLE	EPIC	8
4	6	LOVIN' YOU	MINNIE RIPERTON	EPIC	6
10	7	YOU ARE SO BEAUTIFUL	JOE COCKER	A & M	4
1	8	ME EYES ADORED YOU	FRANKIE VALLIE	PRIVATE STOCK	10
3	9	DON'T CALL US, WE'LL CALL YOU	SUGARLOAF/JERRY CORBETTA	CLARIDGE	8
9	10	EXPRESS	B.T. EXPRESS	ROADSHOW	8
-	11	EMMA	HOT CHOCALATE	BIG TREE	2
5	12	SAD SWEET DREAMER	SWEET SENSATION	ATV	4
19	13	SOMEBODY DONE SOMEBODY WRONG SONG	B.J. THOMAS	ABC	4
11	14	SHAME, SHAME SHAME	SHIRLEY & COMPANY	VIBRATION	6
17	15	POETRY MAN	PHOEBE SNOW	SHELTER	8
18	16	ONCE YOU GET STARTED	RUFUS	ABC	4
20	17	HARRY TRUMAN	CHICAGO	COLUMBIA	4
-	18	WHAT AM I GONNA DO WITH YOU	BARRY WHITE	20th CENTURY	2
-	19	SUPERNATURAL THING, PT. 1	BEN E. KING	ATLANTIC	2
-	20	WALKING IN RHYTHM	BLACKBYRDS	FANTASY	2
HITBOUND		WHO'S SORRY NOW	MARIE OSMOND	MGM	
HITBOUND		AMIE	PURE PRAIRIE LEAGUE	RCA	
HITBOUND		ONLY YESTERDAY	CARPENTERS	A & M	

KIXS ALBUM FEATURES
"PHYSICAL GRAFFITI"............LED ZEPPLIN
"ROCK 'N' ROLL.................JOHN LENNON
"COLD ON THE SHOULDER".........GORDON LIGHTFOOT
"WELCOME TO MY NIGHTMARE"......ALICE COOPER
"REALLY ROSIE"................CAROLE KING
"AN EVENING WITH JOHN DENVER"..JOHN DENVER
"HAVE YOU NEVER BEEN MELLOW"...OLIVIA NEWTON-JOHN

AMERICAN TOP 40

Saturdays 6pm-9pm
and
Sundays 9am-Noon

55 KTSA
HITLIST

Casey Kasem with American Top 40 Countdown, Sunday Nine to Noon on KTSA.

THE KTSA PEOPLE

Bruce Hathaway . . . 6 - 9 a.m. Charlie Browe . . . 6 - 10 p.m.
David Kline . . . 9 - Noon Sam Burke . . . 10 - 2 a.m.
Mike Kelly . . . Noon - 3 John Wagner . . . 2 - 6 a.m.
Lee Randall . . . 3 - 6 p.m. Larry Jackson . . . Anytime

The KIXS (Killeen, Texas) record survey from April 4, 1975 promoted two *AT40* broadcast times, Saturdays at 6 p.m. and Sundays at 9 a.m. *AT40* was heard at the same time on Sundays according to the October 4, 1974 survey from San Antonio's KTSA, which featured Casey Kasem's photograph to publicize the countdown.

VIRGINIA

City	Station	Dates
Appomattox	WTTX	1-8-77 (new); 5-21-77; 10-15-77; 4-29-78; 12-9-78
Bedford	WBLT	3-3-79 (new)
Big Stone Gap	WLSD	1-29-77 (new); 5-7-77; 11-5-77
Charlottesville	WINA	10-28-72 (new); 2-10-73; 3-17-73; 5-26-73; 9-15-73; 12-29-73; 4-27-74; 10-19-74; 4-26-75; 3-27-76; 5-21-77
	WELK	1-21-78 (new)
	WCHV	10-28-78 (new); 7-28-79
Collinsville	WFIC	11-20-76 (new); 11-27-76 (new; mentioned as Kentucky); 2-25-78; 10-21-78; 10-20-79
Danville	WBTM	12-23-72; 3-31-73; 6-16-73; 8-4-73; 12-15-73; 3-2-74
	WBTM	10-13-79 (new)
Emporia	WEVA	1-13-79 (new)
Farnham	WFJC	1-5-74 (new)
Grundy	WNRG	8-28-76 (new); 10-9-76
Lexington	WREL	9-29-73 (new) 11-17-73; 6-8-74; 11-9-74
Lynchburg	WLVA	11-17-73 (new); 5-18-74; 11-30-74; 5-10-75
Martinsville	WMVA	7-3-71 (new, and listed in *Billboard* ad); 8-21-71
Newport News	(see Norfolk, VA)	
Norfolk	WGH	7-3-71 (listed in *Billboard* ad); 7-31-71 (new); 8-28-71; 12-18-71; 1-8-72 (listed in *Billboard* ad); 3-18-72; 11-11-72; 2-17-73; 8-4-73; 12-29-73; 4-13-74; 11-23-74; 7-26-75; 2-28-76; 4-21-79; 5-26-79
Norton	WNVA	11-18-78 (new); 9-1-79
Petersburg	WSSV	4-21-79 (new)
Portsmouth	(see Norfolk, VA)	
Pulaski	WPUV	9-7-74; 12-7-74; 3-29-75; 7-19-75; 9-24-77; 9-9-78; 9-8-79
Richmond	WGOE	2-6-71 (listed in *Billboard* ad); 3-6-71; 6-19-71; 7-3-71 (listed in *Billboard* ad); 10-2-71; 1-8-72 (listed in *Billboard* ad); 6-17-72; 9-9-72; 11-25-72; 2-24-73; 8-4-73; 4-13-74; 1-4-75; 8-2-75; 2-21-76
	WRVQ	4-24-76 (new); 6-25-77; 7-23-77; 4-22-78; 3-3-79
	WRNL	4-14-79 (new)
Roanoke	WFIR	8-4-73; 1-19-74; 2-2-74; 3-30-74; 6-29-74; 1-11-75;
	WFIR	6-19-76 (new); 12-3-77; 4-21-79
	(also see Salem, VA)	
Salem	WBLU	5-29-71 (new); 7-3-71 (listed in *Billboard* ad); 7-31-71; 1-8-72 (listed in *Billboard* ad)
	(also see Roanoke, VA)	
Staunton	WTON	5-4-74 (new); 7-13-74; 8-31-74; 1-25-75; 8-30-75; 2-17-79
Tappahannock	WRAR	6-1-73 (listed in 1973 Vacation Listening Guide; first public acknowledgement as a subscribing station) 12-1-73 (new); 5-25-74; 7-27-74; 2-1-75; 7-26-75; 9-20-75; 2-5-77; 2-10-79
Winchester	WINC	1-8-77 (new); 2-19-77; 6-17-78; 4-21-79; 10-27-79

WASHINGTON

City	Station	Dates
Aberdeen	KGHO	9-9-72 (new); 11-18-72; 3-24-73
Bellingham	KPUG	5-8-71 (new); 7-3-71 (listed in *Billboard* ad); 7-31-71; 9-4-71 (listener question); 12-25-71; 1-8-72 (listed in *Billboard* ad); 3-25-72; 9-2-72; 3-17-73; 6-23-73; 9-1-73; 12-29-73; 5-18-74; 2-22-75; 5-3-75; 10-11-75; 7-10-76; 5-7-77; 3-17-79
Ellensburg	KXLE	5-13-72 (new); 10-7-72 (new); 5-5-73
Forks	KVAC	1-10-76 (new)
Hoquiam	(see Aberdeen, WA)	
Kelso	KLOG	10-21-78 (new); 8-25-79
Longview	KLYK-FM	9-1-73; 11-3-73; 4-20-74
Moses Lake	KSEM	11-5-77 (new); 2-25-78; 9-16-78; 9-15-79
Olympia	KGY	10-27-73; 3-16-74; 8-10-74; 8-31-74; 3-1-75; 6-28-75; 4-17-76; 6-25-77; 6-24-78; 4-14-79
Omak	KOMW	1-13-79 (new); 11-17-79
Pasco	KALE	10-23-71 (new); 1-8-72 (listed in *Billboard* ad)
Seattle	KJR	11-28-70; 1-2-71; 2-6-71 (listed in *Billboard* ad); 7-3-71 (listed in *Billboard* ad); 7-24-71; 10-16-71; 1-8-72 (listed in *Billboard* ad); 2-5-72; 2-26-72; 5-13-72; 7-29-72; 9-2-72; 11-4-72; 2-17-73; 5-5-73; 9-1-73; 11-10-73; 4-13-74; 9-21-74; 9-28-74; 3-8-75; 4-26-75; 10-18-75; 5-1-76; 9-25-76; 2-5-77; 4-9-77; 7-9-77; 8-27-77; 4-29-78; 11-25-78; 2-17-79; 12-15-79

PLAZA

HARDWARE

OPEN EVERY DAY
PLAZA SHOPPING CENTER
WALLA WALLA

FLEENORS
THRIFT STORES
the Special Stores
2028 Isaacs 905 S. 2nd

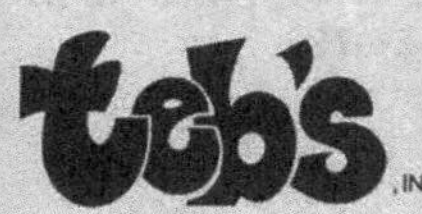

EASTGATE MALL
WALLA WALLA

RCA
MOTOROLA
RADIO SHACK

210 EAST MAIN STREET

STOP IN
AND
LOOK AROUND

1503 E. Issacs Ave.
Walla Walla, Wash. 99362

2nd & Poplar • Walla Walla

AMERICAN TOP 40

WITH
CASEY KASEM
ON

SUNDAY AFTERNOONS
1:00 TO 4:00 P.M.

AMERICA'S FAVORITES FOR THE WEEK OF APRIL 11

1. Disco Lady - Johnnie Taylor
2. Dream Weaver - Gary Wright
3. Lonely Night - Captain & Tennille
4. Let Your Love Flow - Bellamy Brothers
5. Right Back Where We Started From - Maxine Nightengale
6. Dream On - Aerosmith
7. Boogie Fever - Sylvers
8. Only Sixteen - Dr. Hook
9. Sweet Lover - Commodores
10. Golden Years - David Bowie
11. Show Me The Way - Peter Frampton
12. Bohemian Rhapsody - Queen
13. Sweet Thing - Rufus/Chaka Khan
14. December 1963 - Four Seasons
15. There's A Kind of Hush - Carpetners
16. Money Honey - Bay City Rollers
17. Deep Purple - Donny & Marie Osmond
18. Fooled Around & Fell In Love - E. Bishop
19. All By Myself - Eric Carmen
20. Welcome Back - John Sebastian
21. Action - Sweet
22. Love Machine - Miracles
23. I Do, I Do, I Do, I Do - Abba
24. Take It To The Limit - Eagles
25. Tangerine - Salsoul Orchestra
26. Shannon - Henry Gross
27. Livin' For The Weekend - O'Jays
28. Only Love Is Real - Carole King
29. Looking For Space - John Denver
30. Love Fire - Jigsaw
31. Lorelei - Styx
32. You'll Lose A Good Thing - Freddy Fender
33. Fopp - Ohio Players
34. Sara Smile - Daryl Hall & John Oates
35. Strange Magic - Electric Light Orchestra
36. We Can't Hide It Anymore - Larry Santos
37. Tryin' To Get The Feeling Again - B. Manilow
38. Misty Blue - Dorothy Moore
39. Rhiannon (Will You Ever Win) - Fleetwood Mac
40. Hit The Road Jack - Stampeders

IT'S YOUR BANK

DOWNTOWN
EASTGATE

DIAMONDS WITH QUALITY FOR A YOUNG BUDGET!

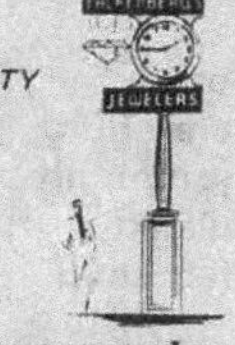

FALKENBERG'S
6 East Main • Walla Walla

EASTGATE MALL • WALLA WALLA, WASH.

FAMOUS BRAND FASHIONS
THAT FIT YOUR NEEDS
THE CUBE
&
THE TIGER SHOP
AT
THE
BON MARCHE
DOWNTOWN - WALLA WALLA

It appears that the KHIT (Walla Walla, Washington) sales department was hard at work to generate *AT40* sponsors based on this April 11, 1976 survey. Listeners who had the survey in hand when the countdown aired Sundays from 1-4 p.m. knew the position of every record on *American Top 40*.

WASHINGTON (cont'd)		
Spokane	**KJRB**	**2-6-71 (listed in *Billboard* ad); 5-1-71; 7-3-71 (listed in *Billboard* ad); 9-25-71; 1-8-72 (listed in *Billboard* ad); 4-29-72; 8-26-72; 11-11-72; 12-2-72; 1-20-73; 5-5-73; 9-1-73; 2-9-74; 3-30-74; 9-7-74; 3-8-75; 5-3-75; 11-29-75; 5-29-76; 10-15-77; 12-3-77; 2-17-79**
Tri-Cities	**KALE**	**3-25-72**
	KALE	**12-22-79 (new)**
Walla Walla	**KHIT**	**4-20-74 (new); 3-15-75; 7-12-75; 11-22-75; 6-19-76; 2-12-77**
Wenatchee	**KMEL**	**3-6-71 (new); 7-3-71 (listed in *Billboard* ad); 9-25-71; 11-20-71; 1-8-72 (listed in *Billboard* ad); 1-29-72; 3-4-72; 3-24-73; 6-23-73; 9-1-73; 11-24-73; 4-27-74; 3-22-75; 7-26-75**
	KWWW	**9-18-76 (new); 10-9-76; 2-26-77; 9-30-78; 9-29-79**
Yakima	**KMWX**	**7-3-71 (listed in *Billboard* ad); 8-7-71; 12-18-71; 1-8-72 (listed in *Billboard* ad)**
	KMWX	**4-23-77 (new); 3-31-79**
WEST VIRGINIA		
Beckley	**WWNR**	**6-3-72 (new); 7-8-72 (new); 7-15-72; 10-28-72; 3-3-73; 8-4-73; 10-27-73; 7-27-74; 10-19-74; 5-17-75; 12-6-75; 10-9-76; 8-27-77; 2-24-79**
Charleston	**WXIT**	**9-13-75 (new); 5-7-77; 9-24-77; 6-24-78; 3-3-79**
Huntington	**WKEE**	**5-29-71 (new); 7-3-71 (listed in *Billboard* ad); 8-14-71; 10-16-71; 11-20-71 (listed in *Billboard* ad as Ashland, KY); 1-8-72 (listed in *Billboard* ad); 4-22-72; 8-19-72; 12-2-72; 3-24-73; 9-22-73; 1-19-74; 2-2-74; 5-11-74; 11-23-74; 5-3-75; 3-13-76; 5-14-77; 10-15-77; 2-10-79**
Keyser	**WKLP**	**3-6-71 (new); 5-22-71; 7-3-71 (listed in *Billboard* ad); 7-31-76 (new); 5-14-77; 12-3-77; 4-28-79**
Logan	**WVOW**	**1-7-78 (new); 2-25-78; 12-9-78**
Morgantown	**WCLG**	**11-17-73; 3-9-74; 7-27-74; 11-9-74; 6-7-75; 1-24-76; 5-22-76; 5-6-78; 7-29-78; 7-28-79**
Parkersburg	**WPAR**	**2-16-74 (new); 11-30-74; 7-19-75; 9-18-76; 6-24-78 (d.j. question); 11-18-78; 3-17-79**
Pineville	**WWYO**	**4-13-74; 12-7-74; 3-29-75; 9-6-75; 3-13-76; 2-12-77; 3-3-79**
Roncevert	**WRON**	**10-23-76 (new); 2-5-77; 4-29-78; 9-23-78; 9-15-79**
Salem	**WVSC**	**1-8-72 (listed in *Billboard* ad); 1-15-72 (new); 2-5-72**
Weirton	**WEIR**	**8-14-76 (new)**
Wheeling	**WNEU**	**9-28-74 (new); 10-12-74; 1-4-75; 7-12-75**
White Sulphur Springs.	**WSLW**	**11-4-72 (new); 11-11-72; 1-27-73**
Williamson	**WBTH**	**10-8-77 (new); 5-6-78; 7-15-78**
	WBTH	**10-21-78 (new); 7-21-79**
WISCONSIN		
Black River Falls	**WWIS**	**1-11-75**
Eau Claire	**WOKL**	**5-4-74 (new); 7-27-74; 1-25-75; 7-12-75; 9-27-75; 5-1-76; 5-7-77; 12-3-77**
	WEAQ	**2-25-78 (new); 1-20-79**
Fond Du Lac	**KFIZ**	**11-27-71; 1-8-72 (listed in *Billboard* ad); 9-9-72; 3-31-73; 8-11-73; 12-29-73; 3-16-74; 2-1-75; 6-21-75**
Green Bay	**WNFL**	**3-31-73 (new); 6-16-73; 9-22-73; 1-26-74; 5-18-74; 7-27-74; 2-15-75; 7-12-75; 10-25-75; 5-14-77; 5-6-78; 9-2-78**
Hartford	**WTKM**	**9-13-75 (new)**
Hayward	**WHSM**	**5-14-77 (new)**
LaCrosse	**WIZM**	**3-3-73 (new); 6-23-73; 8-11-73; 12-29-73; 5-4-74; 7-20-74; 2-22-75; 5-3-75; 3-27-76; 5-14-77; 1-27-79**
Madison	**WYXE-FM**	**6-24-72 (new); 7-15-72; 12-30-72; 1-20-73; 2-9-74; 7-6-74; 3-8-75**
	WWQM	**4-8-78 (new); 3-3-79**
Marinette	**WLOT**	**11-2-74 (new); 6-28-75**
Menomonie	**WVSS**	**10-20-73**
Milwaukee	**WRKR**	**12-20-75 (new); 10-9-76; 2-12-77; 8-27-77; 6-24-78; 11-25-78; 11-17-79**
New London	**WLIH**	**4-12-75 (new)**
Racine	**(see Milwaukee, WI)**	
Ripon	**WCWC**	**1-8-72 (never mentioned in show, listed in *Billboard* ad)**
Sun Prairie	**(see Madison, WI)**	
Two Rivers	**WQTC**	**9-21-74 (new); 3-15-75; 7-26-75; 2-25-78; 9-16-78; 9-15-79**
Waupun	**WGCQ**	**9-17-77 (new); 5-6-78; 8-19-78**
West Bend	**WBKV**	**2-24-79 (new)**
Wisconsin Rapids	**WFHR**	**12-4-76 (new)**

STATE

Market	Calls	Air Date Mentions
WYOMING		
Cheyenne	KRAE	10-14-78 (new); 8-11-79
Gillette	KOLL	1-15-77 (new); 12-3-77; 6-24-78; 11-18-78; 11-10-79
Kemmerer	KMER	1-18-75 (new); 8-2-75; 10-18-75; 5-15-76; 11-27-76
Lander	KDLY	8-18-79 (new)
Laramie	KOWB	10-15-77 (new); 2-25-78; 9-9-78; 9-8-79
New Castle	KASL	9-11-71 (new); 10-30-71; 1-8-72 (listed in *Billboard* ad); 1-15-72
	KASL	7-8-78 (new; late welcome from 6-3-78 start); 4-7-79
Rawlins	KRAL	8-19-78 (new); 5-12-79; 11-17-79
Rock Springs	KVRS	6-22-74 (new); 8-3-74; 3-22-75
	KRKK	2-7-76; 5-1-76; 2-5-77; 5-12-79
Torrington	KGOS	1-15-77 (new); 2-12-77

INTERNATIONAL (North America)

CANADA		
Hope, British Columbia	CKGO	5-24-75 (new); 10-25-75; 6-12-76; 12-4-76
Grand Forks, British Columbia	CKGF	11-1-75 (new)
Leamington, Ontario	CHYR	8-2-75 (new); 11-15-75; 2-14-76
Lethbridge, Alberta	CJOC	3-20-71 (new); 7-3-71 (listed in *Billboard* ad); 11-6-71; 11-13-71 (listed in *Billboard* ad)
Medicine Hat, Alberta	CHAT	3-27-71 (new); 7-3-71 (listed in *Billboard* ad); 11-13-71 (2x: radio & listed in *Billboard* ad); 1-22-72
Montreal, Quebec	CKGM	8-25-79 (new)
New Glascow, Nova Scotia	CKEC	10-8-77 (new); 1-28-78; 6-23-79; 10-27-79
Prince Albert, Saskatchewan	CKBI	7-8-72 (new); 9-29-73; 6-8-74; 6-22-74 (new); 6-14-75 (new); 6-12-76 (new); 3-19-77 (new); 4-22-78; 10-7-78; 1-13-79; 4-14-79; 7-28-79; 11-3-79
Red Deer, Alberta	CKRD	4-21-73 (new); 4-28-73 (new); 9-29-73
Sarnia, Ontario	CKJD	8-16-75 (new); 12-20-75
Sydney, Nova Scotia	CHER	11-15-75 (new); 2-28-76
MEXICO		
Acapulco	XHSE	3-20-76 (new)
Ciudad Acuna	XHPL	4-28-79 (new)
Guadalajara, Jalisco	XEHL	11-8-75 (new); 5-15-76
Mexico City	XHBST	3-20-76 (new)
Monterrey	XHSRO	3-20-76 (new)
	XHMN	3-18-78 (new)
	Stereo Siete	5-27-78
	XHMN	3-31-79; 12-1-79
Cuernavaca	XHCT	9-27-75 (new)

THERE JUST MAY BE A HUNDRED REASONS WHY THIS WEEKLY THREE-HOUR RADIO PROGRAM GETS BIGGER AND BIGGER, MARKET AFTER MARKET.

2.	KACY	OXNARD	28.	WCBM	BALTIMORE
3.	KAFY	BAKERSFIELD	29.	WCRO	JOHNSTOWN
4.	KCPX	SALT LAKE CITY	30.	WFLI	CHATTANOOGA
5.	KELI	TULSA	31.	WHFM	ROCHESTER
6.	KEYN	WICHITA	32.	WIBR	BATON ROUGE
7.	KEYS	CORPUS CHRISTI	33.	WGAR	CLEVELAND
8.	KHYT	TUCSON	34.	WGOE	RICHMOND
9.	KIMN	DENVER	35.	WILK	WILKES BARRE
10.	KINT	EL PASO	36.	WIST	CHARLOTTE
11.	KIRL	ST. LOUIS	37.	WJTO	BATH
12.	K-JOY	STOCKTON	38.	WKBR	MANCHESTER
13.	KJR	SEATTLE	39.	WKDL	CLARKSDALE
14.	KJRB	SPOKANE	40.	WKNX	SAGINAW
15.	KMEN	SAN BERNARDINO	41.	WLOX	BILOXI
16.	KNUZ	HOUSTON	42.	WMEX	BOSTON
17.	K-POI	HONOLULU	43.	WNIO	WARREN
18.	KRIZ	PHOENIX *2/21/71	44.	WNOX	KNOXVILLE
19.	KRLA	LOS ANGELES	45.	WORC	WORCESTER
20.	KQEO	ALBUQUERQUE	46.	WPGC	WASHINGTON, D. C.
21.	KTAP	AUSTIN	47.	WRNC	RALEIGH
22.	KTSA	SAN ANTONIO	48.	WSAR	FALL RIVER
23.	WAIR	WINSTON-SALEM	49.	WSIV	PEORIA
24.	WABY	ALBANY	50.	WTSN	DOVER
25.	WAMS	WILMINGTON	51.	WTHI	TERRE HAUTE
26.	WASK	LAFAYETTE	52.	WVIC	LANSING
27.	WBBO	FOREST CITY	53.	WWWW	DETROIT

Here's Number One:

Casey Kasem—Host each week on American Top 40.

Casey's distinctive voice, style and approach to pop music is what has made American Top 40 the hottest syndicated music show on radio. Each week, Casey joins our team of pop musicologists/ writers to count down the nation's 40 best-selling records based on advance statistics supplied by *Billboard Magazine*. Result? A tried and tested programming device becomes an absorbing, fast-paced, captivating documentary on American music... right now.

Here's 52 more:

Stations that carry AMERICAN TOP 40 quickly become the biggest fans of Casey and of the program. And it's this station support and promotion of American Top 40 that has helped to bring the program so far so fast.
So here's fifty-two important reasons :
(as of January 1, 1971)

And more:

Ratings. October-November ARB, we love you. Los Angeles, Washington, D.C., Boston and Cleveland reports, for example, show that American Top 40 has improved stations' time periods by an average gain of 64% over like-time periods in the April-May ARB. Even in the highly competitive Los Angeles market, KRLA boosted their 9-Noon Sunday time slot 69%.

Flexibility. Here's a big reason that *both* program directors *and* sales managers like American Top 40. An ingenious device called the split logo allows station ID's, commercials and news with minimum loss of program continuity. Stations solve weekend schedule hang-ups with a pre-recorded program that fits their station sound like a glove.

Program costs. Just two minutes of air per hour for top 100 market stations and an additional $13 per hour for smaller market stations. A steal. And affordable when even most small-market stations report total sellout of spots at premium, special-program rates.

More reasons? Plenty. Maybe even more than a hundred. And they're yours for the asking, along with a free demo. So ask. Tom Rounds, Executive Producer, American Top 40, Watermark, Inc., 931 N. La Cienega, Los Angeles, California 90069. Telephone (213) 659-3834.

AMERICAN TOP 40
Division of Watermark, Inc.

This advertisement, which featured the call letters and city of all 53 *AT40* subscribers, appeared in the February 6, 1971 edition of *Billboard Magazine*.

INTERNATIONAL (Cont'd)

AUSTRALIA

City	Station	Dates
Adelaide, South Australia	5KA	8-18-73 (new; mentioned as West Australia); 3-23-74 (Sister Janet Mead's home); 10-12-74; 2-8-75; 4-19-75; 9-27-75; 4-17-76; 9-18-76; 12-11-76; 7-16-77
Albany, Western Australia	6VA	2-14-76; 2-12-77; 7-9-77; 11-4-78
Alice Springs, Northern Territory	8HA	2-19-77 (mentioned as New Territory); 7-16-77 (mentioned as 8AH); 7-29-78; 10-14-78
Armidale, New South Wales	2AD	10-23-76 (new); 1-22-77; 7-23-77; 8-12-78
Bathurst, New South Wales	2BS	9-10-77 (new); 8-19-78; 12-15-79 (new)
Bega, New South Wales	2BE	3-3-79; 5-5-79
Berri, South Australia	5RM	8-17-74 (mentioned as South Australia); 11-2-74 (mentioned as Riverland); 5-31-75 (Riverland); 11-1-75 (mentioned as River Murray); 11-25-78; 5-5-79 (new); 10-6-79
Brisbane, Queensland	4BK	8-12-72; 11-11-72; 12-9-72; 1-27-73; 9-29-73; 1-19-74; 1-18-75; 4-26-75; 2-7-76
	4KQ	8-13-77 (new)
Bunbury, Western Australia	6TZed	7-24-76 (new); 2-26-77
Bundaberg, Queensland	4BU	8-27-77 (new); 12-16-78; 6-2-79
Cairns, Queensland	4CA	5-14-77 (new); 7-30-77
Canberra, New South Wales	2CA	3-6-76; 12-11-76
Colac, Victoria	3CS	10-19-74; 5-3-75
Deniliquin, New South Wales	2QN	9-13-75
Dubbo, New South Wales	2DU	4-9-77 (new); 7-30-77; 8-27-77 (new); 6-23-79
Geraldton, Western Australia	6GE	8-6-77
Gladstone, Queensland	4CD	7-21-79 (new)
Goldberg, New South Wales	2GN	6-17-78
Gosford, New South Wales	2GO	3-20-76; 5-8-76; 3-12-77; 8-20-77; 6-24-78
Grafton, New South Wales	2GF	5-14-77 (new); 6-3-78
Griffith, New South Wales	2RG	3-5-77; 8-13-77; 9-29-79
Gunnedah, New South Wales	2MO	3-26-77; 8-27-77; 5-27-78; 4-21-79; 10-20-79
Hobart, Tasmania	7HT	4-21-79 (new); 9-22-79; 11-17-79
Horsham, Victoria	3LK	1-25-75; 5-10-75
Inverell, New South Wales	2NZed	11-20-71 (new)
Kalgoorlie, Western Australia	6KG	6-1-73 (listed in 1973 Vacation Listening Guide; first public acknowledgement as subscribing station); 4-30-77; 9-3-77; 5-20-78
Launceston, Tasmania	7LA	3-26-77; 9-10-77
	7EX	7-29-78 (new; mentioned as 7XE); 10-21-78 (7XE); 10-28-78 (corrected); 5-12-79
Lismore, New South Wales	2LM	7-15-72
Mareeba, Queensland	4AM	2-28-76
Melbourne, Victoria	3KZed	11-13-71 (listed in *Billboard* ad); 12-4-71; 3-25-72; 4-29-72; 7-8-72; 9-9-72; 11-25-72; 1-27-73; 3-17-73; 5-19-73; 6-1-73 (listed as 3AK in 1973 Vacation Listening Guide); 6-9-73; 9-1-73; 11-24-73 (mentioned as 2KZed; Helen Reddy's hometown); 1-5-74 (Helen Reddy's hometown); 2-9-74; 2-23-74; 4-6-74; 6-1-74; 10-19-74; 2-15-75; 4-12-75; 1-24-76
	3DB	4-2-77 (new); 9-17-77; 5-6-78; 8-26-78; 3-31-79; 6-23-79; 8-18-79; 9-8-79; 11-3-79
Merredin, Western Australia	6MD	10-30-76 (new); 1-15-77; 9-24-77; 3-25-78; 9-23-78; 12-2-78
Maryborough, Victoria	3CB	4-2-77
Murray Bridge, South Australia	5MU	4-23-77
Murray Valley, South Australia	5PM	2-5-72; 5-27-72; 9-29-73; 1-26-74; 3-9-74; 10-1-77 (mentioned as 5RM); 3-18-78
Murwillumbah, New South Wales	2MW	12-9-78 (new); 4-14-79; 7-14-79
Nambour, Queensland	4NA	7-9-77 (new); 10-8-77; 3-11-78; 12-16-78; 9-1-79; 11-17-79
Newcastle, New South Wales	2KO	11-20-71 (new); 3-4-72; 11-4-72; 1-27-73 (no city mentioned); 10-15-77; 2-25-78; 6-9-79
Northam, Western Australia	6AM	10-29-77; 1-21-78
Nowra, New South Wales	2ST	1-18-75; 5-24-75
Orange, New South Wales	2GZed	11-20-71 (new); 2-26-72; 2-17-73; 1-19-74; 2-2-74
Parkes, New South Wales	2PK	1-14-78 (new); 4-14-79
Perth, Western Australia	6KY	9-4-71 (new); 11-13-71 (listed in *Billboard* ad); 11-27-71; 4-1-72; 5-6-72; 8-5-72; 11-25-72; 1-27-73; 9-8-73 12-14-74 (new); 7-12-75
	6PM	4-30-77; 11-5-77; 2-18-78; 9-30-78; 11-11-78; 3-24-79; 12-1-79

AUSTRALIA (cont'd)

City	Station	Dates
Port Augusta, South Australia	**5AU**	**2-5-72; 6-10-72; 10-21-72; 5-12-73; 7-14-73 (mentioned as Spencer Gulf); 9-7-74 (Spencer Gulf); 9-21-74 (Spencer Gulf); 10-26-74 (Spencer Gulf); 11-2-74 (Spencer Gulf); 6-14-75 (Spencer Gulf); 3-13-76; 4-16-77; 10-22-77; 11-26-77 (Spencer Gulf); 1-7-78; 9-16-78 (mentioned as Whyalla); 5-26-79 (Whyalla); 8-25-79 (Whyalla, S. Australia)**
Port Hedland, Western Australia	**6NW**	**12-15-79 (new)**
Rockhampton, Queensland	**4RO**	**7-31-76 (new); 5-7-77; 11-19-77**
Sale, Victoria	**3TR**	**10-22-77 (new); 9-2-78; 2-17-79; 5-19-79; 10-27-79**
Shepparton, Victoria	**3SR**	**10-26-74; 11-2-74; 6-7-75**
Swan Hill, Victoria	**3SH**	**5-14-77**
Sydney, New South Wales	**2UE**	**11-13-71 (listed in *Billboard* ad); 11-20-71 (new); 3-11-72; 4-29-72; 6-17-72; 8-26-72**
	2UW	**10-11-75 (new); 9-4-76; 11-6-76; 1-8-77; 1-29-77; 12-3-77; 1-14-78; 7-15-78; 2-3-79; 12-15-79**
Tamworth, New South Wales	**2TM**	**10-23-76 (new); 5-14-77; 12-10-77; 4-15-78**
Taree, New South Wales	**2RE**	**7-9-77 (new); 12-17-77; 1-28-78; 12-8-79**
Toowoomba, Queensland	**4AK**	**6-14-75 (new); 3-27-76; 9-11-76; 5-21-77**
Townsville, Queensland	**4AY**	**12-7-74 (new); 7-19-75; 5-28-77; 4-8-78; 9-9-78**
	4TO	**6-2-79 (new)**
Wagga Wagga, New South Wales	**2WG**	**11-20-71 (new; mentioned as Wagga); 2-1-75 12-22-79 (new)**
Warragul, Victoria	**3UL**	**8-31-74; 11-23-74; 6-28-75; 5-1-76**
Warrnambool, Victoria	**3YB**	**11-23-74; 7-12-75; 12-20-75; 12-4-76; 2-4-78; 4-14-79; 7-21-79**
Wollongong, New South Wales	**2WL**	**10-30-76 (new); 3-4-78**
Young, New South Wales	**2LF**	**10-9-76 (new)**
	2GL	**12-15-79 (new)**

NEW ZEALAND

City	Station	Dates
Auckland	**Radio Hauraki/1XA**	**5-20-72; 9-2-72; 10-21-72 (Casey's boat); 12-23-72; 2-17-73; 5-19-73; 9-29-73; 12-15-73; 4-20-74; 7-6-74; 7-20-74; 11-16-74; 5-24-75; 1-31-76; 4-10-76; 7-31-76; 12-18-76; 4-30-77; 4-29-78; 7-8-78; 8-26-78; 10-7-78; 2-24-79; 4-7-79; 7-21-79; 11-10-79**
Christchurch	**Radio Avon/3XA**	**1-5-74; 6-15-74; 11-16-74; 5-31-75; 8-2-75; 12-6-75; 8-7-76; 1-15-77; 4-23-77; 12-17-77; 7-22-78; 11-25-78; 3-24-79; 4-28-79; 7-28-79; 10-13-79**
Dunedin	**4XO**	**10-7-72 (new); 11-4-72; 2-10-73 8-6-77 (new); 12-9-78; 5-19-79**
Hamilton	**1ZedH**	**9-23-72 (new); 2-10-73; 4-13-74; 8-24-74; 11-30-74; 4-12-75**
	Radio Waikato	**8-28-76 (new); 1-22-77; 4-16-77; 9-10-77; 6-10-78; 8-5-78 10-28-78 (mentioned as 1XW); 4-21-79; 8-18-79**
Masterton	**2ZedD**	**11-25-78 (new); 5-12-79; 8-11-79**
New Plymouth	**2ZedP**	**6-2-73 (new); 1-12-74; 3-30-74; 12-7-74; 3-29-75 12-16-78 (new); 1-27-79; 6-30-79**
Palmerston North	**2ZedA**	**12-7-74; 3-29-75; 4-26-75**
	2ZedA	**11-18-78 (new); 5-26-79**
Rotorua	**1ZedC**	**12-16-78 (new); 6-2-79; 12-15-79**
Taumarunui	**1ZedU**	**4-21-79 (new)**
Taupo	**1ZedA**	**7-26-75 (new); 2-12-77 12-16-78 (new)**
Timaru	**3ZedC**	**1-5-74 (new); 8-24-74; 1-4-75; 5-17-75 12-16-78 (new); 4-28-79; 7-14-79**
Wanganui	**2ZedW**	**7-26-75 (new) 12-9-78 (new)**
Wellington	**2ZedM**	**6-2-73 (new); 1-26-74; 3-16-74; 6-15-74; 12-14-74; 5-3-75; 2-7-76; 12-11-76; 4-9-77; 8-20-77; 3-25-78; 9-15-79; 12-1-79**
Whakatane	**1XX**	**9-2-72 (new); 11-4-72; 2-10-73; 1-12-74; 3-23-74; 12-14-74 (new); 7-19-75; 6-19-76; 10-30-76; 4-2-77; 7-30-77; 9-16-78; 10-21-78; 6-9-79**
Whangarei	**1ZedN**	**9-14-74; 9-21-74; 1-4-75; 4-19-75 7-29-78 (new; mentioned as Radio Northland); 11-18-78**

INDONESIA

Bandung, Java	Radio Leidya	3-6-76 (new)
Denpasar, Bali	Radio Yudha	5-28-77
Jakarta, Java	Radio Kejayaan	3-6-76 (new)
Malang, Java	Radio K.D.S.8.	3-6-76 (new)
Medan, Sumatra	Alnora	(listed only in the 1977 Listening Directory)
Palembang, Sumatra	Radio Elita	1-29-77
Semarang, Java	Radio Merci	3-6-76 (new)
Surabaya, Java	Radio Merdeka	6-26-76; 8-28-76; 6-18-77; 9-24-77; 2-11-78
Yogyakarta, Java	Retjo	(listed only in the 1977 Listening Directory)

JAPAN

(no city mentioned)	Far East Network	7-21-73
Sapporo	JOTF	11-9-74; 3-1-75; 6-14-75
Yokohama/Tokyo	JORF/Radio Kanto	9-23-72 (new); 10-14-72; 11-25-72 (Happy B-Day to Radio Atago); 12-2-72; 12-30-72; 2-10-73; 3-17-73; 5-19-73; 6-9-73; 6-16-73; 8-25-73; 2-9-74; 4-6-74; 5-18-74; 7-6-74; 9-7-74; 11-2-74; 11-9-74; 3-8-75; 8-2-75; 9-13-75; 11-22-75; 8-21-76; 12-18-76; 6-4-77; 8-27-77; 11-26-77; 6-17-78; 9-2-78; 11-11-78; 2-10-79; 6-9-79; 9-22-79

PHILIPPINES

Bacolod City	DYMG	4-14-79 (new); 9-1-79
Cebu City	DYXC	5-5-79 (new)
Iloilo	DYXI	4-14-79 (new); 8-4-79; 11-10-79
Manila	DWRT	1-13-79 (new); 6-16-79; 9-29-79; 11-24-79 (long distance dedication)
Ozamiz	DXSY	4-28-79 (new); 12-8-79
Quezon City	DZBM	(listed only in the 1977 Listening Directory)
	DGRD	5-27-78

OTHER

Agana, Guam	Stereo 95 (cable)	11-4-72 (new); 1-13-73; 8-18-73
	KUAM	5-3-75 (new); 11-22-75; 4-3-76; 8-21-76; 5-20-78; 3-17-79; 12-22-79
American Forces Radio Stations Network (350)		7-17-71 (new); 7-31-71; 9-8-73; 3-30-74; 8-23-75; 3-6-76; 8-7-76; 9-4-76; 12-18-76; 1-8-77; 1-7-78; 10-20-79
American Forces - USS Constellation-At-Sea		8-13-77
American Forces - USS Enterprise-At-Sea		9-24-77
Christiansted/St. Croix, Virgin Islands	WSTX	10-21-72; 1-13-73; 4-14-73; 8-18-73; 10-20-73; 6-1-74; 6-22-74; 2-15-75; 5-17-75; 11-29-75; 5-1-76; 2-19-77; 10-29-77; 2-25-78; 3-17-79; 12-22-79
Frankfort, West Germany	AFN	7-21-73 (Armed Forces Radio Network - West Germany); 1-18-75
Guatemala City, Guatemala	TGZQ	4-6-74
	Radio Exclusiva	8-10-74 (new); 11-23-74; 5-10-75; 8-16-75; 10-11-75; 1-10-76; 7-10-76; 8-28-76; 6-25-77; 10-29-77; 3-4-78; 12-16-78; 3-17-79; 11-17-79
Hong Kong, China	Commercial Radio	6-12-71 (new); 7-3-71 (listed in *Billboard* ad); 9-18-71; 11-20-71 (listed in *Billboard* ad); 3-18-72; 6-3-72; 8-19-72; 11-4-72; 3-3-73; 6-23-73; 9-15-73; 1-26-74; 5-11-74; 6-29-74; 11-9-74; 2-22-75; 6-7-75; 8-30-75; 9-20-75; 9-18-76; 6-11-77; 10-8-77; 4-15-78; 9-9-78; 11-4-78; 1-20-79; 5-5-79; 9-8-79
Johannesburg, South Africa (see Swaziland)		
Montevideo, Uruguay, South America	CX-50/Radio Independencia	5-19-79 (new); 8-25-79; 11-3-79; 12-15-79
Oranjestad, Aruba, Netherland Antilles	Voice of Aruba	1-10-76 (new); 8-14-76; 11-13-76; 5-7-77; 8-6-77; 10-7-78
Pago Pago, American Samoa	WVUV	5-10-75 (new); 10-18-75; 9-11-76; 6-18-77; 5-6-78; 3-24-79; 12-22-79
Panama City, Panama	Radio Fabulosa	4-27-74 (mentioned as Guatamala)
Ponce, Puerto Rico	WZAR	6-8-74 (new)

OTHER (cont'd)

Port-of-Spain, Trinidad	**Radio 610**	**3-27-71 (new); 4-3-71; 7-3-71 (listed in *Billboard* ad); 9-18-71; 11-13-71; 1-8-72 (listed in *Billboard* ad); 1-29-72; 4-22-72; 10-28-72; 1-13-73; 8-11-73; 1-5-74; 4-6-74; 4-27-74; 1-11-75; 3-8-75 (re-new); 7-26-75; 10-25-75; 7-24-76; 10-16-76; 3-19-77; 7-16-77; 6-24-78; 8-12-78; 10-14-78; 6-9-79; 8-11-79; 10-6-79**
Rarotonga, South Pacific	**Cook Island Broadcasting**	**6-10-78 (new); 9-30-78; 10-28-78; 1-6-79**
San José, Costa Rico	**Radio Top 12**	**11-22-75 (new); 9-4-76; 12-3-77; 2-4-78; 12-9-78; 3-17-79**
San Juan, Puerto Rico	**WBMJ**	**5-22-71 (new); 7-3-71 (listed in *Billboard* ad); 8-14-71; 10-30-71 (listener question); 12-11-71; 12-25-71 (listed in *Billboard* ad); 4-1-72**
	WRAI	**3-1-75; 7-26-75**
	WHOA	**1-21-78 (new); 10-28-78; 6-23-79; 10-20-79 (Hato Rey)**
San Salvador, El Salvador, Central America		
	YSLN	**2-7-76 (new); 11-26-77**
Seoul, South Korea	**TBC Radio**	**5-4-74 (new); 11-16-74; 5-17-75; 12-13-75**
	Tong Yang Broadcasting	**3-15-75**
Singapore, Malaysia	**Rediffusion**	**6-12-71 (new); 7-3-71 (listed in *Billboard* ad); 9-18-71; 11-20-71; 12-25-71 (listed in *Billboard* ad); 1-29-72; 4-8-72; 5-13-72; 6-24-72; 7-29-72; 11-11-72; 1-20-73; 3-10-73; 5-5-73; 6-9-73; 9-15-73; 1-12-74; 5-4-74; 6-21-75; 9-6-75; 1-17-76; 5-22-76; 10-23-76; 3-26-77; 7-23-77; 6-3-78; 3-10-79; 11-24-79**
Suva, Fiji	**Radio Fiji**	**7-3-71 (listed in *Billboard* ad); 7-24-71; 11-20-71 (listed in *Billboard* ad); 4-15-72**
Swaziland	**Swazi Radio**	**10-21-72; 12-23-72; 5-19-73; 9-29-73; 1-19-74; 2-2-74; 4-6-74; 5-4-74; 1-11-75; 8-9-75; 11-8-75**
Tehran, Iran	**Iran National Radio**	**10-9-76**
	NIRT	**2-5-77; 5-21-77; 9-17-77; 3-11-78**
Tel Aviv, Israel	**Voice of Peace**	**(listed only in the 1977 Listening Directory)**

CONFESSIONS OF AN *AT40* ENTHUSIAST

Pete Battistini

****

Chapter 1 - LIFE BEFORE THE 1970's

****

Touched By Radio

In the summer of 1965, as a ten-year-old, I discovered Top 40 music on the radio for the first time. While vacationing at the home of my aunt and uncle in Olney, Illinois, I learned that my cousins enjoyed listening to Top 40 radio station KXOK in St. Louis. And for three weeks that summer, three records received a great deal of airplay on KXOK. Over and over and over again. Or so it seemed. Those three records – Herman's Hermits' *I'm Henry The Eighth, I Am*, The Rolling Stones' *I Can't Get No Satisfaction* and Sam The Sham's *Wooly Bully* - seemed to be on the radio all the time.

After I returned to my home in Merrillville, Indiana, I was thrilled to find the same records getting airplay on radio station WLS in Chicago. My reaction was positive because of the music's familiarity.

A few weeks later, on Labor Day weekend, a family activity brought my cousins & I back together again. I mentioned to one cousin that I had found a great radio station which played records just like that station in St. Louis. I explained that WLS in Chicago played the same music as KXOK. She was a few years older than I was, and I was determined to make an impression with her. However, her comment to me in return carried enough weight for me to stop listening to WLS and music on the radio. What did she say? She told me that WLS wasn't a very good radio station. And that's all she had to say to sway this 10-year-old away from music, and back to baseball cards and reading *Famous Monsters of Filmland* magazines.

Transistor Identity

Three years later, during the summer of 1968, I met some new friends. Weather permitting, we were at Merrillville's Meadowdale Pool every day. And in between pool announcements, the public address system's microphone sat in front of a transistor radio tuned to WLS, with music blasting all over the pool area out of a little speaker.

Most often, the music was background noise. But Top 40 music is alluring, and has a seductive side. And with WLS' playlist repetition, I heard records being played over and over again. And some of them were great. There was one afternoon that I swear I heard The Amboy Dukes' *Journey To The Center Of The Mind* four times while at the pool. And I loved that record. It turned out to be the first 45 single I ever bought.

At some point that summer, I discovered my parents' little-used, red transistor AM radio and started listening to it, day in and day out. As I became more familiar with the "sound" of WLS -- the jingles, the disk jockeys, the commercials, I became more and more familiar with the music and the records they played. And one particular jingle that was periodically used identified the week's #1 record. I had, however, trouble identifying voices of the disk jockeys.

I remember asking a friend once if he could tell the disk jockeys apart. I heard their names from time to time, but their deep voices all sounded the same to me.

In early August, I reluctantly went off to camp for a week. I hated it. Up until then, summer was going great. New friends meant new activities. But it was my parents' wish for me to go to camp. And I hated it. The only positive memory I have about going was taking my radio. Listening to WLS, as often as time allowed, was my only connection to home, friends and the music I was learning to enjoy. Though it seemed to be an eternity, camp lasted only one week and I was home again. But I hated it.

This experience created a bond to radio listening -- it became personal activity. Radio entertainment is unique because it is programmed for one individual, one listener. It is designed for one person to listen to music, the latest news, a sporting event, a presidential address, respond to someone else's opinion or a commercial message. Since the early 20th century, it's this premise that has lured millions of people to radio listening. For me, it was the music.

During August and September, whenever there was a new #1 record on WLS, I was enticed to buy each 45 single -- The Rascals' *People Got To Be Free*, Jeannie C. Riley's *Harper Valley P.T.A.* and The Beatles' *Revolution/Hey Jude*. There was something significant about being #1 and starting a record collection with songs peaking at the top. But this habit had a short life. The Beatles' double-sided 45 was in the #1 slot for a long time and was replaced by Gary Puckett & the Union Gap's *Over You*. Although Gary Puckett made it to #1, I drew the line on that one and didn't buy it. The song was a bit too sappy for a 13-year-old male. Bring on The Crazy World of Arthur Brown screaming "I am the god of hell fire...and I bring you *Fire!*" That's more like it.

It got to the point where the transistor radio came on when I got home from school every day. And time after time, I ran its battery down until the sound was so distorted, and its volume so weak, that I held it to my ear so I could hear my favorite records.

<u>Saving Survey Sounds</u>

I heard occasional on-air references to WLS' Top 40 Hit Parade record survey, a listing of all of the songs played on the 'Big 89.' WLS was 890 AM, which accounted for the Big 89 nickname. But it wasn't until I was with some friends at a downtown Gary, Indiana record store that I came across an actual copy of one sitting on a cash register counter top, and free for the taking. It was dated December 30, 1968.

But I was disappointed. Recent disk jockey mentions about the station's Hit Parade at that time promoted a complete listing of WLS' year-end Big 89 of 1968 printed on the back side of the current survey. However, the back of the first survey I obtained promoted their on-air New Year's Eve Party. I had missed the Big 89 list by one week.

There were two things that intrigued me about WLS' broadcast of the Big

89 of 1968. First, between Christmas and New Year's Day, the station randomly and repetitiously played all 89 records listed on their year-end survey, interspersed with current hit parade selections. I heard many of these for the first time. Records like John Fred's *Judy In Disguise*, The Lemon Pipers' *Green Tambourine* and Paul Mauriat's *Love Is Blue* were hit records from earlier in the year. These songs, and those previously familiar to me like The Amboy Dukes' only hit, were receiving heavy airplay that week. A hit parade countdown with echoes from a year gone by. I do not recall actually hearing the Big 89 in countdown order as much as I remember the repetition of the year's best records.

The other intriguing aspect was the fact that a friend of mine had a mini reel-to-reel tape recorder which used recording tapes three inches in diameter. He tape recorded some of his favorites from the Big 89 right off of the radio. What a great idea to capture the sound of 1968, with the ability to play and replay any record off of the radio without having to go out and buy it. I then realized that there was a chance that records I liked -- and could not afford to buy -- may never get played on the radio again. I placed myself in a self-appointed role of caretaker of once popular but forgotten songs played on the radio -- it was my job to save these recordings from being forgotten forever. Well, at least I thought it was my job.

Taping a song off of the radio would give *me* an opportunity to preserve it. In addition, tape-recorded songs from the radio did not skip like a record playing on a phonograph. With a 30-minute reel of tape, I could have 8-10 songs recorded onto tape, for less than $1.50. I was sold. I had to have a tape recorder. I begged my mother to let me buy one right away -- with her money, of course. I needed to have it before WLS' Big 89 year-end extravaganza was over. Unfortunately, it wasn't meant to be. I had just received a new transistor radio for Christmas. And there was no way that I could get a tape recorder too. As it turned out, I had to wait until April when I received a $40 Panasonic cassette tape recorder for my 14th birthday.

But I had discovered the WLS Hit Parade. And the best I could do to preserve the sound was to write down the song titles and artists every week, in order, when they featured a Top 10 record countdown.

As many Saturdays as possible in 1969, I walked nearly a mile to catch the city bus that ran from Merrillville to downtown Gary to obtain WLS' weekly survey. And when I got downtown, I walked a lot more. Within a six-block area, three or four record stores kept the surveys on their counter top. If one store didn't have the latest list, I would go to the next one. And I would take one every week and save it. In fact, for months I kept them folded inside of my wallet until there were too many to fold. To this day I still have every one, crease marks and all.

Eye Can Hear The Music

My survey collection was abruptly interrupted in June as a result of an eye accident. The summer began with me confined to bed for six weeks. A

bandage over both eyes resulted in my inability to leave home -- mainly for recovery reasons, but partly because I didn't want any of my friends to see me. However, I had my radio and tape recorder to keep myself occupied. When the radio was on and a record that I wanted to record began playing, I scrambled, scurried and stumbled blindly to my dresser, feeling my way as I pushed the right buttons to turn on the recorder and tape the song.

My recording system, by the way, was somewhat clumsy. But it was all that I had. My portable tape recorder had a plug-in microphone. And to tape records, I placed the mike in front of the speaker of a portable transistor radio. Both sat on top of my bedroom dresser. Recording a three-minute record under those conditions made the quality of the recording vulnerable to my seven-year-old brother's noise-making intrusions. Yet I still managed this way to fill hours of tapes with songs off of the radio.

And during my eye injury recovery, I missed many weeks of collecting the record surveys. I was grateful, however, that this form of entertainment required only the use of my ears. It gave me a deeper appreciation of radio listening. In fact, like the camp experience, this strengthened my radio listening bond. No, actually it did more than that. It forever solidified it.

National Exposure

In the fall of 1969, ABC-TV introduced a weekly program called *The Music Scene,* hosted by comedian David Steinberg and featured recording artists performing their best-selling records. Occasionally Steinberg made references to an enlarged copy of a national hit parade from a magazine called *Billboard*. The hit parade was actually a listing of *Billboard*'s Hot 100. A *national* hit parade survey....hmmmm.

By coincidence, I came across a copy of *Billboard*, dated December 6, 1969, at a downtown Gary magazine shop. I thumbed through it and discovered the Hot 100 list. There it was! Steam's *Na Na Hey Hey* was at #1. The magazine also contained a best-selling list of LPs, 8-tracks, 4-tracks and cassette tapes, the best-selling soul records, country & western records, easy listening records, full-page ads for all kinds of new record releases and more. While looking at it, I deliberated its purchase. If I decided to buy it, I could use it for reference the next time *The Music Scene* came on television. The Hot 100 even had musical note markings next to records listed on the chart, highlighting the artists who had appeared or were scheduled to appear on the TV show. The cost for *Billboard* was $1.25. No hesitation here -- I bought it.

At the time, my dad owned a retail business in Gary's Glen Park area. And his store was on the way home from my visits to downtown, making it convenient for me to periodically get off the bus and stop by. On the occasion of my first *Billboard* purchase, I stopped in to see him. Upon seeing that I purchased a magazine called *Billboard*, my dad immediately picked it up and examined it. Not knowing what *Billboard* was, and with me coming from downtown Gary, he probably thought the title made reference to a girlie publication! But it passed his inspection.

And just like going downtown to pick up WLS' Hit Parade, buying *Billboard* became a part of my weekly music ritual.

Read My Lyrics

And speaking of music-related magazines, every month I purchased another one called *Hit Parader* which, ironically, contained no hit parade. But it *did* contain song lyrics. Remember, I couldn't tell one disk jockey on the radio from the next one? How about understanding song lyrics? You gotta be kidding.

A few examples of song lyrics I had trouble with included one of the three I heard on KXOK in 1965. I misunderstood part of the Rolling Stones' *Satisfaction*, where they sing "....I can't get no......" I thought that they were singing "...I said heck no...." Hey, I was only 10 years old. A couple of other examples of misinterpreted lyrics were from the summer of '68. I thought that the title to the Ohio Express' *Down At Lulu's* was *Got A New Look*. And the Moody Blues' *Tuesday Afternoon* was *June, Say I Do*. Honest. I thought the Moody Blues' record was about a guy trying to get his girlfriend named June to marry him. As far as lyrics go, *Hit Parader* magazine helped set me straight.

****

Chapter 2 - 1970

****

'Smart Aleck Little Kid' Makes The Big Time

In January 1970, another Chicago radio station became a player. WCFL, 1000 AM, which had discontinued a record survey a couple of years earlier, started producing their own weekly hit parade again. Also available at record stores, they were typically found next to WLS' survey. And like WLS, WCFL's weekly survey consisted of 40 records. Record surveys were a promotional tool for radio stations. It gave listeners, and potential listeners, something to *see* from a medium based on sound. Surveys also helped identify current record titles and artists. And seeing WCFL's survey was enough for me to develop a regular habit of flipping-the-dial back and forth between WCFL and WLS, in search of one of my favorite songs.

A notable event regarding my pursuit of surveys took place in April when I sent a note to WLS' afternoon personality Larry Lujack, and he read it on the air as the 'Klunk Letter of the Day.' I had written to him asking why his picture had not appeared recently on the station's record survey.

Reading the letter along with his on-air response went as follows:

".....time now for the Klunk Letter of the Day.....comes from Gary, Indiana....the kid's name is Peter......writes in a childish scrawl....Dear Mr. Lujack comma, when is your picture going to appear on that stupid WLS survey? Each week I go to my favorite record shop hoping to find your foolish picture on it. Each week I see all the other clucks from the Big Dumb 89 with their pictures on it. The reason I want to see it on the survey is because I ran out of pictures for the dartboard and I don't........................Oh, Peter. You know, there's few things in life that I can hack less than some smart aleck little kid.....and you certainly fall into that category. Plus you're certainly not very creative or original. I've heard that dartboard line in requests for pictures a zillion times, along with, you know, the liner for the bottom of the canary cage, and all the others. I've heard 'em. However comma, rejoice Peter, for I bring you glad tidings, baby. The picture on the WLS survey is a rotation thing. See, this week I think its Art Roberts, and the week before it was Joel Sebastian. Uh, you see, I missed a turn. A few weeks back I had to relinquish my last turn for that shot of my mother which appeared on the survey. Remember that one? Mother Lujack? On the front of the survey, and she was shown there in the rocking chair with her granny glasses, and the....one of the dirty books that she pushes at that hardcore pornography store she runs in Boise. But, next week it's my turn again, and next week's WLS Hit Parade will feature a never-before-published, action shot of me, uh, on-the-air. At the top of it says 'Larry Lujack Reads Klunk Letters.' Uh, actually I think the day this picture was taken I was giving my Groundhog Day's Address To The Nation. But, uh, I'm sure you'll want to glom onto one of these......better get into the record stores early, these will certainly go like hotcakes, and probably become collector's items like the, uh, survey with shot

of my mother. Some collectors are already paying $60 - $65 for that one of my mother....."

I could not believe that he read my letter. But thank goodness I had a tape recorder to preserve it.

More Than Forty Records

In May, I participated in a statewide bowling tournament in Anderson, Indiana. While traveling near Indianapolis, we happened to come across station WNAP-FM on the car radio. The only thing I recall hearing was a feature they referred to as a 'capsule countdown.' In countdown order, from #10 to #1, the station played extremely brief portions of all ten records along with a jingle identifying its position. It came and went quickly. I was impressed. How creative. Why couldn't WLS or WCFL do that? Why weren't they doing it? WNAP was cool. I also managed to obtain a few record surveys from radio station WHUT, a Top 40 outlet in Anderson. There were a few records on their survey that I had never heard before, including The Who's *The Seeker*, *I Call My Baby Candy* by The Jaggerz and Van Morrison's *Come Running*. I had some familiarity with the artists' music, but these were unknown records to me.

'Charting' My Course

And speaking of unknown records. After closer inspection of Chicago's radio station record surveys, one thing that I had discovered was that there were a lot of records on *Billboard*'s Hot 100 list -- and a few on WLS and WCFL's surveys -- that I had never heard before. I had never heard the record, and in many cases, I had never heard of the artist. Although I regularly listened to two major-market Top 40 radio stations, both were basically playing the same records.

In reviewing *Billboard*'s Hot 100 list, I often wondered what certain records sounded like. Some examples included The Cuff Links follow-up single record to *Tracy*, titled *When Julie Comes Around*. In addition, there was the curiously-titled *Je T'Aime...Moi Non Plus* by Jane Birkin & Serge Gainsbourg, The Kinks' *Victoria*, Aretha Franklin's version of *Son Of A Preacher Man* and *Theme Music From 2001: A Space Odyssey* by the Berlin Philharmonic. All were Hot 100 records I would have liked to have heard on the radio just once but never did.

Thanks to WCFL's playlist, however, I had the opportunity to hear a few Hot 100 records that never received airtime on WLS. Some of those included Crow's *Cottage Cheese*, which peaked at #56 on *Billboard*, and Elephant Memory's *Mongoose*, which peaked at #50. Poco's *You Better Think Twice* peaked at #72, and Blue Mink's *Our World*, peaked at #64. All received a respectable amount of WCFL airplay. And I liked every one.

WCFL gave airtime to a record called *Cold Turkey* by John Lennon's Plastic Ono Band. WLS never touched it. But I liked it and bought it. This is one that I

didn't tape record off of the radio -- I bought the record. It was loud, raunchy and rebellious, a good 'teen-ager' record. Concurrently, WCFL was playing Joe Cocker's *She Came In Through The Bathroom Window.* I still love that record. Again, WLS never touched it. I had begun to develop an obvious listening preference for WCFL.

Another reason for WCFL as my station of choice involved their method to introduce new records to listeners. Beginning in February 1970, at approximately 25 minutes past every hour, listeners heard a "hit bound" jingle followed by a new record. Using the latest WCFL record survey as reference, I was often there with my tape recorder recording a new song. I knew that if I couldn't identify it by using the survey, more than likely it was a hot, new record. And having the most recent copy of *Billboard* nearby, I knew the hottest and latest releases. WCFL's once-an-hour debut record procedure pointed out to me that they were on top of new records. And that helped satisfy my appetite for knowing up and coming hits. Although not every record they played made the national Top 40, I enjoyed and appreciated this debut process. As a result, WCFL exposed me to a greater variety of music. Most people who grew up in Chicago and surrounding states remember listening to WLS much more than WCFL -- WLS had the reputation as the Midwest's biggest Top 40 radio station. However, as far as I was concerned, WCFL was the better station.

With WCFL and WLS giving airplay to many of the same records, and most of those found in *Billboard*'s Top 40, there was little that I could do to hear any lower-ranking Hot 100 records, unless I went out and bought them. And that was not an option. Hearing these unknown records was not a real priority - I was only 14. But I was curious to know what they sounded like. With my taste in music maturing, I had discovered an appreciation for diversity.

<u>More Buttons To Push</u>

My interest in music variety was also expanded by tuning into other radio stations. Once, while pursuing WLS & WCFL radio station record surveys, I came across a Top 37 hit parade survey for Gary station WLTH. Their playlist consisted of 37 records determined, most likely, by their 1370 AM dial position. The WLTH survey was not that much more uncommon than their giant Chicago counterparts. But they still managed to squeeze in a few unknown records, and so I listened to WLTH on occasion. One example of an uncommon record on WLTH's list was Duke Baxter's *Everyone Knows Matilda*, which climbed to #52 on the Hot 100. Clearly not a best seller and it never received airplay on WLS or WCFL, but I enjoyed it.

Chicago station WGRT, 950 AM, with a radio dial position right between WLS & WCFL, was one of the Windy City's premiere soul music stations. I tuned in occasionally, sometimes by accident. At a few minutes before the top of each hour, WGRT played "the top two soul sounds in Chicagoland" from their record survey. Nowhere else could I have heard Barbara & The Uniques' *There It Goes Again*, which peaked on *Billboard* at #91. But it went to #1 on

WGRT and I liked it. In addition, WGRT was the only radio station where I heard Rufus Thomas' *Breakdown* even though it peaked at #31 on *Billboard*. It reached #1 on WGRT's survey and I liked that one enough to buy the record. Listening to WGRT helped me to develop an indescribable appreciation and enjoyment of soul music.

Top 40 - More Or Less, part one

It's worth noting that, ironically, when the radio program *American Top 40* went on the air the weekend of July 4, 1970, WLS' Hit Parade consisted of 40 records. Three weeks later, the station dropped 10 records from their survey, making WLS a Top 30 station. It's possible to speculate that WLS did not sign up as an *AT40* affiliate in 1970 because of the pending Top 30 Hit Parade change. But that would have likely been just one of a hundred reasons. By 1973, their weekly record survey had been reduced even further to the "Big 8+9." After WCFL beat them in the ratings, WLS expanded their playlist again, eventually to a survey comprising of 45 records.

It's interesting to note that WLS eventually became an *AT40* station, but not until 1982. The station had three or four opportunities during the 1970s to add *AT40* to their programming but apparently station management failed to see the program's benefits until it was forced on them by their network. Because ABC Radio Enterprises, owner and operator of WLS, had purchased *AT40*'s parent company, Watermark Inc., a year earlier, it was extremely likely that the station was mandated to accept the program. Opportunity was there in 1970, 1971, 1972, 1973, 1974 and 1979 for WLS to obtain the show. If the station really wanted the program, why did they wait until ABC's purchase of Watermark? Just a rhetorical wonder.

Top 40 - More Or Less, part 2

Due to an expanding three minute average playing time on single 45 records in 1970, many Top 40 stations across the country were also cutting their playlist to 25 or 30 records. Many of those opted to play the long version of a popular hit record that was found on an LP. In fact, four songs in the Hot 100's Top 10 from December 19, 1970 had popular LP versions with expanded running times – Santana's *Black Magic Woman* (5:11), Chicago's *Does Anybody Really Know What Time It Is?* (4:33) and George Harrison's popular double-sided *My Sweet Lord* (4:39)/*Isn't It A Pity* (4:46). In addition, many stations were making airtime available for other album cuts. Playing tracks from LPs, which added selections from a hit album to a station playlist, was an accepted FM programming trend, and a growing direction on AM radio.

I enjoyed one way WCFL handled airplay of long versions of popular records. Every evening at 11:10, air personality Bob Dearborn selected an LP version of an oldie and played it as part of a feature he called 'long gold.' He included everything from the 5:26 version of Tommy James & The Shondells' *Crimson & Clover* to the

21:30 version of Rare Earth's *Get Ready.* More commonly heard on FM stations, these versions were rarely played on AM radio.

Having A Merry Little Christmas

The year ended with attempts to tape record WLS' Big 89 and WCFL's Top 40 for 1970. Because my recorder was on the blink -- from too much use -- I borrowed a friend's tape recorder to capture both countdowns. Ironically, both were broadcasted simultaneously on Christmas Day -- WLS' year-end review started at 2 p.m. and WCFL's began at 4 p.m. With the year-end surveys in hand, and tape recorder nearby, I knew what record was going to be played next. And I monitored both countdowns by flipping the dial back and forth.

****
Chapter 3 - 1971
****

FM Is Fine Medium

In early 1971, I discovered FM radio: WBBM-FM in Chicago -- a Top 40 station intertwined with LP cuts and an occasional rock oldie. It quickly became one of my favorite stations. The beauty of WBBM and most other FM rock 'n' roll stations at the time was that their disk jockeys talked very little, the station played three or four records in a row without interruption - not even jingles - and they always played the longer version of a hit record airing on AM stations. And, like most other FM stations, WBBM broadcasted in crystal-clear stereo. It was ideal for tape recording. As an added benefit, with LP cuts getting significant airplay on FM, I became exposed to new artists and many soon-to-be-released 45s. An example of one of those made-for-FM records was King Crimson's *The Court of the Crimson King.* It was never a WLS or WCFL playlist item but it *did* reach the Hot 100, peaking at #80. Some radio stations were playing it and listeners must have been buying it.

The Hot 100 Rules

Because of the cost, I bought *Billboard* on an every-other-week basis. Fortunately, I knew of three places to buy it, so if I missed an issue I wanted, I occasionally found two or three back issues on a magazine rack somewhere. I enjoyed watching the national chart movements of various records and often reviewed the Hot 100 to see how many songs were familiar to me. If there was anything extraordinary about a particular Hot 100, like The Beatles' *Let It Be* debuting at #6, and George Harrison's chart climb from #72 to #13 with *My Sweet Lord,* I made sure I bought a copy.

Typically buried in *Billboard*'s Radio-TV Programming section, I noticed an occasional advertisement or article promoting a national countdown radio show, based on the Top 40 from the Hot 100. It sounded like an interesting concept, but to my knowledge, it was not heard on any radio station in my area.

One reason why I enjoyed a hit parade countdown of records was, with advance access, I knew the order that records were going to be played and approximately when they would air. If I wanted to hear or tape record a song, I could make an educated guess as to its approximate air time. I knew when a radio station would play, for example, Rare Earth's *I Know I'm Losing You.* It was advantageous to have the recording tape rolling when that particular song started because it had a cold, *a cappella* introduction.

Of course, this raises an interesting yet baffling contrast. I could never understand why TV stations could tell you a week in advance what programs will be televised and when, but radio stations never knew, or never could tell you, what records they were going to play one week, or even one day in advance. From a broadcasting outsider, it was and still is an interesting paradox. I can imagine what television would be like if it was based upon

viewer requests. What a mess! To this day, with fragmented music formats and umpteen consultants sending a playlist edict to radio stations based on the same list of 200 songs that every other consultant's computer research is recommending, I'm still not sure if I understand this particular logic of radio.

But another reason why I enjoyed listening to a countdown was the variety of music it offered. True Top 40 radio, which no longer exists, had a little of everything. With numerous generic categories, Top 40 records were classified as either rock, easy listening, country & western, soul, instrumental, classical, novelty, comedy, religious, spoken word, unusual or just weird. I believe that The Pipkins' *Gimme Dat Ding* and Dave & Ansel Collins' *Double Barrel* fell into the 'weird' category. Top 40 radio stations offered a little of everything, providing listeners with a mix of recordings that most assuredly offered variety.

With a hit parade countdown program, and survey in hand, I *knew* what records were going to be played and when. And I felt privileged.

Not Another Local Countdown

It was Easter Sunday, April 11. Our family had traveled to Terre Haute to visit my grandmother for the weekend. After church, we went back to her house for our Easter gathering. And after an early lunch, we lounged while watching TV, reading the paper and visiting. I brought my portable radio with me to eliminate any boring moments.

There were two Top 40 radio stations in Terre Haute at the time -- WTHI-AM 1480 and WBOW-AM 1230. And, like WLS & WCFL, I tuned backed and forth to find the best music they had to offer. As usual, I tuned out commercials and ramblings like news and weather. Jingles amused me but I wanted music. Interestingly, the jingles used by the Terre Haute stations sounded exactly like the ones used at WLS & WCFL. Little kids emulating the big kids.

Upon closer listening when I tuned into WTHI that afternoon, the disk jockey on the air made a reference that "....Van Morrison's *Blue Money* was at #30 on this week's survey." Because I had developed a habit of writing down position numbers on record hit parades heard on the radio, I thought I would listen a little longer to this particular countdown. But I had no intention, however, of writing down the chart positions for the best-selling records in Terre Haute, Indiana. Chicago, yes, but not Terre Haute.

As I continued to listen, I picked up on a few words from the disk jockey hosting the countdown. Words like "...Hollywood..." and "....national countdown..." I wondered whether this could have been that Top 40 countdown program I had been reading about in *Billboard*. Since I didn't have a copy of the magazine with me and I didn't bring my tape recorder with me, I decided to write down record titles and their positions so I could verify, if possible, what I heard when we returned home. And once we got home I compared the list I wrote with *Billboard*'s list. They matched. As it turned out, I was listening to the radio program *American Top 40* for the first time. And, of course, the disk jockey was Casey Kasem.

WTHI, with studios four blocks from my grandmother's house, carried *AT40* from 12-3 p.m. on Sundays. Before we left for home that afternoon, and before I knew what I was listening to, I decided to walk to the station, taking my transistor with me. With a tradition that started about the same time as rock & roll, many radio stations had a disk jockey window where listeners could actually watch the disk jockey at work from the sidewalk along the street. WTHI had one as well. But upon my arrival, there was no one in the window. In fact, there was no one in the deejay's chair and no one talking into the microphone when the countdown was on the air. I recall thinking that maybe this guy was on tape. In addition, while listening to my first *AT40* broadcast, I do not recall ever hearing Casey mention his name. I was too caught up in the countdown - listening to what record was in what chart position. And besides, I still had a hard time differentiating between disk jockey voices on the radio.

<u>A "Challenge" Climbs To #1</u>

OK, let's evaluate the situation. I found a national, weekly Top 40 countdown radio program based on *Billboard*'s survey, in an out-of-the-way city. It addressed my desire to hear records that received little or no airplay on Chicago's Top 40 stations, to hear new artists, and new music. And it gave me that privileged feeling of knowing what record was to be played next, and when. It was just like the record survey I picked up off the record store counter, except chart movement was orally interpreted, not visually. Great! I discovered a weekly hit parade program on the radio, where I had advance access to the list of every record, and an opportunity to hear recognized and, quite often, unrecognized music. I discovered a radio program that played every record on the survey, whether it was good or bad, whether it was new or old. Terrific!! It became obvious to me that the radio program *American Top 40* provided a consistent outlet to hear new or rarely-played records that I could not hear anywhere else on the radio. Outstanding!!!

But wait a minute. This program was heard every week on an AM radio station in Terre Haute and, obviously, there was a problem. I did not *live* in Terre Haute or anywhere near it. I had become aware of a radio program that I greatly wanted to listen to every week but couldn't. How was I going to hear this program? Terre Haute was a three-hour drive from home and I was too young for a driver's license.

However, I came up with a few ideas. The first one, unfortunately, didn't work. I tried unsuccessfully to tune into WTHI's frequency from Merrillville at that same time the following Sunday. And many Sundays after that. Their signal, unfortunately, just wasn't that strong. I was out of luck. The second option didn't work either. Every weekend, I scanned the AM radio dial for music I knew was in *Billboard*'s Top 40, straining my ears many times through all kinds of static. And whenever I came across a Top 40 record on a distant station, I waited for its ending to see if I may have stumbled once again onto *American Top 40.* But, record after record, station after station, and week after week, I came up with nothing.

A positive result of this however, was that I now became more aware of records making *Billboard*'s Top 40. Each week, even though I couldn't hear *AT40*, I knew what was being played. But, once again, there were many records in the national Top 40 that were not getting played on any radio station in Chicago or elsewhere. I became frustrated because I knew of a record's Top 40 appearance but I was not able to hear it on the radio. One of the biggest examples of seeing-but-not-hearing was Les Crane's *The Desiderata*. It peaked at #8 in *Billboard*'s Top 10 in December 1971. But it never received airplay in Chicago on WLS, WCFL or WBBM-FM. In fact, until I obtained a vinyl LP copy of a 1971 *AT40* broadcast six years later, I never had the opportunity to hear *The Desiderata*. I failed to understand why this record never received Top 40 airplay in Chicago. Another example was Harry Chapin's 1972 classic, six-minute story of *Taxi*. It never received airtime on WLS or WCFL. Too long? Too bad. It was in *Billboard*'s Top 40 for more than two months, and got plenty of FM airplay in Chicago. It was one more reason for my growing preference for FM over AM. And another reason why I wanted to hear *AT40* every week.

It got to a point where I guess I resented someone else telling me what records they thought I wanted to hear on the radio. I wanted to decide. Give me the opportunity to hear the record, and let me be the judge. *AT40* played every record that reached *Billboard*'s Top 40, and that's about as democratic, and about as close as you can get to eliminating the bias of a radio station's program or music director, whose responsibility was to decide - and perhaps dictate - what record would or would not get station airplay.

<u>Seen But Not Heard</u>

On occasion, news of *American Top 40* was published in *Billboard*. For example, in the August 28, 1971 issue, *AT40* was the subject of an article titled, "*American Top 40* From Barter To $$$." The basis of the article announced that *AT40* would no longer be available to subscribing radio stations without cost. National 'network' commercials were being dropped from the show and, from that point on, the program's broadcast rights would be sold outright to radio stations at a cost to them based on their market size. As a result, all advertising heard during the program would be sold by each individual station, with the station keeping all dollars generated from the program's local advertising sales. Accompanying this article were various photographs of the Watermark studios, including one of Casey at the microphone. But another one of the photographs quickly grabbed my attention. It pictured *AT40* executive producer Tom Rounds placing a pin on a map of the United States. The map contained numerous pins, all representing cities where *AT40* was heard. Upon closer inspection of the map, I noticed that there was absolutely nothing around the Chicago area. But four or five pins marked different parts within the state of Indiana. One was not far from Lake Michigan and appeared to be close to home.

So it was back to scanning the AM dial. What station carried *AT40* so

close to me? I was certain that it was Top 40-formatted WAKE in Valparaiso. The program would have been a natural for them. I called WAKE and learned that they did not run the show. Years later I discovered that radio station WJVA in South Bend was the station represented on the map.

Inside The Radio

During its infancy stages, from July 1970 until October 1971, the show was offered at no charge to most radio stations. In exchange, the station agreed to air all 'network' commercials which were incorporated into the program. In addition, there was time available during each of the program's three hours for the station to sell local advertising. Prior to October 1971, subscribing stations had a no-cost, high-quality weekend program with an opportunity to turn an easy profit. But the news announced in August of a cash-only arrangement forced many subscribing stations into a decision -- keep the show and pay for it or drop it altogether. During the early days, the Watermark staff attempted to sell the program in two ways: 1)to radio stations, and 2)to 'network' commercial sponsors who bought program advertising time. It was an uphill battle trying to simultaneously convince many major and medium market radio stations, along with national sponsors, to give it a chance. They managed to quickly get the show on the air in cities such as Boston, St. Louis and Washington, D.C. And they signed network sponsors including MGM Records, Dentyne and Yamaha Motorcycles.

But one possible reason the program was kept off the air in many markets -- and off of many radio stations -- was due to the music content. With *AT40*, records were played in order from #40 to #1, with no regard to whether they were good or bad. And some of them *were* bad. Rejection responses from radio station general managers and program directors likely included "....I don't want some of the national Top 40 records played on my station....." or ".....our listeners don't respond well with some of those records......." or "...there are records in national Top 40 that do not fit within our Top 40 format........" or "...many records on *Billboard*'s chart are too old, they hang onto them too long....." or "we're not Top 40, we're a Top 25 station..." and so on. Another battle for Watermark was to convince radio stations to accept syndicated radio programming on a weekly basis. For some program directors, a radio station that accepted syndicated programming meant a loss of control, a surrendering of sorts to the work of another programmer. Many program directors had used the radio syndication market before, but typically on a one-time basis only with *The History of Rock & Roll* being the most familiar. Beyond a public affairs program, it was not common to see syndicated programming on a weekly basis.

And because of these factors, Watermark's marketing & sales efforts to sell the show to national sponsors were impeded. National sponsors wanted numbers and they just weren't there. In fact, by July 1971 and one year on the air, *AT40* was carried in only 15 of the Top 25 markets. But while 15 out of 25 was apparently not enough for network advertising, it *was* a major accomplishment for a one-year-old syndicated radio program. Unfortunately,

major market station commitments -- crucial for the program's survival -- were difficult to secure. The program was popular in cities of all sizes but it was new and with a fragmented network and weak national market share -- all built around less valuable weekend airtime -- it was a tough sell to a national advertiser.

Sign 'Em Up

When a major market station was secured, it wasn't always rated at #1 or #2. For example, *AT40* began airing in October 1970 in Los Angeles on AM giant KRLA where Casey Kasem had worked for years. But the show did not last there and a year later ended up on lower-rated KGBS. In New York City, it first debuted in May 1971 on another lower-rated station, WPIX-FM, which carried the show through 1977.

And it took two years after the program's debut before a radio station in Chicago made the decision to carry it. The good news was that the station was a Top 40, industry-regarded powerhouse -- WCFL. The bad news was its airtime. When WCFL began airing *AT40* in June 1972, even the most loyal WCFL listeners likely never heard it. It ran on Saturday night/Sunday morning from 1 - 4 a.m. A few months later, someone must have realized an unfortunate scheduling mistake had been made and consequently changed its airtime. The new time? It was moved one hour to 2 - 5 a.m. Undoubtedly, the WCFL sales department never knew of Casey Kasem's ability to draw an audience. In fact, they likely never knew his program was on their station. With no promotion outside of its own airtime, *AT40* lasted there only six months.

But the *AT40* staff kept at it. In their hearts they knew that they had a radio formula that worked and with dedication, perseverance, patience and a quality product, it would succeed. And eventually it did.

Super Marketing

Watermark occasionally ran *AT40* trade advertisements in *Billboard* mentioning some of their subscribers. A series of weekly *AT40* advertisements ran from November 1971 until January 1972 that listed every subscribing affiliate radio station from around the country, state by state. From Alabama (WGSV in Guntersville) to Wyoming (KASL in New Castle), Watermark was marketing *AT40* to other radio stations and the ads were a good way to get attention. With the ads wisely placed in *Billboard*'s Radio-TV section, perhaps call letter name dropping was a method to solidify existing station relationships while subtly sending a message to potential subscribers -- your name can be here.

It was from these series of ads that I learned that radio station WASK in Lafayette, Indiana was an *AT40* affiliate. One Saturday afternoon, I tuned to 1450 AM, WASK's frequency. The static was oh-so present but I faintly heard the call letters and a jingle for *The History of Rock & Roll* syndicated program. I knew I was on the right track. Unfortunately, I later learned that *AT40* was heard on WASK on Saturday and Sunday nights. I was 75 miles away from

Lafayette and nighttime reception was out of the question.

No Pomp, Just A Circumstance Advance

Graduation was now at hand. No, not yet from high school. It was graduation from one recording technique to another, just in time for year-end taping. I purchased a dandy little combination AM/FM stereo cassette recorder from Sears. The beauty of this unit gave me the ability to tape record and preserve records directly from the radio, including music broadcasted in stereo on FM. No more recording with a microphone placed in front of a radio's speaker. No more wires, no more background noise. Although in retrospect it may appear to be miniscule, this was a big deal for me. I had elevated my recording standards.

More National Exposure

In an effort to expose myself to new music, I had decided to listen to other radio stations. I began scanning the AM dial at night exploring and seeking out other Top 40 radio stations around the Midwest and around the country, with the sole intention of learning what records were being given airplay. From our northwest Indiana home in Merrillville, I listened to many stations and a lot of static. But there were a few with signals strong enough that resulted in fairly decent reception including Little Rock's KAAY and San Antonio's WOAI. When I should have been studying, I spent many evenings tuning into WLS, WCFL, WBBM, KAAY and WOAI. On occasion, I could hear WNBC and WABC, both out of New York City, and CKLW from Windsor, Ontario. There were many other stations, but only these had Top 40 formats with consistent, listenable radio transmission signals.

I sent a note to KAAY's evening personality Jonnie King along with a few WLS surveys and promotional Tooth Fairy peel-off stickers that the station used to hype the comical, syndicated radio series. He returned the favor with a note and a few of KAAY's record surveys. Obtaining KAAY's surveys gave me an idea.

The Survey's In The Mail

In early December 1971, I went to the public library and searched through the Yellow Pages telephone directories of various cities in an effort to obtain radio station information -- call letters and street addresses. Reading *Billboard* helped me to know some of the top-rated, Top 40 stations around the country. I consequently sent postcards to many medium and large market stations and asked each to send a copy of their year-end hit parade survey of the biggest records of 1971.

My motive was to learn what records had made each station's year-end list, and to make comparisons of record popularity city-by-city, and region-by-region. I could then integrate this information with records listed on the Chicago surveys and *Billboard*'s national list. While it was not exactly the most common activity for a 16-year-old, surveying radio station record surveys had

become a hobby. In addition to perusing other stations' hit parade lists, I also enjoyed reading additional information the surveys provided -- various tidbits of station information including names and photos of their disk jockeys, station advertising, announcements, and whatever they wanted to bring to the attention of listeners. I hoped to see something in print on a station's record survey promoting the *American Top 40* radio program. But I never did during this time.

The response to my postcard request was great. I had received nearly two dozen 1971 year-end surveys from Top 40 stations around the country including KRUX in Phoenix, WTIX in New Orleans, KYA in San Francisco and WPOP in Hartford. Response, I felt, was so good that I did it again in 1972 & 1973. But receiving all of these surveys furthered my attention toward a year-end hit parade countdown. And in regards to tape recording any 1971 music review, I decided to tape all of WLS' Big 89 exclusively. It had the most variety, the most records, and I once again had their survey in hand when the countdown began Christmas afternoon at 2 p.m.

****
Chapter 4 - 1972
****

Call To Action

One weekend in March, I participated in another state bowling tournament, this time in Indianapolis. I knew that *AT40* was heard on radio station WIFE, but I didn't know its airtime. While there, I managed to get to Ayr-Way, a local department store, to pick up WIFE's record survey. And I had brought a transistor radio with me to listen to WIFE as much as I could. But there was no mention of *AT40* on the record survey and, while listening, I never heard anything related to the program - either a promotional announcement, or the show itself. Later I would learn that the show was heard on Sunday nights, starting at 7 p.m. But by then, the bowling tournament I participated in had concluded and we had been home for hours.

I finally started subscribing to *Billboard* in April and it was home delivered every Monday, so I was able to review the Hot 100 chart weekly. In addition, I was still scanning the radio dial, but I just could not hear an *AT40* broadcast. This was frustrating.

After seeing numerous *AT40* ads and mentions in *Billboard*, this 16-year-old gathered enough nerve to call Watermark. I wanted to know if there was any radio station near my home that carried *AT40*. I do not remember what I told the telephone receptionist, but I got connected directly to *AT40*'s executive producer, Tom Rounds. I explained to him that I was just a listener, in search of an *AT40* station in Chicago or northwestern Indiana. He pointed out that, in fact, there was no present *AT40* affiliate in Chicago, and that they were trying to find a station there. But there was nothing he could tell me in the way of news of a Chicago subscriber. I believe that he sensed my frustration, however, and he promised to send me a vinyl copy of the show. What?! Really? *Cool!* I was thrilled....excited.......jubilant! What a neat thing for him to do. After I got off of the phone, I immediately grabbed the latest *Billboard,* and checked the current Hot 100 to inspect what records were, and were not, in the Top 40. I couldn't wait to receive it! But I waited and waited. And waited. Two weeks later, and I still waited. Unfortunately, I never received it and, I assume, he never sent it. I didn't have the nerve to call him back and remind him that he promised to send a kid in Indiana a copy of the show. So my next move was to ask a friend of mine who was attending Purdue University in Lafayette to tape record an *AT40* show for me, via WASK. I provided him with a few tapes, and he recorded a portion of the final hour of the program dated May 20, 1972. The recording quality was bad, but at least I had part of *AT40* on tape.

As a side note, I wonder if that call to Rounds inspired extra attention to the Chicago market. A little more than two months later and *AT40* was on the air in Chicago.

Scan No More!

I must have been talking about the program because, a month later, another friend told me he heard it late one Saturday night on a Chicago radio station. Could it be? The following Monday, I called WCFL, the station my friend said he had heard it on, and they verified that it was on the air on Saturday night/Sunday morning, starting at 1 a.m. I checked the calendar to find that the next *AT40* broadcast on WCFL, and the first complete *AT40* show that I would hear would be from the issue of *Billboard* dated July 1, 1972.

Once I confirmed that WCFL was carrying the program, I realized that I needed to make a few preparations. In anticipation, I bought two 90-minute Memorex cassette tapes, at $3.19 each, and had my copy of *Billboard* on my desk. WCFL was set on the radio and, after going out Saturday night for a while, I made sure I was home and wide awake for its 1 a.m. start. Just prior to the show's beginning, I looked at the Hot 100 one more time. Let's see.....the first song I'll hear will be Graham Nash & David Crosby's *Immigration Man*. I liked that record. And since it was #36 the week before, and dropping on the chart, it appeared that this would be its last week in the Top 40. My thoughts then turned to records that had just fallen out of the Top 40 that I won't hear this week. There was Commander Cody's *Hot Rod Lincoln*, Bread's *Diary* and The Moody Blues' *Isn't Life Strange*. They were gone.

But I was ready. The last record before 1 a.m. was playing, and then the WCFL station I.D. began. This was it. I started the tape recorder. Then the *AT40* theme music started. Yes! Finally! I could hear a complete, uninterrupted broadcast of *Billboard*'s current Top 40 records. And I'll have it on tape for future listening. I was 17, and certainly could have been out doing other things. But I had just broken up with my girlfriend, and I didn't have anything else to do. And who cares? This is what I wanted to do. This is where I wanted to be. I was thrilled. Bring on Nash & Crosby.

Casey opened the show.... *"....Hi! And welcome to 'American Top 40.' My name is Casey Kasem, and what I usually do every week about this time is countdown the 40 current best-selling songs in the country. But this week, we're doing a very special show. As I promised, the AT40 staff, headed by our chief statistician Ben Marichal, has ranked the 40 biggest hits of the rock 'n' roll era. The period from 1955 to the present. And this is the day we count them down. In a few moments I'll explain our tabulating procedure, but right now, let's start the countdown of the 40 biggest hits of the past 17 years."*

What?! What's this? A special program? With *old* music?? The #40 jingle played, and Casey introduced a Four Seasons record from 1962. To say that I was disappointed was an understatement. I couldn't believe it. I wouldn't hear this week's Top 40 after all. The regular weekly countdown had been replaced, for this week, with a special countdown. However, I kept my tape recorder running because it was *American Top 40*, so I recorded the entire show. But I still couldn't believe it. To this day, I still have the original recorded-off-the-air tape of that program. And that was the start to a new ritual

for me.......to tape record every weekly edition of *AT40*. By the way, the Four Seasons record that ranked at #40 on that program was *Big Girls Don't Cry*, a record that furthered my awkwardness with song lyrics. I had always thought the title was *Big Girl, Small Fry*!

<u>I'll Take The Blame</u>

In September, a friend and I took a train to Chicago for a shopping trip. This, however, was not a typical shopping trip. It was more like a hunt. Hunting for hard-to-find records, music magazines & publications. Occasional trips like this included record stores, magazine and book stores, and to the observation windows at the studios of WLS & WCFL.

And on this particular trip, the WCFL visit became more interactive. I stopped at the receptionist's desk inquiring about *AT40*. The questions I asked her must've been too inquisitive because she proceeded to pick up the phone, and promptly called what may have been the program director. She got him on the line, and then handed the phone to me. Nervously, I explained that I was a listener of *AT40*, and I wanted to know why it was on-the-air at such an ungodly time of day. I also wanted to know why there was no on-air promotion of the program's existence. And how can it gain listeners if no one knows it's on the air? I wanted the show to succeed on WCFL, but there wasn't even a mention or a picture of Casey Kasem on their weekly record survey. On a rotation basis, all the other disk jockeys had their time slot and photo promoted on it. But never Casey. Why not? In response, his tone of voice was defensive and his answers were not what I wanted to hear. He probably gave the receptionist a verbal lashing after we left for wasting his time with a listener. And, as a result of this pesky kid, I will take credit as the reason WCFL's last *AT40* broadcast was just a few months later at the end of December, right after airing the Top 80 of 1972. As far as WCFL was concerned, Casey Kasem was out, and his syndicated Saturday night/Sunday morning replacement - Wolfman Jack - was in. My guess is, at the time of my visit, this guy probably had *AT40*'s renewal contract on his desk and tore it up immediately after my call.

<u>An Unrecognized Soul</u>

One of my favorite *AT40* special programs was "The Biggest Artists of the Past 5 Years," which was based on the charts from 1967 - 1972 and aired at the end of September.

What was unusual about this program were the artists who ranked at #2 - James Brown, and #3 - Aretha Franklin. I was familiar with a few of their songs, but I did not realize their popularity on the national charts was so strong. In this special program, James Brown ranked higher than at least three major artists who had big records between 1967 and 1972. The Jackson Five had *four #1 records*. Three Dog Night had *two #1 records*. And Creedence Clearwater Revival had *five #2 records*. What made this so unusual was that James Brown's highest ranking record between 1967 and 1972 was *I Got The Feeling*, which peaked at #6. But what brought him to the special's #2 position was the

fact that, between 1967 and 1972, he had 28 Top 40 records! Twenty-eight!!! At the time, I do not think that I could have named more than two of them! And for good reason. Radio stations WLS, WBBM & WCFL, with little exception, were cautious to add any of his records to their playlists. He was hardcore soul. And consequently, I had little exposure to his music. For this special broadcast, the decision makers at *AT40* opted to play *Super Bad*, a James Brown record that peaked at #13 on *Billboard.* But this record was unknown to Chicago Top 40 audiences, including myself. *Super Bad* was one of many James Brown releases that were never added to the playlists of WLS, WCFL or WBBM. In fact, *Super Bad*'s appearance on *AT40* was probably the only time it was heard on WCFL's airwaves. James Brown was beaten in this special by only one recording act, The Beatles, who ranked at #1. And while Aretha Franklin got a little more Top 40 airplay, the justification behind her high ranking was the same - twenty-five Top 40 records between 1967 and 1972. Although I was more familiar with her music, it was still another hard-to-believe chart statistic.

<u>No Production At School</u>

During the fall of 1972, while *AT40* was still on WCFL, I was a high school senior with a curriculum that included a radio broadcasting class at a local vocational-technical school. The school had its own radio station, commercial-free public radio station WGVE -- Gary's Voice of Education -- located at 88.7 FM. Because most of WGVE's on-air programs were pre-recorded on reel-to-reel tape, I was inspired to purchase a 7" reel-to-reel tape recorder for my own use. Reel-to-reel tape recording had a higher quality than cassettes because the recorder provided a selection of tape recording speeds, based on the number of inches-per-second a reel of tape would pass through the machine. And that resulted in a better sound. The faster the tape moved, the better the sound quality. Another reason I bought a reel deck was for convenience. I was able to record an entire *AT40* show onto one 7" reel of tape, instead of two or three cassette tapes. And I recorded many *AT40* programs this way before WCFL pulled it off the air.

Before 1972 closed out, and influenced by my accessibility to WGVE's studios at school, I decided to mimic Casey, and organize my own year-end, Top 40 countdown program. I have often wondered how many others like me were influenced this way. My attempt at a homemade hit parade almost made it to the airwaves. A few of the other radio students at WGVE had their own one-hour, after-school program, where they could play just about any record they wanted. I inquired about the opportunity of having some airtime for a year-end countdown, and was given an initial green light. But there were three steps I needed to take before I could obtain full approval: I needed a list of the top records of the year, I needed a script, and I needed the records.

The first part was done because, weeks before, I had reviewed all of *Billboard*'s 1972 Hot 100 charts, and began my own compilation of the year's Top 100. When time allowed after school, after work and on weekends, I

worked on the script, while seeking the records I needed - either on LP or 45. WGVE was not able to provide the records I needed because all of their material was pre-produced and pre-recorded educational programming - no music. In fact, the students with their own shows actually used their own records. And besides, they were more inclined to play Black Sabbath more often than The Carpenters or the Jackson Five. I purchased a few 45s at record stores, but the popularity of many of 1972's records had passed. Most record stores at that time did not keep an inventory of 45s that were six to eight months old, in order to make room for newer product. And I was struggling to find those records on my list. My only other option was to ask around at school to see if anyone I knew had what I needed.

It was nearly Christmas, and I was running out of time. Because of the short shelf life of a year-end countdown, I needed to have this program on the air by the second week of January. There were some obscure records on my list, including The Chakachas' *Jungle Fever*. And they were nowhere to be found. I had the list. I had the script. But I could not find the needed records and, unfortunately I abandoned the project.

Tracking Tabulations

***AT40*'s 1972 year-end list was different from *Billboard*. *AT40* statistician Ben Marichal compiled the list because of the unavailability of *Billboard*'s chart by the show's production deadline. It is rather ironic that all year *AT40* used *Billboard*'s Top 40, but did not utilize *Billboard*'s year-end survey. (The *AT40* staff compiled their own year-end list again for the Top 40 of 1973 and the Top 100 of 1977.) Of course, Marichal's list was based on *Billboard* and, to his credit, he correctly matched nine of the year's Top 12 records. And either correctly predicted, or was off by only one, two or three positions on 65% of *Billboard*'s Top 80.**

There were, however, two wide distinctions between *AT40*'s list and *Billboard*'s chart. On *AT40* for 1972, Mouth & MacNeal's *How Do You Do* came in at the #61 position, but finished at #25 on *Billboard*. And on *AT40*, The Stylistics' *You Are Everything* was tabulated at #29, while it was not even listed on *Billboard*'s Top 100 year-end chart. Considering that both records' completed chart runs on the Hot 100 within the year-end tabulation period of November 1971 to November 1972, it's difficult to determine why there was such a significant difference.

At this point, I began to notice the various chart positions of the same record on year-end surveys. And in particular, I enjoyed reviewing the final rankings of records on local radio station surveys vs. the positions of the same records on the national survey. For example, both *AT40* and *Billboard* ranked Roberta Flack's *First Time Ever I Saw Your Face* as #1 for 1972. And, to make a radio station comparison, here are a few local charts with the year-end results of various large, medium and small Top 40 markets, and their #1 records for 1972:

city	station	year-end chart contained:	1972's #1 records
Boston	WMEX	100 records	Horse With No Name
Chicago	WLS	89 records	First Time Ever I Saw Your Face
Chicago	WCFL	40 records	American Pie
Davenport, IA	*KSTT	100 records	First Time Ever I Saw Your Face
Hartford	WDRC	100 records	American Pie
Philadelphia	WFIL	100 records	American Pie
Phoenix	KRUX	100 records	I Can See Clearly Now
Pueblo, CO	KDZA	200 records	American Pie
St. Louis	KXOK	63 records	American Pie
San Francisco	KYA	100 records	I Can See Clearly Now
Windsor, ONT.	CKLW	100 records	Lean On Me

KSTT's chart originated from Dick Starr's syndicated year-end countdown, "Opus '72"

And that's not a typographical error. The year-end list of Pueblo's KDZA actually contained 200 records. Here's how five randomly selected records finished in 1972's year-end surveys:

	AT40	Billboard	WMEX	WLS	WCFL	KSTT	WDRC	WFIL	KRUX	KDZA	KXOK	KYA	CKLW
Ben	#22	20	23	18	23	21	83	73	6	28	20	7	44
Anticipation	#n/l	73	n/l	67	n/l	77	45	n/l	n/l	116	n/l	n/l	n/l
Burning Love	#40	48	48	31	21	38	13	32	56	34	50	51	90
Layla	#63	60	58	n/l	n/l	58	47	78	n/l	91	n/l	n/l	88
Scorpio	#16	43	n/l	n/l	n/l	96	63	49	n/l	35	28	72	n/l

n/l = not listed

Many unscientific conclusions can be drawn from this observation, including the wide differences of positions posted by *Ben*. From #6 for the year in Phoenix, to #83 in Hartford, its popularity was all over the charts. And the national ranking of *Scorpio* on *AT40* and *Billboard* does not seem to reflect its overall local popularity, as indicated here. But as pointed out, these are random and unscientific conclusions.

Gone But Not Forgotten

Regarding an effort to tape record any Chicago year-end countdown in 1972, I had no interest. I was no longer obtaining the weekly record surveys, and so I had no advance list for WLS or WCFL. All I did, out of curiosity and for future reference, was to write down the records reaching WLS' 1972 Big 89. Other than sending postcards to Top 40 stations in 1972, and again in 1973, my interest in recording - on paper or on tape - local year-end countdowns had ended. I was now only interested in the national chart. And in regards to the national chart, an interesting observation about *Billboard*'s Top 100 for 1972 -- it's a good thing that *AT40* did not use the complete list of 100 records for their year-end show because Casey and staff would have been looking for a "lost" record. *Billboard*'s original published list contained only 99 records, somehow

inadvertently leaving out the record in position #89. And finally, with WCFL's last *AT40* broadcast airing on December 30, 1972, it's interesting to note here that Casey answered a question on-the-air from a Chicago listener during the January 20, 1973 program. But more than likely, the letter writer never knew it.

Unfortunately, here we go again. No *AT40* outlet in the Chicago area.

****

Chapter 5 - 1973

****

No Gain - Much Pain

After WCFL dropped *AT40*, I contacted Tom Rounds on behalf of WGVE, inquiring about the possibility of the show airing on "Gary's Voice of Education." In response, he sent a packet of *AT40* marketing materials to me, which included a reel-to-reel tape containing a sample *AT40* program, in hopes that WGVE would pick up the show. However, the station manager could not justify paying $28 a week for the rights to broadcast *AT40* -- the cost to carry *AT40* at the time for non-commercial, educational radio stations. If I had the money -- I would have gladly paid for it.

A couple of weeks later, one Saturday night in late January, I drove my parents' car to Lafayette, and to radio station WASK. I wanted to hear the show and hoped to get an inside look at the program being placed on the air. But I went unprepared and, upon my arrival at WASK, their engineer would not allow me, a stranger, to enter the station. And I couldn't blame him. But driving into Lafayette, and on my way out again, I heard part of a show, so it wasn't a total waste of time. Later in 1973, I will use this lesson to open a door for me.

So it was back to scanning the AM dial at night, looking for an *AT40* broadcast. One Sunday evening, I came across Casey's voice. Wow! I finally did it! I found a distant broadcast of *AT40*. But where was it originating from? The signal was filled with static but I managed to finally hear the call letters and city. It was KOIL in Omaha, Nebraska. The next day, I sent a note to KOIL's program director. I wanted to let him know that I heard his station while in northwest Indiana, to let him know of my interest in the show, and ask about *AT40* in relation to KOIL. In response, he sent a reply with information about *AT40* and KOIL. Unfortunately, due to the static and an unreliably faint signal, it was not possible to listen to the show every week.

One Friday evening in March, I again went through the motions of scanning the AM dial, hoping to find a static-free signal and an *AT40* broadcast. And there it was! Well, at least an *AT40* broadcast. I picked up the show coming out of Paducah, Kentucky on station WDXR. Another faint and static-filled signal, but Casey was there, Friday evenings from 7-10 p.m. I tuned in when I could for a few weeks to follow, even attempting to tape record it once or twice. But the static made it too difficult to listen to it for more than a few minutes at a time.

A few weeks later, in Richmond, Indiana, I participated in another state bowling tournament. And this time I brought a determination to find an *AT40* broadcast, along with my radio/cassette recorder. I managed to find some time to listen to the radio and scan the dial. (Does that surprise you?!) Stations that I could hear were Indianapolis' WIFE faintly during the day and nothing at night, CKLW Detroit/Windsor, WOWO in Fort Wayne and a few others. But it was WTUE out of Dayton that caught my interest, an FM Top 40 station with a great

signal. I listened to it whenever possible and I was oh-so-hopeful that I would hear an *AT40* promo or a portion of the show. *AT40* had just begun stereo broadcasts -- each program was recorded in mono until then -- and would have fit in well with WTUE's format. But again, no Casey.

Going Hollywood

Not long after I graduated from high school in June, I noticed a small write-up in *Billboard* explaining that *AT40* was going to be heard in a new Gene Hackman movie titled *Scarecrow.* The devoted *AT40* listener -- and would-be listener -- that I was, I went to see the movie. And I learned that the show did not have a big part in the movie. It was strictly background sound.

But what fascinated me about the movie's *AT40* broadcast was that Casey was heard playing Aretha Franklin's 1968 record *House That Jack Built.* I wasn't sure whether *House That Jack Built* was ever played on an *AT40* program, but I had my doubts. (And as a result of program research, it turns out that it never was heard within an *AT40* show.) What was used in *Scarecrow* was part of a special recording Casey and Watermark produced exclusively for the Warner Brothers movie. Adding to the irony, not only had *AT40* never played the record *House That Jack Built*, but the scene in the movie where *AT40* is heard playing on the radio took place in contemporary Detroit. At the time, and in fact from 1971 - 1978, *AT40* had no affiliate station in Detroit.

Rolling Up My Shirt Sleeves

And by summer, there was still no *AT40* station in Chicago. However, unknown to the Watermark staff in charge of marketing the program, I was trying to help get it back on the air. I contacted Chicago's Top 40 & LP-formatted WBBM-FM and Top 40-automated WMAQ-FM inquiring about the possibility of an association with *AT40*. A woman I spoke to at WMAQ sounded very pleased to hear from me but they never acquired the show. Interestingly, WBBM eventually *did* pick up *AT40* -- six years later.

Encounter With Somebody's WIFE

One of my most memorable displays of enthusiasm for *AT40* occurred on Sunday, July 22. Just before I graduated from high school in June, I began working part-time on Sundays at Gary radio station WWCA. At some point on a Sunday evening not long after that, I called radio station WIFE, the *AT40* affiliate in Indianapolis. I talked to the guy who engineered *AT40* and asked him if it would be OK for me stop by the station one Sunday while *AT40* was on the air. I am not certain what ran through his head at the time of my request but perhaps he noticed that I was an up & coming radio person in Gary, Indiana, looking to make some contacts. Or perhaps he was interested in having his ego stroked due to his position at a medium market station. Or both. Either way, he was happy to accommodate my visit to the WIFE studios.

Also at the time, I was preparing to attend Indiana State University in Terre Haute in the fall, majoring in radio/TV. And since my grandmother lived

there, I would have the opportunity to visit her more often.

In preparation of my WIFE visit, I made arrangements to take my sister with me to Terre Haute to stay a day or two with our grandmother. And we drove in our parents' car to Terre Haute the afternoon of July 22. My plans were to arrive at my grandmother's house and show some interest in taking time to explore the ISU campus. Upon arriving, I dropped my sister off and told my grandmother that I wanted to drive to ISU and look around. And so I left. But without telling my sister, my grandmother or my parents, I drove directly from Terre Haute to downtown Indianapolis -- right to the WIFE studios at 1440 N. Meridian Street. I had made arrangements to stop by, and watch the engineer place *AT40* on the air. It hit the airwaves at 7 p.m. I left Terre Haute about 5:15, and arrived at the station about 6:30. My contact there - his name long forgotten – didn't arrive until 6:55. After a quick introduction, we hurriedly went into the main studio, which also had one of those disk jockey observation windows that looked out onto Meridian Street, a major Indianapolis thoroughfare. He grabbed the *AT40* box, which contained three LPs and engineer cue sheets.

When *AT40* dropped network commercials in 1971, another change impacting radio stations was made. Until then, the pre-recorded program was distributed on three reel-to-reel tapes, with each reel representing one hour of the three-hour show. Along with the program came engineer's cue sheets which contained a song title and artist rundown and broadcast timing information, alerting the station's engineer when to insert a local commercial in the program's broadcast. In October 1971 however, the program began arriving at radio stations in a boxed set with cue sheets and LPs.

And so the WIFE engineer pulled out the first record, placed it on the turntable, cued it up and, as an oldie by the group Chicago began to fade, he hit the station I.D., started the *AT40* record and Casey was on the air in Indianapolis, introducing the #40 record. Once he got settled at the controls and made the necessary notations to the station's on-air log, we rushed back to a production studio where he prepared some sort of promo or commercial announcement.

We returned to the main studio a few minutes later just in time for a commercial break. But then something unusual occurred. He sat down, reached for one of the volume controls and faded out Gladys Knight's #39 record *before* Casey's outcue closed the segment. He then placed a local commercial on the air. I was surprised. I couldn't believe what I had just witnessed. Less than ten minutes into the program, and he *butchered* it! As an *American Top 40* purist -- one who appreciates what Casey has to say before and after each record in the Top 40 -- I was astonished. If I was a regular WIFE listener and had tape recorded the show off of their station every week, I truly would have made a pest of myself to station management due to this inexcusable program editing. And, like WCFL, I would have been responsible for WIFE dropping the show!!

After he finished the commercial break and got the program started again, I commented to him that I didn't think he was supposed to edit the show

like he did. His response was that "WCFL did it all the time." Admittedly, the engineer at WCFL had done it occasionally, but from someone who had heard -- and tape recorded -- every show on WCFL, I knew the edits were infrequent and I told him. And I don't think that I earned any points with him. Consequently, I didn't get anywhere when I asked him to dub a copy of the show onto tape for me. "No, sorry, man. Can't do it.....too busy." Regrettably, I never thought to ask if I could have the actual records or what WIFE did with old copies of the show. My thought at the time was that the station just kept them.

By 7:45, a little more than an hour after I arrived in Indianapolis, I was on my way back to Terre Haute, listening to *AT40* and hoping my grandmother wasn't too worried. From where she lived, it was about 12 blocks to the ISU campus. I could have walked there. But I drove, and was gone nearly four hours.

<u>Another Act Of Preservation</u>

A couple of weeks later, I decided to take it upon myself to obtain a taped copy of the show. My uncle and his family lived in Lafayette, and I called them to place an unusual request – to drive to their home and set up my recorder to tape an *AT40* Sunday night broadcast. The starting time of the program -- 9 p.m. -- made my appeal come across that much more unusual and, of course, it would be midnight before I left. But it was OK with them. I am certain that they thought I was a little mixed up with my priorities. I convinced a friend to drive with me to keep me company. He understood. He *knew* I was mixed up!

<u>College Calls And Countdown Walls, part 1</u>

If you are wondering if I decided to attend school in Terre Haute because *AT40* was heard there on WTHI, where it still wasn't heard in Chicago, the answer is no. I knew *AT40* was not on the air anymore in Terre Haute from an experience a year earlier.

I had driven to Terre Haute one weekend to visit the ISU campus in September 1972. At the time, the program was still on the air on WCFL. With a dedication to recording *AT40* every week, I brought my radio & cassette recorder with me to my grandmother's house, where I stayed. It was Saturday afternoon, September 30 when I arrived.

One of my first objectives was to call WTHI and ask what time *AT40* came on. Their response was that WTHI no longer carried the program. What?! Oh no! How am I going to record it? There was only one thing I could do. It came on at 1 a.m. in Chicago and WCFL's signal was 50,000 watts -- strong enough to be heard in Terre Haute at night. So I stayed up until 4 a.m. recording a static-filled, fading signal. Not only was I not too pleased about this arrangement but my grandmother wasn't too happy either. Every hour or so after midnight she came downstairs to the living room where I had my radio set up, reminded me what time it was and told me to go to bed. And every time I assured her that it wouldn't be too much longer. But there was no way that I was going to tell her at 1:30 that I knew I would be up until 4 a.m. And I got the job done.

College Calls And Countdown Walls, part 2

In September 1973, after developing a routine for college classes and regular visits to my grandmother, I had the opportunity to assess the formats of Terre Haute's radio stations. WTHI-AM had changed from Top 40 to an 'adult rock' format, leaving only one Top 40 station in town -- WBOW. I made an appointment with their program director, Jim McKnight, in an attempt to convince him that WBOW should be an *AT40* station. And I tried. We talked for 45 minutes. Here I was again, unbeknownst to Watermark, making an effort to market the show. Right or wrong, one of my arguments with McKnight was that the show performed well in the ratings in college towns, pointing out that *AT40* was heard on WASK in Lafayette, home to Purdue University, and on WERK in Muncie, where Ball State University was located. But my appeal fell on deaf ears.

Like WBBM however, WBOW eventually picked up *AT40* -- two years later. Unfortunately, I was long gone from Terre Haute and I suspect McKnight was too.

College Calls And Countdown Walls, part 3

Since I spent a great deal of time scanning the AM dial prior to living in Terre Haute and quite a bit of time doing the same while at school, I was inspired to write a five-page paper for a broadcasting class, based on this experience, titled "The Policies of AM Station Allocations and Frequencies." The paper's content was even more boring than the title. But I had all this radio knowledge of call letters, markets, frequencies, nighttime kilowatts, etc. In this regard, it proved to be productive use of time because, for my first college paper, I earned a B.

Columbus Discovered

Still in Terre Haute, I was fortunate to find another *AT40* outlet while scanning the dial. One Sunday afternoon, I came across Casey on a radio station in Columbus, Indiana -- WCSI, 1010 AM. They ran it from 3:00 - 6:00 p.m. My roommate was not around when I discovered it, and I had to leave the dorm before he returned. So I placed a note on the radio we shared, with instructions to NOT change the radio's dial position. When we caught up with each other later, his first comment to me was, "...find Casey?" He knew that I had.

So Many Shows, So Little Time

I left Indiana State and Terre Haute in December, with a couple of things in mind. I decided that I held a preference to work and generate income instead of fulfilling an education. And I thought I could retrace my steps where I left off in August, if possible, and try and obtain the jobs I had in radio and retail.

But before I left school, I befriended a guy from Indianapolis. He agreed to tape record *AT40*'s 1973 year-end show for me, from radio station WIFE, once

he was home for the holidays. Even though I knew of WIFE's editing of *AT40*, I gave him a reel-to-reel tape, a few dollars for postage, my mailing address, and instructions to tape record it -- start-to-finish -- including commercials.

Because I had a chance to faintly hear the program every week on WCSI, and because of an *AT40* full-page advertisement in *Billboard* earlier in the year which detailed 1973's special December programs, I knew there were actually two year-end specials -- an all-time Christmas music countdown and the year's Top 40. He agreed to record the year-end show, but I wondered if it was possible to obtain a copy of the Christmas program. Could arrangements be made to get it recorded off of the radio? Where there's a will, there's a way.

The semester ended by the third week of December and I returned home to northwestern Indiana for the holidays. Once home, I made arrangements to drive to Lafayette on Saturday, December 29 to visit my uncle and his family. I am almost ashamed to say that the family visit was secondary, because I came prepared to tape the Christmas program. And as I drove into the Lafayette area, I turned on WASK only to hear a promo for the year-end show, which was to air later that day. What?! Oh no. Another disappointment. I wanted the Christmas program.

WASK typically would air a new *AT40* program on Sunday night, and repeat the same show the following Saturday night. And I thought I had timed my visit where I could record the Christmas special, which was dated December 22, on its repeat night. After arriving, I called the station and asked them why the Christmas show would not be heard. Their explanation was simple -- it was after Christmas and they were not playing any more Christmas music. They played the Top 40 for 1973 instead, and in fact, would play that special three times. So I ended up having two recorded-off-of-the-radio copies of the year-end show. However, there was good news -- WASK's version was complete, not like WIFE's edited version. A week later, I received the WIFE tape. For a nighttime broadcast with a weak signal, its quality was fair at best. But at least I had a copy of an *AT40* broadcast on WIFE, program edits and all.

****

Chapter 6 - 1974

****

If Taping *AT40* Is Wrong, I Don't Want To Be Right

By spring, I retrieved both jobs I that had given up the previous August - one at Gary radio station WWCA, and the other at a local supermarket. Still interested in *AT40*? You bet! In fact, I visited a friend from high school who was attending Purdue University in Lafayette. And yes, I took my radio and tape recorder with me. And yes, I recorded a show while I was there. In fact, I left it there with a request for her to record the following week's program, which was "The Most Extraordinary Top 40 British Artists" special.

Still hopeful that *AT40* would return to Chicago, in May I called what seemed to be an emerging Top 40 station - WDHF-FM. It had an easy listening format, which had evolved into Top 40. When I called, I do not think I talked to anybody there beyond the receptionist. But I obtained the information I wanted. WDHF would become an *AT40* affiliate with a 9 a.m. broadcast beginning Sunday, June 9. Finally. The show is back in Chicago. And on the air at a decent time. *And in stereo.*

Feeling good because it was spring, I decided to buy a new stereo receiver and reel-to-reel tape deck. (I know, I know.......I lean toward the bizarre.) Happily, it was a time to begin the weekly ritual of taping *AT40* programs.

Flipping Over An Elvis Production

During the 1960's and early 1970's, *Billboard* occasionally listed both sides of an artist's Hot 100 record -- the 'A' side and the 'B' side. For both to be listed indicated that each side of the 45 single was getting radio station airplay. But not many Top 40 stations, however, played both sides of an artist's double-sided record. However, when double-sided records reached the Top 40, Casey and *AT40* did a good job of playing, or at least mentioning, the other side of a popular 45. And during the early 1970's, when flipsides charted, many times it was an Elvis Presley record.

And speaking of Elvis.......In September, I sent a letter to Casey and *AT40*. It was prior to the upcoming Top 10 "Producers of the 1970's" special, and contained the question -- *Who produces Elvis Presley records?* Although my name was never mentioned in answer to a question on the show, I wrote and asked the Elvis Presley question once before in 1972. And to be honest, I really didn't care who produced his records. I thought that the question was a unique one to ask, however, and that it was a clever way to get my name on the air. And it could have been answered as a part of the upcoming Producers special. But with the many records Elvis released during the early 1970's - fourteen reaching the Top 40, and eight of those listed as double-sided singles, he did not appear in that special program.

To give proper credit, my inspiration to ask the question about Elvis' producer came from the Hot 100. Many of Presley's Hot 100 records had "(not listed)" in the space designed for the record producer's name. To the best of my knowledge, the question was never asked by another listener and the producer information was never provided. And to this day I still don't know who produced Elvis Presley's records. And to this day, I still don't care.

<u>BUT IT WAS MY IDEA!</u>

There was more to this particular letter, however, than the Elvis Presley question. In fact, an unconfirmed result of this correspondence became something quite noteworthy. In addition to the question, I made a program suggestion that eventually became reality. I recommended, for *AT40*'s upcoming 5th anniversary on July 4, 1975, that the first program be repeated. And that's exactly what happened. Unfortunately, I have never been able to confirm that my letter -- submitted nearly a year before the repeat broadcast of the first show on *AT40*'s fifth anniversary -- inspired the idea. I wish I could take credit for it.

****

Chapter 7 - 1975

****

Hang Forty

At the beginning of this section of the book, I indicated that I attempted to resist the urge of being a fanatic. However, another *AT40*-related experience may have pushed me into that category. In July 1974, Casey took a week off of hosting *AT40* to take an acting role in an episode of the TV show, *Hawaii Five-O*. For me, that was enough to consider taking a vacation to Hawaii. By January 1975 I decided to go and started making plans -- either with someone or alone. At the time, I was in a growth stage of independence and individuality and I was comfortable with the idea of going without someone. And in June I went and went alone.

Of course there is a great deal to see and do in Hawaii, but I also packed my radio/cassette recorder for any down time. I could not resist the urge to scan the AM dial for radio stations outside of Hawaii. I had heard that the signal of Chicago's WLS was strong enough to be heard in different parts of the world at night. I tried to tune it in at different times, but could not hear it while in Hawaii.

While there, I also made it a point to contact radio station KKUA, the *AT40* affiliate in Honolulu. The music director invited me to the station and introduced me to a few station personnel. While touring their studios, I spied a few copies of *AT40* on a record shelf, some of which were marked "emergency show." I inquired about those and was told that they were used in case of a problem with the program's regular weekly mail delivery. A request for an extra copy went unfulfilled. *AT40* had a Sunday morning air time in Honolulu, and I arrived in Hawaii late Sunday afternoon. I had missed the opportunity to record a program on KKUA, but I ended up with a copy of KKUA's *AT40* on-air promo, and a great vacation.

A New Set Of Reels

A week later I was home and Casey was promoting the next special -- a repeat broadcast of the first program -- on the 5th anniversary of the show. The first show. From the summer of 1970. *The First Show.* Three hours loaded with records -- in countdown order -- from one of my prime adolescent years. Recording and preserving this show was a must. And I could not risk missing this show because of faulty stereo equipment. My reel-to-reel recorder was malfunctioning occasionally and, for this special broadcast, I decided that it was time for another upgrade. I liked the reel-to-reel concept so well that I decided to buy a 10½" reel deck, an Akai GX600D. What a machine. The tape reels -- like a huge cassette tape without the casing -- provided twice the sound quality and recording time. And if I desired, I could actually record two three-hour *AT40* shows onto one tape. Even though the cost for 10½" reel tapes was $10 each, I was determined to continue my weekly ritual to record and preserve each program.

****
Chapter 8 - 1976
****
WIFE Search

In early 1976, I decided to make an attempt to network with other *AT40* listeners. As unusual as my hobby of tape recording *AT40* shows was, I had hopes that perhaps there were others who, like me, had an interest of preserving the program every week. And since WIFE in Indianapolis had carried the show since 1971, wouldn't it be great if I could locate someone who had tape recorded and preserved some of the 1971 programs? In February, I placed a 'wanted to buy' classified ad in the *Indianapolis Star* that read "Attention American Top 40 Fans. I'm looking for persons interested in sending tapes of old programs to me. For more info write Pete Battistini, 6909 Pennsylvania Street, Merrillville, Ind. 46410." After receiving no response, I further understood that, indeed, I had an unusual hobby.

Double The Pleasure

A spring 1976 vacation led me to Fort Lauderdale, and an opportunity to hear *AT40* on the radio twice in the same day but on different radio stations. From Delray Beach, I was able to listen to the show on WJNO-FM in West Palm Beach, and later on Miami's WGBS-AM. I was aware of *AT40*'s market exclusivity for radio stations -- only one radio station in one market could own the broadcast rights -- yet I wondered how I could hear it, from a licensing agreement standpoint, on two stations with crossover signal patterns. Nevertheless, *AT40* twice in one day was a pleasant oddity.

A Low Point In Chicago - Part 1

Chicago's WDHF aired the show from 1974 until early 1979 -- nearly five years. A couple of low points for *AT40* during that time included an April 1976 time change, which moved *AT40*'s Sunday morning start time from 9 a.m. to 7 a.m. The week prior to the change, on-air promos during the show called "attention Casey Kasem fans", and tried to explain and justify the change. The announcement reasoned "....many people get up earlier in the summertime......" In reality however, WDHF was soon to change call letters and, in doing so, was making a Sunday morning overhaul. To appeal more to the masses, they discontinued public affairs programming between 7 - 9 a.m., and used the ratings success of *AT40*'s final hour to kick start their generic Sunday programming of repeating playlist records every two hours. But in spite of the fact that the first 7 a.m. airing of *AT40* went commercial free -- which made it easy for me to edit the commercials out because there weren't any -- this was not a move that I favored. I knew of *AT40*'s airtime on other stations and few, if any, were airing it at 7 a.m. on Sundays. Shades of WCFL! Of course, when fall arrived and listeners stopped 'getting up earlier,' there was no reversal to the old time slot. It stayed there until WMET (formerly WDHF) dropped the show.

A Low Point In Chicago - Part 2

Another low point was WDHF's handling of "The Fourth of July's Greatest Hits" bicentennial special, which the station never aired. In honor of the USA's 200th birthday, *AT40* designed a unique special that spotlighted #1 records from every July 4th holiday spanning the previous 40 years. Working in chronological order, Casey played the #1 record from July 4, 1937, the #1 record from July 4, 1938, and so on. Like other *AT40* specials, promotion for this program began -- about a month in advance -- in early June. A few promos for the special were aired on WDHF before station management caught on and put the brakes on the announcements. By the time the show dated June 19 hit the air on WDHF, all references to the July 4th special were edited out. In fact, the week before the special was to air there was no *AT40* program whatsoever on WDHF. During *AT40*'s regular time slot, and in between airing regular playlist records, a station announcer explained that they were "...having technical difficulties with the show, and we'll try and get it on the air...." But it never made it on the air that week. As it turns out, the station "postponed" the airing of the June 26 program and played it on Sunday, July 4th in place of the special with -- once again -- all promotional bicentennial special announcements edited out. To the average listener, there was no noticeable difference because most records were on the chart both weeks. The #1 record was even the same. And unless you followed *Billboard*'s chart, you probably were not aware of any change that WDHF had made. The station's management did not miss any detail. In addition to removing all of the promos, they even edited out the chart date that Casey typically mentioned in the show's closing, eliminating any reference to an 'old' chart.

Even at an early hour on a Sunday morning, WDHF's management obviously went out of their way to not air this special. The station would have no part of a program airing music from the 1930's, 1940's or the 1950's. Perhaps a decision had been made that the station would either offend or permanently lose listeners. Is that possible? Even at 7 a.m. on Sunday morning? For a station that was so concerned about alerting 'Casey Kasem fans' when changing the program's airtime just two months earlier, they pulled the rug out on listeners with this one.

"Great Britain's Top 40"

Whenever I wrote a letter to *AT40*, the purpose was not always question-related. Like in 1974, I made a few program suggestions. One special program suggestion I made was to use *Billboard*'s source of Great Britain's weekly top single records for a one-time countdown of England's Top 40. Part of my reasoning echoed from a 1972 special where, for one week, *AT40* suspended the Hot 100 list and counted down selections from *Billboard*'s Top 40 albums from the Top 200 LP chart. In the summer of 1976, The Beatles recordings were being re-released and were all over the chart in England. Casey counting down Great Britain's Top 40 would have been a good July 4, 1976 Bicentennial special -- a 200th year anniversary British invasion.

For The Record

In September, I came across a classified advertisement in *Billboard* that mentioned that 125 *AT40* programs were available for sale. I read it twice before I realized what it said. *AT40* programs on LP? *For sale?!* At that point, the ad was three or four weeks old and I thought for sure that I was out of luck and that the 125 programs had been sold. When I contacted the seller, I was told that, until my call, there had been no response to the ad. *Yes!* Until this time, I never had the opportunity to actually handle, not to mention own, an actual radio station copy of an *AT40* program. However, the ad changed that and I realized what a find this was. And what really made this exciting was that I had the opportunity to obtain copies of shows that I had never heard before -- programs from 1971, 1972, 1973 & 1974. After receiving a boxed, 3-LP *AT40* show from March 1973, for example, it made up for the radio static that I tolerated to in order to hear it on Paducah's WDXR. I made arrangements to obtain every show that was available -- regular weekly countdowns, special programs, and even shows hosted by a guest when Casey Kasem was away. I continued, however, my weekly ritual to record the program off the air. Indeed, I was a loyal listener!

***American Top 40* On The Road**

There were a few occasions where taping the program at home was not an option due to circumstances that took me away from my stereo while *AT40* was on the air. The most awkward taping experience, which gave friends an opportunity to gently ridicule my hobby, was New Year's Eve 1976. WMET was airing the program's Top 100 year-end countdown from 4 p.m. to midnight. Since a party took me to a friend's apartment that night, I didn't want to miss any of the year-end show which the station would air only one time. Earlier that afternoon, I disconnected my stereo components -- receiver and tape deck -- and took them over to his apartment in preparation of recording the program there. Explaining the purpose of the equipment and periodic reel-to-reel tape changes brought attention to my Top 40 loyalty. And I took some ribbing. So my hobby was a little different -- that didn't bother me.

Also, occasionally I worked as an engineer Sunday mornings at station WWCA. And, loyal as I was, I would pack up my receiver and reel tape deck and take them to the station with me. In between placing one-hour-in-length gospel programs on the air at the station, I would listen to *AT40* and edit out commercials as I recorded it. The station was located on the fourth floor of a bank building in downtown Gary and setting up my receiver there meant getting a great FM radio signal from a location that was almost within eyesight of Chicago's skyline.

I'll Take 40 Shares

And with all this interest in *AT40* and seeing its growth over the years, I decided that perhaps I should look into its parent company, Watermark Inc. As

much time and effort that I spent with *AT40*, I concluded that I should own stock and be part owner of Watermark. I contacted a broker and asked him to find out about obtaining Watermark shares. I recall talking to him two or three times about his unsuccessful attempts to find out something about the company. I told him all I could about it, but to no avail. It turned out to be a private company and public stock sales were not possible. Too bad for me. A little over five years later, Watermark Inc. was sold to ABC Radio Enterprises for an estimated $5 million. Again, too bad for me!

****
Chapter 9 - 1977
****

Buddies & Bee Gees

I had a few friends who followed *Billboard*'s Hot 100 chart changes every week like I did. It got to the point where we attempted to predict the following week's Top 40 -- what songs would debut, what were the fastest chart climbers and, of course, we took a guess at the #1 record.

One of these friends, also a regular *AT40* listener, once accused the program of fabricating stories that Casey told. It was a rare occasion when Casey's stories appeared farfetched and bordered unbelievable but, once in a while, it happened. The story that confirmed, in his mind, that fiction writers were at work was an incident involving a story about the Bee Gees. During the March 5 program, Casey related how the Bee Gees' recording career was saved in 1975 by the sound of a rickety old bridge in Florida. The Brothers Gibb apparently traveled over it every day on their way to a studio and recording session. And it supposedly inspired the beginning instrumentation to the successful record *Jive Talkin'*. *Jive Talkin'* became a #1 record and its success saved the Bee Gees' career. In my friend's eyes, *AT40* had stooped to a ridiculous low. The point of the story was the sound of a rickety old bridge made *Jive Talkin'* a #1 record. The sound of a bridge made *Jive Talkin'* a #1 record??? Admittedly, the story *did* sound unusual and exaggerated.

Special Women Are Weak

During the 1970's, the *AT40* staff produced many special programs including the "Greatest Disappearing Acts of the Rock Era", "Top 40 Records from 1968-1973" and the "Beatle Years 1964-1970." There were a few years where there were actually four or five specials released. My least favorite was the "Top 40 Girls of the Rock Era", which aired over the July 4th weekend. It was based on 40 records that were dedicated to, or inspired by women. A few examples of the special's records included Dawn's *Say, Has Anybody Seen My Sweet Gypsy Rose*, Dion's *Runaround Sue* and Debbie Reynolds' *Tammy*, which was the special's #1 song. But I did not understand its purpose. My guess is that it was supposed to be a 'fun to listen to' special. But, even as a loyal listener, I just didn't get it. It wasn't entertaining to listen to and I considered the theme for this special to be weak.

We Have A Winner

At some point in September or October, I learned that radio station WBOW in Terre Haute was giving away their vinyl copy of *AT40* to a listener every week. All it took to win one was to send in a specially-marked postcard and they would include it in a weekly drawing. I decided not to send in a postcard. Instead, I sent 25. After two months went by, I had not heard a word.

Surely, with 25 entries, I should have won at least *once.* After all, this was Terre Haute, not Chicago. So I called the station and learned from music director Larry Joseph that the promotion had been discontinued due to music licensing agreements. But he remembered my cards arriving all at once. I proceeded to briefly explain my interest in the show and, on a one-time basis, he sent a copy of *AT40* to me. The postcard promotional giveaway would prove to be successful for me again in 1979.

What's Your Point?

I got the year-end chart bug again in 1977 and decided to make an attempt at predicting the year's Top 100 using *Billboard*'s standard point system. My objective was to match *Billboard*'s year-end list, record-by-record. But in order to do that, I needed to start with the exact week beginning in November 1976, and award points to every record for each week it was on the chart through a specified week in November 1977. As once explained to me, year-end charts were tabulated with an 'upside down' point system in relation to the Hot 100. In other words, the first week a record is on the Hot 100, and if it is in position #100, it received one point. If it moved to #99 the following week, it received two more points, giving it a three-point subtotal. And if it jumped to #30 the following week, it would receive an additional 70 points, and so on. Number one records supposedly received 100 points for being at #1, plus an additional 100 'bonus' points for its top-of-the-chart ranking. Once a record fell off the chart, a point total was determined based on its chart performance. So the longer a record was on the chart, and the higher it climbed, the more points it earned during its chart run.

I took every record that made the Top 40 in 1977, and a few that didn't, and determined their point totals. But for some unknown reason, my goal to match *Billboard*'s Top 100 list for 1977 was not achieved. In fact, there were only a handful of records from my list whose year-end position actually matched with *Billboard*. But I was not alone. For the year-end countdown shows for 1972, 1973 and 1977, the *AT40* statistical staff -- professional chart experts -- created their own list, giving Casey a non-*Billboard* chart to work from for each of those year-end programs. And, other than the #1 record and a few exceptions, their list never matched *Billboard*'s either.

In 1972, I sought to gain some attention with my homemade year-end list by going on the radio with it. But the best I could do in 1977 was to post it at a local Camelot Music record store where I was a manager.

****
Chapter 10 - 1978
****

Spring To Life

There were times before where the Top 40 lacked a flavor of excitement. The music from the spring of 1977, for example, was drab. Forgettable records like Shalamar's *Uptown Festival*, Hot's *Angel In Your Arms* and the Wilton Place Street Band's *Disco Lucy* were representative of a boring time period for music. A lot of disco, a lot of ballads. And boredom. There did not seem to be anything that I would consider exciting in regards to *American Top 40.* I enjoyed seeing unusual chart movement and statistics, and interesting debut records. And I especially enjoyed seeing an obscure or unusual record receive national recognition and airplay. Other than Silvetti's *Spring Rain* and Olivia Newton-John's *Sam*, the spring of 1977 lacked all of that.

But the spring of 1978 was a different story. For the record industry, 1977 & 1978 were outstanding years. And I believe the most exciting time for music during that time was in March, April & May 1978. The soundtrack to the movie *Saturday Night Fever* was red hot. At one point in fact, on *Billboard*'s chart of March 25, there were six records in the Top 40 from the movie's soundtrack. More music-related movies were being released, with soundtrack cuts and title songs soon-to-be abounding in the Top 40. They included Frankie Valli's *Grease*, Steely Dan's *FM* and Love And Kisses' *Thank God Its Friday*. And Debby Boone's *You Light Up My Life* -- music from the movie of the same name -- had just completed ten weeks at #1. With the Academy Awards ceremony set for early April, it was perfect timing for *AT40*'s special program, "*AT40* Goes To The Movies", which ranked the biggest Top 40 singles from movie soundtracks. In contrast to the "Girls" special, I considered this program to be an excellent show.

Add a few personal favorites to the Top 40, like Parliament's *Flashlight* and Van Halen's *You Really Got Me*, and it was an electrifying time period for music. Unusual chart movement and interesting debut records were added reasons why I looked forward to listening to *American Top 40*.

I also had established correspondence with former *AT40* statistician Ben Marichal and in August made arrangements to fly to California to meet him. He even had arranged for me to sit in on a taping of *AT40*. Unfortunately, a family matter brought me back home before I had a chance to get to the Watermark studios. I enjoyed, however, the opportunity to examine some of his *AT40* files which contained a great deal of background information.

Fleetwood Mac Attack

But by mid-1978, I began to lose interest in the music and, after four years, I became burned out from taping every weekly show. It was not fun any longer. Repetitious airplay of a few artists, such as Fleetwood Mac and The

Eagles, and the continuous airplay of a few records, such as The Emotions' *Best Of My Love* and Andy Gibb's *I Just Want To Be Your Everything* was all I needed to seriously diminish enjoyment of Top 40 radio. To this day, I still cannot listen to The Eagles' *Hotel California*, Billy Joel's *Just The Way You Are*, and practically *anything* by Fleetwood Mac. Another reason why I enjoyed tape recording and re-playing *AT40* broadcasts offered a no repetition rule -- never within the countdown would you hear the same record twice in three hours. Perhaps there was a different version, but never the same record. However, a change was in the air.

<u>Move On</u>

It may have been a combination of the music's repetition, disco overkill, and my realization that there are more important things in life than the weekly Top 40. It was that logic that reinforced the message that I needed to make a change. Add in another factor -- I learned that *AT40* would expand from three hours to a four-hour program. The logic behind that decision was twofold -- an opportunity for all involved -- Watermark, radio stations and advertisers -- to increase sales and, second, a need for more program airtime because of an ever-increasing single record playing time, which had plagued *AT40* for most of the 1970's. The expansion from three to four hours meant generating additional advertising revenue through a 33% increase of program airtime, playing the full length of a record, a few oldies, and Casey relating more stories. *Everyone* benefited.

But quite honestly, I was not fond of *AT40*'s expansion from three hours to four, which began with the show dated October 7. Four hours just seemed to be a long time to be chained to a radio and tape recorder. And the visualization of 'being chained' made me realize that taping *AT40* every week was no longer appealing. Putting things in perspective, I guess that shackled image was no different from spending four or five hours all day Saturday & Sunday watching football, basketball or baseball on television. And millions of people do that every week. However, it was time to move on and I permanently disassociated myself from Top 40 music, Top 40 radio and from weekly tapings of *AT40*. It was a bittersweet turning point because I still had interest in the program but not the music -- certainly this created a philosophical contradiction. Just as I ended my weekly tape recording ritual -- prior to the first four-hour show -- my subscription to *Billboard* was about to expire. The time was right to adjust my life's priorities.

****

Chapter 11 - 1979

****

Re: Postcards & Re: Play

Although I had re-enrolled in college, I discovered that Top 40 radio was still alluring, and I could not stay away. I noticed a blurb in the May 30, 1979 edition of the *Chicago Tribune* that *AT40* was heard Sunday mornings on WBBM-FM, from 8 a.m. to noon. I couldn't resist tuning in at least once to hear how they were presenting the show and learn if it had changed since I had last heard it eight months earlier. Because I had shut down my interest in new music, I listened long enough to hear Casey come in and out of a commercial segment, but I did not recognize the music. However, I did hear something unusual and appealing during a commercial segment. WBBM was giving away their weekly copy of *AT40* to listeners who sent in a postcard for a once-a-week drawing. Hey! I've done this before! Needless to say, I mailed in 25-30 postcards. A few weeks later, my name was announced on the air as a winner, unbeknownst to me, and I received a copy of the June 30 program along with a congratulatory note from the station.

But the affiliation between WBBM & *AT40* really aroused my curiosity. One reason was due to WBBM's laid back, young adult music format. The Top 40 music scene in 1979 was layered with disco and rock tunes, many of which were not regularly played on WBBM. The likes of Carly Simon and Dan Fogelberg were the station's norm. And the exceptions were many artists heard on *AT40* -- Cheap Trick, Donna Summer and Kiss. WBBM must have recognized however, *AT40*'s sales potential and its attraction to new listeners. The other peculiarity involving WBBM was the re-playing of the final two hours of *AT40* on Monday nights from 10 p.m. to midnight. I'm not certain what their motive was but it was refreshing to see the show getting additional, non-weekend airplay and attention.

An *AT40* Subscription

While my current interest in *AT40* at that point had waned, I was still concentrating on a continued effort to obtain unwanted radio station copies of *AT40*. In my quest to locate old copies of the show, I came across a program director of an *AT40* station. And we worked out an arrangement where, once a month, I obtained the four most recently aired programs. This arrangement literally gave me a subscription to *AT40*, which went on for about a year. Although I was acquiring programs from 1979, I never listened to them. When they arrived, I inspected each and stored them away.

Stats Off To You!

But by the end of 1979, the chart bug was biting again. Rather than air the annual Top 100 for the year, I learned that *AT40* had produced two specials -- the

"Top 50 of 1979" and the "Top 50 of the 1970's."

I could not let the 1970's fade away without one last review and I decided to create my own Top 40 list of the decade. I went though all the *Billboard* magazines that I had saved -- hundreds of them from 1970-1978 -- and determined the list's candidates. And that wasn't too difficult. I took all the #1 records from every year and determined which ones had the greatest number of weeks on the chart as well as the greatest number of weeks at #1. But I was not expecting any of my statistics to match *AT40's* chart. In fact, the only way that I could produce data on 1979 records was by reviewing the radio-station-copy cue sheets that accompanied *AT40* shows that I had in my collection.

My plan for this list was not for radio broadcast or for record store posting. This time I decided to send it to Casey & *AT40,* prior to the airing of their year-end specials. I never received any kind of acknowledgment or response after I sent it but I suspect at the very least that their statistician compared my list to theirs. And without a doubt, I enjoyed going through the charts one last time.

<u>It's The Write Time</u>

Finally, in addition to compiling the decade-ending list, I sent letters in December to many radio stations who had carried the program during the early 1970's. I wrote to approximately 15 or 20 stations, seeking a historical perspective of *AT40* in relation to their station, including information about an *AT40* start date, whether they kept copies of the program once it aired, and day & times of its airing. The few responses I received were very informative.

****

Chapter 12 - A SLICE OF LIFE AFTER THE 1970's

****

Switching Gears

With the exception of Top 40 and contemporary rock music, my radio station listening preferences had latched onto nearly every radio format including classical music and all-news stations. I preferred listening to all-oldies radio, however there was no such station in the Chicago area in 1980. It got to the point where just scanning the dial was entertaining. (I know, I know......get a life. Well, I was trying!)

The 1980's began for me just like the 1970's ended -- with a distant interest in *AT40*. A few months into the new year and I tuned into WBYG-FM in Kankakee, Illinois where the program was heard on Sunday afternoons. WBYG, with a Top 40 and album-oriented format sprinkled with oldies, carried the show from 1-5 p.m. And it was somewhat ironic that I could receive WBYG's signal in Merrillville. I now had the ability to hear *AT40* on Sunday mornings over WBBM-FM and on Sunday afternoons on WBYG. With the struggle years earlier in trying to find a radio signal -- anything -- to hear *AT40*, I now could regularly hear it twice on Sunday on two different radio stations. But I no longer had the desire to listen.

Call Me A Loaner

In late May 1980, I heard an on-air reference to an upcoming all-oldies weekend on WBYG and I called program director Bill Taylor with an idea. With an oldies weekend scheduled for the week before the July 4th holiday, and because *AT40*'s 10th anniversary was approaching, I suggested that he consider replaying *AT40*'s first show that weekend -- the 5th anniversary repeat broadcast that originally aired on July 4, 1970 -- in place of the current Top 40. And if interested, I would be happy to lend my LP copy of the program to WBYG. He thought it was a great idea.

A week in advance to this special weekend, WBYG heavily promoted the oldies weekend, and the broadcast of the first *AT40*. Once the weekend arrived, and just prior to the start of the show, a WBYG personality introduced *AT40* and provided on-air credit to me for lending the show to them. Upon its completion, I was once again acknowledged. There were hundreds of stations that aired this program in July 1975, but WBYG may have been the only radio station to re-broadcast the first show on *AT40*'s 10th anniversary.

****

Chapter 13 - CONCLUSION

****

Attitude, Influence & Responsibility

Many people have been critical of Casey's style, delivery and image, including many of his peers. He was, and perhaps still is, an easy target. In fact, I recall hearing WLS' Larry Lujack once make an on-air reference to Casey as "a twink." And Rick Dees mocked Casey for years, both as a Top 40 countdown competitor and because of Casey's overall on-air demeanor.

Quite frankly, the image of Casey that comes through on *American Top 40* may likely be the opposite image of actor Clint Eastwood. Behind the *AT40* microphone, his easy-to-listen-to radio voice, inflection and style are upbeat, positive and points to a heartfelt concern for others. Through *AT40*, he has told hundreds, perhaps thousands, of human interest stories about everyone from recording artists who made it big on the national charts to Long Distance Dedication letter writing listeners looking for a song of hope or a song of love. If there was a story to be told, Casey was the one to tell it. And because many recording artists have tainted images -- drug use, violent tempers, anti-society behavior and suicidal tendencies -- it's easy to identify their negative side. But through *AT40*'s researchers and Casey's distinctive storytelling, the program has highlighted factual, uplifting stories about the positive aspect, outcome or outlook of those same artists that would be heard nowhere else.

Indeed, Casey's positive, caring attitude drew listeners to *AT40* and was just one of many reasons why *AT40* flourished during the 1970's. And that became an add-on reason why I was so enthusiastic about it. Casey Kasem is influential.

Beyond the countdown, Casey has used this image, his position and influence to lead many social campaigns and causes. His community-mindedness and charity support has advanced organizations such as Mothers Against Drunk Driving, Project Hunger and MDA. In fact, he recorded special radio public service announcements for each of those nonprofit groups and included them in *AT40* broadcasts for radio station use.

In an August 1980 article from *The Oregonian* (Portland, OR), Dan Hortsch wrote that Casey "wants his show to be a 'force for good,' to offset 'some of the things done on radio that I'm not particularly proud of - some of the language, some of the records, the philosophies from deejays with ego problems.'" *Chicago Tribune* writer Eric Zorn wrote on January 31, 1983 that Casey "sounds like your sunny next door neighbor. When he waxes enthusiastic about the record coming up or the granola fruit bar he wants you to buy, it comes off as though he really means it, not at all hip and sassy." And an article by Pat Dooley in the February 13, 1983 edition of *Grit* newspaper quoted Casey as saying "I'm not a goody-two-shoes, but at the same time I feel when you have millions of people listening to what you have to say, you

have a responsibility as a citizen, as a human being, to send out positive vibrations whenever you can avoid the negative ones."

To this day, I enjoy listening to *AT40* shows - in their entirety - from the 1970's. It's unfortunate that many records that reached the Top 40 back then do not receive airplay today. Many oldies bring back memories, but listening to an *AT40* show from the past actually brings back the time period. And when listening to old programs, I usually dig up a show from the past that matches the present time period. That is, I may listen to a show from December 1973 during the month of December.

By starting in July 1970 on seven radio stations, *AT40* finished the decade of the 1970's with more than 600 subscribing stations, all over the United States and throughout the world. *AT40* became an industry-respected, syndicated radio program phenomenon, heard by millions of listeners.

And during the 1970's, I was much more than a radio listener. I was an *AT40* enthusiast.

****

Chapter 14 - AND FINALLY..................

****

After many years of assembling and compiling a collection of *AT40* programs, my objective to obtain a copy of every show was finally completed in 2003. But apparently my aggressiveness to get to the front of the collector line created, at times, a direct and unstoppable reputation.

An observer to my pronounced obsession, fellow program collector and good friend Bob Moorhead, decided that my antics and dealings were noteworthy. Below are his re-written lyrics to a 1979 record that he emailed to me, and a few other collectors, in January 2000. Unfortunately, I've lost track of Bob and was unable to include any *AT40* memory from him for this text. But I could not overlook his comment on my enthusiasm. Thanks, Bob.

A story...or song...to Pete

Ol' Pete went down to the southern states
He was lookin' for some shows to steal.
He was in a bind
Cause he was way behind
He was willin' to make a deal.
When he came across this old store
Goin' out of business, cause everything was hot.
And ol' Pete jumped on a hickory stump
And said "Store, let me tell you what.
I guess you didn't know it
But I'm a Casey collector too.
And if you care to take a dare
I'll make a bet with you.
Now you got some pretty good shows there
But give ol' Pete his due.
I've been collectin' Casey
So let's not get hasty
I think I got more shows than you."
The store said "My name's Johnny,
And this might blow your nose,
But I'll take your bet,
You're gonna regret
Cause you ain't gettin' these shows."
Johnny lock them doors and hide them records fast
Cause Hell's broke loose in Georgia
And ol' Pete deals in cash.
But if he wins, he'll get them shiny Casey Kasem shows
But if he fails...I strongly suggest you lock your doors!

ACKNOWLEDGEMENTS

ALL DISPLAY MATERIALS AND ILLUSTRATION PIECES, INCLUDING THE FOLLOWING, ARE FROM THE PRIVATE COLLECTION OF PETE BATTISTINI

Radio station surveys:

KBYR Anchorage, Alaska
KBBC Phoenix, Arizona
KERN Bakersfield, California
WAMS Wilmington, Delaware
KPOI Honolulu, Hawaii
WASK Lafayette, Indiana
WIFE Indianapolis, Indiana
KBEQ Kansas City, Missouri
KIRL St. Louis, Missouri
KOIL Omaha, Nebraska
KIXS Killeen, Texas
KTSA San Antonio, Texas
KHIT Walla Walla, Washington

Radio station testimonials:

KCRA Sacramento, California
WKFM Syracuse, New York
WQOK Greenville, South Carolina
WCOR Lebanon, Tennessee

LPs:

Paul Frees and the Poster People (MGM Records)
Cyrus (Elektra Records)

REPRINT PERMISSION GRANTED FOR THE FOLLOWING:

American Top 40 advertisements:

Radio Station Comments & Testimonials (9-5-70)
The Hottest 10 Minutes... (6-5-71)
Growing Station List... (11-13-71)
52 Specials... (2-3-73)
...Announces 52 Specials (1-19-74)
Disappearing Acts Special... (3-8-75)
...Moving Burgers (5-3-75)
1977's Top 100 Special... (11-12-77)
4-Hour Countdown... (8-5-78)
Summer Special... (6-9-79)
There Just May Be A Hundred Reasons Why... (2-6-71)
Just Put New York... (7-3-71)
Casey Is Selling Shoes... (3-18-72)
Much More Than Music... (7-21-73)
Casey Joins KLOM... (2-2-74)
...Builds Higher Ratings (4-19-75)
ARB Results... (7-31-76)
1978 Specials... (2-4-78)
Secrets Revealed... (4-28-79)

American Top 40 articles:

...Gets 26 Stations, Billboard Magazine (10-10-70)
...From Barter to $$$, Billboard Magazine (8-28-71)
Watermark Promo LP Deal, Billboard Magazine (7-31-71)
Watermark to Disk, Billboard Magazine (10-23-71)

American Top 40 marketing booklets:

1971, 1972, 1974, 1978

American Top 40 listener directories:

1976, 1977, 1978, 1979

American Top 40 memos:

*ARB ratings
*ratings
*My Ding-A-Ling warning
*upcoming special
*flash....alert....urgent
*last ARB
*listening guide/upcoming special
*idea input
*American Country Countdown
*playing cards
*idea bank
*upcoming specials
*Earth shaking events
*Casey's Annual Disappearing Act
*authentic station IDs
*Casey tubes again!
*new jingles, listening directory, ratings
*programming year-end specials
*extra special program copies
*1974 Top 100 8-hour conversion
*Robert W. Morgan, guest host
*1975 specials
*No No Song warning/next special
*Disappearing Acts promos
*first program repeat promos
*Fight The Power/Tush warnings
*Wink Martindale, guest host
*Jerry Bishop, guest host
*1976 specials
*Bicentennial special promos
*error in Bicentennial special
*Beatles special
*shipping of year-end specials
*Bruce Phillip Miller, guest host
*1978 specials
*program ratings
*last 3-hour show
*4-hour debut/new closing theme
*Only The Good Die Young warning
*1978 Top 100 8-hour conversion
*error in 1-6-79 program
*Top 3 recap
*Superman warning
*1979 specials
*Bumper Morgan, guest host/Roxanne warning
*American Top 40 yearbook
*Gordon Elliott, guest host
*Disco special promos
*Casey/TV, Ain't Love A Bitch & disco story warnings
*Listening Directories, Station IDs, Upcoming Special
*The Killing of Georgie/Telephone Man warnings
*Paradise By The Dashboard Light warning
*Dave Hull, guest host
*surprise special
*format change
*Kodachrome warning
*hand-written Jungle Fever warning
*going stereo
*questionnaire results
*station listening guide

American Top 40 program script cards:

British Hits special; 8-24-74 program; Robert W. Morgan show; 8-19-78 program

American Top 40 photograph:

Double Dozen LP set
deck of playing cards
set of 10" reel-to-reel tapes from 1971
3LP box set from 1971
cover of year-end Top 40 of 1973 special countdown LP box

American Top 40 miscellaneous:

American Top 40 (Uncle Sam) logo
Top 80 of 1970 mailer
Program cue sheet from 5-1-71 special
Soon........Stereo flyer

American Top 40 article:

American Top 40 to WCFL, Billboard Magazine (7-15-72)

BIBLIOGRAPHY
(from the private collection of Pete Battistini)
BOOKS, MAGAZINES & MISCELLANEOUS

__________. American Top 40 Gets 26 Stations. *Billboard Magazine*, Billboard Publications, Inc., New York: October 10, 1970

__________. American Top 40 to WCFL. *Billboard Magazine*, Billboard Publications, Inc., New York: July 15, 1972

__________. From Barter to $$$. *Billboard Magazine*, Billboard Publications, Inc., New York: August 28, 1971

__________. Watermark to Disk. *Billboard Magazine*, Billboard Publications, Inc., New York: October 23, 1971

Durkee, Rob. American Top 40, The Countdown of the Century. New York: Schirmer Books. 1999.

Kasem, Casey. Casey's Corner, *SPEC Magazine*. New York: 16 Magazine, Inc. September 1971.

Kasem, Casey. Casey's Corner, *SPEC Magazine*. New York: 16 Magazine, Inc. October 1971

INTERVIEWS & QUOTES

Rich Appel, August 22, 2003
Fred Baur, September 3, 2003
Doug Bowden, October 22, 2003
Rob Durkee, August 20, 2003
Claude Hall, October 6, 2003
Bill Hergonson, August 27-September 23, 2003
Richard "Uncle Ricky" Irwin, August 21, 2003
Ron Jacobs, October 2, 2003
John Jayne, August 21, 2003
Casey Kasem, September 28, 2003
Jim Kiehle, September 18, 2003
Tom Konard, April 1, 1982 and April 8, 1982
Debbie Kruger, September 23, 2003
Shannon Lynn, September 5, 2003
Carl Mann, February 16, 2004
Rick Martinez, September 6, 2003
Larry McKay, December 14, 2003
Chuck Miller, October 22, 2003
Bob Moorhead, January 21, 2000
Steve Orchard, August 22, 2003
Ken Ott, August 23, 2003
Tom Rounds, September 30, 2003
Lanny Springs, August 22, 2003
Art Vuolo, September 24, 2003
Kurt Youngmann, September 3, 2003

SPECIAL RECOGNITION AND CREDIT

Don Bustany	Ron Jacobs	
Casey Kasem	Tom Rounds	
Rich Appel	Tom Berg	Doug Bowden
Steven Camhi	Jeff Dible	Frank Douglas
Rob Durkee	Claude Hall	Gene Hallahan
Bill Hergonson	Jim Kiehle	Scott Lakefield
Todd Lucas	Shannon Lynn	Ben Marichal
Rick Martinez	Mark McGehee	Bob Moorhead
Darryl Morden	Ron Muth	Ken Ott
Jerome A. Peterson	Daniel Shulman	Lanny Springs

Kraig Kitchin and Premiere Radio Networks **VNU Business Media**

Paul Gruwell, artist of AT40's "Uncle Sam" logo

****

INDEX

ABOUT THE AUTHOR

Pete Battistini was born in Gary, Indiana in 1955. Thirteen years later he picked up his first radio station record survey – a Top 40 listing of WLS' (Chicago) Hit Parade. This lead to a fascination with artist and music variety typically found in Top 40 radio and in Top 40 countdowns. In 1971, Battistini heard Casey Kasem's *American Top 40* for the first time and was instantly captivated.

He has accumulated one of the largest collections of *American Top 40* memorabilia, including an *AT40* promotional poster seen here that he obtained from former WICB (Ithaca, New York) general manager Gene Hallahan.

His enthusiasm for Casey Kasem's radio show carried over into a desire to document *AT40* program information, the 1970s in particular. Much of that data is presented in this text. Additions, changes or suggestions to this text are welcomed by the author.

Contact Pete Battistini at at40@aol.com

Printed in the United States
By Bookmasters